ON THE THIRD PART
OF THE SECRET
OF FÁTIMA

BY

KEVIN J. SYMONDS

EN ROUTE BOOKS & MEDIA

En Route Books & Media

5705 Rhodes Avenue, St. Louis, MO 63109

Contact us at contactus@enroutebooksandmedia.com

© En Route Books & Media, 2017

Cover design by TJ Burdick

Cover image credits:

Bruegel, Pieter, The Procession to Calvary (1564) via Wikimedia Commons: https://commons.wikimedia.org/wiki/File:Pieter_Bruegel_(I)_-_The_Procession_to_Calvary_(1564).jpg

Callahan, Dennis, Our Lady of Fatima- Pilgrim Statue, via Flikr CC: https://flic.kr/p/jbrzKC

Cavalleri, Ferdinando, Corpus Christ Procession with Pope Gregory XVI in the Vatican via Wikimedia Commons: https://commons.wikimedia.org/wiki/File:Corpus_Christi_Procession_with_Pope_Gregory_XVI_in_the_Vatican.jpg

Paperback ISBN: 978-1-950108-23-7

E-book ISBN: 978-0-9988940-6-5

Nihil Obtat granted by Fr. Randy Soto, S.Th.D.,

Pontifical Gregorian University, Rome, Italy

In accordance with CIC 827, permission to publish has been granted on April 5, 2017 by Bishop-Elect Msgr. Mark S. Rivituso, Vicar General, Archdiocese of St. Louis. Permission to publish is an indication that nothing contrary to Church teaching is contained in this work. It does not imply any endorsement of the opinions expressed in the publication; nor is any liability assumed by this permission.

Printed in the United States of America

On the Third Part of the Secret of Fátima

This book by Kevin J. Symonds provides a well-researched and fascinating study of the many questions and controversies concerning the third part of the secret of Fátima. This study includes many new insights gathered from the 2013 biography of Sister Lúcia written by the Carmelite Sisters of Coimbra, Portugal. Symonds treats the critics of the Holy See's account of the Fátima secret—Fr. Gruner, Fr. Kramer, Br. François de Marie des Anges, C. Ferrara, A. Socci, et al.— with respect and fairness, even though he does not hesitate to expose the flaws of their scholarship. Symonds' book also contains some valuable texts in the appendix, such as Cardinal Ottaviani's 1967 allocution on Fátima; a 1994 interview with Archbishop Capovilla, and a transcript of the June 26, 2000 Vatican Press Conference on the secret of Fátima. For those wishing an in depth examination of the third part of the Fátima secret—and one not based on suspicion and conspiracy theories—this is the book to read.

—Robert L. Fastiggi, Ph.D. Professor of Systematic Theology,
Sacred Heart Major Seminary, Detroit Michigan,
former President of the Mariological Society of America,

In his latest work, *On the Third Part of the Secret of Fátima,* Kevin J. Symonds offers a valuable contribution to the literature about this aspect of the message given by Our Lady to Lúcia, Francisco and Jacinta one hundred years ago. With so much interest in the Third Part of the Secret (or "The Third Secret," as some writers employ), our author presents a useful summary and analysis as well as pertinent documents that are not often seen in English. This reviewer is grateful for those sources, the recommendation concerning the Biography of Sister Maria Lúcia of Jesus and the Immaculate Heart penned by the Carmelites of Coimbra entitled, *A Pathway Under the Gaze of Mary* and Mr. Symonds' plausible contention

and exhortation: "We are entering into a new period of the history of Fátima and we ought to be celebrating this fact, not engaging in seemingly endless controversies."

— Monsignor Charles M. Mangan,
Office of the Marian Apostolate,
Diocese of Sioux Falls,

Symonds has done a very thorough job in getting to the bottom—insofar as it is possible—of the various confusions and conspiracy theories on the subject of the Third Secret, making a compelling case that what the Vatican published in 2000 was the whole text of it as written by Sr Lúcia. No doubt the debate will continue, but the clarity and intellectual honesty of Symonds' work, with copious reference to the relevant sources in their original languages, will be of enormous assistance for scholars in the future who wish to understand this tangled affair.

—Dr. Joseph Shaw,
Research Fellow at St. Benet's Hall, England

CONTENTS

Dedicated to Drs. Andrew Minto & Stephen Hildebrand

—ACKNOWLEDGEMENTS—

I would like to thank the following people for their assistance in the writing of this book:

The staff of the Sanctuary of Fátima Archives; Mr. Robert Tunmire (Waco, TX); Dr. Robert Fastiggi (Detroit, MI); Dr. William A. Thomas (Ireland); Dr. Jason Bourgeois and the Faculty & Staff of the International Mariological Research Institute (Dayton, OH); Deacon Robert "Bob" Ellis (New Jersey); Mrs. Barbara Ernster (Minnesota); The Staff of the Moody Library at Baylor University (Waco, TX); Mr. Donal A. Foley (England); Mr. John Preiss (Hanceville, AL); The Franciscans at the Shrine of St. Maximilian Kolbe (Marytown, IL); Mrs. Rose Lawson at the Kenrick-Glennon Seminary Library (St. Louis, MO); The Staff of the Pius XII Memorial Library (St. Louis, MO).

The translators: Mr. Tony Verhallen, Mr. Mark Waterinckx, Mr. Nathan Dean, Mr. Bryan Gonzalez, Mr. Richard Chonak, Dr. Daniel Nodes, and Dr. Andre Villeneuve.

—Introduction—

"There is nothing better to provoke curiosity and interest among persons than that which is intentionally kept hidden.... [T]he secret [of Fátima] *has been one of the most subtle yet discreet means the Maternal Heart of Our Lady used to draw to herself the attention of so many men."*

—F. Stein, *Rally*, February, 1960

The history of the Catholic Church in the twentieth century has yet to be written. It is, however, an undeniable fact that such a history cannot be without reference to the apparitions of Our Lady in Fátima, Portugal. From May-October, 1917, Our Lady appeared to three Portuguese children in Fátima: Lúcia dos Santos, Jacinta and Francisco Marto. The latter two were cousins to Lúcia and died within three years of the apparitions' end (October, 1917). Lúcia became a nun (first a Dorothean, then a Carmelite) and lived until February 13, 2005.

During the six apparitions, Our Lady made some requests. Among them was for Russia to be consecrated to the Immaculate Heart of Mary, and for the spread of a new devotion called the Communion of Reparation of the Five First Saturdays. Also, during the July 13, 1917 apparition, Our

Lady communicated a secret in three parts to the children. The first two parts were published by the end of 1941. The third, as we shall see, was revealed much later.

The present book grew out of research from my book *Pope Leo XIII and the Prayer to St. Michael*. I had discovered a link between Pope Leo's vision and the requests of Our Lady of Fátima and was exploring this connection. Between January and February, 2015, I was talking with Deacon Bob Ellis of the World Apostolate of Fatima, USA Inc. (WAF-USA). WAF-USA had obtained the English translation rights to a new biography of Sr. Lúcia entitled *A Pathway Under the Gaze of Mary*. I sought permission to place an English translation of a chapter from this biography in my book.

At one point of our conversation, Deacon gave me an idea to write an essay on a Fátima-related matter. That essay was completed (though never published) if memory serves, by the end of February or April, 2015. Coinciding with this essay were two articles that I wrote for the web site *Catholic Stand* entitled *Is There a "Fourth Secret" of Fatima?* (February) and a book review of *A Pathway Under the Gaze of Mary* (April). What I did not realize at the time was how these writings would become the basis for an entire and new book project.

As I continued to read the Carmelites' biography of Sr. Lúcia, I discovered that it was a gold mine of information. Based upon published and unpublished manuscripts of Sr. Lúcia, as well as the Sisters' own recollections, the biography cast new light on the history of Fátima. In fact, some of its revelations were quite astonishing, especially when they touched upon old controversies. As I reflected upon the biography, there were a couple of observations that arose.

One of the most important observations was that the history of Fátima is not known, much less understood, in its entirety. This history is still being written. If it is still being written, what value do statements have that presume absolute certitude on some controversial matter? Before his death

in February, 2016, Richard Salbato of *Unity Publishing* once stated to me that Sr. Lúcia said shortly before her death, "If Fátima were an 800-page book, we'd only be on page 400." While I have not verified independently this statement, *A Pathway Under the Gaze of Mary* in some ways proves it.

As my book attempts to demonstrate, very little research is available in the English language which critically assesses Fátima and its major interlocutor, Sr. Lúcia. Much of what we know on Fátima comes from her pen, and a little-appreciated rule in the Church's theology of private revelation is to look at the recipient(s) of the revelation. Their background is examined and assessed so as to provide a fuller picture to the events that are claimed. What was Lúcia's spiritual life like? What kind of person was she throughout the years? How did she grow in the spiritual life? How did this growth affect her understanding and promotion of Our Lady's call at Fátima?

A Pathway Under the Gaze of Mary places us in close communication with the "human" side of Sr. Lúcia from the perspective of those who lived with her. We see this "human" side, but we are also afforded a *very* rare glimpse into the depths of her spiritual life and her beautiful soul. This life Sister *fiercely* guarded and protected with all of her strength. She took this so seriously that, as the biography reveals, Sr. Lúcia even risked the displeasure of Bishop da Silva when she wrote to the Holy Father to request entrance to the Carmel.

Regretfully, the publication (in Portuguese) in 2013 of the biography went almost unnoticed in the English-speaking world. This changed when a passage of the book was brought to light, first in Italian then into English, which touched upon the matter of the third part of the secret. Many of us in the English-speaking world (myself included) learned of the biography through a questionable report. We were introduced to the book before it could be properly understood as a beautiful encounter with the magnanimous soul of Sr. Lúcia.

Ever a contentious subject, the third part of the secret of Fátima has long been mired in controversy. I invite the reader to learn about this his-

tory in chapter one of the present book. For the moment, it suffices to say that speculation, hype, and theories have surrounded the third part of the secret for a very long time. The publication of the text on June 26, 2000 even had the *opposite* intended effect as it created even more questions. In 2015, I attempted to address some of these matters in the articles mentioned earlier.

From these articles, I decided to write on matters pertaining to the third part of the secret of Fátima. For over a year I have studied and examined various matters on this subject. I have been greatly assisted by research in libraries, and even the archives of the Sanctuary of Fátima. Many of my findings are present within the pages of this book, though not every question is addressed. I would like to point out one area in particular, namely the claims of Dr. Solideo Paolini on statements attributed to Cardinal Capovilla.

Paolini, an Italian Fatimologist, claims to have received significant information from Cardinal Capovilla, the former private secretary to Pope John XXIII. Capovilla was present when the Holy Father opened the envelope containing Sister Lúcia's text on the secret. Capovilla allegedly indicated to Paolini that there was a second, unrevealed text. This claim was promoted by Italian journalist Antonio Socci in his book *The Fourth Secret of Fatima* in 2006. In 2016, Robert Moynihan of *Inside the Vatican* magazine claimed a similar story from Capovilla. I do not examine these claims in this book for the following reasons:

1. An in-depth examination of Paolini's claim requires extensive work in Italian. Little time and my capacity with this language prohibit a fair assessment of Paolini's works.

2. I have made attempts to communicate with Dr. Moynihan. He has, to date, made little effort to engage me on the topic of his own conversation with Capovilla. I learned that Moynihan was ill and perhaps is behind in personal correspondence.

3. Cardinal Capovilla died in 2016 having attained to 100 years of age.

His death means that time must pass for his affairs to be settled.

4. The Italian journalist Giuseppe de Carli claimed in 2010 to have a private letter from Capovilla that denied Paolini's story. De Carli himself died shortly after making this admission.

From these facts, I conclude that the matter is best left to competent historians and archivists.

Concerning any other area of importance that is not addressed in these pages, I ask the reader to consider the sheer vastness of the topic at hand. I am one man and a comprehensive treatment of the topic is best performed by a panel of experts. Speaking within the context of the English language, I appear to be one of the *very* few willing to "take the bull by the horns" and provide a treatment on the subject. My book is thus to be understood as an *attempt* to address some difficulties associated with the third part of the secret of Fátima.

Many things within these pages may be surprising to the reader. The history of the third part of the secret is re-examined, an action deemed necessary in the light of the revelations present within *A Pathway Under the Gaze of Mary. Much* recourse to original language sources has been performed as some disputed matters are resolved by this recourse. Facts are presented in a sober and critical manner. If one is looking for exaggerations that grossly mischaracterize Our Lady's call, then this book will be of no help. It is intended for *serious* study of Fátima and the third part of its secret.

The nature of the topic herein discussed is highly specialized and presents a narrow focus. Others in the Church have also taken an interest in the topic and written about it. I am grateful to them for their efforts, even if we may disagree on some finer details. A body of literature has been formed that must be treated if justice is to be done. Regretfully, there is not much by way of critiques or responses to this literature, at least in the English language. Some good questions have been raised over the years, while other questions or assertions may not be as viable. If during

my examination of the facts I come across as harsh towards any particular group, I am to be read as critiquing from charity. No ill will or polemics are intended.

My debt is tremendous to all those who have helped me with this book and I am grateful to them. Some do not want to be named, but God will reward them. I wish to thank Dr. Andrew Minto in particular who taught me both the how and the value of critically assessing manuscripts. I also wish to give a special thank you to Juan Antonio Hernandez Fuentes for his invaluable and painstaking assistance. Indeed, thank you to everyone from the bottom of my heart for your willingness to carry this burden with me, for the glory of God and His Immaculate Mother!

-Kevin J. Symonds
May 13th, 2017
Our Lady of Fátima

—1—
FÁTIMA AND ITS SECRET:
A HISTORY

"Do not tell this to anyone. Yes, you may tell Francisco."
—Our Lady of Fátima, July 13, 1917

One of the most controversial aspects of the history of the apparitions of Our Lady in Fátima, Portugal is the secret given to the three visionaries on July 13, 1917. From within the first month of it being communicated unto the present moment, this topic has been the cause for much ink to be spilled. The present chapter aims to provide a history of the secret to serve as a backdrop for subsequent chapters from which to make observations. To this end, we will keep in mind—though not exclusively—the following questions:

1. Who are the main contributors in the discussions on the third part of the secret of Fátima?
2. What are the arguments of said contributors?
3. Are there underlying biases/prejudices to the arguments?
4. How do these arguments impact the discussion on the history and interpretation of the secret of Fátima (in all its parts)?

The apparitions of Our Lady to Lúcia dos Santos, Francisco and Jacinta Marto from May-October, 1917 are the center of the present discus-

sion.[1] On July 13, 1917, the Virgin Mary revealed specific information to the children popularly known as the "secret."[2]

I. The Secret of Fátima: A History

Once word of the "secret" spread, it became a thing of curiosity to people. For now, it suffices to say that the initial news of a secret having been communicated piqued the curiosity of many. It attracted unwanted attention to the children wherein they were sought-after, interrogated, and even persecuted. They were kidnapped in August, 1917 by the local Administrator and an attempt was made to extract the secret.[3]

Ascribing an exact date for the end of this initial period is difficult.[4] We can say that it had ended around the deaths of Francisco (April, 1919) and Jacinta (February, 1920) and the relocating of Lúcia in 1921. Lúcia was, in this year, sent to an orphanage in the Portuguese city of Porto and educated by the Sisters of St. Dorothy (the Dorothean Sisters), herself eventually entering the Order.[5] Her name in religion was Sr. Dores (we

---

1   The prior apparitions of the Angel of Portugal to the visionaries are not considered here. The reason for this being that the children mostly kept silent about these apparitions and thus nothing public came of them. It was not until much later that Sr. Lúcia revealed them in her writings. We will also not consider other apparitions unless they have some bearing on the history of the secret.

2   The term was used immediately by the visionaries after the secret was communicated in response to people asking them questions about the apparition.

3   Cf. Dr. Antonio Maria Martins, S.J., *Memórias e Cartas de Irmã Lúcia*. (Porto, Portugal: Simão Guimarães, Filhos, LDA, 1973), 263-265. Hereafter *Memórias e Cartas de Irmã Lúcia* followed by page number.

4   The children had prophesied that a miracle would be given on October 13, 1917. After the occurrence of this miracle, there were continued interrogations both from the curious as well as ecclesiastical authorities (as was the duty of the latter to do).

5   During Lúcia's educational years and then her time in the Dorotheans, it was nearly impossible to keep hidden the knowledge of her identity (despite

shall continue to refer to her as Lúcia or Sr. Lúcia for the sake of convenience).

A. Sr. Lúcia—The Sole Surviving Seer

Prior to entering (and during) the religious life, Sister Lúcia remained in communication with the competent ecclesiastical authorities, particularly the Bishop of Fátima, H.E. José Alves Correia da Silva. From about 1921 to 1935 one will find that information about the events at Fátima was in its nascent stages. Lúcia was, at the end of February, 1920 the sole remaining witness to the apparitions. This fact left her as the one authoritative source on earth for the content, understanding and dissemination of the message of Fátima.[6]

The historical record demonstrates that Lúcia largely left the dissemination of the message to the ecclesiastical authorities.[7] Interpretations of said message also similarly appear to be left to their purview except

---

people's best efforts). See Fr. Robert J. Fox and Fr. Antonio Maria Martins, S.J., *The Intimate Life of Sister Lucia.* (Alexandria, South Dakota: Fatima Family Apostolate, 2001), 100ff.

6   Just prior to leaving Fátima for the last time, Our Lady appeared to Lúcia in April, 1921 to fulfill a promise made that she (Our Lady) would appear in Fátima "yet a seventh time." See: Carmelo de Santa Teresa – Coimbra, *Um Caminho sob o Olhar de Maria: Biografia da Irmã Lúcia de Jesus e do Coração Imaculado, O.C.D.* (Coimbra, Portugal: Edições Carmelo, 2013), 120-122. Hereafter *Um Caminho sob o Olhar de Maria* followed by page number. During this apparition, the Blessed Virgin confirmed that it was the Will of God for Lúcia to follow the directive of the Bishop.

7   Cf. the 1946 interview between Sr. Lúcia and Fr. Jongen as relayed in Frère François de Marie des Anges, *Fatima: Tragedy and Triumph.* (Buffalo, New York: Immaculate Heart Publications, 1994), 207. Hereafter *Fatima: Tragedy and Triumph* followed by page number. See also the French edition of this book entitled *Fatima Joie Intime Événement Mondial.* (Saint-Parres Lès Vaudes, France: Éditions de la Contre-Réforme Catholique, 1991), 385. Hereafter *Fatima Joie Intime Événement Mondial* followed by page number.

when it pertained to factual information.[8] Lúcia, meanwhile, having been relocated relatively soon after the end of the apparitions in 1917 allowed time for the authorities to get affairs in order (i.e., sort out the events, handle logistics, conduct proper investigations, etc.). Gradually, word of the events at Fátima spread from their Portuguese origins to other locales, most notably the French, Italian, Flemish, and English speaking areas as we will see later.

Concerning the events of 1917, Lúcia was under an order from the Blessed Virgin herself *not* to reveal the secret given in July, 1917.[9] The secret (along with later apparitions that expounded or fulfilled elements of the earlier apparitions) was only revealed later on.[10] Added to this fact is an often underrated aspect of Sr. Lúcia's personality, namely a general reluctance or hesitation for her to reveal her various supernatural experiences except under direct obedience to the competent ecclesiastical authority.

From the outset, then, one must make a critical observation: the message of Fátima would be revealed *gradually* over time from the sole surviving witness. It is thus imperative for any researcher or scholar on Fátima to exercise discretion and patience when it comes to interpretation. There is a tendency within contemporary biblical scholarship that believes "earlier is better." The same principle cannot be said of Fátima.

Between 1921 and 1935, Lúcia received further apparitions of Jesus and Mary. Most notable are the apparitions in Tuy (1929) and Pontevedra (1925). These apparitions expounded upon the devotion to the Immaculate Heart (the Five First Saturdays), as well as the request for the Holy Father

---

8   For more on this matter, see *Um Caminho sob o Olhar de Maria*, 136-144. See also the events during what took place when the book *Jacinta* was being written.

9   *Memórias e Cartas de Irmã Lúcia*, 341.

10   This fact was criticized by Fr. Edouard Dhanis in 1944/1945 as we will later see.

to consecrate Russia to the Immaculate Heart of Mary.[11] We shall not discuss these aspects of the message of Our Lady at any great length as our focus concerns the secret of Fátima, particularly its third part.

Outside of various letters and other writings (i.e. interrogations, reports), there was little written by Lúcia between 1917-1935 that provided a narrative or insight into the events of 1917.[12] This lacuna began to be filled shortly after September 12, 1935 when the corpse of Jacinta was exhumed and a picture was sent to Lúcia. She was so excited to receive this picture that she wrote a letter to Bishop da Silva about Jacinta. This letter inspired the Bishop to order Lúcia to write down her memories of Jacinta.[13]

Between 1935 and 1941, Lúcia produced four documents that covered many aspects of the message of Fátima, each one known individually as the *First Memoir*, the *Second Memoir*, etc.[14] The first, on Jacinta, was produced by December 25, 1935. The second was composed in November, 1937 and covered the history of Lúcia's life and the apparitions. The third came on August 31, 1941 and it provided further details on Jacinta's life. Finally, the fourth was written by December 8, 1941 in which Lúcia wrote further details at the prompting of the Bishop.[15]

The *Memoirs* of Lúcia would prove to be a boon for scholars and devotees alike.[16] As was stated above, there was arguably a lacuna of informa-

---

11   *Um Caminho sob o Olhar de Maria*, 168-172, 198-200.

12   Cf. Fr. Louis Kondor, SVD (edit.), *Fatima in Lucia's Own Words: Volume One*. (Fatima: Portugal: Secretariado dos Pastorinhos, 2005), 33. Hereafter *Fatima in Lucia's Own Words: Volume One* followed by page number.

13   *Memórias e Cartas de Irmã Lúcia*, 1.

14   A few decades later, Lúcia composed two further writings known as the fifth and sixth *Memoirs*.

15   Ibid., 1, 83, 215, 241.

16   For a survey on the relationship of Fátima and Mariology in the twentieth century, see Stefano de Fiores, *Il Segreto di Fatima: Una luce sul futuro del mondo*. (Milano: San Paolo Edizioni, 2008), 18-24.

tion available to the public on the events of 1917 direct from the seer's own hand. Lúcia's *Memoirs* served to fill this gap. Though they were a boon, they did not contain every detail—a fact that would continue to interest various parties for the next several decades. According to the best information available at this time, the reason why some details were left out is because Lúcia expressed reluctance to discuss her experiences.[17] Moreover, in at least one other place, she did not have permission from heaven.[18]

B. The Secret and Sr. Lúcia's *Memoirs*

For the purposes of the present history and its relationship to the third part of the secret of Fátima, it is necessary to dive into some of the material presented in Lúcia's *Memoirs*. Concerning the events of 1917, Lúcia spreads details throughout all four *Memoirs*. On the parts touching upon the "secret," the first real allusions to it can be found in the first *Memoir*.

In said *Memoir*, Lúcia halts her narrative on Jacinta at one point in order to tell the Bishop that some details touch upon the secret and she will proceed cautiously.[19] After this note, the narrative on Jacinta largely concerns her processing of the vision of hell and her heroic sacrifices for sinners up to her death in 1920. Still, however, Lúcia provides scanty information about the "secret" of July, 1917. In fact, very close to the end of the first *Memoir*, Lúcia relays one of the last words from Jacinta: never to reveal the secret.[20]

Within the next two years, Bishop da Silva came to believe that there

---

17   Cf. Joaquin Maria Alonso, C.M.F., *The Secret of Fatima: Fact and Legend.* (Cambridge, Massachusetts: The Ravengate Press, 1979), 15-18, 26-32, 61-62, 88-89, 98. Hereafter *The Secret of Fatima: Fact and Legend* followed by page number.

18   Cf. *Um Caminho sob o Olhar de Maria*, 266-268.

19   *Memórias e Cartas de Irmã Lúcia*, 33.

20   Ibid., 79.

was more to be said about Fátima.[21] He ordered Lúcia to write more in depth. This concerned her as she was careful to guard the secret.[22] After relaying details of her early life and family, Lúcia revealed that she had received apparitions of the Angel of Portugal prior to the ones of Our Lady.[23] Shortly thereafter, Lúcia begins to discuss the apparitions of Our Lady in 1917.[24] The apparition of July is not covered in much detail.[25] It finishes with details of the lives of the children post October 13, 1917 and when Lúcia left Fátima.

In the third *Memoir*, composed in 1941, Lúcia begins to describe the secret in *much* greater detail. Asked to provide more information on Jacinta, Lúcia writes that she believes heaven gave her permission to reveal (at least partially) the secret.[26] In discussing the secret, Lúcia prefaces the description by saying that the secret comprises three parts, but she is only relaying the first two. Lúcia describes these two parts as follows in her third *Memoir*:

> The first part is the vision of hell[!]
>
> Our Lady showed us a great sea of fire which seemed to be under the earth. Plunged in this fire were demons and souls in human form, like transparent burning embers, all blackened or burnished bronze, floating about in the conflagration,

---

21   Cf. the letter from Fr. Fonseca to Bishop da Silva in *Fatima in Lucia's Own Words: Volume One*, 65.

22   Cf. *Memórias e Cartas de Irmã Lúcia*, 87. Here, Lúcia makes known her obedience but that it is difficult as there is a part of her that wants to keep secret some details.

23   Ibid., 111-121.

24   Ibid., 127-165.

25   Ibid., 139.

26   Ibid., 217, 219. As to why she did not reveal it sooner, see Lúcia's own explanation on pages 233-235 of *Memórias e Cartas de Irmã Lúcia*.

now raised into the air by the flames that issued from within themselves together with great clouds of smoke, now falling back on every side like sparks in a huge fire, without weight or equilibrium, and amid shrieks and groans of pain and despair, which horrified us and made us tremble with fear. The demons could be distinguished by their terrifying and repulsive likeness to frightful and unknown animals, all black and transparent. This vision lasted but an instant. How can we ever be grateful enough to our kind heavenly Mother, who had already prepared us by promising, in the first Apparition, to take us to heaven. Otherwise, I think we would have died of fear and terror.

We then looked up at Our Lady, who said to us so kindly and so sadly:

"You have seen hell where the souls of poor sinners go. To save them, God wishes to establish in the world devotion to my Immaculate Heart. If what I say to you is done, many souls will be saved and there will be peace. The war is going to end: but if people do not cease offending God, a worse one will break out during the Pontificate of Pius XI. When you see a night illumined by an unknown light, know that this is the great sign given you by God that he is about to punish the world for its crimes, by means of war, famine, and persecutions of the Church and of the Holy Father. To prevent this, I shall come to ask for the consecration of Russia to my Immaculate Heart, and the Communion of reparation on the First Saturdays. If my requests are heeded, Russia will be converted, and there will be peace; if not, she will spread her errors throughout the world, causing wars and persecutions of the Church. The good will be martyred; the Holy Father will have much to suffer; various nations will be annihilated. In the end, my Immaculate Heart will triumph. The Holy Father will consecrate Russia to me, and she

shall be converted, and a period of peace will be granted to the world".[27]

Thus, the first two parts of the secret of Fátima pertained to 1) the vision of hell, and 2) the devotion to the Immaculate Heart of Mary and the prediction of World War II. Nothing is herein relayed about the third part of the secret.

Shortly after receiving Lúcia's third *Memoir*, Bishop da Silva ordered her to write down further details about the apparitions of the Angel of Portugal and those of Our Lady. Lúcia complied with this request and composed the fourth *Memoir*. Although charged to write about the aforementioned apparitions, Lúcia begins the fourth *Memoir* at length about Francisco.[28] After relaying details of Francisco's life, Lúcia then turns to the topic of the apparitions of the Angel of Portugal and those of Our Lady.

Lúcia prefaces said topic with a note about the circumstances as to how she was ordered to write the fourth *Memoir*, indicating her disposition to silence and that it is only by obedience that she writes.[29] It had been recommended to the Bishop that Lúcia write down everything, keeping nothing hidden. This would, of course, entail writing about the third part of the secret.[30] More on this matter is relayed in a separate chapter of the present book, thus we will only relay here the general story.

Lúcia was not ordered to write down the third part of the secret, a fact which made her rejoice.[31] In beginning her task, she wrote: "I begin,

---

27   Congregation for the Doctrine of the Faith, *The Message of Fatima*. (Vatican City: Libreria Editrice Vaticana, 2000), 15-16. Hereafter referred to as *The Message of Fatima* followed by page number. See also *Memórias e Cartas de Irmã Lúcia*, 219-221.

28   *Memórias e Cartas de Irmã Lúcia*, 247-313.

29   Ibid., 315-317.

30   Cf. *Fatima in Lucia's Own Words: Volume One*, 135.

31   *Memórias e Cartas de Irmã Lúcia*, 317.

then, my new task to fulfill your orders and the wishes of Rev. Galamba. Except for the secret that I must not reveal now, I will tell everything else. Consciously, I will omit nothing. I suppose that it is possible I may forget some little worthless details."[32] From there, she further discusses first the apparitions of the Angel of Portugal, then the apparitions of Our Lady.[33]

As the present history concerns the secret (and its third part thereof), what is of interest to us are any remarks from Lúcia on the July, 1917 apparition. Lúcia provides the narrative of this particular apparition but this time she includes details that were not present in the third *Memoir*.[34] One detail, a phrase (italicized below), has been highly controversial and *directly* affects the present discussion on the third part of the secret. Lúcia wrote:

> [Our Lady said] "To prevent this, I will come to ask the consecration of Russia to my Immaculate Heart, and the Communion of reparation on the first Saturdays. If they listen to my requests, Russia will be converted and there will be peace. If not, she will scatter her errors throughout the world, provoking wars and persecutions of the Church. The good will be martyrized, the Holy Father will have much to suffer, and various nations will be annihilated. In the end my Immaculate Heart will triumph. The Holy Father will consecrate Russia to me and it will be converted and a certain period of peace will be granted to the world. *In Portugal the dogma of the Faith will always*

---

32   Ibid.

33   Ibid., 317-329 (for the apparitions of the Angel of Portugal); 329-353 (for those apparitions of Our Lady).

34   Ibid., 337-343. These further details are characterized as "some annotations" by the Congregation for the Doctrine of the Faith in its document *The Message of Fatima* (page 4). This characterization has been criticized (cf. Christopher Ferrara, *The Secret Still Hidden*. [Pound Ridge, New York: Good Counsel Publications, 2008], 54).

be kept, etc. Tell this to no one. Francisco, yes, you may tell him..." (emphases mine).[35]

What does the above italicized phrase mean? Where is it situated within the narrative of Our Lady? Lúcia places it at the end of the second part of the secret on the devotion to the Immaculate Heart. Is it thus meant to be with the second part or is it the *incipit* (beginning) of the third? For our purposes, once all of the *Memoirs* were composed and given to Bishop da Silva, they could be published. According to the journalist Antonio Socci, the first two parts of the secret were revealed as follows:

> The first two parts of the Secret, unfortunately in an incredibly "retouched" form that favored the USSR for political and war-related reasons, were published in April 1942 in the fourth edition (printed in Vatican City) of the *Marvels of Fatima* by Padre [Luigi] da Fonseca, a Portuguese Jesuit of the Pontifical Biblical Institute in Rome. This work contained ample selections from the four Memoirs of Lucia. In May 1942 Don Luigi Moresco published *The Madonna of Fatima* with the same "retouched" version of the first two parts of the Secret. Finally, on October 13 of the same year the complete and correct text of the Memoirs was published in Portugal in the third edition of the book *Jacinta*, with the approval of Jose Galamba de Oliveira and the semi-official approval of the Portuguese Church, but always in a non-official manner, so to speak.[36]

Much interest, however, remained on the question of the third part

---

35   *Memórias e Cartas de Irmã Lúcia*, 341.

36   Antonio Socci, *The Fourth Secret of Fatima*. (Fitzwilliam, New Hampshire: Loreto Publications, 2009), 27-28. See also Joaquín María Alonso, CMF, *História da Literatura sobre Fátima*. (Fatima, Portugal: Edições Santuário, 1967), 28-33.

of the secret, which continued, arguably, from the end of 1941/early 1942 to the present (2017). During this time, one can specify various periods wherein the interest in the third part of the secret would manifest. These periods are as follows: 1941-1944; 1944-1960; 1960-2000; 2000-2005; 2005-Present. The reason for the difference of interest in these periods is based upon various developments in the history of the third part of the secret. It would complicate this history to detail precisely every aspect of each period. Instead, a basic picture will be painted and details left to the forthcoming chapters.

II. The Secret of Fátima: 1941-1944
The Third Part of the Secret Committed to Paper

After Lúcia completed the fourth *Memoir*, it appears that her decision not to reveal the third part of the secret was respected. Bishop da Silva was not amenable to the idea of plying it from her by a direct order and this was the only way by which the third part would have been communicated.

The situation changed, however, in 1943 when Lúcia became ill. Subsequent medical treatments either further impaired her health or gave her some temporary relief. There was a growing concern over whether she would survive the illness. It was out of this concern that Bishop da Silva was advised to order Lúcia to write down the third part of the secret, lest she take it with her to the grave. The Bishop acquiesced to the idea but did not issue a direct order, instead leaving her with the *option* of doing so. This situation changed when the Bishop later issued a second and direct order.[37]

Lúcia struggled to obey Bishop da Silva, but finally came to write the document on January 3, 1944.[38] It was subsequently sealed in an envelope. On the outside of this envelope was an important note from Lúcia.

---

37   *The Secret of Fatima: Fact and Legend*, 35-42.

38   *Um Caminho sob o Olhar de Maria*, 266-267.

She wrote that Our Lady *expressly* ordered that the envelope was not to be opened until 1960. Moreover, the opening was to be done by the Bishop of Leiria or the Cardinal Patriarch of Lisbon.[39] Not trusting the envelope to the postal service, apparently for security concerns, Lúcia waited until June, 1944 to hand it to the Titular Bishop of Gurza (Dom Manuel Ferreira da Silva) who in turn gave it to Bishop da Silva.[40] For his part, the Bishop kept safe the document in the archive of the Diocese of Leiria until 1957.[41]

III. The Secret of Fátima: 1944-1960
Speculation and Growing Anticipation

This second period entailed commentary and speculation upon the contents of the sealed envelope. Gradually, word had spread that Lúcia had written down the third part of the secret. People were writing about this fact and had stated that the envelope was to be opened in 1960.[42] This claim was understood to mean not just simply "opened" and "read" but also that its contents were to be divulged to the public in that year. Expectations grew as the year 1960 approached but then something unexpected happened.

Between February and April of 1957, the third part of the secret was transferred to Rome.[43] The transfer happened by way of (then) auxiliary Bishop João Venancio Pereira of the Diocese of Leiria handing it and other documents on Fátima to the Papal Nuncio, Archbishop (later Cardinal) Fernando Cento in Lisbon who, in turn, passed it on to the Holy Office.[44]

---

39   Ibid., 266.

40   Ibid., 273-277.

41   *The Secret of Fatima: Fact and Legend*, 41-48.

42   Ibid, 43, 52-55.

43   Ibid., 48-49.

44   Ibid., 50. There is some debate over two dates that have been given for the exact date of the transfer. Frère Michel de la Sainte Trinité, basing himself

There has been some speculation and debate about the reasons for this transfer, with doubts being expressed by notable Fátima scholars.[45]

Towards the end of the 1950s, there was a notable event related to the history of the third part of the secret. On December 26, 1957, a Mexican priest named Fr. Agustín Fuentes Anguiano met with Sr. Lúcia at her convent in Coimbra, Portugal.[46] Five months later, on May 22, 1958, Fuentes gave a conference in Mexico. During the conference, he remarked upon his meeting with Sr. Lúcia. These remarks were published in Spanish in October, 1958 and then in English in June, 1959.[47] Fuentes' account contained some statements he attributed to Sr. Lúcia that were quickly denied and condemned by the Diocese of Coimbra (despite the fact that it had

---

upon Fr. Joaquín María Alonso, gives the date of April 16 (cf. *The Whole Truth About Fatima. Volume III: The Third Secret.* [Buffalo, New York: Immaculate Heart Publications, 1990], 501 note 39. Hereafter *The Whole Truth About Fatima: Volume III* followed by page number). Archbishop Bertone, in his introduction to the Vatican's booklet *The Message of Fatima* (4), states that the date of the transfer was April 4, 1957. When one looks at the reference by Frère Michel to Fr. Alonso, we find an *unsourced* claim from Alonso on the date of April 16 (Fr. Joaquín María Alonso, "De Nuevo el Secreto de Fátima," *Ephemerides Mariologicae* 32, Fasc. 1 [1982]: 86). How seriously, then, should one take the date provided by Alonso?

45   Frère Michel discusses the story of the transfer from within a hermeneutic of suspicion and conspiracy (see Frère Michel de la Sainte Trinité, *The Whole Truth About Fatima. Volume III*, 479-484; 490-499). It should be noted that in his 1967 Allocution, Cardinal Ottaviani stated that the request for the transfer of the text to Rome was for its protection. This explanation did not appear to convince Fr. Alonso (cf. *The Whole Truth About Fatima: Volume III*, 483-484).

46   Joaquín María Alonso, C.M.F., *La Verdad sobre el Secreto de Fatima: Fátima sin mitos.* (Madrid, Espana: Centro Mariano, 1976), 103-106. Hereafter *La Verdad sobre el Secreto de Fatima: Fátima sin mitos* followed by page number. The account of this meeting is better known in the English language through a French translation given in Frère Michel de la Sainte Trinité, *The Whole Truth About Fatima: Volume III*, 503-522.

47   *Fatima Findings* (June, 1959), page 1.

been supported by the Bishop of Leiria).[48] Fuentes' account agitated the heightened expectations of the public on the third part of the secret.

It was also during this time period of 1944-1960 that one of the most significant developments occurred in the history of Fátima. Publishing Sr. Lúcia's *Memoirs* afforded people a closer look into the events of 1917, but they also gave rise to criticisms. In 1945, a Jesuit scholar named Fr. Edouard Dhanis published a book in the Flemish language entitled *On the Apparitions and Secret of Fatima: A Critical Contribution.*[49] This book was a compilation of two articles that he wrote for the publication *Streven* in 1944.[50] The topic of both publications was to provide a critical examination of Fátima.

Dhanis' book (and articles) has never received a complete translation into the English language.[51] Information about it, along with *partial* translations, largely comes to an English-speaking audience through other sources who provide quotations from Dhanis' work(s).[52] According to

---

48   *Novidades*, 4 July 1959 (Lisboa), #74.

49   *Bij de verschijningen en het geheim van Fatima: een critische bijdrage.* (Brugge-Brussel: De Kinkhoren, 1945).

50   Cf. Fr. Robert Graham, S.J., *Profezie di Guerra: Fatima e la Russia nella propaganda dei belligeranti dopo il 1942* (La Civiltà Cattolica, Year 132 [1981], Volume 4, Issues 3151-3156, page 23). Graham cites the periodical entitled *Streven XI* (1944), 129-149; 193-215. He also points out that Dhanis wrote another article entitled *A propos de «Fatima et la critique»* in the publication *Nouvelle Revue Théologique* LXXIV (1952), 580-606.

51   Some of Dhanis' general criticisms were expressed in the English language through his Jesuit confrere C.C. Martindale in his book *The Message of Fatima*. (London: Burns Oates and Washbourne Ltd, 1950).

52   Arguably, what is known of it in the English-speaking world largely comes through the French writer Frère Michel de la Sainte Trinité. Many of Frère Michel's writings on Fátima have been translated into English. For his treatment of Fr. Dhanis, see Frère Michel de la Sainte Trinité, *The Whole Truth About Fatima, Volume I: Science and the Facts*. (Buffalo, New York: Immaculate Heart Publications, 1989), 381-524. Hereafter *The Whole Truth About Fatima: Volume I* followed by page number. For a more complete list of other publica-

at least one of these sources, Dhanis proposed a "thesis" on Fátima that distinguished between what is called "Fatima I" and "Fatima II." The distinction between the two is essentially "old" Fátima (I) and "new" Fátima (II).[53] Dhanis accepted as authentic the events of 1917, but expressed reservations concerning later events, developments or descriptions.

A distinctive characteristic in Dhanis' writings was to question the memory of Sr. Lúcia.[54] Dhanis wrote a new article in 1952 in the French language entitled *On «Fatima and Criticism»* which was a response to some criticisms that his book had received. In this article, Dhanis wrote that Sr. Lúcia may have engaged in an "unconscious fabrication" when writing her *Memoirs* about events that occurred twenty years prior:

> All things considered...it is not easy to state precisely what degree of credence is to be given to the accounts of Sister Lucy. Without questioning her sincerity, or the sound judgment she shows in daily life, one may judge it prudent to use her writings only with reservations....Let us observe also that a person can be sincere and prove to have good judgment in everyday life, but have a propensity for unconscious fabrication in a certain area, or in any case, a tendency to relate old memories of twenty years ago with embellishments and considerable modifications.[55]

---

tions that discuss Dhanis' book and/or thesis, see Karl Rahner, *Visioni e profezie: mistica ed esperienza della trascendenza.* (Milano: Vita e Pensiero, 1995), 38 (second edition).

53   *The Whole Truth About Fatima: Volume I,* 394, 396.

54   Ibid., 401-403.

55   Ibid., 402. Frère Michel cites the article "On Fatima and Criticism" in the periodical *Nouvelle Revue Théologique* (1952), 583-584. Dhanis' article is originally titled in French, "A propos de «Fatima de la critique»." This article responded to criticism from Fr. Luigi Gonzaga da Fonseca in a book entitled *Fatima y la Critica* (Santander, 1952). This book was originally published in the Portuguese periodical *Brotéria*.

Dhanis' thesis caused much scholarly debate.[56] For our aims, we must ask whether Dhanis' writings affected the history of the third part of the secret.

The history of the third part of the secret *is* affected by the logical consequence of Dhanis' writings. For now, if events after 1917 were affected by "unconscious fabrication" from Sr. Lúcia, then the third part would likewise come under this characterization. Written in 1944, the reliability of the text and/or its supernatural character would be scrutinized, or even discredited.[57] If it can be discredited, then an argument can be made for its contents not to be heeded. One is then forced to ask who will be influenced by and adhere to Dhanis' critical observations and their pursuant logic. This question will arise once more when we look at some later history.[58]

---

56   Fr. Joaquín María Alonso wrote about these events (*História da Literatura sobre Fátima*. [Fatima, Portugal: Edições Santuário, 1967], 35-51). Hereafter *História da Literatura sobre Fátima* followed by page number. For another summary of the debate after 1944/1945, see: José Barreto, "*Edouard Dhanis, Fatima e a II Guerra Mundial*," *Brotéria* 156, January (2003): 13-22. This article is available on the Internet from the *Brotéria* publication: <http://broteria.pt/images/books/pdf/Janeiro_2003.pdf> (Accessed 8 March, 2016). The former Jesuit, Fr. Malachi Martin, described Fr. Dhanis as being a "stalwart conservative" (Malachi Martin, *The Jesuits*. [New York, New York: Simon & Schuster, 1987], 269).

57   Cf. *The Whole Truth about Fatima: Volume I*, 403-404.

58   There is some question about the *precise* influence of Dhanis' thesis in Rome. Frère Michel, using a hermeneutic of suspicion and controversy, argues for a decisive influence (*The Whole Truth About Fatima: Volume III*, 274-277; 327-329; 389-395; 407; 495-499). His argument appeared to have been given credence in the year 2000 when the Vatican released the text of the third part of the secret on June 26 of that year. Cardinal Ratzinger, in his *Theological Commentary*, cited Dhanis. This one citation appears to be indicative of Dhanis having had some enduring influence in Rome concerning Fátima, despite the various responses collated by Fr. Alonso cited above. Finally, the best efforts of some writers notwithstanding, there appears to be conflicting or circumstantial evidence that Dhanis' writings deeply impacted the opening and release to the public of the third part of the secret from 1960 onward.

IV. The Secret of Fátima: 1960-2000
The Vatican Withholds Publication

The expectations of the publication of the third part of the secret came to naught in early February, 1960. The A.N.I. (*Agência Nacional de Informação*) published a short news article dated the eighth of that month written by an unnamed United Press International (UPI) reporter.[59] Based upon information obtained from unspecified "Vatican circles," the reporter wrote that the Vatican "most likely" would never release Lúcia's text and three reasons were provided.[60] The reaction to this news was mixed, and in accordance with one's interest on the subject. For devotees of Fátima, the news was not well-received. Other people, such as certain scholars and even some ecclesiastics, were indifferent.[61]

The article appeared to have adopted a skeptical tone. It stated that "Although the Church recognizes the apparitions of Fátima, she does not desire to take the obligation [to] guarantee the veracity of the words that the three pastorinhos said that the Virgin Mary had directed to them."[62] One cannot help but wonder if the writings of Fr. Dhanis were behind such a highly skeptical statement. There is, however, little to no definitive

---

59   This news article has elsewhere been described as a "press release." This term appears to be slightly misleading as it was not issued by any ecclesiastical authority and contains information that appears to be based upon rumors circulating in the Vatican. We shall endeavor to discuss this matter more at length in a later chapter.

60   The Portuguese original is very difficult to obtain in its original publication, but it was reproduced by Sebastião Martins dos Reis in his book *O Milagre do Sol e o Segredo de Fátima: Inconsequências e especulações*. (Porto: Edições Salesianas, 1966), 127-128. Hereafter *O Milagre do Sol* followed by page number.

61   Cf. *The Whole Truth About Fatima: Volume III*, 573-620.

62   *O Milagre do Sol*, 128. There are legitimate questions about the author of this article and his or her sources which may have a bearing on interpreting the A.N.I. article.

evidence for this theory and remains a matter of dispute.

The decision of the Vatican not to publish the text had the effect of causing further speculation upon the third part of the secret. One of the more reasonable speculations that was said to be endorsed by the Cardinal Patriarch of Lisbon (Manuel Cerejeira) was the idea that the third part must have pertained to something very serious otherwise it would have been released.[63] Such speculations were not lacking because not only did the Vatican never issue an official statement on the matter in 1960, it was generally silent on the matter. The first time any major Vatican authority figure addressed the public on the matter was in 1967.

On February 11, 1967, Alfredo Cardinal Ottaviani, the Prefect of the Sacred Congregation for the Doctrine of the Faith (CDF, formerly the "Holy Office"), delivered an Allocution at the Antonianum in Rome.[64] His remarks were delivered *ex tempore* though he did have a prepared text. Owing to his status as the Prefect of the CDF, Ottaviani's Allocution was the most authoritative statement on the matter. He provided details as to how Sr. Lúcia's text was transferred to Rome as well as how Pope John XXIII (r. 1958-1963) read the document and made the decision not to disclose it.

The information from the Cardinal's Allocution was added to by subsequent statements from other people for the next thirty-three years.[65] His

---

63   *The Whole Truth About Fatima: Volume III*, 589 and 667.

64   *Acta Pontificiae Academiae Marianae Internationalis vel ad Academiam quoquo modo pertinentia. Volume 4.* (Romae: Pontificia Academia Mariana Internationalis, 1967), 44-49. An earlier Allocution, dated May 13, 1955 and delivered in the Cova da Iria (Fátima), from Cardinal Ottaviani sheds some light on his 1967 Allocution. See: *Lumen: Revista de Cultura do Clero* 19 (Maio-Junho,1955), 264-268. This text is reproduced in English in the appendices of the present book.

65   There have been a few unofficial accounts of how the decision came about. The first is the Allocution given by Cardinal Ottaviani. The next was a statement by Pope John XXIII's private secretary, Archbishop (later Cardinal) Loris Capovilla in 1977, then interviews in 1978, 1994/1995, ca. 1997/1998,

words, however, would be taken very seriously owing to his status and the fact that he read Sister's text. He had a fundamental role in shaping the discussion on the third part of the secret for decades to come.

A. Fátima, Communism and *Aggiornamento*

Regardless of the Vatican's silence, it is clear that "fervor" over the third part of the secret was present among the public. This fervor kept alive the third part in people's minds, for good or for ill.[66] Around the time of the non-release of the third part was the announcement by John XXIII of his intention to convoke an Ecumenical Council (Vatican II).[67] The orientation of this Council, according to John XXIII, was to "update" (*aggiornamento*) the Church, and offer mercy to the world and not condemnation.[68]

This orientation raised concerns over the response of the Church to Communism. Previous Popes displayed open opposition towards it. After seeing its concrete manifestation in Russia from 1917 onward and the horrible atrocities it brought, Pius XI (r. 1922-1939) warned the Catholic faithful against it most especially in his Encyclical *Divini Redemptoris*.[69] Twelve years later, Pius XII (r. 1939-1958) declared through the Holy Of-

---

2000 and finally in 2006/2007.

66   As theories and speculations grew, people became highly influenced by these ideas and anticipation grew. One author even attempted to divine significance out of expressions on Sr. Lúcia's face (see *Fatima: Tragedy and Triumph*, 203-204)! This particular example concerns the question of the consecration of Russia. It demonstrates, however, the overall point, namely the lengths that people underwent in order to justify certain interpretations of the message of Fátima.

67   *Acta Apostolicae Sedis* 51 (1959), 65-69.

68   Cf. Pope John XXIII's opening speech at the Second Vatican Council entitled *Gaudet Mater Ecclesia* in *Acta Apostolicae Sedis* 54 (1962), 786-795.

69   *Acta Apostolicae Sedis* 29 (1937), 65-106.

fice that Catholics could not collaborate with Communists.[70] In all, Catholics were always to be on guard against Communists as they were wicked and perverse, and sought to subvert the Christian moral and social order.

For its part, the message of Fátima is intimately connected with the Church's struggle against atheistic Communism.[71] In July, 1917, Our Lady made known her intention to request at a future point the consecration of Russia to her Immaculate Heart in order to save this country and to avoid the spread of the errors inherent to atheistic Communism to the rest of the world.[72] This intention was fulfilled in 1929 by a successive apparition of Our Lady to Lúcia in Tuy (Spain), but which went unheeded by the Holy Father (Pius XI).[73] His successor, Pius XII, twice attempted the consecration (1942 and 1952 respectively) but it was not done as specified by Our Lady.[74] By the end of the pontificate of Pius XII, time had been afforded to Russia to spread its errors and they quickly did so.

At the election of John XXIII to the Papacy in October, 1958, the world appeared to be in a dire situation with Communism. John, however, took a stunning course of action. He *reversed* his predecessors' policy by entering into dialogue with Communist officials. This policy became known as *Ostpolitik* ("East Politics").[75] His policy reversal was met with utter exasperation by the Abbé Georges de Nantes, founder of the Little Brothers of the

---

70   *Acta Apostolicae Sedis* 41 (1949), 334.

71   For a good expounding upon this connection, see the Allocution of Cardinal Cerejeira in *La Documentation Catholique* 49 (March 19, 1967), columns 546-552.

72   Cf. *Memórias e Cartas de Irmã Lúcia*, 341.

73   *Um Caminho sob o Olhar de Maria*, 198-199.

74   See *Acta Apostolicae Sedis* 34 (1942), 313-325; *Acta Apostolicae Sedis* 44 (1952), 505-511. As to these acts not being done according to the specifications of Our Lady, cf. *Um Caminho sob o Olhar de Maria*, 198-206.

75   *Fatima: Tragedy and Triumph*, 55-79.

Sacred Heart community and the "League of Catholic Counter-Reform."[76]

Writing from France, the Abbé de Nantes was deeply concerned that the heresy of Modernism that had been condemned by Pope St. Pius X in 1907 had reached the "highest summits of the Church."[77] Moreover, he was horrified that the new orientation of John XXIII included a lack of willingness to condemn Communism both prior to and during the Second Vatican Council.[78] The message of Fátima with its clear and unequivocal warning against Communism, confirmed by the miracle of the sun in October, 1917, would become a rallying point for the Abbé.

The subsequent claim arose from the Abbé de Nantes' organizations that Rome has essentially rejected Fátima.[79] Over the years, this claim

---

76   For a synopsis of the Abbé Georges de Nantes, see the short biography about him entitled "Fidei Defensor" on his League of Counter-Reform's web site: <http://crc-internet.org/our-founder/fidei-defensor/> (Accessed 1 January, 2016).

77   See Pius X's Encyclical *Pascendi Dominici Gregis* in *Acta Sanctae Sedis*, 40 (1907), 593-650. For the Abbé de Nantes' concern about Modernism and the Church, see: <http://crc-internet.org/our-doctrine/catholic-counter-reformation/for-the-church/3-founding-league-crc/> (Accessed 1 January, 2016). See also the influence of the Abbé on Frère François in *Fatima: Tragedy and Triumph*, 267, 287.

78   Cf. *Fatima: Tragedy and Triumph*, 48-50, 58-74. Most of these pages are the telling of events from Frère François. It is, however, to be noted that he published the French original under the auspices of the Abbé de Nantes who would never have published the book if he did not agree with its contents. For a more balanced critique of Communism and the Second Vatican Council, see Michael Davies, *Pope John's Council*. (Kansas City, Missouri: Angelus Press, 2007), 233-255.

79   One can see examples of this train of thought in various forms in the literature. See *Fatima: Tragedy and Triumph*, 55, 74, 81ff. The Abbé de Nantes also appears to have taken *much* interest in the third part of the secret. Basing himself upon the fact that the text was not released in the year 1960 as was the public expectation, the Abbé wrote in his *Book of Accusations Against Paul VI* (1973):

Your silence can have no other result...on the true Message of Fatima,

(amid other Fátima-related themes) became prominent in the literature published under the auspices of the Abbé and his organizations.[80] As we will see further below, there were two important people that became the focal points for the Abbé's rallying cry, namely Frère Michel of the Holy

---

soon after your pilgrimage, than to transform into terrible reality the threats of new punishments which form beyond doubt the essence of the Third Secret, if only by analogy with the first two. If it is not allowed to know the terrible fate with which it is threatened by Heaven, the world will not become converted, and will drift unchecked into a mire of filth and a bath of blood. There will be a Third World War, Communism will spread its persecutions, atomic war will bring its untold ravages, and there will come the Great Apostasy of Christians. And because they have not received the warning and been called to conversion, the peoples will lose not only their lives but also their faith.

The Abbé de Nantes then continued this theme by presenting his opinion that Sr. Lúcia wanted to speak with Paul VI privately to request that the third part of the secret be released. He wrote:

As the wishes of Heaven do not change, I believe that Sister Lucy wanted to implore the Pope, the other day, to make known to the world the warnings of Our Lady and that, perhaps, she had been charged with making this request as a sort of final appeal, an ultimatum. The cup is overflowing, iniquity has reached its fill. It is absolutely vital that the entire Church should be made aware into what abyss of sin mankind is sinking

(<http://crc-internet.org/further-information/liber-accusationis/in-paulum--sextum/fatima-profaned/> [Accessed 13 July, 2016]).

80   Two notices were issued by the Congregation for the Doctrine of the Faith concerning the Abbé. The first instance was in August, 1969 in *L'Osservatore Romano* and was translated into French for the periodical *La Documentation Catholique* 66 (1969), pages 794-796. The second notice was issued on May 13, 1983 and published in *L'Osservatore Romano* (May 16/17, 1983 edition, page 2). Both documents are available on the Vatican's web site: <http://www.vatican.va/roman_curia/congregations/cfaith/doc_doc_index_it.htm> (Accessed 1 January, 2016).

Trinity and Frère François de Marie des Anges.[81]

The Abbé's concern for the direction of the Church coincided with the date of 1960 that Sr. Lúcia stipulated the envelope containing the third part could be opened. Between the text not being revealed, and the concerns over the orientations of John XXIII, the Abbé supported the idea that the third part of the secret referred to an apostasy in the Church.[82] This theory would grow and come to influence other influential people who were gravely concerned about Communist infiltration.[83] The warnings present in the message of Fátima against atheistic Communism thus became a living hope for people who shared similar (if not the same) concerns with the Abbé de Nantes.[84] Our Lady's warning is a part of her message, they

---

81   For a stark example of the Abbé's denunciation of *Ostpolitik*, see *Fatima: Tragedy and Triumph*, 284-285. For an intriguing discussion on the effects of the efforts of the Abbe and other like-minded individuals, see Fr. Joaquín María Alonso, "De Nuevo el Secreto de Fátima," *Ephemerides Mariologicae* 32, Fasc. 1 (1982): 93. Hereafter *De Nuevo el Secreto de Fátima* followed by page number. See also *Fatima 50* (January, 1968, number 9, page 17 [p. 32 for a summary in English]), Fr. Alonso names a few publications that subscribe to the idea that Fátima is "anti-conciliar, anti-ecumenical, reactionary, retrograde and triumphalistic." He specifies them as «*Réforme*», «*Nuovi-Tempi*» and «*Les Informations Catholiques Internationales*».

82   *The Whole Truth About Fatima: Volume III*, 623ff. No statement is being made on the merits of this theory in the present book.

83   Cf. Christopher Ferrara, *False Friends of Fatima*. (Pound Ridge, New York: Good Counsel Publications, 2012), 86. Hereafter *False Friends of Fatima* followed by page number. Dr. Alice von Hildebrand, wife of the late Dr. Dietrich von Hildebrand, made a public statement which touched upon this very matter. See the article entitled "Alice von Hildebrand Sheds New Light on Fatima" available on the Internet web site *One Peter Five*: <http://www.onepeterfive. com/alice-von-hildebrand-sheds-new-light-fatima/> (Accessed 14 May, 2016).

84   Dr. Joaquín Navarro-Valls gave an interview with the periodical *Corriere della Serra* (18 May, 2000). Navarro-Valls was asked about the impending publication of the third part of the secret and "anti-ecumenical" groups. Navarro-Valls responded:

The publication of the prophecy will not imply at all a papal support

argued, and it was being rejected by the Vatican in favor of *Ostpolitik*.[85]

It is here that our attention turns from the French speaking world to the English. In this world, and for our topic, there is one person in particular that merits attention. This person is Fr. Nicholas Gruner, the founder of the "Fatima Center" and its publication *The Fatima Crusader*.[86] For our purposes, it suffices to say that Gruner engaged in various efforts at promoting Fátima that had a noticeable impact on the English-speaking world.[87]

Fr. Gruner's efforts included publishing the above-mentioned period-

---

of anti-ecumenical traditionalism, which had illegally appropriated some aspects of the message of Fátima, speculating in a millenarian tone on one's presumptions, but not the actual content of the unpublished text. The decision to publish it comes, in fact, from the conviction that one cannot leave Fátima hostage to a partisan position. When it will be known, every aspect of the message of Fátima will regain the right balance, and together will be better understood by all (translation by Kevin J. Symonds).

This interview was reproduced in PDF format on Dr. Navarro-Valls' personal web site in both PDF format as well as a transcription: <http://www.navarro--valls.info/cms/index.php/en/component/content/article.html?id=4> (Accessed 5 December, 2015).

85   Another name, used by the Abbé de Nantes himself, for those who question *Ostpolitik* in the light of Fátima (cf. *Fatima: Tragedy and Triumph*, 161; *Fatima Joie Intime Événement Mondial*, 358) is "Fatimists" (*fatimistes*).

86   An entire biography on Fr. Gruner has been made available by his Fatima Center and so there is no need to recount his life in great detail (Christopher A. Ferrara and Francis Alban, *Fatima Priest*. [Pound Ridge, New York: Good Counsel Publications, 2013]. Hereafter *Fatima Priest* followed by page number). Fr. Gruner passed away on April 29, 2015 and his Requiem Mass was celebrated by Bishop Bernard Fellay, the successor to Archbishop Marcel Lefebvre as head of the Society of St. Pius X (SSPX). See *The Fatima Crusader*, Summer 2015, Issue 112 and <http://sspx.org/en/news-events/news/fr-gruner-requiescat--pace-8151> (Accessed 1 January, 2016).

87   For an alternative, and more objective view to the life and work of Fr. Gruner, see Michael W. Cuneo, *The Smoke of Satan*. (New York: Oxford University Press, 1997), 45-46, 81-87, 134-152 (see also the citations on pages 188, 195, 202-205).

ical *The Fatima Crusader*, as well as offering talks, lectures and organizing conferences on the message of Fátima. At first, these efforts largely included literature on the consecration of Russia and how Pope John Paul II needed to fulfill this request in order to obtain world peace. This focus was modified, however, from the year 2000 onward as we will see further below.[88]

There was some collaboration between the Abbé de Nantes and Fr. Gruner. This collaboration involved the persons and figures of two members of the Abbé's Little Brothers of the Sacred Heart community, Frère Michel of the Holy Trinity and Frère François de Marie des Anges. The Abbé de Nantes had charged Frère Michel in 1981 with studying and writing extensively on the history of Fátima.[89] The results of this study were published in a lengthy three-volume work in French entitled *Toute la Vérité sur Fatima* between 1983 and 1985, of which the third installment is particularly relevant to our purposes.[90] The above volumes were rendered into English and published by Gruner as *The Whole Truth About Fatima*.[91]

For his part, Frère François became more involved in this work on Fátima after Frère Michel left the Little Brothers community in 1989. The Abbé de Nantes had ordered Frère François to continue the unfinished work of Frère Michel (a fourth volume on Fátima).[92] The work of Frère François concerning Fátima largely revolved around an abridged version of Frère Michel's work and was entitled *Fatima: Joie Intime Événement Mondial* in 1991. This was translated into English in four

---

88   Cf. *Fatima Priest*, 231.

89   Cf. *Fatima: Tragedy and Triumph*, v.

90   Frère Michel de la Sainte Trinité, *Toute la Vérité sur Fatima: Le Troisième Secret (1942-1960)*. (Saint-Parres lès Vaudes, France: Renaissance Catholique Contre-Réforme Catholique, 1985). Hereafter *Toute la Vérité sur Fatima: Volume III* followed by page number.

91   *The Whole Truth About Fatima: Volume III,* 601ff.

92   *Fatima: Tragedy and Triumph*, vii-ix.

volumes by 1994 and was also published by Fr. Gruner, the fourth of which pertains directly to our purposes and is entitled *Fatima: Tragedy and Triumph.*

Between Frère Michel and Frère François, combined with the promotional efforts and literature of Fr. Gruner, an influential body of literature in English on Fátima began to grow. There appears to have been no serious study done in English by competent historians on Fátima that either assesses the impact of this literature or provides scholarly criticism of it in its totality.[93] Based, however, upon the literature of Fr. Gruner's Fatima Center, one receives the distinct impression that Frère Michel certainly had an unmistakable influence.[94] This influence is due to Frère Michel's ability to gather various sources (from a number of languages) into a specific narrative, one that involves a hermeneutic of suspicion and conspiracy.[95] It also raises, however, a question on the reliability of a "translation of a translation."[96]

---

93   Frère François provides notes of praise from respected authorities on Fátima in *Fatima: Tragedy and Triumph*, v-vii. He also discusses one particular attempt to criticize Frère Michel by Fr. Antonio Maria Martins (see *Fatima: Tragedy and Triumph*, vi, 289-290). Concerning criticism, there was a point made by Antonio Socci regarding a faulty translation in Frère Michel (cf. *The Fourth Secret of Fatima*, 95). Finally, there was the effort of Tarcisio Cardinal Bertone in 2007 to attempt an explanation of some matters pertaining to the third part of the secret with his book *L'Ultima Veggente di Fatima: I Miei Colloqui con Suor Lucia.* (Milano: Rai Eri Rizzoli, 2007).

94   Much of the literature from about 1985 onward from Gruner's Fatima Center will refer to Frère Michel.

95   Examples of this hermeneutic are given in later chapters of the present work.

96   Frère Michel's books were composed in the French language. His sources were not always in this language and yet the quotes are given in French. When his three volumes were translated into English, how were the sources treated? Did the translator, John Collorafi, consult the original texts to amend his English translation or did he simply go by the French text of Frère Michel?

V. The Secret of Fátima: 2000-2005
The Third Part of the Secret Revealed and Questioned

In May, 2000, Pope John Paul II was in Fátima for the beatification of Francisco and Jacinta Marto. On May 13, after the Mass of Beatification, Cardinal Angelo Sodano, the Vatican Secretary of State, announced that the Holy Father had decided to release the third part of the secret. Sodano gave its contents *in brevis* and further stated that it would be published in its entirety under the auspices of the CDF.[97] This publication took place on June 26, 2000 during a press conference by Joseph Cardinal Ratzinger and Archbishop Tarcisio Bertone (Prefect and Secretary respectively of the CDF), with the Holy See Press Office director, Dr. Joaquín Navarro-Valls. A booklet was issued entitled *The Message of Fátima*.[98]

The publication of the third part of the secret in *The Message of Fatima* raised many questions. The text of the third part (as well as the accompanying statements, documents and *Theological Commentary*) was subject to what can only be called severe scrutiny by some journalists and other writers. At the helm of these, at least in the English-speaking world, was Fr. Nicholas Gruner and his Fatima Center. Gruner disbelieved that the secret had been fully revealed and quickly accused the Holy See of a cover-up.[99]

From the year 2000 onward, Gruner believed there was a "new urgency" for his organization to devote more attention to the third part of the

---

97   *The Message of Fatima*, 30-31.

98   For some commentary on this booklet from a non-polemical source, see the essay by José Jacinto Ferreira de Farias, "Les révélations privées dans la vie de l'Église, À propos du «Message de Fatima» de la Congrégation de la Doctrine pour la Foi (26 Juin 2000). Analyse et Interprétation." *Apparitiones Beatae Mariae Virginis in Historia, Fide, Theologica*. (Città del Vaticano, Pontificia Academia Mariana Internationalis, 2010). 59-76, especially 69-75.

99   Cf. *The Fatima Crusader*, Issue 64 (Summer, 2000). This issue is available online: <http://www.fatimacrusader.com/cr64/toc64.asp> (Accessed 1 January, 2016).

secret.[100] Gruner theorized that the "entire" secret had not been divulged to the public.[101] Three arguments in particular put forth by Gruner and his associates stand out. The first was the phrase discussed earlier, namely "In Portugal the dogma of the Faith shall always be kept etc." Much of the argumentation in this initial period surrounded the "etc" and how "incomplete" the phrase sounded.[102]

Secondly, Frère Michel wrote that the third part of the secret comprised 20-25 lines.[103] The text released by the Vatican was a little over 60. The contradiction made significant Frère Michel's observation, which became important for Gruner and his associates in their arguments. Third, and finally, the last principle argument was that there must be a "second text" with an explanation from the Blessed Virgin on the text released in 2000. The foundation for this argument was essentially that it made no sense for the Blessed Virgin to give a vision without providing an explanation when she had done so in the previous two parts.[104]

---

100   Cf. *Fatima Priest*, 231.

101   In the Summer 2000 issue of *The Fatima Crusader*, Gruner argued for two documents and that "security problems" may be to blame for the "missing" second text. See "The Other Manuscript: What To Do About It!" available online: <http://www.fatimacrusader.com/cr64/cr64pg08.asp> (Accessed 1 January, 2016).

102   See another interview in the Summer 2000 issue of *The Fatima Crusader* with Fr. Gruner entitled "The 3rd Secret Vision Explained." This interview is available online: <http://www.fatimacrusader.com/cr64/cr64pg18.asp> (Accessed 1 January, 2016). See also the article by Fr. Paul Kramer in the same issue of *The Fatima Crusader* entitled, "Third Secret Revealed But Not All Of It!" The article is available online: <http://www.fatimacrusader.com/cr64/cr64pg28.asp> (Accessed 1 January, 2016).

103   *The Whole Truth About Fatima: Volume III*, 707. The French text reads, "De fait, elle se rendait sûrement compte que par ces vingt lignes elle allait lancer dans l'histoire de l'Église, dans l'histoire du monde, un évènement d'une portée formidable" (*Toute la Vérité sur Fatima: Volume III*, 474).

104   Cf. Christopher A. Ferrara, *The Secret Still Hidden*. (Pound Ridge, New York: Good Counsel Publications, 2008), 51. See also Antonio Socci, *The*

In 2002, many supporting arguments for the theory of a second text were organized into a book entitled *The Devil's Final Battle* by Gruner's long-time associate Fr. Paul L. Kramer.[105] In this book, Kramer details most, if not all, of the prior two years of argumentation, evidence and theories as to why the text released by the Vatican could not be the "entire" secret. This book was subsequently translated into several languages and underwent a revision in the year 2010 with over 100 pages added.[106]

VI. The Secret of Fátima: 2005-Present Controversy Continues

We come at last to the final period of the history of the third part of the secret of Fátima. The year 2005 saw the deaths of both Sr. Lúcia and Pope John Paul II within two months of each other (February 13 and April 2 respectively). Also, published this year was the writing of an Italian researcher named Dr. Solideo Paolini entitled *Fatima. Do not Despise the Prophecy: Reconstruction of the Unpublished Part of the Third Secret*.[107] Paolini would become a catalyst in the debate on Fátima owing largely to a later interview with a witness to a key moment in the history of the third part of the secret.

Fourth Secret of Fatima. (Fitzwilliam, New Hampshire: Loreto Publications, 2009), 66.

105   Fr. Paul L. Kramer, *The Devil's Final Battle*. (Terryville, Connecticut: The Missionary Association, 2002). Hereafter *The Devil's Final Battle* followed by page number.

106   Fr. Paul L. Kramer, *The Devil's Final Battle: Our Lady's Victory Edition*. (Terryville, Connecticut: The Missionary Association, 2010).

107   *Fatima. Non Disprezzate le Profezie. Ricostruzione della Parte non Pubblicata del Terzo Segreto.* (Segno, 2005). Copies of this book are now nearly impossible to obtain. Note that Paolini is mentioned here in this present history insofar as he served as a catalyst for the events that arose at this time. The merits of his claims are not examined.

During the summer of 2006, Paolini spoke with the personal secretary to Pope John XXIII, Archbishop (later Cardinal) Loris Capovilla. Capovilla was present when the late Pope opened the envelope and read its contents in August, 1959. He was the last living witness to this moment and his testimony carried much import. Paolini claims that Capovilla indicated to him there was more to the third part of the secret than was released in June, 2000.

Such a testimony, if true, would surely be a boon for those who questioned the Vatican. Paolini, however, remained little noticed until his works were brought out into the mainstream Italian media through the work of the journalist and "Vaticanista" Antonio Socci. For reasons his own, Socci decided to investigate the matter of an alleged second text of the third part of the secret. He published his findings in the book *Il Quarto Segreto di Fatima* in November, 2006.[108] This book was subsequently translated into English in 2009 as *The Fourth Secret of Fatima*.[109]

As a part of his examination into the claims of a second text, Socci went over various writers such as Frère Michel, Fr. Gruner and Fr. Kramer. He also obtained a copy of Paolini's 2005 book and incorporated discussion of it.[110] It is clear that even while Socci questions some of the arguments, he concludes there is, in fact, another text to the third part of the secret. He places a lot of weight and credibility upon Paolini's work and asks why such questions were not being openly addressed by the ecclesiastical authorities.[111]

---

108   Antonio Socci, *Il Quarto Segreto di Fatima*. (Rizzoli, 2006). Hereafter *Il Quarto Segreto di Fatima* followed by page number. This book underwent a second edition in March, 2010 by BUR Saggi. This author is in possession of the second edition.

109   Antonio Socci, *The Fourth Secret of Fatima*. (Fitswilliams, New Hampshire: Loreto Publications, 2009). Hereafter *The Fourth Secret of Fatima* followed by page number.

110   *The Fourth Secret of Fatima*, 129-167.

111   Ibid., 1-5; *Il Quarto Segreto di Fatima*, 11-14.

Socci's *The Fourth Secret of Fatima* posed a notable challenge. Not only was Socci a mainstream Italian journalist, he had, up to that point, enjoyed a good relationship with the new Vatican Secretary of State, Tarcisio Cardinal Bertone. Socci's book essentially took the arguments out of a select circle of people and put the matter before the general public who respected his work. That public was beginning to ask questions.

Against these events, Cardinal Bertone published his own book. His involvement with the booklet *The Message of Fatima* placed him in a unique position to address the matter at hand. Bertone, with the help of Italian journalist Giuseppe De Carli, published the book *L'Ultima Veggente di Fatima: I Miei Colloqui con Suor Lucia* in May, 2007. This book was subsequently translated into English in 2008 as *The Last Secret of Fatima*.[112]

The book is a long dialogue between the Cardinal and De Carli wherein questions and answers are provided on Fátima and other subjects. While some intriguing details come out during the course of their dialogue, it did not satisfy Fr. Gruner, his associates and others. In fact, it could be argued that the opposite effect occurred by the raising of *more* questions.

As part of the promotion for the book, in May, 2007, Cardinal Bertone appeared via teleconference on the popular Italian TV program *Porta a Porta* with host Bruno Vespa and a panel (including Giuseppe De Carli). Bertone fielded questions from Vespa and the panel. The Cardinal also did something heretofore never done in the history of the third part of the secret. He had brought with him the text of Lúcia's document enclosed in the famous envelope.[113] He revealed them, one by one *on camera* for all to

---

112   Cardinal Tarcisio Bertone, *The Last Secret of Fatima*. (New York: Doubleday, 2008).

113   It is imperative to note that Bertone revealed there were two envelopes with inscriptions from Lúcia. The second contained the text of the third part of the secret and this envelope was contained within another envelope. Both envelopes and the text were within a larger envelope sealed by Bishop da Silva. The existence of two envelopes was not a detail previously known in the history or the literature.

see. Again, however, it is possible to argue that this teleconference raised more questions than answers.[114] Bertone, later in 2007, then appeared at the Urbaniana in Rome where he gave a talk and presented a video interview between Giuseppe De Carli and Archbishop Capovilla.

In 2008, an associate of Fr. Gruner's, attorney Christopher Ferrara, published a book of his own entitled *The Secret Still Hidden*.[115] In this book, Ferrara attempts to advance the thesis of a second text of the third part of the secret by questioning the Vatican. There has never been a formal response from the Holy See on this particular book, though a second edition of Bertone/De Carli's book was published in 2010 with some corrections that, in effect, addressed some points found in *The Secret Still Hidden*.[116]

Also in 2010 and as part of the promotion of the second edition of the book, Giuseppe De Carli attended a conference organized by Fr. Gruner. He was asked questions by an audience eager to have the opportunity to speak to a close collaborator of Bertone's.[117] De Carli passed away a few months later.[118] Also, as was noted earlier, 2010 is the year wherein Fr.

---

114   Socci responded to Bertone in *Dear Cardinal Bertone: Who Between You and Me is Deliberately Lying?* This article is reproduced in *The Devil's Final Battle* (2010), 372-376.

115   Christopher A. Ferrara, *The Secret Still Hidden*. (Pound Ridge, New York: Good Counsel Publications, 2008).

116   One such point concerns the discussion over a question of the number of sheets. In the 2007 edition of Bertone's book, the plural ("sheets") was used. In the 2010 edition, this word was changed to the singular ("sheet"). Giuseppe De Carli was asked about this change in 2010 during a conference in Rome organized by Fr. Gruner. De Carli responded that he and Bertone consulted the notes Bertone had written down and realized a change needed to be made. See the pamphlet from Christopher Ferrara entitled *The Secret Still Hidden: Epilogue*. (Good Counsel Publications, 2010), 40-45. Hereafter followed by page number. This pamphlet is available online in PDF format: <http://www.secretstillhidden.com/pdf/epilogue.pdf> (Accessed 2 January, 2016).

117   *The Secret Still Hidden: Epilogue*, 4-8, 10.

118   Ibid., 62-63.

Kramer issued the second edition of his book *The Devil's Final Battle*.

A further noteworthy piece of the history of the third part of the secret from the year 2010 was Pope Benedict XVI's Apostolic Voyage to Fátima. During the course of this Voyage, Pope Benedict made a couple of remarks that caused some discussion.[119] In the year 2000, Cardinals Sodano and Ratzinger (Benedict) asserted that the events foretold in the secret "now seem part of the past...."[120] Questions arose as to whether or not Ratzinger, now as Pope Benedict, repudiated this position.

The first remark came during the flight to Portugal on May 11, 2010. Fr. Federico Lombardi, the Vatican's press director, asked the Pope two particular questions about Fátima. The first was on the meaning of Fátima for the Church today. The second concerned whether or not it was possible to extend the meaning of the third part of the secret "to other sufferings of the Church today for the sins involving the sexual abuse of minors."[121]

Pope Benedict's response to the first question indicated that above all else, Fátima was a call to "ongoing conversion, penance, prayer, and the three theological virtues: faith, hope and charity." In this call Fátima continues to have meaning. Benedict responded to the second question in terms of continued attacks against the Church and the Pope from both outside as well as inside the Church. Finally, during his homily on May 13 in Fátima, Benedict remarked that, "We would be mistaken to think that Fatima's prophetic mission is complete."[122] From these statements, people wondered at how to

---

119   <http://w2.vatican.va/content/benedict-xvi/en/speeches/2010/may/ documents/hf_ben-xvi_spe_20100511_portogallo-interview.html> (Accessed 14 May, 2016). Hereafter *Benedict XVI May 2010 Interview*. See also his homily of May 13, 2010 in *Acta Apostolicae Sedis*, 102 [2010], 324-327.

120   Cf. *The Message of Fatima*, 9, 31, 43.

121   *Benedict XVI May 2010 Interview*. Also, according to the Eternal Word Television Network (EWTN), the interview was conducted in Italian: <http:// www.ewtn.com/library/papaldoc/b16portflght.htm> (Accessed 14 May, 2016).

122   "Iludir-se-ia quem pensasse que a missão profética de Fátima esteja concluída" (*Acta Apostolicae Sedis*, 102 [2010], 324-327).

reconcile the two seemingly opposing positions from 2000 and 2010.[123]

In the year 2013, the Carmelite Sisters of the Convent of St. Teresa in Coimbra, Portugal published a biography of Sr. Lúcia entitled *Um Caminho sob o Olhar de Maria*. It was translated into English and published on April 13, 2015 by the World Apostolate of Fatima, USA, Inc. under the title *A Pathway Under the Gaze of Mary*. This biography contained new information on the life of Sr. Lúcia, including how she wrote down the third part of the secret.

The Carmelites' biography revealed that there was indeed more to the third part of the secret than was released in the year 2000. The Sisters, however, were careful to note that this was not because of an alleged Vatican conspiracy. The matter was over a hitherto unknown command given to Sr. Lúcia by Our Lady on or around January 3, 1944 not to reveal "what is given to you [Sr. Lúcia] to understand of its significance."[124] This revelation caught the attention of Antonio Socci who wrote about it on his web site.[125] Socci's article was subsequently translated by Christopher Ferrara and published in the fall 2014 edition of *The Fatima Crusader*.[126]

---

123   For an example of how people were interpreting Pope Benedict's words, see the article "Fatima for Today: A Response" by Christopher A. Ferrara in *The Fatima Crusader*, (Summer 2011), Issue 99, pages 43-55.

124   *Um Caminho sob o Olhar de Maria*, 266.

125   See his article entitled, *Novita' Apocalittiche da Fatima (L'Ultim Mistero: Il Silenzio delle Suore, ma Chi Tace…) of August 17, 2014. This page is available from the Internet Archive Wayback Machine: <https://web.archive. org/web/20140820000910/http:/www.antoniosocci.com/2014/08/novita-apocalittiche-da-fatima-lultimo-mistero-il-silenzio-delle-suore-ma-chi-tace/> (Accessed 19 October, 2016).

126   *The Fatima Crusader* (Fall 2014), Issue 110, pages 22-26. Unfortunately, the article contains an erroneous claim on page 23 that reads "Now, 60 years later, Sister Lucy's biography reveals that there truly is a missing text which explains the vision of the 'Bishop dressed in White.'" The biography states that Sr. Lúcia was ordered *not* to write down what she understood of the vision she received on July 13, 1917. How, then, could there be a "missing text" when Sister was ordered to the contrary?

Regretfully, the revelation about Our Lady's command had been mistranslated in the English translation of *Um Caminho sob o Olhar de Maria*. This fact was discussed on June 12, 2015 by Christopher Ferrara in an article for the Fatima Center's web site entitled *"World Apostolate of Fatima" Hides Our Lady of Fatima's Words in English Translation of New Lucia Biography*.[127] In his article, Ferrara cast the mistranslation within a hermeneutic of suspicion and conspiracy, insinuating a deliberate cover-up by the World Apostolate of Fatima, USA Inc. (WAF-USA).[128]

Ferrara's article received two responses. The first was issued later in June by the Executive Director of WAF-USA, Mr. David Carollo, entitled *A Respectful Response to Mr. Christopher Ferrara*.[129] The second response was by this author in an article that appeared on July 5 on the web site *Catholic Stand* entitled *In Defense of the World Apostolate of Fatima*.[130] Ferrara replied to Carollo on July 9 in an article entitled *A Respectful Reply to David Carollo*.[131] Ferrara followed up this article with a response to this author on August 24 in an article entitled: *Bio-gate: Some Further Developments*.[132] The last known public word on this dispute came from

---

127   <http://fatima.org/perspectives/ts/perspective743.asp> (Accessed 12 March, 2016).

128   Ironically, while pointing out the mistranslation on the part of WAF-USA, Ferrara himself, *twice*, mistranslated the text.

129   <http://wafusa.org/a-respectful-response-to-mr-christopher-ferrara/> (Accessed 12 March, 2016). Unfortunately, Mr. Carollo states that the biography was published in May, 2015. This was an error as the book was published in April.

130   <http://www.catholicstand.com/waf-usa-defense/> (Accessed 12 March, 2016).

131   <http://www.fatimaperspectives.com/ts/perspective749.asp> (Accessed 13 March, 2016).

132   <http://www.fatimaperspectives.com/ts/perspective767.asp> (Accessed 13 March, 2016).

Ferrara during a conference in Washington, D.C. in September, 2015.[133]

In April, 2016, a little-noticed development in the present history occurred. The French writer Yves Chiron published the latest edition of his periodical *Aletheia*.[134] In this edition, Chiron revealed that he wrote a letter to Benedict XVI on the subject of Fátima and received a reply. Chiron stated that Benedict wrote to him the following, "a fourth secret of Fátima does not exist. The published text is entire and there exists nothing else."[135] News of this letter, however, did not reach the English-speaking world prior to the following development.

In May, 2016, the ninety-ninth anniversary month of the first apparition of Our Lady in Fátima, a series of noteworthy articles on or touching upon the third part of the secret of Fátima were published. On May 12, the web site *One Peter Five* published an article entitled *Alice Von Hildebrand Sheds New Light on Fatima*.[136] In this article, an E-mail from Dr. von Hildebrand (dated May 6, 2016) is discussed and prefaced by an editorial by Fr. Brian Harrison of St. Louis, Missouri.

Von Hildebrand's E-mail discusses her and her husband's relationship with Bella Dodd, a former Communist who admitted to the von Hildebrands in 1966/1967 that there were no less than four Cardinals who were working at the Vatican for Communism. Based upon the opening

---

133   A video of this talk was made available on *YouTube*: <https://www.youtube.com/watch?v=7OIyqzjuiU8> (Accessed 13 March, 2016).

134   *Aletheia: Lettre d'informations religieuses*. n° 245, XVIIe année, 4 avril 2016. This edition was placed online at the *Academia* web site: <https://www.academia.edu/24046882/Fatima_LIle_Bouchard_Dozule> (Accessed 3 August, 2016). Chiron is respected for his work on Pope St. Pius X (*Pope St. Pius X, Restorer of the Church*. [Kansas City: Angelus Press, 2002]). He has also written on apparitions (*Enquête sur les apparitions de la Vierge*. [Perrin-Mame, 1995]).

135   The French text reads, "un quatrième secret de Fatima n'existe pas. Le texte publié est intégral et il n'existe rien d'autre."

136   <http://www.onepeterfive.com/alice-von-hildebrand-sheds-new-light--fatima/> (Accessed 27 May, 2016).

paragraph of the original E-mail from von Hildebrand, Fr. Harrison's accompanying editorial framed Dr. von Hildebrand's E-mail within the context of the third part of the secret of Fátima. Within this context, the speculation arose once again concerning the matter of there being more to the third part of the secret than what was revealed in May/June, 2000.[137]

Three days later another article appeared on *One Peter Five* on May 15 by Dr. Maike Hickson entitled *Cardinal Ratzinger: We Have Not Published the Whole Third Secret of Fatima*.[138] In this article, Dr. Hickson relays a phone conversation that she had with Fr. Ingo Dollinger, a friend of Benedict XVI. Hickson reiterates a claim from Fr. Dollinger that was revealed by Fr. Paul Kramer in 2009, namely that Benedict, as Cardinal Ratzinger, had told Dollinger that there was more to the third part of the secret than what was revealed in 2000. This story quickly circulated around the Internet and the Holy See issued a denial on May 21, 2016.[139] On the same day of the denial, Steve Skojec, the editor of *One Peter Five*, issued his own response to the denial in which he questioned the Vatican's statement.[140]

On May 17, this author published an article which questioned Fr. Dollinger's claim.[141] Three discrepancies were pointed out over Doll-

---

137   It is possible to argue that the full impact of the 2013 Carmelites' biography had not been fully realized by this time.

138   <http://www.onepeterfive.com/cardinal-ratzinger-not-published-whole--third-secret-fatima/> (Accessed 27 May, 2016).

139   <http://press.vatican.va/content/salastampa/it/bollettino/pubblico/2016/05/21/0366/00855.html> (Accessed 27 May, 2016).

140   <http://www.onepeterfive.com/on-fatima-story-pope-emeritus-benedict-xvi-breaks-silence/> (Accessed 27 May, 2016). *One Peter Five*, on November 18, 2016, published a follow-up article from Dr. Hickson wherein she revealed a private letter she composed to Pope Emeritus Benedict XVI. She does not address the letter of Benedict XVI to Chiron: <http://www.onepeterfive.com/private-letter-pope-emeritus-benedict-xvi-revealed/> (Accessed 19 November, 2016).

141   <https://kevinsymonds.com/2016/05/17/fatima-and-fr-dollinger-a-response/> (Accessed 27 May, 2016).

inger's claim. The first discrepancy notes that there are different versions of Dollinger's claim, one from 2009 and the other from Hickson in 2016.[142] The second area of concern is that Dollinger's claim contradicts an authentic letter from Sr. Lúcia in which she comments on the Second Vatican Council. The third area concerns an unresolved question pertaining to the 2013 biography of Sr. Lúcia mentioned earlier. Shortly after the publication of this article, Fr. Paul Kramer published a response on his *Facebook* account.[143] His response was followed up by this author with an expanded version of his article.[144]

Further developments occurred in this history from May to July, 2016.[145]

---

142   It is interesting to note that two sources cited by this author which discuss these differing versions are also referenced by Steve Skojec in his response to the Vatican's denial. One will find these references in the section under his first question on the "semantics" of the denial. Web links to the sources are provided, first in the words "an interview with Fr. Paul Kramer in *Fatima Crusader* in May of 2009." The second link is in the words "he had heard this same story from a priest." Skojec does not respond to the substance of this author's article.

143   <https://www.facebook.com/paul.kramer.1023611/posts/1216582278387181> (Accessed 28 May, 2016). Hereafter *Kramer Response 2016.*

144   <https://www.academia.edu/25807772/A_Response_to_Fr._Dollinger_on_F%C3%A1tima> (Accessed 3 August, 2016). To date, Fr. Kramer has not responded to this expanded article. This article has since been removed in view of the impending publication of the present book.

145   Though not considered in depth in the present chapter, author Joanna Bogle wrote a couple of articles on Fátima that were published on the Internet. The first appeared on June 1 on the *Catholic World Report* web site and was entitled *The Boring Third Secret of Fatima*: <http://www.catholicworldreport.com/Blog/4819/the_boring_third_secret_of_fatima.aspx> (Accessed 13 August, 2016). She then issued a follow-up article on July 29 in the *Catholic Herald* publication (print and online): <http://www.catholicherald.co.uk/issues/july--29th-2016/no-benedict-xvi-hasnt-been-brainwashed/> (Accessed 13 August, 2016). To this latter article, Christopher Ferrara issued a three-part response on his *Fatima Perspectives* column on the web site of the *Fatima Center*: <http://fatimaperspectives.com/ts/perspective878.asp> (Accessed 13 August, 2016). For the other two articles, substitute the numbers "878" with "879" and "880"

In late May, Cardinal Capovilla died. This news caused a resurgence of interest in his involvement in the history of the third part of the secret of Fátima. In particular, Dr. Robert Moynihan of *Inside the Vatican* magazine, published a *Letter* (#48, 2016) that reflected upon a meeting he had with Capovilla toward the end of the year 2006.[146] During this meeting, Moynihan recounts, Capovilla told him that there was an envelope with Capovilla's handwriting on it with a dictated note from John XXIII. This claim is significant as this envelope was *not* produced by Cardinal Bertone in May, 2007 on the *Porta a Porta* program, nor has the Vatican ever published it.

This non-disclosure led to speculation that said envelope contains the alleged missing text of the third part of the secret, i.e. the "fourth secret" of Fátima as labeled by Socci. Moynihan's *Letter* was part one of the story, with part two (*Letter* #49) published on July 29.[147] Concerning this follow-up, Moynihan wrote that Capovilla led him to believe there was "some other version of the Third Secret," one that was "different from the one that was revealed and published."

In-between the publication of *Letters* 48 and 49, Yves Chiron published another edition of *Aletheia* (#247) dated June 5 that was reported on by the web site *TradiNews*.[148] This edition contained the entirety of the letter of Benedict XVI to Chiron. In this article, Chiron discusses the

---

respectively.

146   <http://insidethevatican.com/news/newsflash/letter-48-2016-passing--capovilla> (Accessed 3 August, 2016).

147   <http://insidethevatican.com/news/newsflash/letter-49-2016-russia> (Accessed 3 August, 2016). Hickson composed an article published on August 8 on *One Peter Five* that discussed this Moynihan's *Letters*: <http://www.onepeterfive.com/robert-moynihan-keeps-fatima-questions-alive/> (Accessed 14 December, 2016). Prior to this article, she published an article to support the character of Fr. Dollinger: <http://www.onepeterfive.com/profile-the-life-of-dr--ingo-dollinger/> (Accessed 14 July, 2016). This author issued a response to this last article on his *Facebook* profile.

148   <http://tradinews.blogspot.com/2016/06/yves-chiron-aletheia-pour-en--finir-avec.html> (Accessed 3 August, 2016).

developments that occurred in the previous month in the light of his letter from Benedict. He critiques these developments, adding at the end a serious note that re-reading Ratzinger's *Theological Commentary* from the year 2000 "would be more useful and profitable, intellectually and spiritually, than to listen to the 'pure inventions, absolutely false' of Dollinger, Socci, and others."[149] A rough translation into English of this letter was published on June 8.[150]

In the last few months of 2016, there appeared two more noteworthy articles. In October, the Brazilian author Dr. Antonio Borelli Machado gave an interview with the publication *Catolicismo*.[151] Among other things, Dr. Borelli discussed the reason why the third part of the secret was not revealed in the year 1960. He took a remark of Cardinal Ratzinger during the June, 2000 press conference to advance an argument that Our Lady's vision did not harmonize with the vision of Pope John XXIII for the Second Vatican Council.[152] Later, in November, 2016, Dr. Maike Hickson published another article about Fátima entitled *A Private Letter to Pope Emeritus Benedict XVI Revealed*.[153] As the title implies, this article

---

149   Ibid. The French text reads, "Relire ce Commentaire théologique serait plus utile et profitable, intellectuellement et spirituellement, que prêter l'oreille aux « pures inventions, absolument fausses » des Dollinger, Socci, et autres."

150   <https://kevinsymonds.com/2016/06/08/chiron-and-fatima/> (Accessed 3 August, 2016). This author discovered Chiron's prior issue of *Aletheia* from April and brought that to the attention of the English-speaking world as well. The translation received some notoriety through the web site *Spirit Daily* on June 10, 2016: <http://www.spiritdaily.net/A69Popethirdsecret.htm> (Accessed 3 August, 2016).

151   *Catolicismo* N°790 (Outubro, 2016), 10-21. The interview is entitled: "Mensagem de Fátima: Por que o 3° Segredo de Fátima não foi divulgado em 1960?"

152   See the English translation available online: <http://www.pcpbooks. net/email17.html> (Accessed 5 December, 2016).

153   <http://www.onepeterfive.com/private-letter-pope-emeritus-benedict- -xvi-revealed> (Accessed 19 November, 2016).

revealed a personal letter that she composed to Benedict requesting that he fully reveal the secret.[154] The first quarter of 2017 saw some continued discussion from *One Peter Five* on the Fr. Dollinger story. [155]

To date, the above is a rough historical outline of the events involving the third part of the secret of Fátima. In the following chapters, we shall endeavor to discuss specific aspects of this history in order to bring to light some of the more controversial aspects of this history and, hopefully, lay these to rest. We shall begin by discussing one of the most prominent arguments, namely the number of the lines of text.

---

154   She neglects to mention in this article the letter of Benedict to Yves Chiron.

155   Cf. Dr. Maike Hickson's article, "A Further Confirmation of Father Dollinger's Claim about Cardinal Ratzinger and Fatima" dated March 10th: <http://www.onepeterfive.com/confirmation-father-dollingers-claim-cardinal-ratzinger-fatima/> (Accessed 28 April, 2017). See also Steve Skojec's article "Our Top Ten Posts of 2016 from December 28th, 2016: <http://www.onepeterfive.com/top-ten-posts-2016/> (Accessed 28 April, 2017).

—2—
HOW MANY LINES OF TEXT?

"[Lúcia] wrote on a sheet, in the Portuguese language...."
—Alfredo Cardinal Ottaviani, February 11, 1967

Among the arguments against the Vatican's booklet *The Message of Fatima* there is one in particular that stands out more prominently.[1] This argument concerns the number of the lines of text of the third part of the secret that is presented in the booklet.[2] Over sixty lines of text are presented. Prior to the year 2000, there was a belief that the text was comprised of some 20-25 lines. The present chapter seeks to address the difference presented in *The Message of Fatima* booklet from that of the popular belief.[3]

---

1   Cf. Christopher Ferrara, *The Secret Still Hidden*. (Pound Ridge, New York: Good Counsel Publications, 2008), 21, 69, 79, 90-94, 124, 140-144, 159-160, and 201. Hereafter *The Secret Still Hidden* followed by page number.

2   Congregation for the Doctrine of the Faith, *The Message of Fatima*. (Vatican City: Libreria Editrice Vaticana, 2000). Hereafter referred to as *The Message of Fatima* followed by page number.

3   In September, 2015, this author published an article entitled *Cardinal Ottaviani on the Third Secret of Fatima*: <http://www.catholicstand.com/ottaviani-fatima-secret/> (Accessed 6 December, 2015). The article was preceded by another article in February, 2015 entitled *Is There a "Fourth Secret" of Fatima?* (<http://www.catholicstand.com/fourth-secret-fatima/> [Accessed 6 December, 2015]).

It is argued that the facts became mixed up and the sources not consulted (or at least not carefully).[4]

I. How Many Lines? 1960-2000

The question of who claimed there were 20-25 lines for the third part of the secret of Fátima requires an introduction. In the history of Fátima, there have been a number of key and influential people and events. One of those events was the expected revelation of the third part of the secret in the year 1960. When, in 1944, Sr. Lúcia wrote down the third part, she sealed it in an envelope and wrote instructions on said envelope. Those instructions were that by the express order of Our Lady, the contents of the envelope were not to be opened until 1960 or upon her (Sister's) death. The Cardinal of Lisbon or the Bishop of Fátima were specified as being able to open it.[5]

Between 1944 and 1960, word had spread that the third part was written down and to be opened in 1960. A general expectation arose

---

4   I am grateful to Dr. Antonio Borelli and his insightful article *Some Friendly Reflections for the Clarification of a Debate*:
<https://web.archive.org/web/20140211073510/http:/www.lepantofoundation.org/wp-content/uploads/2010/05/Friendly-Reflections_Lepanto03.pdf> (Accessed 5 December, 2015). Hereafter *Friendly Reflections* followed by page number. For some criticism of Borelli's article, see Christopher Ferrara's response:
<http://www.fatima.org/news/newsviews/ferraraexpose.pdf> (Accessed 22 December, 2015).

5   Fr. Joaquín María Alonso, C.M.F., *The Secret of Fatima: Fact and Legend*. (Cambridge: The Ravengate Press, 1979), 44-45. Hereafter *The Secret of Fatima: Fact and Legend* followed by page number. It should also be noted that since the appearance of Cardinal Bertone on the *Porta a Porta* Italian program in May, 2007, the public has now seen the text of Sr. Lúcia written on the envelope concerning the date of 1960. Further, this author's use of the word "envelope" (singular) is not used with prejudice to the fact that Bertone revealed *two* envelopes (plural).

among Catholics that the text would be published.[6] The Pope in 1960 was Pope John XXIII. The Holy Father had read the text at Castel Gandolfo in August, 1959. About 6 months later, in February, 1960, an article appeared in Portuguese media stating that the secret was not going to be published.[7]

Disbelief and dismay arose among Catholics around the world. Despite efforts by various ecclesiastical officials (and perhaps others), the third part of the secret remained unpublished.[8] This fact was discussed by Cardinal Ottaviani himself in a famous Allocution on the occasion of a 50th anniversary celebration of the apparitions of Our Lady at Fátima. This Allocution is partly why there is confusion over the number of lines of text, thus it necessitates some discussion.

A. The 1967 Ottaviani Fátima Allocution

From 1960-1967, the general expectation, as was said above, was that the third part of the secret was to be released. The repeated appeals for its release would not cease.[9] In the midst of this climate appeared Cardinal Ottaviani's Allocution on February 11, 1967 at the Antonianum in Rome. Originally to be delivered as a prepared speech, the Cardinal made

---

6   *The Secret of Fatima: Fact and Legend*, 52-54.

7   Ibid., 55-56. See also: Sebastião Martins dos Reis, *O Milagre do Sol e o Segredo de Fátima: Inconsequências e especulações*. (Porto: Edições Salesianas, 1966), 127.

8   Frère Michel de la Sainte Trinité, *The Whole Truth About Fatima. Volume III: The Third Secret*. (Buffalo, New York: Immaculate Heart Publications, 1990), 601ff. Hereafter *The Whole Truth About Fatima, Volume III* followed by page number. The original French text is: Frère Michel de la Sainte Trinité, *Toute la Vérité sur Fatima: Le Troisième Secret (1942-1960)*. (Saint-Parres lès Vaudes, France: Renaissance Catholique Contre-Réforme Catholique, 1985). Hereafter *Toute la Vérité sur Fatima: Le Troisième Secret* followed by page number.

9   *The Secret of Fatima: Fact and Legend*, 49-56; *The Whole Truth About Fatima, Volume III*, 578-620.

remarks *ex tempore* in Italian which were recorded, transcribed, and published in a larger volume of *Acta* (Acts) of the Pontifical International Marian Academy (PAMI).[10]

As our discussion of the Allocution at this point primarily concerns the question of the number of lines of text, discussion of the Allocution is left to the next chapter. It suffices to say that at no point did Cardinal Ottaviani mention the number of lines of the third part of the secret. Just how the claim began that Ottaviani spoke on the number of lines of text shall be examined later in this chapter. In the meantime, in addressing this matter, it is important to continue forward in the timeline of events. Much ink was spilled from the years 1960-2000 that speculated upon the contents of the secret and we find the origin of the 20-25 lines of text in the mid-1980s.

B. Frère Michel and the Number of Lines of Text

After modestly researching available materials in various sources, it is necessary to begin with the writings of Frère Michel de la Sainte Trinité. Frère Michel is primarily known in the English-speaking world for his three-volume work on Fátima. According to his contemporary Frère François de Marie des Anges:

> In the month of June 1981 in Brittany, after preaching a day of
> recollection on the Fatima revelations, our Father Superior the
> Abbé Georges de Nantes, entrusted a member of his commu-

---

10   Cf. *Acta Pontificiae Academiae Marianae Internationalis vel ad Academiam quoquo modo pertinentia. Volume 4.* (Romae: Pontificia Academia Mariana Internationalis, 1967), 44-49. Marco Tosatti provides a partial Italian text in his book *Il Segreto non Svelato.* (Casale Monferrato, AL: Piemme, 2002), 84-85. He cites his source as the magazine "Fatima" (year 1, number 7, November 13, 1967). In fact, this reference is to a Portuguese translation available in the periodical entitled *Fatima 50* (Year 1, No. 7, November 13, 1967), pages 14-16.

nity, Brother Michael of the Holy Trinity, to resume his studies in a scientific and exhaustive manner in a work presenting the apparitions and the requests of Our Lady [of Fátima] as well as the meaning of Her Message for our times; in short, everything on Fatima. Brother Michael immediately began drafting this monumental work which merited the title: "The Whole Truth About Fatima."[11]

This "monumental work" was a three-volume set of books in the French language under the title *Toute la Vérité sur Fatima*. According to Frère François, the first volume was released in March 1983 and given the subtitle "Science and the Facts." The second volume came in January, 1984 with the subtitle "The Secret and the Church." Finally, the third volume was published in July, 1985 and subtitled "The Third Secret."[12] Frère François himself made his own literary contribution on Fátima that are described as summaries of Frère Michel's three-volume set.[13]

Between 1989 and 1990, the three volumes of *Toute la Vérité sur Fatima* were published in English translation (the translator was John Collorafi) under the title *The Whole Truth About Fatima*. These three volumes

---

11   Frère François de Marie des Anges, *Fatima: Tragedy and Triumph*. (Buffalo, New York: Immaculate Heart Publications, 1994), v. Hereafter *Fatima: Tragedy and Triumph* followed by page number.

12   Ibid. There was a proposed fourth book, but Frère Michel left the Little Brothers community in 1989 for the *Grande Chartreuse* Carthusian monastery in France where he remains today. He is known as Dom François-Marie Velut. In 2012, he was elected to be the Minister General of the Order, but had to step down for reasons of health in 2014. For some general information, see: <http://www.quies.org/DFMVelut.pdf> (Accessed 19 October, 2016).

13   The French title is *Fatima Joie Intime Événement Mondial*. (Saint-Parres Lès Vaudes, France: Éditions de la Contre-Réforme Catholique, 1991). The English titles are as follows: (Book 1) *Fatima: The Astonishing Truth*; (Book 2) *Fatima: Mary's Immaculate Heart and Your Salvation*; (Book 3) *Fatima: The Only Way to World Peace*; (Book 4) *Fatima: Tragedy and Triumph*.

have become a foundational text and are highly regarded by various circles of Catholics. They enjoy this status because, as Frère François explained, the books give an exhaustive treatment on Fátima. Frère Michel manages to organize countless sources from different languages in order to weave together a comprehensive story on the events of Fátima and its history.[14]

Much can be said about Frère Michel's impressive work. Our interest, however, is in the third part of the secret and the question of the number of its lines of text. According to the observation made by Dr. Borelli in his article *Friendly Reflections*, the originator of the 20-25 lines claim is Frère Michel (p. 10).[15] Just what, when and how Frère Michel made the claim remains a point of contention so let us look at the facts.

The claim that the third part of the secret comprises 20-25 lines goes back to a specific story relayed by Frère Michel. This story involves a particular incident when the envelope containing the third part was sent to Rome in 1957.[16] According to Frère Michel, he received directly from the former Bishop of Leiria-Fátima, João Venancio, the following information on February 13, 1984 in Fátima:

> Bishop Venancio related once he was by himself, he took the
> great envelope of the Secret and tried to look through it and see
> the contents. In the bishop's large envelope, that of Lucy, and
> inside this envelope an ordinary sheet of paper with margins on

---

14   The story is "comprehensive" because of how it marshals many sources together in order to give basic facts and a timeline on Fátima. The question of Frère Michel's accuracy or bias to that narrative is another matter. For an example of one writer's questioning Frère Michel's accuracy, see Antonio Socci, *The Fourth Secret of Fatima*. (Fitswilliams, New Hampshire: Loreto Publications, 2009), 95. Hereafter *The Fourth Secret of Fatima* followed by page number. While Frère Michel's work is helpful, it is even more beneficial to consult and verify his sources.

15   *Friendly Reflections*, 10.

16   *The Whole Truth About Fatima, Volume III*, 481; *Toute la Vérité sur Fatima: Le Troisième Secret*, 321.

each side of three quarters of a centimeter. He took the trouble to note the size of everything. Thus the final Secret of Fatima was written on a small sheet of paper.[17]

The reader will observe that nowhere above does Frère Michel make a comment about the lines of text that comprises the secret. The closest that he comes to saying anything about it was his remark about the size of the paper, saying that it was "ordinary," "small," and had margins. Remember too that Bishop Venancio could not view the contents directly enough to read any text and make a copy. Why does Frère Michel make no mention of the lines of text when relaying the story from Bishop Venancio? The answer is as shocking as it is clear: Venancio never said it.

There are two pieces of evidence for the above assertion. The first is that Frère Michel *does* elsewhere comment about the lines of text. In Volume III of *The Whole Truth About Fatima*, he remarks later, "As a matter of fact, Sister Lucy surely realized that by writing these twenty [little] lines, she was inaugurating an event which would have a formidable impact in the history of the Church and the world."[18] This is all Frère Michel

---

17   According to the French text of 1985:

Mgr Venancio raconte qu'une fois seul chez lui, il prit la grande enveloppe du Secret et qu'il essaya de voir, par transparence, quel en était le contenu. Dans la grande enveloppe de l'évêque, il discerna une enveloppe plus petite, celle de Lucie, et à l'intérieur une feuille ordinaire, avec trois quarts de centimètre de marge de chaque côté. Il prit le soin de noter la taille de tout cela. L'ultime Secret de Fatima est donc écrit sur une petite feuille de papier.

The English translation herein given is based upon the third French edition of this particular volume (April-May of 1986). These dates will be significant as we shall see.

18   *The Whole Truth About Fatima, Volume III*, 707. The French text reads, "De fait, elle se rendait sûrement compte que par ces vingt lignes elle allait lancer dans l'histoire de l'Église, dans l'histoire du monde, un évènement d'une portée formidable" (*Toute la Vérité sur Fatima: Le Troisième Secret*, 474). One would have to ask how Frère Michel could possibly have known the mind

states on the matter and he does not give an explanation for this number. It appears to be *his own* speculation that is not developed further in Volume III, but which was developed shortly after the book was published.[19]

The second piece of evidence dates to November 24, 1985. On this date Frère Michel gave a talk in French at the Augustianum in Rome.[20] This talk was turned into an article that was printed in English and distributed by Augustine Publishing Company in September, 1986.[21] The talk itself was delivered nine months after Frère Michel spoke with Bishop Venancio in Fátima, and about three to four months after the first French edition of the third volume of *The Whole Truth About Fatima* was published. On page eight of the English text, Frère Michel states, "We thus know that the Third Secret is not very long, probably 20 to 25 lines, that is to say,

---

and intention of Sr. Lúcia to make this remark.

19   In his book *Fatima: Tragedy and Triumph*, Frère François accounts the same story about Bishop Venancio as was quoted above. However, he adds the following line at the end, "The final Secret of Fatima, written on a small sheet of paper, is therefore not very long. *Probably twenty to twenty-five lines, that is almost the same length as the Second Secret*" (emphases mine). *Fatima: Tragedy and Triumph*, 45. There is an endnote for this quotation and Frère François cites volume three, page 379 of *The Whole Truth About Fatima*. As we have seen, this citation is bogus.

20   It appears as though his talk might have been delivered in the French language. A copy of the French text was published as *Le Troisième Secret de Fatima.* (Sherbrooke, Québec: Éditions Kolbe, Inc., 1987). Hereafter *Le Troisième Secret de Fatima* followed by page number. This is the version in the possession of this author. Also, it appears as though the conference at which Frère Michel delivered his talk was the same as that chaired by Fr. Nicholas Gruner entitled "Is the 1985 Extraordinary Synod the Last Opportunity for World Peace?" (cf. Francis Alban and Christopher Ferrara, *Fatima Priest.* [Pound Ridge, New York: Good Counsel Publications, 2013], 79).

21   Brother Michel de la Sainte Trinité, *The Third Secret of Fatima.* (Chulmleigh, United Kingdom: Augustine Publishing Company, 1986). In *Friendly Reflections* (10), Dr. Borelli notes that the talk was printed in May, 1986 in the publication *La Contre-Réforme Catholique*, no. 222, page 4).

about the same length as the Second Secret."[22] It is important to analyze this statement as Frère Michel here said a lot in a few words.

First, let us remember that the source of Frère Michel's information is reputed to be Bishop Venancio—the very one who measured the contents of Sr. Lúcia's envelope. As was asked earlier, if Venancio claimed 20-25 lines of text, why did Frère Michel not include such a precious detail in the July/August 1985 (first edition) printing of volume three during the narrative on Venancio? It is an unlikely argument to say that Frère Michel did not have time to get the information to press, or even that he forgot about it. The fact is that he relayed everything else on the above story about Bishop Venancio in his book. Moreover, if it is a question of adding the statement in a later French edition, why did the English translation—itself based upon the *third* French edition published in April/May 1986—not include this information?

Secondly, it is important to note the adverb "probably" (*probablement*). The very nature of the word does not have the mark of certainty. It sounds more like speculation and one must ask who is the one speculating—Bishop Venancio or Frère Michel? It is unclear where Venancio ends and Frère Michel begins. Moreover, there are no quotation marks, which further complicates the matter.

Thirdly, there is a consideration on the nature of a book and a talk. Given the first two observations, what appears to have happened is that Frère Michel was speaking more openly in his talk. This is not an uncommon phenomenon for authors when they are presenting materials from their book(s). It is easy to embellish details or add one's personal thoughts to established facts. The text from Frère Michel's talk reads well in this way.

In the end, the observation of Dr. Borelli is correct. The origin of the belief that the third part of the secret of Fátima comprises 20-25 lines of text can be attributed accurately to Frère Michel. From 1985 to the present,

---

22   In the French text we read: "Nous savons ainsi que le troisième Secret n'est past très long. Probablement vingt à vingt-cinq lignes..." (*Le Troisième Secret de Fatima*, 12).

many people understood Frère Michel not as *speculating*, but rather to be *relaying a fact* from Venancio through Frère Michel.[23] As we said above, however, whether it was Frère Michel or the Bishop who made such speculation is not entirely clear. Finally, in either case, it must be remembered that speculation is not established fact.

In the absence of any contradictory evidence—and it could only be truly contradicted by publishing the text itself—Frère Michel was never challenged nor questioned. He was simply taken for granted and his proposition had time to settle in people's minds. Meanwhile, there were no quotation marks, and the French adverb *probablement* indicates uncertainty. Whether Frère Michel was representing Bishop Venancio or interjecting his own understanding is not clear.

Having established the origin of the 20-25 lines of text, it remains to show how this notion was used in the period after the publication of the third part of the secret. From May/June 2000 onward, the claim began to manifest itself more concretely. Let us look at the history more in depth.

II. How Many Lines? 2000-Present

On May 13, 2000, the Holy Father, Pope John Paul II, was in Fátima to beatify Sr. Lúcia's cousins, Francisco and Jacinta.[24] At the end of the Mass on May 13, Angelo Cardinal Sodano, the Vatican Secretary of State, announced that the third part of the secret of Fátima was going to be re-

---

23   One source from 1985 to 2000 includes: Frère François' *Fatima: Tragedy and Triumph*; Sources from 2000 to the present include: Fr. Paul Kramer, *The Devil's Final Battle.* (Good Counsel Publications, 2002); Antonio Socci, *The Fourth Secret of Fatima.* (Fitswilliams, New Hampshire: Loreto Publications, 2009); Christopher Ferrara's, *The Secret Still Hidden.* It should be noted that the number of lines of text was never contested until after June, 2000 when the Vatican released Sr. Lúcia's text. This seems to be a very good reason why a paucity of references exists from 1985-2000.

24   *Acta Apostolicae Sedis* 92 (2000), 708-712.

leased. "In order that the faithful may better receive the message of Our Lady of Fatima," the Cardinal said, "the Pope has charged the Congregation for the Doctrine of the Faith with making public the third part of the secret, after the preparation of an appropriate commentary."[25]

The faithful would not have to wait long. The Vatican held a press conference on June 26, 2000. In attendance was Joseph Cardinal Ratzinger as Prefect for the CDF; Archbishop Tarcisio Bertone as Secretary for said Congregation, and Dr. Joaquín Navarro-Valls the Vatican press office director. During the conference, both Cardinal Ratzinger and Archbishop Bertone delivered remarks while information was given to the assembled journalists.[26] After their remarks, there was a question and answer period and then the end of the conference.

The information given to the journalists was the booklet *The Message of Fatima*. This booklet contained the text of Sr. Lúcia on the third part of the secret as well as accompanying documents and the promised *Theological Commentary* from Cardinal Ratzinger. It is unnecessary to go into the details here. It suffices to say that it was hoped that the publication of the third part would put to rest the rumors and speculations that had arisen. Unfortunately, it had the opposite effect, as veteran Vatican-watcher John Thavis wrote:

> This initiative [in the year 2000 of publishing the third secret of Fátima] to set the record straight after decades of secrecy and ominous speculation not only failed to convince many Catholics, but ended up spawning a small industry of books and videos speculating about a Vatican cover-up. The third secret of Fatima was the Vatican equivalent of Area 51: any attempt at an official explanation was bound to ignite new conspiracy theories.[27]

---

25   *The Message of Fatima*, 30-31.

26   <http://press.vatican.va/content/salastampa/it/bollettino/pubblico/2000/06/26/0407/01462.html> (Accessed 4 August, 2016).

27   John Thavis, *The Vatican Prophecies*. (New York, New York: Vi-

A. An "Unofficial" Narrative

Over the course of the years 1960-2000, there many theories, hypotheses and speculations on the third part of the secret. These things titillated audiences and expectations were quite high and would not easily be dismissed after such a long period of fermentation. These speculations were largely negative in nature as the obvious question was "if it was a good thing, why would the Vatican not release it for everyone?"[28] Another popular theory was that the secret involved a crisis in the Church and was connected with the Second Vatican Council.[29] Cardinal Ratzinger himself touched upon this connection (not the crisis) during the June, 2000 press conference.[30]

---

king, 2015), 7. For some further information, see Tarcisio Cardinal Bertone, *The Last Secret of Fatima*. (New York: Doubleday, 2008), 45, 67-68. Hereafter *The Last Secret of Fatima* followed by page number.

28   The Cardinal Patriarch of Lisbon, Cardinal Cerejeira, is attributed with having made a remark to this effect (cf. *The Whole Truth About Fatima, Volume III*, 667).

29   Cf. *The Fatima Crusader*, Summer 1990, Issue 33, article entitled "Apostasy in the Church." This article is available online: <http://fatima.org/crusader/cr33/cr33pg14.asp> (Accessed 5 December, 2015).

30   The remark was made in response to a question from a journalist during the question and answer session at the end of the press conference. Ratzinger was less conspiratorial in his explanation. He said:

> ... .In the 1960s we are at the threshold of the Council, this great hope to find a new positive relationship between the world and the Church and also to open up a bit the closed doors of Communism, in...even in the time of Pope Paul VI still we digest, so to speak, the Council with so many problems that this text would not have had its proper placement... (....Nel '60 siamo alla soglia del Concilio, questa grande speranza di trovare una nuova relazione positiva tra mondo e Chiesa e anche di aprire un po' le porte chiuse del Comunismo, nel...stesso ancora nel tempo di Papa Paolo VI ancora siamo in digestione, per così dire, del Concilio con tanti problemi che questo testo non avrebbe avuto un suo collocamento corretto...) [Text transcribed from the video of the conference].

When the Vatican released the text, Ratzinger stated in his *Theological Commentary* that the text may be "disappointing or surprising after all the speculation it has stirred."[31] The text of the secret as written by Sr. Lúcia did not describe nuclear fall-outs, the second coming of Christ, nor explicit words prophesying some future event(s). It was largely descriptive and pictorial. There was no heavenly explanation of the individual elements by Sr. Lúcia, though a letter from her was partially reproduced in which she explained the overall vision. People could make of these individual elements what they wanted, even with the *Commentary* provided by Ratzinger and other supporting documentation. As there was no great heralding of doom, this would be the very thing used to "ignite the fire" about which Thavis wrote.

Almost as quickly as the booklet was read, there arose an outcry and disbelief of "*That's it?!*" among some people.[32] The criticisms began to change—*but only slightly*. It was no longer claimed that the Vatican is "covering-up" the secret; the claim became the Vatican is covering-up the *entire* secret.[33] The idea came quickly that there *must* be more to the secret that treated the last phrase from the fourth *Memoir* of Sr. Lúcia, namely "In Portugal the dogma of the faith shall always be preserved etc."[34] From

---

See also Dr. Borelli's interview in *Catolicismo* Nº790 (Outubro, 2016), 10-21.

31   *The Message of Fatima*, 32.

32   Cf. Christopher Ferrara, *False Friends of Fatima*. (Pound Ridge, New York: Good Counsel Publications, 2012), 95. Hereafter *False Friends of Fatima* followed by page number. Fr. Nicholas Gruner expressed similar sentiments in the Summer, 2000, Issue 64 edition of *The Fatima Crusader*. See "The 3rd Secret Vision Explained" <http://www.fatimacrusader.com/cr64/cr64pg18.asp> (Accessed 5 December, 2015).

33   Cf. <http://www.fatima.org/essentials/opposed/cvrup2.asp> (Accessed 5 December, 2015).

34   For an early example of this outcry, see the July-August, 2000 article by Fr. Fabrice Delestre, SSPX entitled *Revelation of the Third Secret of Fatima or Curtailed Revelation*. <http://www.sspxasia.com/Newsletters/2000/July-Aug/

the years 2000-2006 the above idea was spread and further developed. More authors took up their pens and wrote on the question of the above phrase as well as the number of lines of text.[35]

Within this milieu appeared in the year 2002 Fr. Paul Kramer's book *The Devil's Final Battle*.[36] This book was a compilation of various writings and speeches that had been written by Fr. Kramer (and at least one other) over the years and which were edited or revised to be in book format.[37] In chapter four of *The Devil's Final Battle*, Kramer makes a statement relevant to the question of the number of lines of text. After quoting Frère Michel's story in *The Whole Truth About Fatima* on Bishop Venancio examining the envelope, Kramer then adds discussion of the lines of text. He writes, "The evidence further shows that this single sheet of paper contained some 20-25 lines of text. On this point the testimonies of Sister Lucy, Cardinal Ottaviani, Bishop Venancio, Father Alonso, Frère Michel and Frère François all agree...."[38] In support of his point, Kramer then provides three quotes and citations—two works of Frère Michel and one by Frère François.

Delestre-3rd-Secret.htm> (Accessed 17 July, 2015). While the focus of this essay is not the above phrase, it is important to note that the phrase became a rallying point. The phrase sounded incomplete without another one that continued the thought, or so the idea went.

35   Antonio Socci cites a few of these authors throughout his book *The Fourth Secret of Fatima*. As to the question of the reason for the incomplete phrase, some discussion of this is provided in my article *Is There a 'Fourth Secret' of Fatima?* The evidence suggests that, at least as of January 3, 1944, it was the Will of God that Sr. Lúcia not reveal what she understood of the vision. Whether or not this means there were more words of Our Lady after the "etc" is still a debated matter.

36   Fr. Paul L. Kramer, *The Devil's Final Battle*. (Good Counsel Publications, 2002). Hereafter *The Devil's Final Battle (2002)* followed by page number. This first edition was followed by a second in 2010 under the same title.

37   *The Devil's Final Battle (2002)*, vii. The "principle" sources are listed on page ix.

38   Ibid., 29.

Kramer providing only three quotes and citations when he named six separate individuals in support of his point is most curious. The way that the book reads (as quoted above), Kramer gives the appearance that *all six* individuals testified that there were 20-25 lines of text. He does not provide a single citation from four of the above-named individuals (Sr. Lúcia, Fr. Alonso, Bishop Venancio and Cardinal Ottaviani).[39] Moreover, as Kramer phrases himself, there is a *direct* claim that Cardinal Ottaviani made a statement about the number of lines of text. From where did Kramer get this information? Owing to a good paper trail in *The Devil's Final Battle*, and the availability of some of the sources on the Internet, one can quickly reconstruct Kramer's sources and discover the answers.

In the preface to the book, Kramer lists the "principle" sources he consulted to write *The Devil's Final Battle* (ix). The first source is an article by Andrew M. Cesanek entitled *Are There Two Original Manuscripts on the Third Secret?* This article appeared in *The Fatima Crusader*, Issue 64, Spring 2000 and appears to be the first article that postulated the existence of two texts.[40] Cesanek lists several "facts" in his article, the fourth of which provides the exact same three quotes that are provided by Kramer on page 29 of *The Devil's Final Battle*. There is, however, a noted difference between the two writers. We have seen above how Kramer prefaces the three quotes. For his part, Cesanek prefaces the quotes with the words:

> As a result of the evidence cited in Fact #3 regarding the Third Secret being written on just one single sheet of paper, as provided by the testimonies of Sister Lucy, Cardinal Ottaviani, Bishop Venancio, and Father Alonso, Frère Michel and Frère

---

39   Later, in chapter twelve, Kramer will again reiterate the question of the lines of text but says nothing about Ottaviani (page 148).

40   <http://www.fatimacrusader.com/cr64/cr64pg03.asp> (Accessed 5 December, 2015).

François both agree that the text of the Third Secret contains only 20 to 30 lines...."

The difference is clear. Cesanek clearly names *four* people who testify to a single sheet of paper upon which the third part of the secret was written. He then makes it clear that based upon *that* testimony, Frère Michel and Frère François "agree" on the 20-25 lines of text. Cesanek does *not* say Ottaviani (or the other 3 individuals) stated that there were only 20-25 lines of text.

We must make a further observation on the above matter. *The Internet Archive Wayback Machine* (hereafter *Wayback Machine*) provides helpful tools for researchers who wish to look at web sites as they existed many years ago. As Kramer's book is available for free on the Internet, *The Devil's Final Battle* is accessible via the *Wayback Machine* in its Italian translation. According to the *Wayback Machine*, the earliest record of chapter four of Kramer's book is dated to August 22, 2004.[41] Upon examining the text that we have seen in English, it is clear that Kramer states the exact same in Italian.[42] The importance of this Italian translation shall be discussed later.

From the above observations, it appears as though Kramer simply made a notable error in the editing of his book.[43] The precise influence of this error

---

41   <http://www.devilsfinalbattle.com/it/ch4.htm> (Accessed 6 December, 2015).

42   Ibid. The Italian reads, "Altri elementi provano ulteriormente che questo singolo foglietto di carta conteneva circa 20-25 righe di testo. *Su questo punto le testimonianze di Suor Lucia, del Cardinale Ottaviani, del Vescovo Venancio, di Padre Alonso, di Frère Michel e di Frère François coincidono tutte*... (emphases mine)." An English translation would read, "....On this point [the 20-25 lines of text] the testimony of Sr. Lúcia, Cardinal Ottaviani, Bishop Venancio, Fr. Alonso, Frère Michel and Frère François all coincide...."

43   This conclusion is reinforced by the fact that on page 148 (as we noted previously) Kramer provides the same three quotes but prefaces them with a more accurate presentation of their content.

upon the reader cannot be calculated, but we can speculate upon the *very real possibility* that there would be an influence given the relative popularity of Kramer's book. In the meantime, it is important to point out that the discussions on the interpretation of the third part of the secret (and the debates over the text) were not considered "mainstream." There was not as much pressure on the Vatican to respond. This changed, however, in 2006.

B. The Third Secret Discussions—Antonio Socci

Antonio Socci is a respected Vatican journalist. He was even on good terms with the new Secretary of State, Tarcisio Cardinal Bertone, under Pope Benedict XVI. Shortly after the death of Sr. Lúcia on February 13, 2005, Socci found himself reading an article by another popular Italian journalist, Vittorio Messori.[44] This article questioned the text of the third part of the secret released in June, 2000. Because of Messori's prominence as a writer, Socci took this concern with some measure of gravity. In his own words:

> Therefore I reacted to the new article by Messori with a journalistic polemic in which I defended with a sword the rightness of the Vatican … attacked the writer and liquidated all of his "dietrologies" concerning unpublished documents. Certainly, I knew that after the fateful revelation of the Third Secret in 2000, doubts, suspicions, rumors, and critical observations had begun to circulate within the curial environment, and that they had found public expression in traditionalist circles. But I had never paid attention to the traditionalist publications because I believed that they originated from a burning disappointment over a Secret that negates all of their "apocalyptic" forecasts.[45]

---

44   Cf. *The Fourth Secret of Fatima*, 1-5.

45   *The Fourth Secret of Fatima*, 2.

Sometime after the above story, Socci began to look more seriously into the matter. He observed that the arguments against the Vatican on the third part of the secret "have never been analyzed, confronted, and confuted by the ecclesiastical party...." Socci says that this "did not seem right."[46] He began his own investigation and found himself questioning the Vatican.

Because of his status as a mainstream Italian journalist, Antonio Socci provided some credibility to the arguments for a Vatican cover-up. He collected his findings and published them in book form called, in Italian, *Il Quarto Segreto di Fatima* which was published in November, 2006. In 2009 this book was published in English translation as *The Fourth Secret of Fatima*.

For its part, *The Fourth Secret of Fatima* attempted an objective view of the facts behind the third part of the secret of Fátima. Socci gave credit where credit was due, debunked some of the theories and chastised the polemics employed by various writers. For our purposes, Socci looks at the question of the number of lines of text (pages 143-153, English edition). It is clear that Socci accepts the postulation of 20-25 lines of text as coming from Bishop Venancio, which, as we have seen, is in question. He does not, however, connect the postulation as having come from Cardinal Ottaviani.

For the above and other reasons described in *The Fourth Secret of Fatima*, Socci came out in favor of the general position held by Gruner *et al.* concerning the third part of the secret. This position included the 20-25 lines of text claim. Owing to his respect as a journalist, and one outside the mold, Socci effectively posed a challenge to the Vatican. The profile of the claim to a cover-up had been significantly raised by Socci's entry into the discussion. The Holy See was hard-pressed to respond, and it did so.

---

46   Ibid, 2-3.

C. Cardinal Bertone and Giuseppe De Carli:

Having been involved in the publication of *The Message of Fatima* in 2000, and now the Cardinal-Secretary of State, Cardinal Bertone defended the Vatican. That defense began when noted Italian journalist, Giuseppe De Carli and Cardinal Bertone were at a conference in Genoa.[47] De Carli proposed to Bertone that they do a book together about Sr. Lúcia, an idea in which Bertone showed interest. The two sat down for this project, which resulted in the book entitled *L'Ultima Veggente di Fatima*: *I Miei Colloqui con Suor Lucia*, published in May, 2007.[48] The book was subsequently translated into English by the publisher Doubleday in 2008 under the title *The Last Secret of Fatima*.[49]

The claim of 20-25 lines of text now largely became centralized on the person of Cardinal Bertone. The first serious mention in his book on this claim would be in an exchange between the Cardinal and De Carli in the chapter entitled *One Envelope, One Secret* (*Non sono mai esistite due buste e due segreti*).[50] De Carli states to Bertone the following:

> Alfredo Cardinal Ottaviani stated that the Secret was written on a single sheet of paper. So we would be talking about twenty to twenty-five lines in toto, whereas the text presented in the press room of the Holy See on June 26, 2000, consisted of sixty-two lines. In other words, it added up to four pages, not one....[51]

---

47 *The Last Secret of Fatima*, 1-3.

48 Tarcisio Bertone con Giuseppe De Carli, *L'Ultima Veggente de Fatima*. (Milano: Rai Eri Rizzoli, 2007). Hereafter *L'Ultima Veggente* followed by page number.

49 There is a lot of interesting material in Bertone's book. The reader is reminded that our purposes here concern the matter of the alleged 20-25 lines of text.

50 *The Last Secret of Fatima*, 63; *L'Ultima Veggente di Fatima*, 75.

51 *The Last Secret of Fatima*, 63. The Italian text (p. 75) reads, "Il cardi-

In the above quote, we see that De Carli is clearly under the impression that the single sheet of paper mentioned by Ottaviani contains 20-25 lines of text.

How De Carli came to the above conclusion is not specified but one strong possibility exists.[52] A few lines earlier, De Carli mentions the book *Il Segreto non Svelato* (*The Secret not Revealed*) by the Italian journalist Marco Tosatti. In the book, Tosatti clearly discusses the number of lines of text.[53] In making his argument, he cites the alleged Bishop Venancio statement of 20-25 lines of text.[54] As we saw, this belief comes from Frère Michel.

The question of De Carli's source aside, we also see in the above quote that Bertone is given the direct opportunity to respond to this claim of the lines of text. The Cardinal's response is given amid an explanation of how one obtains access to the documents in the former Holy Office (now Congregation for the Doctrine of the Faith). To the remark about Ot-

---

nale Ottaviani affermò che il «Segreto» era vergato su un unico foglio di carta. Venti, venticinque righe in tutto, mentre quello presentato nella sala stampa della Santa Sede il 26 giugno 2000 era di sessantadue righe. Quattro pagine, appunto. Sono piccoli e flebili indizi, non provano o non mettono in crisi nulla."

52   It is also possible that De Carli read Kramer's book *The Devil's Final Battle* in Italian.

53   Marco Tosatti, *Il Segreto non Svelato*. (Casale Monferrato, AL: Piemme, 2002), 109-110.

54   Tosatti wrote:

Always based on the "reading" against the light of the Auxiliary of Leiria [Bishop Venancio] the text appeared formed of about 25 lines written by hand (while Monsignor Loris Capovilla, secretary of Pope John XXIII, in the interview to the aforementioned author spoke of "four or five short pages by hand") [Sempre in base alla «lettura» controluce della ausiliare di Leiria il testo appariva formato da circa 25 righe scritte a mano (mentre monsignor Loris Capovilla, segretario di Giovanni XXIII, nell'intervista alla autore già citata parlava di «quattro o cinque paginette a mano»)]. Tosatti, 109.

It is also of interest that Tosatti, on page 111, references both the Cesanek article mentioned earlier, as well as *The Fatima Crusader*. His influences are clear.

taviani, Bertone replies simply, "So I'm not sure what Cardinal Ottaviani was talking about" (according to the Doubleday translation).[55] Between the Italian and English texts, there are some notable observations.

The first observation is the translation itself. The Italian text reads, "Le parole del cardinale Ottaviani non so a cosa si riferiscano." A literal translation is "The words of Cardinal Ottaviani I do not know to what they refer" or in more idiomatic English, "I do not know to what the words of Cardinal Ottaviani refer." The Doubleday translation comes across a bit harsh-sounding towards Ottaviani when the Italian text does not necessarily communicate such an intention.

The second observation notes an ambiguity on the part of De Carli. He makes two statements back-to-back and does not make distinctions. The first statement is the direct claim that Ottaviani stated that the text of the third part of the secret was written on a single sheet of paper. The second statement is the 20-25 lines of text. Did De Carli also intend this second statement to be attributed to Cardinal Ottaviani? There is a noted difference between the Italian original and the Doubleday translation which affects the answer to this question.

The English suggests a break in thought which is not necessarily in the Italian text. The Italian reads, "Il cardinale Ottaviani affermò che il «Segreto» era vergato su un unico foglio di carta. Venti, venticinque righe in tutto, mentre quello presentato nella sala stampa della Santa Sede il 26 giugno 2000 era di sessantadue righe...." A more literal translation would be, "Cardinal Ottaviani affirmed that the "Secret" was written on a single sheet of paper. Twenty, twenty-five lines in all, whereas the one presented in the press hall of the Holy See [on] June 26, 2000 was 62 lines...."

De Carli's question in Italian to Bertone appears to indicate continuity in thought between the remark on the single sheet of paper and the lines of text. This is apparent in that after the first period, De Carli continues on

---

55   *The Last Secret of Fatima*, 64. "Le parole del cardinale Ottaviani non so a cosa si riferiscano" (*L'Ultima Veggente di Fatima*, 76).

to say "twenty, twenty-five lines, etc." without words prefacing them to indicate a break in thought. The Doubleday translation adds words prior to the number of lines, thus indicating a break in thought.

Did De Carli intend to treat the two statements (i.e. one sheet of paper and 20-25 lines) separately or as one? The best indicator of a response to this question is how Bertone responded to it. After hearing the two statements, Bertone says simply, "I do not know to what the words of Cardinal Ottaviani refer" (my translation). To what was Bertone referring, the first statement, the second or both? The answer to this question is itself not entirely clear, but is not thereby to be dismissed.

Perhaps the best answer to that last question is found in the observation that Bertone does not make a distinction with De Carli. He does not say in response, "It is important to make a distinction here. Ottaviani never spoke on the number of lines of text, only about a single sheet of paper." Instead, Bertone appears to accept De Carli's assertion as he does not challenge it. The reader is left with the impression that Bertone presumed De Carli was accurately presenting a statement by Cardinal Ottaviani.

Accepting the assertion without question is later going to affect *deeply* Bertone's defense. After the De Carli interview, the question of the 20-25 lines of text will arise again and in a much more pronounced manner.

D. Cardinal Bertone and the *Porta a Porta* Interview

In late May, 2007, Cardinal Bertone appeared via teleconference on the popular Italian television program *Porta a Porta* with host Bruno Vespa and a panel of guests (De Carli included).[56] The episode was rich with important

---

56 Unfortunately, there was no transcript of this program and the video is not easy to obtain. This author, however, has watched the full one hour and 30-minute program and can verify the sequence of events herein described. A transcript of this program has been made and is available in the appendices to the present book. As to exact statements, I am relaying them as found in Chris-

content, up to and including Cardinal Bertone revealing for the first time on camera, the envelope(s) containing Sr. Lúcia's text and the text itself. Important for our consideration is how that text clearly showed a single sheet of paper, but now it was seen that the paper had been folded into squares.[57] In these squares are the lines and text that were reproduced in June, 2000.

The above detail was a significant development because it was never previously revealed. When the Vatican released the text in 2000 there was an impression from the reproductions that there were four separate sheets.[58] This impression was never directly addressed by the Vatican until Bertone's (who appears to address *indirectly* the matter) appearance on *Porta a Porta*. This development changed the entire discussion because now there was a clearer answer for the 62 lines as opposed to 20-25.

For some reason, however, Bertone did not capitalize on this significant detail. Had he talked about it during the program, combined with the earlier distinction over what Ottaviani did and did not say, then the matter would have easily been resolved. Instead, Bertone offered an *alternative* explanation on the *Porta a Porta* program that led to further criticism.

E. Alternative Explanations

On the program, Bertone was asked by Marco Politi about the lines of text in connection with Ottaviani.[59] In response, Bertone stated, "To me it was a little amazing that Cardinal Ottaviani had said categorically a

---

topher Ferrara, *The Secret Still Hidden*. (Pound Ridge, New York: Good Counsel Publications, 2008), 140-154.

57   See also *Friendly Reflections*, 9.

58   See also *Friendly Reflections* (9-10) in which Dr. Borelli explains Portuguese writing customs at the time of the writing down of the third part of the secret. Also, Bertone's revelation may also explain why, as Tosatti (109) notes, Capovilla mentioned four or five pages of handwritten text.

59   Cf. *The Secret Still Hidden*, 140-141.

sheet of 25 lines..."[60] The Cardinal went on to state, "...it may be that he had given a rather hasty summary [of the Secret], that he was mistaken. I don't believe that this element is so convincing as to say that there exists a sheet of paper (*foglio*) of 25 lines respecting the other of around 60 lines."[61] Lastly, Bertone offered a theory that Ottaviani counted only two pages instead of the four.[62]

In its totality, Bertone's explanations were quickly decried as implausible. The objection was right but for the wrong reason(s) as these were largely conspiratorial in nature. Thus, the characterization was wrong but the implausibility of Bertone's theory was correct.[63] After the *Porta a Porta* appearance, various other events took place on the matter of the 20-25 lines of text. It is not necessary to explain all of them as they will all revolve around the same fundamental point, namely ignorance of what Cardinal Ottaviani and Frère Michel/Bishop Venancio actually said.

The only thing this author deems worthy of mention is the publication in October, 2007 of Dr. Antonio Borelli's *Friendly Reflections* essay in which he discussed the number of lines controversy among other points. Sometime in the first half of the year 2010, Christopher Ferrara, issued a challenge to *Friendly Reflections*.[64] In the light of all that has been exam-

---

60   *The Secret Still Hidden*, 141.

61   Ibid., 142.

62   Ibid., 143.

63   The implausibility of Bertone's theory became a weapon of choice in polemics against the Vatican. For example, see *The Secret Still Hidden*, to say nothing of countless other writings, talks, and lectures that attacked Bertone's theory.

64   <http://www.fatima.org/news/newsviews/ferraraexpose.pdf> (Accessed 6 December, 2015). See pages 17-20, and 36-37 of this PDF document. Christopher Ferrara opens up his response with an attack and polemic on Borelli's character. This is a simple case of the pot calling the kettle black. Ferrara himself engages in *numerous* polemics with people and organizations against which he is in an adversarial posture. This fact is so apparent throughout Ferrara's literary output that this author does not believe it necessary to provide any

ined, it is now clear that Ferrara did not see the possibility that Cardinal Bertone simply accepted an assertion without proof.[65] In fact, Ferrara himself makes the same error as he takes Bertone's words at face value!

F. One Final Consideration

While acknowledging that there were facts rooted in even further past events, this chapter has demonstrated that any *serious* discussion and questioning over Ottaviani and the lines of text began around the year 2006 with the publication of Antonio Socci's book *Il Quarto Segreto di Fatima*. One can draw a line from this book to Bertone's responses in *L'Ultima Veggenti di Fatima* and his appearance on *Porta a Porta*. The line continues further to Ferrara's book *The Secret Still Hidden*, onward. It is apparent that a *specific and clear* citation was not produced. Note the words "specific and clear." Ferrara alone provides his readers with some measure of a citation, but it is incomplete or questionable.[66] On page 21 of *The Secret Still Hidden*, there is a footnote (52). This footnote references both Frère Michel (*The Whole Truth About Fatima: Volume III*, pages 479-481) and Frère François (*Fatima: Tragedy and Triumph*, page 45). As we have seen, these two citations are questionable.

Additionally, in footnote 52, Ferrara provides mention of the "renowned Mariologist" Fr. Rene Laurentin in support of the 20-25 lines of text claim. Ferrara also cites Bertone's testimony in *The Last Visionary of*

---

particular citation.

65   Accepting Bertone's testimony with respect to Cardinal Ottaviani is understandable. Bertone *is* representing the Vatican and he is the Secretary of State. It is not unreasonable to expect Bertone to be familiar with the facts from having researched it, and, in Bertone's case, being an intimate part of the story.

66   Cf. *The Secret Still Hidden*, pages 21, 69, 79, 90-94, 124, 140-144, 159-160, and 201. See also pages 39-40 of the PDF "Epilogue" to *The Secret Still Hidden* written sometime around or after 2010 available online at: <http://www.secretstillhidden.com/pdf/epilogue.pdf> (Accessed 6 December, 2015).

Fatima and the *Porta a Porta* interview. Concerning the latter, we have discussed Bertone's testimony above. As concerns the mention of Laurentin, Ferrara does not provide a citation.

Lastly, it is in the year 2013 that a reference is given from Ferrara that indicates the 1967 Allocution of Cardinal Ottaviani at the Antonianum is the source of the 20-25 lines of text claim.[67] Even then the reference simply reads, "a single page of some 25 lines of text (sources: Bishop Venancio [1959] and Cardinal Ottaviani [1967]." Can there be another reference from Ottaviani in the year 1967 other than his 1967 Allocution? If there is, it is unknown in the available literature on Fátima.

III. Conclusion

This chapter has endeavored at length to present significant facts on the question of the number of lines of text that comprise the third part of the secret of Fátima. From those facts, it appears that Bertone's own explanations on this topic can be charitably understood as a misguided effort based upon the information he then possessed. Bertone appears to have accepted as fact an assertion that was both questionable and unclear, to the detriment of his own defense of the Vatican. It is to be hoped that the information herein presented will bring to close at least one part of the ongoing controversy behind said part of the secret.

---

67   Francis Alban and Christopher Ferrara, *Fatima Priest*. (Pound Ridge, New York: Good Counsel Publications, 2013), 232. A similar presentation of the matter can be found in Ferrara's book *False Friends of Fatima*, 91, 96.

—3—
THE 1967 ALLOCUTION
OF CARDINAL OTTAVIANI

"May we then listen to what the Holy Virgin is telling us from Fátima: lift up your heads, for your redemption is at hand."
—Alfredo Cardinal Ottaviani, February 11, 1967

In the previous chapter, we mentioned the 1967 Allocution of Cardinal Ottaviani in relation to the number of lines of text in the third part of the secret of Fátima. There is, however, more to be said about this Allocution and the present chapter endeavors to do so. We shall discuss first the historicity of the Allocution, followed by its reliability and then a question about a remark the Cardinal made concerning for whom the third part was intended.

I. The Textual Tradition of the Allocution

The Allocution was delivered in Italian by Ottaviani on February 11, 1967 at the Antonianum in Rome. It was then incorporated into a larger volume of *Acta* (Acts) of the Pontifical International Marian Academy (PAMI).[1] According to a footnote at the end of the first page, the Allocu-

---

1   *Acta Pontificiae Academiae Marianae Internationalis vel ad Academiam quoquo modo pertinentia. Volume 4.* (Romae: Pontificia Academia Mariana

tion was placed in the Archives of PAMI and given the protocol number 208/67.[2] At the end of the document was a note by the editor(s) of the *Acta*. This note relays that the transcription was made from the recording (*registrazione*) of the Cardinal's discourse. It says:

> Transcription made from the recording of the discourse of His Eminence and Most Reverend Cardinal Alfredo Ottaviani, Pro-Prefect of the Sacred Congregation of the Doctrine of the Faith, held on February 11, 1967 in the great hall "Maria Assunta" of the Pontifical Ateneo Antonianum, on the occasion of the Roman celebration organized by the Pontifical International Marian Academy in preparation for the V Mariological Congress and the XII International Mariological [Congress].[3]

The Allocution was also published in French and Portuguese translations. The French translation was published by a well-known French periodical entitled *La Documentation Catholique* (LDC) in 1967.[4] With-

---

Internationalis, 1967), 44-49. Hereafter *Acta Pontificiae Academiae Marianae Internationalis* followed by page number. This volume is a standard publication for PAMI and so it did not attract much attention in the larger populous.

2   Ibid., 44.

3   Ibid., 49. The Italian text reads:

(1) (Trascrizione effettuata da registrazione del discorso di Sua Em.za Rev.ma il Card. Alfredo Ottaviani, Proprefetto della S.C. della dottrina della fede, tenuto l'11 Febbraio 1967 nell'Aula Magna « Maria Assunta » del Pont. Ateneo Antoniano, in occasione della celebrazione romana, organizzata dalla Pont. Accademia Mariana Internazionale in preparazione al V Congresso Mariologico e XII Mariano Internazionale).

The above note is important as it clearly states that it is a *transcription* of the words of the Cardinal, including his off-the-cuff remarks. It is not a simple reproduction of his prepared text.

4   *La Documentation Catholique*, 19 mars (1967), T. 64, numéro 1490,

in the writings of Frère Michel and those influenced by him, the French translation became the basis for most references to the Allocution. The reason for this development was due to the fact that the translation was cited (and commented upon) in the third volume of *The Whole Truth About Fatima* by Frère Michel.[5] Once Fr. Gruner published Frère Michel's book in English, the Allocution became more widely accessible.

The French translation provided four very helpful footnotes by the editor(s) of LDC. The first of these notes provided some context for the Allocution. It notified the reader of some critical information pertinent to how the Allocution was delivered and how the French translation was made. Concerning the first point, LDC stated the following:

> We have translated this discourse from the audiotape recording of the Cardinal's address. A (much shorter) written text was given to the press, but the Cardinal, whose sight is not good, spoke without text. The spoken text is notably different from the written text. We indicate by notes some passages from the written text that are not found in the spoken text. The subtitles are ours.[6]

---

columns 541-546. Hereafter *LDC* followed by year and column number.

5   Frère Michel de la Sainte Trinité, *The Whole Truth About Fatima. Volume III: The Third Secret.* (Buffalo, New York: Immaculate Heart Publications, 1990), 721-732. Hereafter *The Whole Truth About Fatima, Volume III* followed by page number. We will also have recourse to the original French text of this book (*Toute la Vérité sur Fátima: Le Troisième Secret.* [Saint Parres lès Vaudes, France: Renaissance Catholique Contre-Réforme Catholique, 1985]. Hereafter *Toute la Vérité sur Fátima: Le Troisième Secret* followed by page number).

6   The original French text reads as follows:

> Nous avons traduit ce discours d'après l'enregistrement au magné-tophone du discours du cardinal. Un texte écrit avait été remis à la presse (beaucoup plus court), mais le cardinal Ottaviani, dont la vue est très faible, a parlé sans texte, de sorte que le texte prononcé est sensiblement différent du texte écrit. Nous indiquons en note quelques

The above tells us that Ottaviani came to the Antonianum with a pre-pared text. He did not, however, keep to his text and made off-the-cuff remarks at various intervals. A copy of the prepared text was issued to people present to hear the Cardinal speak. What became of these copies is not clear, though it appears a copy was printed in the publication *La Madre di Dio*.[7]

In its translation, LDC noted a few places where the Cardinal's *viva voce* differed from his prepared text. These notes were the other three footnotes and contained the prepared text (in French) with some commentary from LDC.[8] As to how the French translation was made, note that LDC wrote in the first footnote that they possessed a recording of the Allocution. For good measure, the editor(s) of LDC added subheadings on their own authority.

Concerning the Portuguese translation, it was placed in the short-lived periodical entitled *Fatima 50*.[9] It was the fourth of a series of articles on the secret of Fátima that were written by Fr. Joaquín María Alonso, the Sanctuary's Archivist. He prefaced it with a brief introductory note that, among other things, attempts not to foment curiosity (*nem tão pouco para fomenter uma curiosidade*) while asking if the Cardinal's remarks may hold a clue to the content (*conteúdo*) of the text. According to Alonso, the translation was a literal one made from the Italian transcription available by PAMI, even to the point of the translation being against Portuguese language preferences.[10]

---

passages du texte écrit qui ne se retrouvent pas dans le texte prononcé. Les sous-titres sont de notre redaction (*LDC*, 1967, 541).

7   *La Madre di Dio*, Anno XXXIV, No.3 (March, 1967), 16-18. Hereafter *La Madre di Dio* followed by page number.

8   In the amended text presented in Appendix A of the present book, these references were retained as they provide useful information.

9   *Fatima 50* (Year 1, No. 7, November 13, 1967), pages 14-16. Hereafter *Fatima 50* followed by date and page number.

10   Alonso wrote, "...daí certas expressões que gostaríamos de escrever

II. The Reliability of the Allocution

In the previous chapter, we saw that the 1967 Allocution of Cardinal Ottaviani is celebrated for its (alleged) statement on the 20-25 lines of text. Believing this claim favors the argument that the Vatican is hiding another text on the third part of the secret. In the midst, however, of this dependence upon Ottaviani's Allocution, it appears as though an inconvenient truth is neglected, namely the *serious* criticisms of the Allocution by Frère Michel.[11]

The scholarship of Frère Michel, the reader is reminded, is held in high regard by many leading advocates for a second text. The problem, however, is that whereas there is a desire to uphold the Allocution in favor of a second text of the third part of the secret, Frère Michel considered the Allocution to be highly suspect. He accuses the Cardinal of "falsehoods" that were abusing, deceiving, and shamefully misleading the faithful.[12] Was he just in doing so?

A. Assessing Frere Michel's Criticisms

If one were to assess critically the various observations made by Frère Michel, one will find that he was not always accurate. For example, he criticizes a remark attributed to Ottaviani in the French translation about Francisco and Jacinta being the brother and sister of Sr. Lúcia when they were her cousins. Frère Michel wrote:

No, this is not a simple slip of the tongue: in three places the Cardi-

---

à nossa maneira de tradutores correctos para o português mas que preferimos deixar com o sabor do idioma original e que foi feita sobre o texto literal italiano..." (*Fatima 50*, November 13, 1967, page 14).

11   *The Whole Truth About Fatima, Volume III*, 721-732; *Toute la Vérité sur Fátima: Le Troisième Secret*, 483-492. Frère Michel refers his readers to the very severe criticisms of Fr. Freire (see note 1 on page 483 of the French text).

12   Ibid., 732. See also the remarks at the end of page 721. *Toute la Vérité sur Fátima: Le Troisième Secret*, 483 & 492.

nal will state that Jacinta and Francisco are Lucy's *little brother and little sister!* This shows how much attention and care the Prefect of the Holy Office — who in 1956-1957 had requested the Bishop of Leiria for all Lucy's writings, to examine them — had taken to inform himself about Fatima events![13]

A comparison of the French text utilized by Frère Michel with the Italian shows a translation error.[14] The Cardinal did *not* refer to Francisco and Jacinta as Sr. Lúcia's brother and sister.[15]

In another place, however, Frère Michel questions the Cardinal's understanding of who was the intended recipient of the third part of the secret.[16] His observations on Ottaviani's claims have merit. Ottaviani claims

---

13   *The Whole Truth About Fatima, Volume III,* 723); *Toute la Vérité sur Fátima: Le Troisième Secret,* 485. Ironically, the same remark on "attention and care" can here be said of Frère Michel who failed to consult the Italian original even though it had been available since 1967 in the *Acta.*

14   *Acta Pontificiae Academiae Marianae Internationalis,* 44. The Italian text is, "L'uno riguardava Lucia nei suoi sentimenti familiari più intimi, la predizione che *Francesco e la sorellina Giacinta* sarebbero presto volati nel cielo" (emphases mine). Compare this with the French text (LDC 1967, 541-542): "L'un concernait les sentiments familiaux les plus intimes de Lucia, la prédiction que *son petit frère Francesco et sa petite soeur Giacinta* s'envoleraient bientôt pour le ciel" (emphases mine).

15   A comment is necessary on the reliability of the Italian transcription. How faithful or accurate was the transcriptionist(s)? Was anything added, subtracted, or emended? At this time, the question of the reliability of the transcription cannot be addressed in full. An audio or video recording of good quality has not been provided to the public that can be used to check the accuracy of the transcription. Despite this drawback, one can compare the Italian to the French translation, which also claims to be based upon a recording of the actual address. This author has performed such a comparison and discovered that although some differences exist with respect to *expression* and some *details*, the two texts agree *structurally* in all but one place. Thus, there is strong evidence to support that the Italian and French texts are indeed based upon the remarks delivered *ex tempore* by Cardinal Ottaviani.

16   *The Whole Truth About Fatima, Volume III,* 725, 728-729; *Toute la Vérité sur Fátima: Le Troisième Secret,* 488ff.

that the third part (what he calls the "secret message") was destined (*destinato*) for the Holy Father. In the Italian text, the Cardinal stated:

> The public Message of Fátima is what matters. The secret matters, this matters to the Holy Father to whom it was destined [*Importa « il Segreto », importa questo al Santo Padre a cui era destinato*]. He was the recipient [*Egli era il destinatario*]. And if the recipient [*destinatario*] has not decided to say, "This is the moment to reveal it to the world", we must stick to his wisdom who has wanted it kept secret.[17]

The Cardinal's discussion revolves around his understanding, usage and development of the Italian words *importa*, *destinato* and *destinatario* into the point he wishes to make.[18] A careful study of this part of the Allocution leads one to question if the *viva voce* nature of the Cardinal's address is affecting the formulating of his thought. The Cardinal appears to struggle when he says, "The secret matters, this matters to the Holy Father...etc."[19]

---

17   *Acta Pontificiae Academiae Marianae Internationalis,* 47.

18   *Importa* is a form (third person singular present indicative) of the verb *importare. Destinato* is a past participle of *destinare*, and *destinatorio* is a masculine noun. The French translation employs equivalent words (*importe, destiné, destinataire*).

19   In the Italian text in the *La Madre di Dio* (17) article, Ottaviani's text is:

Ma con insoddisfatta curiosità ed ansia il mondo cerca di scrutare quale sia il segreto che la Madre di Dio confidò alla Veggente; se è un segreto, come si può pretendere che esso sia rivelato? a meno che Quegli che doveva esserne il destinatario ed il custode, non avesse stimato giunto, dopo il 1960 — data rimessa alla prudenza ed alla saggezza dell'Augusto Pontefice — il momento di svelarlo.

Il contenuto del Messaggio, ricordato fedelmente e poi scritto di propria mano dalla Veggente di Fatima, viene custodito ancora nel segreto del cuore di Lucia, né d'altra parte, chi ne è in possesso ed ha l'autorità di disporre, ha giudicato opportuno svelarlo.

For his part, Frère Michel is not as concerned about the first two words as he is about the third (*destinatario*/*destinataire*). This word is clear: the receiver of a message. At face value, within the context of the written text of the third part of the secret, Ottaviani's choice of words conflicts with the facts. The note placed on the envelope by Sr. Lúcia does not mention the Holy Father. Thus, on a literal level, the Cardinal would be incorrect as the envelope was not addressed to the Pope. It is possible, however, to understand Ottaviani a little differently, a discussion of which we shall defer to the next section.

For now, whether or not the Cardinal deserved such serious accusations from Frère Michel is a matter for debate. It is, however, undeniable that Frère Michel was correct at the core—the Cardinal made some notable gaffes in his Allocution. These gaffes are significant enough that anyone who wishes to cite the Allocution needs to proceed with great caution.[20] An example of where such caution should be exercised can be found in Christopher Ferrara's book *The Secret Still Hidden*.

On page 23, there is a sub-section entitled *The Secret contains difficult Portuguese expressions*. In this sub-section, Ferrara provides a discussion of what happened when the third part of the secret was opened by Pope John XXIII. He presents two different versions of events, one by Archbishop Loris Capovilla and the other by Cardinal Ottaviani. Both stories differ in some details (specified by Ferrara, but unnecessary to detail for our purposes).[21]

In making his case for another text of the third part of the secret, Fer-

---

It is clear that Ottaviani was clearly struggling to express his point.

20   Cf. *The Whole Truth About Fatima, Volume III*, 557.

21   Frère Michel notes the contradiction concerning whether or not Mgr. Tavares was consulted for translation purposes (*Toute la Vérité sur Fátima: Le Troisième Secret*, 487). Let us here ask ourselves an important question. If there are two texts, both from the pen of Sr. Lúcia, why would John XXIII need help with one but not the other? Did Sister suddenly write differently between 1944 and 1957 for some unknown reason?

rara reads these differing stories as evidence of a second text. Concurring with a conclusion of Antonio Socci on this matter, Ferrara writes, "These two opposed affirmations...can be explained by holding that the matter treats of two different readings of two different texts."[22] "Can be explained" is subjective; the question is *should* they be explained in this manner?[23]

If Cardinal Ottaviani made notable errors in the Allocution, is it not also possible to explain Ottaviani's version of events as similarly flawed?[24] This question requires some examination by competent persons and no strict conclusion is intended to be reached at this time. Our intent in this section is only to raise a question for further reflection and consideration.

III. Ottaviani, the Third Part of the Secret and the Holy Father

Cardinal Ottaviani's remarks on the intended recipient of the text touch upon a sensitive point of contention.[25] Ottaviani claims that the secret mattered (*importa*) to the Holy Father. According to the account written by Sr. Lúcia herself in her personal diary, it was the express will of Our Lady that the secret be opened and/or read by the Bishop of Leiria or

---

22   *The Secret Still Hidden*, 23. An early interview with Capovilla is presented in the appendices to the present book for comparison purposes. The reader is reminded that Capovilla was an eyewitness whereas Ottaviani was consulted *after* the fact.

23   One could argue that the notion of two texts did not exist when Frère Michel was researching and writing on Fátima. Thus, he did not foresee this possibility. This notion, however, does not factor well that the Cardinal was speaking *viva voce* and that his gaffes were more than likely rooted in this fact.

24   On how Ottaviani could have made such gaffes, consider Roberto de Mattei, *The Second Vatican Council: An Unwritten Story*. (Fitzwilliam, New Hampshire: Loreto Publications, 2012), 535. Contrast his depiction with Yves Congar, *My Journal of the Council*. [Collegeville, Minnesota: Liturgical Press, 2012], 829-830).

25   *The Whole Truth About Fatima, Volume III*, 465-479.

the Cardinal Patriarch of Lisbon.[26] Moreover, it was clear during Cardinal Bertone's appearance on the *Porta a Porta* program in May, 2007 that Sr. Lúcia wrote on the envelope that it was Our Lady who specified the recipients of the envelope; the Holy Father was not specified.[27]

As we elsewhere observed, Rome asked for copies of all documents and the original text was sent to Rome.[28] A copy was *not* made and kept in the Chancery of the Diocese of Leiria. The opportunity was thus lost for the specified members of the Portuguese hierarchy to open and reveal the third part of the secret. Was the text of the third part intended by heaven to be forwarded to Rome and given to the Holy Father? Frère Michel gives negative indications in this regard.[29]

---

26   Carmelo de Santa Teresa – Coimbra, *Um Caminho sob o Olhar de Maria: Biografia da Irmã Lúcia de Jesus e do Coração Imaculado, O.C.D.* (Coimbra, Portugal: Edições Carmelo, 2013), 273-275. Hereafter *Um Caminho sob o Olhar de Maria* followed by page number.

27   It must be noted, however, that this fact is not to be read outside of the principle of subsidiarity within the hierarchy of the Church. It would have been an egregious error if the Holy Father were to have requested the document and it was denied him simply because it fell outside of the literal words of Our Lady. Let us remember as well that the Holy See had requested *copies*, not the originals, of the documents.

28   *The Whole Truth About Fatima, Volume III*, 53, 480-481; *Toute la Vérité sur Fátima: Le Troisième Secret*, 320. It is true to say that the recipient/custodian of the document was the Bishop of Fátima. To say, however, that he was the recipient/custodian of the document is not quite the same as saying it was "destined" for him. In other words, it is not the same to say that the third part of the secret was *about* him.

29   *The Whole Truth About Fatima, Volume III*, 465-479. In addition to this, Frère Michel later uses the person of Fr. Dhanis as a figurehead of blame to attribute conspiratorial motives to authorities in Rome who requested the document be forwarded to the Holy See (cf. *The Whole Truth About Fatima, Volume III*, 495-499). His discussion, however, is sheer speculation. Not one direct reference is provided that proves a conspiratorial motive. He does not appear to value much the fact that the responsibility for this matter lay with Bishop da Silva in his unwillingness to make a copy of the document. Finally, Frère Michel curiously passes over an important reference to the Holy Father in his discussion

A. Ottaviani and the Recipient of the Message

As the above discussion pertains to the Allocution of Cardinal Otta-viani, there is an observation to be made. The observation concerns what Cardinal Ottaviani meant when he claimed that the third part of the secret matters/pertains (*importa*) to the Pope to whom it was destined (*destinato*). Given the facts, it appears as though there are differing interpretations of the Cardinal's remarks and we shall discuss these presently.

One interpretation is literal and holds that Ottaviani meant the document was addressed to the Pope.[30] In other words, Sr. Lúcia wrote it down and from the beginning wanted it sent to the Holy Father. The issue here is that Sister *clearly* wrote that the envelope was to be opened by the Bishop of Leiria or the Cardinal Patriarch of Lisbon. There is no mention of the Holy Father.

Another interpretation is not as literal. It envisions Ottaviani's words as meaning that the third part of the secret *pertained* to the Holy Father, i.e. that it was *about* him. If it was about him, then it is not inconceivable that he would withhold the text. A premise for this interpretation is the apparent struggle that Ottaviani had in formulating his thought, delivered *viva voce* as we have seen, and thus is not meant to be understood in a strict fashion.

Let us look at Ottaviani's respective statements that touch upon the matter at hand. They are as follows in English translation (followed by the page number in which they appeared in the *Acta*) and numbered in the order in which the statements appear:

---

on the famous 1957 meeting of Fr. Fuentes with Sr. Lúcia (cf. *The Whole Truth About Fatima, Volume III*, 503-522). Here, Sister is reported to have said that it was the will of Our Lady for the Pope to know the third part of the secret.

30   *The Whole Truth About Fatima, Volume III*, 177, 721, 725, 728-729. It is necessary to point out that Frère Michel himself makes the distinction (on page 711) that the document was not *addressed* to the Holy Father, but that it was *about* him. He makes a very similar observation on page 177 of the same book.

[1] The world has lent its ear to the message of Lúcia, that message which is past the private aspect, the family, over to the part which concerned the whole world — the message invited to prayer and penance the entire world —, it contained the third part of those things the Most Holy Madonna confided. And these things had been confided not for herself [Lúcia], not for the world—at least for now—but for the Vicar of Jesus Christ [45].[31]

[2] Also, what did Lúcia do to obey exactly the Most Holy Virgin? She wrote on a sheet [of paper], in the Portuguese language, that which the Holy Virgin had asked her to tell the Holy Father [45].[32]

[3] The envelope containing the "Secret of Fátima" was given closed to the Bishop of Leiria, and, although Lúcia said he could read it, he did not want to read it. He wanted to respect "the Secret" out of reverence for the Holy Father. He sent it to the Apostolic Nuncio, then Msgr. Cento, today Cardinal Cento, who is present, and who faithfully handed it to the Congregation for the Doctrine of the Faith, who had requested it... [46].[33]

---

31   The Italian text:

Il mondo ha prestato orecchio al messaggio di Lucia, quel messaggio che oltre alla parte privata, familiare, oltre alla parte che riguardava tutto il mondo — il messaggio invitava a preghiera e penitenza tutto il mondo —, conteneva la terza parte delle cose che aveva confidato la Madonna Santissima. E queste gliele aveva confidate non per sé, non per il mondo — subito almeno —, ma per il Vicario di Gesù Cristo.

32   The Italian text: "E allora che ha fatto essa, per ubbidire appunto alla Vergine Santissima? Ha scritto in un foglio, in lingua portoghese, quello che la Madonna le ha detto di dire al Santo Padre."

33   The Italian text:

La busta contenente il « Segreto di Fatima » fu dal Vescovo di Leiria presa chiusa, e quantunque Lucia avesse detto che lui poteva leggerlo, non volle leggerlo. Volle rispettare « il Segreto », anche per riverenza al Santo Padre. Lo mandò al Nunzio apostolico, allora Mons. Cento,

[4] .... The public Message of Fátima is what matters. The secret matters, this matters to the Holy Father to whom it was destined. He was the recipient. And if the recipient has not decided to say, "This is the moment to reveal it to the world", we must stick to his wisdom who has wanted it kept secret [47].[34]

[5] But what matters, as I said, is that we know to conform our life, our actions and our activities to that which is the spirit of the public Message, because Lúcia was charged not only to transmit to the Pope the Secret Message but also to publish and make known to all the world the public message, a message which is contained in these words: prayer and penance [47]![35]

In order to understand best the Cardinal, it is recommended to read Ottaviani's entire Allocution in context (provided in the appendices to this book). We will, however, proceed to examine the above five statements.

Overall, it is undeniable that Cardinal Ottaviani's remarks are very "papal-centric." His discussion on publishing the text revolves around the person and will of the Pope. This "papal-centrism" is the cause for much

---

ora Cardinal Cento, qui presente, e questi lo rimise fedelmente alla Congregazione della dottrina della Fede, che glielo aveva chiesto....

34   The Italian text:

Il Messaggio pubblico di Fatima è quello che importa. Importa « il Segreto », importa questo al Santo Padre a cui era destinato. Egli era il destinatario. E se il destinatario non si decide a dire: « questo è il momento di farlo noto al mondo », dobbiamo lasciare alla sua saggezza che esso resti segreto.

35   The Italian text:

Ma quel che importa — come dicevo — è che noi sappiamo uniformare la nostra vita, le nostre azioni, le nostre attività a quello che è lo spirito del Messaggio pubblico, perché Lucia fu incaricata non soltanto di mandare al Papa il Messaggio Segreto, ma anche di pubblicare e fare noto a tutto il mondo il Messaggio pubblico, messaggio che si rinchiude in quelle parole: preghiera e penitenza.

of the criticisms of Ottaviani's Allocution. In the first two statements, as well as the fifth, he comes across as meaning that the third part of the secret was supposed to go [exclusively] to the Holy Father. There is, however, no known record that:

1. Our Lady confided the third part of the secret to Sr. Lúcia for the Pope,
2. the Virgin asked Sister to tell the third part to the Holy Father, and
3. Sr. Lúcia was charged to transmit the third part to the Pope.

On these counts, and unless further information can be provided, Ottaviani was *clearly* and *factually* mistaken.[36]

Ottaviani makes a further error in the third statement wherein he claims the Bishop of Leiria decided against reading the secret "out of reverence for the Holy Father." There is nothing in the historical record that warrants this interpretation of events. According to all available documentation, Bishop da Silva simply did not want to accept the burden of the knowledge contained within the text.[37] Nowhere in the available documentation is "regard for the Holy Father" mentioned by the Bishop, though it is believed that da Silva would have been glad to be relieved of the document by a higher authority.[38]

Upon coming, however, to the fourth statement, Ottaviani makes a subtle shift.[39] He stated, "The secret matters, this matters to the Holy Father to whom it was destined...." Moreover, the past participle *destinato* indicates that the Cardinal was not stating the secret was written to the Holy Father. Otherwise, the Cardinal would have said "addressed." The

---

36   Ottaviani may have drawn upon his own memories or knowledge gained from the archives of the Congregation for the Doctrine of the Faith.

37   See the summary in *The Secret of Fatima: Fact and Legend*, 44-49. See also John Haffert's remarks in his book *Dear Bishop!* (Washington, New Jersey: AMI International Press, 1982), 4, and 122.

38   Cf. *The Whole Truth About Fatima, Volume III*, 52-53.

39   Frère François (*Fatima: Tragedy and Triumph*, 245) and Frère Michel (*The Whole Truth About Fatima, Volume III*, 728-729) caught Ottaviani's subtle shift.

word he *did* use conveys that the third part was *about* the Pope. If it was *about* him, then, in the Cardinal's opinion, it is within the Pope's prerogative to reveal it or not.

The Italian text is clear: Ottaviani revealed that the third part of the secret contained a prophecy pertaining to the Holy Father.[40] The revelation of the text in the year 2000 adds weight to this observation. The text of the vision published in 2000 portrays a "bishop dressed in white." It is stated that Sr. Lúcia claimed (in response to a question) this person is the "principal figure" of the vision.[41] Let us look at the relevant text:

> ....And we saw in an immense light that is God: 'something similar to how people appear in a mirror when they pass in front of it' a Bishop dressed in White 'we had the impression that it was the Holy Father'. Other Bishops, Priests, men and women Religious going up a steep mountain, at the top of which there was a big Cross of rough-hewn trunks as of a cork-tree with the bark; before reaching there the Holy Father passed through a big city half in ruins and half trembling with halting step, afflicted with pain and sorrow, he prayed for the souls of the corpses he met on his way; having reached the top of the mountain, on his knees at the foot of the big Cross he was killed by a group of soldiers who fired bullets and arrows at him, and in the same way there died one after another the other Bishops, Priests, men and women Religious, and various lay people of different ranks and positions. Beneath the two arms of the Cross there were two Angels each with a crystal aspersorium in his hand, in which they gathered up the blood

---

40   Cf. *The Whole Truth About Fatima, Volume III*, 711. Frère Michel was astute to observe this fact, though he framed it in scathing terms against the Cardinal.

41   *The Message of Fatima*, 28.

of the Martyrs and with it sprinkled the souls that were making their way to God.[42]

Sister's May 12, 1982 letter to the Holy Father in which she summarizes the vision confirms the above text. She wrote:

The third part of the secret refers to Our Lady's words: 'If not [Russia] will spread her errors throughout the world, causing wars and persecutions of the Church. The good will be martyred; the Holy Father will have much to suffer; various nations will be annihilated' (13-VII-1917).[43]

If the principal figure of the vision is the Pope, then the third part of the secret concerns him (though not exclusively). This fact was unknown to all parties other than Sr. Lúcia until the envelope was opened by John XXIII. Let us imagine the event for a moment. After 15-16 years of anticipation and speculation, the third part of the secret was now opened. Pope John reads it and learns that it portrays a Pope being shot and killed.

It is a fact that the warnings of Our Lady at Fátima are intimately bound up with the struggle of the Church with Communism and atheism. It is not a leap of logic to connect the attack on the Pope with this struggle. What was Pope John to do? Pope John Paul II, in 1980, is *alleged* to have remarked in Fulda, Germany the following, "Given the seriousness of the contents, my predecessors in the Petrine office diplomatically preferred to postpone publication so as not to encourage the world power of Commu-

---

42   Ibid., 21.

43   Ibid., 8-9. It is clear from the above texts that the third part refers to what happens if Russia were afforded the opportunity to spread her errors.

nism to make certain moves."[44] This remark was denied by the Vatican.[45]

The question of its veracity aside, there is a good point in it. To notify the world that the Mother of God prophesied one or more representatives of Communism would attack the Pope is the equivalent of putting a target on the Papal cope and cassock. What Pope is voluntarily going to submit himself to such a fate? Let us consider an observation made by Fr. Stanley Jaki:

> In retrospect it should not be difficult to see why it was most prudent not to make public the text of the Third Secret. Its early publication would have prompted not a few to suspect a conspiracy against the Pope whenever he traveled, and he traveled much and at times in truly perilous circumstances. Conspiracy theories would not have failed to be given political twists to the enormous harm of the Pope's pastoral mission. Apocalyptic scenarios would have been concocted. Visionaries would have popped up in great numbers, news about "apparitions" would have been generated in even greater numbers. Hysteria might have ruled when humble, quiet service of God was alone called for.[46]

The prophecy was conditional based upon the response of the Church to Our Lady's requests. By 1960, the Popes had failed to fulfill them and Russia's errors had spread. Of course, to some people, the above reasoning would not matter. Their argument rests upon the fact that Our Lady

---

44   <http://www.fatima.org/thirdsecret/fulda.asp> (Accessed 24 December, 2015). This remark was published in the German magazine *Stimme des Glaubens* in October, 1981 (according to the citation).

45   The remark was denied by Cardinal Ratzinger during the June 26, 2000 press conference. This author does not intend to contradict this denial.

46   Fr. Stanley Jaki, *The Sun's Miracle, or of Something Else?* (New Hope, Kentucky: Real View Books, 2000), 4. Contrast this statement with Christopher Ferrara's statement on the year 1960 and the third part of the secret in *False Friends of Fatima* (Pound Ridge, New York: Good Counsel Publications, 2012), 96.

stated that the envelope be opened in 1960 by the Bishop of Leiria or the Cardinal Patriarch of Lisbon. The decision, however, not to make a copy and forward the original to Rome effectively removed the matter from the Portuguese hierarchy.

In the light of the above observations, it becomes more intelligible as to why Cardinal Ottaviani spoke of the third part of the secret with such strong "papal-centrism." He revealed that it had something to do *with* the Pope. Thus, to Ottaviani, if the prophecy was *about* the Pope then it was *meant for him* and the Cardinal's discussion revolved around this point. Unfortunately, owing to his own statements, the Cardinal was subjected to severe criticism. It is yet one more reason why his Allocution must be weighed carefully before drawing any conclusions such as the existence of a second text.

—4—
THE MYSTERIOUS DATE
OF 1960

"Why only after 1960? Was it Our Lady who fixed that date?"
—Archbishop Tarcisio Bertone, April, 2000

The message of Fátima is beautifully simple, yet its history is re-grettably not without controversy.[1] One of those controversies concerns a note that Sr. Lúcia put on the envelope containing the third part of the secret of Fátima.

When Sr. Lúcia wrote down the third part of the secret on January 3, 1944, she placed the writing within an envelope and sealed it. On the outside of the envelope she wrote in Portuguese that it was by the "ex-press order of Our Lady" (*por ordem expreça de Nossa Senhora*) that it be opened "in 1960" by the Cardinal Patriarch of Lisbon or the Bishop of Leiria. Catholics eagerly awaited the impending opening of the envelope. When it was decided not to publish its contents, the speculations grew over the course of 40 or so years. The present chapter seeks to address a discrepancy over the date of 1960.

---

1   The reader is encouraged to read this author's article that offers more background on this matter: <http://www.catholicstand.com/fourth-secret-fati-ma/>.

I. Why 1960? The Tale of Two Cardinals

In his 1967 Allocution, Cardinal Ottaviani revealed that he met with Sr. Lúcia in 1955 at her convent in Coimbra, Portugal.[2] During the course of his meeting with her, he asked why she put this date on the envelope. Her answer, according to the Cardinal, was, "Because then it will appear more clear."[3] If we fast-forward about 30 or so years, this matter comes up again in a stunning fashion. After the release of the third part of the secret in June, 2000 by the Congregation for the Doctrine of the Faith (CDF), conspiracy theories continued unabated by the document's publication. In the years 2000, 2001 and 2003, Tarcisio Bertone went to speak with Sr. Lúcia to obtain clarifications.[4]

The first interview was on April 27, 2000 and an account of the event

---

2   During his pilgrimage to Fátima in 1955, Cardinal Ottaviani delivered an Allocution at the Cova da Iria. This text has been translated and placed in the appendices of the present book as it provides some helpful information to understand better his later Allocution of 1967.

3   *Acta Pontificiae Academiae Marianae Internationalis vel ad Academiam quoquo modo pertinentia. Volume 4.* (Romae: Pontificia Academia Mariana Internationalis, 1967), 45. The Italian text is, "Domandai a Lucia: perché? — il perché di quella data. Ed essa mi rispose: « perché allora apparira " mas claro' (più chiaro) »." To the best of anyone's knowledge (or at least in accordance with the numerous books consulted), Sister never further clarified publicly this matter even if she made some remarks about the third part of the secret itself (not the date). This is until the new biography was published in 2013. Discussion on this point is provided later in the present chapter.

4   For a summary of the meeting in 2001 see: <http://www.ewtn.com/library/CURIA/CDFLUCIA.HTM>.

On a personal note, this author was in college at the time of the second meeting in 2001. It was right after the September 11 attacks in New York. Rumors were spreading that Sister Lúcia told people to pray. If memory serves it was because some disaster was coming upon us all. People went to their dorms to pray. According to a contact in Coimbra, Michael Brown of *Spirit Daily* reported the actual story:
<https://web.archive.org/web/20011016121838/http://www.spiritdaily.com/coimbra.htm> (Accessed 4 August, 2016).

was published on June 26, 2000 in the booklet *The Message of Fatima*.[5] Bertone states that he asked Sister to clarify the date of 1960 on the envelope. According to *The Message of Fatima*, the exchange went as follows:

> Before giving the sealed envelope containing the third part of the "secret" to the then Bishop of Leiria-Fatima [in 1944], Sister Lucia wrote on the outside envelope that it could be opened only after 1960, either by the Patriarch of Lisbon or the Bishop of Leiria. Archbishop Bertone therefore asked: "Why only after 1960? Was it Our Lady who fixed that date?" Sister Lucia replied: "It was not Our Lady. I fixed the date because I had the intuition that before 1960 it would not be understood, but that only later would it be understood. Now it can be better understood. I wrote down what I saw; however it was not for me to interpret it, but for the Pope.[6]

Bertone's claim that Sr. Lúcia said it was she who fixed the date was not in keeping with her own note on the outside of the envelope. People were

---

5   Congregation for the Doctrine of the Faith, *The Message of Fatima*. (Vatican City: Libreria Editrice Vaticana, 2000), 28-29. Hereafter referred to as *The Message of Fatima* followed by page number.

6   *The Message of Fatima*, 29. The Italian text reads:

Poiché Suor Lucia, prima di consegnare all'allora Vescovo di Leiria-Fatima la busta sigillata contenente la terza parte del « segreto », aveva scritto sulla busta esterna che poteva essere aperta solo dopo il 1960, o dal Patriarca di Lisbona o dal Vescovo di Leiria, Sua Ecc.za Mons. Bertone le domanda: « perché la scadenza del 1960? È stata la Madonna ad indicare quella data? ». Suor Lucia risponde: « Non è stata la Signora, ma sono stata io a mettere la data del 1960 perché secondo la mia intuizione, prima del 1960 non si sarebbe capito, si sarebbe capito solo dopo. Ora si può capire meglio. Io ho scritto ciò che ho visto, non spetta a me l'interpretazione, ma al Papa » (Congregazione per la Dottrina della Fede, *Il Messagio di Fatima*. [Vatican City, 2000], 29).

quick to question this apparent discrepancy and continually did so over the next several years.[7] During this time, Sister herself died in February, 2005.

In 2006, Bertone, now Cardinal Secretary of State for Pope Benedict XVI, addressed the continued questions over his account of his meetings with Sr. Lúcia. He was interviewed by Italian journalist Giuseppe De Carli in 2006 and this interview was published first in Italian called *L'Ultima Veggente di Fatima* (2007) and then in English as *The Last Secret of Fatima* (2008).[8]

During the interview, the question of the date of 1960 on the envelope arose. Giuseppe De Carli asked about it and Bertone responded as follows:

> As the date approached, certain people thought that something extraordinary was bound to happen. I asked Sister Lucia: "Why only after 1960? Was it Our Lady who fixed that date?" She replied: "It was a decision that I took on my own initiative. First, I thought that 1960 lay sufficiently far in the future from when I wrote down the Secret (which was in 1944). Second, I thought I would be dead by then, so that the last obstacle to publishing and interpreting it would be removed. Our Lady didn't tell me anything on this score."[9]

---

7   The next two meetings between Bertone and Sr. Lúcia did not pertain to the question of fixing the date on the envelope (or at least Bertone never mentioned if he discussed this matter again with Sister in 2001 and 2003). This is why these two meetings are not herein discussed.

8   The title of the English translation is different from the Italian. The Italian is *L'Ultima Veggente di Fatima* ("The Last Visionary of Fatima") and this more accurately describes the contents of the book which is about the person of Sr. Lúcia.

9   Tarcisio Cardinal Bertone, *The Last Secret of Fatima*. (New York: Doubleday, 2008), 80. Hereafter *The Last Secret of Fatima* followed by page number. The Italian text is:

> All'avvicinarsi della data qualcuno pensava che in quell'anno doves-se accadere qualcosa di straordinario. Ho chiesto a suor Lucia: «È

De Carli pushed the Cardinal for his opinion on the matter and received the following reply:

> Sister Lucia's explanation is plausible, but I understand that it may not be completely satisfying. The distance between 1944 and 1960 probably suggested to her mind a remote horizon, a period of time long enough for the meaning of the vision to be understood. It was a fictitious date, and Lucia admitted as much with disarming frankness.[10]

In the above, the Cardinal only reiterates what Sr. Lúcia told him personally; he does not resolve the apparent discrepancy. Because of this, the

---

stata la Madonna a suggerirle questa data, a indicarle una scadenza così precisa?». Lei ha risposto: «È stata una decisione mia perché ritenevo che il 1960 fosse una data lontanissima dalla stesura del "Segreto" del 1944 e perché pensavo di essere già morta in quell'anno, dunque sarebbe stato tolto l'ultimo ostacolo all'interpretazione e alla divulgazione del "Segreto". La Madonna non mi ha comunicato nulla al riguardo» (Tarcisio Bertone con Giuseppe De Carli, *L'Ultima Veggente di Fatima*. [Milano: Rai Eri Rizzoli, 2007], 92. Hereafter *L'Ultima Veggente di Fatima* followed by page number).

10   Ibid. The Italian text is:

Le parole di suor Lucia offrono una plausibile spiegazione, ma capisco che non possa essere completamente appagante. L'arco di tempo che va dal 1944 al 1960, probabilmente, segnava per lei un orizzonte remoto, un arco temporale sufficientemente ampio per la comprensione del senso della visione. Era una data fittizia e Lucia l'ha confessato con disarmante candore (*L'Ultima Veggente di Fatima*, 92).

In May, 2010, *L'Ultima Veggente di Fatima* was re-published as *L'Ultimo Segreto di Fatima* (Milano: Rai Eri Rizzoli, 2010). A comparison of the preceding quotes with the new edition shows that the first sentence of the second quote was edited. It now reads, "Non possiamo sovrapporre delle interpretazioni complicate a quanto ha candidamente dichiarato suor Lucia, ma capisco che non possa essere del tutto appagante" (p. 102). In English, "We cannot superimpose complicated interpretations to what Sister Lucia has stated candidly, but I understand that it may not be completely satisfying."

challenges to the Cardinal's account of his meeting with Sister continued unabated.

In May, 2007, Cardinal Bertone gave an interview with the Italian program *Porta a Porta*.[11] For this interview, the Cardinal came prepared with Sister Lúcia's envelope and the paper whereupon she wrote the third part of the secret. He opened it, on camera, and demonstrated to the audience what it looked like, what it said, and answered questions.

The *Porta a Porta* interview made it plain for all to see that Sr. Lúcia did write on said envelope that it was Our Lady who expressly ordered when it was to be opened. Vespa, before the program ended, asked the Cardinal about this fact.[12] Bertone's answer again reiterated his previous interview with Sr. Lúcia of April, 2000 which did not satisfy his critics.

---

11   A portion of the interview is available on *YouTube*: <https://www.you-tube.com/watch?v=AhB4WQtiBAE> (Accessed 4 August, 2016). *Catholic News Agency* carried a short report on its web site: <http://www.catholicnewsagency.com/news/cardinal_bertone_shows_original_letter_containing_third_secret_of_fatima_on_tv/> (Accessed 4 August, 2016).

12   From a transcript of the program, the exchange went as follows in Italian:

> Bruno Vespa: Ma no, ma prima, scusi Eminenza, Lei ha detto "Suor Lucia dice che Nostra Signora le ha detto non prima del '60"…
>
> Cardinal Bertone: Sì.
>
> Bruno Vespa: Quindi una prescrizione della della Vergine.
>
> Cardinal Bertone: Sì, della Vergine però io ho chiesto "ma è stata proprio la Madonna che ha ordinato di non aprire la busta prima del '60 o è stata lei che ha messo questa data?" e Suor Lucia mi ha risposto letteralmente così "son stato io che ho messo questa data, la Madonna non voleva che si conoscesse il segreto", questo è un punto fermo, no, anche se lei si è decisa a scriverla con il permesso della Madonna, poi si è decisa a scriverlo e a consegnarlo come segreto che non venisse pubblicato, no, ma disse "son stato io perché pensavo che il 1960 fosse un termine sufficiente per poter aprire poi la busta" e disse anche "io pensavo già magari di essere morta e allora devo essere più coinvolta nel terzo segreto", queste sono le parole che ha detto Suor Lucia.

In 2005, Sr. Lúcia died but did any hope of obtaining a clarification die with her? The publication of the biography of Sr. Lúcia by the Carmelite Sisters of Coimbra has revealed some very interesting facts.[13] The biography suggests that there was more going on in the heart of Sr. Lúcia than was previously known or understood. The biography offers two particular facts on this matter for our interest. The first is what appears to be a previously unpublished letter of Sr. Lúcia to Pope Pius XII. The other is an explanatory note offered by the Coimbra Sisters.

The letter to Pius XII is dated June 6, 1958. In this letter, Sr. Lúcia gives an explanation for the 1960 date. She states that it is in the 1960s that Communism will reach its zenith (*o comunismo atingirá o ponto máximo*).[14] In making this comment, Sister appears to connect the threat of Communism with the third part of the secret and the date of 1960. This connection is deliberate. If the date of 1960 was arbitrary and strictly in relation to how Sr. Lúcia thought she was going to be dead by then, why is she predicting in 1958 the zenith of Communism would occur in the 1960s?[15] It seems as though such questions were anticipated by the Carmelite Sisters.

---

13   Carmelo de Santa Teresa – Coimbra, *Um Caminho sob o Olhar de Maria: Biografia da Irmã Lúcia de Jesus e do Coração Imaculado, O.C.D.* (Coimbra, Portugal: Edições Carmelo, 2013). Hereafter *Um Caminho sob o Olhar de Maria* followed by page number.

14   *Um Caminho sob o Olhar de Maria,* 256.

15   On this specific point it is important to note that it was clear by 1958 Sr. Lúcia was not going to die of the illness afflicting her in 1944. It is entirely probable that Sister's thinking on the matter changed because of this fact. The question then is how would Sister have been able to connect the date of 1960 with Communism? It would appear as though some understanding was given to her about the vision (cf. *Um Caminho sob o Olhar de Maria,* 266). It is a known fact that Sr. Lúcia received later communications throughout her life which even Cardinal Bertone acknowledged (*The Last Secret of Fatima,* 83).

A. Truthful, Yet Evasive

Immediately after providing the above letter, the Sisters discuss why Sr. Lúcia fixed the 1960 date.[16] They explain it as Sister wanting to avoid the revelation of the new encounter with Our Lady on January 3, 1944.[17] Sr. Lúcia truly thought she was going to die, and her health *was* very precarious. Thus, according to the Sisters, when asked about the matter, Sr. Lúcia answered in terms of how she thought she was going to die before 1960.

The answer put forward by the Sisters is consistent with the known details of Sr. Lúcia's interior life. It is a well-documented fact that she did not like to reveal the secrets of her interior life. For instance, consider the fact that there are several *Memoirs* that Sister wrote touching upon some aspect of Fátima. Part of the reason why there are so many was because Sr. Lúcia wrote out of obedience and her religious superiors suspected that she was hiding details. She was ordered to write down more, and then still more, all the while Sister was at some pain to do so. Consider her own words:

> I think, Your Excellency, that I have written everything that you have told me to write for now. Until now, I did all I could to hide the more intimate parts of the apparitions at Cova da Iria. Whenever I spoke about them, I always touched on them lightly, so that I would not unveil what I wanted so much to reserve. But since now, obedience has obliged me, here it goes; and I remain like a skeleton stripped of everything, even of life itself, an exposition in the National Museum, reminding the visitors of the misery and nothingness of all that passes. Thus stripped, I will be on exposition in the World Museum, reminding those who pass, not of the misery

---

16   *Um Caminho sob o Olhar de Maria,* 256-257.

17   For more on this, see my article: <http://www.catholicstand.com/fourth-secret-fatima/>. See also *The Last Secret of Fatima,* 83.

and the nothingness, but of the greatness of the Divine Mercy.[18]

Sister's personal history on how she answers questions also provides a clue. She stated in her fourth *Memoir* the following:

Almost all the interrogators have been impressed for when I am being questioned, I lower my eyes and concentrate in such a way that I do not seem to pay attention to the question that is being asked. Sometimes some of them even repeat the question, thinking that I did not hear them. To Mr. Antero de Figueiredo I answered that I was remembering what happened regarding the question that was being asked. Of course it was so, but the real motive for my silent behavior was that I was searching in my conscience with the assistance of the Divine Holy Spirit *for an answer which, without revealing the facts, would be in accordance with the truth* (emphases mine).[19]

Even Cardinal Bertone revealed Lúcia was evasive with her answers on further conversations with Our Lady. The Cardinal stated:

I'm convinced that Sister Lucia continued to have conversations... with Our Lady. She had them for decades, all throughout the eighties and beyond. During our meetings, she referred to a whole sequence of dates between 1985 and 1989....In general, she would wait until

---

18   Dr. Antonio Maria Martins, S.J., *Memórias e Cartas de Irmã Lúcia.* (Porto, Portugal: Simão Guimarães, Filhos, LDA, 1973), 365. Hereafter *Memórias e Cartas de Irmã Lúcia* followed by page number.

19   Fr. Robert J. Fox, edit. *Documents on Fatima & Memoirs of Sister Lucia.* (Fatima Family Apostolate, 2002), 449. Hereafter *Documents on Fatima* followed by page number. This is also demonstrated in an incident relayed by Sister Maria Celina de Jesus Crucificado, OCD, *Our Memories of Sister Lucia.* (Coimbra, Portugal: Carmelo de Coimbra, 2005), 10. Hereafter *Our Memories of Sister Lucia* followed by page number.

she was certain of something before confirming it in writing. But so long as she had the slightest doubt, she preferred to remain silent. *Sister Lucia was evasive about her continuing conversations with Mary, and she would change the subject whenever it was brought up.* Her community and her prioress, who observed her at close range for decades, came to the conclusion that visions were not at all a rare occurrence with her. The cell of a Carmelite nun holds secrets that the rest of us will discover only in heaven (emphases mine).[20]

It is clear from the above texts that 1) Sr. Lúcia was reluctant to discuss the events that happened to her, and 2) she would find ways to be truthful, yet evasive. This insight into Sister's interior life is an interpretive key to understanding the controversy at hand as we shall see below.

Based upon the above, if Sr. Lúcia was privy to another revelation on January 3, 1944, it is not inconsistent for her not to want to reveal it. If she was not asked by her superiors to do so, nor asked the more fundamental question of whether she had even received another revelation, then Sister was at liberty not to divulge this information. The question that must then be asked is how successful was Sr. Lúcia in giving evasive yet truthful responses?[21]

---

20   *The Last Secret of Fatima*, 83. The Italian text reads:

Io sono convinto che suor Lucia abbia avuto ancora dei colloqui... Li definisca come vuole: apparizioni, visioni, locuzioni interiori con la Madonna. Li ha avuti per decenni, li ha avuti per tutti gli anni Ottanta e anche dopo. Lei, nei nostri incontri, ha solo citato alcune date, tutte a cavallo fra gli anni 1985 e 1989, come se cercasse di capire dalla sua Celeste Interlocutrice se ciò che era stato fatto rispondeva a un superiore disegno. Quando era sicura scriveva e confermava. Se v'era un minimo dubbio taceva. Su questa questione suor Lucia era sfuggente, evasiva, passava a conversare di altro. La sua comunità e la sua superiora, osservandola e vivendo vicino a lei per decenni, si sono convinte che le visioni non fossero cosi rare. La cella di una carmelitana serba segreti che solo in cielo scopriremo (*L'Ultima Veggente di Fatima*, 95).

21   What appears to be necessary is a good study on the life and character of

B. Some Challenges

While the explanation from the Coimbra Sisters is consistent with the facts of Sr. Lúcia's life, it also provides some challenges that must be addressed through careful thinking and research.

The first challenge is that the explanation offered by the Sisters for the 1960 note does not account for the proverbial pink elephant in the room. If Sr. Lúcia did not want to discuss the vision she received on January 3, 1944, what did she think was the logical conclusion at which people would arrive upon seeing the note on the envelope? Sister could only know of an express command from Our Lady by a supernatural communication.

Could it be that Sister simply did not foresee this logical deduction? Perhaps she did not think too much of the matter at the time. The envelope *was* originally intended for the Cardinal Patriarch of Lisbon and the Bishop of Leiria. It might be that Sister saw this as an "in-house" and thus confidential affair that would not assume any significance. It is also plausible that Sister attached no significance at the time because she thought she would be dead by 1960. Finally, perhaps all of the above are factors and have some convergence with one another.

The second challenge posed by the Coimbra Sisters' explanation is the statement revealed by Cardinal Ottaviani (quoted earlier). If the third part of the secret would appear "more clear" by 1960, how does this harmonize with the reasoning that Sister thought she would be dead by 1960? Why did she not just say to Ottaviani "I thought I'd be dead by then?" It is clear that, at least as of 1955, Sister had more in mind than just the concern of dying.

Concerning this second challenge, it must be noted that while it is

---

Sr. Lúcia. In the English-speaking world, such studies are few and far in-between as much of the literature revolves around statements from Sister about the events in or related to the 1917 apparitions of Our Lady in Fátima. This fact makes sense as Sister was the last surviving visionary and it was important to get her testimony as thoroughly as possible. The 2013 Carmelite biography itself presents fresh and significant contributions to our knowledge of Sr. Lúcia's character.

an important statement, Cardinal Ottaviani only relayed a few words from Sr. Lúcia. He did not give a transcript of his meeting with her. It is within the limits of reason and common sense to hold the idea that there was a context to her remarks and that, looking at the Cardinal's quote, he does not provide it. What we have are a few isolated words that are used for the purposes of the greater point the Cardinal makes in his Allocution.

For the purposes of a thorough investigation, a few words are not much by which to go. Further research would be necessary so as to arrive at a more conclusive assessment. In the meantime, it is fitting not to make more of Ottaviani's quote than what is absolutely necessary.[22] For now, it suffices to say that it agrees with Bertone's statement from the year 2000—that the third part of the secret would not be understood until/ would be clearer by 1960.

The third challenge is in Cardinal Bertone's rendition of Sr. Lúcia's conversation with him. As indicated in the quotations given earlier, Bertone has rendered the conversation a couple of different ways. In *The Message of Fatima*, the account of Bertone's April 27, 2000 conversation was published. The text, again, was as follows:

Archbishop Bertone therefore asked: "Why only after 1960? Was it Our Lady who fixed that date?" Sister Lucia replied: "It was not Our Lady. I fixed the date because I had the intuition that before 1960 it would not be understood, but that only later would it be understood. Now it can be better understood. I wrote down what I saw; however it was not for me to interpret it, but for the Pope."

---

22   Sr. Lúcia seemed to think more of the date than what she apparently let on later to Bertone. This, of course, poses the question "why did she apparently think differently with Ottaviani than with Bertone?" Technically she did not think differently with him as Bertone originally reported in 2000 that Sr. Lúcia spoke about the secret not being understood until 1960. We do not know everything she said to Ottaviani.

In his interview with Giuseppe De Carli, Bertone renders the conversation as follows:

> I asked Sister Lucia: "Why only after 1960? Was it Our Lady who fixed that date?" She replied: "It was a decision that I took on my own initiative. First, I thought that 1960 lay sufficiently far in the future from when I wrote down the Secret (which was in 1944). Second, I thought I would be dead by then, so that the last obstacle to publishing and interpreting it would be removed. Our Lady didn't tell me anything on this score.[23]

The differing accounts are apparent.

In the first quotation, Sr. Lúcia is explicitly credited with having said "It was not Our Lady. I fixed the date...etc." Nothing is said about her death having been a factor in the 1960 date. This changes, however, in the second quotation. The explicit wording "It was not Our Lady" and "I fixed the date" is slightly modified to the more indirect phrasing, "It was a decision that I took on my own initiative."[24] There is no mention of Our Lady. Bertone then adds to this the discussion of how Sr. Lúcia thought she was going to die and this addition agrees with the answer given by the Coimbra Sisters.

Though consistent in his claim that Sister stated it was *she* who fixed the date, Bertone then gives two apparently contradictory details in his above two accounts of his conversation. These details concern the remark

---

23   It is not clear what Sr. Lúcia was referring to here (as herein presented by Bertone) when she said, "Our Lady didn't tell me anything on this score." Is Sr. Lúcia referring to whether or not she (Sister) was going to die, or did she mean to say that it was not Our Lady who told her to put the date of 1960 on the envelope? The grammar is not clear and the answer to this question could help to resolve the larger question at hand, namely why fix the date of 1960 on the envelope?

24   There appears to be no real difference here except in the directness of language.

from April, 2000 about Sister fearing that the text would not be "understood" and then the later remark about Sister thinking she would be dead by 1960. Which account is more accurate, the one made in April, 2000, the summer, 2006, or is it possibly both?[25]

There are only a handful of people yet living who can answer that last question. Moreover, until the discrepancy in Bertone's statements is fully addressed, there is going to be legitimate debate on the matter. This debate will surround the merits of Bertone's recounting of an unrecorded conversation versus an account of the 1944 events written by Sister herself.[26] In the meantime, how do we reckon the differences between these two accounts? A thought comes to mind.

C. Stream of Consciousness

The meeting of April, 2000 does not appear to have been recorded with cameras or an audio recording device, though the Bishop of Leiria-Fátima was present to act as witness and assist with the languages in which the meeting was conducted (Portuguese and Spanish).[27] Bertone admits that he is "not tremendous in either language" but that nevertheless the conversation was "perfectly comprehensible."[28] Additionally, Bertone took some private notes of the meeting, as he later revealed, which served as the basis for the publication of the account in June, 2000 by the CDF.[29]

---

25   If it is both, then Bertone would have to harmonize the statements by providing a more complete rendition of that aspect of the conversation.

26   *Um Caminho sob o Olhar de Maria*, 266.

27   *The Last Secret of Fatima*, 30.

28   Ibid.

29   *The Last Secret of Fatima*, 35-36; See also Christopher A. Ferrara, *False Friends of Fatima*. (Pound Ridge, New York: Good Counsel Publications, 2012), 180-182 It would be a great help to be able to compare these notes with the published account.

Based upon the above information, a picture begins to form of the conversation. Bertone only took notes; he did not make a transcript. Even though Bertone took notes of his conversation with Sr. Lúcia and these influenced the official account of June, 2000, there was more that was said between them. The memory of that conversation is stored in Bertone's mind and is subject to what will here be called the "stream of consciousness."

All of us see the events of our lives in a sort of continuum. Because of this continuum, individual events take on greater or lesser meaning depending on time, place, circumstance or simply what one values.

For Cardinal Bertone, his meeting with Sr. Lúcia on April 27, 2000 can be nothing less than a momentous event of his life. He knows the context of the conversation that he had with her and enjoys the ability to pull from it when necessary in a given moment later in time. Based upon this, in the course of a presumably unscripted interview (with Giuseppe De Carli), it is completely understandable for Bertone to recall various facts and tell-tale phrases that did not make it into the official account.[30]

The problem, however, with the "stream of consciousness" is that it is not always the most reliable. Memories fade; our mind confuses facts or reshapes our memories with the passage of time. In the case of Cardinal Bertone, over six years had passed from his April, 2000 meeting with Sr. Lúcia and his interview with De Carli. During that time, Bertone underwent some life changes, such as becoming Secretary of Vatican City State.

At the end of the day, this "second challenge" ultimately rests upon the accuracy of Bertone's memory, what notes he took and—with all due respect—his linguistic abilities in Spanish and Portuguese self-described as "not tremendous." All of these factors are subject to (what is coincidentally discussed in *The Last Secret of Fatima*) the Scholastic axiom, "quid-

---

30   This interview appears unscripted, at least at the point herein discussed. If it was not unscripted, de Carli would have quoted the 2000 account. Moreover, there is a footnote that openly acknowledges this discrepancy (*The Last Secret of Fatima*, 168).

quid recipitur, ad modum recipientis recipitur" (Whatever is received, is received according to the condition of the one who receives it).[31]

In the light of what we know of Sr. Lúcia's propensity to be truthful yet evasive, what were her *exact* words to Bertone in April, 2000? This is a question to which we may never know the answer with certitude due to the lack of a full recording or transcript of the meeting. As it pertains to Bertone, what we have are differing accounts from the same source, but ones that agree on a central point—that it was Sr. Lúcia herself who said to Bertone that it was she, not Our Lady, who specified the date of 1960 for the envelope.[32] Given the facts, one ought not to be so quick to judge Bertone.

D. A Failing Memory?

There is one final consideration concerning this mystery of the date of 1960 affixed to the envelope. What if Sr. Lúcia's memory simply failed her?

By April, 2000, Sr. Lúcia was 93 years old and suffering from physical ailments not uncommon to a woman of her age.[33] She is remembering an event that took place some 56 years earlier at a time of her life when she was quite ill and there was talk of her death. It is reasonable to consider the possibility that Sister's memory in April, 2000 might not have recalled accurately the events of January 3, 1944 as well as it once could. It must also be noted that elsewhere, Sr. Lúcia's recalling of facts has been proven demonstrably inaccurate.[34]

---

31   Ibid, 40.

32   The real question is why would Sr. Lúcia give this answer to Bertone in April, 2000? It clearly does not square with the information that she wrote in her private diary *O Meu Caminho* (My Way) and on the outside of the envelope in 1944.

33   *Our Memories of Sister Lucia*, 23.

34   Cf. Fr. Robert J. Fox and Fr. Antonio Maria Martins, S.J., *The Intimate Life of Sister Lucia.* (Alexandria, South Dakota: Fatima Family Apostolate,

II. Conclusion

In conclusion, the matter of the discrepancy of the 1960 date on the envelope containing the third secret of Fátima is intimately bound up within the person and character of Sr. Lúcia. She was reluctant to speak of supernatural events in her life and she would answer questions about any such event truthfully but evasively. Even when under direct orders by her religious superiors, Sister obeyed with some difficulty.

Within the above dynamic is bound the apparent contradiction between statements made by Cardinal Bertone and those that are published in the Carmelites' biography *Um Caminho Sob o Olhar de Maria*. The published testimonies of Bertone are consistent with respect to the question he asked Sister ("Was it Our Lady who fixed the date?"). Bertone, however, is not consistent in relaying how she answered him and this is important given Sister's reluctance to speak on these matters.

Doubt and mistrust of Bertone's account continue in the face of the now published words of Sr. Lúcia on the matter. In order to arrive at a more definitive answer, further information/clarifications are required on the part of key persons while they yet live. Scholarly examination of important records and texts is also necessary. In the meantime, the explanation offered by the Coimbra Sisters—that Sr. Lúcia did not want to reveal the new vision given in 1944—appears to have merit.

2001), 70, 82-83. See also *The Last Secret of Fatima*, 29; *Our Memories of Sister Lucia*, 23. This observation should be balanced with the claim that Sr. Lúcia was blessed with a good memory of the events of Fátima. Sister herself even acknowledges this, citing a general theological premise that supernatural things are better remembered than things within the natural order (cf. *Memórias e Cartas de Irmã Lúcia*, 353).

—5—
THE MEETING OF FR. FUENTES WITH SISTER LÚCIA

"The chastisement from heaven is imminent."

—Fr. Agustín Fuentes Anguiano, May, 1958

On December 26, 1957, a Mexican priest named Fr. Agustín Fuentes Anguiano met with Sr. Lúcia at her convent in Coimbra.[1] Fr. Fuentes was, at the time, working on the cause of beatification for Francisco and Jacinta. Later, on May 22, 1958, Fuentes gave a conference to religious sisters in Mexico. During the conference, he remarked upon his meeting with Sr. Lúcia, giving quotes and messages he attributed to her. The conference was later published in Spanish and then issued in English translation in the United States.

---

1   Joaquín María Alonso, C.M.F., *La Verdad sobre el Secreto de Fatima: Fátima sin mitos.* (Madrid, Espana: Centro Mariano, 1976), 103-106. Hereafter *La Verdad sobre el Secreto de Fatima: Fátima sin mitos* followed by page number. The book was translated into English in 1979. See: Fr. Joaquin Maria Alonso, C.M.F., *The Secret of Fatima: Fact and Legend.* (Cambridge: The Ravengate Press, 1979), 108-113. Hereafter *The Secret of Fatima: Fact and Legend* followed by page number. The account of this meeting is better known in the English language through a French translation given in Frère Michel de la Sainte Trinité, *The Whole Truth About Fatima. Volume III: The Third Secret.* (Buffalo, New York: Immaculate Heart Publications, 1990), 503-522. Hereafter *The Whole Truth About Fatima, Volume III* followed by page number.

Present within Fuentes' conference were some remarks that touched upon the third part of the secret of Fátima. Some of these remarks were on the activity of Satan in the world and a chastisement from heaven. The Diocese of Coimbra issued a public condemnation, one that was supported by Sr. Lúcia herself, and Fuentes' account was discredited by leading authorities on Fátima.[2] Fuentes' local Ordinary, Archbishop Manuel Pio Lopez of the Archdiocese of Vera Cruz, defended him.[3]

In 1976, Fr. Joaquín María Alonso, the archivist for the Fátima Sanctuary, published a defense of Fuentes' account in his book *La Verdad sobre el Secreto de Fatima: Fátima sin mitos*.[4] This was a startling action as Alonso had previously been one of the authorities who believed the account to be discredited. After providing an extensive quote from Fuentes' original Spanish text, Alonso gives three reasons as to why he believed the account should be considered as authentic.[5] Alonso's overall reasoning is that there is a *genuine* account and *exaggerated* accounts, which the Diocese of Coimbra did not distinguish. Moreover, he claims that there is nothing objectionable to faith and morals.

After the account was defended by Alonso, it was seen as authorita-

---

2   Cf. *The Whole Truth About Fatima, Volume III*, 549-551. As we shall see, Fr. Alonso criticized this condemnation, claiming that it did not differentiate between the authentic text from spurious versions of it. According to the Portuguese journalist Aura Miguel, the condemnation was issued by the Auxiliary Bishop of Coimbra, Manuel de Jesus Pereira (Aura Miguel, *Totus Tuus: Il segreto di Fatima nel pontificato di Giovanni Paolo II*. [Castel Bolognese, Italia: Itaco, 2003], 134). Fr. Gruner stated that the author of the condemnation is unknown (Nicholas Gruner, *Crucial Truths to Save Your Soul*. [Buffalo, New York: Immaculate Heart Publications, 2014], 104).

3   *Hacia los altares* (1959) Septiembre-Octubre (#5), 23-29.

4   *La Verdad sobre el Secreto de Fatima: Fátima sin mitos*, 107ff.

5   Ibid., 108-109. Fr. Alonso also observes the fact that the Diocese of Leiria had also approved the original account before it was published.

tive and authentic by Frère Michel and other writers.[6] Its theme of chastisements from heaven (among others) became a hallowed and integral component within their writings (and interpretation) on Fátima. Owing to this fact, we shall herein discuss Fuentes' account of his meeting and Fr. Alonso's defense of it. The purpose of this discussion is to see if the condemnation issued by Coimbra stands after Fr. Alonso's defense. Finally, we shall consider this discussion within the larger examination of the third part of the secret of Fátima and make some tentative conclusions.

I. The Textual Tradition and a Critique

Owing to the convoluted nature of the matter, it is necessary to establish the genuine account of Fuentes' meeting with Sr. Lúcia. Fr. Alonso specifies that there are two authentic texts, namely the Spanish original and an English translation. He considers that the Spanish is "more original" (*más original*), but accepts the English as authentic.[7] Unfortunately, he does not name where these texts can be located. Frère Michel, however, notes that the English translation was published in a newsletter entitled *Fatima Findings* in its June, 1959 edition.[8]

A. The English Translation

The above edition of *Fatima Findings* provides an account of how the publication came into possession of the text. The note reads:

---

6   Fr. Joaquín María Alonso, "De Nuevo el Secreto de Fátima," *Ephemerides Mariologicae* 32, Fasc. 1 (1982): 93. Hereafter *De Nuevo el Secreto de Fátima* followed by page number.

7   *La Verdad sobre el Secreto de Fatima*, 103.

8   *The Whole Truth About Fatima, Volume III*, 522 (note 7). A copy of this edition of *Fatima Findings* was obtained from the Fátima Sanctuary by this author.

The following Conference was given in Spanish on May 22, 1958 at the Mexican Motherhouse of the Missionary Sisters of the Sacred Heart and of Our Lady of Guadalupe. It was sent to the Editor of FATIMA FINDINGS early in February [1959], but he deferred publication until its authenticity could be clearly established. In proof of its authenticity we now have: 1) the following letter of Rt. Rev. Abbot M. Columban Hawkins, O.C.S.O. of Lafayette, Oregon; 2) the signed copy by Father Fuentes himself of this English translation of the Conference attesting to its accuracy; 3) the copy of "HACIA LOS ALTARES" of October, 1958, published by Father Fuentes with the Ecclesiastical approbation of Don Manuel Anselmo Sanchez, Vicar General of Vera Cruz, containing all the facts stated in the Conference in even fuller detail.[9]

The above note is very helpful for a number of reasons, the first of which is that it provides the name of the publication that published the Spanish original. It also states that the English translation was signed by Fuentes himself in order to attest to its accuracy.

Concerning the English translation, there are two notes on page one concerning the translator. The first remark is from Abbot Hawkins who wrote:

The text of the conference is a translation from the original Spanish delivered on May 22nd, 1958 at the Mexican Mother-house of the Missionary Sisters of the Sacred Heart and Our Lady of Guadalupe. Father Fuentes has signed his name to this

---

9   *Fatima Findings* (June, 1959), 1. This author was able to obtain various editions of *Hacia los altares* dating between the years 1958-1961. When one reads the table of contents pages, one finds that the "ecclesiastical approbation" by Don Sanchez is not just about this specific article from the October, 1958 edition of *Hacia los altares*. It is a general approbation given to the publication as a whole.

translation as being exact; he understands English well but does not speak it. A Benedictine Sister, a friend of mine in Mexico City, interviewed Father Fuentes on my behalf. She is competent in both English and Spanish and is entirely trustworthy. I enclose a copy of the pertinent part of her letter to me.[10]

After the Abbot's letter a second note followed which appears to be a note from the editor of *Fatima Findings* about the Sister mentioned above. Whether or not the note was based on her letter to the Abbot is unclear. It reads:

The Sister who interviewed Father Fuentes in regard to this translation in behalf of Abbot Columban was born and raised in the United States and has been teaching in Mexico City for a number of years—hence, she is a complete master of both English and Spanish. She is moreover highly conscientious and most trustworthy. The English text which follows was submitted by her to Father Fuentes in a personal interview. Father Fuentes signed the translation stating that it agreed exactly with the Spanish original. Above is the Conference which we publish with Father Fuentes' permission and approval.[11]

B. The Spanish Text

The Spanish text was originally published in *Hacia los Altares* in October, 1958. Unfortunately, this publication is *extremely* difficult to obtain as it is a localized publication and not readily available elsewhere.[12] Fr.

---

10   Ibid.

11   Ibid.

12   After reviewing the copies of *Hacia los altares* from 1958-1961, one can see why this publication is difficult to obtain. The publication has the feel of

Alonso, however, states that he was in possession of both the Spanish original and the English translation.[13] He provides, as we said earlier, a lengthy (and incomplete) citation of what appears to be the Spanish original. At this time, it is the only copy available to the larger public as Alonso's book is more readily accessible.[14]

C. Subsequent Translations

Alonso's book was translated into French and English in the year 1979.[15] The French translation of Fuentes' account appears between pages 91-94; the English translation appears between pages 109-110. These translations, however, appear to have been largely neglected after the publication of Frère Michel's study in French entitled *Toute la Vérité sur Fatima*.[16]

---

being the production of a private publishing enterprise undertaken by Fr. Fuentes who, it must be noted, was its Director. The impression is given that it was a "cottage industry" publication, though one supported by the local Ordinary of Jalapa, Mexico with the *imprimatur*.

13   *La Verdad sobre el Secreto de Fatima*, 103. He wrote, "Poseemos dos textos «auténticos» de esa conferencia, uno en español y otro en inglés." He then notes that the English text is an "abbreviated" (*abreviada*) version of the Spanish original.

14   Owing to this fact, whatever is said at this time of the Spanish text must be understood as being tentative. Alonso indicated in some places that he abbreviated the quotation. Nevertheless, there is something to be said for taking the text as Alonso presented it when examining how he defended it.

15   R.P. Joaquim Maria Alonso, *La Vérité sur le Secret de Fatima*. (Paris: Téqui, 1979). Hereafter *La Vérité sur le Secret de Fatima* followed by page number.

16   Frère Michel de la Sainte Trinité, *Toute la Vérité sur Fatima: Le Troisième Secret (1942-1960)*. (Saint-Parres lès Vaudes, France: Renaissance Catholique Contre-Réforme Catholique, 1985), 336-338. Hereafter *Toute la Vérité sur Fatima: Volume III* followed by page number. The reason for this neglect appears to be the sheer influence of Frère Michel's study, especially as it was promoted by Fr. Gruner.

A comparison between the French text of the third volume of Frère Michel's study with the French text published by Téqui in 1979 reveals some differences either of style or omission. For an example of omission, the 1979 Téqui text relays the remark attributed to Sr. Lúcia about how the Pope and the Bishop of Fátima did not want to know the third part of the secret.[17] It omits, however, the reason for this, which was "so as not to be influenced" which was in the Spanish text.[18] Frère Michel restored the remark.[19]

Later, the translator (John Collorafi) of Frère Michel's study on Fátima appears to have made his own translation based upon the French text in Frère Michel.[20] This observation is made from a comparison of the existing texts in *Fatima Findings* and Fr. Alonso's book.

D. Critiquing the Genuine Texts

When we look at the English text from *Fatima Findings* and compare it with the Spanish that Alonso quoted, we see that the English was not a line-for-line translation.[21] Comparing what we *do* have, it is apparent that a comment made by Alonso describing the English as "abbreviated" (*abreviada*) was rather generous.[22] If one goes in the order in which the

---

17   *La Vérité sur le Secret de Fatima*, 91.

18   *La Verdad sobre el Secreto de Fatima*, 104, "...para no influenciarse."

19   *Toute la Vérité sur Fatima: Volume III,* 336.

20   *The Whole Truth About Fatima, Volume III*, 504ff.

21   This fact forces one to question Abbot Hawkins' claim that Fr. Fuentes stated the English translation published in *Fatima Findings* to be an "exact" copy. Did he make this claim or was that Abbot Hawkins' understanding based on the fact that Fuentes signed the translation? The text indicates that Fuentes made the statement to the translator who, presumably, relayed it to the Abbot who then wrote the note to the editor of *Fatima Findings*. Perhaps Fuentes meant that the translation captures the heart of what he said in Spanish, not necessarily a word-for-word translation.

22   *La Verdad sobre el Secreto de Fatima*, 103.

texts begin and end, it is not possible to follow them exactly parallel with each other. There are too many notable differences, thus we shall endeavor to discuss critically these texts.

First, it is difficult to provide a complete assessment of the respective texts as Alonso did not provide the entire Spanish. He indicated in five places that there was further text by some ellipses in parentheses. What were these texts? How closely did the English translation follow this missing information? Without the text as it appeared in *Hacia los Altares*, these questions cannot be answered. Thus, when the Spanish text is referenced below, it is to be understood from the perspective of "as presented by Alonso."

In the English translation from *Fatima Findings*, the text is organized into fourteen paragraphs (going by indentation). The Spanish is ten. For easy referencing, we shall refer to these paragraphs in the order in which they appear and by number. It is not noted whether or not the English translator ordered the text into fourteen paragraphs or whether that was the choice of the editor of *Fatima Findings*. We leave this question open, taking at face value the ordering of paragraphs as they appeared in the publication.

The first two paragraphs of the English text are an opening by Fr. Fuentes that is not found in the Spanish.[23] The first correlation between the two texts is Fuentes' observation of Sr. Lúcia in the convent (Spanish-1/ English-3). The English text notes simply that Sister received Fuentes "full of sadness." The Spanish is more detailed and slightly dramatic, "I encountered her in her convent very sad, pale and emaciated" (*La encontré en su convento muy triste, pálida y demacrada*). The English then has a note about Sr. Lúcia's actual age versus how she appears that is not in the Spanish, and no note from Alonso is given here as to a possible omission.

Paragraph four (English) continues paragraph one of the Spanish, which are words attributed to Sr. Lúcia. There is a very large section of the

---

23   Alonso gives no indication of an omission of any introductory text.

Spanish (¿Qué falta, Padre...nos dijo) that is omitted in the English. Both paragraphs, however, end on the same note about many nations disappearing. Here, Alonso indicates with ellipses some omitted text in the Spanish. Either there was more to this paragraph or there was a new one(s). Also, the translator took the first line of the second paragraph (Spanish) about the devil and made it the last line of the fourth in the English. This act presents a problem because the Spanish has more detail critical to understanding this statement. They, too, are words attributed to Sr. Lúcia.

Paragraphs five to seven of the English are presented as more dialogue from Lúcia. These are entirely omitted in the Spanish. As noted above, this is quite possibly the text that was omitted as indicated. Some trace-lines on consecrated souls are pulled from paragraph two of the Spanish and placed in paragraph seven of the English.

Paragraph eight (English) corresponds to paragraph three of the Spanish. The translator, however, presents it as a summary (except for one quote attributed to Lúcia) by Fr. Fuentes of what he claims Sr. Lúcia told him. The Spanish portrays it as a direct quote from her. There are also some additions by the translator, such as mention of the Miraculous Medal, that are not found in the Spanish. Here, however, in the Spanish is the second ellipses. It is possible that there was further text upon which the translator based her work.

Alonso presents the fourth paragraph in the Spanish as an isolated line (ending with the third ellipses) about the vision of hell being what sanctified Francisco and Jacinta. This line was placed toward the end of paragraph eight in the English. Meanwhile, the fifth and sixth paragraphs (this last one contains the fourth ellipses) in the Spanish are then omitted in the English.

Paragraph nine (English) is paragraph seven of the Spanish. The translator, however, presents the text as a summary of Sister's dialogue by Fuentes whereas the Spanish is presented by Alonso as a direct quote. Also, a sizeable discussion in the Spanish that discusses sin against the

Holy Spirit was omitted in the English. Immediately following this omission is paragraph eight in the Spanish. This paragraph is a singular line about prayer and sacrifice being the remedy for the ills facing the world. The remark is presented by Alonso as Fuentes' own thought which expresses a point that Sr. Lúcia made to him. The fifth and final ellipses from Alonso ends this paragraph.

Paragraphs ten and eleven in the English are not in Alonso's presentation of the Spanish. This may be explainable by the aforementioned last ellipses. The translator then does something perplexing with paragraph twelve (English). The paragraph is mostly comprised of a quote attributed to Lúcia about not expecting the Holy Father to summon the faithful to do penance. This text, however, appeared in paragraph six of the Spanish.

Paragraph thirteen (English) is primarily an exhortation by Fuentes to pray the Rosary. There is one quote that is attributed directly to Sr. Lúcia which is found in paragraph nine of the Spanish. Finally, paragraph fourteen (English) is a concluding exhortation by Fuentes that is not provided by Alonso. The last paragraph (ten) of the Spanish text is not clear whether or not it is Sr. Lúcia or Fr. Fuentes speaking. Moreover, there is a line about the message of Fátima having a "second part" that referred to the Holy Father. This remark was placed by the English translator as the first line of paragraph eleven.

These critical observations indicate some very notable differences between the two texts. From these differences, questions arise pertaining to the proper understanding and interpretation of Fuentes' account. We shall return to this notion later in this chapter. For now, we shall look at and critique how Fr. Alonso himself examined and/or defended Fuentes' account.

II. Fuentes' Account "Rehabilitated?"

Fr. Alonso's reversal of his prior stance on Fr. Fuentes' account of his meeting with Sr. Lúcia was a notable development. As the account is

now considered authentic by many people, doubt exists as to the status and/or validity of the Diocese of Coimbra's condemnation. In an attempt to address this question, we shall look at Fr. Alonso's individual points. They were:

1. Fuentes' account corresponds in its essentials to what he heard from Sr. Lúcia. To this Alonso adds two caveats:

   a. First: Fuentes embellished for oratorical purposes and falsely characterized the remarks as a message to the world from Sr. Lúcia (Alonso claims this was not her intention).[24]

   b. Second: what Fuentes published corresponds to things said by Sister in her numerous published writings.[25]

2. The genuine text contains nothing to warrant the condemnation.

3. There is no differentiation of genuine from sensationalized texts.

A. Reason One: The "Essentials" of Fuentes' Account

Fr. Alonso's first point is that what Fuentes relays corresponds in its essentials (*en lo esencial*) from what he heard from Sr. Lúcia.[26] In a

---

24   Ibid. The Spanish texts reads, "Porque aunque esté mezclado con consideraciones oratorias del predicador…" and "Tal vez el defecto principal consista en haber presentado esos textos en boca literalmente de Lucía…."

25   *The Secret of Fatima: Fact and Legend*, 112; *La Verdad sobre el Secreto de Fatima: Fátima sin mitos*, 108. Regretfully, Alonso does not make specific comparisons.

26   While we herein question Fr. Alonso's claim, there is the simple fact that Fuentes points out Sr. Lúcia's letter to the Pope seeking entrance to the Carmel. The Carmelite's biography indicated that she did write such a letter. It is, however, the competence of the Holy See to allow the transfer of one's religious vows to another religious congregation. It is no surprise then for Sister to have written a letter to the Pope. What is, however, noteworthy for our consideration is given the surreptitious nature of how Sister sent the letter to Rome, how did Fuentes get a copy of this letter to be able to quote or paraphrase it? Perhaps he saw a copy in Rome? If so, this is not stated by Alonso. Cf. Carmelo de Santa

way, this is an extraordinary claim. How could Fr. Alonso know what the essentials were of a conversation—to which he was not privy—without having some kind of objective verification? He does not mention that such verification exists, much less claim to possess it. Despite such a lack of evidence, Alonso claims Fuentes' account "certainly" (*ciertamente*) corresponds in its essentials to what he heard from Sister. It could be that Alonso possessed such verification, but if so, why not tell his readers about it in order to satisfy any doubt?

Fr. Alonso proceeds to make a couple of caveats. The first is that he recognizes that Fuentes "may have mixed [the account] with oratorical considerations of the preacher" (*Porque aunque esté mezclado con consideraciones oratorias del predicador...*). He then follows up this observation with another one that the account "may be irregular literary [style]" (*aunque esté arreglado literariamente*]. Alonso adds at the end of these observations that they do not really matter because the content corresponds to public statements Sr. Lúcia made elsewhere (*esos textos no dicen nada que la Hermana Lucía no ha dicho en sus numerosos escritos hechos públicos*). Regrettably, Alonso does not provide his readers with a study of Sister's prior writings with the present statement(s).[27]

At the end of the above observations, Alonso then adds that Fuentes' "principal defect" (*defecto principal*) was to present the text as coming directly out of the mouth of Lúcia herself (*en boca literalmente de Lucía*). Fuentes then labeled it as a "message from Lucia" (*un mensaje suyo*) to the world when she had no such intention (*no tenía esa intención*). Here is, perhaps, one of the most curious parts of Alonso's defense. Sr. Lúcia

---

Teresa – Coimbra, *Um Caminho sob o Olhar de Maria: Biografia da Irmã Lúcia de Jesus e do Coração Imaculado, O.C.D.* (Coimbra, Portugal: Edições Carmelo, 2013), 323-325. Hereafter *Um Caminho sob o Olhar de Maria* followed by page number.

27   Alonso addressed the reasons for such in the beginning of his book. We have elsewhere treated this matter in the present book.

clearly is said to command Fuentes to warn souls about upcoming dangers if Russia is not converted.[28] If Lúcia is commanding Fuentes to tell people what she is saying, how can his account *not* be (or, at least, contain) a message from Lúcia?

It would seem as though Alonso is admitting that Fuentes embellished this part of his meeting. One is then compelled to wonder if Fuentes embellished here, did he do so elsewhere? If so, in what part(s)? Can the average reader be expected to parcel out oratorical embellishments from an exact relaying of a message claimed to be straight from Lúcia herself? The average reader, generally speaking, is not equipped to figure out such things. Thus, behind Alonso's own observation is a question of justice to the average reader who, generally speaking, is justified in taking seriously a message from a man of Fuentes' standing without question. If Alonso's defense is accurate, he has, indirectly, made Fuentes liable to accusations of carelessness and injustice.

B. Reason Two: Coimbra Condemnation Unwarranted

In the second reason that Alonso gives in defense of Fuentes' account, he claims the genuine text does not justify the condemnation from Coimbra. At first glance, Alonso's claim appears to be just as it is only fair to give a person a fair hearing. We shall return to this matter in the next sub-section.

Alonso follows up his claim with his opinion that Fuentes' text contains doctrine that is very apt to edify piously the Christian people (*...contiene una doctrina muy apta para edificar piadosamente al pueblo cristiano*).[29] Here, Alonso seems to pass over without comment the question

---

28   *La Verdad sobre el Secreto de Fatima: Fátima sin mitos*, 104. Fuentes uses the word "Dígales" for the command.

29   *La Verdad sobre el Secreto de Fatima: Fátima sin mitos*, 108.

of its veracity. He focuses upon the doctrinal underpinnings of Fuentes' account, intimating that in it there is nothing contrary to faith and good morals. If, however, the account itself is not accurate, it is, at worst, a lie, a fabrication, presumably (in such a worst-case scenario) to deceive. A best-case scenario is that the account is simply inaccurate owing to some human failure with no malice involved.

Focusing here *only* on the question of doctrinal content presents a myopic vision. It is accurate to say that, on a literal level, one's faith and morals may not be disturbed—strictly speaking—by reading the words. Here, Fr. Alonso essentially stands on a pastoral practice of the Church in matters of private revelation concerning endless human arguments.[30] We are, however, not here discussing a private revelation *per se*. What we are discussing is Fuentes' rendition of a *private conversation* that he had with the visionary of Fátima. The Church's pastoral practice on private revelation does not necessarily apply here.

Let us also consider the fact that people make decisions or receive impressions/understandings based upon such information and warnings as presented by Fuentes. What if it were to be proven beyond a shadow of reasonable doubt that Fuentes' (authentic) account was indeed fraudulent? True, any grace that people obtained through this error is not thereby removed. Nevertheless, there is a risk of people becoming disillusioned or scandalized. Moreover, if Fuentes was wrong, he gave rise to scandal for the authentic message of Fátima, an error that would have *grave* repercussions.

The pastoral situation that arises from these circumstances is something that needs to be more deeply considered by theologians and the pastors of the Church in weighing matters pertaining to private revelation. Alonso does not consider such a need here in favor of a potentially misapplied strict focus upon doctrinal content. This observation may work in the short term, but does not consider the potential long-term effects among the faithful.

---

30   For more on this matter, see the Encyclical *Pascendi Dominici Gregis* (*Acta Sanctae Sedis* [1907], 649).

C. Reason Three: Coimbra Made No Distinction

Fr. Alonso believed that Coimbra did not distinguish between the genuine text of Fuentes from other accounts which distorted it. Alonso wrote:

> The diocese of Coimbra, and through it Sister Lucia, have made no distinction between the genuine text which alone can be justly attributed to Father Fuentes, and the vast "documentation" to which we have already referred. An error of judgment was thus committed, for everything was included in one single all-embracing condemnation.
>
> The proliferation of spurious texts about the Secret of Fatima did not end here, however....[31]

It is true that the condemnation does not mention Fuentes' original Spanish article in *Hacia los Altares*. Coimbra was, however, more specific than Alonso's characterization indicates. Here is the full text of the condemnation:

Note from the Diocesan Curia of Coimbra
Sister Lúcia Denies

Father Agustín Fuentes, postulator of the cause of beatification for the seers of Fátima, Francisco and Jacinta, visited Sister

---

31   *The Secret of Fatima: Fact and Legend*, 112-113. The original Spanish reads:

> La Curia diocesana de Coimbra —y a través de ella la Hermana Lucía— no han distinguido entre el texto genuino, único atribuible al P. Fuentes en justicia, y esa ingente «documentación» aludida. Se há cometido así un error de juicio, confundiéndolo todo en una única y global condena.
> Pero no se terminó ahí la proliferación de textos espúreos en torno al secreto de Fátima... (*La Verdad sobre el Secreto de Fatima: Fátima sin mitos*, 108-109).

Lúcia at the Carmel of Coimbra and spoke to her exclusively about things concerning the process; arriving in Mexico, his country (if we give credit to what *A Voz* of June 22 related, and repeated on July 1 in translation from M. C. de Bragança) [Fuentes] permitted himself to make sensational declarations, of an apocalyptic, eschatological and prophetic character, which he declares that he heard from Sister Lúcia.

Given the gravity of such statements, the Diocesan Curia of Coimbra believed it its duty to make a rigorous investigation into the authenticity of such news which persons too avid for the extraordinary have spread in Mexico, in the United States, in Spain, and finally in Portugal.

For the tranquility of those who, reading the documentation published in *A Voz* and have taken alarm at the thought of fearful cataclysms which (according to such documentation) are to come upon the world in 1960, and still more, in order to put an end to the biased campaign of "prophecies," whose authors, perhaps without realizing it, are provoking a storm of ridicule, not only where they themselves are concerned, but also with regard to things reported as having been said by Sister Lúcia, the Diocesan Curia of Coimbra has decided to publish these words of Sister Lúcia, a reply to questions from someone who by right asked her.

"Father Fuentes spoke with me in his capacity as Postulator for the causes of beatification of the servants of God, Jacinta and Francisco Marto. We spoke only of things related with this subject; therefore, whatever else he refers to is neither exact nor true. I am sorry about it, for I do not understand what good can be done for souls when it is not based on God, Who is the Truth. I know nothing, and could therefore say nothing, about such punishments, which are falsely attributed to me."

The chancery of Coimbra is in a position to declare that Sr. Lúcia, having said up to now all she understood that she had to say [*entendeu que devia dizer*] about Fátima and is found in various books published about Fátima, at least since February of 1955 until now, she has said nothing and therefore authorized no one to bring to the public whatever it might be that could be attributed to her concerning Fátima.

Coimbra, July 2, 1959.

The Diocesan Chancery of Coimbra[32]

The opening paragraph specifies two editions of the Portuguese publication *A Voz* (June 22 and July 1, 1959). It also states the name of the translator (M.C. de Bragança). Then, in the third paragraph, *A Voz* is specified once again as being of particular concern to the Chancery. No other publication is specified by name. From the beginning, the appearance is clearly conveyed that *A Voz* was the primary publication being addressed.

If indeed the focus was upon the articles in *A Voz*, the next logical question is what was published? Alonso indirectly indicated that it published a "spurious" (*espúreos*) version. When one looks up, however, what *A Voz* actually published, what is found is something that is the *exact opposite* of Alonso's characterization. In its June 22, 1959 issue, *A Voz* published on page three a Portuguese translation of the English translation in *Fatima Findings*![33]

---

32   The English translation is taken from *The Whole Truth About Fatima, Volume III*, 549-550. It has been amended in accordance with the Portuguese text that appears in the publication *Novidades*, 4 July 1959 (Lisboa), #74.

33   Consider also that, later in 1967, the Bishop of Coimbra, Ernesto Sena de Oliveira, remarked on this matter. In commenting upon some rumors that had appeared around the year 1967, the Bishop traced their origin back to Fuentes. The Bishop specified *Fatima Findings* in this context. See the article entitled "Refutada pelo Arcebispo-Bispo de Coimbra mais uma interpretação alarmista do texto ainda não conhecido da mensagem de Fátima" in *Arauto* (Bissau), 2 February, 1967, pages 1, 6.

This translation was prefaced and concluded with some remarks from the translator, M.C. de Bragança. These remarks are secondary to the translation which is clearly the main feature of the article. Moreover, Bragança's translation does not appear to be unfaithful to the English text. Fr. Alonso *himself* considered this particular English translation to be authentic (*auténticos*).[34] How, then, could he cast aspersions on it? He must truly not have believed that Coimbra was referring to the translation in *A Voz*. Given how specific Coimbra was in mentioning *A Voz*, how could Alonso miss it?

D. Apocalyptic, Eschatological & Prophetic Remarks

Let us also consider the condemnation's overall objection that Fuentes "permitted himself to make sensational declarations, of an apocalyptic, eschatological and prophetic character, which he declares that he heard from Sister Lúcia."[35] Fr. Alonso argues that Fuentes was distorted by the various publications. That may be true in other publications that we have not here considered. The "authentic" accounts, however, accepted by Alonso *do* contain some striking statements from Fuentes that he attributes to Lúcia. Consider the following elements in the Spanish text:
1. a sickly-looking Sr. Lúcia just prior to the foretold event(s),

---

34   *La Verdad sobre el Secreto de Fatima: Fátima sin mitos*, 103. He wrote, "Poseemos dos textos «auténticos» de esa conferencia, uno en español y otro en inglés. El primero es bastante más largo que el segundo, ya que éste es una traducción abreviada, aunque esencialmente idéntica al primero" (We possess two "authentic" texts of this conference, one in Spanish and another in English. The first is quite a bit larger than the second, since it is an abridged translation, but essentially identical to the first). Noting the contradiction in Alonso's logic is not prejudicial to our earlier discussion on the English text in *Fatima Findings* not being an exact translation.

35   *Novidades*, 4 July 1959 (Lisboa), #74. The Portuguese text is, "[P. Fuentes] permitiu-se fazer afirmações mirabolantes, de sentido apocalyptico, escatológico e profético, que declarou ter ouvido à Irmã Lúcia."

2. an imminent chastisement from heaven,

3. a focus on the year 1960 and the famous third part of the secret (which, we note, the English text presents in more dramatic fashion),

4. the sadness of the Blessed Virgin,

5. a decisive battle between the Virgin and the devil,

6. a great loss of souls (particularly consecrated religious),

7. a call for people not to wait upon Rome to call us to penance,

8. a remark on the decision we must all make for God or the devil.

While the Spanish text does not necessarily overstate its case, Coimbra's characterization of the remarks is accurate. The same is true of the English translation in *Fatima Findings*. The accounts *do* have an "apocalyptic, eschatological and prophetic" character. Consider as well the fact that there was heightened expectation that existed in 1959. The opening and/or publication of the third part of the secret of Fátima was heavily anticipated by many people. Fuentes' remarks had explosive potential to disturb the peace and create alarm. It would make sense for Coimbra to allay this disturbance.

Seen from this perspective, Coimbra's purpose was not necessarily to settle what was genuine from what was not. Its primary concern was to calm a rising panic. The quickest way to accomplish this goal was to go straight to the source, Sr. Lúcia, and ask her about it. As we saw, she denied having spoken of chastisements to Fuentes and that his claims are falsely attributed to her. On the strength of this statement, Coimbra made its own. Let us look at it again:

The chancery of Coimbra is in a position to declare that Sr. Lúcia, having said up to now all she understood [*entendeu*] that she had to say about Fátima and is found in various books published about Fátima, at least since February of 1955 until now, she has said nothing and therefore authorized no one to bring to the public whatever it might be that could be attributed to her concerning Fátima.

The matter is clear. Sister denies talking with Fuentes about chastisements.[36] She has already said what she thought she had to say about Fátima. This information is found in various books that are already in circulation. Since February of 1955 until July, 1959, Sister has said nothing else and has not authorized anyone to speak for her to the public. These statements are a clear refutation even of the authentic versions endorsed by Fr. Fuentes.

While the condemnation from Coimbra is clear, there is one unresolved matter. Who went to Sr. Lúcia about the situation and how was it presented? What questions were asked of her? Coimbra acknowledged the story in *A Voz*. Thus, was its version (itself based on the *Fatima Findings* article) the only one presented to Sister or were there others? The answers to these questions are important. For example, if it was the case that one of the inauthentic versions was brought to her attention and Sister denied it, what does that say for the information presented in the *authentic* texts?

III. A Change in the Story?
Fuentes and the Third Part of the Secret

We have seen how the third part of the secret came to be written. Sr. Lúcia received the secret in July, 1917 but never wrote it down until she was given permission to do so in early January, 1944. She enclosed the text in an envelope and wrote instructions on the outside that it was not to be opened until 1960. The task, she further wrote, of opening the envelope was assigned to the Bishop of Leiria or the Cardinal Patriarch of Lisbon.

---

36   Frère Michel (*The Whole Truth About Fatima, Volume III*, 509) notes a letter that Sr. Lúcia wrote on July 1, 1958 to an unnamed person wherein she mentions that we should pray so as not to be chastised by God. Frère Michel's source is Fr. Antonio Maria Martins, *Fatima: Way of Peace*. (Chulmleigh, England: Augustine Publishing Company, 1989), 80. It is a very short quotation and the context of the remark is not provided. Given this information, it would be imprudent to draw conclusions.

A discrepancy in this history arises from Fr. Fuentes' account of his meeting with Sr. Lúcia that deserves examination. He attributes a remark to Sister pertaining to the people who were permitted to know the third part of the secret. According to Fuentes (through Alonso), Sister stated:

> Father, how much time is there before 1960 arrives? It will be very sad for everyone, not one person will rejoice at all if beforehand the world does not pray and do penance. I am not able to detail further because it is still a secret that, by the will of the Most Holy Virgin, only the Holy Father like (*como*) the Lord Bishop of Fátima were able to know; but they have desired not to know it so as not to be influenced.[37]

Sister is quoted as saying "only" (*solamente*) the Pope and the Bishop of Leiria "were able to know" (*pudieran saberlo tanto*) the secret. Why is there no mention of the Patriarch of Lisbon?[38] Let us propose three possible answers:

---

37   Cf. *The Whole Truth About Fatima, Volume III*, 504. The translation has here been amended to reflect more closely the original Spanish text which reads:

> ¿Qué falta, Padre, para 1960; y qué sucederá entonces? Será una cosa muy triste para todos; y no una cosa alegre si antes el mundo no hace oración y penitencia. No puedo detallar más, ya que es aún secreto que, por voluntad de la Santísima Virgen, solamente pudieran saberlo tanto el Santo Padre como el señor Obispo de Fátima; pero que ambos no han querido saberlo para no influenciarse (*La Verdad sobre el Secreto de Fatima: Fátima sin mitos*, 103-104).

In his book *The Secret Still Hidden* (Good Counsel Publications, 2008, pages 32-33), Christopher Ferrara puts ellipses where the above quote is located.

38   It is noteworthy that Frère Michel does not appear to notice this difference. He also omits another reference to the Holy Father at the very end of the article (as quoted by Alonso). See *Toute la Vérité sur Fatima: Volume III*, 338. The English translation (page 508) maintains the omission.

1. there was a later (and as yet unrevealed) apparition of Our Lady,

2. Sister never said it (or she simply contradicted herself),

3. Fr. Fuentes did not accurately remember what Sr. Lúcia said to him.

If it was the first, why would Our Lady suddenly change her mind? Would the simple fact of the document's transfer to Rome in April, 1957 change the will of heaven? What would such a change indicate, theologically, if heaven is outside of time and the transfer would have been foreknown? Why not simply tell Sister in 1944 to send it directly to the Holy Father?

If the question before us is answered by the second possibility, a question exists on the reliability of Sr. Lúcia. This notion is generally not well-received by those who hold her in high regard. The third possibility, however, is more likely in the light of the dispute that arose after the publication of Fuentes' account. The discrepancy is another reason to question the account.[39]

Let us also ask: outside of a supernatural communication or some notification from the Pope, how could Sr. Lúcia have known that the Holy Father opted not to know the third part of the secret?[40] Clearly, the infor-

---

39   Consider also that Fr. Fuentes' meeting was not recorded. The contents of his meeting are in a hard-to-find article in Spanish that was quoted by Fr. Alonso but which comes to the English-speaking public largely through the French translation in Frère Michel. Cardinal Bertone was *sharply* criticized for not recording his meeting(s) with Sr. Lúcia (cf. Christopher Ferrara, T*he Secret Still Hidden.* [Pound Ridge, New York: Good Counsel Publishing, 2008], 52, 75, 78-81, 89-90, 103, 105, 108, 200). Only *one* case, however, is taken to be beyond doubt. This is a double-standard. See also Fr. Paul L. Kramer, *The Devil's Final Battle: Our Lady's Victory Edition.* (Terryville, Connecticut: Good Counsel Publications, 2010), 188-189, 191, 265-266, 302-303.

40   For his part, Bishop da Silva's unwillingness to read the text is fairly well documented. Moreover, if he was unwilling to read the text, it is not a leap in logic to say that he would not have asked for its contents to be given directly to him *verbally* by Sister. Moreover, by the time of her meeting with Fr. Fuentes (December 26, 1957), Bishop da Silva had been dead for 22 days. If da Silva was already dead, was Sister referring to his successor, Bishop João Venancio? This lament does not seem just. The historical record *clearly* shows that Venan-

mation was now desired to be known. How could Sister, from the cloister of her convent, know enough of Vatican affairs to lament that the Pope decided not to know it when the text had not even been at the Vatican very long? Was she not aware that people were waiting for the year 1960, the year *she* stipulated the text would be "more clear?" If so, why lament the unwillingness of the hierarchy to know the third part of the secret?

Between 1944 and 1960, various writers claimed Sister stated that Bishop da Silva could open the document, read (and publish) it before 1960.[41] If these claims are accurate, then she could have thus been lamenting to Fuentes the fact that the Bishop chose not to do so. The question, again, is to what end? Would da Silva have published it prior to 1960? If so, what does that say for Our Lady's *express* instruction that the envelope could "only" (*só*) be opened in 1960 by the Cardinal or Bishop? Would not the instruction have lost much of its force and reasoning if the date could be disregarded so easily?[42]

---

cio *begged* da Silva, *twice*, to make a copy before forwarding the text to Rome (cf. *The Whole Truth About Fatima, Volume III*, 480). Moreover, the text had been received by Rome in April, 1957, about eight months before the death of Bishop da Silva and Venancio's subsequent succession as the Bishop of Fátima. The decision was not his in this affair and he did what he could to influence da Silva, to no avail.

41   Cf. *The Whole Truth About Fatima, Volume III*, 468-479. For a contradictory opinion, based upon an actual letter of Sr. Lúcia, see: Antonio María Martins, "A Proposito del Secreto de Fatima" *Ephemerides Mariologicae* 36 (1986): 348.

42   Consider also Sr. Lúcia's account of the January 3, 1944 apparition (*Um Caminho sob o Olhar de Maria*, 266). Sister does *not* write that Our Lady said the text could be *published*, rather that the envelope "can only be opened in 1960" (*...que só pode ser aberto em 1960*) by the specified persons. Did Our Lady appear later to Sister and clarify this matter? Were the later declarations attributed to Sr. Lúcia between 1944 and 1960 *her own interpretation* of what Our Lady said? It is noteworthy that in all the sources during 1944-1960 given by Frère Michel on Sr. Lúcia discussing the publication of the text in 1960, not one is directly from Sister herself. Given, however, the amount of evidence, it is more than likely that Sr. Lúcia had stated that it was to be published (cf. April

Perhaps Sr. Lúcia was referring to prior attempts to get the information (be it the text or a living account) to the Vatican? Canon Formigão, one of the earliest authorities on Fátima, once stated in 1946 that Sister might have gone to Rome from Fátima and relay the information to the Holy Father.[43] His discussion, however, was speculative. The context given in the story indicates that while Sr. Lúcia "nurtured" (*alimentou*) the idea of going to Rome, nothing suggests that she was *in fact* going to reveal the third part of the secret to the Holy Father.[44] If it was that important

---

Oursler Armstrong and Martin F. Armstrong, Jr. *Fátima: Pilgrimage to Peace.* [Garden City, New York: Hanover House, 1954] 104).

43   Cf. *The Whole Truth About Fatima, Volume III,* 469.

44   The source of this information is given by Frère Michel as a publication entitled *Stella (The Whole Truth About Fatima, Volume III,* 228). The citation in his endnotes is a little confusing (cf. page 239), but it appears as though Frère Michel is referring to the publication *Stella* as it was quoted by Fr. Sebastião Martins dos Reis in his own book entitled *A Vidente de Fátima DIALOGA e responde pelas Aparições.* (Braga, Portugal: Editorial Franciscana, 1970), 115-116. The Portuguese text reads as follows:

> —Devo deixar estes sítios amanhã, de manhã, não sabendo ainda para onde irei... (I must leave these sites tomorrow morning, not yet knowing where I am going).

> —Lembrámo-nos de que talvez a vidente fosse chamada nesta ocasião a Roma, para expor, ao Santo Padre Pio XII, a terceira parte do «segredo» de Nossa Senhora de Fátima, a que ela se refere nos seus últimos escritos (We remember that perhaps the seer was called on this occasion to Rome, to reveal, to the Holy Father Pius XII, the third part of the "secret" of Our Lady of Fátima, to which she refers in her later writings).

> [*The following text was a footnote—KJS*] É muito provável que o Visconde de Montelo não ignorasse que de facto se pensava numa ida da Vidente a Roma: Iniciaram-se mesmo e facilitaram-se as indispensáveis diligências com esse objectivo, e ela própria alimentou algumas esperanças de êxito, que todavia não chegaram a concretizar--se em definitivo... (It is very likely that the Visconde de Montelo was not ignorant of the fact that, *de facto*, they thought of a trip of the Seer

for him to receive the information (that Sister would lament his willful ignorance in 1957), why did she not write to the Pope, privately, and have it delivered surreptitiously to him, as she did with Fr. Thomas McGlynn in 1947 on the matter of her entrance to the Carmel?[45]

IV. Interpreting Fr. Fuentes' Account: Some Concluding Thoughts

It is clear from the preceding sections that there are many questions surrounding Fr. Fuentes' account of his meeting with Sr. Lúcia. Concerns such as translation difficulties, availability of key documents, presumptions and potentially biased opinions pose many concerns about the account. What, then, are we to make of the matter? Are we to believe that a priest who enjoyed a good reputation and standing would suddenly risk everything by publishing false information?[46] Let us make some observations.

Coimbra's condemnation states that Fuentes "permitted himself to make [*permitiu-se fazer afirmações*] sensational declarations, of an apocalyptic, eschatological and prophetic character, which he declares that he

---

to Rome: They even initiated and facilitated the indispensable measures toward this objective, and she herself nurtured some hope of success, which however did not succeed in materializing in the end).

Frère François speculates that Sr. Lúcia wanted to tell directly to the Pope the third part in 1944 (see Frère François de Marie des Anges, *Fatima: Tragedy and Triumph*. [Buffalo, New York: Immaculate Heart Publications, 1994], 8).

45   Cf. *Um Caminho sob o Olhar de Maria*, 323-325. Sister was reluctant to entrust such deep matters on paper to the postal service, but she did trust clergy, especially Bishops. Why did she not write a document and give it to a Bishop for the Pope?

46   Frère Michel's discussion of the condemnation largely revolves around Fr. Alonso's defense. The former is largely content to claim, using a hermeneutic of suspicion and conspiracy, that the reason for the condemnation was "Roman authorities" ordered it (cf. *The Whole Truth About Fatima, Volume III*, 549-554).

heard from Sister Lúcia." While leaving room for arguments for Portuguese linguistic preferences, why did Coimbra not simply say Fuentes "made" such statements?

To say that he "permitted himself to make" these statements can be interpreted as he was not supposed to discuss such topics, like they were some sort of secret taboo. A subject that is "taboo" does not necessarily mean that its content is untrue; rather it means that there exists a *preference* by authority figures not to speak about it. The subject, in other words, is "well-known" but not spoken.[47] The question is why is it taboo? Moreover, if this reading is correct, how then does one understand the approval from the Bishop of Leiria to Fuentes' account prior to the condemnation from Coimbra?

Let us also consider the overall content of Fuentes' account of his meeting from the Spanish text. Was there anything that was *truly* objectionable in itself? Was there anything not in keeping with the message of Fátima? Is it right and just to look at the matter only from within the perspective of the contents' fidelity to the message of Fátima?[48] To the first two questions, it is possible to make an argument for a connection between the message of Fátima and Fuentes' statements. The last question does not seem to satisfy critical demands which encompass more concerns than just

---

47   Cf. Mark Fellows, *Sister Lucia: Apostle of Mary's Immaculate Heart.* (Immaculate Heart Publications, 2007), 262-263. Fellows bases his argument upon a cordial conversation between Fr. Luis Kondor and David Boyce, the English translator of the Abbé de Nantes' publication *La Contre-Reforme Catholique.* Boyce claims that Kondor used the word "indiscretion" in reference to Fuentes as opposed to "lies" or "fabrications." A conversation self-described as "cordial" and with laughter does not strike one as serious or scholarly. *The Fatima Crusader* published Boyce's account: <http://www.fatimacrusader.com/cr35/cr35pg12.asp> (Accessed 3 November, 2016).

48   Alonso believed that Fuentes' account was edifying to Christians and argued that it did not contain anything new from Sr. Lúcia. Thus, he gives the appearance that his criterion was whether or not the account was faithful to the message of Fátima.

fidelity to content. One must inquire about *veracity* as well. Let us look at chastisements as an example.

Our Lady was very specific about mankind bringing down upon itself the Second World War if it did not repent.[49] War is viewed as a chastisement from God for the sins of man.[50] If there was to be some new war (let us note, the hostilities between Cuba [backed by Russia] and the United States in the early 1960s), then the warning about an "imminent chastisement from heaven" would not be inconsistent with the message of Fátima.[51] This observation, however, does not answer the question of whether Sr. Lúcia *actually* made such statements. Clearly, she objected to the statements attributed to her. Did, therefore, Fuentes simply lie?

To help us answer that last question, let us recall our previous examination of the two "authentic" texts. As we saw, Fr. Alonso held that both the Spanish original and the English translation in *Fatima Findings* were "genuine." Our examination and comparison between the two texts showed that there were some notable differences and liberties taken by the English translator. How much did these liberties affect a proper reading and understanding of Fuentes' account? If there was no proper understanding, did Sr. Lúcia act based upon the information presented to her? If so, once again we ask, *how* and *what* was the information presented to her?[52]

---

49   ˙ Dr. Antonio Maria Martins, S.J., *Memórias e Cartas de Irmã Lúcia*. (Porto, Portugal: Simão Guimarães, Filhos, LDA, 1973), 341.

50   Cf. Fr. Thomas McGlynn, O.P., *Vision of Fatima*. (Boston, Massachusetts: Little Brown and Company, 1948), 90.

51   Let us consider the fact that, according to the Carmelites' biography, Sr. Lúcia told Pope Pius XII that Communism would reach its "high point" in or by the year 1960 (*Um Caminho sob o Olhar de Maria*, 275). Clearly, Sister either knew or suspected that something very grave was going to take place around that year.

52   Raising this question is not intended to question Coimbra's notice. Rather, it is an attempt at clarity in order to understand better the place of Fr. Fuentes' account in the history of the third part of the secret.

Consider as well our discussion on *which* text influenced the Diocese of Coimbra. We observed that the Portuguese translation provided by M.C. de Bragança in *A Voz* appears to have been the one that most influenced Coimbra. However, this text was a translation from the English in *Fatima Findings*. If, as is quite possibly the case, the English translation was notably flawed and negatively impacted a proper understanding of Fuentes' account, how would such a fact affect Coimbra's condemnation?

It seems as though much of the present difficulty can be attributed to the fact that the English translation in *Fatima Findings* was authorized by Fr. Fuentes. The translator took many liberties and he trusted her competency. English was a language that Fuentes was not comfortable speaking, though he was said to have understood it. Perhaps because of his *reading* ability in English, he saw that the essential heart of his conference to the Mexican Sisters was present and authorized it. Nevertheless, the differences between the two texts necessitated a critical eye. Failing to provide it led to a lot of misunderstanding.

In the end, the matter of Fuentes' account of his 1957 meeting with Sr. Lúcia is not clear, leaving us with unanswered questions. It is clear that any questions aside as to fidelity to what Sister actually said, Fuentes' account appeared at a time when there was heightened anticipation on the third part of the secret. His account fed into that anticipation with all of its fears and anxieties. This "indiscretion" on Fuentes' part contributed greatly to damaging his good name and credibility. Given the ongoing controversial nature of this story, an objective reassessment of this area of the history of Fátima needs to be performed—one free from notions of a conspiratorial nature that have (thus far) dominated the discussion within various circles of Catholics.

—6—

SISTER LÚCIA AND A "TERRIFYING" SECRET?

"I have written what you asked me; God willed to try me a little, but finally, this was indeed His will: [the text] *is in an envelope and it is in the notebooks...."*

—Sr. Lúcia, January 9, 1944

One of the most misunderstood aspects in the history of Fátima is the great struggle that Sr. Lúcia experienced in writing down the third part of the secret.[1] The question is *why* did she struggle? The available literature on Fátima indicates two different explanations. The first explanation concerns obedience.[2] The second is that the third part "terrified" Sister.[3] In order to

---

1   Cf. Frère Michel de la Sainte Trinité, *The Whole Truth About Fatima. Volume III: The Third Secret.* (Buffalo, New York: Immaculate Heart Publications, 1990), 37-55. Hereafter *The Whole Truth About Fatima: Volume III* followed by page number.

2   See Joaquin Maria Alonso, C.M.F., *The Secret of Fatima: Fact and Legend.* (Cambridge, Massachusetts: The Ravengate Press, 1979), 35-40. Hereafter *The Secret of Fatima: Fact and Legend* followed by page number.

3   See Antonio Socci, *The Fourth Secret of Fatima.* (Fitzwilliam, New Hampshire: Loreto Publications, 2009), 142, 145-153. Hereafter *The Fourth Secret of Fatima* followed by page number. See also *The Whole Truth About Fati-*

discuss which of the two is more accurate, it is necessary to recount in some depth how the third part came to be written down. For this story, let us turn to one of the most relied upon authorities of Fátima, Fr. Joaquín María Alonso.

I. Obedience or Terror?

In 1976, Fr. Alonso wrote a book in Spanish entitled *La Verdad Sobre el Secreto de Fatima*.[4] This book was subsequently translated into English in 1979 by the Dominican Nuns of the Perpetual Rosary and entitled *The Secret of Fatima: Fact and Legend*. In this book, Alonso attempts, among other things, to discuss how the secret of Fátima came to be written down. First he explains that the secret is best understood as an organic whole in order to show its inner unity.[5] Alonso breaks down the secret for the sake of explanation. He covers the first two parts, saving discussion of the third for its own unit. He opens this discussion in part II (*The Unpublished Part of the Secret*) of the book.

Part II: Chapter I (*The Origin of the Secret*) recounts how the third part of the secret was written down. Fr. Alonso wrote:

> As we have said, the first two parts of the Secret were defin-
> itively written in 1941. Halfway through 1943 Lucia fell ill.
> This led the Bishop of Leiria to order her to write down the
> remainder of the Secret.

---

ma: Volume III, 51; Frère François de Marie des Anges, *Fatima: Tragedy and Triumph*. (Buffalo, New York: Immaculate Heart Publications, 1994), 6, 202. Hereafter *Fatima: Tragedy and Triumph* followed by page number; Christopher Ferrara, *False Friends of Fatima*. (Pound Ridge, New York, Good Counsel Publications, 2012), 91, 101.

4   Joaquin Maria Alonso, C.M.F., *La Verdad Sobre el Secreto de Fatima, Fatima sin mitos*. (Madrid: Centro Mariano, 1976). Hereafter *La Verdad Sobre el Secreto de Fatima* followed by page number.

5   *The Secret of Fatima: Fact and Legend*, 98.

Sister Lucia had always enjoyed good health, except that she occasionally suffered from bronchial trouble. At times this became acute, and she would be sent away for a rest, almost always to one of the peaceful low-lying estuaries of Pontevedra, La Toja or Rianjo.

In the summer of 1943, however, at the beginning of June, she fell sick with pleurisy. At first it seemed to be a mild attack, but almost immediately it became serious. She was running a high temperature....

By July, however, Lucia was recovering, but she soon became worse again as the result of an infection caused by a badly administered injection.

The Bishop of Leiria was concerned about Lucia's health, and even feared for her life. In July he wrote to ask her for notes which were to be used for a new edition of the little book, *Jacinta*, but when he heard of Lucia's relapse, he became anxious. Was Lucia about to leave this world and take her Secret with her? He decided to visit her and order her to write down the still hidden part of the Secret. Lucia had meanwhile contracted another infection, caused in the same way as the previous one, and was confined to bed. In spite of this, the Bishop went to Tuy towards the middle of September and spoke with her. They discussed writing down the remainder of the Secret.[6]

Alonso then discusses the "painful ordeal" that the illness caused Sr. Lúcia and how it was in the midst of this that the secret was written. He relates that Bishop da Silva made an initial request in September, 1943 for Sister to write down the Secret. This request, however, was based upon the condition "if [Sister] wished" (*se eu quiesse*) to do so.[7] As the English

---

6   Ibid., 35-36.

7   *La Verdad Sobre el Secreto de Fatima*, 31.

translation notes, the request "put Lucia in a quandary."[8]

What exactly was the quandary and how did Alonso know this fact? He cites a letter from Lúcia in which she stated the following:

> It seems to me that to write it down is already in a way to disclose it, and I do not yet have Our Lord's permission for that. In any case, as I am used to seeing the will of God in the wishes of my superiors, I am thinking of obedience, and I don't know what to do. I prefer an express command which I can rely on before God, so that I can say in all security, "They ordered me that, Lord." But those words, "if you wish," disturb me and leave me perplexed.[9]

Alonso continues on to write about how the Bishop of Leiria then ordered Sr. Lúcia to write down the third part of the secret. Still torn over whom to obey, Sr. Lúcia wrote to the Apostolic Administrator of Tuy (Spain), Don Antonio Garcia. Alonso summarized the correspondence as follows:

> [Lúcia] told [Don Antonio Garcia] that this order frightened her since, on the one hand, Our Lord had commanded her to say nothing to anyone and, on the other, His representative had told her to write it down. A real struggle was taking place within her. What

---

8   *The Secret of Fatima: Fact and Legend*, 37. These words are not in the Spanish text (31).

9   Ibid. The Spanish text reads:

Que no era, claro está, para ser inmediatamente publicado, sino sólo para quedar escrito. «Pero —añade Lucía— a mí me parece que escribirlo es ya de algún modo revelarlo, y no tengo todavía licencia de Nuestro Señor para ello. De todos modos, como estoy habituada a ver en los deseos de los superiores la voluntad de Dios, estoy mirando a la obediencia, y no sé qué hacer. Prefiero una orden expresa en que me pudiese apoyar delante de Dios, y decir con seguridad: *"Mandaram-mo, Senhor."* Pero esas palabras: "Se a Irma quizesse", me conturban y me dejan perpleja.» (*La Verdad Sobre el Secreto de Fatima*, 31-32).

should determine her decision? Begging Don Antonio to advise her, she added that she had several times wished to obey and had sat down at the table to write, only to find herself unable to do so.... [F]aced with Heaven's perplexing silence, [Lúcia] felt that she had now become a stranger in Our Lord's eyes, and she suffered greatly on this account.[10]

After narrating the above, Alonso discusses what came of this correspondence, how it was communicated, etc. This discussion does not provide very many helpful details for our purposes, except to say that Don Antonio's replies did not reach Sister in a timely fashion (40-41). She had to go without his direction as the letters had been "intercepted" (*interceptadas*) according to Alonso (41-English, 35-Spanish). He then continued the story as follows:

Lucia, without the aid of Don Antonio's letters...wrote to tell him that she had tried several times to write the Secret but was unable to do as she had been commanded. She added that this was certainly not the effect of natural causes. In another of her letters we learn that the Secret had still not been written by Christmas day. However, we also know that by the ninth of January, 1944 the third part of the Secret had been written. Therefore, even though our research up until now has not been able to determine the exact date, we know for certain that between December 25, 1943 and January 9, 1944 the famous final section of the Secret of Fatima, revealed on July 13, 1917, was at last written down by Lucia.

The only problem which still remained was that of finding a good opportunity to place the Secret, with all security, in the hands of the Bishop of Leiria. This took several months. Final-

---

10   Ibid., 39-40.

ly, on June 17, 1944 the Bishop of Gurza, traveling with others who were unaware of the special mission entrusted to him by the Bishop of Leiria, arrived at the border of Spain and Portugal, at a place called Valencia do Minho. Lucia, who had come there from Tuy, gave him the precious document. That same afternoon the happy bearer of the long-awaited letter handed it over to Dom Jose when he and his companions arrived at the Bishop's country residence, *Quinta da Formigueira*, in Braga. The Secret had been written by Lucia on a sheet of paper, placed inside an envelope and sealed up. Later Dom Jose put it into another larger envelope, sealed that also and wrote upon it in his own hand:

This envelope with its contents is to be given to His Eminence, Cardinal Dom Manuel, Patriarch of Lisbon, after my death.

Leiria, December 8, 1945
†Jose, Bishop of Leiria[11]

It is clear from the above story that the struggle within the soul of Sr. Lúcia over writing down the third part of the secret concerned obedience. She had been told by Jesus Himself not to reveal the secret. As a religious, however, bound to obedience, a legitimate order from her superiors was as if it came from God Himself. When ordered to write down the third part of the secret, there arose a conflict within Sister over whom to obey.

From Fr. Alonso's recounting of events, based upon correspondence from Sister, we know that this difficulty was resolved sometime between Christmas, 1943 and January 9, 1944. The details of just how the difficulty was resolved have always been sparse. Despite this fact, it has been for several decades common knowledge that an apparition of Our Lady to Sr. Lúcia resolved the difficulty. Frère Michel collated the data on this

---

11   Ibid., 41-42.

fact, citing as his authorities Canon Martins dos Reis, Fr. Antonio Maria Martins and Fr. Alonso, saying that the apparition of Our Lady occurred on January 2, 1944.[12]

Though the details on the above fact have been sparse, we rejoice that more information has recently become available to the public in the biography of Sr. Lúcia *Um Caminho sob o Olhar de Maria*.[13] Chapter thirteen of this book (*O Segredo Escrito/The Secret Written*) is divided into eight sections. The first three describe how the third part of the secret was written down.[14]

The story of the struggle within Sr. Lúcia's soul as presented in the first two sections agrees with the story provided by Fr. Alonso. More details on the events, however, are given in section three entitled "Our Lady permits that Lúcia writes the secret and gives to her new lights" (*Nossa Senhora permite que Lúcia escreva o segredo e dá-lhe novas luzes*) as to the apparition of Our Lady.[15]

In section three, the Carmelite Sisters quote directly from one of the unpublished manuscripts of Sr. Lúcia, her personal diary, as to when Our Lady appeared. In doing so, they fill in a notable lacuna in the literature on Fátima with a document direct from Sr. Lúcia herself that narrated the event in question. First, it is to be noted that Sr. Lúcia wrote that the date of the apparition was January 3, 1944, not the second of that month.[16]

---

12   *The Whole Truth About Fatima. Volume III*, 47-48, 55.

13   Carmelo de Santa Teresa – Coimbra, *Um Caminho sob o Olhar de Maria: Biografia da Irmã Lúcia de Jesus e do Coração Imaculado, O.C.D.* (Coimbra, Portugal: Edições Carmelo, 2013). Hereafter *Um Caminho sob o Olhar de Maria* followed by page number. The English translation is: Carmel of Coimbra and James A. Colson (trans.), *A Pathway Under the Gaze of Mary*. (Washington, New Jersey: World Apostolate of Fatima, 2015). Hereafter *A Pathway Under the Gaze of Mary* followed by page number.

14   *Um Caminho sob o Olhar de Maria*, 262-267.

15   Ibid., 266-267.

16   Ibid., 266. Noting the difference in dates, Fr. Nicholas Gruner and

Concerning the apparition proper, Sister described the event as follows:

> While I was waiting for an answer, on January 3, 1944, I knelt beside the bed which sometimes served as a writing table, and again I experienced the same without success. What most impressed me was that at the same moment I could write anything else without difficulty. I then asked Our Lady to let me know if it was the Will of God. I went to the chapel at 4 p.m. in the afternoon, the hour that I always made a visit to the Blessed Sacrament [when it is] ordinarily [most] alone. I do not know why, but I liked being alone with Jesus in the Tabernacle.
>
> Then I knelt in the middle, next to the rung of the Communion rail and asked Jesus to make known to me what was His Will. Accustomed as I was to believe that the order of the Superiors was the expression of the Will of God, I couldn't believe that this wasn't. Feeling puzzled and half absorbed under the weight of a dark cloud that seemed to hang over me, with my face between my hands, I hoped without knowing how for a response. I then felt a friendly, affectionate and motherly hand touch me on the shoulder and I looked up and saw the beloved Mother from Heaven. "Do not be afraid, God wanted to prove your obedience, faith and humility. Be at peace and write what they order you, [not however what is given you to understand of

---

James Hanisch have opined that there were *two* apparitions of Our Lady to Sr. Lúcia, one on January 2nd and another on January 3rd, 1944 (*The Fatima Crusader*, Spring 2016, pages 30-39). January 2nd has been customarily held to be the date of this apparition to Sr. Lúcia, largely owing to Frère Michel's citing the authority of Fr. Antonio Maria Martins. Martins himself relied upon the "written declaration" of Mother Cunha Mattos (Sr. Lúcia's superior in Tuy) who stated the date to be January 2nd, 1944 (see *The Whole Truth About Fatima, Volume III*, 55 [endnote 21]). Frère Michel does not provide discussion as to how Mother Mattos gave this date and the new document from Sr. Lúcia addresses the matter more completely.

its meaning]. After writing it, place it in an envelope, close and seal it and write on the outside that this can be opened in 1960 by the Cardinal Patriarch of Lisbon or by the Bishop of Leiria."[17]

The above description straight from the pen of Sr. Lúcia is truly revelatory.[18] It demonstrates *clearly and beyond a shadow of doubt* that the struggle was over obedience, not some "terrifying" content of the secret.

II. The Origin of the "Terrifying" Characterization

We have endeavored to examine the reason for the struggle within Sr. Lúcia over writing down the third part of the secret. It remains to us to discuss the origin of the claim that the third part was "terrifying." The origin of the claim is not necessarily the result of one person, but a confluence of different peoples and events. We shall look at the matter through the eyes of Fr. Alonso who provides a general history for us as well as demonstrates his own role and contribution in this history.

The English translation of Fr. Alonso's *The Secret of Fatima: Fact and Legend* begins with an introduction that was written by an unspecified person or persons.[19] The introduction begins by providing a basic and quick

---

17   *Um Caminho sob o Olhar de Maria*, 266. The English translation is taken from *A Pathway Under the Gaze of Mary*, 243. I have taken the liberty of slightly emending the translation (indicated by the texts in brackets) after consulting the Portuguese original in those places. Also, compare Sister's description of how she wrote down the secret "without difficulty" (*sem dificuldade*) immediately after the vision (*A Pathway Under the Gaze of Mary*, 244) with Frère Michel's description of it being "extremely painful mission" to communicate it (*The Whole Truth About Fatima. Volume III*, 708).

18   For an observation on a peculiar aspect of the history of Fátima related to this new revelation, please consult the chapter entitled "Various Considerations" section titled, "Sr. Lúcia, the "Last Obstacle" to the Third Secret?" of the present book.

19   It may have been the work of the translators, but this is merely conjecture.

synopsis of Fátima and its events. The aim is to discuss the secret communicated to the three visionaries and no time is wasted in getting to that topic. After attaining this objective, the unnamed author(s) wrote the following:

> There is one part of the Fatima message, however, that has never been publicly revealed. It is contained in a sealed letter written by Lucia dos Santos, the only surviving member of the three to whom Our Lady appeared, now a Carmelite nun with the name Sister Mary Lucia of the Immaculate Heart. Lucia had written this letter in late 1943 or early 1944, at the insistence of her ordinary, the Bishop of Leiria. The letter was sealed, its contents known only to Lucia herself, with the instruction that it should be opened "not before 1960." At first the letter was kept in a safe at the bishopric in Leiria, but in [1957] it was removed to the Vatican.
>
> As 1960 approached, the letter containing the Secret became an object of world-wide publicity and curiosity. Noting that previously-published parts of the Fatima message showed that Our Lady had in 1917 foretold both the end of World War I and the coming of World War II, sensation-mongers speculated freely as to what apocalyptic pronouncements the letter might contain.
>
> And so, to a crescendo of excitement and anticipation, 1960 arrived and Lúcia's letter was opened. Pope John XXIII read the letter, showed it to a few close aides, and then ordered it returned to the Vatican Archives—its contents still unrevealed.
>
> The resulting disappointment was unquestionably due to the sensationalism that had preceded the letter's opening. Nevertheless, the sensationalists quickly went to work again, assuring the public that the Pope had not dared to publish the Secret because it was simply too terrifying. (On the other side, of course, were the detractors, who said he had not revealed it because it was just not worth revealing.) The worst effect of all this confu-

sion was that the known parts of Our Lady's message at Fatima were being disparaged and obscured. And that message was far too clear, and too important, for such a thing to happen.[20]

Alonso himself states later in the book:

> I want first to do away once and for all with the mystifications, the caricatures, the hair-raising exaggerations, the cheap and sensational apocalyptic writings which have been produced on the subject of Fatima and its Secret. To achieve this first end, there was only one way to proceed: to tell the truth and nothing but the truth.
>
> But the "truth about the Secret of Fátima" has extremely positive aspects that we also want to highlight. Because Fátima and its secret, if it is not in some way "fearful," is rather absolutely serious when we are faced with the tremendous mysteries of the hereafter [*del más allá*]. And one can confuse the "fearful" with the seriousness of our Catholic faith. Neither ought one to place in ridicule the Acts and the Message of Fátima simply because they announce from a manner absolutely evangelical the more serious truths of our faith.[21]

---

20   *The Secret of Fatima: Fact and Legend*, 1-3. While we do not know the author of the above description, it is hard to believe that Fr. Alonso did not agree with it as he was still alive when it was published under his name and authority. Regardless, it is an accurate description of Alonso's own discussion in the rest of the book.

21   Ibid., 11-12. The original Spanish reads as follows:

> Nuestra intención principal es doble: primero consiste en un intent de acabar para siempre con las mistificaciones, con las caricaturas, con los tremendismos, con la apocalíptica barata y sensacionalista que se he producido, casi comercializado, en torno a Fátima y a su secreto. Para conseguir este primer propósito, sólo había un camino: decir la verdad, nada más que la verdad.
>
> Pero la «verdad sobre el Secreto de Fátima» tiene unos aspectos

It is clear that Fr. Alonso believed that exaggerations concerning the secret of Fátima were present. The historical record indicates that the hype and speculations existed in different phases. The first phase was the period right after the secret was given in July, 1917 and was, arguably, more localized.[22] A second phase, more widespread, can be considered to have taken place after the first two parts were revealed in 1941 and the subsequent committing of the third part to paper in January, 1944. Shortly thereafter, news had reached the public that said part had been written down and was to be opened in 1960. Speculation arose and was furthered by various events. One such event was mentioned by Fr. Alonso that discusses what happened after the secret was given to Bishop da Silva. Alonso wrote:

> The third part of the Secret of Fatima was now in the hands of the Bishop of Leiria. Respecting absolutely the seal of the document, he deposited it in the safe of his chancery. It was never taken out except on very rare occasions, and then merely to be

---

sumamente positivos, que también queremos destacar. Porque Fátima y su secreto, si no es en modo alguno «tremendista», sí que es absolutamente algo serio cuando nos enfrenta con los tremendos misterios del más allá. Y no se puede confundir el «tremendismo» con la seriedad de nuestra fe católica. Ni se debería poner en ridículo a los Hechos y al Mensaje de Fátima simplemente porque anuncian de una manera absolutamente evangélica las verdades más serias de nuestra fe (*La Verdad Sobre el Secreto de Fatima,* 5-6).

The English translation present in *The Secret of Fatima: Fact and Legend* seems not to translate the entire Spanish text of the second paragraph. The translation provided above is more faithful to this text.

22   News had spread that something had been communicated to the children and people made many inquiries about it. The children would not budge, even when kidnapped, imprisoned and faced with bribes and threats in August, 1917 by the Mayor of Ourem, Arturo dos Santos. Cf. Dr. Antonio Maria Martins, S.J., *Memórias e Cartas de Irmã Lúcia.* (Porto, Portugal: Simão Guimarães, Filhos, LDA, 1973), 263-265. Hereafter *Memórias e Cartas de Irmã Lúcia* followed by page number.

gazed at by a few privileged persons. Mr. Pazen, a reporter for *Life* magazine, was permitted to take a photograph of it which *Life* published.

These incidents, and especially their repercussions, have made Fatima "famous," thus constituting one of the more interesting chapters in the history of morbid curiosity on the part of the press and other news media, ready as they always are to jump at anything sensational and spectacular. It is necessary for us to clarify matters in order to free Fatima from the merely human elements which have so often made it appear ridiculous or have deformed it into a caricature which is utterly grotesque.[23]

Finally, one can discern a third phase of exaggerated speculation(s) from about 1960 onward. Alonso devotes two chapters (3 and 4) of part II of his book to this topic. He walks the reader through some of the lead-up to 1960, then shows the reaction to a news article in Portuguese media that revealed the third part of the secret was not going to be published.[24]

---

23 *The Secret of Fatima: Fact and Legend*, 43. The Spanish text reads:

La tercera parte del secreto estaba, finalmente, en manos del señor Obispo de Leiría. Este, respetando absolutamente el sigilo del documento, lo depositó en la caja fuerte de la Curia, de donde no salió sino en rarísimas ocasiones, para ser simplemente, contemplado por fuera por algunos privilegiados. Por ejemplo, fue fotografiado por el reportero de «Life» Mr. Pazen, en donde apareció.

En cambio, las peripecias, y sobre todo las repercusiones, para la «fama» de Fátima constituyen uno de los capítulos más interesantes para la historia de la curiosidad malsana de la prensa y de todos los medios de comunicación, ávidos de lanzarse sobre todo lo sensacional y maravillosista. También aquí es necesario hacer luz para liberar Fátima de adherencias humanas, que tantas veces la han puesto en ridículo, y otras la han deformado en caricaturas grotescas (*La Verdad Sobre el Secreto de Fatima*, 36-37).

24 *The Secret of Fatima: Fact and Legend*, 52-56. Chapter four offers some discussion as to why it was not revealed by ecclesiastical authorities (pages 57-63).

While discussing a hypothesis on the meaning of the third part of the secret, Fr. Alonso makes a surprising statement. He appears to contradict his earlier, carefully laid out version of events as to the nature of the struggle within Sr. Lúcia in writing down the third part of the secret. He wrote:

> Moreover, how are we to understand Lucia's great difficulty in writing the final part of the Secret when she had already written other things that were extremely difficult to put down? Had it been merely a matter of prophesying new and severe punishments, Sister Lucia would not have experienced difficulties so great that a special intervention from Heaven was needed to overcome them. But if it were a matter of internal strife within the Church and of serious pastoral negligence on the part of high-ranking members of the hierarchy, we *can* understand how Lucia experienced a repugnance that was almost impossible to overcome by any natural means.[25]

In short, in order to advance his hypothesis, Alonso appeared willing to believe that "internal strife within the Church" was part of the secret. This strife was so repugnant to Sr. Lúcia that she struggled to write down the third part of the secret. This is a complete reversal of his earlier point which focused upon Sister's religious obedience as the reason for

---

25   Ibid., 82. The Spanish text reads:

Por lo demás, ¿cómo comprender las grandes dificultades de Lucía en escribirlo después de haber escrito otras cosas ya enormemente difíciles? Se se hubiera tratado simplemente de anunciar proféticamente nuevos y grandes cataclismos estamos seguros gue la Hermana Lucía no hubiera sufrido tales dificultades, cuyo vencimiento exigió una especial intervención del cielo. En cambio, si se trata de luchas intestinas en el seno de la misma Iglesia y de graves negligencias pastorals de altos Jerarcas se comprende que Lucía tuviera unas repugnancies casi imposibles de superar naturalmente (*La Verdad Sobre el Secreto de Fatima*, 75).

her struggle. No reason is given why Alonso took such a sudden turn in his thinking.[26]

While the reason for the shift is not clear, it is fair to question the *effect* of Alonso's hypothesis. He wrote that he wanted to do away with the "mystifications" surrounding the third part of the secret. Speculating upon internal strife within the Church is a serious topic, one that is easily abused and quickly taken advantage of, thus necessitating *very* careful study and a sober analysis.[27] Alonso must have viewed his discussion as not contradicting his intended aim. It *is*, after all, reasonable to ponder what Our Lady meant by Portugal preserving the dogma of the Faith. In whatever way that he saw this matter, Alonso did not see the contradiction in his own argument, nor did Frère Michel and others.[28]

---

26   Frère Michel notes that Alonso's position as the official archivist of Fátima allowed him access to Sr. Lúcia. This fact led to the observation that perhaps it was Sister who said something to Alonso and he was surreptitiously broadcasting her view (cf. *The Whole Truth About Fatima. Volume III*, 704-709). This hypothesis, while largely circumstantial, has not been refuted. At the same time, it is not proven.

27   Consider what happens when attempts are made by the media to place one Church representative against another to the detriment of the cause of religion. In his 1915 Encyclical *Ad Beatissimi Apostolorum* (21-22), Pope Benedict XV warned about such measures being used by forces hostile to the Church (cf. Claudia Carlen, IHM (edit.), *The Papal Encyclicals: 1903-1922. Volume III*. [Raleigh, North Carolina: The Pierian Press, 1990], 148). This author recalls the example from March, 2007 involving Sean Hannity and Fr. Thomas Euteneuer. Hannity, a Catholic, was told that he would be denied Holy Communion by Euteneuer on the grounds that Hannity has publicly stated his difference with the Church on one or more doctrines. After this program, Fr. Jonathan Morris went on *Fox News* and stated his disagreement with Fr. Euteneuer. The damage done to a brother priest by this contradiction was not insignificant. See: <https://www.lifesitenews.com/news/on-fox-news-fearless-hli-priest-takes-on-sean-hannity-over-contraception-ha> (Accessed 14 December, 2015). This author has the video of the exchange between Hannity and Fr. Euteneuer.

28   One can see a hint of this in *The Whole Truth About Fatima. Volume III*, 51 (see also pages 706-707). Here, Frère Michel states his belief in the position that whatever was in the third part of the secret surely "frightened" Sr.

In conclusion, that the contradiction was not caught led to further speculations that have led to misunderstanding an important part of Fátima. It is only fair, however, to make an important distinction. The present chapter is composed with the benefit of hindsight. At the time of his writing (1976/1979), Fr. Alonso did not enjoy this benefit. No excuse is here offered for Alonso's contradiction, but we must remember that the available literature on Fátima in his day was not what it is today. Even if, as the archivist of Fátima, Alonso had access to documents not known to the public at that time, he did not have access to everything.

Lúcia and this accounts for the difficulty she experienced in writing it down. This is contradictory to the very evidence that Frère Michel himself provided a few pages prior (36). On this page he *directly* quotes from Sr. Lúcia's *Fourth Memoir* where she *explicitly* states that an order to write down the third part would have put her in a quandary over obedience. To read Sister's own text, see *Memórias e Cartas de Irmã Lúcia*, 315-317. While on page 51 of his book, Frère Michel does not offer discussion of the "frightening" nature of the third part of the secret, it becomes apparent that he upholds the hypothesis of interior strife within the Church (*The Whole Truth About Fatima. Volume III*, 683ff.). The logical conclusion is that if this hypothesis truly *is* the third part of the secret, and Sr. Lúcia was "frightened" by this part, then she would be frightened by the "apostasy."

—7—
THE 1960 PORTUGUESE NEWS ARTICLE

"In 1960."

—Sr. Lúcia

In February, 1960 in Portuguese media, an article was published that concerned the non-release of the third part of the secret of Fátima. This article was met with dismay by devotees of Fátima.[1] There exists, however, few critiques of this article in English. Moreover, it is used to support the notion of a second text of the third part of the secret, thus necessitating a closer examination.[2] The Portuguese text was reproduced by Sebastian Martins dos Reis in his book *The Miracle of the Sun*.[3] The numbers herein

---

1   Frère Michel de la Sainte Trinité, *The Whole Truth About Fatima. Volume III: The Third Secret.* (Buffalo, New York: Immaculate Heart Publications, 1990), 578-591. Hereafter *The Whole Truth About Fatima, Volume III* followed by page number.

2   Christopher Ferrara, *The Secret Still Hidden.* (Pound Ridge, New York: Good Counsel Publications, 2008), 26, 117. See also Ferrara's response (pgs. 12 and 36): <http://www.fatima.org/news/newsviews/ferraraexpose.pdf> (Accessed 23 December, 2015). The present chapter is highly speculative, thus necessitating the reader to view it on its own terms.

3   Sebastião Martins dos Reis, *O Milagre do Sol e o Segredo de Fátima: Inconsequências e especulações.* (Porto: Edições Salesianas, 1966), 127-128. An

added (indicated in brackets) are for the sake of convenience. The Portuguese text with an English translation are as follows:

Portuguese	English Translation
ASSEGURA-SE EM MEIOS DO VATICANO SER PROVÁVEL QUE O "SEGREDO DE FÁTIMA" NUNCA SEJA TORNADO PÚBLICO	VATICAN CIRCLES ASSURE US IT IS LIKELY THAT THE "SECRET OF FÁTIMA" MAY NEVER BE MADE PUBLIC

CIDADE DO VATICANO, 8 — (*A.N.I.*) — É provável que o «Segredo de Fátima» nunca chegue a ser tornado público.

[2] Circulos do Vaticano, altamente fidedignos, declararam agora, ao representante da UNITED PRESS INTERNATI-O-NAL, ser muito provável que a carta, em que a Irmã Lúcia escreveu as palavras que a Virgem Maria dirigiu aos três pastorinhos da Cova da Iria, nunca venha a ser aberta.

[3] Por indicação da Irmã Lúcia, a carta só poderia ser aberta durante o ano de 1960.

VATICAN CITY, 8 — (*Agência Nacional de Informação*) — It is likely that the "Secret of Fátima" will never come to be made public.

[2] Vatican circles, highly reliable, to a representative of the United Press International, now declare [it] to be very likely that the letter, in which Sr. Lúcia wrote the words that the Virgin Mary directed to the three pastorinhos of the Cova da Iria, will never come to be opened.

[3] By indication of Sr. Lúcia, the letter could only be opened during the year 1960.

English translation was provided by Joaquin Maria Alonso, C.M.F., *The Secret of Fatima: Fact and Legend.* (Cambridge, Massachusetts: The Ravengate Press, 1979), 55-56.

[4] Perante as pressões que têm sido exercidas junto do Vaticano, afirmaram os mesmos circulos, — umas, para que a carta seja aberta, e o seu conteúdo revelado ao mundo inteiro; outras, partindo da suposição de que na carta se conteriam vaticínios alarmantes, para que não seja publicada, — o Vaticano resolveu que o texto da carta da Irmã Lúcia não seja revelado, continuando a ser mantido sob rigoroso sigilo.

[5] A decisão das autoridades do Vaticano fundamenta-se nas seguintes razões:

1. —A Irmã Lúcia ainda está viva;
2. — O Vaticano já conhece o conteúdo da carta;
3. — Embora a Igreja reconheça as aparições de Fátima, não deseja tomar o compromisso de garantir a veracidade das palavras que os três pastorinhos disseram que a Virgem Maria lhes havia dirigido.

[4] Confronting the pressures that have been exercised on the Vatican, the same circles affirmed (with some wanting the letter to be opened and its content revealed to the whole world, while others, going by the supposition that within the letter there may contain alarming prophecies, [desire] that it might not be published) the Vatican decided that the text of the letter of Sr. Lúcia may never be revealed, continuing it to be maintained under rigorous secrecy.

[5] The decision of the Vatican authorities is itself based in the following reasons:

1. Sr. Lúcia is still living;
2. The Vatican already knows the content of the letter;
3. Although the Church recognizes the apparitions of Fátima, she does not desire to take the obligation [to] guarantee the veracity of the words that the three pastorinhos said that the Virgin Mary had directed to them.

| [6] Nestas circunstâncias, é muito provável que o «Segredo de Fátima» seja mantido, para sempre, sob absoluto sigilo. | [6] In these circumstances, it is very likely that the "Secret of Fátima" may be maintained, forever, under absolute secrecy. |

Based upon the above texts and their origins, we can make some simple observations:

1. The author of this news article is not given.[4]
2. In paragraph two, the unspecified author cites unnamed "Vatican circles" (*circulos do Vaticano*) as his/her authority for the information presented in the article.
3. The "Vatican circles" spoke to a representative of the United Press International (UPI) to whom was communicated the information about the fate of Sr. Lúcia's text.
4. The author of the article is not specified as the UPI representative.
5. There is mention of the "letter" written by Sr. Lúcia and it is said to contain the "words" of Our Lady to the three visionaries.
6. Concerning the mention of *letter* and *words*, there are no quotation marks, indicating the "Vatican circles" are not being directly quoted.
7. Paragraph four indicates conflicting opinions within the Vatican over

---

4   Fr. Paul Kramer and Christopher Ferrara attribute the article as having been issued by the Vatican (*The Devil's Final Battle*. [Good Counsel Publications, 2010], 54) and *False Friends of Fatima*. (Pound Ridge, New York: Good Counsel Publications, 2012), 78-79). This characterization gives the notice an appearance of authority. This attribution appears to be an error. The article is very explicit in that the author of the piece states that the source of the information was various "Vatican circles." Let us keep all of this information in perspective as the source of the Portuguese text presented above is not the original publication. It is taken from Sebastian Martins dos Reis' book cited above. One must ask whether or not dos Reis neglected to include the name of the author of the article in question.

the fate of the third part of the secret.

8. Finally, there appears to be some contradiction within the document over "opening" (*aberta*) the envelope and "revealing" (*revelado*) it.

From these observations, we must then proceed to ask some questions:

1. Who is the author of this news article?
2. Who are the members of these "Vatican circles?"
3. Is the author of this article the representative of UPI?
   a. If not, what manner of consultation did the author have with this representative?
4. Why was the representative not named?
5. Since there are no quotation marks in paragraph two, what is the origin and provenance of the terms "letter" and "words?"
   a. Was the source an eyewitness to the text read by John XXIII?
   b. Were these terms solely those of the author of this article?
   c. If the terms "letter" and "words" are the author's and not an eyewitness, how much weight should be given these terms in favor of an argument for an alleged second text?

In paragraph five we see the phrase, "...the words that the three pastorinhos said that the Virgin Mary had directed to them." This phrase can also be interpreted similarly as the two terms discussed above. The article appears to present a distinction between "apparitions" and "words" in paragraph five.[5] Moreover, it is not specified by the author that the antecedent of the term "words" is the third part of the secret. It is thus possible to interpret the phrase in a generic "overall" sense of the apparitions of Our Lady in 1917.

---

5   Let us note as well the apparent contradiction between paragraphs two and five. In the former paragraph, it is said that Our Lady *did* communicate something to the three children. Then, in paragraph five, it is stated that the Church does not want to guarantee the words. If the UPI representative is presenting the opinions of people within the Vatican, there appears to be some *notable* disagreement among them.

One must also wonder at some confusion within the article over opening (*aberta*) the letter and revealing (*revelado*) it to the world. Looking at the article objectively, one sees that there is no mention of whether or not the unnamed "Vatican circles" are actually involved with the matter. This fact questions their ability to speak on said matter. In fact, the article slightly feels like a local "gossip corner" for the Vatican.

The first paragraph begins with a broad statement that it appears likely that the third part of the secret will never be made public (*nunca chegue a ser tornado público*). Such a statement is simple enough, but then paragraph two makes reference to the fact of the document being opened (*nunca venha a ser aberta*), not published/revealed. This focus is followed by another reference to *opening* the document in paragraph three. At this point, the author gives the impression that the document in question *has not yet been opened*.[6]

The above impression is continued into paragraph four when the author presents the conflicting opinions among the unnamed "Vatican circles" over what should be done with the document. It is quite clear that these unnamed "Vatican circles" do not know what has been done with the document already, much less its contents. First, the group that wants it revealed is said also to want it "opened." Secondly, the group that does not want it revealed is portrayed as being concerned that the content *may contain* "alarming prophecies." These opinions are either 1) not in keeping with the historical record, or 2) expressive of ignorance (i.e. they have not read the contents).

Pope John XXIII *opened* the still-sealed document, and read it in Au-

---

6   The Portuguese word *aberta* is a feminine adjective referring back to *carta* (letter). A modest investigation in Portuguese dictionaries shows no usage of *aberta* as synonymous with "publish." The author of the article appears to be conflating two different actions, namely "opening" the document and then "publishing" it. The former act, logically speaking, precedes the latter. Strangely enough, the author seems to acknowledge this logical sequence in paragraph four when the debate among the unnamed "Vatican circles" is discussed.

gust, 1959.[7] We can thus reasonably opine that the group who wanted the text opened and revealed may not have known that it was already opened. If true, such would be an indication that this group was not "in the know."[8] As for the second group, if its concern is based upon a simple supposition that the text "*may* contain" (*se conteriam*) alarming prophecies, then we can conclude that they are ignorant of its contents.

In either case, these unnamed Vatican circles appear to be expressing nothing more than their opinion. The only thing it seems that they knew for sure was that the document most likely was not going to be revealed to the public. How they arrived at that conclusion was not mentioned by the author of the article, but the fact that the text was indeed not released confirmed their report to said author.

Paragraph five then proposes another matter that deserves treatment, namely the identity of the "Vatican authorities" (*autoridades do Vaticano*) herein cited. Are these unnamed persons the same as the "Vatican circles" or is it an entirely new and separate group? The author of the article is not clear on this point, but internal evidence suggests it is an entirely new group.

Paragraph five concerns the reasons why the text from Sr. Lúcia was not going to be released as was the general expectation. Three such reasons are given, but it is the second one that interests us the most, namely that "the Vatican already knows the content of the letter." As we have seen above, the group identified as the "Vatican circles" did not seem to know that the letter had been opened and/or what it contained. How, then, would it be possible for the "Vatican circles" group suddenly to know the contents of the letter?

This question is resolved if one reads the article from within the following hermeneutic. Paragraph five is the narration of the author of the ar-

---

7 Congregation for the Doctrine of the Faith, *The Message of Fatima*. (Vatican City: Libreria Editrice Vaticana, 2000), 4.

8 If this group believed the document unopened, how would they know its contents?

ticle who is communicating information given to him/her by the "Vatican circles" (VC) group. This information concerns the decision of another group, identified as "Vatican authorities" (VA) on the fate of Sr. Lúcia's text. Somehow, the decision from VA came to the knowledge of VC who then relayed it to the author of the article.

If the above hermeneutic is correct, there remains one question to answer. How could the VC group state that "the Vatican already knows the content of the letter" and not know that the letter had been opened and read? It is important to note that the statement does *not* claim that the Vatican knows the contents of the letter *from having read the text*. There is, in the historical record, a peculiar incident that may shed some light on this matter.

According to Frère Michel, Fr. Joseph Schweigl of the Russicum in Rome traveled to Coimbra, Portugal to speak with Sr. Lúcia.[9] He was commissioned by Pope Pius XII for this task. It remains a mystery as to what transpired between Fr. Schweigl and Sr. Lúcia as well as what report was given to the Holy See. There are, however, two sources of information on public record that give us some indications. The first source is a report that Fr. Schweigl issued to the Council Fathers at Vatican II.[10] The second is a witness from the Russicum who wrote a private letter to Frère Michel.[11]

Between both sources, we learn that Schweigl was sent to Coimbra with Pius XII's permission to ask 31 questions regarding the consecration of Russia. It appears that while he was there, he had opportunity to speak with Sr. Lúcia about the third part of the secret. Upon his return to the Russicum, Schweigl (according to his confrere, Fr. Cyrille Karel Kozina) made the following statement:

---

9   *The Whole Truth About Fatima, Volume III*, 337-341; 710.

10   Frère Michel (*The Whole Truth About Fatima, Volume III*, 352, endnote 41) cites the document as *Immaculatum Cor Mariae et Russia*, Romae 1963, Pro Patribus Concilii tantum (a four-page typed text). Unfortunately, after some modest research, a copy of this text appears to be very difficult to locate.

11   *The Whole Truth About Fatima, Volume III*, 710.

I cannot reveal anything of what I learned at Fatima concerning the third Secret, but I can say that it has two parts: *one concerns the Pope*. The other, logically – although I must say nothing – would have to be the continuation of the words: *In Portugal, the dogma of the Faith will always be preserved.*" Regarding the part that concerns the Pope, I had asked (our witness [Kozina] continues): "The present Pope or the next one?" To this question Father Schweigl made no reply.[12]

While the above quote has much significance in other contexts, for the purposes of this chapter, the quote provides evidence that Schweigl learned something about the third part of the secret. It is reasonable to state that this knowledge could have gone into his report to the Vatican, which, in turn, means that the Vatican would be privy to knowledge about the third part that might have been hitherto unknown.

To conclude, the above discussion ought to make one ponder how much stock to put in the news article. It presents enough ambiguity that makes it most unwise to turn the article into an argument for the existence of a second text of the third part of the secret of Fátima. Some weight has been given to the terms "letter" and "words" but it is unclear *who* used these terms and, in one case, a question over an antecedent. If a connection could be established between the speaker and the terms, one might be able to make an intelligible argument either way but such is nearly impossible.[13]

---

12   Ibid. The name of Fr. Kozina is given by Frère François de Marie des Anges in his book *Fatima: Tragedy and Triumph.* (Immaculate Heart Publications, 1994), 252.

13   It is "nearly impossible" because as of the time of this book's composition, it is possible that the author of the article is yet living. If this fact is the case and this person was discovered, he or she could answer many questions.

—8—
THE "SILENCING"
OF SISTER LÚCIA

"I thank God for the shelter where they welcomed me, removing me from so many curious views of the poor world. I pity the souls that are there struggling with many difficulties…. Their confidences are so sad, which hinder the good that God could do with them, taking time from me and filling my mind of things that I should disregard."

—Sr. Lúcia, March 26, 1948

One of the most influential claims in the matter of the third part of the secret of Fátima is that Sr. Lúcia was (allegedly) "silenced" by the Vatican.[1] This claim is used with fierce polemics in order to underscore a belief

---

1   For a summary of the matter, see the article entitled *Chronology of Four Cover-up Campaigns* published by Fr. Nicholas Gruner's organization *The Fátima Network*. <http://www.Fátima.org/essentials/opposed/cvrup4.asp> (Accessed 20 December, 2015). See also the article entitled *Reflections on the Silencing of Sister Lucia* in *The Fátima Crusader*, Vol. 89 (Summer 2008). This article is available on the Internet:
<http://www.Fátimacrusader.com/cr89/cr89Pg36.pdf > (Accessed 20 December, 2015). The article is attributed to being from the introduction to the book *Sister Lucia: Apostle of Mary's Immaculate Heart* by Mark Fellows. See also Fr. Nicholas Gruner (et al.), *World Enslavement or Peace...It's Up to the Pope*. (Ontario,

that the Vatican has attempted to de-emphasize the call of Fátima since around the pontificate of Pope John XXIII.[2] Was Sr. Lúcia "silenced" by the Vatican? Recent developments have shed some light on this question.

To begin, it is the opinion of this author that it is not necessary to provide various quotations to establish the claim of the alleged silencing of Sr. Lúcia. The literature on this claim is abundant. Instead, citations to the relevant sources have been provided and left to the reader to research at his or her leisure. It is, however, necessary to say a word about the origin of the alleged silencing. It is not known exactly how the claim originated. What can be stated is that there was one person who, at the very least, promulgated the claim far and wide. That person is Frère Michel who indicates it in the third volume of his *The Whole Truth About Fátima*.[3]

In his rendition of the history of the third part of the secret, Frère Michel discusses the aftermath of the meeting of Sr. Lúcia with Fr. Agustín Fuentes in 1957. He frames the aftermath, as it pertains to the person of

---

Canada: The Fátima Crusader, 1988), 362-367; Fr. Paul Kramer, *The Devil's Final Battle*. (Terryville, Connecticut: The Missionary Association, 2002), 50, 185-205, 249-250, 265; Christopher A. Ferrara, *The Secret Still Hidden*. (Pound Ridge, New York: Good Counsel Publications, 2008), 34-35, 78; Antonio Socci, *The Fourth Secret of Fátima*. (Fitzwilliams, New Hampshire: Loreto Publications, 2009), 103-104; Frère François de Marie des Anges, *Fátima: Tragedy and Triumph*. (Buffalo, New York: Immaculate Heart Publications, 1994), 33-34, 199-200. Frère Michel de la Sainte Trinité, *The Whole Truth About Fátima. Volume III: The Third Secret*. (Buffalo, New York: Immaculate Heart Publications, 1990), 638. Hereafter *The Whole Truth About Fátima, Volume III* followed by page number.

2   *The Whole Truth About Fátima. Volume III*, 555-620. See also Frère François de Marie des Anges, *Fátima: Tragedy and Triumph*. (Buffalo, New York: Immaculate Heart Publications, 1994), 21-34. Hereafter *Fátima: Tragedy and Triumph* followed by page number. Often connected to this claim is an undertone of a dire fear on the part of the Vatican that if Sister were only allowed to speak freely, she would expose the entire Vatican "apparatus." Seen in this light, Sr. Lúcia becomes a heroine coming with the authority of heaven behind her.

3   *The Whole Truth About Fátima, Volume III*, 748-749.

Sister, as her becoming "invisible" (*l'invisible*), and that she "found her-self obliged to a much more rigorous silence..." (*elle se trouva astreinte à un silence beaucoup plus rigoureux*).[4] From then onwards, the impression is given that ecclesiastical authorities essentially deemed Sr. Lúcia as a "wild card" and silenced her.

This silence was especially noteworthy because 1960 and the opening of the third part of the secret was fast approaching. Thus, the notion was that Church authorities wanted Sr. Lúcia silent in an effort to control her and the call of Our Lady because this call conflicted with the *aggiorna-mento* of Pope John XXIII.[5] Frère Michel and those who followed his lead either missed or simply did not give much credence to an important reference in the famous 1967 Allocution of Cardinal Ottaviani. This is most curious, and revealing, as Frère Michel devoted an entire section of his third volume to the Allocution.[6] On page 727 of this volume, Ottaviani is

---

4   *The Whole Truth About Fátima*, 748. The French text is taken from Frère Michel de la Sainte Trinité, *Toute la Vérité sur Fátima*. (Saint Parres les Vaudes, France: La Contre-Réforme Catholique, 1985), 505. The English pre-sented above is this author's own translation from the French.

5   *The Whole Truth About Fátima, Volume III*, 683-720. See also *Fátima: Tragedy and Triumph*, x. Frère François makes a grandiose and extravagant statement that the third part of the secret is of itself "capable of erasing the apostasy in the Church of the last twenty years...." One must wonder whether or not such a characterization made the third part bigger than what it was intended to be. As such hyper-prognostications grew and fed upon themselves, people became victims of their own making. Thus, when the text was released in June, 2000 and it did not meet these expectations, there was going to be much disap-pointment and frustration.

6   *The Whole Truth About Fátima, Volume III*, 721-732. The reader is reminded that Frère Michel makes some good observations such as noting in-consistencies and inexactitudes by Ottaviani. This author himself noted discrep-ancies while translating the Allocution in April/May of 2015. Frère Michel also offers his own interpretations and presumptions. For example, see pages 721 and 635 wherein Frère Michel interprets Ottaviani's address as being the moment when Paul VI chose to make known his mind on the secret. Frère Michel cites no authority that such was Ottaviani's mission. Frère Michel comes across here

quoted on what took place when Sister Lúcia went from being a Dorothean Sister to a Carmelite. In his *prepared* remarks, Ottaviani had written:

> We had to defend the visionary, who became a religious, to escape from the curiosity of the world in a Carmelite monastery in Coimbra where, more than from devotion, the curiosity of many people has sought to draw from [Lúcia] a few words. Despite Lúcia's reserve, these curious ones, eager for mysterious things, have thought to make deductions and have published apocryphal texts of the secret of Fátima, making it into legend. The Congregation for the Doctrine of the Faith had to forbid access to the Coimbra convent where Lúcia prays, remembers, meditates, but does not speak....[7]

In the above quote, Ottaviani makes it *very* clear that Rome forbade access to Sister Lúcia. He does not deny the fact, but the question is *for what reason*? It was, according to Ottaviani, to protect Sister from curiosity seekers. She was, after all, a religious, bound to observe the religious life with all its incumbent rigors and duties, and also to see to her interior

---

in a very acrimonious manner.

7   The above translation is this author's from *La Documentation Catholique* (1967). It is the third footnote, which cites the written text of Ottaviani. Frère Michel had access to the text through the French translation. The Italian text appears to have been published in *La Madre di Dio*, Anno XXXIV, No.3 (March, 1967), 16-18. The text in question reads as follows:

> Si è poi dovuto difendere la Veggente, fattasi suora e sottrattasi alla curiosità del mondo nella raccolta preghiera di un monastero di Carmelitane di Coimbra, dove più che la devozione, la curiosità di molti profani, ha cercato di carpire qualche sua parola. Purtroppo dal riserbo di Lucia gli investigatori, i curiosi delle cose misteriose, hanno creduto fare delle deduzioni, e qua e là, si sono pubblicati testi apocrifi dell'ormai divenuto leggendario segreto di Fátima. E la congregazione posta a difesa della Dottrina della Fede ha dovuto interdire, ai profani ed agli investigatori, l'accesso al Convento di Coimbra, dove Lucia prega, ricorda, medita, ma non parla....

life. Curiosity seeking would only serve to interrupt that observance.[8]

Protecting Sr. Lúcia was confirmed at least *twice* by the Carmelites of Coimbra. In 1991, the Prioress, Mother Maria do Carmo, gave an interview that was published in *O Jornal*.[9] In response to a question about Sr. Lúcia being able to receive visitors, Mother do Carmo responded:

> Cardinals may visit her without authorization of the Holy Father. But even the Bishops may not visit her here, as you know, without special permission from the Holy See. But permit me to tell you something: there are people who believe that Sister Lucy is in a state of seclusion here, and that she does not have the right to speak or to show herself. That is not true; it is she who wishes it thus. First as a Carmelite, then in order to preserve herself from the very great curiosity which is due to the fact that she is the seer of Fátima.[10]

The reader should note that the source of this quotation is Frère François and his book *Fátima: Tragedy and Triumph*.

The second time that the Carmelites made a public statement on this matter was in 2013. In their biography of Lúcia, *Um Caminho sob o Olhar de Maria*, the Carmelite Sisters provide previously lacking details on this part of Sr. Lúcia's life.[11] Chapter Sixteen (*Religiosa Carmelita*/Carmelite Religious) of this biography, delves into Sr. Lúcia's entrance into and life

---

8   Frère Michel says *nothing* in response to this part of Ottaviani's Allocution. Either Frère Michel closely adhered to his own interpretation or he attributed little importance to it given the gaffes the Cardinal made within the Allocution.

9   Cf. *Fátima: Tragedy and Triumph*, 197-200.

10   Ibid., 199. Frère François seems to realize the impact of this statement. He offers his take on it in an attempt to "refute" the Prioress' characterization of the matter (page 199ff). It appears as though he missed her point.

11   Carmelo de Santa Teresa—Coimbra, *Um Caminho Sob o Olhar de Maria*. (Sersilito—Maia, Portugal: Edições Carmelo, 2013), 320-384. Hereafter *Um Caminho Sob o Olhar de Maria* followed by page number.

as a Carmelite.[12] The chapter is broken down into twelve sections, the tenth of which is entitled, *Uma como todas e sempre singular* (One like all and always singular). This section discusses what it was like for Sr. Lúcia to have two roles with their concurrent duties, namely to be both a Carmelite and the seer of Fátima.

As a Carmelite, it was Sister's duty not to attract attention to herself. As the seer of Fátima, she was in constant demand by people from all over the world. How were her two roles to be reconciled? The Carmelites wrote:

> In Carmel she was protected by the strict confinement, and it was not long after she arrived that she savored the absence of such visits. Like any Carmelite she could receive visitors—family members and intimate friends—during normal times, except Lent and Advent.
>
> She wanted to be a religious like everyone else, but as the shepherdess she was unique. As a religious she was equal, and as a Carmelite she had a distinct lifestyle exemplified by love that she strove to live faithfully. At the same time she was the Seer of Fátima, increasingly requested by people from all corners of the earth, which caused her no small amount of suffering.
>
> Those who sought her knocked on the doors of the monastery, and being unsuccessful, they would appeal to Archbishop Ernesto Sene de Oliveira to arrange the favor they wanted.
>
> It was necessary for her to give in sacrificially, and also to the Prioress, who sometimes found it very difficult to protect her. The Archbishop, in spite of himself, had to sign one more permission slip and present the visitor. Each visitor thought an exception should be made especially for him and that it would not affect the life of Sister Lucia or the Community life. They did not consider what it meant for her to receive so many exceptions.

---

12   Ibid., 341-384.

She asked Archbishop Ernesto for help in a letter, confessing how difficult it was to receive so many visits. At the same time she offered this sacrifice, not wanting to lose anything that could be of benefit to the people:

These visits form a small portion of my cross, but they are also a part of the Mission which God has entrusted to me. Not even in Heaven will they leave me alone, but there I will meet them with great pleasure, because there will be no danger of disturbing the union of my soul with God.

Seeing he could not avoid so many requests and to prevent multiple visits, the Archbishop, during a trip to Rome, asked for an authorized standard under the Constitution prescribing that all visitors who were not of her family or more intimate friendships could only be received with permission from the Holy See. With this protection the visits became very rare, since it was more difficult to reach Rome.[13]

Once again, it is very clear that the reason for the "silence" was to protect the interior life and religious observance of Sr. Lúcia. In 1967, Cardinal Ottaviani had indicated what happened in his *ex tempore* remarks while his written remark was more explicit. The Carmelites fill in the details. First of those details is that it was Sr. Lúcia herself who requested the restricted access. Secondly, after a period of time, these requests appear to have become burdensome (both to the Archbishop and to Sister) which resulted in Archbishop Ernesto requesting Rome's intervention on the matter.

---

13   English translation courtesy of Carmel of Coimbra and James A. Colson (trans.), *A Pathway Under the Gaze of Mary*. (Washington, New Jersey: World Apostolate of Fátima, 2015), 342-343. The letter from Sr. Lúcia to the Archbishop, according to a footnote, is dated August 30, 1949. See also the September 29, 1949 letter of Bishop da Silva to Fr. Aparicio wherein he describes what he saw in Sr. Lúcia after he visited her in the Carmel convent (cf. *Fátima: Tragedy and Triumph*, 20).

To conclude this chapter, the restricted access to Sr. Lúcia has been misconstrued. It is undeniable that from the 1950s/early 1960s until her death in 2005 Sr. Lúcia was not much in the public eye. How are we to think of this fact? An objective examination into the matter reveals an alternative story than the interpretation championed by Frère Michel and others. It is more likely that Sr. Lúcia was not "silenced" but rather enjoyed "restricted access" for the sake of her religious observance and spiritual life.

—9—

PORTUGAL AND THE DOGMA OF THE FAITH

"In Portugal the dogma of the Faith shall always be preserved etc."
—Our Lady of Fátima, July 13, 1917

In her fourth *Memoir*, Sr. Lúcia provided a fuller account of the apparition of Our Lady on July 13, 1917. It is from this account that one of the most heavily debated phrases in the history of Fátima has its origin, namely the words of Our Lady "In Portugal, the dogma of the Faith shall always be preserved etc."[1] These words are debated for a number of reasons. The present chapter shall examine one aspect of this debate, namely its placement (and subsequent meaning) within the overall secret of Fátima.

I. Theories on the Phrase

To begin our discussion, it is necessary to remember some background. A general history of the first four *Memoirs* of Sr. Lúcia was provided in chapter one. We will thus pick up the discussion from the question

---

1   Dr. Antonio Maria Martins, S.J., *Memórias e Cartas de Irmã Lúcia*. (Porto, Portugal: Simão Guimarães, Filhos, LDA, 1973), 341. Hereafter *Memórias e Cartas de Irmã Lúcia* followed by page number.

of what happened after Sr. Lúcia wrote the fourth *Memoir* and people had opportunity to read and comment upon the phrase. First, let us remind ourselves of what Our Lady said in July, 1917 as recorded by Sister in the fourth *Memoir*:

> To prevent this, I will come to ask the consecration of Russia to my Immaculate Heart, and the Communion of reparation on the first Saturdays. If they listen to my requests, Russia will be converted and there will be peace. If not, she will scatter her errors throughout the world, provoking wars and persecutions of the Church. The good will be martyrized, the Holy Father will have much to suffer, and various nations will be annihilated. In the end my Immaculate Heart will triumph. The Holy Father will consecrate Russia to me and it will be converted and a certain period of peace will be granted to the world. In Portugal the dogma of the Faith will always be kept, etc. Tell this to no one. Francisco, yes, you may tell him....[2]

Taking a look at the phrase in question and its placement there are a few questions that arise. They are:

1. Were there more words of Our Lady after the "etc.?"
2. Is the phrase in question part of the second half of the secret or the beginning (*incipit*) of the third?
3. If Portugal will preserve the dogma of the Faith, is it implied that said dogma will not be preserved in other countries?
4. How long will Portugal preserve the dogma of the Faith? During what time-frame shall this preservation be done?

Since 1941, scholars have attempted to address these and other questions. As

---

2   Ibid.

to the first question, this is not known with any amount of certitude. It remains an open question and we shall briefly discuss it later in this chapter.

Concerning the second question, this one in particular remains a very vexing question. Over time, two different interpretations have arisen on the placement of the phrase in the overall secret of Fátima. For our purposes, we shall call them the "accepted" and the "debated" interpretations. The "accepted" interpretation is that the phrase in question is the *incipit* (beginning) of the third part. This interpretation is *generally* held by most scholars on Fátima. The "debated" interpretation suggests that the phrase is the end of the second part of the secret. This interpretation has seen some discussion, though it has not gained much traction in the scholarly world. Let us briefly provide a general historical sketch of these interpretations.

A. The "Accepted" Interpretation

From whence does the idea arise that the phrase about Portugal and the dogma of the Faith is the beginning of the third part of the secret? Let us turn to Fr. Joaquín María Alonso. In 1967, Fr. Alonso began a series of articles on the secret of Fátima for the publication entitled *Fatima 50*. This publication began on the 50th anniversary of the apparitions of Our Lady in Fátima. The articles are as follows:

1. *O Segredo de Fátima: Conjuro de Uma Palavra*[3]
2. *O Segredo de Fátima: A Economia da Sua Progressiva Manifestação*[4]
3. *O Segredo de Fátima: A Terceira "Coisa" do Segredo*[5]
4. *O Segredo de Fátima: O Conteúdo*[6]

---

3   *Fatima 50*, number 1, May 1967, pages 30-31, 38-39.

4   *Fatima 50*, number 5, September 1967, pages 23, 28.

5   *Fatima 50*, number 6, October 1967, page 11.

6   *Fatima 50*, number 7, November 1967, pages 14-16.

5. *O Segredo de Fátima: Gravidade e Seriedade*[7]

Later on, in 1976, Fr. Alonso collated much information into his book entitled *La Verdad Sobre el Secreto de Fatima: Fátima sin mitos*.[8] This book was translated into both the French and English languages in 1979, the English translation being done by the Dominican Nuns of the Perpetual Rosary and entitled *The Secret of Fatima: Fact and Legend*.[9] As it was a singular volume on the topic of the secret, and one of the first on this matter from an authoritative source, the contribution of this book was fundamental.

The stated purpose of the book was to provide a "serious study" that is "meant for the average reader."[10] Fr. Alonso did not provide footnotes in the book and he stated two reasons for this decision. First, he did not want to dissuade the "average reader" from the presentation and message of the book. Secondly, there was an anticipated critical edition in Portuguese of various texts and questions on Fátima.[11] It seems as though Fr. Alonso did not want to reinvent the proverbial wheel and simply left the bulk of such important references to the anticipated critical edition of these texts. What Alonso intended for the book overall was:

> I want first to do away once and for all with the mystifications, the caricatures, the hair-raising exaggerations, the cheap and sensa-

---

7   *Fatima 50*, number 8, December 1967, pages 4-5.

8   Joaquín María Alonso, *La Verdad Sobre el Secreto de Fatima: Fátima sin mitos*. (Madrid: Centro Mariano, 1976). Hereafter *La Verdad Sobre el Secreto de Fatima* followed by page number.

9   French: R.P. Joaquim Maria Alonso, *La Verite sur le Secret de Fatima* (Paris: Tequi, 1979). English: Fr. Joaquin Maria Alonso, *The Secret of Fatima, Fact and Legend* (Cambridge: The Ravengate Press, 1979). Hereafter *The Secret of Fatima: Fact and Legend* followed by page number.

10   *The Secret of Fatima: Fact and Legend*, 11.

11   Ibid. While he does not specify *which* critical edition, it is more than likely that Alonso was talking about the several volume series that he himself was working on and which were never published in their entirety.

tional apocalyptic writings which have been produced on the subject of Fatima and its Secret. To achieve this first end, there was only one way to proceed: to tell the truth and nothing but the truth.

But the "truth about the Secret of Fátima" has extremely positive aspects that we also want to highlight. Because Fátima and its secret, if it is not in some way "fearful," is rather absolutely serious when we are faced with the tremendous mysteries of the hereafter [*del más allá*]. And one can confuse the "fearful" with the seriousness of our Catholic faith. Neither ought one to place in ridicule the Acts and the Message of Fátima simply because they announce from a manner absolutely evangelical the more serious truths of our faith.[12]

From there, and speaking for the English translation, the book is divided into three parts, each with their own chapters. Concerning the matter of the placement of the text, Fr. Alonso sets the stage in Part I, chapter two (English edition) for a later discussion. He provides a lengthy quotation from Sr. Lúcia's *Memoirs* (the fourth in particular) on the secret, numbering it into eight paragraphs for easy referencing, and he will refer to these sections as "paragraphs."[13] The phrase that we are examining appears in paragraph seven of Alonso's accounting. It is preceded by the sixth paragraph which is about the triumph of the Immaculate Heart. Before he ends this chapter, he notes that the text was "presented by Lucia only in her fourth Memoir" and

---

12   *The Secret of Fatima: Fact and Legend*, 11-12; *La Verdad Sobre el Secreto de Fatima,* 5-6. See also our citation of this passage in chapter six.

13   *The Secret of Fatima: Fact and Legend*, 21-22; *La Verdad Sobre el Secreto de Fatima,* 14-15 (Spanish edition). Fr. Alonso must be correctly understood with respect to his choice of words. Otherwise, one will receive the wrong impression when later in the same book (79-80) he talks about Sr. Lúcia introducing a new paragraph (*párrafo*). Her original manuscript clearly does not demonstrate that she began a new paragraph. Alonso was speaking about his own division of the text, which, regretfully, easily lends itself to the bias of Sister beginning a "new thought."

that it "contains what most certainly is the third part of the Fatima Secret."[14] He ends Part I (chapter three) mentioning the dots Sr. Lúcia placed in the seventh paragraph.[15] Alonso was mistaken, as Sister did not here use dots.[16]

Part II of *The Secret of Fatima: Fact and Legend* recounts how the third part of the secret was written. As our purpose concerns the placement of the phrase about Portugal and the Faith, we shall restrict our discussion to what Alonso says on this matter. One must go to chapter five before finding such a statement. Alonso wrote:

> All authors have taken into consideration how Lucia, in the fourth Memoir, introduced the famous paragraph with the words: "In Portugal, the dogma of the Faith will always be preserved; etc...."[17] They have deduced as certain that the third "thing" began there. These words introduce the revelation of the third part of the Secret. The phrase most clearly implies a critical state of faith, which other nations will suffer, that is to say, a crisis of faith; whereas Portugal will preserve its faith. That is why Lucia, in the enormous difficulty she experienced in writing this remaining third part,

---

14   *The Secret of Fatima: Fact and Legend*, 25; *La Verdad Sobre el Secreto de Fatima,* 18-19 (Spanish edition). Alonso writes in the Spanish text: "El párrafo séptimo, introducido por Lucía solamente en su Cuarta Memoria, contiene lo que con toda seguridad es la TERCERA PARTE del secreto de Fátima...." It is noteworthy that he does not here say that these words *are the beginning* of the third part of the secret, only that the paragraph itself contains said part. Though it is clear that Alonso read the phrase in question as a new thought, otherwise he would have placed the words at the end of the sixth paragraph.

15   *The Secret of Fatima: Fact and Legend*, 32; *La Verdad Sobre el Secreto de Fatima,* 25 (Spanish edition).

16   Compare Alonso's statement with the handwritten manuscript as found in *Memórias e Cartas de Irmã Lúcia*, 340.

17   [Author note: Fr. Alonso *again* misrepresented the facts. Sr. Lúcia did not begin a new paragraph in her *Fourth Memoir* to introduce the phrase about Portugal and the dogma of the Faith (cf. *Memórias e Cartas de Irmã Lúcia*, 340).]

complained, saying that it was not necessary, for she had already said it so clearly [*porque ya lo había dicho con claridad ahí*].[18]

After the above comment, Alonso promptly ends discussion of the matter until Part II, chapter seven. In this chapter, he builds upon his earlier division of the secret of Fátima into eight paragraphs. He begins to speculate upon the placement of the sixth and seventh paragraphs. Alonso wrote:

Logically it would seem that the sixth section should have come after the seventh, for it speaks of a later "definitive" period, whereas the seventh deals with a preceding "intermediate" period. The reason for this apparent contradiction is simple. When Lucia wrote the first version of the text, the seventh section was not given at all; therefore any allusion to the intermediate period was overlooked. But when she wrote the final version (in December, 1941), and introduced this disquieting section, she departed from the earlier versions already written, and the seventh part has therefore been placed where it is. Both the literary structure of the text, however, and the interpretations that Lucia has given us concerning it make its meaning very clear.[19]

---

18   *The Secret of Fatima: Fact and Legend*, 69-70. The original Spanish text reads:

Todos los autores se han dado cuenta de que Lucía, en la Cuarta Memoria, ha introducido el célebre párrafo: «*En Portugal se conservarán siempre los dogmas de Fe, etc...*» Y han deducido con toda certeza que la tercera «cosa» comenzaba ahí: esas palabras inician ya la revelación de la tercera parte del secreto. Esa frase insinúa con toda claridad un estado crítico de la fe, en el que otras naciones sufrirán en ella, es decir, una crisis de fe; mientras que Portugal salvará su fe. Por eso Lucía, en sus enormes dificultades para escribir ese «resto», se quejaba diciendo que no era necesario, porque ya lo había dicho con claridad ahí (*La Verdad Sobre el Secreto de Fatima*, 64).

19   *The Secret of Fatima: Fact and Legend*, 79-80; *La Verdad Sobre el Secreto de Fatima*, 72 (Spanish edition). The original Spanish is:

In the above text Fr. Alonso attempts to explain a discrepancy within Sr. Lúcia's text concerning the placement of the phrase in question. He specifies a dual period of time, a "definitive" period that is represented in the sixth paragraph and an "intermediate" period indicated by the seventh. Alonso then characterizes the phrase of paragraph seven as "disquieting" (*párrafo inquietante*) apparently because he reads it as interrupting the flow of the dialogue of Our Lady between the two periods. He does not appear to entertain the idea that it may not be as disquieting as he thinks. Thus, in order to explain the alleged disquietude, Alonso focuses solely upon the fact that the phrase in question was added later.[20]

This interpretation forced Fr. Alonso to state that Sister "departed from the earlier versions" (*se ha dejado llevar de las redacciones anteriores*). Alonso here seems to imply that Sr. Lúcia essentially backed herself into a literary corner. Consider when he writes (in the Spanish), *y ha sido colocado «ilógicamente»*. The Dominican Sisters translated this text as

---

El párrafo sexto tendría que venir construido lógicamente detrás del séptimo, puesto que habla de un período «definitivo» posterior, mientras que el séptimo habla de un período «intermedio» anterior. La razón de esta construcción «ilógica» es sencilla: cuando Lucía escribe primero el texto, en otras redacciones anteriores, no figuraba para nada el párrafo séptimo. De ahí que se saltara, omitiéndolo enteramente, toda alusión al período «intermedio». Pero cuando hace la redacción última (diciembre 1941) e introduce ese párrafo inquietante se ha dejado llevar de las redacciones anteriores, ya hechas, y ha sido colocado «ilógicamente». Pero tanto la estructura literaria, tal como está, cuanto las interpretaciones que ha dado Lucía sobre este texto nos dicen claramente su significación.

20   Alonso's questioning will influence Frère Michel's discussion on the same topic (cf. *The Whole Truth About Fatima: Volume III*, 686 and 693 [note 6]). Frère Michel will argue that Sr. Lúcia simply followed her previous writings, and, finding nowhere else to put the phrase, just put it at the end of the text. This interpretation essentially argues that Sister either did not remember the point in Our Lady's discourse wherein the phrase was said or that Sister simply placed the phrase at the end because she did not know what else to do with it. Neither possibility is very appealing.

"...and the seventh part has therefore been placed where it is" though a more literal translation would be, "...and has been placed 'illogically.'"[21] If the phrase has been placed "illogically" by Sr. Lúcia, then one must conclude that Alonso would not believe Our Lady said these words at this point of her discourse.

Following this logic to its natural conclusion, Fr. Alonso must explain the difficulty presented by his interpretation. His explanation, however, cast a questionable aspersion on Sr. Lúcia. Doing so would seem to undermine his entire argument as her testimony is critical if we are to understand—and believe—the events of Fátima. Either Our Lady said the phrase in question at the point in the narration indicated by Sr. Lúcia or she did not.

After the above treatment, Fr. Alonso does not again mention the placement of the phrase in *The Secret of Fatima: Fact and Legend*. Until now, no one apparently questioned Fr. Alonso's interpretation. His work, in fact, heavily influenced Frère Michel, to whom we must now pay some attention for further developments.[22]

In Volume III of his book *The Whole Truth About Fatima*, Frère Michel discusses the phrase on Portugal and the dogma of the Faith.[23] He begins his discussion with a note on the *existence* of the phrase (not its *placement*), Frère Michel observes that the phrase itself, at least among French writers on Fátima, has been little noticed.[24] Second, he understands the phrase to be

---

21   It is also regrettable that Alonso mentions the "interpretations that Lúcia has given us" and yet does not specify what these interpretations, much less where, when how and to whom she communicated them. Alonso writes that she gave them to "us" but he is not clear as to whether he refers to himself or to the general public.

22   The English translation of his *The Whole Truth About Fatima* series has been, arguably, among the most influential texts—the present subject matter included.

23   *The Whole Truth About Fatima, Volume III*, 683ff.

24   Here, Frère Michel cites a number of French authorities but *only* from

the beginning of the third part of the secret.[25] He believes this, it appears, based upon the writings of scholars, especially those of Fr. Alonso.

Concerning the interpretation on the *placement* of the phrase, Frère Michel, makes what he calls "a decisive critical remark."[26] What is this remark? Frère Michel wrote:

> [I]n her third Memoir, written in July-August, 1941, Sister Lucy had been content to mention the existence of a third part of the Secret, but as yet she had said nothing about it. A few months later, in her fourth Memoir, written between October-December, 1941, she decided to say more. She recopied almost word for word the text of the third Memoir, but adding after the final words — «…and a certain period of peace will be granted to the world» — the new sentence: «*Em Portugal se conservara sempre o dogma da fé, etc.*» [In Portugal the dogma of the faith shall always be preserved etc.].[27]

---

this language group. He cites Canon Barthas, Cerbelaud-Salagnac, Rémy, Father Paul, Jean Madiran, Dom Jean-Nesry (*The Whole Truth About Fatima, Volume III*, 693, note 1).

25   Cf. *The Whole Truth About Fatima, Volume III*, 686.

26   Ibid., 684.

27   The original French text reads as follows:

Dans son troisième Mémoire, rédigé en juillet-août 1941, soeur Lucie s'était contentée de mentionner l'existence d'une troisième partie du Secret, mais elle n'en n'avait encore rien dit. Ce fut quelques mois plus tard, dans son quatrième Mémoire, écrit d'octobre à decembre 1941, qu'elle se décida à en dire davantage. Elle retranscrivit alors presque littéralement le texte du troisième Mémoire, mais en ajoutant à la suite des derniers mots — «…et sera donné au monde un temps de paix» — la nouvelle phrase: «*Em Portugal se conservará sempre o dogma da fé, etc.*» (Frère Michel de la Sainte Trinité, *Toute la Vérité sur Fatima: Le Troisième Secret*. 1e [Saint-Parres-Lès-Vaudes, France: La Contre Réforme Catholique, 1985], 458). Hereafter *Toute la Vérité sur Fatima: Le Troisième Secret* followed by page number.

Let us examine for a moment what has been said. Frère Michel begins by mentioning the fact that Sr. Lúcia wrote the third and fourth *Memoirs* by the end of 1941. He makes a distinction on the third part of the secret by saying that she *mentions* (*mentionner*) its existence, but says nothing *about* it (*encore rien dit*), i.e. by way of description. This observation appears accurate.

Despite the accuracy on the above point, there seems, however, to be a presumption on another point. When Frère Michel says "but as yet she had said nothing about it," one can interpret him as *implying* that Sr. Lúcia is going to say something about it. This interpretation is confirmed in the next sentence when Frère Michel writes that "she decided to say more" (*qu'elle se décida à en dire davantage*), the "more" (*davantage*) being a clear implication to referencing the third part of the secret.[28] His interpretation is a presumption and whether or not it is accurate shall be addressed further below.

Between Fr. Alonso and Frère Michel, the matter of the placement of the phrase on Portugal and the Faith largely fell in favor of the phrase being a new thought, and thus the beginning of the third part of the secret. This interpretation influenced later writers who clearly accepted it without much question based largely upon the authority of Fr. Alonso.

While perhaps overly simplified, the above is a rough historical sketch of the "accepted" interpretation of the phrase on Portugal and the Faith. Was this prevailing interpretation correct or was something overlooked? To help us answer this question, let us proceed to the "debated" interpretation.

B. The "Debated" Interpretation

While it is the most popular, the "accepted" interpretation is not beyond

---

28   It is here that we have to ask, is Frère Michel correctly interpreting Sr. Lúcia's text? Did she intend at this point of her writing to speak on the third part of the secret?

question. Not everyone subscribed to the "accepted" interpretation. There was an early scholar on Fátima who seems to have interpreted the phrase on Portugal and the Faith as belonging to the second part of the secret.

Just prior to Alonso's influential writings on the topic, Fr. Sebastião Martins dos Reis offered a minor discussion on the history of the phrase in his book *Síntese Crítica de Fátima: Incidências e Repercussões* (1967).[29] This discussion indicates that he did not understand said phrase to be the beginning of the third part of the secret. After reproducing Sr. Lúcia's text in the main body of the book, dos Reis added a footnote at the end after the "etc." He commented as follows, "Here is placed the third part of the Secret, yet to be revealed (and most likely will never be revealed), and whose first and second part we identify and clarify immediately before...."[30]

Dos Reis says little on the placement of the phrase on Portugal and the Faith in the above text, but he does make an important observation. He identifies the first and second parts of the secret as the text which precedes the "etc." If we take his words at face value, Dos Reis understands that the

---

29   Fr. Sebastião Martins dos Reis, *Síntese Crítica de Fátima: Incidências e Repercussões*. (Porto, Portugal: Edições Salesianas, 1967), 68-69. Hereafter *Síntese Crítica de Fátima* followed by page number. By noting Dos Reis as one early scholar who appeared not to hold to the "accepted" interpretation, it is not the intention of this author to claim that he is the founder of the "debated" interpretation. The idea being advanced is not every scholar or writer on Fátima subscribed to the "accepted" interpretation. At this time, it is not known if Dos Reis later subscribed to this interpretation.

30   The Portuguese text is as follows:

É aqui que se situa a terceira parte do Segredo, ainda por revelar, — e que muito provàvelmente nunca será revelada, — e cuja primeira e segunda parte se identificam e esclarecem imediatamente antes... (*Síntese Crítica de Fátima*, 68-69).

In the next two paragraphs, Dos Reis first refers his readers to his book *O Milagre do Sol e o Segredo de Fátima* for more information. He then gives a basic history of the writing down of the third part of the secret.

phrase about Portugal and the Faith is not the *incipit* of the third part.[31] His observation appears to have gone practically unnoticed.[32]

Thirty-three years later, the logical implication behind Dos Reis' observation (that the phrase must be considered as belonging to the preceding part of the secret) would arise once again. In the year 2000 during the June 26th press conference at the Vatican. Portuguese journalist Aura Miguel posed two questions to Archbishop Bertone on the meaning of this phrase. After posing her first question, she then asked a follow-up question:

> The other question concerns the phrase *"Portugal will always remain* [rimarrà] *the dogma of the faith,"* which until this moment we all interpreted as belonging to the third part of the secret. In fact it is never even been commented on regarding the first and the second [parts] because everyone thought it concerned the third; and it also aroused all these speculations on the end of the world, etc., but now we understand that it has nothing to do with the third part of the secret, I wanted to know, then, how we should think of it, thank you.[33]

---

31   Dos Reis also appears to think there is an implication that in other nations the dogma of the Faith shall not be preserved whereas Portugal shall.

32   Frère Michel quotes from a paragraph of this same section of Dos Reis' book and completely passes over the reference (*The Whole Truth About Fatima: Volume III,* 688)!

33   Aura Miguel's question in Italian was as follows (from the transcript in the appendices in this book):

> L'altra domanda riguarda la frase "*Il Portogallo rimarrà sempre il dogma della fede*" che fino a questo momento noi tutti interpretavano come appartenente alla terza parte del segreto, anzi non si è mai commentato riguardo anche la prima e la seconda perché tutti pensavano che riguardava la terza e ha suscitato anche, anche tutte queste speculazioni sul fin del mundo, eccetera, invece adesso capiamo che non c'entra nulla con la terza parte del segreto, volevo sapere allora come dobbiamo considerarla, grazie.

Bertone responded to both questions. His answer to the second one demonstrates that his opinion was that the phrase belongs to the *second* part of the secret and not the third. He stated:

And then with regard to that other problem, here it is a bit of a particular problem, that of, as she said…of Portugal, it is difficult to say if it relates to the second part, [or] to the third part (certainly it is an addition that Sister Lúcia made in that famous redaction, in a new redaction with the dots, etc.,[34] which would suggest who-knows-what) while on the other hand, when it starts with the precise text (as you have seen that it is a text detached from the first and second part) it begins to refer on the third part of the secret. There's not a stitch, it no longer makes any reference to that expression *"Portugal will preserve the faith,"* so it is hard to say if it belongs to the second or third part: it seems more that it belongs, may belong, to the second part.[35]

Bertone's opinion on the matter was, to say the least, very controver-

---

34   [Author's note: As we stated earlier, Sr. Lúcia did not place dots with the "etc." (cf. *Memórias e Cartas de Irmã Lúcia*, 340).]

35   The Italian read as follows (transcription from the appendices to this book):

E poi riguardo a quell'altro problema, ecco questo è un po' un problema particolare, questo della, come diceva [*incomprehensible*], del Portogallo, è difficile dire se si riferisce alla seconda parte, alla terza parte, certamente è una aggiunta che ha fatto Suor Lucía in quella famosa redazione, in una nuova redazione con i puntini, eccetera che lascerebbero supporre chissà che cosa mentre invece con quando inizia nel testo preciso, come avete visto, che è un testo staccato dalla prima e dalla seconda parte, inizia a riferire sulla terza parte del segreto, non fa più nessuna sutura, non mette più nessun riferimento a quella espressione *"Il Portogallo conserverà la fede"*, e quindi è difficile dire se appartiene alla seconda o alla terza parte, sembra di più che appartiene, appartenga alla seconda parte.

sial. It challenged the "accepted" interpretation of the phrase in question, and, as a Vatican authority, his opinion was noteworthy. The response to his opinion, simply and in large measure, was to reassert the belief that the phrase introduced a new thought. In the words of Fr. Paul Kramer, "... these ten words [...] introduce a new, and incomplete, thought into the Secret of Fatima. The phrase suggests, as every reputable Fatima scholar concludes, that there is more to follow and that the 'etc.' is but a placeholder for the third part of the Secret."[36]

For reasons that we have seen above, it appears better to say that *many* (perhaps even *most*) reputable scholars hold this opinion, not *every* scholar. An assertion, moreover, or even a reassertion that the phrase is a new and incomplete thought (even if accepted by many scholars) is not conclusive evidence of the fact. At best, their opinion must be considered with all respect and seriousness, but it cannot be taken as infallible proof. Moreover, let us ask a simple question, has anyone even tested the "accepted" interpretation? If it is untested, how does one know it is certain?

After Bertone's challenge to the "accepted" interpretation, little work appears to have been done in support of the "debated" interpretation. Taking both interpretations into account, what follows is a critique of the "accepted" interpretation based upon reconsideration of the evidence as well as taking a fresh look at more recent evidence.

---

36   Fr. Paul L. Kramer, *The Devil's Final Battle*. (Terryville, Connecticut: The Missionary Association, 2002), 145. For some evidence of this claim, see *The Secret of Fatima, Fact and Legend*, 69-70. Insofar as Kramer's statement is concerned, the "etc." *is* a placeholder for the third part of the secret. There is also more to follow, though "more" to Kramer appears to mean more *words* of Our Lady. He indicates this further down on page 145 when he wrote, "But the Vatican's June 2000 manuscript of the Third Secret...contains no words of Our Lady...."

II. Critiquing the "Accepted" Interpretation

We remarked in the previous section that an assertion or reassertion is not evidence of a fact. Let us ask a simple question: is there incontrovertible documentation from Sr. Lúcia *herself* for the "accepted" interpretation? Curiously, such documentation is missing and the interpretation in question appears to be the work of scholars. We must then ask whether Sister intended at this point of her writing to speak on the third part of the secret? Let us look at two texts in particular from Sr. Lúcia.

A. First Text—The Fourth Memoir

In chapter one of the present book, we noted that Lúcia was at first not ordered by her superior(s) to write down the third part.[37] A comment that she makes at the beginning of the fourth *Memoir* is particularly relevant to the present discussion. Sister wrote:

> I begin, then, my new task to fulfill your orders and the wishes of Rev. Galamba. Except [the part of the] secret that I must not reveal now, I will tell everything else. Consciously, I will omit nothing. I suppose that it is possible I may forget some little worthless details.[38]

In this text, Sr. Lúcia clearly states that she is *not* going to reveal the third

---

37 *Memórias e Cartas de Irmã Lúcia*, 317.

38 Ibid. The Portuguese text reads:

Começo, pois, a minha nova tarefa, e cumprirei as ordens de V. Ex.ª Rev.ma e os desejos do Senhor Dr. Galamba. Exceptuando parte do Segredo, que por agora não me é permitido reveler, direi *tudo*. Advertidamente não deixarei nada. Suponho que poderão esquecer-me apenas alguns pequenos detalhes de mínima importância.

part. Moreover, we know Sister struggled to write it down.[39]

If the above is true, then we must ask a serious question. If this sentence is the beginning of said part, why, at least in the available literature, is there no record of Sr. Lúcia struggling to write down the phrase? Is there anything—published or not—that even remotely suggests that Sr. Lúcia experienced at least *some* difficulty doing so? If the phrase pertained to the third part of the secret, is it perhaps possible that Sister received permission from heaven to write down this one phrase? To all of these questions, there appears to be no irrefutable evidence in the available literature.

Notice that the word "evidence" is modified by "irrefutable." This is because there is only one argument on this matter which has been seized upon in support of the position that the phrase is the beginning of the third part of the secret, namely that Sister did not write down the phrase in the third *Memoir*. An example of this argument is found in Frère Michel. He reads the fact of the phrase's inclusion in the fourth *Memoir* as *de facto* proof that it is the beginning of the third part of the secret. He wrote:

> Thus we now know the first sentence of the final Secret. This addition is definitely significant. For it is certain that Sister Lucy did not insert it here out of levity, but in the specific intention of showing us, in a veiled manner, the essential contents of the third Secret.[40]

---

39   *The Whole Truth About Fatima, Volume III*, 44-48; Carmelo de Santa Teresa – Coimbra, *Um Caminho sob o Olhar de Maria: Biografia da Irmã Lúcia de Jesus e do Coração Imaculado, O.C.D.* (Coimbra, Portugal: Edições Carmelo, 2013), 262-267. Hereafter *Um Caminho sob o Olhar de Maria* followed by page number.

40   *The Whole Truth About Fatima, Volume III*, 684 (see also 686). The French text reads:
> Ainsi connaissons-nous désormais la première phrase de l'ultime Secret. Cet ajout est à coup sûr significatif. Car il est certain que soeur Lucie ne l'a pas inséré là à la léègere, mais dans l'intention expresse de laisser transparaître, de manière voilée, le contenu essential du troisième Secret (*Toute la Vérité sur Fatima: Le Troisième Secret*, 458).

How does Frère Michel know the mind and intention of Sr. Lúcia? He offers no citation to anything concrete that she said on this matter.

In support, however, of his interpretation, what Frère Michel *does* offer is a remark from Fr. Alonso's book *The Secret of Fatima: Fact and Legend*. Frère Michel interprets this remark as supporting his interpretation. He wrote:

> Indeed in 1943, when Bishop da Silva had asked her to write down the text, and she was encountering insurmountable obstacles in obeying this order, she declared that it was not absolutely necessary to do so, «*since in a certain manner she had said it*». Undoubtedly she was alluding to the ten words discreetly added in December, 1941, to the text of the great Secret — but added so discreetly that almost nobody noticed them. However, they are very enlightening when we stop and think about them.[41]

The words in italics and in the European-style quotation marks are as Frère Michel worded it. There is some confusion with the quotation which needs to be highlighted and assessed. First, the authority cited for these words is page 64 of the Spanish text of Fr. Alonso's *The Secret of Fatima: Fact and Legend*.[42] When one reads what Fr. Alonso wrote, he was not providing a quote from Sr. Lúcia. We have seen this quote already, but here it is once again for the sake of convenience:

---

41   *The Whole Truth About Fatima, Volume III*, 684. The French text reads:

Si bien qu'en 1943, lorsque Mgr da Silva lui eut demandé d'en rédiger le texte et qu'elle rencontrait d'insurmontables difficultés pour obéir à cette ordre, elle déclara un jour que ce n'était pas absolument nécessaire de le faire «*puisque d'une certaine façon elle l'avait dit*». Sans doute faisait-elle allusion aux dix mots discrètement ajoutés en décembre 1941 au texte du grand Secret, mais si discrètement que presque personne n'y prendra garde. Ils sont pourtant très éclairants dès lors qu'on s'y arrête (*Toute la Vérité sur Fatima: Le Troisième Secret*, 458).

42   It is only in the English translation wherein this note appears.

All authors[43] have taken into consideration how Lucia, in the fourth Memoir, introduced the famous paragraph with the words: "In Portugal, the dogma of the Faith will always be preserved; etc...." They have deduced as certain that the third "thing" began there. These words introduce the revelation of the third part of the Secret. The phrase most clearly implies a critical state of faith, which other nations will suffer, that is to say, a crisis of faith; whereas Portugal will preserve its faith. That is why Lucia, in the enormous difficulty she experienced in writing this remaining third part, complained, saying that it was not necessary, for she had already said it so clearly [*porque ya lo había dicho con claridad ahí*].[44]

One will notice in the above quote that Fr. Alonso does not put quotation marks around the "complaint" that he ascribes to Sr. Lúcia. This fact indicates that he was *paraphrasing*. Unfortunately, Alonso does not tell us *where* Sister had expressed this complaint, thus limiting our examination.

Frère Michel wrote that Sr. Lúcia "declared" (*déclara*) these words in 1943, after receiving the order from Bishop da Silva to write down the third part of the secret.[45] While not conclusive, one is left with the *impression* that Frère Michel understood that she made such a declaration to Bishop da Silva. Fr. Alonso, however, points out that during this timeframe of late 1943 there were a number of communications passed between Sr. Lúcia and at least two or three officials (da Silva being one).[46] Alonso does

---

43   [Author's Note: Would that Fr. Alonso had provided citations to these authors!]

44   *The Secret of Fatima, Fact and Legend*, 69-70; *La Verdad Sobre el Secreto de Fatima*, 64.

45   Frère Michel seems to be faithful to Alonso's timeframe and so the general date of 1943 appears to be accurate. The question remains, however, upon what evidence is Fr. Alonso basing this "complaint" [*quejaba*]?

46   *The Secret of Fatima, Fact and Legend*, 37-42. These officials were:

not specify Bishop da Silva as being the recipient of this "declaration."[47]

While the above matter is noteworthy, it is not central to our examination. For our purposes, the *antecedent* of the complaint is what interests us. We shall presume, for the sake of argument, the authenticity of the complaint as stated by Alonso in order to make an observation.[48] Let us ask, to what was Sister referring when she made this complaint? It is clear from his discussion that Frère Michel understood the sentiment to refer to the phrase about Portugal and the dogma of the faith. His interpretation, however, is based upon—as we have seen—an unsourced statement which is not provided in context. Despite these facts, Frère Michel argues that Sister was referring to the phrase on Portugal and the dogma of the faith. For now, we shall defer the discussion on this point until a little further below.

After all that has been said above, we are still left with the question of why Sr. Lúcia left out the phrase in the third *Memoir*. The answer to this question is debatable, but one thing is for sure: it is either a very simple or a complicated answer. Let us propose a simple answer—human error. In other words, perhaps Sister merely forgot it in the third *Memoir*. This answer is not implausible as Sr. Lúcia herself admitted the possibility of a faulty memory. Moreover, we know that in her *Memoirs*, she did not recall everything that transpired during the apparitions.[49]

---

1) Bishop da Silva, 2) Don Antonio Garcia (Apostolic Administrator of Tuy, Spain), 3) Don Jesus Varela (Vicar General to Don Antonio).

47   Moreover, when Frère Michel provided this text, did he intend it to be a quotation from Sr. Lúcia or as a quotation from Fr. Alonso? There is some ambiguity.

48   It is herein accepted by this author on Fr. Alonso's authority that such a "complaint" was made by Sr. Lúcia to someone presumably in authority over her. Accepting this premise is based upon the fact that it is highly unlikely that Fr. Alonso would have made such a straightforward statement if he did not have some documentation attesting to it.

49   Cf. Costa Brochado, *Fátima in the Light of History*. (Milwaukee, Wisconsin: The Bruce Publishing Company, 1955), 130. See also *Documentação Crítica de Fátima: I – Interrogatórios aos Videntes – 1917*. 2ᵉ. (Fátima,

Let us also consider a fact described in chapter one: Sister was reluctant to discuss her experiences and usually did so under obedience. From this motive, we know that Sr. Lúcia would answer a question faithfully without having to give up specific information. Maybe she withheld, at first, this phrase out of a desire to keep one more treasure of her interior life. Consider also her own words from her *Sixth Memoir*:

> I wrote the Memoirs out of obedience to the Bishop of Leiria, D. José Alves Correia da Silva, who asked me, indeed, ordered me to do so. However, I wrote them in the midst of many difficulties, lack of the necessary time and opportunity in which to write something that would be approved of, and recognising at the same time that I did not have the necessary education, which made me think that the manuscript would be no use, and would not be used.
>
> This enabled me to write freely as the various events came back to my mind, without being concerned about order, times, places, and without the time or opportunity to read over and correct what I had written....[50]

B. Second Text—Sr. Lúcia's May, 1982 Letter

The second text which calls into question the "accepted" interpretation is Sister's May, 1982 letter to Pope John Paul II. The letter provides a

---

Portugal: Santuário de Fátima, 2013), 41. Brochado here writes about a little-appreciated event that is taken straight from an original interrogation in 1917 (ca. May 28). Lúcia presented an object to Our Lady who responded that it was "not fitting for heaven." Nowhere in the four *Memoirs* is this event recounted. This event may seem minor or secondary, but it demonstrates that Sr. Lúcia clearly either did not remember everything that transpired or, at least, did not write down some things for her own reasons.

50   Fr. Louis Kondor, SVD (edit.), *Fatima in Lucia's Own Words. Volume II.* (Fátima, Portugal: Secretariado dos Pastorinhos, 2004), 141. See also page 8.

critical hermeneutical key to understanding the vision. Sister clearly states that *the vision pertains to Our Lady's words* on the spread of Russia's errors, the persecution of the Church, martyrdoms, the suffering of the Holy Father and annihilation of various nations. She wrote:

> The third part of the secret refers to Our Lady's words: "If not [Russia] will spread her errors throughout the world, causing wars and persecutions of the Church. The good will be martyred; the Holy Father will have much to suffer; various nations will be annihilated" (13-VII-1917).
>
> The third part of the secret is a symbolic revelation, referring to this part of the Message, conditioned by whether we accept or not what the Message itself asks of us: "If my requests are heeded, Russia will be converted, and there will be peace; if not, she will spread her errors throughout the world, etc.".
>
> Since we did not heed this appeal of the Message, we see that it has been fulfilled, Russia has invaded the world with her errors. And if we have not yet seen the complete fulfilment of the final part of this prophecy, we are going towards it little by little with great strides. If we do not reject the path of sin, hatred, revenge, injustice, violations of the rights of the human person, immorality and violence, etc....[51]

---

51   Congregation for the Doctrine of the Faith, *The Message of Fatima*. (Vatican City: Libreria Editrice Vaticana, 2000), 8-9. Hereafter referred to as *The Message of Fatima* followed by page number. The original Portuguese (reproduced on page 9 of the aforementioned source) is as follows:

> A terceira parte do segredo:—Refere-se às palavras de Nossa Senhora: "Se não, espalhará os seus erros pelo mundo, promovendo guerras e perseguições à Igreja. Os bons serão martirizados, o Santo Padre terá muito que sofrer, vàrias nações serão aniquiladas." (13-VII-1917).
>
> A terceira parte do segredo, que tanto anciais por conhecer, é uma revelação simbólica, que se refere a este trecho do Mensagem, condicionado a se, sim os não, nos aceitarmos ou não o que a Mensa-

If, then, the third part of the secret pertains to these things, it is a self-evident fact that Sr. Lúcia had already written of them by the time she completed her fourth *Memoir*. Thus (and to return to our earlier discussion on this matter), if Sister complained, in 1943, that she had already said what the third part of the secret was, then the antecedent of her complaint could be referring not to the phrase about Portugal and the dogma of the Faith. She could have been referring to her writing about the spread of Russia's errors, persecution and suffering, etc.

Along the lines of the above observations, we must consider the recent revelation in the 2013 Carmelite biography of Sr. Lúcia that there was more information to the third part of the secret.[52] From this revelation aris-

---

gem nos pede: "Se atenderem a meus pedidos, a Russia converterá e terão paz; se não, espalhará seus erros pelo mundo," etc.

Porque não temos atendido a este apelo da Mensagem, virificamos que ela se tem cumprido, a Rússia foi invadindo o mundo com os seus erros. E se não vemos ainda, o facto consumado, o final desta profecio, vemos que para aí caminhamos a passos largos. Se não recuarmos no caminho do pecado, do ódio, da vingança, da injustiça atropelando os direitos da pessoa humana, da imoralidade e da violência, etc.

E não digamos que é Deus que assim nos castiga, mas sim, que são os homens que para si mesmos se preparam o castigo. Deus, apenas nos adverte e chama ao bom caminho, respeitando a liberdade que nos deu; por isso, os homens são responsaveis.

It should be noted that the above is a more literal transcription of the text than the one provided in *The Message of Fatima* which appears to be a polished version: (<http://www.vatican.va/roman_curia/congregations/cfaith/documents/rc_con_cfaith_doc_20000626_message-fatima_po.html> [Accessed 16 August, 2016]). The phrase "...*que tanto anciais* [ansiais] *por conhecer...*" was left out of the transcription. The reason for this omission does not appear to have been provided by the Vatican. The omission was discussed in conspiratorial overtures by Christopher Ferrara (*The Secret Still Hidden*, 59-60). In the light of the general polishing of the text, it is possible that this omission was part of that effort. Why would the redactors omit such a notable phrase? Perhaps they did not understand how Sr. Lúcia used the verb *conhecer* (to know).

52   Carmelo de Santa Teresa – Coimbra, *Um Caminho sob o Olhar de Ma-*

es a question that the "debated" interpretation must address. If there was more information that Sister withheld at the command of Our Lady, is it possible that there were, in fact, more words of Our Lady that followed the phrase about Portugal and the faith?[53] The "debated" interpretation cannot give a definitive answer because the available evidence is not conclusive.

If there were more words of Our Lady, one could conclude that these words continue the phrase on Portugal and the Faith and thus seemingly defeat the position taken by the "debated" interpretation. Such would be, however, a hasty conclusion. If, as the "debated" interpretation holds, the phrase in question belongs to the second part of the secret, *whatever words that may follow afterwards might introduce a new thought.* The simple fact of the matter is that the present discussion is highly speculative and theoretical. Nothing is known with certainty and the possibility herein provided is as plausible as the consideration being examined.

In fact, let us reflect for a moment upon the opening words of Sr. Lúcia's text of the third part of the secret. She wrote, "After the two parts which I have already explained…."[54] How much clearer can Sister be? She clearly states that what she wrote in her *Memoirs* pertains to the first and

---

ria: Biografia da Irmã Lúcia de Jesus e do Coração Imaculado, O.C.D. (Coimbra, Portugal: Edições Carmelo, 2013), 266. Hereafter *Um Caminho sob o Olhar de Maria* followed by page number.

53 As we have written, this revelation was seized upon in defense of the idea that there were two texts written by Sr. Lúcia. This interpretation was unwarranted by virtue of the fact that Our Lady *expressly* told Sister *not* to write down "what is given to you to understand of its meaning." We saw that unless one can prove that Sr. Lúcia was later given permission to write down this information, there can be no possible way that she would have gone against the express will of heaven. As has been well-noted throughout this chapter, Sister agonized about the one piece of information that she did write down. Why would it have been any less with further information that she was expressly told not to reveal?

54 *The Message of Fatima*, 21. The Portuguese text reads, "Depois das duas partes que já expus…" (ibid., 17).

second parts of the secret—*not the third*. This includes the phrase on Portugal and the Faith. Thus, if there were more words of Our Lady that provided an explanation of the vision that is the third part of the secret, these could very well be a separate (albeit related) thought.[55] Seen in this light, the position taken up by the "debated" interpretation is, therefore, intact.

Let us also consider another point by asking a salient question. Our Lady indicated that there was some understanding of the vision that "is given" to Sr. Lúcia. Does the understanding of a prophetic vision come only to the mind of a prophet (or visionary) through intelligible words? St. Thomas Aquinas would answer in the negative to this question. He wrote in his *Summa Theologiae*, "Hence it is evident that prophetic revelation is conveyed sometimes by the mere infusion of light, sometimes by imprinting species anew, or by a new coordination of species."[56]

If a prophetic revelation can be imparted to a soul by the above means, it is not necessary that understanding be presented to the mind of the prophet *only* by intelligible words. The understanding can be supernaturally imparted to the mind of the prophet. In the absence of evidence, how do we know with certainty the manner in which this knowledge was communicated to Sr. Lúcia? Unless she communicated it, this piece of information does not appear to be known at this time. It is thus an open-ended issue, one that may remain as such for an indeterminate amount of time.[57]

---

55   They would be related as the secret is an organic whole.

56   John Mortensen and Enrique Alarcón, (edits.), *Summa Theologiae: Secunda Secundae, 92-189*. (Lander, Wyoming: The Aquinas Institute for the Study of Sacred Doctrine, 2012), 639. The Latin text (taken from the same source) is: *Sic igitur patet quod prophetica revelation quandoque quidem fit per solam luminis influentiam, quandoque autem per species de novo impressas, vela liter ordinatas.*

57   On this point, there is one final consideration. In *Um Caminho sob o Olhar de Maria* (267), there follows immediately after Sr. Lúcia's description of what Our Lady told her in January, 1944, the description of another vision. This vision portrays much destruction. Considering that it followed immediately after Our Lady's instructions to Sr. Lúcia, is it possible that this vision and its meaning

What has been examined above is the argument that the phrase on Portugal and the Faith is to be considered as belonging to the second part of the secret. If this argument is accurate to the mind and writings of Sr. Lúcia, it remains to examine the meaning of the phrase in question in connection to the second part of the secret. After all, even Fr. Alonso thought of it as a "disquieting" text, one that necessitated criticism along literary lines. How, then, is this phrase connected *organically* with the second part (and thus, by extension, the first part)? We shall endeavor to discuss this matter presently.

III. Portugal and the Dogma of the Faith

In his Allocution of February 11, 1967, Cardinal Ottaviani stated that he spoke with Sr. Lúcia in 1955.[58] He specifically revealed that he inquired of her the reason for the date of 1960 that appeared outside of the envelope containing the text of the third part of the secret. Ottaviani relays that Sr. Lúcia told him that the text would be "more clear" (*mais claro*).

Her remark appears to be critical and revelatory. First, let us note that Sister said *mais claro* — which is rendered into English as "more clear" or "clearer."[59] It is deduced from this statement that events up to 1960 would render clearer the text.[60] Events subsequent to that year may shed *further*

---

is what is meant by Our Lady's words "...that which is given to you to understand of its meaning?" It is a question for thought, not one that is expected to be answered at this time.

58   *Acta Pontificiae Academiae Marianae Internationalis vel ad Academiam quoquo modo pertinentia. Volume 4.* (Romae: Pontificia Academia Mariana Internationalis, 1967), 45.

59   Ottaviani does *not* state that she said it would be *completely* clear. The comparative indicates that the text would simply be better understood, not necessarily completely.

60   Frère Michel intimates that it would be clearer *after* 1960 (*The Whole Truth About Fatima, Volume III*, 690). Certainly, there is a post-1960 element

light, but it is clear that Sr. Lúcia believed that events up to that year would demonstrate the message contained within the text. We know from her May, 1982 letter that this message pertained to the spread of Russia's errors, persecution, etc.

To this point, it must be noted that Frère François writes (quoting the Abbé de Nantes) in his book *Fatima: Tragedy and Triumph* that Krushchev declared the year 1960 to be ground zero for the spread of Communism.[61] Sr. Lúcia herself wrote to Pope Pius XII in 1958 saying that Communism would reach its "high point" (*o ponto máximo*).[62] Pius died within six months of the date of this letter and the matter fell to his successor, Pope John XXIII. As we discussed in the first chapter of the present book, John XXIII—for good or for ill—took a more conciliatory approach towards Communism, reversing his predecessors' policy of non-collaboration.[63]

One of the clear messages of Our Lady in Fátima is the warning of future wars if mankind does not repent. She foretold the coming of World War II as "another and worse war" and that there would be an "annihilation" of various nations.[64] The horrors and atrocities of any war is well-

---

to the reasoning behind the date. Further events would only make the text more intelligible. Nevertheless, events *by* 1960 would have had to have transpired for it to have been "more clear" in that year. Christopher Ferrara also observed that the text of the third part of the secret has "absolutely nothing to do with 1960" (*False Friends of Fatima*. Pound Ridge, New York: Good Counsel Publications, 2012), 96. Hereafter *False Friends of Fatima* followed by page number. Ferrara does not appear here to ask whether or not the text may pertain to world events up to 1960.

61   Frère François de Marie des Anges, *Fatima: Tragedy and Triumph.* (Buffalo, New York: Immaculate Heart Publications, 1994), 48, 58.

62   *Um Caminho sob o Olhar de Maria*, 275.

63   It is not our intention to engage in a debate over the rightness or wrongness of John XXIII's revering his predecessors' policy.

64   Frère Michel seems to think that this prophecy was fulfilled in the subsuming of the various nations around Russia into the USSR (*The Whole Truth About Fatima, Volume III*, 64; 121ff.). This is in contradistinction to the view of

known, especially to those who have lived through one, and so it is unnecessary to delve into such descriptions here. What is, however, noteworthy is a little-appreciated fact of war, namely how it affects the *faith and good morals* of people.

Cardinal Ottaviani himself once discussed this very topic. Concerning war during the First Vatican Council (ca. 1870), Ottaviani wrote:

> Now the Fathers at the Vatican Council, being concerned about the spiritual well-being of the Christian people who were beset "rather by terrible destruction" than battles; and, likewise, especially anxious that because of the wars, so many souls were perishing because of the moral evils that both accompany and follow upon battles, did seek from the Supreme Pontiff Pius IX that he establish those things that were needed to persuade men to avoid wars and, at least, to wage them humanely....[65]

Fr. Gruner and at least one of his associates who apparently believe this prophecy has yet to be fulfilled (cf. Fr. Paul L. Kramer, *The Devil's Final Battle: Our Lady's Victory Edition*. [Good Counsel Publications, 2010], x; xiii; 151. Hereafter *The Devil's Final Battle (2010)* followed by page number; see also *False Friends of Fatima*, xi).

65   The Latin reads as follows:
Iam Patres Concilii Vaticani, de salute christianarum plebium anxii «potius horribilibus caedibus» quam proeliis iam tunc oppressarum, itemque maxime solliciti quod, causa bellorum, tot quoque animae essent pereuntes ob mala moralia quae proelia comitantur et subsequuntur, a Summo Pontifice Pio IX petierunt ut necessaria statuerentur quae ad bella vitanda et ad eadem saltem humaniter gerenda, homines inducerent. Ast, insuper... (Alaphridus Ottaviani, *Institutiones Iuris Publici Ecclesiastici. Vol. I. Ecclesiae Constitutio Socialis et Potestas [editio quarta]*. [Typis Polyglottis Vaticanis, 1958], 135). Translation by Dr. Daniel J. Nodes.

For an alternative English translation, see *Blackfriars*. Vol. XXX (September, 1949), number 354, page 418. This translation can be found online: <http://www.catholicapologetics.info/morality/warfare/justwar.htm>j (Accessed 27 October, 2014). See also my book *Pope Leo XIII and the Prayer to St. Michael*. (Boonville, New York: Preserving Christian Publications, 2015), 106ff. Hereaf-

Let us note a couple of key points in Ottaviani's text. First, he says that the Bishops at Vatican I were concerned about the well-being or salvation (*salute*) of Christians. He then draws a line that indicates their well-being can be jeopardized by a "terrible destruction" that besets people by war. What is this terrible destruction? Ottaviani states that war brought "moral evils" which not only "accompany" war, but also follow after. These things made a shipwreck of people's faith, thus jeopardizing their eternal salvation.

If we take Cardinal Ottaviani's observations at face value, it is apparent that war changes a people and/or society.[66] Norman Dodd, an American businessman and member of the Congressional Commission for the study of tax-exempt organizations in the 1950s, discussed this fact in *very* sharp terms in two interviews. The first interview was with Dr. Stan Monteith of *Radio Liberty* in 1980 and the other was in 1982 with G. Edward Griffin. Dodd was unequivocal in his statements that there was a concerted effort on the part of tax-exempt organizations to effect social change in the United States (though with a global agenda), one that was meant to align the country's education system (among other things) with the Soviet (Communist) system.[67] These efforts themselves are deeply rooted in the rise of the error of materialism and secularism that arose strongly in the nineteenth century (with even deeper roots) and continued through the twentieth.

The question becomes "in whose image" shall the society/peoples be formed? A perfunctory glance at contemporary western civilization demonstrates that the West has not advanced toward Christian ideals but rather moved away from them in favor of secularism and atheism (actual

---

ter *Pope Leo XIII and the Prayer to St. Michael* followed by page number.

66   Cf. *Pope Leo XIII and the Prayer to St. Michael*, 104ff.

67   The respective interviews with Norman Dodd are available on *YouTube*. For the 1980 interviews: <https://www.youtube.com/watch?v=EK-4fVyUtHSQ> (Accessed 14 August, 2016); The 1982 interview can be viewed here: <https://www.youtube.com/watch?v=YUYCBfmIcHM> (Accessed 14 August, 2016).

or practical). While these errors existed prior to World War I, they did take on a concrete form in the Russian Revolution of 1917. Russia would then become the champion for atheistic humanism and develop to an even greater degree the errors of the preceding centuries into the twentieth century. Russia was the face of these errors even if they originated elsewhere. She made them her own, enhanced them, and then inflicted them upon the rest of the world, thus they could properly be called "the errors of Russia." Consider some words of Archbishop Fulton J. Sheen from his television program *Life is Worth Living*:

> There is not a single philosophical idea in Communism that did not come from the West. Its philosophy came from Germany, its sociology from France, its economics from England, and what Russia gave it was an Asiatic soul and power and force.[68]

In this broadcast, Archbishop Sheen continued his point with some salient observations about *faith and good morals* in the Western world. He said:

> Communism, then, is coming back upon the Western world because something died in the Western world, namely the strong faith of men in the God that made them. And before Russia's won back again to the Faith, therefore, regard Communism as a kind of a manure, a fertilizer! It is a death that is spread upon the civilizations of the world until the springtime of a newer and better world begins to come into being [to be?]. This is the role of Communism from a divine point of view, before conversion, and then afterward what will it be? When Russia receives the gift of faith, Russia will have a new road and its role then

---

68   To view this program, see the episode available on *YouTube*: <https://www.youtube.com/watch?v=TZAc1A3bYiY> (Accessed 16 August, 2016). See also Christopher Dawson, *The Movement of World Revolution*. (New York: Sheed and Ward, 1959), 17ff; 62ff.

will be to be an apostle to the rest of the world. It will help bring faith to the rest of the world.

Why are we so hopeful about Russia? Why should it be the means of evangelizing nations of the earth? For one reason: Russia has *fire*. It has zeal. Communism has that. The great shame of the world is that we have the truth but we have no zeal; they have zeal but they have no truth! Communism is like a fire that is spreading itself over the world and this fire is already in their hearts! Someday instead of burning downward, that fire will begin to burn upward in a Pentecostal fashion and then it will bring light and peace and joy to men as today it's bringing hate and tyranny and destruction and death! Our Western world lacks that fire. We lack it obviously. Where is the fire of patriotism today? The fire of men were [for?] trying to kindle sparks of love in other men. We in the Western world are rather cold, and dull and apathetic....[69]

Faith and good morals, as established in the Western world by Christianity, was being eroded in favor of atheism and secularism. In order to create this change, significant societal upheavals were necessary and there is no faster way to achieve this goal than through war and crisis (actual or manufactured).[70] If the goal was to effect social change that led people away from Almighty God and His Church, that is certainly a danger

---

69   Ibid.

70   In both of his interviews (mentioned earlier) Norman Dodd specified that ca. 1909, the Carnegie Foundation asked this very question and concluded that no other means can change a society as fast as war. He also states that, after the end of World War I, said Foundation—as was discovered in the minutes of its meetings—did not want the United States to return to pre-war times. It is undeniable that a molding and re-shaping of the United States was taking place, and again we ask *into whose image?*

against which Christians need to be on guard.[71] Thus, Our Lady appeared in Fátima.[72]

It is against this background that we can better understand the words of Cardinal Ratzinger from his celebrated 1984 interview with Vittorio Messori. The Cardinal stated that Our Lady's message in Fátima was "a radical call for conversion, the absolute seriousness of history, the dangers threatening the faith and the life of the Christian, and therefore of the world. And then the importance of the *Novissimi*."[73] It is clear that

---

71   Consider contemporary events, for example, with the billionaire George Soros. E-mails attributed to his Open Society Foundations state that it is looking to take advantage of the so-called "refugee crisis" in order to form and shape Europe in accordance with his societal views: <http://dailycaller.com/2016/08/15/leaked-soros-memo-refugee-crisis-new-normal-gives-new-opportunities-for-global-influence/> (Accessed 16 August, 2016). We also see some form of this influence in the E-mails attributed by *WikiLeaks* to John Podesta concerning the infiltration of the Catholic Church by hostile groups intending to effect social and doctrinal change within the Church. See: <https://wikileaks.org/podesta-emails/emailid/6293> (Accessed 28 October, 2016). Note the use of the word "revolution" in the E-mail.

72   Consider as well the observations of Pope Pius XII in his 1941 Christmas Address (*Acta Apostolicae Sedis* 34 [1942], 10-21). An English translation is available: Vincent A. Yzermans (edit.), *The Major Addresses of Pope Pius XII. Volume II*. (St. Paul, Minnesota: The North Central Publishing Company, 1961), 38-50.

73   The translation is made with the help of a picture reproduction of the text in question on the *Fatima Center* web site. A more complete English translation would be as follows (the *Center's* own translation is not herein used):

> Because, according to the judgment of the Pontiffs, it adds nothing different to what a Christian ought to know from Revelation: a radical call for conversion, the absolute seriousness of history, the dangers threatening the faith and the life of the Christian, and therefore of the world. And then the importance of the *Novissimi*. If it is not published—at least for now—it is to avoid mistaking religious prophecy with sensationalism. But the contents of this "third secret" correspond to the announcement of Scripture and have been reaffirmed in many other Marian apparitions, beginning with Fatima itself in its known

Ratzinger was here interpreting the message of Fátima against a much larger background of sin and error that had (and was presently) invaded the world. These were dangers that threatened the salvation of Christians and against which Our Lady came to warn and call us back to God through prayer, conversion and sacrifice, offering us her Immaculate Heart as a refuge and means to accomplish these things. If we did not do this, the "last things"—the *novissimi*—a Christian will face at the end of his life may see his or her salvation jeopardized.[74]

Having established the deleterious effect of war and crisis on the faith and good morals of a society, perhaps we can assess better the placement of the phrase on Portugal and the Faith. At the time of World War II, Portugal did not enter into the war. According to Sr. Lúcia, this fact was due to the consecration of the country to the Immaculate Heart of Mary by the Portuguese Bishops.[75] Thus this country was spared the horrors and atrocities of the war and, presumably, the effect these would have had upon the Portuguese people. The Catholic Faith remained firm throughout, in other words *the dogma of the Faith was preserved in Portugal.*[76]

Thus, it is entirely plausible that the phrase we have heretofore been

---

contents. Conversion and penitence are the essential conditions for salvation

(cf.: <http://www.fatima.org/thirdsecret/ratzinger.asp> [Accessed 14 August, 2016]).

74   Ratzinger's usage of the term *Novissimi* led to some ink being spilled over the meaning of the term. Frère Michel published his book in French, which translated the original Italian and explained *Novissimi* as *les derniers temps* (the last times). He restricted the meaning of the term. For a more in-depth examination of this matter, see the *Various Considerations* chapter of the present book.

75   *Memórias e Cartas de Irmã Lúcia*, 427, 433, 437-439.

76   World War II may have ended the Nazi and Fascist regimes, but not Communism. It had more power owing to its hold on Eastern Europe (the "Iron Curtain"). Russia could now consolidate its position and further spread her errors across the globe.

discussing can be interpreted as belonging to the second part of the secret of Fátima. Seen in this light, Our Lady was predicting the eroding of the Faith in the world as a result of the spread of Russia's errors, the primary, or, perhaps, the *most effective* means of which would be the proliferation of wars, the sowing of hatred and violence, etc.[77]

The secret of Fátima, in all its parts, is an organic whole. The first part indicates the eternal destination of those who do not repent of their sins and amend their lives before Almighty God. The second part is the remedy that is offered for the errors plaguing mankind, ending in a third part warning about what would happen in this life if mankind did not repent. The third part, according to Sr. Lúcia, concerns Our Lady's words about what would happen if her requests were not heeded. It is a visual description, the interpretation of which we have not been given except in the broad, overall sense indicated by Sr. Lúcia in her May, 1982 letter.[78]

---

77   Archbishop Sheen offered some very insightful remarks on his program *Life is Worth Living*: <https://www.youtube.com/watch?v=rxNC2eW-g7hg> (Accessed 14 August, 2016). Sheen states that the Soviets introduced the concept of the protracted war wherein there are two zones, a "peace" zone and a "war" zone. He described Russia as the "peace" zone and the rest of the world as the "war" zone. He notes that "Russia will not go to war with any other nation until the last war where they will be victorious." The rest of world must be at war, Sheen states, to keep other non-Communist countries fighting so that Russia could come in "for the kill." The fighting makes the warring nations look like they are disturbing the peace, not Russia. He then lists several advantages of keeping other nations warring:

1. **Economic** (warring nations go into debt),
2. **Political** (disturbs the unity of the people),
3. **Psychological** (they convince the other nations that it is not Russia disturbing the peace),
4. **Religious** (there will be some in the area of religion that will identify religion with politics and nothing else).

78   This observation should give us pause when considering the question of whether or not there were words of Our Lady after the "etc." If the phrase belongs to the second part of the secret, then it is possible that Our Lady did not *say* anything else in July, 1917. Instead, she *showed* the visionaries what her

Russia's errors—her godless atheistic materialism—spread, the effect of which would, arguably, have both an exterior *and* interior effect for the Church. The truth of this statement is evident. The Church is not "of" the world but she is "in" it, subject ultimately to Christ, the Lord of history, but also susceptible to the vicissitudes of the age in which she finds herself. Moreover, her Lord can allow her to be chastised through world events. To what degree the Church was affected by the errors of Russia is a *hotly* contested matter.[79]

IV. A General Conclusion

It is clear from the above information that both the meaning and placement of the phrase about Portugal and the dogma of the Faith is a contentious matter. We have seen that there are two schools of thought on the phrase's placement. The first position is that the phrase is the beginning of the third part of the secret. The second position is that it belongs to the end of the second part. There are weighty opinions and questions on either side of the discussion. The position that the phrase begins the third part of the secret enjoys more scholarly support.

While acknowledging their weight and esteemed stature, let us also recall a simple fact. Whether or not these various respected scholars had access to information that has since become available is not clear.[80] One can certainly respect, for example, Fr. Alonso's exhaustive efforts. One must also honor the fact that he was the Fátima archivist for a number of

---

verbal warning was about.

79   In chapter eleven of the present book, we note that Pope Benedict XVI was concerned about the encroaching secularism in Portugal. Sr. Lúcia herself, in a private remark recalled by the Carmelite Sisters, indicated trouble for Portugal with the sin of abortion (cf. *Um Caminho sob o Olhar de Maria*, 67-68).

80   We can say that Fr. Alonso never knew the text that was released in the year 2000.

years and had access to many documents and/or important persons. At this time, however, we do *not* know what exactly he knew about the matter of the placement of the phrase. Thus, there is room for *charitable* discussion and debate.

In the end, it is clear that there are arguments for and against the two primary interpretations on the placement of the phrase "In Portugal the dogma of the faith shall always be preserved etc." The present book does not presume to solve this difficulty, but to provide an alternative assessment of the matter for further study. It remains for scholars on Fátima to examine the matter and discover what, if any, interpretive lines exist to prove either position. This author, regrettably, is not in a position to go into any great depth on the matter but hopes that the present contribution is useful.

—10—

RATZINGER, DHANIS
AND FÁTIMA

*"Because French Jesuit seminaries were considered to be hotbeds
of budding Modernism, in 1948 Jesuit Father General Janssens
sent a stalwart conservative, Belgian Jesuit Edouard Dhanis, to
visit the seminaries and houses of studies in that country."*
—Malachi Martin, *The Jesuits*, 1987

On May 13, 2000, Angelo Cardinal Sodano announced the impending publication of the third part of the secret of Fátima with a *Theological
Commentary*.[1] On June 26, 2000, the publication was done at a press conference in Rome in the booklet *The Message of Fatima*.[2] The *Commentary*
at the end of said booklet was written by Joseph Cardinal Ratzinger, then
Prefect of the Congregation for the Doctrine of the Faith (CDF).

Since the publication of *The Message of Fatima*, there has been a
long, controversial reception of the information presented in this booklet.
Highly critical and polemical articles appeared that discuss the booklet.

---

1   Congregation for the Doctrine of the Faith, *The Message of Fatima*.
(Vatican City: Libreria Editrice Vaticana, 2000), 30-31. Hereafter *The Message
of Fatima* followed by page number.

2   *The Message of Fatima*, 15-16.

The present chapter seeks to focus upon one criticism in particular, namely the influence of the Flemish theologian, Fr. Edouard Dhanis, S.J. upon Cardinal Ratzinger's *Theological Commentary*. We shall look at two specific areas wherein this influence is thought to have been exerted upon Ratzinger, namely on pages 35 and 42.

I. Fr. Dhanis and Fátima: Background

In the first half of the twentieth century, the propagation of the events of Fátima from the year 1917 was still in its early stages. Gradually, word of these events was spread throughout Europe and across the Atlantic into the Americas. By the mid-1940s, the last surviving seer, Sr. Lúcia dos Santos, had written about the events from 1917 in four specific *Memoirs* (generally referred to as the *First Memoir, Second Memoir*, etc.). She had also communicated the secret of Fátima from July, 1917 in writing and in its three parts.

Having written her *Memoirs*, Sr. Lúcia provided the Church with detailed accounts of the events of and surrounding the year 1917 in Fátima. While these were intended to spread the devotion requested by Our Lady in Fátima, the *Memoirs* also afforded to scholars opportunities to criticize Fátima and/or Sr. Lúcia. One such theologian was Fr. Edouard Dhanis of the Jesuits.

Not much is available on Fr. Dhanis in the English language, and much of his writings remain in languages other than English.[3] What concerns us is his involvement with Fátima. Dhanis became involved in the

---

3   Some of the published works of Fr. Dhanis are as follows: *Tractatus de fide*. (Louvain, 1935-1939); *Miracula et resurrection Iesu*. (Rome, Pontificia Universitas Gregoriana, 2^e,1961); *Introductio in problema Christi*. (Rome: Pontificia Universitas Gregoriana, 1962); *Testimonium Iesu de seipso*. (Rome, Pontificia Universitas Gregoriana, 1965); *L'Eglise et les religions*. (Rome, Pontificia Universitas Gregoriana, 1966); *The Supplement to a New Catechism*. (London: Burns & Oates, 1969).

history of Fátima in 1944. In this year, nearing the end of World War II, he wrote a two-part article for the Flemish journal entitled *Streven*. The article itself was entitled *On the Apparitions and Prophecies of Fatima*.[4] The article was later turned into a book in 1945 entitled *On the Apparitions and Secret of Fatima: A Critical Contribution*.[5]

Fr. Dhanis criticized how the events of Fátima were being propagated. For example, in the first part of his 1944 article, Dhanis noted how some literature on Fátima was "devotional" and not always "academic." He wrote:

> In various ways the authors intend their books to serve as devotional [*stichtelijke*] literature. Critically they do not always reach academic standards [*wetenschappelijk*]. We have to admit that sometimes they gloss over disturbing details. Yet, they do provide valuable data, maybe not about those facts themselves, but at least the prevention of them in the most important sources.[6]

Dhanis then raised two questions. These two questions pertained to the reliability of the visionary (in this case, Sr. Lúcia) and whether or not she added—even unconsciously—anything to what she saw. Dhanis wrote:

---

4   *Bij de Verschijningen en de Voorzeggingen van Fatima. Streven XI* (1944) Issue 3, pages 129-149 and Issue 4, pages 193-215. Hereafter *Streven* followed by year, issue and page number(s).

5   *Bij de verschijningen en het geheim van Fatima: een critische bijdrage*. (Brugge-Brussel: De Kinkhoren, 1945).

6   Dhanis wrote:

> Hun boeken zijn in verscheiden opzichten als stichtelijke lectuur bedoeld. Kritisch staan ze niet altijd op wetenschappelijk peil. We zullen moeten vaststellen dat ze storende bijzonderheden wel eens bewimpelen. Maar zij verstrekken ons kostbare gegevens, wel niet altijd over de feiten zelf, dan toch over het voorkomen daarvan in de voornaamste bronnen (*Streven* [1944] Issue 3, page 130). Translation courtesy of Mr. Tony Verhallen.

When historical sources announce extraordinary phenomena and suggest these facts are supernatural, then two questions arise. Are these phenomena proposed in a faithful way? Is the supernatural explanation well-founded? It is not sufficient that a witness with a high moral standing exposes his spiritual findings, to believe that all expressions of his words are correct. Through the years his memories could be changed [*verrijkt*] or idealized [*geïdealiseerd*]. The deformations sometimes are so strong that it seems like a pathological case. But even then the moral pureness and balanced judgment of the witness can remain intact.[7]

Later, in the second part of his article, in a section entitled "General Decision" (*Algemeen Besluit*), Dhanis proposed a distinction with respect to the history of Fátima. He distinguished what can be called "old" Fátima history [*oude geschiedenis*] from "new" Fátima [*nieuwe geschiedenis*] history. He wrote:

---

7   The Flemish text reads:

Wanneer historische bronnen buitengewone verschijnselen vermelden en ze als bovennatuurlijke feiten voorstellen, dan worden als van zelf twee vragen gesteld. Zijn de verschijnselen getrouw weergegeven? Is de bovennatuurlijke verklaring er van gegrond? Het volstaat niet dat een getuige met een hoogstaand zedelijk leven zijn geestelijke bevindingen voorlegt, opdat men al zijn woorden voor de juiste uitdrukking zou nemen van de door hem opgedane ervaring. Door de jaren werden zijn herinneringen misschien gewijzigd, geïdealiseerd verrijkt. De vervorming kan soms zoo sterk zijn, dat men van een min of meer' pathologisch geval zal spreken. Maar zelfs dàn kunnen de zedelijke ongereptheid en het evenwichtig oordeel van den getuige gaaf blijven. Wie met de psychologische vragen weinig vertrouwd is, denkt soms dat men de buitengewone psychische verschijnselen, visioenen bij voorbeeld en openbaringen, gemakkelijk voor al of niet bovennatuurlijk kan uitmaken (*Streven* [1944], Issue 3, page 130). Translation courtesy of Mr. Mark Waterinckx.

It is now possible to develop a sketch that provides a general solution of the Fátima problem. The visions of Our Lady, which the three little shepherds claimed to have received in 1917, appeared to have come through supernatural intervention. The sun miracle, which accompanied the last apparition, guaranteed the visions. Solid witnesses testified to this miracle and it is reasonable to see a miraculous sign in it. Actually, it is not an isolated case. Apart from other atmospheric miracles, Fátima pilgrimages have seen many exceptional healings, some of which have made a great impression. Church approval of the pilgrimages and the apparitions also invites us to consider the visions authentic. *All of this relates to what we call Fátima's old history.* It has its dark spots, but light ultimately wins.

The new Fátima history, the one that relies on Lúcia's reports, demands more reservation… (emphases mine).[8]

In short, Dhanis proposed that the earlier history of Fátima was more reli-

---

8   Dhanis wrote:

Het is nu mogelijk een algemeene oplossing van het probleem van Fatima te schetsen. De visioenen van Onze Lieve Vrouw die de drie herdertjes beweerden in 1917 gekregen te hebben, lijken wel van een bovennatuurlijk ingrijpen voort te komen. Zij worden gewaarborgd door het zonnewonder, dat de laatste verschijning vergezelde. Dit wonder berust op stevige getuigenissen en het is redelijk daarin een miraculeus teeken te zien. Het staat overigens niet alleen. Afgezien van andere atmosferische wonderen, heeft de bedevaart van Fatima talrijke buitengewone genezingen gekend, waarvan sommige een grooten indruk maken. De kerkelijke goedkeuring van de bedevaart en van de verschijningen noodigt ook uit om deze voor authentisch te houden. Dat alles heeft betrekking op wat wij de oude geschiedenis van Fatima noemen. Deze heeft schaduwen, maar beslist overwint er het licht.

De nieuwe geschiedenis van Fatima, degene die berust op de verslagen van Lucia, vergt meer voorbehoud… (*Streven* [1944], Issue 4, 213ff.). Translation courtesy of Mr. Tony Verhallen.

able than the later history as the distance of 20 or so years from 1917 may have affected the memories of Sr. Lúcia. Dhanis' proposition has been termed his "thesis" and became known as "Fatima I" (old) and "Fatima II" (new).[9]

Dhanis' "thesis" became the catalyst for scholarly debate. For our purposes, it is unnecessary to go over in detail this debate, or to take a position.[10] Our focus is whether or not Dhanis' writings (particularly his "thesis") influenced Ratzinger's *Theological Commentary* and if so, how. Before examining this question, some further background history is necessary.

II. The Influence of the Abbé Georges de Nantes

As we noted in chapter one, the Abbé Georges de Nantes was concerned that the heresy of Modernism had reached the "highest summits of the Church."[11] Moreover, he noted the new orientation of Pope John XXIII

---

9   Cf. Frère Michel de la Sainte Trinité, *The Whole Truth About Fatima, Volume I: Science and the Facts.* (Buffalo, New York: Immaculate Heart Publications, 1989), 381-524. Hereafter *The Whole Truth About Fatima: Volume I* followed by page number. The original French is: Frère Michel de la Sainte Trinité, *Toute la Vérité sur Fatima: La Science et les Faits.* (Saint-Parres lès Vaudes, France: Renaissance Catholique Contre-Réforme Catholique, 4ᵉ, 1986),5-102. Hereafter *Toute la Vérité sur Fatima: Volume I* followed by page number. In the French, the discussion on Fr. Dhanis is in the *beginning* whereas it is towards the *end* of the English translation.

10   Fr. Joaquín María Alonso, *História da Literatura sobre Fátima.* (Fátima, Portugal: Edições Santuário, 1967), 35-51; See also his article *Fatima y la Critica* in *Ephemerides Mariologicae* 17 (1967): 392-435; Eloy Bueno de la Fuente, *A Mensagem de Fátima. A Misericórdia de Deus: o triunfo do amor nos dramas da história.* (Fátima, Portugal: Santuário de Fátima, 2014), 115-122.

11   *Pascendi Dominici Gregis* in *Acta Sanctae Sedis*, 40 (1907), 593-650. See also: <http://crc-internet.org/our-doctrine/catholic-counter-reformation/for-the-church/3-founding-league-crc/> (Accessed 1 January, 2016); Frère François de Marie des Anges, *Fatima: Tragedy and Triumph.* (Buffalo, New York: Immaculate Heart Publications, 1994), 267, 287. Hereafter *Fatima: Tragedy and*

for the Catholic Church included an unwillingness to condemn Communism both prior to and during the Second Vatican Council.[12]

We saw that there was a subsequent claim which arose from the Abbé de Nantes and his *Catholic Counter-Reform* (*Le Contre-Reforme Catholique*) that Rome has essentially rejected Fátima. This claim (amid others) became prominent in the literature published under the auspices of the Abbé.[13] The reason for Rome rejecting Fátima, according to the Abbé (*et al.*), was the acceptance in Rome of the "Fatima I/Fatima II" thesis of Fr. Edouard Dhanis. This claim would have a long-lasting influence upon the question being examined in this chapter.

We also noted that Frère Michel of the Holy Trinity and Frère François de Marie des Anges were important writers on Fátima. Frère Michel wrote three-volume works in French entitled *Toute la Vérité sur Fatima*.[14] These volumes were rendered into English and published as *The Whole Truth About Fatima*.[15] Frère François continued this work after Frère Michel

---

Triumph followed by page number.

12   Cf. *Fatima: Tragedy and Triumph*, 48-50, 58-74. Most of these pages are the narrative of events from Frère François. It is, however, to be noted that he published the French original under the auspices of the Abbé de Nantes who would never have published the book if he did not agree with its contents. See also Michael Davies, *Pope John's Council*. (Kansas City, Missouri: Angelus Press, 2007), 233-255.

13   Coupled with this claim was an emphasis upon the third part of the secret of Fátima as it was theorized of being capable of dispelling the ills plaguing the Church.

14   Frère Michel de la Sainte Trinité, *Toute la Vérité sur Fatima: Le Troisième Secret (1942-1960)*. (Saint-Parres lès Vaudes, France: Renaissance Catholique Contre-Réforme Catholique, 1985). Hereafter *Toute la Vérité sur Fatima: Volume III* followed by page number. The English translation is : Frère Michel de la Sainte Trinité, *The Whole Truth About Fatima. Volume III: The Third Secret*. (Buffalo, New York: Immaculate Heart Publications, 1990). Hereafter *The Whole Truth About Fatima: Volume III* followed by page number.

15   *The Whole Truth About Fatima: Volume III*, 601ff.

left the Little Brothers community. In their own turn, these two writers rejected Fr. Dhanis' thesis, Frère Michel going so far as to accuse Dhanis of engaging in Modernism.[16]

We also saw that the information contained in Frère Michel and Frère François were then promoted in the English language by Fr. Nicholas Gruner.[17] These efforts led to an influential body of literature on Fátima, one that will directly affect the reception of the Vatican's booklet *The Message of Fatima*. The question before us in the present chapter is Dhanis' influence on Cardinal Ratzinger's *Theological Commentary*, specifically pages 35 and 42.

III. The Influence of Dhanis on Ratzinger—Page 35:

After the publication of the booklet *The Message of Fatima*, Fr. Gruner and his associates studied it. They did not believe that everything was published and advocated various ideas and theories to explain this belief.[18] These various ideas and theories were organized by Fr. Paul L.

---

16   *The Whole Truth About Fatima: Volume I*, 389; *Fatima: Tragedy and Triumph*, 133.

17   A biography on Fr. Gruner is available (Christopher A. Ferrara and Francis Alban, *Fatima Priest*. [Pound Ridge, New York: Good Counsel Publications, 2013]. Hereafter *Fatima Priest* followed by page number). For an alternative view, see Michael W. Cuneo, *The Smoke of Satan*. (New York: Oxford University Press, 1997), 45-46, 81-87, 134-152, 188, 195, 202-205. Gruner died on April 29, 2015. His Requiem Mass was celebrated by Bishop Bernard Fellay, the head of the Society of St. Pius X (SSPX). See *The Fatima Crusader*, Summer 2015, Issue 112 and <http://sspx.org/en/news-events/news/fr-gruner-requiescat-pace-8151> (Accessed 1 January, 2016).

18   For one example, see *The Fatima Crusader*, Issue 64 (Summer, 2000). This issue is available on the Internet: <http://www.fatimacrusader.com/cr64/toc64.asp> (Accessed 1 January, 2016). To specify only the first two years is not to neglect the years after 2002. This specification is only a means to lead up to the publication of *The Devil's Final Battle*.

Kramer in his book *The Devil's Final Battle* (2002).[19] As the above ideas and theories pertain to the question of Ratzinger's *Theological Commentary*, Gruner and his associates made the observation that there was only one scholar cited by Ratzinger, Fr. Dhanis.[20]

A: Dhanis & the Approval of a Private Revelation

On page 35 of *The Message of Fatima*, Ratzinger quotes from an article written by Fr. Dhanis in 1953 on Fátima entitled *Looking upon Fatima and Assessment of a Debate* (*Sguardo su Fátima e Bilancio di una Discussione*). Referring to him as an "eminent scholar in this field," Ratzinger cites a point that Fr. Dhanis makes about how the "ecclesiastical approval of a private revelation has three elements." These three elements are:

1. the message contains nothing contrary to faith and morals,
2. it is lawful to make it public, and
3. the faithful are authorized to accept it with prudence.[21]

In his own words, Dhanis wrote:

> In summary, ecclesiastical approval of a heavenly communication means three things in regard to it: first, that there is nothing in it contrary to faith and morals; secondly, that it is permitted

---

19   Fr. Paul L. Kramer, *The Devil's Final Battle*. (Terryville, Connecticut: The Missionary Association, 2002). Hereafter *The Devil's Final Battle* followed by page number. This book was later updated in the year 2010.

20   For an example, see a "Summary" written in defense of Fr. Gruner: <http://www.fatima.org/apostolate/defense/vsoaap24.asp> (Accessed 5 July, 2016). This "Summary" was written in May, 2001. The claim that Dhanis is the only scholar cited is questionable. Ratzinger quotes Cardinal Lambertini's famous treatise *De Servorum Dei*. This treatise was published before Lambertini's elevation to the Papacy as Benedict XIV. As such, it was not, at least originally, part of the Papal Magisterium. See also José Barreto, "Edouard Dhanis, Fátima e a II Guerra Mundial." *Brotéria* 156 (January, 2003): 16.

21   *The Message of Fatima*, 35.

to publish it; thirdly, that the faithful are expressly authorized to grant it their assent prudently. Ecclesiastical approval in these matters [*queste materie*] means that and nothing else, because the declarations of the Magisterium in these matters are proportionate to the office that is divinely entrusted to it: it must preserve, interpret and defend the Deposit of Faith, received from Christ and the Apostles. It must do so with the assistance of the Holy Spirit, but without basing its teaching on new revelations. Such approval must be received with respect and obedience....[22]

Citing Dhanis was taken as a *tremendous* affront by Fr. Gruner and/or his associates. They read the Cardinal's *Theological Commentary* with suspicion for two particular reasons. The first is a body of literature catalogued by Fr. Alonso challenging Dhanis. Why was this literature not factored into Ratzinger's *Theological Commentary*? Moreover, why would Ratzinger refer to Dhanis as being an "eminent scholar in this field" when Dhanis had been challenged? Was Ratzinger turning a blind eye to such information, and if so, why?

The second reason is that Dhanis was described by Frère Michel as

---

22   *La Civiltà Cattolica*, 1953, vol. II, p. 397. Hereafter *Dhanis 1953* followed by page number. The original Italian reads as follows:

Riassumendo, l'approvazione ecclesiastica di una comunicazione celeste significa tre cose nei suoi riguardi: primieramente che in essa non vi è nulla contro la fede e i buoni costumi; secondariamente che è permesso di pubblicarla; in terzo luogo che i fedeli sono espressamente autorizzati ad accordarle prudentemente il loro assenso. L'approvazione ecclesiastica in queste materie significa ciò e non altro, perché le dichiarazioni del magistero in queste cose sono proporzionate all'ufficio che gli è divinamente confidato: deve conservare, interpretare e difendere il deposito della fede, ricevuto da Cristo e dagli apostoli, deve farlo con l'assistenza dello Spirito Santo, ma senza fondare il suo insegnamento su nuove rivelazioni. Una tale approvazione dev'essere ricevuta con rispetto e con ubbidienza (translation by Kevin J. Symonds).

the "opponent of Fatima," its "most unyielding and terrible adversary" and its "censor."[23] The intellectual groundwork for rejecting Dhanis goes back to the above-mentioned body of literature against Dhanis' thesis (and Frère Michel's own contributions). There was for the Abbé de Nantes a personal dimension in this matter. Frère François notes that Fr. Dhanis was on a committee (under the CDF) charged with examining the Abbé.[24]

Concerning Ratzinger's making use of Dhanis' 1953 article on Fátima, let us examine the specific quotation in question. The quote says nothing about his Fatima I/Fatima II thesis. The *only* point referenced by Ratzinger is Dhanis' three elements to ecclesiastical approval of a private revelation. These three elements are theologically sound—in fact, they are built, in part, upon the very same Encyclical wherein the heresy of Modernism is condemned! The citation fits *in tandem* to Ratzinger's preceding citation to a famous quote from Cardinal Lambertini on the kind of faith one puts in private revelations. This same quotation from Lambertini appeared in Dhanis' 1953 article.[25]

---

23   Cf. *The Whole Truth About Fatima: Volume I*, 389, 398; *The Whole Truth About Fatima: Volume III*, 389.

24   *Fatima: Tragedy and Triumph*, 133. Two notices were issued by the Congregation for the Doctrine of the Faith (CDF) concerning the Abbé. The first instance appeared in August, 1969 in *L'Osservatore Romano* and was translated into French for the periodical *La Documentation Catholique* 66 (1969), pages 794-796. The second notice was issued on May 13, 1983 and published in *L'Osservatore Romano* (May 16/17, 1983 edition, page 2). Both documents are available on the Vatican's web site for the CDF: <http://www.vatican.va/roman_curia/congregations/cfaith/doc_doc_index_it.htm> (Accessed 1 January, 2016).

25   Quoting from the 1937 Provincial Council of Mechelin (Malines), Dhanis wrote:

Perciò essi cominciano col citare il trattato classico del cardinal Lambertini sulla beatificazione e la canonizzazione: « Bisogna sapere — scrive quegli che stava per diventare il papa Benedetto XIV — che una tale approvazione non è altra cosa che il permesso di pubblicare in vista dell'istruzione e dell'utilità dei fedeli, e dopo un maturo esame. Un assentimento di fede cattolica non è dovuto a rivelazioni

B: Dhanis as an "Eminent Scholar in This Field"

What did Ratzinger mean when he referred to Dhanis as an "eminent scholar in this field?"[26] The antecedent of the words "this field" (*questa materia*) are not clear. *Which* field is not referenced.[27] The Cardinal is either referring to Fátima or another subject. In order to attempt to address this matter, one must step back and look at the passage within the context Ratzinger wrote.

First of note is that the passage is found within the first section of the *Commentary* entitled *Public Revelation and private revelations – their theological status.* Prior to the passage we are examining, Ratzinger mentions Fátima only once, and that is at the very beginning of the section (page 32). The passage citing Fr. Dhanis is at the top of page 35. Outside of naming Fátima in the citation to Dhanis, the Cardinal does not again mention Fátima until the very end—indeed, the *very last* sentence—of this first section of his *Commentary* (page 36). The subject of this first section is clearly on Revelation (Public and private).[28]

Moreover, there is the internal evidence within Dhanis' 1953 article. The citation to page 397 appears within the second section (out of three) within Dhanis' article. This second section is entitled, "The Significance of the Acts of the Authority of the Church" (*Il significato degli atti dell'au-*

---

approvate in tal modo; non è neppure possibile. Queste rivelazioni domandano piuttosto un assentimento di fede umana conforme alle regole della prudenza che ce le presenta come probabili e piamente credibili » (*Dhanis 1953, 396*).

26   Cf. *The Devil's Final Battle*, 103.

27   The Italian text of Ratzinger's *Commentary* reads, "…eminente conoscitore di questa materia…." The official English text from the Vatican translates *di questa materia* as "in this field." This translation is not inaccurate, though perhaps a better one would be "…of this matter."

28   Moreover, the words *questa materia* are feminine, as is the Italian word for Revelation, *rivelazione.*

torità della Chiesa). In this section, he outlines a basic theology of private revelation. To do this he cites the Papal Encyclical *Pascendi Dominici Gregis* of Pope St. Pius X and the decrees of the 1937 Provincial Council of Mechelin (Malines). Dhanis wrote:

> Let us ask ourselves first what is, according to theology, the significance of an approval accorded by the Church granted to apparitions or private revelations. Theologians generally agree in this regard and their doctrine was proposed by the ecclesiastical authority itself. It is indicated by the Encyclical *Pascendi* and was explained by the provincial council of Mechelen in 1937.[29]

Dhanis then continues to develop his thinking by following closely upon the heels of Mechelen's decrees. He wrote:

> We mention first the decrees of this council, which were promulgated by the bishops of Belgium after they were "revised by the Sacred Congregation of the Council and approved by His Holiness Pope Pius XI." Having defined revelation, these decrees distinguish public revelation, entrusted whole to the Church by Christ and the Apostles, and private revelations, of which it is prudent to allow that at times they have been granted in the course of the history of the Church. Furthermore, directly addressing our subject, they declare: "It can happen that the Church may approve of private revelations or apparitions." And

---

29   *Dhanis 1953*, 396. The Italian reads:

Domandiamoci dapprima quale sia, secondo la teologia, la portata di un'approvazione della Chiesa accordata ad apparizioni o a rivelazioni private. I teologi in generale concordano a questo riguardo e la loro dottrina è stata proposta dall'autorità ecclesiastica stessa. Essa è indicata dall'enciclica *Pascendi* ed è stata esposta dal concilio provinciale di Malines del 1937 (translation by Kevin J. Symonds).

they immediately explain the meaning which approvals of such kinds have. Hence, they begin by quoting the classic treatise of Cardinal Lambertini on beatifications and canonizations: "We should know - writes he who was to become Pope Benedict XIV - that such an approval is nothing else than permission to publish in view of instruction and the benefit of the faithful, and after a mature examination. An assent of Catholic faith is not owed to revelations approved in this way; it is not even possible. These revelations seek rather an assent of human faith in keeping to the requirements of prudence which puts them before us as probable and piously credible." After this quotation, the council continues: "So, therefore, the judgment of the Church does not at all present these things to be believed by everyone: it only declares that they are not opposed in any way to faith and good morals, and that there is sufficient evidence to give rise to a pious and prudent assent by human faith." And the council refers in a footnote to an authority higher than its own, the Encyclical *Pascendi*.[30]

Concerning *Pascendi*, Dhanis wrote:

According to this Encyclical, the Church, when she permits that public writings of "pious traditions" may be issued, such as those of "apparitions or revelations," "she does not thereby affirm the truth of the fact," but "she simply does but forbid belief in things for which human arguments are not wanting." The same Encyclical also states: "The devotion based on any apparition, insofar as it regards the fact itself, that is to say insofar as it is *relative*, always implies the condition of the truth of the fact; insofar as it is *absolute*, it must always be based on the truth, seeing that its

---

30   Ibid., 396-397.

object is the persons of the saints who are honored."[31]

From there, Dhanis then provides his three criteria cited above. He then applies the above paragraphs to Fátima over the course of two paragraphs (herein omitted). Upon finishing, Dhanis then wrote:

God has made, in the course of history, the revelation of the Old Testament and the New; this is the public revelation entrusted to the Church and constitutes the object of the Catholic faith. At the time of the prophets of the Old Testament this revelation was accomplished with a succession of partial revelations: perfected by Christ and concluded by his Apostles, it has become the *depositum fidei* (Deposit of Faith), which the Church transmits and explains. The time is therefore ended in which public revelation was formed in successive stages; and there is no more place for that in the world, but only for private revelations. These are not addressed either to the universal Church or to the whole human race, but rather to a particular person or groups of people. They may have a resonance in the whole Church, and a resonance willed by God, if it is conveyed to the person to whom he speaks,

---

31   Ibid., 397. The Italian reads:

Stando a quest'enciclica, la Chiesa permettendo che si redigano scritti pubblici di « pie tradizioni », come sono delle « apparizioni o rivelazioni », « non perciò afferma la verità del fatto », ma « solo non proibisce che si creda, ove a farlo non manchino argomenti umani ». La stessa enciclica dichiara anche: « Il culto di qualsiasi apparizione, in quanto riguarda il fatto stesso, e dicesi *relativo,* ha sempre implicita la condizione della verità del fatto; in quanto poi è *assoluto,* si fonda sempre nella verità, giacché si dirige alle persone stesse dei santi che si onorano ».

Concerning the quotations from the Encyclical, much use is made of the English translation available on the Vatican's web site: <http://w2.vatican.va/content/pius-x/en/encyclicals/documents/hf_p-x_enc_19070908_pascendi-dominici-gregis.html> (Accessed 25 July, 2016).

who has to communicate the content of his revelation.

But that God may speak to the whole Church through the intermediary of ministers who transmit His word addressed to all is one thing; and that He might speak to a person conveying that she must manifest to others the word addressed to her alone is quite another thing. In the first case it calls upon [*interpella*] everyone, at least indirectly, asking for faith, obedience; in the second case, it only calls upon a particular person. God spoke to the whole Church when he announced the Christian revelation by means of the minister of the humanity of Christ, and through that of the Apostles; He spoke to one person when, for example, He addressed St. Margaret Mary Alacoque charging her to spread the devotion to the Sacred Heart. The revelations of Paray-le-Monial are not, if we want to use the terms precisely, a word addressed to the Church of God; God has spoken to the Church and to the world once and for all through His Son and the Apostles. Private revelations can be greatly beneficial, for example, by favoring certain devotions; but they have only a secondary role with respect to public revelation, which alone nurtures the entire Catholic faith. Moreover, they are incomparably less guaranteed than this revelation, toward which converge many reasons to believe. They constitute a domain in which it is difficult to reach much certainty. In addition, they have to be judged in the light of the Catholic faith and of theology, and be treated with a great circumspection. All the masters of the spiritual life teach as a general rule that we should not be inspired by them in our manner of proceeding or in our undertaking except as an ancillary reason, and after having subjected them to a competent examination. Theologians note that the same reserve is observed by the Church hierarchy, by law, when it wishes to permit these revelations. Fr. Fonse-

ca has clearly pointed out: "We know that the Vicar of Jesus Christ in his determinations does not govern himself by private revelations, but by theological reasons. But nothing prevents – it is indeed a historical fact many times proven - that some extraordinary intervention of Heaven, sufficiently verified, may suggest the first idea or give the final impulse to a decision that is recognized already and for superior reasons, as legitimate, suitable, necessary."[32]

Based upon the above information, one is left with the impression that Dhanis was fluent in the Church's theology of private revelation. Moreover, his formulation does not appear to contradict the Church's consistent teaching on private revelation with respect to Public Revelation. One can reasonably concede the possibility that Cardinal Ratzinger views Dhanis as an expert on the theology of Public and private revelation.

We have interior evidence within Dhanis and that of Ratzinger which supports the interpretation that the words "this field" (*questa materia*) are in reference to Revelation. Read in this way, Ratzinger would be referring to Dhanis as being an eminent scholar on the theology of *Public* and *private revelation*. This reading is harmonious with the purpose of the section in which this citation is found. The focus here is not on Fátima *per se*, but rather the Church's theology on Public and private revelation as it *relates* to Fátima.

Dhanis' scholarship on this theology appears to be intimately connected to Fátima.[33] Moreover, we recall that not much of Dhanis' scholarship is in English. What *is* known about him in English has largely come through efforts from Frère Michel and the Abbé de Nantes. Based upon these facts, it is not without reason for one familiar with the history of

---

32   *Dhanis 1953*, 399-401.

33   This perception is not challenged by the present chapter as a study of Dhanis' *entire* body of writings would have to be performed.

Dhanis and Fátima easily to interpret Ratzinger's description of him as referring to his scholarship on Fátima. A more careful look, however, questions this interpretation.

IV. Dhanis & Ratzinger—Page 42

The next alleged influence of Dhanis upon Cardinal Ratzinger's *Theological Commentary* is said to be on page 42 of *The Message of Fatima*. On this page, Cardinal Ratzinger has reached the final part of remarks about the various images present in the vision that is the third part of the secret. Specifically, he is remarking upon the angels gathering up the blood of the martyrs. He opens this final part with the following words, "The concluding part of the 'secret' uses images which Lucia may have seen in devotional books and which draw their inspiration from long-standing intuitions of faith."[34]

Taken at face value, these words appear to imply that Sr. Lúcia essentially fabricated the vision. The reasoning behind this interpretation is clear. If Lúcia was using images that she "may have seen in devotional books," then one must ask what is the source of the vision, devotional books or an objective supernatural vision? If it was the former, then Ratzinger must logically be understood as indirectly accusing Sr. Lúcia of having made up the whole thing.

For those familiar with the history of Dhanis and his critical assessments of Fátima (from the perspective of Frère Michel and the Abbé de Nantes), reading his "thesis" into Ratzinger's above words is not difficult. Dhanis did say that Sr. Lúcia could have, even unconsciously, added elements to what she remembered and it appears as though Ratzinger is affirming this notion. Moreover, clearly Dhanis *did* exert some influence on

---

34   *The Message of Fatima*, 42.

Ratzinger as evidenced by the simple fact that he was cited by Ratzinger.[35]

Thus, we see some reason for interpreting Ratzinger's *Commentary* in the light of Dhanis' writings. If, however, this interpretation is accurate, why would Ratzinger not also provide a citation to Dhanis' "thesis?" Is it that Ratzinger himself was perhaps acting "unconsciously" on information he gleaned from Dhanis' writings? An alternative explanation may exist.

A: Reassessing Dhanis' Influence

We have so far read Ratzinger's above quote in isolation from:
1. the rest of his *Theological Commentary*, and
2. a larger tradition of writings on mystical theology.[36]

When a reader reads the *Commentary* within the above two contexts, some light is shed on Ratzinger's remark. This light is much less conspiratorial and demonstrates a great concern for truth, preciseness and Christian theological history. Let us look at the first way given above—within the text itself.

1.) Within the Text of the Commentary

Before interpreting the specific images of the third part of the secret, Ratzinger prefaces said interpretation with two sections:
1. Public Revelation and private revelations – their theological status

---

35   As an accomplished theologian, Ratzinger may have been familiar with Dhanis' overall work on Fátima. One has to ask how he came to select this *one* article by Dhanis out of hundreds of other scholarly works on the topic (Revelation or Fátima).

36   While Cardinal Ratzinger provides profound theological insights throughout his *Commentary*, he does not provide more citations or a bibliography to the sources of his theological anthropology. This fact makes it difficult for a researcher to check the sources of the Cardinal's thinking and its development.

(pages 32-36), and

2. The anthropological structure of private revelations (pages 36-38). We have already discussed, to some degree, the first section.[37] The second one offers much for our consideration of Ratzinger's later remark on page 42.

Having established the *theological* character of private revelation(s), the Cardinal discusses the working of private revelation(s) *within a subject*, i.e. a "seer" or "visionary" in this case. This discussion is what he calls a "theological anthropology." The focus of this anthropology as it relates to supernatural communications and revelations is significant to the *Commentary*. This significance is in how said communications are *received, understood* and *expressed by* the subject.[38] Ratzinger's discussion must necessarily explain the nature of supernatural communications and their operation in and on the receiver.

It is clear from the above that the Cardinal's theological anthropology will keep in focus two things: 1) the *human* subject, and 2) the interaction of the supernatural upon said subject.[39] From the outset of this discussion,

---

37   By way of summary, Ratzinger explains that Public Revelation and private revelations are related, but distinct. We are obliged to believe in Public Revelation, not private revelation though we would be wise to accept this "help which is offered." It is to this category of "private revelation" that Fátima belongs.

38   Theological anthropology might also take interest in the *effect* that these communications and revelations have upon the human person.

39   The emphasis upon anthropological structure of private revelation is of interest in the contemporary world with the rise of the psychological sciences. Avery Cardinal Dulles once wrote:

Contemporary theologians are conscious of the social and psychological mechanisms at work in visions and auditions. Such phenomena normally occur in a context of faith and of struggle for the faith. The visionaries tend to be eidetically gifted [i.e. blessed with good memory] and emotionally involved. The words and images are normally borrowed from the seers' own memory and past experience. Even an authentic divine revelation is filtered through a human consciousness that influences the choice of words and concepts. One must be cau-

Ratzinger establishes the nature of the supernatural communication given at Fátima in July, 1917. He states that there are "three forms of perception or 'vision'" in theological anthropology:

1. Vision with the senses (exterior bodily perception),
2. Interior perception, and
3. Spiritual vision.

After going through each of these perceptions, Ratzinger concludes that it is the second category to which the secret of Fátima must be ascribed.[40] Before discussing this category, a careful reader should note that Ratzinger does not provide a citation in his *Commentary* to his source(s) for these three categories. It is therefore necessary to take a step back and look at the larger tradition of theological and philosophical writings.

2.) On the Sources of Ratzinger's Thought:
The Larger Tradition of Literature

Over time, the Church's understanding of and vocabulary on mystical phenomena and theology has developed.[41] It is difficult to go over the

---

tious, therefore, in what one attributes to God the Revealer. Special caution is required in evaluating accounts given some time after the apparition, whether by the visionaries themselves or by others reporting what was allegedly said (Avery Cardinal Dulles, S.J., *The Assurance of Things Hoped for: A Theology of Christian Faith*. [New York: Oxford University Press, 1994], 200).

Christian anthropology does not deny the possibility that God communicates private revelation(s) to individual people. It *defends* the supernatural by safeguarding what is supernatural from that which comes from the subject.

40   The question of whether or not Ratzinger was correct in his conclusion is not here addressed. Our focus is on explaining what he *did* write in order to understand better the quote which appears on page 42.

41   Cf. Augustin Poulain, S.J. & Leonora L. Yorke Smith (trans.), *The Graces of Interior Prayer: A Treatise on Mystical Theology*. 10ᵉ (London: Routledge and Kegan Paul Limited, 1951), 539. Hereafter *The Graces of Interior*

history of this development as it spans 2000 years. We shall thus limit our scope to a couple of specific timeframes and/or persons, beginning with that period of time known as the Scholastic era (ca. 1000-1350). From there we shall consider more recent developments from the twentieth century onward.

a: Scholasticism and St. Thomas Aquinas

The Scholastic period contributed to the development of the Church's understanding of many areas of theology and philosophy by synthesizing much of the previous centuries' literature (mystical theology being only one such area). Part of this development was an overall finely-tuned theological and philosophical language. Among the Scholastics is St. Thomas Aquinas and his *Summa Theologiae*.[42] In his *Summa*, Aquinas discusses the nature of prophecy and other extraordinary gifts (*ST* II-II, questions 171-178). He does so, however, within the context of what is today called "theological anthropology."

Prior to the above discussion, Aquinas discusses the human person, looking at questions pertaining to man himself, epistemology, etc (*ST* I-I, questions 75-102). From this examination, he will state later in his discussion on prophecy that there are three cognitive powers within man. He enumerates these as "sense" (*sensus*), "imagination" (*imaginatio*), and "intellect" (*intellectus*).[43]

Prayer followed by page number.

42   Owing to his elevated doctrine and ability of synthesis and summary, Aquinas is highly regarded by scholars and reading him is encouraged even by the Papal Magisterium. See the Encyclical *Aeterni Patris* by Pope Leo XIII (*Acta Sanctae Sedis* 12 [1879], 97-115). English translation in Claudia Carlen, IHM (edit.), *The Papal Encyclicals 1878-1903*. (Raleigh, North Carolina: The Pierian Press, 1990), 17-27.

43   Cf. ST II-II, q. 174, a.1, reply to objection 3). See also *The Graces of Interior Prayer*, 301; Reginald Garrigou-Lagrange, *The Three Ages of the Inte-*

These three cognitive powers correspond to the three "perceptions" that Ratzinger discusses in his *Commentary*. Since the Cardinal eliminates the first and third perceptions in his assessment of the type of vision that occurred in Fátima (1917), it remains to look at what Aquinas says on the second perception, the *interior* ("imaginative") perception as it pertains to prophecy.

Aquinas' *Summa* (II-II, q. 173, a.2) addresses the question of whether or not a prophetic revelation communicated to a prophet is something entirely "new" to the prophet's mind or if it is more simply a new light given to the prophet. In his lengthy response to the objections, Aquinas begins with a quote from Book XII of St. Augustine's *On the Literal Meaning of Genesis* concerning that to which prophecy pertains (intellect).[44] Aquinas wrote:

> As Augustine says (*Gen. ad lit. xii*, 9), *prophetic knowledge pertains most of all to the intellect* [*mentem*]. Now two things have to be considered in connection with the knowledge possessed by the human mind, namely the acceptance or representation of things, and the judgment of the things represented.[45]

---

rior Life. Volume II. (Rockford, Illinois: TAN Books, 1989), 577-578. Hereafter *Three Ages of the Interior Life II* followed by page number. Ratzinger understood these three categories early on in his career as a theologian. See his *The Theology of History in St. Bonaventure.* (Chicago, Illinois: Franciscan Herald Press, 1971), 64-69.

44   Chapter XII of *De Genesi* is a very influential Patristic text in the Church's mystical theology as it provides the tri-partite division on the types of visions. According to G.E. Berrios and Ivana S. Marková, the reference to St. Augustine's division on visions "was to be repeated many times in the history of Christian theology…" (see article entitled "Visual hallucinations: history and context of current research" in Daniel Collerton, Urs Peter Mosimann, and Elaine Perry [edits.], *The Neuroscience of Visual Hallucinations.* [Hoboken, New Jersey: John Wiley & Sons, Ltd, 2015], 6). See also Wendy Love Anderson, *The Discernment of Spirits: Assessing Visions and Visionaries in the Late Middle Ages.* (Tübingen, Germany: Mohr Siebeck, 2011), 31.

45   John Mortensen and Enrique Alarcón, (edits.), *Summa Theologiae:*

Having established the intellect [*mentem*] (and thus knowledge [*cognitionem*]) as that to which prophecy pertains, Aquinas draws the attention of his reader to two points as to what happens with knowledge in the human mind. He specifies these two things are man's 1) accepting/representation (*acceptionem* and *repraesentationem*), and 2) the judgment (*iudicium*) of things (*rerum*).

After specifying these two things, Aquinas explains how things are represented to the human mind. He presents three ways:

> Now things are represented to the human mind under the form of species: and according to the order of nature, they must be represented first to the senses, second to the imagination, third to the passive intellect, and these are changed by the species derived from the phantasms, which change results from the enlightening action of the active intellect.[46]

For things to be represented to the human mind, Aquinas writes, the presentation is done accordingly, in the "order of nature," first to the senses.[47] It can also be presented to man's imagination, then to the passive intellect (one's understanding). Concerning one's imagination, Aquinas observes that there is information ("forms of sensible things") already in it that has been received through the senses.[48] This information can be utilized by

---

Secunda Secundae, 92-189. (Lander, Wyoming: The Aquinas Institute for the Study of Sacred Doctrine, 2012), 637. Hereafter *ST II-II* followed by page number. The corresponding Latin texts are also from the same source.

46   *ST II-II*, 637.

47   St. John of the Cross appears to build upon this idea of the senses and knowledge. See E. Allison Peers (trans.), *Ascent of Mount Carmel*. Book II, Chapter III, verse 2. (Garden City, New York: Image Books, 1958), 168ff.

48   For some discussion on knowledge and imagination, see chapter 17 (*From Sensation and Imagination to Understanding and Wisdom*) from Vivian Boland, OP, *St. Thomas Aquinas*. (London: Continuum International Publishing Group, 2007).

God in a prophetic utterance. Aquinas wrote:

> Now in the imagination there are the forms of sensible things
> not only as received from the senses, but also transformed in
> various ways, either on account of some bodily transformation
> (as in the case of people who are asleep or out of their senses),
> or through the coordination of the phantasms, at the command
> of reason, for the purpose of understanding something. For just
> as the various arrangements of the letters of the alphabet con-
> vey various ideas to the understanding, so the various coordi-
> nations of the phantasms produce various intelligible species of
> the intellect.[49]

After a discussion about judgment on a prophecy, Aquinas then
addresses how sensible forms are presented to the prophet's mind.[50] He
specifies three: 1) externally through the senses, 2) imaginary forms, and
3) those that are brought to the prophet's mind by existing forms but coordinated by divine action (i.e. a supernatural impulse). In his own words:

> Now sensible forms are divinely presented to the proph-
> et's mind, sometimes externally by means of the senses—
> thus Daniel saw the writing on the wall (Dan 5:25)—some-

---

49   *ST II-II*, 637-638.

50   It is worthwhile to point out that in his discussion on the judgment of
prophecy, Aquinas says that it is not to be reckoned as a prophecy if the mind of
the subject is not enlightened as to the matter being represented (...*non est talis
censendus propheta, nisi illuminetur eius mens ad iudicandum*....). This observation is because "judgment is the complement of knowledge" (*quia iudicium
est completivum cognitionis*). Aquinas' teaching here may shed some light on the
question as to when Sr. Lúcia received the meaning (*significado*) of the vision
that is the third part of the secret of Fátima. Either she received it in July, 1917
or at an unspecified time afterward. For a basic synopsis of this question, see
endnote iv of my article: *In Defense of the World Apostolate of Fatima* <http://
www.catholicstand.com/waf-usa-defense/> (Accessed 13 July, 2016).

times by means of imaginary forms, either of exclusively Divine origin and not received through the senses (for instance, if images of colors were imprinted on the imagination of one blind from birth), or divinely coordinated from those derived from the senses—thus Jeremiah saw the *boiling caldron...from the face of the north* (Jer 1:13)—or by the direct impression of intelligible species on the mind, as in the case of those who receive infused scientific knowledge or wisdom, such as Solomon or the apostles.[51]

Aquinas then summarized his point: "Hence it is evident that prophetic revelation is conveyed sometimes by the mere infusion of light, sometimes by imprinting species anew, or by a new coordination of species."[52]

Finally, in the answers to the objections presented at the beginning of Question 173 Article 2, Aquinas is more direct as to the action of a divine influence (supernatural impulse) upon the mind of a prophet. These replies indicate that Aquinas accepts the notion that within the imagination of man there exists forms and objects which can be used by God for the purposes of prophecy. These forms and objects are coordinated by divine influence in order to point to "intelligible truths" (*intelligibiles veritates*) beyond the mind of man, requiring the assistance of supernatural light (*necessarium est auxilium supernaturalis luminis*). He wrote:

> **Reply Obj. 1:** As stated above, sometimes in prophetic revelation imaginary species previously derived from the senses are divinely coordinated so as to according with the truth to be revealed, and then previous experience is operative in the

---

51   *ST II-II*, 638.

52   *Sic igitur patet quod prophetica revelation quandoque quidem fit per solam luminis influentiam, quandoque autem per species de novo impressas, vela liter ordinatas* (*ST II-II*, 639).

production of the images, but not when they are impressed on the mind wholly from without.

Reply Obj. 2: Intellectual vision is not effected by means of bodily and individual images, but by an intelligible image. Hence Augustine says (*De Trin.* Ix, 11) that *the soul possesses a certain likeness of the species known to it.* Sometimes this intelligible image is, in prophetic revelation, imprinted immediately by God, sometimes it results from pictures in the imagination, by the aid of prophetic light, since a deeper truth is gathered from these pictures in the imagination by means of the enlightenment of the higher light.

Reply Obj. 3: It is true that man is able by his natural powers to form all kinds of pictures in the imagination, by simply considering these pictures, but not so that they be directed to the representation of intelligible truths that surpass his intellect, since for this purpose he needs the assistance of a supernatural light.[53]

Aquinas makes it clear that there are different ways that God acts upon the mind of a prophet when it concerns prophecy. For our purposes, one of those ways is that God can make use of information in the mind of a prophet, his imagination, that had been obtained through the senses.[54] This

---

53   *ST II-II*, 639.

54   Part of the issue, it seems to this writer, with understanding the concept of *visio imaginativa* is the word "imaginative." There is a technical meaning in Aquinas and a common usage. On this point, Fr. Poulain made a helpful observation. He wrote:

> In French…it is the custom to say imaginary locutions and visions, following the Latin. If I make this change [imaginary to imaginative] it is because in our language the word imaginary nearly always means a flight of the imagination; it applies to things that are entirely non-existent, while imaginative means an act of the imagination, but one that is not inordinate. The word *imaginary* is often wrongly understood by

information is used by God to direct the mind of a prophet (what Aquinas calls "divinely coordinated" [*divinitus ordinantur*]). The information is then "directed to the representation of intelligible truths" that surpass the intellect of the prophet.[55]

Aquinas' theological anthropology corresponds to what Ratzinger writes on this subject in his *Theological Commentary*. It is, nevertheless, only one part of the puzzle as there is one further consideration.

b: Nineteenth and Twentieth Century Developments

From about the mid-nineteenth century to the present, there have been some developments in or affecting the Church's mystical theology.[56] We shall point out the rise of the psychological sciences as a primary consideration.

---

the uninstructed in these matters, because they take it in the everyday sense (*The Graces of Interior Prayer*, 299).

55   It is helpful to note that Fr. Poulain identifies five causes of error in a private revelation (*The Graces of Interior Prayer*, 323). He lists them as follows:

1. Faulty interpretations of revelations or visions,
2. Ignorance of the fact that historic events are often given with approximate truth only,
3. The mingling of human activity with supernatural action during the revelation,
4. The subsequent, but involuntary, modifications made by the person who receives the revelation, and
5. Embellishments by secretaries or compilers of the Life [i.e. writings].

Having looked at the observations made by Fr. Dhanis, it is clear that he was concerned about the third and fourth causes. It is also noteworthy that Poulain was one of Dhanis' sources (*Streven* [1944] Issue 3, pages 130, 131, 142; Issue 4, pages 210, 211, 212).

56   For some helpful background information, see the entry on "Mysticism" by T. Corbishley and J. E. Biechler in: Thomas Carson & Joann Cerrito (edits.), *The New Catholic Encyclopedia (Second Edition). Volume 10.* (Detroit, Michigan: Gale, 2003), 111-117 (particularly 115).

Within the context of a traditional Catholic examination, the question of mysticism and associated phenomena is addressed by various theological methods and structures. Proper theology is a necessary guiding light, but it was never the *sole* criterion by which the Church examined said phenomena. For example, in her processes for beatification and canonization, there has been some surprise at how thorough the Church's examinations are.[57] This impression is not simply about the theology that goes into such scrutiny, but also the Church's dependence upon other disciplines.

In the nineteenth century, the error of materialism was spreading within many western European countries and even into the Americas.[58] Materialism denied the existence of a non-material (i.e. "spiritual") world, thus anything supernatural (and, by association, preternatural) was subjected to the highest scrutiny if not ridicule. Education became an all-encompassing effort as it was largely believed that educating the mind of man would free him from "superstition."

Within the framework of materialism, the natural sciences would become an important focus within academia. Questions pertaining to the spiritual life of man were generally disfavored by adherents to materialism and anything said to be "supernatural" must, of necessity, have a natural explanation. In short, God was dethroned and man placed at the center of things. Thus, an impetus was given for the favoring/rise of various disciplines known as the "social sciences." These include areas such as psy-

---

57   Cf. John Thavis, *The Vatican Prophecies*. (New York, New York, Viking, 2015), 186-188. In this book, Thavis recounts the journey of Jacalyn Duffin, author of *Medical Miracles: Doctors, Saints, and Healing in the Modern World*. She wrote this book after ten years of research in the Vatican Archives.

58   For some considerations on Spiritualism in this history, see this author's article entitled *St. Michael and Spiritualism: A Hidden History?* <http://www.catholicstand.com/michael-spiritualism-hidden-history/>; *The Graces of Interior Prayer*, ix, 365-366. Generally speaking, some people desired to address the rising tide of rationalism and materialism that was overtaking western countries. They sought answers in the spiritual world, leading to some attention being given to various phenomena such as "table-rappings," poltergeists, etc.

chology, sociology, social studies, anthropology, etc.

Traditionally, theology and what is today called psychology, have been utilized in matters pertaining to mystical theology and associated phenomena.[59] This relationship was forced to undergo some changes in the light of the development of the social sciences from the nineteenth century onward.[60] Nevertheless, the fundamental link between these two disciplines has remained intact. Owing to this fact, various theologians have taken advantage of the developments in the social sciences in order to fine-tune the Church's processes of discerning alleged mystical phenomena.

One of the more famous theologians who took up this issue was Karl Rahner. In 1964 there appeared in English his book entitled *Inquiries*.[61] Five topics are discussed in this book, the second of which is entitled *Visions and Prophecies*. By the mid-1960s, there had already been a number of developments between the social sciences and mystical theology. Rahner, effectively, provides a summary of some of those developments

---

59   Arguably, one of the more well-known examples of this close association can be seen in the Church's Rite of Exorcism from 1614. Included in this Rite was a list of various rubrics. The third one is of particular interest to us as it clearly demonstrates that the Church requires prudence and discernment in verifying that the matter is one of possession and not a psychological ailment. See Philip T. Weller, *The Roman Ritual. Volume II.* (Boonville, New York: Preserving Christian Publications, 2013), 169.

60   The "changes" are largely due to the hostility and often venomous hatred displayed by the "free-thinkers" of the nineteenth and early twentieth centuries. They believed in the division between faith and reason. Their methodology was "charged" with many errors and anti-Catholic rhetoric. Catholics cannot accept the rejection of the supernatural, which, as we have said, was a fundamental premise of materialism. For a description of the general trends of the nineteenth century, see René Fülöp Miller, *Pope Leo XIII and Our Times.* (London: Longmans, Green and Co., 1937), 1-36.

61   Karl Rahner, *Inquiries.* (New York, New York: Herder and Herder, 1964). Hereafter *Inquiries* followed by page number. Fr. Stefano de Fiores seems to suggest a potential connection between Ratzinger and Rahner (cf. Stefano de Fiores, *Il Segreto di Fatima: Una luce sul futuro del mondo.* [Milano: San Paolo Edizioni, 2008], 15-16).

while adding his own unique perspective to the matter.[62] There is no need to recount his essay at any great length or depth and the reader is instead referred to his essay as a whole.

It is imperative to note that one of those areas of fine-tuning pertains to imaginative visions. We have seen in Aquinas' *Summa Theologiae* a foundation for a Christian anthropology. Our interest in this foundation was his writing on the nature of the supernatural impulse upon the mind of the prophet (which incorporates a theological viewpoint as well as philosophical). The social sciences, however, contribute to this knowledge by looking more in depth as to how this relationship works within the context of the human person.

In the light of these developments, Rahner indicates that imaginative visions can be caused either by a natural or a supernatural force.[63] One is, therefore, required to exercise caution and discernment before declaring something to have a supernatural character. It is not one single criterion, but rather a convergence of many that will provide a profile of the cause for the phenomenon.[64] This observation will become important further below.

---

62   There are two sources that come across as particularly influential to Rahner (*Inquiries*, 90). These are the work of A. Brenninkmeyer entitled *Traitement pastoral des névrosés* (Paris, 1947) and C.M. Staehlin, *Apariciones* (Madrid, 1954). Fr. Dhanis also appears to have influenced Rahner (cf. *Inquiries*, 95, 122, 153, 155-157, 168, 172). Rahner states on page 95 that Fr. da Fonseca's response to Dhanis "seems too unsympathetic towards a sober criticism based on the results of modern psychological research." For his part, Fr. Alonso criticizes Staehlin's book as having an "inadequate method of dealing with extraordinary phenomena in the Church" one that "totally fails" (...*envolvida num método inadequado de tratar os fenómenos extraordinários na Igreja...falha totalmente* [Joaquín María Alonso, CMF, *História da Literatura sobre Fátima*. (Fatima, Portugal: Edições Santuário, 1967), 44-45]). See also his article *Fatima y la Critica* in *Ephemerides Mariologicae* 17 (1967): 415-422.

63   Cf. *Inquiries*, 123-124. Rahner treats the question of a vision (imaginative) with natural causes but which contributes to the edification of the alleged visionary.

64   This theme of "convergence" was utilized by the CDF in *Normae S.*

It appears the link between the social sciences and the Church's doctrine on imaginative visions has undergone a little-appreciated development. This development, however, is one that has a significant impact on understanding Cardinal Ratzinger's *Theological Commentary* and deserves further study. What is necessary for the purposes of the present chapter is to formulate the basic fact of this development's existence and note that it appears to offer an alternative interpretation of the Cardinal's *Theological Commentary*.

3.) Returning to Ratzinger's *Theological Commentary*

After identifying interior perception as his primary focus, Ratzinger discusses the specifics of this perception.[65] He begins with the straightforward statement, "Interior vision does not mean fantasy, which would be no more than an expression of the subjective imagination. It means rather that the soul is touched by something real, even if beyond the senses."

It is clear in the above quote that Ratzinger does not believe the vision shown to the seers at Fátima to be a fantasy or contrived. In fact, he declared, indirectly and in theological terms, quite the opposite. He upholds that the seers were "touched by something real" that was "beyond the senses." The question, however, is how this having been "touched" by something "beyond the senses" is communicated to the three children and their expression of it.

Congregationis. In its "indicative and not exhaustive" criteria for discerning alleged private revelations (*Acta Apostolicae Sedis*, 104 [2012], 497-504, particularly page 502).

65   This discussion comes after a remark that for the visionary, "this perception certainly has the force of a presence, equivalent for that person to an external manifestation to the senses." Further discussion of the Cardinal's remarks on the individual words and images of the third part of the secret necessarily revolves around this specification of interior perception as the type of communication.

Before explaining how it is expressed, Ratzinger first points out a "limitation" that is found with interior perceptions/visions. This discussion is important because it is another side to interior perceptions which must be highlighted in order to understand more concretely the words and images of the third part of the secret of Fátima. This limitation the Cardinal identifies as the "subjective element" that is "always present" in this perception. He writes, "We do not see the pure object, but it comes to us through the filter of our senses, which carry out a work of translation."

With respect to interior visions, this subjectivity is "more evident," Ratzinger continues, and the visionary "sees insofar as he is able, in the modes of representation and consciousness available to him." Moreover, the person "shares in an essential way in the formation of the image of what appears. He can arrive at the image only within the bounds of his capacities and possibilities." The visions themselves are then "influenced by the potentialities and limitations of the perceiving subject."

Finally, if the reader did not get his point, Ratzinger summarizes the theological anthropology that he has developed. He writes that the images are, "a synthesis of the impulse coming from on high and the capacity to receive this impulse in the visionaries…." Concerning this synthesis of the visionary and the divine impulse, Rahner wrote:

> In the actual "point" at which God first affects the soul lies deeper, behind the faculties of sense-perception, if it leads primarily to a contact and union of man's spirit with God and thus to the scene of the real work of grace, then it becomes understandable and natural that the echo in man's sensibility of this interior and pivotal process will not be governed exclusively by the process itself, *but will also be influenced by all the other dispositions of the visionary* which are unconnected with this divine influence, such as elements of phantasy, patterns of perception, selective attitudes of expectation due to religious train-

ing, or the historical situation, or aesthetic taste, etc.

The content of the imaginative vision then…will inevitably represent the joint effect of the divine influence plus all the subjective dispositions of the visionary (emphases mine).[66]

We see in the text of the third part of the secret a helpful example of the Cardinal's point and observations.

In the description of the angels sprinkling the figures in the vision, Sr. Lúcia used the Portuguese word *regador* to refer to the object used to sprinkle the blood. *Regador* quite literally means a "watering can."[67] Are we to believe that an angel used a mundane object as a watering can to sprinkle the blood of the martyrs? Certainly not as it is very unbecoming and would, in fact, call into question the character of the vision. This is not a fitting ecclesiastical term and so the English translator(s) rendered it as "*aspersorium*."[68]

If one were to look at the text in question from Sr. Lúcia using only a theological lens, one would have to conclude that there is no supernatural origin. It employs what is ridiculous at face value. To avoid having to make this conclusion, one is then necessarily forced to look at the circumstances of the visionary and this is where the anthropological component of private revelation offers assistance. Sr. Lúcia's shepherdess upbringing was still prominent at the time she wrote down the text in 1944 at age 36. Though she had learned to read and write, this is not the same as having

---

66   *Inquiries*, 144-145.

67   Elbert L. Richardson, Maria de Lourdes Sá Pereira and Milton Sá Pereira (edits.), *McKay's Modern Portuguese-English and English-Portuguese Dictionary*. (New York: David McKay Company, Inc., 1943), 151.

68   *The Message of Fatima*, 21. The Italian translation rendered it as "con un innaffiatoio di cristallo nella mano..." (Congregazione per la Dottrina della Fede, *Il Messaggio di Fatima*. [Citta del Vaticano: Supplemento a L'Osservatore Romano, numero 147 del 26-27 giugno 2000]), 21. For more of a detailed linguistic study of Sr. Lúcia's writing, see Antonio Socci, *The Fourth Secret of Fatima* (Fitzwilliams, New Hampshire: Loreto Publications, 2009), 229-236.

received a *refined* education.[69]

Sr. Lúcia used the best word she knew, even as a grown woman, to describe the object held by the angels. Some interpretation was necessary—a filter, if you will—that the anthropological component of private revelation addressed. In so doing, one does not conclude that a literal watering can was used by an angel to sprinkle the blood of the martyrs. One concludes that Sr. Lúcia "saw" the object but lacked the word necessary to identify it accurately and used the closest one she knew. This is an example of the "subjective disposition" of the visionary in conjunction with the divine impulse acting upon her.

To summarize the preceding discussion, Cardinal Ratzinger upholds as supernatural the vision seen by the seers of Fátima. What they saw was communicated in an interior vision, which is an objective supernatural reality with a strong subjective component. That subjective component is that the subject (i.e. "visionary") receives the supernatural vision in accordance with his or her own "capacities and possibilities." In other words, the vision is filtered through one's subjective experiences such as education and understanding.[70]

An underlying component of this discussion is that Cardinal Ratzinger bases himself upon another observation from Aquinas. Aquinas taught, "For it is clear that whatever is received into something is received according to the condition of the recipient" (*Summa Theologiae* Ia, q. 75, a. 5).[71] Things of the supernatural are not always easy to translate into human language, as

---

69   Cf. Carmelo de Santa Teresa – Coimbra, *Um Caminho sob o Olhar de Maria: Biografia da Irmã Lúcia de Jesus e do Coração Imaculado, O.C.D.* (Coimbra, Portugal: Edições Carmelo, 2013), 128-138.

70   See also Ratzinger's discussion on this very point in May, 2010 as Pope Benedict XVI during his flight to Portugal: <http://w2.vatican.va/content/benedict-xvi/en/speeches/2010/may/documents/hf_ben-xvi_spe_20100511_portogallo-interview.html> (Accessed 14 May, 2016).

71   John Mortensen and Enrique Alarcón, (edits.), *Summa Theologiae: Prima Pars, 50-119.* (Lander, Wyoming: The Aquinas Institute for the Study of Sacred Doctrine, 2012), 216. See also Cardinal Tarcisio Bertone, *The Last Secret of Fatima.* (New York: Doubleday, 2008), 40-42.

251

the history and tradition of the Church have long demonstrated.[72] Consider Sr. Lúcia's own words from her *Third Memoir* about the events of July, 1917:

> ...Keeping silent has been a great grace for me. What about the revelation of hell? *I can't even find the exact words to explain its reality. What I say is nothing, it only gives a vague idea of it.* What would have happened if I had said one thing this time and another that time trying in vain to explain myself. I might have caused such a confusion of ideas as, perhaps, to hinder God's work. For this very reason I thank God and find that He does everything well.
>
> Ordinarily God causes an interior and exact discernment of their meaning to accompany His revelations. *But I don't dare to speak about this for fear of being led by my imagination, which, in my opinion, can very easily happen.* Jacinta seemed to have this discernment to an extremely high degree (emphases mine).[73]

After explaining the nature of interior visions, only then does Ratzinger explain the individual components of the vision that is the third part of the secret. As we indicated earlier, he goes through most of the vision before his remark on the images that Sr. Lúcia may have seen from devotional books.[74] Having examined both Ratzinger's theological anthro-

---

72   Cf. Pope St. Gregory the Great, *Moralia in Job, Volume I, Parts I and II.* (Ex Fontibus Company, 2012), 9-10.

73   Dr. Antonio Maria Martins, S.J., *Memórias e Cartas de Irmã Lúcia.* (Porto, Portugal: Simão Guimarães, Filhos, LDA, 1973), 235. Hereafter *Memórias e Cartas de Irmã Lúcia* followed by page number.

74   At the time of the vision in July, 1917, Sr. Lúcia apparently did not know how to read. Her illiteracy is implied by the very command of Our Lady for Lúcia to learn to read (...*e que aprendam a ler*) during the June, 1917 apparition (*Memórias e Cartas de Irmã Lúcia*, 335). This fact gives cause for one to ask the following question, how could Sr. Lúcia have described the vision in terms of images she may have seen in a devotional book when she was clearly

pology and some potential sources behind it, the intention behind the remark may be clearer.

Ratzinger clearly could not have been accusing Sr. Lúcia of inventing the vision. That would contradict his earlier upholding of the vision as supernatural. What he *does* is offer an explanation that appears to be deeply rooted in the Church's mystical theology, including more recent developments. Ratzinger explains that Sr. Lúcia may have seen such images in a devotional book, and, then, while experiencing a supernatural impulse, God made use of (i.e. "divinely coordinated") the images already in her mind. Describing the vision in this way is not the same to say that the *origin* of the vision came from devotional books.

In the larger perspective, the origin of the vision would have come with the supernatural impulse that Sr. Lúcia received in July, 1917. God, however, would have then "coordinated" the existing images in her mind "so as to accord with the truth to be revealed" thus making "previous experience [sic] operative in the production of the images..." (ST II-II, q. 173, a. 2).[75]

---

illiterate at the time of the communicating of the vision?

The reader is encouraged to keep in mind a couple of points. First, Ratzinger specifies *images* (*immagini*) not *words* that Lúcia may have seen. Secondly, Lúcia herself wrote about how her mother, Maria Rosa, was a respected person in the community and a catechist (*Memórias e Cartas de Irmã Lúcia*, 93-95). Lúcia even provides a quote from her mother (Ibid., 93) which indicates that her mother had a number of books about faith stories and the lives of the Saints. It is *possible* that at least some of these books may have contained images. Even if they did not, Maria Rosa may have been quite capable of using the things around her to provide illustrations in her catechesis.

75   Aquinas further states in the passage a possibility that images can be given to the mind of a prophet entirely from outside of his imagination. He wrote, "...but not when they are impressed on the mind wholly from without." Though Ratzinger speaks hypothetically ("...may have seen" [*può avere visto*]), it would be difficult to accept the notion that the Cardinal encompasses the possibility of the images being given to Sr. Lúcia "entirely from without." For some further considerations on this point, see *Inquiries*, 146. Rahner discusses the impossibility "in principle" of separating the "content of a vision" from a "seer's subjective limitations."

If one understands the *Theological Commentary* of Cardinal Ratzinger in the above light, it is possible to look differently at the influence of Dhanis than was previously assumed. There is a larger tradition of literature on mystical phenomena which includes more recent developments in the social sciences.

While beyond our present scope, even a cursory glance at Dhanis' own writings demonstrate that he himself was influenced by that same larger tradition and subsequent developments. He then applied these things to the case of Fátima for what appeared to be the first time.[76] Dhanis thus established himself (unwittingly) as the founder of critical scholarship on Fátima.[77]

Theologians are to keep sober and critical eyes upon mystical phenomena as part of their evaluation. It is not surprising, therefore, if Dhanis becomes a "filter" or "prism" through which later writers will apply critical methodology with respect to Fátima. It is undeniable that Ratzinger's citation on page 35 of *The Message of Fatima* is a clear indication of Dhanis' influence. The question is, however, *how much* influence did he exert upon Ratzinger on page 42? It does not appear as though he exerted any more than what can be considered reasonable from one accomplished theologian to another.

V. Conclusion

This chapter has sought to examine the claim that the Jesuit priest, Fr. Edouard Dhanis, influenced in two places the *Theological Commentary* of Joseph Cardinal Ratzinger on the message of Fátima. We have seen that indeed, there was some influence exerted by Dhanis upon Ratzinger.

---

76   The present chapter does not seek to address the accuracy of his criticisms.

77   In making his critical observations, Dhanis made himself a target. Insofar as his scholarship is concerned, it could be applied to any other case. Why such responses were issued against Dhanis, Rahner offers some perspective (*Inquiries*, 89-94).

This influence is in the concrete fact that he was cited *once* by the Cardinal in the *Commentary* on a matter pertaining to a larger theology of private revelation expressed by Dhanis. Nothing of the Jesuit's controversial Fatima I/Fatima II "thesis" was cited or necessarily expressed by Ratzinger.

Ratzinger's *Theological Commentary* displays a deep perspective on the theology of private revelation. It is clear from the preceding examination that there is a larger tradition of literature on this theology. Ratzinger may have composed his *Commentary* from this larger tradition. In support of this position, we have employed the writings of St. Thomas Aquinas on anthropology and prophecy in his *Summa Theologiae*. These writings clearly incorporate important and delicate Scholastic terms and venues, developed by later writers.

If Dhanis were to have influenced Ratzinger's *Commentary* any further than the one and only citation to him, such might not be as significant as has been previously thought. Fr. Dhanis' own writings on private revelation appear to be intimately affected by the larger tradition of literature on the topic. If Ratzinger also were to have written from this larger tradition, it is not unreasonable to expect these two theologians drawing upon the same source(s) to have points of agreement. Thus, one may be able to speak in terms of a "proximate" and "remote" influence of the Jesuit upon Ratzinger.

On a final note, the fact is reiterated that there is some room for scholarly debate on the writings of Fr. Dhanis. There exists little of his writings in the English language for study and competent persons with an interest in the topic are encouraged to assist English-speaking theologians. While the present chapter does not seek to be an exhaustive treatment of the matter, it is hoped that an impetus has been provided for further charitable discussion and debate. Meanwhile, Ratzinger has said more about Fátima that has raised some notable questions. We shall endeavor to examine these remarks in the next chapter.

—11—
POPE BENEDICT XVI
AND FÁTIMA

"We would be mistaken to think that Fatima's prophetic mission is complete."

—Pope Benedict XVI, May 13, 2010

Upon the death of Pope John Paul II in April, 2005, Cardinal Ratzinger succeeded him as Pope Benedict XVI. In 2010, Benedict made an Apostolic Voyage to Portugal. During this Voyage, the Holy Father made some comments that some people understood as Benedict "repudiating" a position he held in the year 2000.[1] In this year, Benedict, as Cardinal Ratzinger, stated in his *Theological Commentary* that the events contained in the

---

1   For an example of this characterization, see Christopher A. Ferrara, *The Secret Still Hidden: Epilogue* (Canada: Good Counsel Publications, 2010), 46ff. Hereafter *The Secret Still Hidden: Epilogue* followed by page number. This is a little booklet meant to serve as an epilogue to Ferrara's larger work entitled *The Secret Still Hidden*. The booklet is also available on the Internet: <http://www.secretstillhidden.com/pdf/epilogue.pdf> (Accessed 23 May, 2016). See also the article entitled "Pope Benedict XVI Vindicates Fatima Center" in *The Fatima Crusader* 95 (Summer 2010), pages 3-10. This article is available online: <http://www.fatimacrusader.com/cr95/cr95pg3.pdf> (Accessed 23 May, 2016). See also pages 11-15 of this same edition for an article by Antonio Socci entitled "So There Was a 'Fourth' Secret After All."

third part of the secret have been fulfilled.[2] In 2010, Benedict stated that it is a mistake to think that the prophetic message of Fátima is completed.[3]

Did Benedict repudiate his earlier statement? The present chapter endeavors to look at this question. To begin, it is necessary to recount what took place in the year 2000, then to look at the events of 2010.

I. The Disclosing of the Secret—May/June 2000

On May 13, 2000, Pope John Paul II was in Fátima for the Beatification of Jacinta and Francisco Marto. At the end of the Mass, Cardinal Angelo Sodano, announced (in Portuguese) the impending release of the third part of the secret. He proceeded to give a synopsis of the contents of the third part, during which the Cardinal made the following statement:

> The successive events of 1989 led, both in the Soviet Union and in a number of countries of Eastern Europe, to the fall of the Communist regimes which promoted atheism. For this too His Holiness offers heartfelt thanks to the Most Holy Virgin. In other parts of the world, however, attacks against the Church and against Christians, with the burden of suffering they bring, tragically continue. Even if the events to which the third part of the "secret" of Fatima refers now seem part of the past, Our Lady's call to conversion and penance, issued at the start of the twentieth century, remains timely and urgent today.... [4]

---

2   Congregation for the Doctrine of the Faith, *The Message of Fatima.* (Vatican City: Libreria Editrice Vaticana, 2000), 43. Hereafter referred to as *The Message of Fatima* followed by page number.

3   *Acta Apostolicae Sedis* 102 (2010), 327.

4   *The Message of Fatima*, 31. The original Portuguese, to which we shall occasionally refer, is as follows:

Depois, os acontecimentos de 1989 levaram, quer na União Soviética

The line for our consideration is "Even if the events...etc."

On the surface, it would seem that the Cardinal was relegating Fátima to the past. For if the events that pertained to the third part of the secret already happened then there is nothing further to be said, no further expectation of future events. About a month and a half later, in his *Theological Commentary* on the text, Cardinal Ratzinger affirmed the assertion. The Cardinal wrote:

> And so we come to the final question: What is the meaning of the "secret" of Fatima as a whole (in its three parts)? What does it say to us? First of all we must affirm with Cardinal Sodano: "... the events to which the third part of the 'secret' of Fatima refers now seem part of the past". Insofar as individual events are described, they belong to the past. Those who expected exciting apocalyptic revelations about the end of the world or the future course of history are bound to be disappointed. Fatima does not satisfy our curiosity in this way, just as Christian faith in general cannot be reduced to an object of mere curiosity. What remains was already evident when we began our reflections on the text of the "secret": the exhortation to prayer as the path of "salvation for souls" and,

---

quer em numerosos Países do Leste, à queda do regime comunista que propugnava o ateísmo. O Sumo Pontífice agradece do fundo do coração à Virgem Santíssima também por isso. Mas, noutras partes do mundo, os ataques contra a Igreja e os cristãos, com a carga de sofrimento que eles provocam, infelizmente não cessaram. Embora os acontecimentos a que faz referência a terceira parte do « segredo » de Fátima pareçam pertencer já ao passado, o apelo à conversão e à penitência, manifestado por Nossa Senhora ao início do século vinte, conserva ainda hoje uma estimulante actualidade...(<http://www.vatican.va/roman_curia/congregations/cfaith/documents/rc_con_cfaith_doc_20000626_message-fatima_po.html> [Accessed 14 May, 2016]).

likewise, the summons to penance and conversion.[5]

In the above text, Cardinal Ratzinger affirms (*dobbiamo affermare*) the assertion expressed by Cardinal Sodano that the events referred to in the third part of the secret now seem to be part of the past. Notice, however, between the two statements of Sodano and Ratzinger that both Cardinals do not end their respective discussion on a conclusive note. They continued by doing the *exact opposite*. They discuss what "remains" of the Fátima message, citing Our Lady's exhortation (*esortazione*) to prayer and her call (*apelo/richiamo*) to prayer, penance and conversion.

At the heart of the respective texts of both Cardinals is prophecy. Therefore, it is important to offer a cursory examination on the nature of prophecy as much of the Cardinals' discussion (particularly Ratzinger's) hinges around this point.[6] First, let us define "prophecy."

---

5   *The Message of Fatima*, 43. The Italian text reads as follows:

Siamo così giunti ad un'ultima domanda: Che cosa significa nel suo insieme (nelle sue tre parti) il « segreto » di Fatima? Che cosa dice a noi? Innanzitutto dobbiamo affermare con il Cardinale Sodano: « ... le vicende a cui fa riferimento la terza parte del « segreto » di Fatima sembrano ormai appartenere al passato ». Nella misura in cui singoli eventi vengono rappresentati, essi ormai appartengono al passato. Chi aveva atteso eccitanti rivelazioni apocalittiche sulla fine del mondo o sul futuro corso della storia, deve rimanere deluso. Fatima non ci offre tali appagamenti della nostra curiosità, come del resto in generale la fede cristiana non vuole e non può essere pastura per la nostra curiosità. Ciò che rimane l'abbiamo visto subito all'inizio delle nostre riflessioni sul testo del «segreto»: l'esortazione alla preghiera come via per la « salvezza delle anime » e nello stesso senso il richiamo alla penitenza e alla conversione (Congregazione per la Dottrina della Fede, *Il Messaggio di Fatima*. [Vatican City: L'Osservatore Romano, 2000], 43. This is a copy distributed by *L'Osservatore Romano* as a supplement to this publication [number 147, June 26-27 June, 2000]).

6   Though Cardinal Sodano does not use the word "prophecy" in his announcement of May 13, 2000, the topic is, undoubtedly, present insofar as Sodano is talking about the third part of the secret. The present chapter includes

A: The Nature of Prophecy

Contemporary western culture facilitates one to think of prophecy solely in terms of the foretelling of future events. The Catholic tradition, however, offers a broader view. For example, according to the definition of prophecy given by St. Thomas Aquinas, prophecy is not simply the telling of future events. Rather, it "...first and chiefly consists in knowledge, because, to wit, prophets know things that are far *(procul)* removed from man's knowledge [*cognitione*]" (*Summa Theologica* II:II q. 171, a.1).[7]

Aquinas' explanation characterizes prophecy as knowledge given to a person by God that is beyond his or her capacity to know. This knowledge *could* pertain to specific future events, but is not, strictly speaking, consigned *only* to such demonstrations. It could also be, for example (and as is demonstrated by the apparitions of Our Lady in 1917), that knowledge of the state of deceased persons could be communicated.[8] Such knowledge is certainly "far removed" from anything man can know on earth unless it is communicated by supernatural means.

Cardinal Ratzinger appears to build his discussion on prophecy from the above broader Catholic tradition. In his *Theological Commentary*, Ratzinger discusses both the place and nature of prophecy in the Church. After clarifying the nature of private revelation with respect to Divine Revelation, Ratzinger states the following:

Sodano with Ratzinger's more complete discussion of prophecy for the sake of convenience, while recognizing that Ratzinger's *Commentary* is of more interest to the topic.

7 John Mortensen and Enrique Alarcón, (edits.), *Summa Theologiae: Secunda Secundae, 92-189.* (Lander, Wyoming: The Aquinas Institute for the Study of Sacred Doctrine, 2012), 610.

8 Dr. Antonio Maria Martins, S.J., *Memórias e Cartas de Irmã Lúcia.* (Porto, Portugal: Simão Guimarães, Filhos, LDA, 1973), 331. Hereafter *Memórias e Cartas de Irmã Lúcia* followed by page number

In every age the Church has received the charism of prophecy, which must be scrutinized but not scorned. On this point, it should be kept in mind that *prophecy in the biblical sense does not mean to predict the future but to explain the will of God for the present, and therefore show the right path to take for the future.* A person who foretells what is going to happen responds to the curiosity of the mind, which wants to draw back the veil on the future. *The prophet speaks to the blindness of will and of reason, and declares the will of God as an indication and demand for the present time. In this case, prediction of the future is of secondary importance.* What is essential is the actualization of the definitive Revelation, which concerns me at the deepest level. The prophetic word is a warning or a consolation, or both together. In this sense there is a link between the charism of prophecy and the category of "the signs of the times", which Vatican II brought to light anew: "You know how to interpret the appearance of earth and sky; why then do you not know how to interpret the present time?" (*Lk* 12:56). In this saying of Jesus, the "signs of the times" must be understood as the path he was taking, indeed it must be understood as Jesus himself. To interpret the signs of the times in the light of faith means to recognize the presence of Christ in every age. In the private revelations approved by the Church—and therefore also in Fatima—this is the point: they help us to understand the signs of the times and to respond to them rightly in faith (*emphases mine*).[9]

In the above discussion, Ratzinger is employing the broader understanding

---

9   *The Message of Fatima*, 36. See also Ratzinger's discussion in his *Jesus of Nazareth: From the Baptism in the Jordan to the Transfiguration*. (San Francisco: Ignatius Press, 2007), 1-8.

of prophecy. He speaks in terms of how it explains "the will of God for the present" and thus points out "the right path to take for the future."[10]

Our Lady did not appear in Fátima in order to foretell future events. Her primary aim was to call wayward men back to the Gospel of her Son. She revealed future events insofar as they pertained to this call. She begins from the start of her appearances (May, 1917) with the request that the children come every thirteenth of the month and to ask if they are willing to offer (sacrifice) themselves for God.[11] Each subsequent appearance confirms this call and we see its manifestation in the lives of the children as they underwent many sufferings.[12]

Having established a foundation for understanding how prophecy is used and/or understood by Cardinals Sodano and Ratzinger, one must next examine their interpretation of the third part of the secret. Before doing so, let us remember that prophecy is primarily about communicating to man's knowledge what is the will of God for the present; it is not intended to be restricted only to the predicting of future events.

B: Prophecy and the "Events" of Fátima

It is clear from their respective discussions that both Sodano and Ratzinger interpret the "events" (*os acontecimentos/singoli eventi*) shown by Our Lady in the third part of the secret as pertaining to events taking place in the twentieth century.[13] It is clear that intimately connected with this interpretation is the belief that the Pope is the principal figure of the

---

10   Fr. Nicholas Gruner himself affirmed this understanding of prophecy in his preface to Christopher Ferrara's book *False Friends of Fatima*. (Pound Ridge, New York: Good Counsel Publications, 2012), xvi-xvii.

11   *Memórias e Cartas de Irmã Lúcia*, 331-333.

12   Cf. *Memórias e Cartas de Irmã Lúcia*, 113, 127, 129ff.

13   Cf. *The Message of Fatima*, 41 & 43.

vision.[14] Moreover, the assassination attempt of May 13, 1981 is interpreted as being the *culmination* of the image in the vision of an attack against the Pope.[15]

In the above interpretation, the Cardinals appear to change slightly their discussion to include the "future" component of prophecy. These "events" are future events insofar as they were shown to the children in 1917 when said events had not yet come to pass. At the revealing of the third part of the secret in the year 2000, the impact of these events was significantly lessened.[16] The impact of the text having been lessened with the passage of time is why Ratzinger wrote the following at the beginning of his *Theological Commentary*:

A careful reading of the text of the so-called third "secret" of

---

14   *The Message of Fatima*, 28.

15   *The Message of Fatima*, 29, 31-32, 40-42. The word "culmination" is herein chosen in order to reflect the fact that the assassination attempt does not necessarily "fulfill" the vision. In her May, 1982 letter to the Holy Father, Sr. Lucia herself indicated that there may yet be more to the secret (*The Message of Fatima*, 9).

16   This observation is important because of the earlier observations of Sodano and Ratzinger who, speaking at the end of the twentieth century, refer to the prophesied events as now seeming to be part of the past (cf. *The Message of Fatima*, 31 & 43). In 1917, the events had not yet occurred in their fullness. Both Cardinals employ the hypothetical language of "seems" (*pareçam pertencer* in the Portuguese and *sembrano ormai appartenere* in the Italian), though Ratzinger goes a step further and states unequivocally that the specific prophesied events of the third part of the secret are now fulfilled. Ratzinger, after quoting Sodano in Italian translation from the Portuguese, continues in his own words to specify that "Insofar as individual events are described, they belong to the past" (*Nella misura in cui singoli eventi vengono rappresentati, essi ormai appartengono al passato*) and thus removes any doubt as to where he at least stands on this particular point. It is also to be noted that Sodano prefaced his words with the Portuguese conjunction *embora* (translated by the Vatican as "Even if" when a more literal translation would be "although"), and Ratzinger leaves out mention of this conjunction in his citation.

Fatima, published here in its entirety long after the fact and by decision of the Holy Father, will probably prove disappointing or surprising after all the speculation it has stirred. No great mystery is revealed; nor is the future unveiled. We see the Church of the martyrs of the century which has just passed represented in a scene described in a language which is symbolic and not easy to decipher.[17]

A hasty reading of Ratzinger would be to mistake his point on how "no great mystery is revealed" or having the "future unveiled" as saying that the third part of the secret does not predict the future, or even that they still pertain to future events.[18] These comments are meant to be understood from the perspective of the year 2000 when said events were interpreted—rightly or wrongly—as having been fulfilled. Reading Ratzinger in this way is confirmed at the end of his *Commentary* when he writes about the events belonging to the past.[19]

Though the Cardinals appear on this point to be speaking of prophecy in its restricted sense, this is not to the exclusion of the broader definition. The broader definition is presented in that both Cardinals recognize that the message of Fátima, and even in the third part of the secret, is primarily about penance and conversion. This aspect contains the will of God being manifested to the mind of man, namely that man is to convert and do penance for his sins. As this aspect of the message relates to the call of the Gospel, it is timeless and thus not restricted to a specific historical period.

---

17   *The Message of Fatima*, 32.

18   For a modest example of the latter reading of Pope Benedict's words, see *The Secret Still Hidden: Epilogue*, 46-47. It should also be noted that even though Ferrara clearly states on page 47 that he is providing only the "relevant" parts of the Pope's response, there is much subjectivity as to what was "relevant." Ferrara leaves out much of the preceding text that provided context to the remarks quoted by Ferrara.

19   Ibid., 43.

It is based upon the above critical distinction between "future events" and the "call to prayer and penance" that much of the Sodano/Ratzinger interpretation depends. To be clear, we are specifying the assertion that the events in the third part of the secret "seem" to pertain to the past. As to whether or not the prophesied events have taken place, the Cardinals are simply either correct or incorrect. If the former is the case, then there is no question—the prophecies contained within the third part of the secret have been fulfilled.[20] If the latter is true, then the question is re-opened as to the fulfillment of the events foretold in the vision.

C: Events of Fátima Fulfilled?

Sr. Lúcia, in her May, 1982 letter to Pope John Paul II, clearly states that the vision pertains to the spread of Russia's errors, the persecution of the Church and the suffering of the Holy Father—events that did take place in the twentieth century. She wrote:

> The third part of the secret refers to Our Lady's words: "If not [Russia] will spread her errors throughout the world, causing wars and persecutions of the Church. The good will

---

20   The presentation given within the book *The Message of Fatima* provides internal evidence for the claim that the third part of the secret pertains to events of the twentieth century. This is explicitly given on page 28 where it says, "[Sr. Lúcia] repeated her conviction that the vision of Fatima concerns above all the struggle of atheistic Communism against the Church and against Christians, and describes the terrible sufferings of the victims of the faith in the twentieth century." The editor of *The Message of Fatima*, however, does not provide the reader with a precise quote. Also of note is the lack of a citation to a reference when Sr. Lúcia had made such a statement in the past (i.e. when we are told that she "repeated her conviction"). These are not, however, insurmountable obstacles, nor should they be read from a hermeneutic of suspicion and conspiracy. This hermeneutic displays lack of trust and is, indirectly at least, an accusation directed at ecclesiastical Authority of its having malicious intent and a deliberate will to deceive the public.

be martyred; the Holy Father will have much to suffer; various nations will be annihilated" (13-VII-1917).

The third part of the secret is a symbolic revelation, referring to this part of the Message, conditioned by whether we accept or not what the Message itself asks of us: "If my requests are heeded, Russia will be converted, and there will be peace; if not, she will spread her errors throughout the world, etc.".

Since we did not heed this appeal of the Message, we see that it has been fulfilled, Russia has invaded the world with her errors. And if we have not yet seen the complete fulfilment of the final part of this prophecy, we are going towards it little by little with great strides. If we do not reject the path of sin, hatred, revenge, injustice, violations of the rights of the human person, immorality and violence, etc....[21]

Furthermore, as Ratzinger wrote in his *Commentary*, "the interpretation offered by Cardinal Sodano" was put to Sr. Lúcia who stated that it "corresponded to what she had experienced and that on her part she thought the interpretation correct."[22]

While the Sodano/Ratzinger interpretation enjoys some notable support, it is also true that there are open questions. In keeping with truth, people are free to examine the facts and form their own opinion but there

---

21   *The Message of Fatima*, 8-9.

22   Ibid., 39. Also on this page are two sentences that now appear to contradict new information that has arisen concerning what Sr. Lúcia knew and understood of the third part of the secret. Cardinal Ratzinger states "Sister Lucia responded by pointing out that she had received the vision but not its interpretation. The interpretation, she said, belonged not to the visionary but to the Church." As we have elsewhere discussed, Sr. Lúcia may have received some understanding of the vision's meaning. To explain the apparent discrepancy, one would be wise to look at Ratzinger's statement and ask whether or not it was Ratzinger's thought or a statement by Sr. Lúcia when it is noted she was "pointing out that she had received the vision, etc."

is one matter which is not treated at length by Sodano and Ratzinger.[23] If we take Sr. Lúcia's May, 1982 letter at face value, then she has effectively provided a hermeneutical key to understand better (though, perhaps, not completely) the vision. She states that it pertains to the spread of Russia's errors, the persecution of the Church and the suffering of the Holy Father.[24]

From this hermeneutical key arises a question: do the *effects* of Russia's errors having been spread still affect the world in the twenty-first century?[25] The question poses a dilemma. If someone were to answer that said errors still do affect the world today, how can one say that the events

---

23   Cardinal Sodano quickly acknowledges this matter at the beginning of the earlier-cited text. He said:

> The successive events of 1989 led, both in the Soviet Union and in a number of countries of Eastern Europe, to the fall of the Communist regimes which promoted atheism....In other parts of the world, however, attacks against the Church and against Christians, with the burden of suffering they bring, tragically continue.

Sodano restricts his remarks to the fall of Communism beginning in 1989 *in the Soviet Union and in a number of countries of Eastern Europe*. He does *not* state a global collapse of the regime (as is evidenced by China and Cuba, for example). He is, indirectly at best, acknowledging that Communism itself is not a thing of the past. This indirect admission provides ground to question the Sodano/Ratzinger interpretation herein being discussed.

24   In his *Theological Commentary*, Cardinal Ratzinger reports that Sr. Lúcia had stated that she was never given an interpretation of the vision (*The Message of Fatima*, 39; see also page 29). If she was never given an interpretation, how, then, did she know that it pertained to Our Lady's words about the spread of Russia's errors? This question may be answered in the fact that Sister was given some understanding of it according to a journal entry written by Sister and published in 2013 (Carmelo de Santa Teresa – Coimbra, *Um Caminho sob o Olhar de Maria: Biografia da Irmã Lúcia de Jesus e do Coração Imaculado, O.C.D.* [Coimbra, Portugal: Edições Carmelo, 2013], 266).

25   To this end, Christopher Ferrara poses a thoughtful question on pages 74-75 of his book *The Secret Still Hidden* (Pound Ridge, New York: Good Counsel Publications, 2008). Hereafter *The Secret Still Hidden* followed by page number.

are fulfilled when it would appear that they are still *being* fulfilled/playing out? On the other hand, if one were to answer that we are *not* affected today, how does one explain the continued wars and persecutions of the Church and of the Holy Father?[26] Are such events connected to the spread of Russia's errors or is this an unwarranted presumption? In total, these are questions that must be addressed by Fátima scholars.

In the end, what appears to be the difficulty with the above reading of Sodano and Ratzinger is whether or not one agrees with their assertion that the specific prophecies are fulfilled. Regardless of one's take, one thing is clear: at no time does either Cardinal say that Fátima *per se* is "over." Fátima *is still part of the life of the Church* in that we are exhorted to prayer and conversion. In this light, it is erroneous to claim that either Cardinal consigned Fátima to the proverbial "dustbin of history."[27] In fact, they did the *exact opposite* and actually kept alive the heart of the call of Fátima. In so doing, they corrected an error that emphasizes the prophecies of Fátima on future events to the detriment of its call to repentance and the salvation of souls.[28]

---

26   The fact that Russia has spread her errors is not in question as such did happen historically, thus this prophecy would be fulfilled. The question remains, however, as to the *continued effect* in the world of these errors. If the effect continues, then there would appear to be an *ongoing* character to this specific prophecy, thus questioning the Sodano/Ratzinger interpretation. Ratzinger may have foreseen this potential difficulty. It is possible that his statement "Insofar as *individual events* are described, they belong to the past" (*emphases mine*) could be understood as qualifying in nature.

27   See the remark in an article by Iain Colquhoun entitled "The Impending World Crisis" in *The Fatima Crusader* (Spring 2010), Issue 94, page 57. See also *The Secret Still Hidden*, 65. One must be careful to make a distinction between the assertion of Sodano and Ratzinger that the events foretold in the third part of the secret have taken place from the assertion of their critics that they have consigned Fátima to the "dustbin of history." To the former, as we've said above, there are some open questions but to the latter there is no debate.

28   Conversely, the Cardinals also sent a subtle message to the "progressivism" tendency (as discussed by Fr. Alonso) that Fátima's message of prayer

Having examined the respective remarks by Cardinals Sodano and Ratzinger in the light of the Catholic understanding of prophecy, we are now in a position to discuss the remarks of Pope Benedict XVI in May, 2010 to which we shall now turn our attention.

II. *Pope Benedict XVI* & Fátima—*May 11, 2010*

In May, 2010, Pope Benedict travelled to Portugal on an Apostolic Voyage during which he visited Fátima. The first significant event of this Voyage was the Papal interview aboard the plane on May 11.[29] The Vatican spokesman, Fr. Federico Lombardi, S.J. posed some questions to the Holy Father. During this question and answer session, the topic of Fátima was raised. The exchange began with the following question from Fr. Lombardi:

Thank you, and now [we] come to Fatima, in some way the culmination, even spiritually, of this visit. Your Holiness, what meaning do the Fatima apparitions have for us today? In June 2000, when you presented the text of the third secret in the Vatican Press Office, a number of us and our former colleagues were present. You were asked if the message could be extended, beyond the attack on John Paul II, to other sufferings on the part of the Popes. Is it possible, to your mind, to include in that

and conversion remains and, by implication, ought to be fulfilled in their own lives.

29   This interview does not seem to have been included in the Holy See's official journal, the *Acta Apostolicae Sedis*. It was, however, transcribed and made available on the web site of the Holy See, translated from the original Italian into several languages: <http://w2.vatican.va/content/benedict-xvi/it/speeches/2010/may/documents/hf_ben-xvi_spe_20100511_portogallo-interview.html> (Accessed 14 May, 2016). For the claim that the interview was conducted in Italian, the Eternal Word Television Network (EWTN) stated such on its web site: <http://www.ewtn.com/library/papaldoc/b16portflght.htm> (Accessed 14 May, 2016).

vision the sufferings of the Church today for the sins involving the sexual abuse of minors?[30]

First of note is the precise question that is posed to Pope Benedict. The Holy Father is asked two questions that are related to each other (the second being an elaboration of the first and with a specific example). The questions are:

1. "[W]hat meaning do the Fatima apparitions have for us today?"
2. "Is it possible…to include in that vision [the third part of the secret] the sufferings of the Church today for the sins involving the sexual abuse of minors?"

Both questions depend upon each other for proper context. It is clear, however, that Fr. Lombardi is asking the Holy Father to give his opinion on whether or not the vision of the third part of the secret of Fátima—as it was revealed in the year 2000—could have relevance to later events in the 21st century. Lombardi specifies the sexual abuse of minors as an example.[31]

Pope Benedict's response to the questions is interesting as it is consistent with his previous statement on the third part of the secret as given

---

30   <http://w2.vatican.va/content/benedict-xvi/en/speeches/2010/may/documents/hf_ben-xvi_spe_20100511_portogallo-interview.html> (Accessed 14 May, 2016). The Italian original reads as follows:

> Grazie, e ora veniamo a Fatima, dove sarà un po' il culmine anche spirituale di questo viaggio. Santità, quale significato hanno oggi per noi le Apparizioni di Fatima? E quando Lei presentò il testo del terzo segreto nella Sala Stampa Vaticana, nel giugno 2000, c'erano diversi di noi e altri colleghi di allora, Le fu chiesto se il messaggio poteva essere esteso, al di là dell'attentato a Giovanni Paolo II, anche alle altre sofferenze dei Papi. E' possibile, secondo Lei, inquadrare anche in quella visione le sofferenze della Chiesa di oggi, per i peccati degli abusi sessuali sui minori?

31   Let us remember that the sexual abuse of minors by members of the clergy in the Catholic Church was not a phenomenon that occurred solely in the 21st Century. The revelations of such abuse largely concern accusations made against members of the clergy from events that transpired in the 20th Century.

in June, 2000. His response is somewhat lengthy and so we shall break it down into parts. First, Benedict prefaced his remarks as follows:

> Before all else, I want to say how happy I am to be going to Fatima, to pray before Our Lady of Fatima. For us, Fatima is a sign of the presence of faith, of the fact that it is precisely from the little ones that faith gains new strength, *one which is not limited to the little ones but has a message for the entire world and touches history here and now, and sheds light on this history* (*emphases mine*).

These opening remarks provide some initial context to the rest of the response. Here, Pope Benedict makes the point that at Fátima one's faith can find "new strength" in the example of Bls. Jacinta and Francisco (and arguably, Sr. Lúcia). This fact is something that affects the present moment.

Does this mean that from the onset of his remarks that the Holy Father is already repudiating his position from June, 2000? Not necessarily. This first remark can be understood as emanating from the "prayer and conversion" aspect of Our Lady's message. This understanding is rooted in the fact that Benedict explicitly states that Fátima is a "sign of the presence of faith" and holds up the example of the shepherd children to demonstrate his point.

Pope Benedict then continued his remarks as follows:

> In 2000, in my presentation, I said that an apparition – a supernatural impulse which does not come purely from a person's imagination but really from the Virgin Mary, from the supernatural – that such an impulse enters into a subject and is expressed according to the capacities of that subject. The subject is determined by his or her historical, personal, temperamental conditions, and so translates the great supernatural impulse into his or her own capabilities for seeing, imagining,

expressing; *yet these expressions, shaped by the subject, conceal a content which is greater, which goes deeper, and only in the course of history can we see the full depth, which was – let us say - "clothed" in this vision that was accessible to specific individuals (emphases mine).*

In the above text, Pope Benedict discusses the impact of a supernatural impulse upon a person. There is the subjective disposition of the recipient meeting with the objective content of the impulse and how the recipient expresses this meeting is dependent upon his or her capabilities. The Holy Father is basing himself upon a principle from St. Thomas Aquinas which is cited in matters of private revelation. Aquinas taught, "For it is clear that whatever is received into something is received according to the condition of the recipient" (*Summa Theologiae* Ia, q. 75, a. 5; Ia, q. 12, a. 4).[32]

Aquinas' principle leaves much room for human considerations but Benedict does not spend much time on this point. As quickly as he touches upon this observation, he then swiftly moves to point out the depth of the supernatural. It is not always easy to express the supernatural in human terms. Pope St. Gregory the Great highlighted this notion centuries ago in his *Moralia in Job*. In expressing the burden of a specific spiritual task, Gregory lamented his own weakness. Gregory wrote:

....I lifted up the eyes of my mind to the Bestower of all gifts [James 1, 17], waiving my scruples, I fixed my thoughts on this, that what an affection flowing from the hearts of my brethren enjoined upon me, could not certainly be impossible, I despaired, indeed, of being a match for these things, but, stronger for my very despair of myself, I forthwith raised my hopes to

---

32   John Mortensen and Enrique Alarcón, (edits.), *Summa Theologiae: Prima Pars, 50-119.* (Lander, Wyoming: The Aquinas Institute for the Study of Sacred Doctrine, 2012), 216, 367. See also Cardinal Tarcisio Bertone, *The Last Secret of Fatima.* (New York: Doubleday, 2008), 40-42.

Him, by Whom the tongue of the dumb is opened, Who *maketh the lips of babes to speak eloquently*, [Wisd. 10, 21], Who has marked the undistinguished and brute sayings of an ass with the intelligible measures of human speech. What wonder, then, that a simple man should receive understanding from Him, Who whenever He willeth, utters His truths by the mouths of the very beasts of burthen? Armed then with the strength which this thought supplied, I roused mine own drought to explore so deep a well; and though the life of those, to whom I was compelled to give my interpretation, was far above me, yet I thought it no harm if the leaden pipe should supply streams of water for the service of men.[33]

For his part, Pope Benedict says that history shows us the "full depth" of what was shown to select individuals. In other words, supernatural light is given to these individuals for purposes known to God; others watch things unfold in time.[34] Consider the following example from the life of Sr. Lúcia.

---

33   Pope St. Gregory the Great, *Moralia in Job, Volume I, Parts I and II.* (Ex Fontibus Company, 2012), 9-10.

34   The Holy Father will return to this thought during his homily on May 13 in Fátima. Pope Benedict remarked:

Brothers and sisters, in listening to these innocent and profound mystical confidences of the shepherd children, one might look at them with a touch of envy for what they were able to see, or with the disappointed resignation of someone who was not so fortunate, yet still demands to see.... [God] has the power to come to us, particularly through our inner senses, so that the soul can receive the gentle touch of a reality which is beyond the senses and which enables us to reach what is not accessible or visible to the senses. For this to happen, we must cultivate an interior watchfulness of the heart which, for most of the time, we do not possess on account of the powerful pressure exerted by outside realities and the images and concerns which fill our soul (cf. Theological Commentary on *The Message of Fatima*, 2000). Yes! God can come to us, and show himself to the eyes of our heart

At the outset of World War II, the sign promised by Our Lady was given in January, 1938—the famous aurora borealis.[35] Fr. Jongen interviewed Sister in February, 1946 and inquired after her specifying Pius XI in her *Memoirs* as being the Pope under whom the war would begin. Sr. Lúcia remarked the following, "The annexation of Austria was the occasion for it. When the Munich accord was signed, the sisters were jubilant, because the peace seemed to be saved. I knew better than they did, unfortunately."[36]

After explaining the above and furthering his point with the example of the Popes suffering, Pope Benedict then mentioned what is the important part of the message of Fátima. He said:

Consequently, I would say that, here too, beyond this great vision of the suffering of the Pope, which we can in the first place refer to Pope John Paul II, an indication is given of realities involving the future of the Church, *which are gradually taking shape and becoming evident*. So it is true that, in addition to [the] moment indicated in the vision, there is mention of, there is seen, the need for a passion of the Church, which naturally is reflected in the person of the Pope, yet the Pope stands for the Church and thus it is sufferings of the Church that are announced. The Lord told us that the Church would constantly be suffering, in different ways, until the end of the world. *The important thing is that the message, the response of Fatima, in*

(<http://w2.vatican.va/content/benedict-xvi/en/homilies/2010/documents/hf_ben-xvi_hom_20100513_fatima.html> [Accessed 26 May, 2016]. Hereafter *Benedict XVI May 13, 2010 Homily*).

35   *Memórias e Cartas de Irmã Lúcia*, 341.

36   Frere Michel de la Sainte Trinite, *The Whole Truth About Fatima. Volume II: The Secret and the Church*. (Buffalo, New York: Immaculate Heart Publications, 1989), 696.

substance is not directed to particular devotions, but precisely to the fundamental response, that is, to ongoing conversion, penance, prayer, and the three theological virtues: faith, hope and charity. Thus we see here the true, fundamental response which the Church must give – which we, every one of us, must give in this situation (*emphases mine*).

Notice that Benedict touched upon the images of the vision contained in the third part of the secret. He gave, however, the weight of his remarks to Our Lady's call to conversion and penance and the living out of faith, hope and charity. Doing such, as we have seen, is entirely consistent with his statements made in his *Theological Commentary* in the year 2000.

Moreover, in speaking about the realities in the vision "gradually taking shape and becoming evident," Benedict can be understood not as referring to the Church in 2010, but within the timeframe of the twentieth century. Speaking from the perspective of 1917 when the vision was given, the "realities" therein expressed *would* involve the future of the Church over the course of said century. To read Benedict any other way would necessarily mean that he was, in fact, repudiating his earlier position from the year 2000. As we have seen so far, his consistency with his *Theological Commentary* would not allow for such an interpretation.

What is more striking is Benedict's statement that "particular devotions" are not the focus. It was at Fátima that Our Lady expressed heaven's desire for the devotion to the Immaculate Heart to be employed as the remedy for the problems facing the world and the Church.[37] This

---

37   In his book *Fatima: Tragedy and Triumph* (pages 117-118), Frère François de Marie des Anges made comments that questioned the emphasis of the Popes on the "penance" theme. He argues that Pope Paul VI was following the theses of Fr. Edouard Dhanis. Certainly, after the revelation of the text in the year 2000 with its description of the angel shouting "penance!" three times, one can question Frère François' characterization, and, perhaps, better understand why the Popes have emphasized this theme.

may not, however, be as striking when one looks at what Our Lady said to the three visionaries.

In the July 13, 1917 apparition, Our Lady first showed them hell and then explained what they saw saying that "You have seen hell where the souls of poor sinners go. To save them God wishes to establish in the world the devotion to my Immaculate Heart...."[38] The Blessed Virgin is clear: establishing the devotion to her Immaculate Heart is done in mind *with the salvation of souls*. Salvation is given to one who is truly repentant, does penance and amends his or her life, i.e. conversion. The way of Our Lady's Immaculate Heart is offered to this end.[39]

In the last part of his response, Pope Benedict makes what is a very

---

38   Dr. Antonio Maria Martins, S.J., *Memórias e Cartas de Irmã Lúcia*. (Porto, Portugal: Simão Guimarães, Filhos, LDA, 1973), 219. Hereafter *Memórias e Cartas de Irmã Lúcia* followed by page number.

39   Theologians have discussed what is the essential call of Fátima. To this end, different aspects have been highlighted such as the devotion (or the consecration to) the Immaculate Heart, penance, etc. (cf. Stefano de Fiores, *Il Segreto di Fatima: Una luce sul futuro del mondo*. (Milano: San Paolo Edizioni, 2008), 57-62. Identifying the "essential" call is important within the controversy over the third part of the secret. Frère François states, for example, that reducing Fátima to penance does injustice to the devotion to the Immaculate Heart as requested by Our Lady.

For this author's part, it seems that the essential call is that of the Gospel, namely the salvation of souls from eternal damnation. The Immaculate Heart of Mary is offered as a path to this end. This could not be, however, *unless* it is combined with the timeless call of Christ to repentance (Matt. 4:16-17) as the Son of Man came to save the lost (Matthew 18:11; Luke 19:10). Mankind, lost in the sins of atheism, liberalism and materialism had lost sight of God. The words of Pope Benedict XVI in his homily of May 13, 2010 in Fátima are especially pertinent here:

> At a time when the human family was ready to sacrifice all that was most sacred on the altar of the petty and selfish interests of nations, races, ideologies, groups and individuals, our Blessed Mother came from heaven, offering to implant in the hearts of all those who trust in her the Love of God burning in her own heart... (*Benedict XVI May 13, 2010 Homily*).

serious remark concerning the sin in the Church today in relation to the call of Fátima on conversion and penance. He says:

As for the new things which we can find in this message today, there is also the fact that attacks on the Pope and the Church come not only from without, but the sufferings of the Church come precisely from within the Church, from the sin existing within the Church. This too is something that we have always known, but today we are seeing it in a really terrifying way: that the greatest persecution of the Church comes not from her enemies without, but arises from sin within the Church, and that the Church thus has a deep need to relearn penance, to accept purification, to learn forgiveness on the one hand, but also the need for justice. Forgiveness does not replace justice. In a word, we need to relearn precisely this essential: conversion, prayer, penance and the theological virtues. This is our response, we are realists in expecting that evil always attacks, attacks from within and without, yet that the forces of good are also ever present and that, in the end, the Lord is more powerful than evil and Our Lady is for us the visible, motherly guarantee of God's goodness, which is always the last word in history (*emphases mine*).

To begin, it is important to remember that Benedict is responding to the question from Fr. Lombardi which asks about the meaning of the Fátima apparitions for today and if the vision of the third part of the secret could include the sufferings of the Church today.[40] Benedict's response implies

---

40   In the year 2003, Benedict (as Cardinal Ratzinger) discussed this matter with Raymond Arroyo of the Eternal Word Television Network (EWTN). When asked if the third part of the secret could refer to a future Pope, Ratzinger replied:

We cannot exclude that this is clear. Normally, the private visions

an affirmative answer.

First, Benedict connects this sin with the call of Fátima to conversion, thus drawing upon the point made in his *Theological Commentary* from the year 2000. He then does something that he did not do explicitly in his *Commentary*. The Pope describes this sin as attacks not only from outside of the Church, but also "from the sin existing within the Church." At first glance, this distinction gives the appearance that Pope Benedict has questioned his own assertion from 2000 that the events shown in the vision have come to pass. If we can learn from this vision that there are attacks upon the Pope both from without and within the Church, and these attacks are happening in 2010, how can one *not* conclude that the foretold events have yet come to pass?

Such a conclusion is not necessarily a given from the literal sense of what the Holy Father was saying in his interview. Pope Benedict did *not* say that these attacks in 2010 pertain to the third part of the secret.

---

are limited to the next generation, and even Lucia, and all those in Fatima were convinced that in the time of one generation this would be realized. So, the immediate content of the vision is this, I would say. And it is expressed in a vision in an apocalyptic language. It is clear in all the visions, we do not have an historical language, as a report on television, that we have a visionary, symbolic language. We can understand this is indeed an indication of the crisis of the Church in the second part of the last century and in our time. But, even if the immediate sense of this prophecy, this vision is always in the next generations; it has also sense for future times. We cannot exclude – even I would say, we have to wait for, that even in other times we'll have similar crises of the Church and perhaps also similar attacks to a Pope

(<https://www.ewtn.com/library/ISSUES/RATZINTV.HTM> [Accessed 19 October, 2016]).

See also the response of Cardinal Ratzinger to Bishop Hnilica in Salvatore M. Perrella, "Il 'Messaggio di Fatima' della Congregazione per la Dottrina della Fede (26 giugno 2000). Interpretazioni contemporanee." *Marianum* 74 (2012): 341.

Rather, he was drawing upon the basic fact that attacks against the Pope (and the Church) come in every age. This point was indirectly indicated by Ratzinger during the press conference in the year 2000 (as Lombardi pointed out). At that time, he was asked the following question by the French journalist Guillaume Goubert of the periodical *La Croix*: "I want to know if you can say that this message concerns only the past, that the vision is now finished and that there is no, so to speak, danger for the future."[41] Ratzinger responded as follows:

> I think so because naturally martyrdom is a reality present in all ages and in this sense naturally concerns the future. There is no century without martyrdom but here it is a very specific history, a history of persecution, of violence, of destruction of cities, of the human being. I think this world of destruction, of violence, of wars culminating finally in the attack on the present pope is the concrete content of this positive vision that does not indicate the path of future history, that indicates martyrdom as a fact of this century, indicates that the connection to martyrdom must be penance, conversion, to give love strongly against the force of violence. It certainly does not indicate other events; it indicates one thing in this sense as permanent for history—that there will always be martyrdom because there will always be hate and love is always the only force that can confront this problem and overcome the force of hate.[42]

---

41   "Vorrei sapere se si può affermare che questo messaggio concerne solo il passato, che la visione è ormai compiuta e che non c'è, per così dire, pericolo per il futuro" (from the transcript of the conference available at the end of the present book).

42   Penso di sì perché naturalmente il martirio è una realtà presente in tutti i secoli e in questo senso concerne naturalmente anche il futuro, non c'è secolo senza martirio ma qui si tratta di una storia molto specifica, di una storia di persecuzione, di una storia di violenza, di una storia di distruzione delle città,

Pope Benedict, in 2010, uses the occasion afforded him by the present discussion to illustrate his point from June, 2000.

In this context, Benedict then makes a more direct connection with Fátima when he says that, "...the Church thus has a deep need to relearn penance, to accept purification, to learn forgiveness on the one hand, but also the need for justice. Forgiveness does not replace justice. In a word, we need to relearn precisely this essential: conversion, prayer, penance and the theological virtues."

For Pope Benedict to discuss the topic of purification in relation to Fátima is not unreasonable. Fr. Lombardi *specifically* asked the Holy Father about the sexual abuse of minors within the context of the vision of the third part of the secret. Consider also that just prior to his election in 2005, Pope Benedict, as Cardinal Ratzinger, spoke about the "filth" in the Church. While reflecting on the ninth station of the *Via Crucis* at the Colosseum in Rome, Ratzinger said the following:

> What can the third fall of Jesus under the Cross say to us? We have considered the fall of man in general, and the falling of many Christians away from Christ and into a godless secularism. Should we not also think of how much Christ suffers in his own Church? How often is the holy sacrament of his Presence abused, how often must he enter empty and evil hearts! How often do we celebrate only ourselves, without even realizing

---

dell'essere umano, penso che questo mondo delle distruzioni, delle violenze, delle guerre culminante finalmente nell'attentato al papa attuale è il contenuto concreto, positivo di questa visione che non indica il percorso della storia futura, ci indica il martirio come fatto di questo secolo, ci indica che la corrispondenza al martirio deve essere la penitenza, la conversione, dare forza all'amore contro la forza della violenza; altri avvenimenti certamente non indica, indica una cosa in questo senso anche permanente per la storia, che il martirio ci sarà sempre perché l'odio ci sarà sempre e l'amore è sempre l'unica forza che può affrontare questo problema e superare le forze dell'odio (from the transcript of the conference available at the end of the present book).

that he is there! How often is his Word twisted and misused! What little faith is present behind so many theories, so many empty words! *How much filth there is in the Church, and even among those who, in the priesthood, ought to belong entirely to him! How much pride, how much self-complacency!* What little respect we pay to the Sacrament of Reconciliation, where he waits for us, ready to raise us up whenever we fall! All this is present in his Passion. His betrayal by his disciples, their unworthy reception of his Body and Blood, is certainly the greatest suffering endured by the Redeemer; it pierces his heart. We can only call to him from the depths of our hearts: Kyrie eleison – Lord, save us (cf. *Mt* 8: 25) (*emphases mine*).[43]

Ratzinger's comment about the "filth" in the Church is largely interpreted to be a reference to the clerical scandals, which, at that time had been in the news for about three years.[44] It is, thus, not surprising for Ratzinger, now as Pope Benedict, to continue this theme after being asked about the matter *directly* from Fr. Lombardi. As it pertains to the third part of the secret of Fátima (which was posed to the Holy Father by Lombardi), one can here understand Pope Benedict as saying that the call of Our Lady of Fátima to conversion and penance can help the Church in the here and now to address the matter of the clerical abuse scandal.

To summarize, Pope Benedict XVI did not repudiate his prior statements, nor "re-open" the case on the third part of the secret. His statements are in harmony with his *Theological Commentary* from the year 2000 and not against it. Concerning the precise remarks about the suffering of the

---

43   <http://www.vatican.va/news_services/liturgy/2005/via_crucis/en/station_09.html> (Accessed 16 May, 2016).

44   Cf. Gregory Erlandson and Matthew Bunson, *Pope Benedict XVI and the Sexual Abuse Crisis.* (Huntington, Indiana: Our Sunday Visitor, 2010), 29, 153.

Popes and the Church from forces both within and without the Church, Benedict was simply misinterpreted. His remarks were influenced by the question as it was posed to him by Fr. Lombardi and were built upon prior remarks made during the press conference in June, 2000.

III. *Pope Benedict XVI &* Fátima—*May 13, 2010*

Finally, there was a second and more controversial remark made by Pope Benedict in Fátima. During his homily on May 13, the Holy Father remarked that "We would be mistaken to think that Fátima's prophetic mission is complete."[45] When one reads the Holy Father's remarks not just in the context of the homily in question but also the entirety of statements made during the Apostolic Voyage, a picture comes into focus. This picture provides us with important reference points that help us to understand better Benedict's remark. Let us look at the context of the homily itself, which is comprised of nine paragraphs.

The first paragraph begins with quoting from the reading taken from Isaiah 61:9, "Their descendants shall be renowned among the nations [...], they are a people whom the Lord has blessed." The Pope takes the first half of this verse and applies it to the assembly gathered in Fátima. He states that he has four reasons for coming to Fátima. The second half of the verse is then interpreted in paragraph two in terms of identifying the people whom the Lord has blessed. After this interpretation, Benedict then moves to explain in the third paragraph how God "offers a future to his people: a future of communion with himself."

In this explanation of God and our communion with Him, Benedict

---

45   *Acta Apostolicae Sedis* 102 (2010), 327. The Portuguese text is, "Iludir-se-ia quem pensasse que a missão profética de Fátima esteja concluída." English translation available on the Vatican's web site: <http://w2.vatican.va/content/benedict-xvi/en/homilies/2010/documents/hf_ben-xvi_hom_20100513_fatima.html> (Accessed 26 May, 2016).

then makes a significant identification and reference. He identifies Our Lady as the "resplendent daughter" of God's people, saying that she "did not view herself as a fortunate individual in the midst of a barren people, but prophecied for them the sweet joys of a wondrous maternity of God...." This is an important hermeneutical key because the Holy Father uses the word "prophecied" and thus provides us with a reference point for his later remark which we are examining.

Immediately after providing this important key, Benedict then discusses in paragraph four how Fátima is proof of Our Lady's prophecies of "sweet joys." He specifies that pilgrims will return to Fátima in 2017 (some seven years from the date of the present homily) and uses the imagery of Our Lady as "the Teacher who introduced the little seers to a deep knowledge of the Love of the Blessed Trinity and led them to savour God himself as the most beautiful reality of human existence." There is a deep mystical significance being referenced here by Pope Benedict by which he is reminding people of the deep communion to which we are called as Christians.[46]

---

46   The theme of communion was touched upon by Pope Benedict from the outset of his Voyage to Portugal. At the airport in Lisbon on May 11, 2010, Benedict stated:

> ....As for the event that took place 93 years ago, when heaven itself was opened over Portugal – like a window of hope that God opens when man closes the door to him – in order to refashion, within the human family, the bonds of fraternal solidarity based on the mutual recognition of the one Father, this was a loving design from God; it does not depend on the Pope, nor on any other ecclesial authority: "It was not the Church that imposed Fatima", as Cardinal Manuel Cerejeira of blessed memory used to say, "but it was Fatima that imposed itself on the Church."
>
> The Virgin Mary came from heaven to remind us of Gospel truths that constitute for humanity – so lacking in love and without hope for salvation – the source of hope. To be sure, this hope has as its primary and radical dimension not the horizontal relation, but the vertical and transcendental one. The relationship with God is constitutive of the human being, who was created and ordered towards God; he seeks truth by means of his cognitive processes, he tends towards the good

To illustrate this mystical union, the Holy Father points out the examples of Bls. Jacinta and Francisco and their love for God. From this example, and in paragraph five, the Pope then touches upon and responds to the temptation to be envious of the little shepherds "for what they were able to see." Benedict reminds his audience that God "has the power to come to us" but that this transpires when "we…cultivate an interior watchfulness of the heart." In other words, all Christians are called to cultivate within their hearts an abode where God may dwell. Where God dwells, we experience Him and it is not far from anyone to cultivate such a dwelling place.

The focus of the Christian life, the Holy Father indicates in paragraph six, is on Jesus Christ. He entered into human history and it is upon this that "our hope has a real foundation" which both "belongs to" and "transcends" history. About this hope, Benedict then asks three questions meant to provoke people into asking themselves how well they cultivate the dwelling place of God in their hearts. After posing this matter for the consideration of the faithful, the Holy Father then returns to Isaiah 61:9 in paragraph seven. He re-casts the verse against his point on hope and sacrifice, holding up again the example of the shepherd children of Fátima.

Immediately following the above is the next paragraph (eight) and the statement "We would be mistaken to think that Fátima's prophetic mission is complete." Was Benedict repudiating his assertion from the year 2000? No, he was not, and, in fact, was once again very consistent with it. To understand this consistency, we must return to what Benedict said

---

in the sphere of volition, and he is attracted by beauty in the aesthetic dimension. Consciousness is Christian to the degree to which it opens itself to the fullness of life and wisdom that we find in Jesus Christ. The visit that I am now beginning under the sign of hope is intended as a proposal of wisdom and mission (*Acta Apostolicae Sedis* 102 [2010], 339-340). English translation courtesy of the Vatican web site: <http://w2.vatican.va/content/benedict-xvi/en/speeches/2010/may/documents/hf_ben-xvi_spe_20100511_accoglienza-ufficiale.html> (Accessed 23 May, 2016).

earlier in paragraph three. Our Lady came to Fátima to tell mankind of the "sweet joys" of God and that this comes through suffering, prayer and sacrifice for the conversion of sinners.

If we recall the earlier definition of prophecy from St. Thomas Aquinas, we know that prophecy is not just about future events but about knowledge "far removed" from the mind of man. To come to Fátima and remind mankind of the "sweet joys" of God is a prophetic utterance to a world that was forgetting its God. This is the very purpose of private revelation, as Benedict himself had pointed out in his *Commentary*, to "help [Christians] live more fully by [the Gospel] in a certain period of history."[47]

Understanding Pope Benedict's usage of the term "prophetic" in this larger sense is further affirmed by remarks he made later the same day to the Bishops of Portugal. On this occasion, Benedict remarked on the "prophetic dimension" of the Christian life stating:

> *You maintain a strong prophetic dimension*, without allowing yourselves to be silenced, in the present social context, for "the word of God is not fettered" (2 Tim 2:9). People cry out for the Good News of Jesus Christ, which gives meaning to their lives and protects their dignity. In your role as first evangelizers, it will be useful for you to know and to understand the diverse social and cultural factors, to evaluate their spiritual deficiencies and to utilize effectively your pastoral resources; what is decisive, however, is the ability to inculcate in all those engaged in the work of evangelization a true desire for holiness, in the awareness that the results derive above all from our union with Christ and the working of the Holy Spirit (*emphases mine*).[48]

---

47   *The Message of Fatima*, 34. See also the *Catechism of the Catholic Church*, paragraph 67.

48   *Acta Apostolicae Sedis* 102 (2010), 344-347. English translation courtesy of the Vatican web site: <http://w2.vatican.va/content/benedict-xvi/en/

Recall what was said in the *Theological Commentary* on the nature of prophecy. Ratzinger wrote, "The prophet speaks to the blindness of will and of reason, and declares the will of God as an indication and demand for the present time. In this case, prediction of the future is of secondary importance."[49]

In a later interview with the German journalist Peter Seewald, Pope Benedict further clarified his remarks from May, 2010. Asked specifically about his understanding and/or devotion to Our Lady in the context of Fátima, the Holy Father gave some very revealing answers that further support the thesis we have been examining. Commenting upon Our Lady's role in the Scriptures and early Church history, Benedict comments "...God has never ceased to use her as the light through which he leads us to himself."[50] He then proceeds to discuss the example of Our Lady's appearance in Mexico to St. Juan Diego. Building upon an observation of Cardinal Newman on the development of faith, Benedict says:

> Faith develops. And part of this development is precisely the increasing emphatic interventions by which the Mother of God enters the world as a guide along the right path, as a light from God, as the Mother through whom we are also able to know the Son and the Father in turn. God, in other words, has given us signs. In the very midst of the twentieth century. In our rationalism, and in the face of the rising power of dictatorships, God shows us the humility of the Mother, who appears to little children and speaks to them of the essentials: faith, hope, love, penance. It therefore makes sense to me that people find win-

---

speeches/2010/may/documents/hf_ben-xvi_spe_20100513_vescovi-portogallo. html> (Accessed 23 May, 2016).

49   *The Message of Fatima*, 36.

50   Pope Benedict XVI, *Light of the World: A Conversation with Peter Seewald.* (San Francisco, California: Ignatius Press, 2010), 164. Hereafter *Light of the World* followed by page number.

dows here, as it were. In Fatima I witnessed the presence of hundreds of thousands of people whose eyes, you might say, had regained the ability to see God, through all the barriers and enclosures of this world, thanks to what Mary had said to little children in Fatima.[51]

In the light of the above, it is possible to understand the Holy Father as not attempting to use the term "prophetic" in its restricted sense (predicting future events). Read in this way means that he was employing the term in its broader sense of communicating knowledge "far removed" from the mind of man.[52] Christians share in the mission of Christ as priest, prophet and king (CCC 783, 785). Christians are prophets in that they preach the Gospel and its supernatural values to a world that often does not know, understand and appreciate them—i.e. the "blindness of will and of reason" in order to declare "the will of God." That "blindness," as the Pope said to Seewald, was wrapped up in rationalism and the dictatorships of the twentieth century.

In order to testify to the supernatural, Christians need to cultivate that life within their own hearts. Pope Benedict had earlier pointed out the necessity of being in communion with God but that we often do not cultivate such in our hearts. "Mankind," Benedict continues in paragraph eight, "has succeeded in unleashing a cycle of death and terror, but failed in bringing it to an end...." Benedict ends his homily on the following note in paragraph nine:

At a time when the human family was ready to sacrifice all that was most sacred on the altar of the petty and selfish interests of nations, races, ideologies, groups and individuals, our Blessed

---

51   Ibid.

52   Communicating knowledge to the mind of men does not necessarily imply "new" knowledge.

Mother came from heaven, offering to implant in the hearts of all those who trust in her the Love of God burning in her own heart. At that time it was only to three children, yet the example of their lives spread and multiplied, especially as a result of the travels of the Pilgrim Virgin, in countless groups throughout the world dedicated to the cause of fraternal solidarity. May the seven years which separate us from the centenary of the apparitions hasten the fulfilment of the prophecy of the triumph of the Immaculate Heart of Mary, to the glory of the Most Holy Trinity.

Lastly, Pope Benedict clarified further his remarks in Fátima to Peter Seewald. The latter asked the Pope, *directly*, about his remarks on the completeness of the prophetic mission of Fátima. The Pope was asked, "Does the fulfillment of the message of Fátima really still lie in the future?"[53] To this question, the Holy Father responded as follows:

There are two aspects of the message of Fatima that have to be distinguished. On the one hand, there is a particular event, which is recounted in forms typical of visionary experience, and, on the other hand, there is the fundamental significance of the event. I mean, the point was not to satisfy some curiosity. If that had been the case, it would have been logical for us to publish the text much sooner. No, the purpose was to allude to a critical point, a critical moment in history, by which I mean the whole power of evil that came to a head in the major dictatorships of the twentieth century—and that in another way is still at work today.[54]

---

53   *Light of the World.*, 165.

54   [Author's note: It appears as though to Benedict's mind there is a distinction between the major dictatorships of the twentieth century and the power of evil. It is the latter which is still at work in the world and uses new tools for its purposes.]

On the other hand, the answer to this challenge is also an important point here. This answer does not consist in great political actions, but, when all is said and done, it can only come from the transformation of the heart—through faith, hope, love, and penance. In this sense, the message is precisely not a thing of the past, even though the two major dictatorships have disappeared. The Church continues to suffer, and a threat still hangs over man, so the quest for the answer continues as well, which means that the indication Mary has given us retains its validity. Even now there is tribulation. Even now, in every conceivable form, power threatens to trample down faith. Even now, then, there is need for the answer about which the Mother of God spoke to the children.[55]

The above quote clearly demonstrates that the Holy Father was approaching the topic of the prophetic mission of Fátima from the perspective of the broader Catholic tradition on prophecy.

Pope Benedict's comment about the transformation of the heart may also provide an important key as to his previous statement (quoted above) on hastening the triumph of the Immaculate Heart of Mary. First, we must ask what are the Immaculate Heart of Mary and its triumph. Pope Benedict presented his understanding of these in his *Theological Commentary* in the year 2000. Concerning the Immaculate Heart, he wrote:

In biblical language, the "heart" indicates the centre of human life, the point where reason, will, temperament and sensitivity converge, where the person finds his unity and his interior orientation. According to Matthew 5:8, the "immaculate heart" is a heart which, with God's grace, has come to perfect interior unity and therefore "sees God". To be "devoted" to the Immaculate Heart of Mary means therefore to embrace this attitude of

---

55   Ibid., 165-166.

heart, which makes the *fiat*—"your will be done"—the defining centre of one's whole life. It might be objected that we should not place a human being between ourselves and Christ. But then we remember that Paul did not hesitate to say to his communities: "imitate me" (*1 Cor* 4:16; *Phil* 3:17; *1 Th* 1:6; *2 Th* 3:7, 9). In the Apostle they could see concretely what it meant to follow Christ. But from whom might we better learn in every age than from the Mother of the Lord?[56]

Ratzinger clarifies what it means for the individual Christian to have an immaculate heart. He says it is a heart which "has come to perfect interior unity and therefore 'sees God.'" In the Blessed Virgin Mary, this perfect interior unity was brought to its highest possible degree. Thus, for Christians to be "devoted" to Our Lady's Immaculate Heart necessitates them, as Ratzinger wrote, "to embrace this attitude of heart" that makes her "yes" to God the "defining centre of one's whole life" in imitation of Our Lady.

Having explained the nature of the Immaculate Heart, what is its "triumph" spoken of by Our Lady at Fátima? Speaking largely in spiritual terms, Ratzinger states later in his *Commentary*:

I would like finally to mention another key expression of the "secret" which has become justly famous: "my Immaculate Heart will triumph". What does this mean? The Heart open to God, purified by contemplation of God, is stronger than guns and weapons of every kind. The *fiat* of Mary, the word of her heart, has changed the history of the world, because it brought the Saviour into the world—because, thanks to her *Yes,* God could become man in our world and remains so for all time. The Evil One has power in this world, as we see and experience

---

56 *The Message of Fatima*, 39.

continually; he has power because our freedom continually lets itself be led away from God. But since God himself took a human heart and has thus steered human freedom towards what is good, the freedom to choose evil no longer has the last word. From that time forth, the word that prevails is this: "In the world you will have tribulation, but take heart; I have overcome the world" (*Jn* 16:33). The message of Fatima invites us to trust in this promise.[57]

Ratzinger interprets Our Lady's promise of a "triumph" of her Heart in spiritual terms. He is consistent, as Pope Benedict, with this interpretation in his call for the hastening of Our Lady's prophecy of her Immaculate Heart's triumph. In 2000, Ratzinger indicates that the Immaculate Heart will triumph when devotion to her instills that same "flame of love" in her Heart to the hearts of her devotees. This, too, is a prophetic utterance in that it is also part of the call of Our Lady for people to return to God.

Peter Seewald asked Pope Benedict about the "hastening" of the triumph of the Immaculate Heart of Mary. The question posed to the Holy Father by Seewald was whether or not Benedict "thinks that within the coming seven years the Mother of God could actually appear in a manner that would be tantamount to a triumph." Pope Benedict clarified his meaning, stating:

I said that the "triumph" will draw closer. This is equivalent in meaning to our praying for the coming of God's Kingdom. This statement was not intended—I may be too rationalistic for that—to express any expectation on my part that there is going to be a huge turnaround and that history will suddenly take a totally different course. The point was rather that the power of evil is restrained again and again, that again and again the power of God himself is shown in the Mother's power and keeps

---

57   *The Message of Fatima*, 43.

it alive.

The Church is always called upon to do what God asked of Abraham, which is to see to it that there are enough righteous men to repress evil and destruction. I understood my words as a prayer that the energies of the good might regain their vigor. So you could say the triumphs of God, the triumphs of Mary, are quiet, but they are real nonetheless.[58]

From his answer, one can see that Benedict has a spiritual interpretation of the "triumph" of the Immaculate Heart of Mary. This interpretation conflicts with another, more literal one that holds a literal world-wide era of peace will be given once the Holy Father consecrates Russia.[59]

Our purpose in this chapter has been to examine Pope Benedict's statement on Fátima and its prophetic mission. From the indications given above, the Holy Father appears to refer to how Our Lady continues to call people to the "sweet joys" of God. In this capacity, she acts as a prophetess who tells of the hidden designs and mysteries of God. These things are not readily perceived by the human mind except through supernatural grace, cultivated within the dwelling place of the heart of individual Christians.

It is clear from all that has been said above that Pope Benedict XVI was not intending to open up discussion on unfulfilled prophesies, much less to repudiate his position from the year 2000. On the contrary, we have seen that he remained consistent between the years 2000 and 2010. Apart from the question of his consistency, there is yet one final matter concerning Pope Benedict and Fátima that shall be addressed in the following chapter.

---

58   *Light of the World*, 166.

59   For various examples of this interpretation, see Fr. Nicholas Gruner *et al.*, *World Enslavement or Peace…It's Up to the Pope.* (Fort Erie, Canada, *The Fatima Crusader*, 1988). The focus of the present chapter is not the question of this consecration. No comment will then be given on the matter except to say that one is, after study and reflection, free to disagree or not with Ratzinger's understanding of the triumph of the Immaculate Heart of Mary as stated at Fátima.

—12—
Fr. Dollinger and Fátima

"...it is well known that in passing from a trustworthy witness to another a tale keeps growing."

—Fr. Albert R. Bandini

On May 15, 2016, an article written by the writer Dr. Maike Hickson was published that questioned whether or not the third part of the secret of Fátima was released in its entirety.[1] The article recounts a phone conversation between her and Fr. Ingo Dollinger of Brazil. Dollinger, a friend of Pope Emeritus Benedict XVI, claims that Benedict told him there was unpublished material in relation to the third part of the secret. Hickson states that the "unpublished" material allegedly talks about a "bad Council" and a "bad liturgy." The article presents some difficulties which shall be examined in the present chapter.[2]

---

1 <http://www.onepeterfive.com/cardinal-ratzinger-not-published-whole-third-secret-fatima/> (Accessed 27 May, 2016). Hereafter *Hickson-Dollinger*.

2 The present article is an expansion of an earlier on that appeared on this author's personal web site:
<https://kevinsymonds.com/2016/05/17/fatima-and-fr-dollinger-a-response/> (Accessed 30 May, 2016).

I. First Difficulty: Differing Versions

To begin, as Dr. Hickson notes in her article, Fr. Dollinger's claim has been available to an English-speaking audience for several years. It was put into print by Fr. Paul Kramer and the Fatima Center founded by the late Fr. Nicholas Gruner. One can find it in issue 92 (Spring 2009) edition of *The Fatima Crusader* in the article entitled *The Secret Warned Against Vatican Council II and the New Mass.*[3] When one compares Fr. Kramer's version with Dr. Hickson's, there are noted differences between them. In the 2009 version, Fr. Kramer provided the following account:

> When Pope Benedict was still Cardinal Ratzinger, around 1990 he revealed to his friend that in the Third Secret of Fatima Our Lady warns not to change the liturgy: literally, not to mix extraneous foreign elements into the Catholic liturgy.
>
> [*Author's Note: Kramer then discussed the Liturgy. It is here omitted.*]
>
> So we have Cardinal Ratzinger himself stating to a close personal friend that these warnings were given by Our Lady in the Third Secret of Fatima not to change the Mass in precisely the manner that Pope Paul VI changed the Mass.[4]

---

3   <http://www.fatimacrusader.com/cr92/cr92pg7.pdf> (Accessed 27 May, 2016). Hereafter *Kramer-Dollinger* followed by page number (as this is a PDF file).

4   *Kramer-Dollinger*, 9, 10. Kramer continues the narrative on page 10 to include an anecdotal story. He writes:

> ....the German theologian who I am referring to went back to the country in South America where he was Rector of a seminary and he explained to a young priest what Cardinal Ratzinger had related to him. And precisely when he related that Our Lady warned against changing the Mass and there would be an evil Council in the Church, the both of them saw a plume of smoke coming up from the floor. Now it was a marble floor. This could not be anything of a natural

In contrast to the above, Dr. Hickson writes that "Father Dollinger unexpectedly confirmed over the phone the following facts." She then gave the "facts" as follows:

> Not long after the June 2000 publication of the Third Secret of Fatima by the Congregation for the Doctrine of the Faith, Cardinal Joseph Ratzinger told Fr. Dollinger during an in-person conversation that there is still a part of the Third Secret that they have not published! "There is more than what we published," Ratzinger said. He also told Dollinger that the published part of the Secret is authentic and that the unpublished part of the Secret speaks about "a bad council and a bad Mass" that was to come in the near future.

In Kramer's version, the (alleged) conversation between Ratzinger and Dollinger takes place around the year 1990. Dr. Hickson, however, states that Fr. Dollinger told her that the conversation took place "not long after" the publication of the third part of the secret in June, 2000. Hickson neglected to report the fact of this earlier conversation from the year 1990.[5]

Concerning this matter, Fr. Paul Kramer issued a clarification on his *Facebook* account. He wrote:

> There is in fact no [discrepancy] whatsoever. The only difference

---

phenomenon. Both the young priest and the old German Rector were so impressed they drew up a dossier and sent it to Cardinal Ratzinger.

To date, this dossier about the incident has not been produced.

5   In the original article, this difference was noted because Hickson neglected to mention the story of the 1990 conversation between Ratzinger and Dollinger. This conversation added context to the later conversation and was a key piece of the story. It was pointed out only to demonstrate the inconsistency in which the matter of Dollinger's claim appears to be manifesting. Kramer seems to have misunderstood the intention. This confusion has been cleared up in the present writing.

is that my account was more complete. Dr. Hickson reports on a conversation that Dr. Döllinger had with Cardinal Ratzinger not long after the June 26, 2000 publication of the vision of the Third Secret. I also reported on that conversation;[6] but I also mentioned how that conversation referred back to an earlier conversation between Döllinger and Ratzinger around 1991. Dr. Hickson only fails to mention that there were two conversations, and that the latter refers back to the earlier conversation.

I spoke at length with Dr. Döllinger. Döllinger related to me that he had spoken with Cardinal Ratzinger some time shortly after the publication of the vision of the 3rd Secret. I have already reported on this years ago in issue no. 92 of the Fatima Crusader....[7]

---

6   [*Author's Note: Fr. Kramer refers to page ten of his 2009 article about a follow-up conversation between Ratzinger and Dollinger. Kramer wrote*:

Then on June 26, 2000, Cardinal Ratzinger published for the world the document [on the Third Secret] containing the vision of a "bishop in white", claiming that the entire Secret is set forth in this document....

The elderly German priest, Ratzinger's long-time personal friend, took note of the fact that when this vision of the Third Secret was published it did not contain those things, those elements of the Third Secret that Cardinal Ratzinger had revealed to him nearly ten years earlier. The German priest — Father Döllinger — told me that his question was burning in his mind on the day he concelebrated with Cardinal Ratzinger. Father Döllinger said to me, "I confronted Cardinal Ratzinger to his face." And of course he asked Cardinal Ratzinger, "how can this be the entire Third Secret? Remember what you told me before?"

Cardinal Ratzinger was cornered. He didn't know what to say and so he blurted out to his friend in German, "Wirklich gebt das der etwas" which means "really there is something more there," meaning there is something more in the Third Secret. The Cardinal stated this quite plainly.]

7   <https://www.facebook.com/paul.kramer.1023611/

Fr. Kramer's explanation is that there is no discrepancy between his and Dr. Hickson's account, only that his is "more complete." At face value, this appears to be the case as Hickson does not talk much about the earlier conversation from around 1990/1991. Thus, his account is truly "more complete" with respect to his inclusion of the conversation from the early 1990s.

The issue at hand, however, is that while Kramer's account discusses two alleged conversations, Dr. Hickson puts more information in the year 2000 conversation between Ratzinger and Dollinger than did Fr. Kramer. Thus, if Kramer's version is "more complete," why did he not mention that Ratzinger told Dollinger that the "unpublished" material mentioned a "bad Council" and a "bad Mass?" Kramer does not use the adjective "bad" in his 2009 article.

Did Dollinger neglect to mention this important statement to Fr. Kramer? If so, how could he possibly do such given the gravity of these words? Is it that Fr. Kramer neglected to report them? These questions remain unanswered, yet they provide us with an opportunity to examine another difficulty.

II. Second Difficulty: The Alleged Words of Our Lady

Both versions of Dollinger's claim differ in what was allegedly said by the Blessed Virgin about the Second Vatican Council and the Mass. In Kramer's version, there is no mention of a "bad Council" or a "bad Mass" as in Hickson's account, only that there was allegedly a call from Our Lady "not to change the liturgy." There is a difference between the two statements, each with different possible conclusions.

Kramer's version presents a call not to change the Liturgy. This is

---

posts/1216582278387181> (Accessed 28 May, 2016). Hereafter *Kramer Response 2016*.

a more benign, non-condemnatory warning. Hickson's version has a *specific description* of the Second Vatican Council and the Ordinary Form ("Novus Ordo") liturgy as "bad." This description is a graver statement as it indicates a particularly damning heavenly judgment upon the character of the Ecumenical Council and Ordinary Form. Such a damning judgment would be a welcome admission to anyone who questions the Council and its effects within the Church. If, on the other hand, Our Lady only issued a simple warning "not to change the liturgy," there is not quite the same dramatic indictment of the Council itself.[8]

Earlier, we asked whether Dollinger neglected to tell such serious words to Fr. Kramer. It is possible that there was more from Dollinger's year 2000 conversation with Ratzinger than what Fr. Kramer relayed. While possible, and though more subjective, one should consider the tone and tenor of Hickson's recounting of her phone conversation. Her report gives the impression that Dollinger, in 2000, was told this information by Ratzinger *for the first time.*

The above characterization comes across when Hickson relays Ratzinger's alleged remark to Dollinger about a "bad council and a bad Mass." What would be the sense in repeating it if Dollinger already heard it ten or so years prior? Was it merely to remind Dollinger? If so, how could this be, considering that Dollinger was the one who *confronted* Ratzinger in the first place? If he was the one to confront, he was more than likely *not* the one to have forgotten what was said ten or so years prior. Let us consider that Dr. Hickson prefaced her account by saying that she was relaying the "following facts." Perhaps she or Fr. Dollinger simply confused the order of these "facts?" At this time, there has been no clarification.[9]

---

8   It is a different shade of meaning, though the general intent would be the same: changes to the Liturgy of the Roman Church would be a bad idea.

9   Kramer omits clarifying the question of the words about an allegedly "bad" Council and Mass in his *Kramer Response 2016.*

Consider also a statement by a commenter under Hickson's article.[10] The commenter claims to have heard a slightly different story:

> I am Brazilian, and I talked with a priest, who had Fr. Dollinger as professor in the seminary. He told me, and it was about 2003 or, 2004, Fr. Dollinger told him the words of Our Lady were, "don't change the Mass, don't call a Council".

If we take the above comment seriously, then we have an even further discrepancy in the story.[11] Following upon the difference in statements, it is one thing to use the adjective "bad" for the Second Vatican Council and the Liturgy. It is quite another to issue a call *not* to convene an Ecumenical Council or change the Mass, as the character of the above comment demonstrates.

While the name of the Brazilian priest is unspecified, it appears as though the priest is Fr. Rodrigo Maria, a diocesan priest incardinated in the Diocese of Ciudad de Leste, Paraguay.[12] He left a statement on the web site *Fratres in Unum* in which he relays his interaction with Fr. Dollinger.[13] This statement agrees with the above commenter on that Our Lady (allegedly) did *not* say the Council and Mass were "bad." Rather, a call was issued *not* to convene a Council. In the words of the statement:

---

10 <http://www.onepeterfive.com/cardinal-ratzinger-not-published-whole-third-secret-fatima/#comment-2677802041> (Accessed 27 May, 2016).

11 See also <http://www.onepeterfive.com/on-fatima-story-pope-emeritus-benedict-xvi-breaks-silence/> (Accessed 27 May, 2016).

12 Cf. <http://www.padrerodrigomaria.com.br/sobre/> (Accessed 7 August, 2016).

13 <https://fratresinunum.com/2016/05/23/onepeterfive-responde-ao-desmentido-da-sala-de-imprensa-da-santa-se-dollinger-confirma-dialogo/#comment-120365> (Accessed 7 August, 2016). This author has confirmed the comment's authenticity.

[Dollinger] told me that knowing many mystical souls of his time, one of them told him about the contents of the third part of the secret, which seemed to explain the current situation of the Church [as well as the] silence and prevarication of the Ecclesiastical Authorities about the issue. He told me that, according to this mystical soul, the content of the third part of the secret was essentially these words: "There will come a council, through which apostasy will enter the Church ... tell the Pope not to hold the Council" ... when Fr. Dollinger asked Cardinal Ratzinger if such was really the content of the secret the Cardinal went silent (because according to the explanation of Fr. Dollinger, the Cardinal was bound by oath not to speak out about the issue) ... after Fr. Dollinger asked the Cardinal why he did not disclose the content of the third part of the secret, the response of his Eminence was, "Because it's too late."[14]

By all appearances, it seems as though the proverbial game of telephone is playing itself out. When one looks at the matter carefully, there is not found a statement from Dollinger himself. Every statement, thus far released to the public, has been through people who claimed to have spo-

---

14   The original Portuguese (from the above citation) is as follows: Disse-me que tendo conhecimento com muitas almas místicas de seu tempo, uma delas lhe falou sobre o conteúdo da terceira parte do segredo, que parecia explicar a atual situação da Igreja, bem como o silêncio e a tergiversação das autoridades eclesiásticas a cerca do tema. Ele me disse que, segundo essa alma mística, o conteúdo da terceira parte do segredo seriam essencialmente essas palavras: "Virá um Concílio, por meio do qual a apostasia entrará na Igreja...diga ao Papa que não faça o Concílio"...quando o Pe. Dollinger perguntou ao Cardeal Ratzinger se era realmente esse o conteúdo do segredo o Cardeal silenciou(porque segundo explicou Pe. Dollinger o Cardeal estava obrigado por juramento a não pronunciar-se a cerca do tema)...depois o Pe. Dollinger perguntou ao Cardeal porque não se divulgou o conteúdo da terceira parte do segredo e a resposta de sua Eminência foi: "Porque agora é tarde demais".

ken with Dollinger. The contradictory nature of these accounts is enough to cast doubt upon how well Dollinger is being represented.

At least as it pertains to the question of the Second Vatican Council, there may be a resolution of the matter when we look at a third difficulty—this one involving documents from Sr. Lúcia *herself*.

III. Third Difficulty: Sr. Lúcia on Vatican II

Fr. Kramer and Dr. Hickson both agree on a central point: that there is more to the third part of the secret of Fátima.[15] For the sake of argument, if the remark on a "bad" Council and a "bad" Mass is accurate, then Fr. Dollinger has apparently *directly* contradicted Sr. Lúcia herself.[16]

One of the more notable Fátima scholars was a priest named Fr. António Maria Martins, S.J. In 1973, he published a book entitled (in Portuguese), *Memórias e Cartas da Irmã Lúcia* (Memoirs and Letters of Sr. Lúcia). This book reproduces the four famous *Memoirs* of Sr. Lúcia and includes several of her available letters at the time. One of those letters, dated September 16, 1970 to Mother [Maria José] Martins, has a truly revelatory line from Sr. Lúcia in light of the present discussion with Fr. Dollinger.

Writing on the Rosary, Sr. Lúcia makes a comment about the Second Vatican Council. She wrote:

The simple remembrance of the mysteries in each decade is another radiance of light supporting the smoking torch in the souls. This is why the devil had moved against it such a great

---

15   This area from the original article has been slightly amended after further reflection upon Kramer's and Hickson's versions.

16   In a comment under Hickson's article, she was asked what German word was used in her conversation with Fr. Dollinger to describe the Council and Mass. She responded that Father used the word "schlecht" which simply means "bad" <http://www.onepeterfive.com/cardinal-ratzinger-not-published-whole-third-secret-fatima/#comment-2678211641> (Accessed 17 May, 2016).

war. And the worst part is that he had deluded and deceived souls of great responsibility for their position. They are blind men leading blind men. They pretend to base in the Council and do not realize that the Holy Council ordered them to preserve all the practices that in the course of years had been fostered in honour of the Immaculate Virgin Mother of God. The prayer of the Rosary or five decades is one of the most important and according to the decrees of the Holy Council and the orders of the Holy Father one we must maintain.[17]

---

17   Fr. António Maria Martins, S.J., (edit.), *Memórias e Cartas da Irmã Lúcia*. (Porto, Portugal: Simão Guimarães, Filhos, LDA, 1973), 454. The Portuguese text is:

> ....A simples recordação dos mistérios em cada dezena é mais um raio de luz a sustentar nas almas a mecha que ainda fumega.
> Por isso o demónio ihe tem feito tanta guerra! E o pior é que tem conseguido lludir e enganar almas cheias de responsabilidades pelo lugar que ocupam!... São cegos a guiar outros cegos!... E querem apoiar-se no Concilio, e não vêem que o Sagrado Concilio ordenou que se conservem todas as práticas que no decorrer dos anos se vêm praticando em honra da Imaculada Virgem Mãe de Deus, e que a oração do santo Rosário ou Terço é uma das principais a que, em face do ordenado pelo Sagrado Concilio e pelo Sumo Pontifice, estamos obrigados, isto é, devemos conservar.

Sr. Lúcia did not specify a Council document or order of the Holy Father. The reader is asked to consider the following as potential sources: *Sacrosanctum Concilium* 13, and *Lumen Gentium* 66-67. The Apostolic Exhortation *Recurrens Mensis October* (*Acta Apostolicae Sedis* 61 [1969], 649-654). An English translation is available online: <http://campus.udayton.edu/mary/resources/documents/prayingrosary.html> (Accessed 2 June, 2016). See also Paul VI's General Audience of October 8, 1969: <http://w2.vatican.va/content/paul-vi/it/audiences/1969/documents/hf_p-vi_aud_19691008.html> (Accessed 2 June, 2016). English translation of this audience can be found at: <http://campus.udayton.edu/mary/prayers/popepaul.html> (Accessed 2 June, 2016). See also Sister Lucia, *"Calls" From the Message of Fatima*. (Fátima, Portugal: Secretariado dos Pastorinhos, 2001), 266-272.

In the above, Sr. Lúcia makes a contrast. This contrast is between those who are "deluded," "deceived," "blind," and who "pretend" to base their teachings in the Council from what the Council itself said. This contrast implies that the Council is not deluded, deceived, or blind. One must therefore ask in what sense Sr. Lúcia refers to the Second Vatican Council as a "holy" or "sacred" [*Sagrado*] Council. There is a notable discrepancy between the clear meaning here and the Council being "bad" (*schlecht*) as allegedly described by Our Lady.[18]

In response to this discrepancy, Fr. Kramer issued some comments on his *Facebook* account. He wrote:

> (There is no "discrepancy". There is no contradiction. What there is, is possibly only some apparent inconsistency (on the part of Sr. Lucia) at most...
>
> Assuming (hypothetically) that Sr. Lucy wrote those words, the most that one can say is that there is possibly some inconsistency between what she says in her letter, and Our Lady's words which she wrote in the secret. People can be inconsistent. That is an effect of human weakness and fallibility. However, the use by Sr. Lucy of the adjective "holy" in reference to the Council in her letter does not logically contradict or oppose Our Lady's use of the expression "evil council" in the Secret. In some ways one can say the council was holy. In other ways it can be said to be evil. Furthermore, the fact that Sr. Lucy would use the words "holy council" in one qualified sense does not in any way logically deny or oppose Our Lady's words in the Secret that referred to the "evil council" in some

---

18   Known to this author are remarks about this letter of Sr. Lúcia's made by Frère François de Marie des Anges in his book *Fatima: Tragedy and Triumph* (Buffalo, New York: Immaculate Heart Publications, 1994), 111, 114. As these remarks pertain to the current discussion, they do not appear to have any bearing.

other very specific respect. There exists no logical opposition, because the modifying words are not applied to the term by the same person in the same manner and in the same respect. Thus, there is really no real "discrepancy" or any logical inconsistency at all....

Fr. Kramer continues, but let us examine what has been stated so far.

First, Fr. Kramer is not clear in his text, "...Assuming (hypothetically) that Sr. Lucy wrote those words...." Was he referring to Fr. Dollinger's claim of what she wrote for the third part of the secret or Sister's letter to Mother Martins? To whichever one he was referring, what *is* clear is that Kramer denies that there is any (real) discrepancy between what Sr. Lúcia allegedly wrote about the third part of the secret from what she later wrote to Mother Martins.

To advance his assertion, Kramer first distinguishes between "discrepancy" and "contradiction" from "inconsistency." He develops this idea by postulating that Sr. Lúcia was speaking in a "qualified sense" when using the word "holy." Between these two assertions (and depending upon how one resolves the ambiguity), Kramer may also have cast doubt that Sr. Lúcia wrote the letter to Mother Martins when he uses the words "assuming" and "hypothetically." We shall treat these two assertions and the insinuation in the above order.

A. First Assertion: "Discrepancy" or "Inconsistency?"

Concerning Kramer's first assertion, distinguishing between discrepancy/contradiction and inconsistency, this is nothing more than semantics. If Lúcia wrote one thing and then stated another, then that is a contradiction. She has "spoken against" (*contra + dico*) herself, and, logically, denied something that she has written (even if indirectly). Why would Kramer distinguish between these words? Without making a statement as

to Kramer's motives, one *can* examine the practicality of his argument.

The *practical effect* of distinguishing between these words downplays the impact of the contradiction. Dollinger's claim (in whichever version) must be upheld as credible.[19] It indicts very damningly some people as well as vindicates others who have contested the Vatican over the third part of the secret of Fátima. Both here and in his other writings Kramer indicates he *wants* such indictments.[20] Anything that challenges this indictment must be re-characterized, downplayed and presented to the audience as a plausible alternative. There is no real argument here, only a question of semantics.

B. Second Assertion: Human Weakness & Qualified Sense

Kramer advances his argument to state that it is only "possibly some inconsistency." He justifies this alleged possibility by an appeal to human weakness. In other words, Sr. Lúcia (allegedly) heard Our Lady describe as "bad" the Second Vatican Council and the Ordinary Form liturgy. From sheer human weakness, however, Sr. Lúcia declares the Council (at least) to be "holy" (*sagrado*). This alleged "weakness" is quite a different characterization of Sr. Lúcia than the one given by Kramer in his book *The Devil's Final Battle*.[21]

Between the pages of this book, we meet a Sr. Lúcia who was cho-

---

19   This observation is without prejudice to the question of *which* claim from the differing versions is being defended. The fact is that Fr. Dollinger has, generally speaking, indicted the Second Vatican Council and the Ordinary Form liturgy.

20   Cf. Fr. Paul L. Kramer, *The Devil's Final Battle*. (Terryville, Connecticut, Good Counsel Publications, 2002), 216-245. Hereafter *The Devil's Final Battle* followed by page number.

21   Fr. Paul L. Kramer, *The Devil's Final Battle: Our Lady's Victory Edition*. (Good Counsel Publications, 2010). Hereafter *The Devil's Final Battle (2010)* followed by page number.

sen by God to be a "witness" who "we can know for certain" is "worthy of belief." This credibility is due to a Divine stamp of approval via the miracle of the sun.[22] Moreover, Lúcia was, apparently, bold enough at ten years of age to ask the Mother of God for a miracle to prove her claims, and withstood the threat of being boiled in oil so as to uphold what Our Lady *ordered* her to do.[23]

Human beings are not perfect; Kramer is correct in this fundamental fact as he would also be to point out that this "Divine stamp" does not necessarily guarantee infallibility later in life. This sudden appeal, however, to human weakness becomes suspect when it appears to suit conveniently his argument. Moreover, it undermines the credibility of the sole witness whom God left on earth to tell the story of Fátima in its plenitude.

Kramer then provides an alternative explanation as to why Our Lady (allegedly) said one thing and Sr. Lúcia another. Kramer attempts to address the law of non-contradiction and argues for a "with respect to" position. In other words, "with respect to *some elements*" the Council is "holy"

---

22   Ibid., 1. This characterization is even more serious considering Sr. Lúcia's own claim that Jesus told her in response to her concerns over her education, "Não fiques triste. Não estudarás, mas dar-te-ei a Minha Sabedoria. A Mensagem fica ao cuidado da Minha Hierarquia" (Do not be sad. You will not study, yet I give you my Wisdom. The Message is in the care of my Hierarchy) (Carmelo de Santa Teresa – Coimbra, *Um Caminho sob o Olhar de Maria: Biografia da Irmã Lúcia de Jesus e do Coração Imaculado, O.C.D.* [Coimbra, Portugal: Edições Carmelo, 2013], 138. Hereafter *Um Caminho sob o Olhar de Maria* followed by page number). If Jesus promised to give His Wisdom to Sr. Lúcia, one is left to ponder further why she would use the adjective *sagrado* if Our Lady said otherwise.

23   Ibid., 4, 17. We are also expected to pity Sr. Lúcia and be outraged because she was allegedly a captive witness to a "Vatican apparatus" (see *The Devil's Final Battle (2010)*, chapter 11 "Muzzling and Hiding the Witness"). This "captive witness" theme may not hold under scrutiny as the letter to Mother Martins appears to have been unscripted and not forced by any ecclesiastical authority. Moreover, as we shall see momentarily, its veracity was upheld by Sr. Lúcia herself in 1986.

but "with respect to *other* elements" the Council is "evil." Thus, his contention is that Sr. Lúcia was speaking in a "qualified sense." This is, however, a matter of interpretation, one that is dangerously close to *eisegesis*, not *exegesis*. One could make arguments for individual "good" and "bad" elements within the Council documents. The question before us, however, is was this qualification intended by Sr. Lúcia when she wrote the 1970 letter to Mother Martins?

There appears to be *no indication* in said letter that Sr. Lúcia was attempting to speak in a "qualified sense." Consider the following observations. First, Sr. Lúcia did not state that she was speaking in a qualified manner. Second, she was writing freely and openly to a friend and fellow religious from her time with the Dorothean Sisters. Third, there was no reason for Lúcia to include the adjective *sagrado* in this letter if she did not mean it. The word is gratuitous. It underscored, however, her point on the devotion of the Rosary in particular and assisted in her refutation of the error that the Ecumenical Council was to blame for this devotion not being propagated.

Fourth, and finally, let us also consider that for Our Lady to call the Council and Mass "bad" is itself not a balanced qualification. Rather, it is a unilateral adjective describing the Council and Mass overall as bad. Why would Sr. Lúcia refer in a "qualified sense" to the Council as "holy" if Our Lady herself qualified it *unequivocally* as "bad?" Would Sr. Lúcia think that she knew better than the Blessed Virgin?

As indicated earlier, Fr. Kramer continued his response. He wrote further:

> So to Symond's question...we can reply that Mr. Symonds is somewhat disingenuous in his overly simplistic thinking that the alleged "discrepancy" between Sr. Lucy's words "holy council" in her letter somehow renders the expression in Our Lady's words "evil council" in the Secret problematic or im-

possible. That is patently doltish reasoning.

The fact remains that Cardinal Ratzinger did attribute the words "evil council" to the text of [the] Third Secret, since he made this disclosure not only to Dr. Döllinger, but to another priest as well, who was later elevated to the dignity of archbishop. That archbishop told a priest who is well known to us that Cardinal Ratzinger had revealed some contents of the Secret to him, specifically the statement about the evil Council.[24]

Given what has been said previously, there are only a couple of things that need to be said about this text.

First, what has been attempted in this chapter is to present the facts and provide an honest, objective assessment of them. Questions are posed in order to arrive at a greater understanding of the subject at hand. This matter is not one of ill will or polemics, but a sincere search for the truth.[25] It is clear that there are open questions with respect to the third part of the secret, many of which have been posed by people like Fr. Kramer over the years.[26] These questions deserve answers.

In the light of all the confusion brought by the differing versions of Fr. Dollinger's claim, Fr. Kramer might consider naming the above-referenced Archbishop and priest. They might be able to explain exactly *what* was said by Fr. Dollinger (though we'd still have others representing him,

---

24   If, as Fr. Rodrigo Maria claimed he heard from Dollinger, Ratzinger was bound by an oath not to say anything, why would he speak on the matter to this unmentioned Archbishop?

25   To learn Kramer's view of polemics, see *The Devil's Final Battle (2010)*, 154.

26   It is quite possible that some of these questions will not be answered until all the documents about Fatima have been published. It is to be noted that Sr. Lúcia (who was known to express reluctance in talking about her supernatural experiences) lived a very long life and left behind various unpublished writings. These are to be studied and published with due care by the competent authorities.

not Dollinger himself). Moreover, at least to the question of whether Fr. Dollinger spoke in terms of a "bad" Council and Mass to Fr. Kramer, the fact that Kramer does not contradict it (apparently defending it even) leads to an interesting question. Why did Kramer not reveal these words earlier? He has accused the Holy See of impropriety, yet he stands open to the same accusation!

C. Insinuation: Doubting the Authenticity

Depending on how one reads Kramer's ambiguity, he may have cast some doubt on the authenticity of the 1970 letter to Mother Martins when he used the words "assuming" and "hypothetically."[27] Did Sr. Lúcia, in fact, write this letter? Indeed, she did, and not only did Sister write it, she confirmed its authenticity on March 16, 1986. She confirmed it in a letter to a Mother King, intended for a Msgr. Joseph A. Cirrincione. Monsignor published this information in a booklet co-authored with Thomas A. Nelson entitled *The Rosary and the Crisis of Faith*. Reproduced in this booklet is a copy of the 1986 letter in its Portuguese original with an accompanying English translation.[28]

IV. Fourth Difficulty: The Source

Another, and final, difficulty concerns an open question of the source for these alleged comments of Sr. Lúcia about a "bad" Council and Mass. Were these remarks in a written document or were they a verbal state-

---

27   If Kramer cast doubt upon Sister's letter, this would be perplexing given that in the 2002 edition of his book *The Devil's Final Battle* (119), Kramer quotes from this same letter (through Frère Michel) as if it were authentic.

28   Msgr. Joseph A. Cirrincione and Thomas A. Nelson, *The Rosary and the Crisis of Faith*. (Rockford, Illinois: TAN Books and Publishers, Inc., 1986), 12-13.

ment from Sr. Lúcia? The Kramer and Hickson versions do not specify this information (the one attributed to Fr. Rodrigo Maria states that it was another alleged mystic, not Lúcia, who spoke to Dollinger on the contents of Lúcia's letter).

This question is an important observation because of critical information published in the biography of Sr. Lúcia, *Um Caminho sob o Olhar de Maria*. From this biography, we now know that Our Lady had commanded Sr. Lúcia in 1944 *not* to write down what was given her to understand of the significance of the third part of the secret.[29] There is some debate over the precise meaning of this command from Our Lady, but one thing is clear: Sr. Lúcia may have understood more of the third part of the secret than what she may ever have said publicly.[30] For now, if there was further information given to Sr. Lúcia, then to date, the *status quaestionis* is: did Sr. Lúcia ever write down this information, and, if so, when, why, and to whom? No one has answered the question and it is where matters currently stand.

In conclusion, there remain open questions about the differing versions of the claim of Fr. Dollinger. No one appears to have a singular, well-defined version of events and there appears to be no direct statement from Fr. Dollinger. The lack of unity alone deeply affects the credibility of Dollinger's claim, which, conversely, questions which "claim" is authentic. To date, there has been no definitive attempt at resolving these questions, though the Holy See has issued a denial.[31] The matter remains in question and ought to be examined further with the greatest of scholarly

---

29   *Um Caminho sob o Olhar de Maria*, 266.

30   There is some question as to whether or not her May, 1982 letter to Pope John Paul II contains all or part of her understanding of the third part of the secret (cf. Congregation for the Doctrine of the Faith, *The Message of Fatima*. [Vatican City: Libreria Editrice Vaticana, 2000], 8-9).

31   <http://press.vatican.va/content/salastampa/it/bollettino/pubblico/2016/05/21/0366/00855.html> (Accessed 30 May, 2016).

care and precision. This author remains open to further evidence and discussions in a free, non-polemical environment for the honor of God and Our Lady.

—13—
VARIOUS CONSIDERATIONS

"Há pessoas que nunca estão contentes! Não se faz caso."
—Sr. Lúcia

There are some specific matters concerning the third part of the secret of Fátima that the present chapter addresses. These matters do not necessarily warrant an entire chapter for treatment and so they are collected and sectioned off here according to topic for ease of reading.

I. Two Dates, Two Texts?

Among the theories in favor of the existence of a second text of the third part of the secret there is one that purports to answer the question of when Sr. Lúcia allegedly wrote down the two texts. Fr. Paul Kramer formalized this theory in his book *The Devil's Final Battle*.[1] As presented in

---

1   Fr. Paul Kramer, *The Devil's Final Battle*. (Good Counsel Publications, 2002), 148-149. Hereafter *The Devil's Final Battle* (2002) followed by page number. The argument is also contained the second edition of this book: Fr. Paul Kramer, *The Devil's Final Battle*. (Good Counsel Publications, 2010), 231-232. Hereafter *The Devil's Final Battle* (2010) followed by page number. See also Antonio Socci, *The Fourth Secret of Fatima*. (Fitzwilliams, New Hamp-

this book, the theory is based upon two dates around when the third part of the secret was written, namely January 3 and January 9, 1944.

The theory states that the text released by the Vatican in the year 2000 bears the date of January 3, 1944. There was, however, a letter that Sr. Lúcia also wrote to Bishop da Silva bearing the date of January 9, 1944 and quoted by Fr. Joaquin Maria Alonso. Looking at these dates, Kramer asks:

> Considering that Sister Lucy had finally written down the Secret after an apparition of the Blessed Mother, why would she not have immediately informed Bishop da Silva as soon as the document was ready, given the Mother of God's assurance that it was God's will that she deliver the document? Why would Sister Lucy, trained in obedience, wait *another* six days after obeying *Heaven's command* to write down the Third Secret—from January 3 to January 9—before informing her bishop? From this we may conclude that the text of the Third Secret was not ready until January 9, 1944 or very shortly before.
>
> This difference of dates lends further support to the existence of two documents: one containing the vision, completed on January 3, 1944; the other containing Our Lady's words which explain that vision, completed on or very shortly before January 9, 1944 (emphases Kramer's).[2]

The Carmelite Sisters indirectly addressed the question of the two dates in their biography of Sr. Lúcia, *Um Caminho sob o Olhar de Maria.*

The Sisters state that Sister was only able to write letters on Sun-

---

shire: Loreto Publications, 2009), 142. Hereafter *The Fourth Secret of Fatima* followed by page number; Christopher Ferrara, *The Secret Still Hidden.* (Pound Ridge, New York: Good Counsel Publications, 2008), 138. Hereafter *The Secret Still Hidden* followed by page number.

2   *The Devil's Final Battle* (2002), 149; *The Devil's Final Battle* (2010), 232.

days.[3] January 9, 1944 was a Sunday and, according to the journal of Sr. Lúcia (quoted in the Carmelites' 2013 biography), the apparition of Our Lady is indicated as January 3—not the second—making Monday the day of the apparition.[4] It thus makes perfect sense as to why there was nearly a week between writing down the secret (January 3) and when she wrote a letter to Bishop da Silva about it (January 9). Her letter was a cover letter. Moreover, as the document containing the third part of the secret was not a letter in the formal sense of the word, Sr. Lúcia was able to compose it on a Monday.[5]

There is one final consideration on Kramer's theory. In the light of the information provided by the Carmelites, it is impossible for Sr. Lúcia to have written two texts of the third part of the secret on these dates. The reason for this is because Our Lady made the distinction between a vision and its meaning. Sister was told that she could write the former, but not the latter. Sr. Lúcia wrote in her personal diary:

> While I was waiting for an answer, on January 3, 1944, I knelt beside the bed which sometimes served as a writing table, and again I experienced the same without success. What most impressed me was that at the same moment I could write anything else without difficulty. I then asked Our Lady to let me know if it was the Will of God. I went to the chapel at 4 p.m. in the

---

3   Carmelo de Santa Teresa – Coimbra, *Um Caminho sob o Olhar de Maria: Biografia da Irmã Lúcia de Jesus e do Coração Imaculado, O.C.D.* (Coimbra, Portugal: Edições Carmelo, 2013), 274. Hereafter *Um Caminho sob o Olhar de Maria* followed by page number.

4   Sr. Lúcia states that after the full force of the supernatural had passed, she went without delay to write down the third part of the secret. How much time had passed is not specified.

5   It is important to note that the January 9, 1944 letter appears to have been revealed in its entirety by the Carmelite Sisters (cf. *Um Caminho sob o Olhar de Maria,* 274).

afternoon, the hour that I always made a visit to the Blessed Sacrament [when it is] ordinarily [most] alone. I do not know why, but I liked being alone with Jesus in the Tabernacle.

Then I knelt in the middle, next to the rung of the Communion rail and asked Jesus to make known to me what was His Will. Accustomed as I was to believe that the order of the Superiors was the expression of the Will of God, I couldn't believe that this wasn't. Feeling puzzled and half absorbed under the weight of a dark cloud that seemed to hang over me, with my face between my hands, I hoped without knowing how for a response. I then felt a friendly, affectionate and motherly hand touch me on the shoulder and I looked up and saw the beloved Mother from Heaven. "Do not be afraid, God wanted to prove your obedience, faith and humility. Be at peace and write what they order you, [not however what is given you to understand of its meaning]. After writing it, place it in an envelope, close and seal it and write on the outside that this can be opened in 1960 by the Cardinal Patriarch of Lisbon or by the Bishop of Leiria."[6]

Based upon the above information, it appears as though to continue to defend the position of the two dates/two texts theory within this context of the January dates would be a mistake.[7]

---

6   Ibid., 266. The English translation is taken from: Carmel of Coimbra and James A. Colson (trans.), *A Pathway Under the Gaze of Mary*. (Washington, New Jersey: World Apostolate of Fatima, 2015), 243. Hereafter *A Pathway Under the Gaze of Mary* followed by page number. The translation is slightly emended (indicated by the texts in brackets) after consulting the Portuguese original in those places.

7   Kramer admits on page 149 of *The Devil's Final Battle* (2002; page 232 of the 2010 second edition) that this theory is "dependent upon circumstantial evidence." In defense of the theory, he cites the "anti-Fatima establishment" as having "blocked publication" of some important works of Fr. Alonso. This claim is questionable given the simple fact (as stated above) that Fr. Alonso ap-

II. Letter or Writing?

Related to the above theory is the matter of whether or not Sr. Lúcia wrote a letter on January 3 or January 9, 1944.[8] Antonio Socci gives a basic summary in footnote 247 (chapter 4) of his book *The Fourth Secret of Fatima*:

> Monsignor Venancio, in the note deposited in the archives of the sanctuary of Fatima, speaks of this folio as a "letter." Therefore, the "Fatimites" have deduced from this that the Third Secret is written in the form of a letter addressed to Bishop da Silva. This would be a very important particular because the text of the vision published by the Vatican in 2000, on the contrary, does not at all have an epistolary form.[9]

Indeed, this apparent discrepancy is noteworthy as there is an obvious mental image and understanding that comes to mind with the word "letter." Let us remember, however, some key points.

The first is that Sr. Lúcia was not a scholar. She was a simple and humble nun whose earliest formation revolved around being a shepherdess. This characterization is not to insinuate that Sister was just a rustic from the hills and not credible.[10] Rather, it is necessary to place her upbringing and

---

peared to have the letter from Sr. Lúcia to Bishop da Silva. The points made here also address a new claim that appeared in the spring 2016 edition of Fr. Nicholas Gruner's *The Fatima Crusader* (pages 30-39) by a James Hanisch that argues for two apparitions to Sr. Lúcia, one on January 2 and the other on January 3, 1944.

8   See *The Devil's Final Battle* (2002), 151-153.

9   *The Fourth Secret of Fatima*, 145.

10   For a description of the person and character of Sr. Lúcia, see the portrayal by Canon Galamba in Frère François de Marie des Anges, *Fatima: Tragedy and Triumph*. (Buffalo, New York: Immaculate Heart Publications, 1994), 16-18. Hereafter *Fatima: Tragedy and Triumph* followed by page number.

formation within a healthy context because doing so assists in understanding her style and manner of expression.[11] Let us recall the helpful example from chapter ten of the present book that illustrates this point.

In the description of the angels sprinkling the figures in the vision with the blood of the martyrs, Sister used the word *regador* to refer to the object used to sprinkle the blood. *Regador* literally means a "watering can."[12] This is not a fitting ecclesiastical term and so the translator(s) rendered it as "*aspersorium*" in the English.[13] It is to be remembered that Sr. Lúcia wrote this text in 1944 at the age of 36 and had learned to read and write by that time. It is apparent that her shepherdess upbringing was still very prominent and Sister used the best word she knew to describe the object.[14]

From the above example, one can reasonably conclude that it would be wise to take Sr. Lúcia's formation and manner/style of expression into

---

11   Among the literature on Fátima there appears the theme of "exalting" Sr. Lúcia to great heights in order to uphold her as a credible witness. While it is most surely necessary for Sister to be credible, it is also equally important not to make her more than she was. For a balanced portrayal of Sr. Lúcia, written by one who lived with her, see Sister Maria Celina de Jesus Crucificado, OCD, *Our Memories of Sister Lucia.* (Coimbra, Portugal: Carmelo de Coimbra, 2005). See also the discussion entitled "Lucia's Literary Qualities" in Fr. Louis Kondor, SVD (edit.), *Fatima in Lucia's Own Words* (Fatima: Portugal: Secretariado dos Pastorinhos, 2005), 10-13.

12   Elbert L. Richardson, Maria de Lourdes Sá Pereira and Milton Sá Pereira (edits.), *McKay's Modern Portuguese-English and English-Portuguese Dictionary.* (New York: David McKay Company, Inc., 1943), 151.

13   Congregation for the Doctrine of the Faith, *The Message of Fatima.* (Vatican City: Libreria Editrice Vaticana, 2000), 21. Hereafter *The Message of Fatima* followed by page number. The Italian translation rendered it as "con un innaffiatoio di cristallo nella mano..." (Congregazione per la Dottrina della Fede, *Il Messaggio di Fatima.* [Citta del Vaticano: Supplemento a L'Osservatore Romano, numero 147 del 26-27 giugno 2000]), 21. Hereafter *Il Messaggio di Fatima* followed by page number.

14   See also *The Fourth Secret of Fatima*, 229-236.

account. If one was to base him- or herself upon a singular word and read or apply too much meaning into the word, one could be headed down a very narrow path that does not understand the greater picture.

While taking a slightly different angle to the above observation, Antonio Socci questioned the gravity of the word "letter." In the same footnote referenced above (247), Socci looks at the available literature and notices a difference in the usage of the word *even by other authorities*. He writes:

> But is this [lack of epistolary form] certain? In this case the witnesses who confirm the information furnished by Monsignor Venancio are also innumerable.... However, the expression "letter" could also have a generic sense. In fact, the term was used by John Paul II himself even for the text of the vision revealed in 2000, which is not in letter form. Writing to Sister Lucia (*TMF*, p. 27), the Pope says: "your handwritten letter containing the third part of the 'secret'". And on the following page in the account concerning her meeting with Monsignor Bertone, one reads: "That which is in the letter contains the third part of the Secret." In this case "letter" is synonymous with "envelope." It is difficult, therefore, to know whether Lucia, when she speaks of "letter addressed to the Bishop of Fatima," intends to say that the Secret is in epistolary form.[15]

---

15   *The Fourth Secret of Fatima*, 145. It should be noted that Socci cites five authorities on the word "letter," the last of which was Cardinal Ottaviani in 1991. The other references are all dated prior to 1959/1960 when the text was read by Pope John XXIII. How could it be possible for these people to specify the nature of the document's contents before it was even opened? They had to be dependent upon some prior description from an authoritative source, and, most likely, that source was Sr. Lúcia. Socci himself cites a 1946 interview between Fr. Jongen and Sr. Lúcia in which she specifies "...in a letter addressed to the Bishop of Fatima" as one of his five sources. For a similar take on the matter, see Marco Tosatti, *Il Segreto non Svelato*. (Casale Monferrato, AL: Piemme, 2002), 114.

III. "Tell This to No One"

Towards the end of the July, 1917 apparition, and after the communication of the secret (in all its parts) to the children, Sr. Lúcia writes that Our Lady told the children "Tell this to no one. Yes, you may tell Francisco."[16] These words of Our Lady have been taken to refer only to the third part of the secret.[17] As Fr. Alonso points out, however, the secret of Fátima in all its parts is meant to be considered as a whole.[18]

To interpret the words "Tell this to no one" as referring exclusively to the third part of the secret is to divide unnecessarily the secret in all its parts. Moreover, it is a clear violation of the historical record. It is clear from all sources that the children understood Our Lady to mean the *entire* secret was not to be divulged.[19] We read about what happened during their kidnapping in August, 1917 as one clear example, not to mention the numerous references to Sr. Lúcia keeping silence about the secret over the course of many years. She only revealed the secret gradually and when told to do so under religious obedience.

---

16   Dr. Antonio Maria Martins, S.J., *Memórias e Cartas de Irmã Lúcia.* (Porto, Portugal: Simão Guimarães, Filhos, LDA, 1973), 341. Hereafter *Memórias e Cartas de Irmã Lúcia* followed by page number.

17   *The Devil's Final Battle* (2002), 145; *The Devil's Final Battle* (2010), 228.

18   Joaquin Maria Alonso, C.M.F., *The Secret of Fatima: Fact and Legend.* (Cambridge, Massachusetts: The Ravengate Press, 1979), 35, 65-71, 93-94. Hereafter *The Secret of Fatima: Fact and Legend* followed by page number.

19   For a summary, see *The Secret of Fatima: Fact and Legend*, 15-18, 26-32, 61-62, 88-89, 98. See also Tarcisio Cardinal Bertone, *The Last Secret of Fatima.* (New York: Doubleday, 2008), 42-43. Hereafter *The Last Secret of Fatima* followed by page number.

IV. The Prioress of Carmel Alludes to a Second Text?

On April 10, 2015 Christopher Ferrara published an article entitled *More Explosive News from the Convent in Coimbra*.[20] This article speculates that the Prioress of the convent of St. Teresa in Coimbra, Portugal alluded to an unpublished text of the third part of the secret of Fátima.

According to Ferrara, this speculation arose from two letters sent by Solideo Paolini to said convent in an effort to consult the personal writings of Sr. Lúcia or, if this was not possible, to at least have a question answered. These letters went unanswered until October, 2014 when Paolini received what is described by Ferrara as a "scanty note" from the Prioress. Ferrara writes that the Prioress stated, "it is not possible for now to consult the documents you request. In its time, everything will be published." Ferrara wrote on this statement:

> Paolini notes the obvious and totally devastating point: "The Vatican has told us everything was published, but the prioress of the convent says everything *will* be published." Paolini also notes the Prioress' resounding silence in response to his specific question whether the two unpublished sources contain further references to the Third Secret (emphasis author's).[21]

---

20   <http://www.fatimaperspectives.com/ts/perspective722.asp> (Accessed 22 December, 2015). Hereafter *Ferrara: More Explosive News*. This article cites a video entitled "Fatima, le ultime novità" on *YouTube* posted by the organization "Associazione San Michele Arcangelo" on March 11, 2015 <https://www.youtube.com/watch?v=rZP_MoWKYAQ> (Accessed 22 December, 2015). The *YouTube* description is given as follows in Italian for this video, "Il conferenza del secondo ciclo "Il trionfo del Cuore Immacolato", organizzato dall'associazione San Michele Arcangelo. [R]elatore: dott. Solideo Paolini, fatimologo. Perugia, Sala della Vaccara di Palazzo de' Priori, 7 Febbraio 2015." In English: "The conference of the second cycle "The Triumph of the Immaculate Heart," organized by the St. Michael the Archangel association. Spokesman: Dr. Solideo Paolini, Fatimologist. Perugia, Sala della Vaccara di Palazzo de' Priori, February 7, 2015."

21   *Ferrara: More Explosive News.*

The Prioress' "scanty" note was interpreted by Paolini to refer to the third part of the secret. It is, however, quite possible to interpret the note in terms of the documents themselves. There are only two sentences given to us. The subject of the first sentence concerns the documents that were requested by Paolini and the impossibility to fulfill this request. The second sentence reveals the reason for this impossibility, namely that the documents in question will be published at an unspecified point in time.

The Prioress indicates (though does not directly state) that there is no reason for Paolini to examine the unpublished documents because *they will be published in the future.* She was speaking about the unpublished documents of Sr. Lúcia, in this case her private journals, not an alleged second text of the third part of the secret. Thus, Paolini *et al.* misinterpreted the Prioress' statement. Her statement, although related by topic, was not about the Vatican's statement that everything has been published concerning the third part of the secret but rather her statement was about the specific request of Paolini to examine the unpublished journals of Sr. Lúcia.

V. Sr. Lúcia: the "Last Obstacle" to the Secret?

In his book *The Last Secret of Fatima,* Cardinal Bertone attributed a peculiar remark to Sr. Lúcia.[22] He claimed that in a meeting with him, Sister referred to herself as the "last obstacle" in regards to the publication of the third part of the secret. This remark has received some criticism from Christopher Ferrara.[23] While it is a peculiar remark, it does not appear to be uncharacteristic of Sr. Lúcia.

It is a well-known and established fact that Sister was very reticent to discuss the supernatural graces and communications that were given to

---

22 *The Last Secret of Fatima,* 80.

23 *The Secret Still Hidden,* 103-106.

her. Fr. Alonso discusses this fact at some length.[24] Given that there are more documents written by Sr. Lúcia, such as her diaries, it is reasonable to say that such things would never have been published while she lived. It follows then that for Sister to describe herself as the "last obstacle" concerning the third part of the secret is not unreasonable.

VI. Fátima, Ratzinger and the Novissimi

In 1984, Joseph Cardinal Ratzinger gave an interview with the Italian journalist Vittorio Messori. The interview was published in the magazine *Jesus* in its November 11, 1984 issue.[25] It was later published by Ignatius Press as *The Ratzinger Report: An Exclusive Interview on the State of the Church.*[26]

During the course of the interview, the subject of Fátima was raised and Messori inquired about the third part of the secret.[27] Between the Italian version in *Jesus* and the English in *The Ratzinger Report*, there appeared a noted discrepancy, namely what appeared to be an editing of Ratzinger's remarks on Fátima and the third part of the secret. This discrepancy was noticed and commented upon in *The Fatima Crusader.*[28] The following is

---

24   *The Secret of Fatima: Fact and Legend*, 15-18, 26-32, 61-62, 88-89, 98.

25   <http://www.fatima.org/thirdsecret/ratzinger.asp> (Accessed 3 January, 2015). Hereafter *Ratzinger 1984 Interview*.

26   Joseph Cardinal Ratzinger and Vittorio Messori, *The Ratzinger Report*. (San Francisco: Ignatius Press, 1986). Hereafter *The Ratzinger Report* followed by page number.

27   Ibid., 109-110.

28   See *Ratzinger 1984 Interview* above. Present in the online version of this article, the discussion is prefaced with the following remark, "Cardinal Ratzinger said in the same interview that the Secret also refers to 'the importance of the *Novissimi* [the Last Times / the Last Things]....'" Someone at the *Fatima Center* understood the difference but its significance appears to have been overlooked. Moreover, the annotation in brackets predates Socci's book

a comparative English translation of the original Italian as found in *The Fatima Crusader* with this author's own.[29] Some annotations are added by the magazine (marked by italics) in its version:

Fatima Center Translation	Alternate Translation
[...] "Why has it [the third part of the secret] not been revealed?" *(To this the Cardinal gave the following most instructive reply:)*	"Why was it not revealed?"
"Because, according to the judgement of the Popes, it adds nothing *(literally: 'nothing different')* to what a Christian must know concerning what derives from Revelation: i.e., a radical call for conversion; the	Because, according to the judgment of the Pontiffs, it adds nothing different to what a Christian ought to know from Revelation: a radical call for conversion, the absolute seriousness of history, the dangers

by about two years: <http://web.archive.org/web/20041212221505/http://www.fatima.org/thirdsecret/ratzinger.asp> (Accessed 3 January, 2016).

29   *Ratzinger 1984 Interview.* According to the picture reproduction of the article, the Italian text reads:

> [...] «Perché non viene rivelato?» «Perché, stando al giudizio dei Pontefici, non aggiunge nulla di diverso a quanto un cristiano deve sapere della rivelazione: una chiamata radicale alla conversione, l'assoluta serietà della storia, i pericoli che incombono sulla fede e la vita del cristiano e dunque del mondo. E poi, l'importanza dei Novissimi. Se non lo si pubblica – almeno per ora – è per evitare di far scambiare la profezia religiosa con il sensazionalismo. Ma i contenuti di quel "terzo segreto" corrispondono all'annuncio della Scrittura e sono ribaditi da molte altre apparizioni mariane, a cominciare da quella stessa di Fatima, nei suoi contenuti noti. Conversione, penitenza, sono condizioni essenziali alla salvezza»...

absolute importance of history; the dangers threatening the faith and the life of the Christian, and therefore of the world. And then the importance of the 'novissimi' *(the last events at the end of time)*. If it is not made public - at least for the time being - it is in order to prevent religious prophecy from being mistaken for a quest for the sensational *(literally: 'for sensationalism')*. But the things contained in this 'Third Secret' correspond to what has been announced in Scripture and has been said again and again in many other Marian apparitions, first of all that of Fatima in what is already known of what its message contains. Conversion and penitence are the essential conditions for 'salvation'."

threatening the faith and the life of the Christian, and therefore of the world. And then the importance of the *Novissimi*. If it is not published—at least for now—it is to avoid mistaking religious prophecy with sensationalism. But the contents of this "third secret" correspond to the announcement of Scripture and have been reaffirmed in many other Marian apparitions, beginning with Fatima itself in its known contents. Conversion and penitence are the essential conditions for salvation.

In these remarks, Ratzinger made mention of the *novissimi* in connection with Fátima. In 1991 Fr. Gruner published Ratzinger's remark in English in *The Fatima Crusader* (#18). This translation was accompanied by a commentary from Fr. Joseph de Ste. Marie of the Abbé de Nantes' community.[30] Fr. Joseph discussed the *novissimi* in terms of the events at the end of time, citing what he called a "classical theological treatise"

---

30   This translation and commentary is available online: <http://fatima. org/crusader/cr18/cr18pgS4.asp> (Accessed 3 January, 2016).

entitled *De Novissimis*. Fr. Joseph failed to specify the author or date of this publication.

This interpretation of Ratzinger's remark is questionable. In Catholic theology, the *novissimi* do not refer only to the events at the end of time. It also refers to the four last things, namely death, judgment, heaven and hell.[31] The discrepancy was noticed by Italian journalist Antonio Socci in his *The Fourth Secret of Fatima*. He wrote:

> Second point: The alleged disappearance of a reference to the "end times" and to the "events predicted in Sacred Scripture" can be contested. This criticism arises in reality from an error, inasmuch as in *Jesus* Ratzinger had not at all said that Fatima has to do with the "end times," but rather confirms the "importance of the *Novissimi*." The *Novissimi*, in Catholic doctrine, are not the end times, but rather the "last things" that is, death, judgment, Heaven, and hell. Besides, in the Pauline monthly [*Jesus* magazine] the prelate did not at all link the Third Secret to "events predicted in Sacred Scripture," but to the "prophecy of Scripture" which has an entirely difference significance. He said in fact: "The contents of the 'Third Secret' correspond to what is announced in Scripture and what has been repeated many times in Marian apparitions." Then he explained, "Conversion, penance, are essential conditions for salvation."
>
> This gross misunderstanding was already found in the study by Frère Michel [*The Whole Truth About Fatima: Volume III*, pages 818-824], where the text in *Jesus* is reported in French, and the translation of these two points is erroneous. It is probably from there that the other "Fatimists" arrived at the

---

31   Cf. Fr. Alexio Maria Lépicier, *Tractatus de Novissimis*. (Parisiis: P. Lethielleux, 1921). See also Joseph Ratzinger, *Eschatology: Death and Eternal Life*. (Washington, D.C.: The Catholic University of America Press, 1988).

error, having taken the translated text as accurate. This considerable error could have been discovered quickly because the original page from *Jesus* was photographically reproduced and published in millions of copies by *The Fatima Crusader* no. 37, Summer 1991. The same photo was published in another volume of "Fatimist" orientation, the book by Father Kramer, at page 275, where one can check in Italian the Cardinal's authentic text. The episode, at least on these two points, demonstrates that a more or less theological polemic against the Vatican is based on an error of translation and imprecision.[32]

Socci makes it very clear in the above text that there is more to the word "novissimi" than what Frère Michel discussed in *The Whole Truth About Fatima*.[33] Regretfully, Socci takes his point too far and this was noticed by Fr. Paul Kramer.[34] Socci restricts the meaning of *novissimi* to mean only the four last things when it is clear in Catholic theology that the word can also refer to the events at the end of time.

---

32   *The Fourth Secret of Fatima*, 96.

33   Frère Michel may have taken the French translation from *la Contra-Reforme Catholique* (number 206, December, 1984, page 6). This periodical is issued under the auspices of the Abbé de Nantes. One can find the citation on page 553 of the French version of *Toute la Verite sur Fatima, Volume III*. According to this source, the periodical rendered the Italian ("E poi, l'importanza dei Novissimi") into French as "Et puis l'importance des derniers temps" (and then the importance of the last times). The French words "derniers temps" (last times) restricted the meaning of *novissimi*, hence the apparent confusion over Ratzinger's remark.

34   *The Devil's Final Battle* (2010), 34-25. It must also be pointed out that in his effort to correct Socci, Kramer also made a slight gaffe. He says that "the theological term *novissimi* is the Italian rendering of the same term in Latin: *novissimis*." *Novissimis* is the dative or ablative plural case and it is not customary to refer in conversation to a Latin word in these cases, but rather the nominative. It would have been more accurate to say *novissimus* (singular) or *novissimi* (plural).

One is thus forced to ask in what sense was Ratzinger using the term? Given that his last statement ("conversion and penitence are the essential conditions for salvation") touches upon one's salvation, one is forced to consider that Ratzinger was thinking about one's particular death, judgment and destination (heaven or hell). If this reading is correct, then Fr. Joseph wrongly assigned an apocalyptic character to Ratzinger's words.

In the light of the text released by the Vatican in June, 2000, it becomes clear as to why Ratzinger would focus upon conversion and penance. The Angel pictured therein cries out "Penance!" three times.[35]

VII. Bishop da Silva and the Third Part of the Secret

When Sr. Lúcia wrote down the third part of the secret and sealed it in an envelope, she also wrote some instructions on the exterior of the envelope.[36] These instructions, written in Portuguese, were "By the express order of Our Lady, this envelope may be opened in the year 1960 by His Excellency the Lord Cardinal Patriarch of Lisbon or by the Most Excellent Reverend Lord Bishop of Leiria."

It is important to make the observation to whom the envelope and its contents were addressed—the Bishop of Leiria and the Cardinal Patriarch of Lisbon. It was these two men that Sr. Lúcia wrote that Our Lady said

---

35   *The Message of Fatima*, 21. Frère François questions the reasons why Paul VI spoke about the message of Fátima in terms of penance (*Fatima: Tragedy and Triumph*, 117ff). It seems to this author that Paul VI may have been subtly revealing a portion of the third part of the secret.

36   While some controversy exists over these instructions, we shall not endeavor here to get into said controversy and will only give a brief summary in this note. In May of 2007, on the popular Italian program *Porta a Porta*, Cardinal Bertone publicly displayed for the first time ever on camera the envelope and the instructions written by (then) Sr. Lúcia. The camera zoomed in on the Portuguese text and it was clear that Sister wrote that Our Lady said the envelope was not to be opened until 1960 and only by the Bishop of Leiria or the Cardinal Patriarch of Lisbon.

were the ones to open the envelope and read its contents. This order was not followed and herein lays one of the most underrated aspects of the history of the third part of the secret of Fátima.

The third part remained safe in the chancery office of the Diocese of Leiria from 1944-1957. Word had spread during this time that Sister had written down the secret and that it was in the possession of Bishop da Silva. Furthermore, word had also reached the public that there was a date of 1960 attached to the document. A general expectation arose among the public that the secret was going to be published in 1960. The nearer this date approached, expectations grew.[37]

In the mid-1950s, an order went out from the Vatican to the Chancery of Leiria. That order was to send copies of all the manuscripts of Sr. Lúcia to Rome.[38] Naturally, the question arose over whether or not to send the envelope with the third part of the secret. This question was put to a Vatican official and the Diocese was told in no uncertain terms that the secret was *especially* to be sent.[39]

Bishop da Silva, himself very close to death, was asked twice by his auxiliary Bishop, João Venancio, to make a copy of the text before sending the secret to Rome. Da Silva refused, citing that it was not yet 1960.[40] Venancio, reluctantly, accepted da Silva's decision and passed the envelope

---

37 These expectations and the fallout from their not being met are recounted by Frère Michel in *The Whole Truth About Fatima, Volume III*, 525-620.

38 *The Secret of Fatima: Fact and Legend.* (Cambridge: The Ravengate Press, 1979), 48.

39 *The Whole Truth About Fatima, Volume III*, 480. Frère Michel prefaces his remarks by saying that he heard the facts of the story direct from Bishop Venancio himself. Bishop Venancio was, according to Frère Michel, the one entrusted with the task of organizing the copies to be sent to Rome.

40 *The Secret of Fatima: Fact and Legend*, 49. Fr. Alonso paints a benign picture of Bishop da Silva's intention with the third part of the secret. Contrast this characterization with Frère Michel who paints a dramatic picture of Bishop da Silva's relationship to the third part in general (*The Whole Truth About Fatima, Volume III*, 52-53).

and its contents to the Papal Nuncio, Msgr. Cento (later Cardinal) who himself gave it to the Holy Office in April, 1957.[41]

When it was decided not to reveal the third secret in 1960, there was a lot of disappointment among Catholics. Theories, hypotheses and conjectures abounded as to why the text was not published.[42] Unfortunately, some of these conjectures became bound up within much rhetoric and polemics (and, arguably, anger) over how "cheated" people felt. People felt the need to assign blame and, since Rome held the text, the Vatican was perceived to be at fault. This was to the detriment of the historical record.

The fact is that it was Bishop da Silva's decision not to make a copy that led to the secret not being released in 1960. Our Lady's express order was for the envelope to be opened in 1960 by the Bishop of Leiria or the Cardinal Patriarch of Lisbon. According to the best evidence available, she did not say it was to be opened by the Holy Father in that year. If the Bishop of Leiria or the Cardinal Patriarch of Lisbon had opened at least a copy of the text, history as we know it would quite possibly have been altered.[43]

VIII. Cardinal Sodano and the Third Part of the Secret

It took many by surprise when Angelo Cardinal Sodano revealed to the world that the third part of the secret was going to be released.[44] He even revealed that to which it pertained and stated it was going to be pub-

---

41   *The Secret of Fatima: Fact and Legend,* 47-49. See also *The Whole Truth About Fatima, Volume III,* 481.

42   *The Whole Truth About Fatima, Volume III,* 525-620.

43   The reader is to note that we speak here of *copies*. We are not advocating the withholding of the text from the Holy Father. If anyone withheld the text, it would have been morally wrong owing to the Holy Father's right of universal jurisdiction.

44   *The Message of Fatima,* 30-31.

lished in June by the Congregation for the Doctrine of the Faith (CDF).[45] What exactly was Sodano's role in the publication of the text?

When the Cardinal revealed the impending publication of the secret, he also offered an interpretation. When the interpretation was given, Sodano became the public "face," as it were, of the interpretation. To him was directed most (perhaps all) of the criticisms of said interpretation. Among these criticisms were two in particular. The first was that Sodano was trying to downplay the secret by offering a "preventative" interpretation.[46] The second criticism was that Sodano, as the Vatican Secretary of State, had no authority over the faithful to issue such an interpretation.[47] In other words, it was not within his competency or prerogative as the Secretary of State under the stated terms of his office.[48]

For good or for ill, Sodano became the public face of the interpretation that accompanied the Vatican's publishing of the third part of the

---

45   Said Congregation did, in fact, release the text with accompanying documents and a commentary by Joseph Cardinal Ratzinger (later Pope Benedict XVI).

46   *The Fourth Secret of Fatima*, 39 (see also Christopher Ferrara, *False Friends of Fatima*. [Pound Ridge, New York: Good Counsel Publications, 2012], 100. Hereafter *False Friends of Fatima* followed by page number). This criticism made some sense as the Cardinal spoke about an interpretation prior to publishing Sister's text. It may be irresponsible, however, for the Church to publish a vision without comment.

47   Francis Alban with Christopher Ferrara, *Fatima Priest*. (Pound Ridge, New York: Good Counsel Publications, 2013), 228. Hereafter *Fatima Priest* [2013] followed by page number. See also *The Secret Still Hidden*, 233; *False Friends of Fatima*, 104.

48   *Acta Apostolicae Sedis*, Vol. 80 (1988), 841-934. The section on the Secretary of State is found on pages 870-872. This Apostolic Constitution is available in Latin on the Vatican's web site: <http://www.vatican.va/archive/aas/documents/AAS-80-1988-ocr.pdf> (Accessed 22 December, 2015). An English translation is also available on the Vatican's web site: <http://w2.vatican.va/content/john-paul-ii/en/apost_constitutions/documents/hf_jp-ii_apc_19880628_pastor-bonus.html> (Accessed 22 December, 2015).

secret. Seven years later, however, there was a small yet profound revelation that would change this aspect of the discussion. In his book *L'Ultima Veggente di Fatima*, Cardinal Bertone revealed a detail that shed some light as to what happened with respect to the decision to publish the third part of the secret of Fátima. De Carli inquired about Sodano's divulging of the text, directly asking Bertone the following question, "Had the CDF prepared Cardinal Sodano's remarks beforehand?"[49] Bertone replied:

> Of course. The prefect of the Congregation [for the Doctrine of the Faith] and his staff worked out the basic interpretive approach to the message. They also made it clear that at some point they would produce a special document to comment on the Fatima event in its historical and theological context.[50]

The above revelation was a small yet profound admission in the history of the third part of the secret of Fátima. Whereas Sodano had become the public face of the interpretation of the secret (and, in fact, spoken of as if he was its originator), Bertone essentially states that such a description is mistaken. It was Cardinal Ratzinger and his staff who "worked out the basic interpretive approach to the message."

In answering thus, Bertone answered the second criticism stated earlier, namely "on what authority" did Sodano issue the interpretation? The answer is that he was acting as the mouthpiece for the CDF whose competency it is to handle matters of private revelation.[51] This makes sense as, after the

---

49   *The Last Secret of Fatima*, 73; Tarcisio Bertone con Giuseppe De Carli, *L'Ultima Veggente de Fatima*. (Milano: Rai Eri Rizzoli, 2007), 85. Hereafter *L'Ultima Veggente* followed by page number.

50   *L'Ultima Veggente*, 85. For emphasis, it should be noted that in the Italian, Cardinal Bertone says to De Carli's question "Senza dubbio" ("without a doubt"). This statement is emphatic.

51   See also Salvatore M. Perrella, "Il 'Messaggio di Fatima' della Congregazione per la Dottrina della Fede (26 giugno 2000). Interpretazioni contem-

reorganization of the Roman Curia by Pope Paul VI in 1967, the Secretary of State was placed second (after the Pope), followed by the CDF.[52] It should also be made clear that according to Dr. Joaquín Navarro-Valls, then director of the Holy See's press office, Pope John Paul II himself did not announce the text because the Pope was "personally involved."[53]

Concerning the first criticism, the "preventative interpretation," we must reassess it in the light of Bertone's admission. Prior to this admission (and arguably long afterwards), there was a connotation—if not a straight-forward denotation—of a conspiracy.[54] The essential argument was that Sodano tied Ratzinger's hands in the latter's *Theological Commentary*. Ratzinger was then forced (if nothing else by public opinion) to adopt Sodano's interpretation as a Cardinal opposing another Cardinal publicly would reflect badly on the Church. The logical conclusion to this thought was that the Catholic faithful were thus not given an *authentic* interpreta-

---

poranee." *Marianum* 74 (2012), 303ff.

52   See the Apostolic Constitution *Regimini Ecclesiae Universae* of August 15, 1967 in *Acta Apostolicae Sedis* Vol. 59 (1967), 885-928.

53   New York Times, "Vatican Discloses 'Third Secret' of Fatima" by Alessandra Stanley. May 14, 2000. Available on the Internet: <http://partners.nytimes.com/library/world/global/051400pope-fatima-secret.html> (Accessed 2 December, 2015). See also <http://thecabin.net/stories/051400/wor_0513000079.html#.WCRp6forLIU> (Accessed 10 November, 2016). Moreover, if the argument is to be taken seriously that Sodano did not enjoy the authority to issue such an interpretation, one must also consider that Pope John Paul II was sitting right next to Sodano as the announcement was made. If the Holy Father had a problem with this arrangement, why did he not stop it? Christopher Ferrara characterizes this scene as Sodano inducing the Holy Father to adhere to his (Sodano's) "Party Line" (*False Friends of Fatima*. [Pound Ridge, New York: Good Counsel Publications, 2012], 100). His characterization is offensive to the dignity of the Holy Father and not in keeping with the facts.

54   Cf. *The Devil's Final Battle*, viii, 1-3, 90-112. See also Chapter 4 (*Something is Missing*) in *The Secret Still Hidden* (pages 49-71). Pages 73-75, 78-80, 99, 106, 108-109, 147-148, 204 of this book also continue the discussion of Sodano's interpretation.

tion. The harsh rhetoric and polemics against Cardinal Sodano were nothing more than an attempt to pillory him, even to *ad hominem* attacks. This pillorying continued even after Bertone's revelation.[55]

IX. When Did Pope John Paul II Read the Secret?

One of the arguments for a second text of the third part of the secret of Fátima concerns a statement by Archbishop Bertone in *The Message of Fatima*. On page five of this document, Bertone gives a reconstruction of the timeline from when Pope John Paul II was shot on May 13, 1981 to the time when the third part of the secret was returned to the Archives of the CDF (August 11, 1981). Antonio Socci recounts this timeline on pages 136-138 (English edition) of his book *The Fourth Secret of Fatima*.

In short, the argument holds that Bertone contradicted himself on the dates. He states that the Holy Father requested the text of the third part of the secret be brought to him in the hospital and that he received it on or around July 18, 1981. Yet, as Socci notes, Bertone also discusses how the Pope thought of consecrating the world to the Immaculate Heart of Mary on June 7, 1981 based upon his reading of Sr. Lúcia's text. The obvious question is how can the Pope be inspired to consecrate the world to the Immaculate Heart of Mary from reading the third part of the secret of Fátima

---

55   Ferrara used the Fr. Marciel Maciel scandal to portray Cardinal Sodano as being corrupt (Cf. *Fatima Priest* [2013], 228-229). Additionally, there is at least one other item from Bertone's book that Ferrara appears to have missed. In *The Secret Still Hidden* (63-64). Ferrara discusses briefly the question of the 1984 consecration of the world to Our Lady's Immaculate Heart. He takes the opportunity to attack a note in *The Message of Fatima* (page 8) that cites a letter from Sr. Lúcia dated November 8, 1989. Ferrara identifies the letter as one addressed to a Mr. Walter Noelker. Bertone, however, states in *The Last Secret of Fatima* (82) that the letter in question was to the Pope, not Walter Noelker (see also *L'Ultima Veggente*, 94). Whether or not Bertone might have been mistaken is a good question, but as the facts stand at this time, it appears as though Ferrara missed this revelation.

in July for an event that happened five or so weeks prior in June?

The above is a good question and the anachronism is certainly glaring. Prior to publishing their theory, none of the advocates for a second text went back to verify the Italian text of *The Message of Fatima* on this point with the English translation published by the Holy See. A comparison of these texts shows that a notable mistranslation exists that may have a bearing upon the meaning of the text.[56] The Italian text in question is:

> Giovanni Paolo II, da parte sua, ha richiesto la busta contenente la terza parte del « segreto » dopo l'attentato del 13 maggio 1981. Sua Eminenza il Card. Franjo Seper, Prefetto della Congregazione, consegnò a Sua Ecc.za Mons. Eduardo Martinez Somalo, Sostituto della Segreteria di Stato, il 18 luglio 1981, due buste: – una bianca, con il testo originale di Suor Lucia in lingua portoghese; – un'altra color arancione, con la traduzione del « segreto » in lingua italiana. L'11 agosto seguente Mons. Martinez ha restituito le due buste all'Archivio del Sant'Uffizio.
>
> Come è noto Papa Giovanni Paolo II pensò subito alla consacrazione del mondo al Cuore Immacolato di Maria e compose egli stesso una preghiera per quello che definì « Atto di affidamento » da celebrarsi nella Basilica di Santa Maria Maggiore il 7 giugno 1981, solennità di Pentecoste, giorno scelto per ricordare il 1600° anniversario del primo Concilio Costantinopolitano, e il 1550° anniversario del Concilio di Efeso. Essendo il Papa forzatamente assente venne trasmessa la sua allocuzione registrata. Riportiamo il testo che si riferisce esattamente all'**atto di affidamento**....[57]

---

56   This author maintains that *The Message of Fatima* was composed originally in the Italian language. It is from this perspective that the following observations are made.

57   *Il Messaggio di Fatima*, 5.

The English translation issued by the Vatican reads:

> John Paul II, for his part, asked for the envelope containing the third part of the "secret" following the assassination attempt on 13 May 1981. On 18 July 1981 Cardinal Franjo Šeper, Prefect of the Congregation, gave two envelopes to Archbishop Eduardo Martínez Somalo, Substitute of the Secretariat of State: one white envelope, containing Sister Lúcia's original text in Portuguese; the other orange, with the Italian translation of the "secret". On the following 11 August, Archbishop Martínez returned the two envelopes to the Archives of the Holy Office.
>
> As is well known, Pope John Paul II immediately thought of consecrating the world to the Immaculate Heart of Mary and he himself composed a prayer for what he called an "Act of Entrustment", which was to be celebrated in the Basilica of Saint Mary Major on 7 June 1981, the Solemnity of Pentecost, the day chosen to commemorate the 1600th anniversary of the First Council of Constantinople and the 1550th anniversary of the Council of Ephesus. Since the Pope was unable to be present, his recorded Address was broadcast. The following is the part which refers specifically to the Act of Entrustment....[58]

It is clear that in the above English translation, the appearance is given of the anachronism in the timeline. Let us therefore dive into the Italian text.

The first observation comes from how the second paragraph ties together with the first. The impression is clearly given to the reader that they are two connected thoughts. This impression comes through the participle "consecrating." The Italian word, however, is *consacrazione*, which is a noun, not a participle. A more accurate translation of this first phrase, then, would be, "As is known, Pope John Paul II thought immediately *to the*

---

58   *The Message of Fatima*, 5.

consecration of the world to the Immaculate Heart of Mary...."

Consacrazione read properly as a noun with its article "to the" (*alla*) immediately restores the sense of the passage. Bertone is saying that after reading the third part of the secret in July, the Holy Father *thought back to the consecration* he had already done back on June 7, 1981 in the light of what he had just read. In other words, John Paul II was beginning to reflect more deeply upon the message of Fátima and it is clear that he wanted to be more explicit (as Bertone specifically states later on page 5 into page 6 after the quote from the Act of Entrustment) with the consecration than he had been in his "Entrustment" of June 7, 1981.

The rest of the sentence appears to have been accurately translated. Unfortunately, Bertone does seem to become very unclear. He discusses the fact of John Paul II having himself composed a prayer for the June Act of Entrustment. Bertone's grammar gives the impression that the Holy Father wrote said prayer *after* reading the third part of the secret. This impression is given because Bertone continues the narrative with a coordinating conjunction "and" (*e* in the Italian), giving the impression of a continuation of time. In other words, that the Holy Father in July thought back to his Act of Entrustment of June 7, 1981 *and* that he composed a prayer at the same time in July. Despite the obvious grammatical difficulty and the impression that it gives, the fact of the above-mentioned mistranslation makes it easier to accept an alternate explanation of Bertone's discussion.

In the corrected translation, it is clear that Bertone was talking about what the Holy Father had realized in July, 1981 after reading the third part of the secret. John Paul II realized that his Act of Entrustment from the previous June *the prayer of which he himself had composed* was insufficient to what Our Lady had specified. If one were to issue a corrected translation of the original Italian text from *The Message of Fatima*, it would look like the following:

As is known, Pope John Paul II thought immediately to the

consecration of the world to the Immaculate Heart of Mary and he himself composed a prayer which he called [an] "Act of Entrustment" to be celebrated in the Basilica of Santa Maria Maggiore on June 7, 1981, the Solemnity of Pentecost, the day chosen to commemorate the 1600th anniversary of the First Council of Constantinople and the 1550th anniversary of the Council of Ephesus. The Pope being forcedly absent, his recorded Allocution was broadcasted. We publish the text which refers specifically to the Act of Entrustment....

—Epilogue—

The preceding pages have attempted to address some controversial matters concerning the third part of the secret of Fátima. We provided a broad history of Fátima and its secret, focusing especially upon the third part. This history was necessary in order to establish a basic historical timeline of facts and events. From this timeline, we were able in subsequent chapters to discuss some specific matters in more detail.

What we have seen overall from the materials in this book can be summarized as follows. Over the course of several decades, a specific body of literature arose that has attempted to interpret Our Lady's call at Fátima. This body of literature in a number of places approached the topic from what has been herein called a "hermeneutic of suspicion and conspiracy." Within this hermeneutic, we saw that the person of Sr. Lúcia was placed in opposition to ecclesiastical authorities, who, it is believed, attempted to silence her in favor of the "vision" of the Second Vatican Council initiated by Pope John XXIII.

The above is an excellent dramatic story of two contrasting "visions." It is, however, not beyond questioning. Some key errors were noted ranging from matters of mistranslations to incautious readings of texts. Others concerned the unavailability of key texts and the dependency upon

interpretations of those texts. A fairly wide-ranging host of issues has been demonstrated as being potential reasons for a misunderstanding of the call of Our Lady at Fátima.

As much as there are debatable points within this literature, it would be equally a mistake to dismiss the literature in its entirety. There are some observations which deserve treatment. For example, it is believed that Our Lady predicted in the third part of the secret an apostasy. We saw that this interpretation largely surrounded the phrase about Portugal and the dogma of the Faith and connected the statement to the Second Vatican Council.

If, however, the "debated interpretation" of the phrase is accurate, Our Lady may have been referring more generally to the deleterious effects of war upon faith and good morals both in society and the Church. If true, what would have been the effect of this erosion of faith in relation to the Council? Pope John's intention was to renew the Faith and give it a new impetus in our times. Paul VI, however, began to see problems with the interpretation and/or implementation of the Council.

Classifying the good from the bad in the above-mentioned literature is a comprehensive effort. It requires the hands of a surgeon utilizing the utmost of caution and scholarly reserve so as not to exacerbate a delicate situation. Such an effort should be undertaken for the good of souls. Many people have been influenced by the ideas contained within the aforementioned literature. Those so influenced are becoming increasingly distrustful of ecclesiastical authority and risk falling into a sectarian spirit.

We cannot here explain or resolve the various reasons for this distrust, but it is clear that the Church faces a *serious* pastoral situation. As these reasons pertain to the subject of this book, Fátima is perceived as vindicating the distrust. The authority of the Church will continue to be undermined so long as people continue to believe in a cover-up with Fátima. Without a firm, pastoral, and comprehensive study of the matter from the competent ecclesiastical authority, the debate will continue. What then of the call of Our Lady at Fátima to pray, make sacrifices and reparation

as she specified? Will it be fully heeded or will people be too preoccupied with controversies?

As we have attempted to demonstrate in the preceding pages, the history of Fátima is still being written. So long as Sr. Lúcia lived, we would never know that history in its plenitude. In truth, we still do not. Why then, one could ask, would heaven have Sister remain on earth for so long before going to her eternal reward? The answer is debatable, but as Sister herself wrote in her private diary, it was to serve God. What the precise nature was of that service remains to be seen.

One could *very* safely state that at least part of that service was to pray and make sacrifices for sinners and reparation to the holy Hearts of Jesus and Mary. Arguably, the "hidden life" of Sr. Lúcia is not well known. It may very well provide an interpretation of Fátima, a "catechesis" if you will, of Our Lady's call and how to live it. We are entering into a new period of the history of Fátima and we ought to be celebrating this fact, not engaging in seemingly endless controversies.

In short, there are some good and questionable aspects of the aforementioned body of literature on Fátima. We must not "throw the baby out with the bathwater." The competent ecclesiastical authority may wish to address this fact for the good of souls and to renew the call of Our Lady at Fátima to devotion to her Immaculate Heart as the means offered to lead us to God. We have attempted in this book to provide a fairly comprehensive examination of the facts. While not definitive, it is hoped that this book may serve as an initial step forward into this exciting new period of Fátima's history.

What follows are several appendices to various documents referenced in this book.

—Appendix A—
1955 and 1967
Allocutions of the Most Eminent Lord Cardinal Alfredo Ottaviani on Fátima

Message of Fátima*

Allocution of His Eminence Cardinal Ottaviani in the Cova da Iria[1]

May 13, 1955

It is with deep emotion that I am today among you and will speak to you. Although I come from Rome, from the city of Christian wonders, the capital of the Kingdom of God on earth, I feel, in this corner of the world, overwhelmed by the grandeur of the scenery, invaded by emotion. Here, as in Lourdes, there is a mysterious presence; It makes itself felt in the air that breathes, it is almost seen in the light of the sun that enlightens us. It is the presence of the Mother.

Who did not sense, on returning home, the footsteps of his mother?

---

1   * Address delivered at the Cova da Iria, at the solemn Pontifical Mass on May 13, by the Most Eminent Lord Cardinal A. Ottaviani, who came from Rome for the purpose of blessing the Banner of the Basilica of Fátima.

At the time of his visit, His Eminence wrote these words that express his high appreciation for the historical mission of our country: "A history of human civilization without Portugal would be inconceivable, as a history of the Church in the last centuries without Portugal would be inconceivable."

Lumen: Revista de Cultura do Clero 19 (Maio-Junho,1955), 264-268.

Although one can no longer behold her with the eyes of the body, she is filling everything with her mystical presence. Thus, this place, where Our Lady was visibly present and sensibly spoke. We no longer see Her, but we still feel her perfuming everything and everyone with softness and sweetness. It is her house. And if it is hers, it is also ours, because the house of the mother is the house of the children. It is this, in essence, my dear pilgrims, the emotion that I experience, arriving here with so many others; It is this, doubtless, what you experience. We all consider ourselves to be in our home, in the place where the Virgin appeared, in the place where the Mother of God spoke.

In this environment, therefore, one can speak only of Mary, other subjects cannot be treated except those with which she has dealt. Even if I wanted to, it would be impossible to deviate from her message. It is this upon which we must meditate, it is this that we must try to put into practice.

First of all, my brethren, we must see God always present and operative in history.

It is true that the world, both the great world of nature and the small world of our passions, tries in all ways and by all means to divert us from God. But we must overcome one and the other and not obscure the eyes of the soul. We must see God alive in the history of man.

Under the veil of mystery, Our Lady wanted to show us something special for which God is preparing us. This is the certainty that He gave us, notwithstanding the pessimism to which the sadness of the present times could drag us.

In fact, the days we have been through cannot be darker nor more bitter. Sometimes iniquity reaches such refinements of atrocity that our heart almost despairs and feels like exclaiming with the prophet: *Rise up, why do you sleep, O Lord?* Why do you not attend to our tribulations? *Why do You turn Your Face from us?* [Psalm 43:23-24] Have you no longer the heart of a Father? Did you abandon us? But if He abandons us, to whom shall we turn?

Well, Our Lady gave us proof here in Fátima that God always looks at us with eyes of mercy and is never as present as when He seems absent. She told us that God is a Father and cannot abandon the children. That He prepares times for us that are so much more joyful than those sad ones through which we have lived. The Mother of God told us to look on high: *Look up, and lift up your heads, for your redemption is at hand* (Luke 21, 28.). But we continue to keep them low. We are preoccupied only with the earth; We love nothing else except transitory things. And if we see nothing but the earth, if we consider ourselves no more than a piece of dust, no wonder that we do not see God? No wonder, if we fall into despair?

It is written: *Blessed are the pure of heart, for they shall see God* (Matt. 5:8). Our heart is not pure; this is why we do not see God.

What does it mean to purify the heart, except to "do penance" to clear consciences and restore Christian customs in the individual, in families, in society, in this society that is headed for ruin?

The preaching of the prophets was essentially an invitation to penance. The first exhortation of the New Testament is: *repent; repent, for the kingdom of God is near, God's Kingdom is approaching* (Matt 3:2, 3:8; 4:17). The Apostles' preaching began with the same invitation (Acts 2:8). The Holy Fathers, the Doctors of the Church, and the Saints, throughout the centuries, did not preach unless [it was] about penance. And, to confirm such a high doctrine, the Mother of God herself, the Most Holy Virgin, has brought us here to this blessed land of Fátima, sanctified by her with her virginal feet. It is the last call of God's mercy, a supreme invitation to penance.

Unfortunately, my brothers, *there is no one who does penance ... they have not known how to blush* (Jer. 8:6, 9-12).

They presumed and presume to save the peoples: "peace, peace, when there was no peace" [Jer. 8:11], they cry out for peace and there is no peace.

To do penance, fundamentally, means to change hearts, to become

a new creature; Concerning children of man becoming children of God, living according to His Law, citizens of His Kingdom. Doing penance, in short, means living a Christian life.

And in what way do we live? Does there exist today in the world a truly Christian people, in all Catholic manifestations? Has not the number of Christians diminished appallingly?

In our cities, how many good Christians are there, even among those who confess to be Christian? What a formidable reality!

Considering this state of affairs, the necessity of penance assumes such proportions that it must be considered identified with salvation itself. *If we do not do penance, we shall fall into the hands of the Lord* (Eccle. 2:23).

Now, according to the prophet, the hands of God must be regarded as the hands of the artist who molds his figures, who, from the clay, makes them and undoes them at his good pleasure; He can form and destroy us when He wills and how He wills. *Behold as clay in the hand of the potter so you are in my hand* (Jer. 18: 6).

Only penance can make the hands of God, hands that form and create and not destroy and break.

The experience of the years plagued with angst, in which our generation has lived, will it not be sufficient? The sad fruit of the apostasy of man from all that is God will it have taught us nothing? The joy had disappeared, a whole series of miseries had fallen upon us. Neither did Jerusalem in the days of her desolation suffer so much. Even today, how many Christians lie trampled under the Satanic wrath of the enemies of God!

To the Most Holy Virgin our Mother, who in this place has spoken to us, we—gathered here from all parts of the world—respond courageously as good children. Let us say to her with the energy of the prodigal son: Yes, Mother, *in a spirit of humility and in a contrite heart*, with a spirit contrite and humbled we promise you to renew our life, to return to God as He wants, to be worthy of the name of Christians and of saying to Him, "Our Father who art in heaven."

Will we be faithful to this purpose?

Departing from Fátima, we will also carry in our soul the memory of the exhortation that the Most Holy Virgin made to us, inviting us not only to penance but also to prayer. She, the kind Mother, came to remind us that prayer is the means to attain grace that makes us faithful to the purpose formulated here with Christ, for the renewal of Christian customs in ourselves, in families and in society.

Jesus told us that without Him we can do nothing (John 15:5). Therefore, the Celestial Mother came once again to invite her children, I would better say, *insist* with them that they pray and pray much. Her virginal hands, when She appeared, were entwined with the Rosary. Oh, this admirable devotion of the Rosary, which we must take from here to be more rooted in the soul!

We will not leave this place without having purified our conscience by the Sacrament of Penance, without confirming our intentions with the grace that emanates from the Eucharistic Bread, which we receive almost at the hands of Mary; nor will we leave this blessed land without carrying her image well-carved in the eyes of the spirit; her image, I repeat, that will forever remind us of the ineffable sweetness and propitiatory power of the Holy Rosary. This prayer is, undoubtedly, the most universal and at the same time the most intimate of all. What church is there where the Holy Rosary is not recited collectively? Where is there a family of true Christian traditions that does not pray at night this prayer? Who is there who does not carry the Rosary with him? What son did not see the Rosary constantly in the hands of his mother? And in the fingers of those who die, when their arms are drawn over their breasts, are not the Rosary beads always intertwined?

It seems like a prayer of little importance for its simplicity, but it contains within itself qualities and excellences not easy to describe.

It has the value of prayers in litany form, which takes advantage of the repetitions to penetrate more and more into the heart. It uses the most

august formulas, which are the Our Father, the Hail Mary, the Glory Be. It makes continually present as a breath and palpitation of the soul the main mysteries of the life of Jesus intertwined with Mary's joys, sorrows and glories. It has the merit of oral and mental prayer, of individual devotion as well as the prayer of large crowds. It is, finally, the prayer of the greatest victories of Christianity over the enemies of Christ and the Church.

O noble and generous sons of the glorious Lusitanian land! O pilgrims of those nations who were so admirably represented in Lepanto, you can never forget the admirable action of the Rosary in that victory!

And you, in particular, sons and heirs of those heroic discoverers, whose sacrifice and heroism have given to Christian civilization lands hitherto unknown, imagine how many Portuguese mothers, how many wives, how many sisters, how many daughters in this fortunate land and in hours of anguished expectation for their intrepid sailors, did they not hasten the splendorous triumph of the civil and Christian enterprise with the Rosary beads in their hands, the Hail Mary on the lips and a sad prayer in the soul!

Now the Most Holy Virgin, showing herself here at Fátima with the Rosary, has indicated to us that this is the weapon with which She, the conqueror of all heresies, wants us to beg the Lord the deliverance from the horrendous evils that torment the world invaded by materialism, which tries to reduce the whole of humanity to slavery and the most tremendous oppressions.

The distressing example of how much half of Europe is suffering, oppressed by the tyranny of Communism, the cry of pain of so many martyrs, so many confessors of the faith, who beyond the Iron Curtain are paying with prison, with forced labor or with blood itself, their fidelity to Christ, to the Church, to the Pope, have these not yet convinced us of the necessity of the Holy Crusade proclaimed by the Supreme Pontiff for a better world?

In this place, the heavenly Mother spoke to us, she repeated the prophetic invitation *reconciliamini Deo*, be reconciled to God! That is why

all of us, in this place and in this solemn moment, implore her mighty intercession:

O Mother of God and our Mother, restore peace between us and God, for only when we have made peace with God, will human co-existence be more joyful.

Only when each of us is better will the world be better. Inspire us, Most Holy Mother, and help us to be better. From morning to evening we make projects and invent ways to improve living conditions, and we do not want to understand that the only way to achieve everything is to be good.

O Mother of Jesus and our Mother, that in this place of blessing you have assured us that God is with us if we are with Him, behold us, by Your grace, at Your feet. Tell Him, in our name, that we want to be with Him in life and death, in time and in eternity. As He is God with us, all Father all to His children, so we forever want to be entirely His, to live with Him the same life.

Children, brothers of His Only Begotten, heirs of His glory. Amen.

Allocution of His Eminence Cardinal Ottaviani at the Athenaeum February 11, 1967

About the Question of the "Secret of Fátima"

If it is a secret, how could I reveal the Secret?

At any rate, I will address some questions that concern the "Secret of Fátima," as Fr. Balic said very well [...*come ha detto benissimo il P. Balic*].

The first time that I was in Fátima was in 1955. As I climbed the slope that would take me to the Cova da Iria, I was already edified by the piety, the spirit of sacrifice and prayer which so many children of the people gave me, going up the slope, burdened from the weight of carrying provisions and all that they needed to pass the holy night commemorating the event of October 13, 1917.

When I arrived up there, at the Cova da Iria, it seemed to me that I was entering my Mother's house. I seemed to hear my mother say to me, "Prayer, penance!"

All these good people, the thousands upon thousands of people who passed the night outside in prayer and songs, songs and prayers, while the glow of thousands of candles lit up the large square in front of the Basilica, all these people truly gave me the impression that they understood well the spirit of the Message of Fátima.[2]

The Most Holy Virgin, in setting her virginal foot on the land of the Cova da Iria and thereby sanctifying it, in her conversation with little Lúcia, confided to her three messages. One concerned Lúcia in her more intimate family sentiments [...*nei suoi sentimenti familiari più intimi...*], the prediction that Francisco and [his] younger sister Jacinta will soon fly away to heaven [*la predizione che Francesco e la sorellina Giacinta sarebbero presto volati nel cielo*]. The prophecy was verified in a short time. There in the Basilica, now constructed in the Cova da Iria, on the right and left of the main altar, you see the tombstone of the place where the mortal remains of Jacinta and Francisco await the day of the glory of the resurrection while their souls are blessed in heaven. When I asked Lúcia what she wanted to say to the Holy Father, she had a sentiment that moved me, thinking to Francisco and his younger sister [...*ebbe un sentimento che mi commosse, pensò a Francesco e alla sua sorellina*]: "Tell the Pope to advance quickly the cause of beatification."

---

2   [La Documentation Catholique (LDC) Note 2:] We read in the written text: "This immense crowd in prayer did not ask to know the mysterious secret of Fátima. It was already in possession of the most essential secret, one that is engraven in the soul of anyone reading attentively the Gospel—the secret of the scale [ladder?] of heaven, whose degrees are called prayer and penance (Nous lisons dans le texte écrit: "Cette immense foule en prière ne demandait pas à connaître le mystérieux secret de Fatima. Elle était déjà en possession du secret le plus essentiel, celui qui est gravé dans l'âme de quiconque lit attentivement l'Évangile: le secret de l'échelle du ciel, dont les degrés s'appellent prière et pénitence").

We hope that the wish of Lúcia will be fulfilled as soon as possible.

There, I was saying, in the Cova da Iria, it feels like being in the house of the Mother, as if to hear the voice of the Mother who repeats: Prayer and penance.

The world has lent its ear to the message of Lúcia, that message which is past the private aspect, the family, over to the part which concerned the whole world — the message invited to prayer and penance the entire world —, it contained the third part of those things the Most Holy Madonna confided. And these things had been confided not for herself [Lúcia], not for the world—at least for now—but for the Vicar of Jesus Christ.

And Lúcia has kept the secret. She has not spoken, as far as one tried to make her speak. Yes, "Secrets of Fátima" circulate that are attributed to her. Do not believe them! Lúcia has kept the secret.[3]

---

3   [LDC Note 3:] The written text: We had to defend the visionary, who became a religious, to escape from the curiosity of the world in a Carmelite monastery in Coimbra where, more than from devotion, the curiosity of many people has sought to draw from [Lúcia] a few words. Despite Lúcia's reserve, these curious ones, eager for mysterious things, have thought to make deductions and have published apocryphal texts of the secret of Fátima, making it into legend. The Congregation for the Doctrine of the Faith had to forbid access to the Coimbra convent where Lúcia prays, remembers, meditates, but does not speak. We even created a Blue Army that gives an interpretation and a special tone to the mystery of the secret, this is to say a thing that one cannot interpret because one does not know."

In his weekly press conference of February 23, 1967, Mgr. Vallainc declared that if, at the last moment, Cardinal Ottaviani decided not to name the Blue Army it is because he feared that mentioning it to a public that is very sensible to nuances might not go over too well. In other words, it might have been interpreted as a slight on the activities of the Blue Army, contrary to the intention of the Congregation for the Doctrine of the Faith (*La Croix*, 26-27 February, 1967) (Texte écrit: «On a dû défendre la voyante, devenue religieuse, et la soustraire à la curiosité du monde dans un monastère de carmélites à Coimbre où, plus que la dévotion, la curiosité de nombreux profanes a cherché à tirer d'elle quelques paroles. Malgré la réserve de Lucia, ces curieux, avides des choses mystérieuses, ont cru pouvoir faire des déductions, de sorte que ça et là ont été publiés des textes apocryphes du secret de Fatima transformé en légende. La Congrégation

Also, what did Lúcia do to obey exactly the Most Holy Virgin? She wrote on a sheet [of paper], in the Portuguese language, that which the Holy Virgin had asked her to tell the Holy Father [...*quello che la Madonna le ha detto di dire al Santo Padre*].

The message was not to be opened before 1960. I asked Lúcia, Why? — The why of this date. And she replied to me, "Because then it will appear '*mas claro*' (more clear)." This is what makes me think that the Message was of a prophetic tone, precisely because in prophecy—as seen in Sacred Scripture—there is the veil of mystery. Prophecies are not in a generally open language, clear, comprehensible to all. Exegetes are today still interpreting prophecies of the Old Testament. And what to say, for example, of the prophecies contained in the Apocalypse? Indeed, [Lúcia] said, in 1960 it will appear more clear.

The envelope containing the "Secret of Fátima" was given closed to the Bishop of Leiria, and, although Lúcia said he could read it, he did not want to read it. He wanted to respect "the Secret" out of reverence for the Holy Father. He sent it to the Apostolic Nuncio, then Msgr. Cento, today Cardinal Cento, who is present, and who faithfully handed it to the Congregation for the Doctrine of the Faith, who had requested it, to avoid that something so delicate, destined not to be given to the public [...*destinata a non esser data in pasto al pubblico*...], should, for whatever reason, even fortuitous, come into foreign hands. "The secret" came; it arrived carried

---

pour la doctrine de la foi a dû interdire aux profanes et aux curieux l'accès du couvent de Coimbre où Lucia prie, se souvient, médite, mais ne parle pas. On a même créé une Armée bleue qui donne une interprétation et un ton spéciaux au mystère du secret, c'est-à-dire à une chose qu'on ne peut pas interpréter parce qu'on ne la connaît pas.

Dans sa conférence de presse hebdomadaire, le 23 février, Mgr Vallainc a déclaré que si, à la dernière heure, le cardinal Ottaviani s'est décidé à ne pas nommer l'Armée bleue, c'est qu'il craignait que cette mention ne fût interprétée par un public peu sensible aux nuances, comme un blâme des activités de l'Armée bleue, contrairement à l'intention de la Congrégation pour la doctrine de la foi, [La Croix, 26-27 février 1967]).

to the Congregation of the Doctrine of the Faith, and, closed, as it was, was given to John XXIII. The Pope opened it, opened the envelope, and read it. And, although in Portuguese, he afterwards said to me that he had understood entirely the text. Then he himself put in another envelope "the Secret," sealed it, and sent it in one of those archives that are like a well, into which goes down deep the paper [...*nel quale va giù la carta profonda...*], black, black, and no one sees anything. Therefore, it is difficult to say where "the Secret of Fátima" might be now.

However, what is important, and what needs to be imparted to the world is that which is contained in the public Message, has become universal, spread throughout the world and, thanks be to God, received with attention by the entire world. It is another thing then to know if the whole world has put it [the message] into action, according to the desires of the Most Holy Madonna who has exhorted us to prayer and penance to avoid those sanctions that in the divine book of Providence are expected for a world that corresponds so badly to the gifts of the Lord's grace.

To guard Lúcia better — because you can imagine how many journalists, also how many good priests who had the desire to write something on the "Secret of Fátima" went to tempt her — she retired to the convent; Lúcia was truly exemplary in this matter, she did not speak.

Do not believe those who say that they have heard this or that from Lúcia. I who had the grace and gift to read the text of the Secret - though I am secretive as well because I am bound by secrecy - I can say that everything that circulates — a few days ago, a provincial newspaper spoke of the text and gave the text of the "Secret of Fátima" — is fantasy. You can be quite sure that the real Secret is kept in such a way that no one can set eyes upon it. Therefore, nothing else remains so act according to that which is public [*Dunque non rimane altro quindi che regolarsi secondo quello che è pubblico*]. The public Message of Fátima is what matters. The secret matters, this matters to the Holy Father to whom it was destined. He was the recipient [*Importa « il Segreto », importa questo al Santo Padre a cui*

era destinato. Egli era il destinatario]. And if the recipient has not decided to say, "This is the moment to reveal it to the world", we must stick to his wisdom who has wanted it kept secret.

But what matters, as I said, is that we know to conform our life, our actions and our activities to that which is the spirit of the public Message, because Lúcia was charged not only to transmit to the Pope the Secret Message [*…perché Lucia fu incaricata non soltanto di mandare al Papa il Messaggio Segreto…*] but also to publish and make known to all the world the public message, a message which is contained in these words: prayer and penance.

It was the repetition of these [words] that the Madonna had already said in Lourdes. Today, as we commemorate the feast of the apparition of the Most Holy Virgin in Lourdes, we need to unite these two manifestations of the goodness of Mary who descended from heaven, and put her virginal foot on the earth to sanctify it and also to guide it towards better paths. We must seek to ensure, with our actions, prayers, our example, with all Christian virtue that we ought to exercise, in a special way with prayer and with penitence, to make the Message of Fátima have the effects for which it was commissioned [*mandato*] to the world.

It was also underlined the connection of the Message of Fátima with the conditions of the Church in certain regions where she feels the weight of persecutions, where people fight against religion.

This is the Message there, — first in that public aspect — It is the message also of hope, of conversion, and this too can be hastened by the prayers of all the devoted ones of the Most Holy Virgin of Fátima.

Yes, on this day precisely in which we celebrate a Marian feast, that of the apparition in Lourdes, we must turn to the Immaculata, who appeared in Fátima as in Lourdes, because she gives to the world the consolation to see realized the wishes that are in the heart, in the mind, in the prayer, in the breath and sigh of every Christian.

It is quite true that persecution still exists. There are still some coun-

tries that are under the heel of the persecutor, the despot. There are some regions that are annihilated, scattered with scaffolds, the cross and prisons - prisons that are sanctified by many martyrs - but we must hope.[4]

Already certain signs, like the dawn — I wish to say — of new situations, are beginning to emerge. Maybe I am optimistic, but it seems to me that the Most Holy Madonna inspires us to have faith [*fiducia*]. If she descended from heaven, sanctified with her virginal foot the lands of France and Portugal, as well as so many other lands where she appeared, then she also did it to encourage us.

We hope that the signs which are in conformity with this hope that one can have from the Message of Fátima, because if the Madonna appeared, she certainly appeared to tell us that we may have to suffer - as she had predicted the sufferings of the war of which we all were witnesses and

---

4   [LDC Note 4:] We read in the written text: "We spoke much about links between the secret of Fátima and the formidable and agonizing situation of the Church in the numerous regions of the world. [In these regions is] where hell unleashed its wrath against all that is holy and divine, and where the persecutor—even if he wears the gloves of diplomacy and employs honeyed language of peace—tries to extend on the entire world a domination that he already has over vast territories, spread the cross, scaffolds, and prisons sanctified by many martyrs.

But the trust which is inspired by the message of Fátima (also in the public part) makes us scrutinize, in this second half of the 1960s, in a serene abandon to Providence, the first clue—although still unclear—of a future establishment of the things of the world in the peace and kingdom of Christ" (On lit dans le texte écrit : "On a beaucoup parlé de liens entre le secret de Fatima et la situation redoutable et angoissante de l'Église dans de nombreuses régions du monde où l'enfer a déchaîné son ire contre tout ce qui est saint et divin, et où le persécuteur - même s'il prend les gants de la diplomatie et emploie le langage mielleux de la paix - essaie d'étendre sur le monde entier une domination qu'il exerce déjà sur des territoires immenses, semés de croix, d'échafauds et de prisons sanctifiées par tant de martyrs.

"Mais la confiance dont est inspiré le message de Fatima, également dans la partie publique, nous fait scruter, en cette deuxième partie des années 1960, dans un serein abandon à la Providence, les premiers indices - bien qu'encore nébuleux - d'une future instauration des choses du monde dans la paix et le royaume du Christ").

victims — but she was also here in the world to give hope.

She is the mother of faith. We all know to invoke her as mother, "the entire reason of my hope, my trust." Well, since she gives us this hope, let us pray that she may obtain that which is in the heart, in the desire of all that the Reign of Christ may soon come "your Kingdom come"; the Reign of Christ, in the peace of Christ.

The telltale signs that are already in some clues of evolution in certain countries [*I segni rivelatori ci sono in alcuni indizi già di evoluzione in certi paesi...*], of the successes of this ecumenism, that always brings peoples closer together, including those who are not Catholics, but rightly claim the Christian name [*...di successi di quell'ecumenismo, che affratella sempre più i popoli anche di quelli che non sono cattolici, ma si vantano e giustamente si vantano del nome cristiano...*] — the signs of acceptance of all the actions that the Holy Father does for peace — just yesterday he was saying to me [*...proprio ieri mi diceva...*], naturally with the reserve that I must keep — of other additional steps most recently taken in these days to facilitate the solution to the Vietnam conflict. If, as I say, there are so many signs that are given to hope that the Most Holy Virgin on this 50th anniversary of the events of Fátima, will wish to give some sign of her kindness for her children, she will want to give some new hope to the Christian world, then we must say: let us welcome this patronage of the Most Holy Madonna; let us hasten the fulfillment with prayer.

And then we can say that the Madonna tells us from Fátima: "raise your heads — raise, raise your head — for your redemption is at hand."

And our response is with a cry, *Fiat! Fiat!*

Addendum

The following texts are the Italian that appear to be the original written text from Ottaviani. They were published in the periodical La Madre di

Dio.[5] *They correspond with the footnotes in* La Documentation Catholique.

LDC Note 2:

Quella immensa folla orante non chiedeva di conoscere che cosa contenesse il misterioso Segreto di Fatima. Era già in possesso del più essenziale segreto, che è inciso nell'anima di ogni attento lettore del Vangelo: il segreto della Scala del Cielo, i cui gradini si chiamano preghiera e penitenza.

LDC Note 3:

Si è poi dovuto difendere la Veggente, fattasi suora e sottrattasi alla curiosità del mondo nella raccolta preghiera di un monastero di Carmelitane di Coimbra, dove più che la devozione, la curiosità di molti profani, ha cercato di carpire qualche sua parola. Purtroppo dal riserbo di Lucia gli investigatori, i curiosi delle cose misteriose, hanno creduto fare delle deduzioni, e qua e là, si sono pubblicati testi apocrifi dell'ormai divenuto leggendario segreto di Fatima. E la congregazione posta a difesa della Dottrina della Fede ha dovuto interdire, ai profani ed agli investigatori, l'accesso al Convento di Coimbra, dove Lucia prega, ricorda, medita, ma non parla. Si è perfino creata una così detta Armata Azzurra che dà uno speciale tono ed una speciale interpretazione al mistero del Segreto, ad una cosa, insomma, che non si può interpretare perché non è nota.

LDC Note 4:

Si è parlato molto di una connessione del Segreto di Fatima con la tremenda ed angosciosa situazione della Chiesa in ampie zone del mondo, dove l'inferno ha scatenato le sue ire contro tutto ciò che è santo e divino e da dove il persecutore, pur nei guanti della diplomazia e nel linguaggio mellifluo della pace, tenta di estendere su tutto il mondo quel dominio che ha già sterminate terre, seminate di croci, di patiboli e di carceri, santificate da tanti martiri.

Ma la fiducia che ispira a questo proposito, anche nella parte pub-

---

5   *La Madre di Dio*, Anno XXXIV, No.3, March, 1967, pages 16-18.

blica, il Messaggio di Fatima, ci fa scrutare, con sereno abbandono alla Provvidenza, i primi sebbene ancor nebulosi indizi che già si delineano in questo scorcio di anni dopo il 1960, di un futuro assetto delle cose del mondo nella pace di Cristo, nel Regno di Cristo.

—APPENDIX B—

INTERVIEW OF ARCHBISHOP LORIS CAPOVILLA WITH MARCO RONCALLI

1994

The following is an interview given by Archbishop (later Cardinal) Loris Capovilla to Marco Roncalli. It appeared in the Italian language in the book: John XXIII in the Record of His Secretary Loris F. Capovilla. Interview by Marco Roncalli with unedited documents[1]

It is herein presented in the light of the discussion of Cardinal Ottaviani's version of events pertaining to Pope John XXIII opening the envelope containing the third part of the secret of Fátima.

RONCALLI AND APPARITIONS

Q. What attitude did Pope John maintain in regard to miracles, as well as Marian apparitions and revelations?

A. It's obvious. He professed the whole Catholic faith, which includes the possibility of miracles, extraordinary intervention and God's direct intervention. He was very devoted to Our Lady but he was not a facile advocate of apparitions, or a prejudiced and suspicious denier [of them]. He proved

---

1   *Giovanni XXIII Nel ricordo del segretario Loris F. Capovilla Intervista di Marco Roncalli con documenti inediti.* (Milano: San Paolo, 1994), 112-118.

it several times; He gave it a nod in the synodal discourses to the clergy of Rome in 1960. A short essay by that didactic oratory was enough to penetrate his soul by a priest who sought essentials and warned against certain "vagueness of special devotions".

[Here was a discussion on a specific case. It is omitted--KJS]

THE SECRET OF FÁTIMA

D. Pope John and the secret of Fátima. He witnessed on this matter that he is satisfied by what has been printed. You never kept secrets from the Pope on this issue? While it is true that if the gospel already contains everything you should not be interested in revelations, on the other hand,, as recalled by Luciani, in the Gospel is also the verse "signs shall follow them that believe" (Mark 16:17) ...

R. Pope John often conversed with me on Fátima and his attitude on this issue was never different from that he maintained about other supernatural events: he was characterized by a calm and balanced disposition, neither prone to suggestion nor to devastating criticism ...

D. For example?

R. In the beginning of 1959, the new Cardinal Fernando Cento pronounced in Portugal that the Churches asked his opinion on a planned radio message that Sister Lúcia would address the world. The pope gave the answer to the competent bodies, without trying to influence them. But for his part, I think that he preferred silence.

D. What do you know of that sealed envelope containing the autograph of Sister Lúcia dos Santos, in which the third part of the so-called secret would be contained? Exactly to whom the package was addressed?

R. In regard to that there was never any pronouncement. Sister Lúcia sent

the document [*memoriale*] to Pius XII during the years 1954-1956.[2] I do not know exactly. I do not know the reaction of Pius XII who passed it to the Holy Office. Nothing more was heard from the Pope's household. This document was not found in the cabinet [*stipetto*] where Pius XII kept reserved parcels, something that may suggest that he may not even have wanted to read or open it.[3] I forget the exact header of the envelope, but I remember that John XXIII, to the proposal made to him (I cannot say by whom) to read it postponed it until August 1959; ten months after his election.[4] He took the envelope from the hands of Father Paul Philippe, commissioner of the Holy Office on Monday 17 August, at Castel Gandolfo. He said he would open and read it in the presence of his confessor Monsignor Cavagna, the next Friday. He was very unhurried. He read the document, but as the text appeared here and there very difficult to understand due to the phrases in the Portuguese dialect, he had it translated by Monsignor Paolo Tavares, who was Portuguese and a clerk of the Secretary of State (later Bishop of Macau).[5] I was present. They were made partakers of the heads of the Secretariat of State and the Holy Office, and

---

2   [KJS Note: Capovilla was mistaken. Sr. Lúcia never sent the document to Pius XII.]

3   [KJS Note: Whether or not this cabinet was the one photographed by Robert Serrou is unclear. If it was, then Capovilla's story seems to indicate that at some point between the photograph being taken and Pius' death, the envelope was passed to the Holy Office.]

4   [KJS Note: Capovilla forgetting the header of the envelope could suggest that he forgot the note from Sr. Lúcia about 1960. This fact may explain Capovilla's later remark precisely about this date. Note that he does not specify Bishop da Silva's envelope or Sr. Lúcia's. Capovilla was, however, consistent in not remembering the header of the envelope/dossier as is demonstrated in an *earlier* interview with Fr. Alonso that appeared in *Madre di Dio*, 45 (5), May 1978, pages 14-15.]

5   [KJS Note: The reader is reminded of our discussion in chapter nine of the present book on some of the difficulties presented in Sr. Lúcia's Portuguese text.]

other persons, such as Cardinal Agagianian.

Q. So you were there too. And who else besides Tardini, Ottaviani, Parente, Philippe, Samore, Raimondo Verardo?[6] Is there anyone still alive?

A. To my knowledge the only one living is bishop Angelo Raimondo Verardo who is retired and was at the Holy Office in common life with Father Philippe. There may be some official of the Curia, at the time associated to one or other of the Department Heads.

Q. And then?

E. After the reading, John XXIII dictated to me his note that was attached to the envelope. The note certifying that the pope had taken note of the content and remitted to the other (to his successor?) the task to make some pronouncement.

Q. So no comment?

R. Nothing then, nor later. He took the envelope in the Vatican. No one spoke to him, nor did the Holy Office ask where he had gone to finish the document. It was in a drawer of the desk in the bedroom. That is where Paul VI unearthed it.

D. In 1960, the belief spread that the pope would have to reveal the secret, and instead he decided not to?

A. It is not that John XXIII did not want to know. The fact is that no one spoke to him, no one mentioned this deadline for the simple fact that the text of which he had taken note did not contain and does not contain any explicit reference to 1960, or in subsequent years.[7]

---

6   [KJS Note: It is interesting to point out that Antonio Cardinal Samorè was the principal episcopal consecrator of Angelo Cardinal Sodano in 1978: <http://webdept.fiu.edu/~mirandas/bios1991.htm#Sodano> (Acceesed 21 December, 2016).]

7   [KJS Note: It is unclear at this time why Capovilla would have made this remark. It is clear from the envelope that contained Sr. Lúcia's text that

D. Did the knowledge of the "secret" in some way influence the Pope? Is there any truth in relation to what has been disclosed, supposedly: the conversion of Russia, the end of communism, and the like?

A. At no conversation and in no writings of John XXIII is there a reference to the envelope. But he spoke repeatedly of the Fátima events and of spiritual movement which had broken out that he had pondered with his own eyes in 1956, during his pilgrimage to the Portuguese sanctuary.

D. After Pope John, Paul VI also read the document?

A. Of course. He asked me what opinion, if I had any, I had made about his predecessor. And my answer concerning the reserve of John XXIII stressed: "I will do the same."

Q. And John Paul I?

A. I do not know anything. But regardless of the "secret" you know that Luciani had a meeting with Sister Lúcia on July 11, 1977 thirteen months before being elected pope. The interview with the nun left him deeply troubled. I did not speak of the "secret." It seems that she had predicted his rise to the throne of Peter.[8]

---

there was a date of 1960 attached to it. Thus, either Capovilla's memory failed him or, perhaps, he was making a distinction between "opening" and "publishing" the text to the world. There is no note about "publishing" on the envelope. This explanation, however, appears to go against the literal sense of the passage and thus is inconclusive.]

8   Cfr. Camillo Bassotto, « Il mio cuore è ancora a Venezia » (Albino Luciani), Venezia 1990, pp. 113-119. The author writes:

One of the decisive moments of the life of Albino Luciani occurred in Fátima. He told Don Germano (Pattaro), "On the last day, before leaving me, Papa Luciani spoke to me of his conversation with Sister Lúcia ... 'A fact that has troubled me for a whole year' he said to me. 'I took away the peace and spiritual tranquility. Since that day I have never forgotten Fátima. That thought had become a burden on the heart. I tried to convince myself that it was just an impression. I prayed to forget. I wanted to confide to some dear person, to my brother Edward, but I did

D. This also happened with Cardinal Roncalli; the Venetian times foretold the papacy by a French seer, a certain Gaston Bardet who had divined the name he would assume as pontiff ...

A. Yes. And the patriarch Roncalli had answered Bardet with his autograph writing: "... Jesus tells me to say that your [*lei*] intentions are pure and holy, but that you [*lei*] are under the threat of a grave and dangerous hallucination" and "his predictions merit the words 'Get behind me, Satan' ...."

Q. You had disclosed this episode only in 1976 when it appeared in the book of Pier Carpi "The Pope John prophecies" with the types of Edizioni Mediterranee. *Not long ago I reviewed that book at newsstands ...*

A. The thing does not thrill me at all. When it came out in 1976, the book was a sensation and was immediately translated into several languages. He described - as some know - a mysterious initiation of Archbishop Roncalli to the order of "the Rose Cross" [Rosicrucians]. For a while it was discussed. And every now and then there are those who returned to the subject. Of all this a very simple explanation can be made. The *agenda roncalliana* in 1935 and the daily Mass register—the reference point for the alleged prophecies—exclude that Archbishop Roncalli was "initiated" to the secret order of "the Rose Cross" or any secret society and he even less has practiced "spiritual exercises" to be admitted. So we are faced with an unprecedented deception and it arouses just painful amazement at the outrageous attempt to wrap the person and of Pope John and the service in the coils of magic and divination, whereas he should recognize the title of "prophet" in the literal sense, a man and a priest who speaks in the name of another, the faithful interpreter of the gospel.[9]

---

not succeed. That thought was too big, too awkward, too contrary to my whole being, it was not credible. Now the prediction of Sister Lúcia has come true, I'm here, I am the Pope.'"

9   Cfr. *L'Osservatore Romano*, 15-16 novembre 1976 e 23 dicembre 1976.

Q. Let's go back to the secret of Fátima. Even Pope John Paul II has examined [it]*? Does he know where the secret envelope can be found today?*

A. I cannot answer to the two questions, but I know the devotion of John Paul II to Our Lady of Fátima.

Q. What is your opinion of the whole thing?

A. The reading of the signs is very difficult. I would say of them what *Lumen Gentium* states of charisms: "They ought to be received with thanksgiving and consolation, but the judge of their genuineness and their use belongs to the Ecclesiastical Authority, which is responsible above all not to extinguish the Spirit, but to test all and hold fast to what is good."[10]

---

10   *Lumen Gentium*, 12.

—APPENDIX C—

TRANSCRIPT OF THE JUNE 26, 2000 VATICAN PRESS CONFERENCE ON THE THIRD PART OF THE SECRET OF FÁTIMA

The following transcript is in the Italian language with an English translation. It was transcribed by a professional transcription company in the United States based upon an audio recording of the proceedings. The transcription was then reviewed by this author and two translators where it was further reviewed for accuracy. Where text is unclear, these areas are marked in brackets. Some remarks are contained herein and are also in brackets.

Dr. Joaquín Navarro-Valls:

Come sapete, per espressa decisione del Santo Padre Giovanni Paolo II, viene reso pubblico il messaggio di Fátima, comprensivo del segreto confidato ai tre pastorelli nelle apparizioni della Madonna del 1917 nella Cova da Iria a Fátima. In particolare, oggi viene pubblicato nella sua integralità il testo

Dr. Joaquín Navarro-Valls:

As you all know, by an express decision of the Holy Father John Paul II, the message of Fátima is being made public, including the secret confided to the three little shepherds, in the apparitions of the Madonna in 1917 at the Cova da Iria at Fátima. In particular, today the text of the third part of the

della terza parte del segreto, un segreto comunicato ai veggenti nelle apparizione del 13 luglio 1917 e messo per iscritto da Suor Lucía, l'unica testimone sopravvissuta, il 3 gennaio 1944, vale a dire circa 27 anni dopo. E fu scritto, come lei stessa dice, per ordine di Sua Eccellenza il vescovo di Leiria e della Santissima Madre.

Di questo testo esiste un unico manoscritto, lo stesso che in riproduzione fotostatica viene pubblicato oggi insieme ad una traduzione dal portoghese. Questo testo di Suor Lucía è stato custodito dal 1957 nell'archivio segreto del Sant'Uffizio o Congregazione per la Dottrina della Fede ed è stato letto almeno da tre Papi: Giovanni XXIII, Paolo VI, e Giovanni Paolo II.

Pochi giorni dopo l'attentato del 1981, Giovanni Paolo II aveva chiesto che gli fosse portata in ospedale la busta contenente la terza parte del segreto. In occasione della beatificazione

secret is being published in its entirety, a secret communicated to the seers in the apparitions of 13 July 1917 and put in writing by Sister Lúcia, the one surviving witness, on 3 January 1944, that is to say, about 27 years later. And it was written, as she herself says, at the order of his Excellency the Bishop of Leiria and of the Most Holy Mother.

A single manuscript exists of this text, which is being published today in a photostatic reproduction, together with a translation from the Portuguese. This text by Sister Lúcia has been, since 1957, in the custody of the Secret Archive of the Holy Office, or the Congregation for the Doctrine of the Faith, and it has been read by at least three Popes, John XXIII, Paul VI, and John Paul II.

A few days after the attack in 1981, John Paul II had asked that the envelope containing the third part of the secret be brought to him in the hospital. On the occasion of the beatifica-

poco più di un mese fa, vi ricordate, di Francesco e di Giacinta, gli altri due testimoni delle apparizioni di Fátima.

Il Santo Padre decise di rendere pubblica anche la terza parte del segreto e incaricò il Cardinal Angelo Sodano Segretario di Stato, di darne comunicazione, e ciò avvenne a Fátima alla presenza del Papa il 13 maggio scorso.

Le apparizioni di Fátima si iscrivono nella serie di segni soprannaturali che percorrono tutta la storia umana. Il messaggio che proviene da Fátima nella sua, nel suo insieme è ampiamente conosciuto, mancava soltanto conoscere il testo della cosiddetta terza parte del segreto ed è questo testo che oggi abbiamo rilasciato ai giornalisti. Il Santo Padre ha voluto che questa pubblicazione integrale venisse accompagnata da un commento teologico-pastorale del Cardinale Joseph Ratzinger, Prefetto della Congregazione per la Dottrina della Fede, e da una intro-

tion a little more than a month ago, you recall, of the other two witnesses of the apparitions of Fátima – Francisco and Jacinta.

The Holy Father decided to make the third part of the secret public also, and assigned Cardinal Angelo Sodano, Secretary of State, to make the announcement, which took place at Fátima in the presence of the Pope this past 13th of May.

The apparitions of Fátima are enrolled in the series of supernatural signs that run through all of human history. The message that originates from Fátima, as a whole, is widely known; the only thing lacking was to know the text of the so-called third part of the secret, and it is this text which we have released to journalists today. The Holy Father desired that this integral publication be accompanied by a theological- pastoral commentary by Cardinal Joseph Ratzinger, Prefect of the Congregation for the Doctrine of the Faith, and a historical introduction by Mon-

duzione storica di Monsignor Tarcisio Bertone, segretario della stessa Congregazione. Questi due interventi ci permetteranno di inquadrare correttamente la totalità del messaggio di Fátima.

Saluto i telespettatori che oggi ci seguono da casa, per loro e per tutti coloro interessati mi permetto di ricordare che il testo integrale del messaggio di Fátima è disponibile in più lingue a partire dalle ore dodici sul sito interno del Vaticano.

Allora adesso la parola a Sua Eccellenza Monsignor Tarcisio Bertone per la, per questa introduzione storica.

[Here were the presentations by Bertone & Ratzinger. These were provided by the Vatican and are thus not transcribed here.]

signor Tarcisio Bertone, secretary of the same Congregation. These two interventions will allow us to frame the totality of the message of Fátima correctly.

I greet the television viewers who are following us today at home; for them and for all who are interested, I'll take the liberty to note that the full text of the message of Fátima is available in multiple languages starting at 12 o'clock on the internal site of the Vatican.

Now, then, the floor belongs to his Excellency Monsignor Tarcisio Bertone for the, for that historical introduction.

[Here were the presentations by Bertone & Ratzinger. These were provided by the Vatican and are thus not transcribed here.][1]

---

1   <http://press.vatican.va/content/salastampa/it/bollettino/pubblico/2000/06/26/0407/01462.html> (Accessed 1 November, 2016).

Navarro-Valls:

Grazie, Eminenza. Adesso il torno delle domande. Vedo che ci sono molte [...]. Cominciamo da questa parte. [.....] poi accanto. Come, al solito, vi prego di introdurre con il nome della testata.

Luigi Accatoli:

Sono [Luigi] Accatoli, "Corriere della Sera". Chiedo all'Arcivescovo Bertone: riguardo alle notizie certe della sua introduzione, vedo che si riferisce al Papa attuale che legge la terza parte del segreto dopo l'attentato. Io credevo di sapere, ho scritto, quindi sono un po' timoroso che avesse conosciuto la terza parte del segreto subito dopo l'elezione a Papa e che l'avesse richiesta per rivederla dopo l'attentato, essendo al Gemelli. Chiedo se questa mia presunzione, presunta informazione può essere anche essa notizia certa o se va smentita.

Navarro-Valls:

Thank you, Eminence. Now it is time for the questions. I see that there are many [...]. Let's begin from this side. [....] then across. As usual, I ask you to introduce [your questions] with the name of your newspaper.

Luigi Accatoli:

I am [Luigi] Accatoli, "Corriere della Sera". I am asking Archbishop Bertone: regarding the "confirmed news" in your introduction, I see that you make reference to the current Pope, who read the third part of the secret after the attack. I used to believe that I knew – (then) I wrote – so I am a little afraid – that he had learned the third part of the secret shortly after his election as Pope and that he had asked to see it again after the attack, while he was at the Gemelli. I'm asking if my assumption, assumed information, can also be [part of] that "confirmed news" or if that is not the case.

Bertone:

Mi sembra che dalle informazioni certe, orali e di archivio, la Sua presunzione non è notizia certa. Le altre sono notizie certe – mi dispiace doverlo dire.

Navarro-Valls:

Può specificare un po' di più lo stesso tema?

Bertone:

Cioè, cioè: il Santo Padre Giovanni Paolo II ha letto per la prima volta il testo della terza parte del segreto di Fátima dopo l'attentato, dopo aver richiesto il testo essendo all'ospedale Gemelli.

Navarro-Valls:

Tornielli?

Andrea Tornielli:

Andrea Tornielli del Giornale. Volevo chiedere al Cardinale Ratzinger se c'è qualche elemento in più, come si arriva all'identificazione del vesco-

Bertone:

It seems to me that – from the known information, oral and in the archives – your assumption is not a piece of confirmed news, and the others are confirmed news. I'm sorry to have to say it.

Navarro-Valls:

Can you be a little more specific about that topic?

Bertone:

That is, that is, the Holy Father John Paul II read the text of the third part of the secret of Fátima for the first time after the attack, after having asked for the text while he was at the Gemelli hospital.

Navarro-Valls:

Tornielli?

Andrea Tornielli:

Andrea Tornielli from the "Giornale". I wanted to ask Cardinal Ratzinger, eh, if there is some further element: how do you reach the identification

vo vestito di bianco con Papa Wojtyla. Siccome qui abbiamo un Papa che cade ucciso, e la, la visione è simbolica e per stessa ammissione della, di Suor Lucía questa immagine è allo specchio, se non potesse essere interpretata come una visione più ampia che riguarda un po' la storia di tutti i papi di questo secolo, ehh ricordo anche l'attentato che ha subito Paolo VI.

Invece all'Arcivescovo Bertone volevo dire, nella nota introduttiva storica il passaggio su Papa Giovanni è molto sintetico e si dice che Papa Giovanni ha restituito la busta sigillata al Santo Uffizio. Ora, l'Arcivescovo Loris Capovilla, suo segretario, in libri, interviste, testimonianze e documenti vari dice che invece il Papa trattenne questa busta, e mettendola in un tiretto della sua scrivania, e che lì fu trovata da Paolo VI dopo che questi l'aveva richiesta e non l'aveva trovata, eh non l'aveva trovata e l'aveva richiesta; tanto che, racconta, fu

of the bishop clothed in white with Pope Wojtyla? Since here we have a Pope who is slain and falls, and the, the vision is symbolic, and by the very admission of, of Sister Lúcia, that image is the mirror – if it couldn't be interpreted as a broader vision that relates somewhat to the history of all the popes of this century; eh, I also remember the attack made on Paul VI.

In turn, I wanted to say to Archbishop Bertone: in the introductory historical note the passage on Pope John is very brief and it says that Pope John returned the sealed envelope to the Holy Office. Now, Archbishop Loris Capovilla, his secretary, says instead in books, interviews, testimonies, and various documents that the Pope retained the envelope, placing it in a drawer in his desk, and that it was found there by Paul VI after he had asked for it, and they didn't find it, eh, they didn't find it, and he had asked for it; so that, Capo-

chiamato lui stesso, Capovilla, per dire a Paolo VI dove questa busta si trovava. Volevo chiedere se era possibile chiarire anche questo, grazie.

Ratzinger:

Forse subito, subito questo.

Bertone:

Sì. Dunque, dagli archivi e da una annotazione precisa di Giovanni XXIII che è stata anche pubblicata, risulta che lui ha ricevuto la busta dal commissario del Sant'Uffizio Padre Philippe. L'ha trattenuta presso di sé, l'ha letta, naturalmente l'ha letta, poi l'ha risigillata, e l'ha rimandata al Sant'Uffizio con la decisione di non pubblicarla perché si poneva nel '59 la domanda: "pubblichiamo" o "non pubblichiamo". Eravamo alla vigilia del 1960, quella data fatidica che sembrava così importante. Il Papa ha letto, ha risigillato e ha rimandato e, Monsignor Capovilla, proprio, ha rimandato la busta sigillata, così risulta dai

villa recounts, he himself was called to tell Paul VI where the envelope was. I wanted to ask if it could be possible to clarify also this; thank you.

Ratzinger:

Maybe right now, right now this answer.

Bertone:

Yes, So, from the archives, and from a precise note by John XXIII which has also been published, it is clear that he received the envelope from the commissioner of the Holy Office, Fr. Philippe. He kept it himself, he read it – naturally he read it – then he resealed it, and sent it back to the Holy Office with the decision not to publish it, because in '59 the question arose, "do we publish it" or "not publish it"; we were on the eve of 1960, that fateful date which seemed so important. The Pope read it, he resealed and sent it back, and Monsignor Capovilla himself sent the envelope back sealed, as is clear from our archives. That

nostri archivi. Che poi abbiano tenuto una nota, non il testo, non la busta sigillata contenente il manoscritto di Suor Lucía, questo non risulta assolutamente perché è ritornata nell'archivio del Sant'Uffizio, [....] che abbiano trattenuto una nota riportando qualche parte del terzo segreto, può darsi, nel cassetto, eccetera, ma non la busta sigillata, così dai nostri archivi.

Ratzinger:

Alla prima parte della domanda posso rispondere brevemente che naturalmente un tale testo simbolico permette un margine di interpretazione e non una assoluta identificazione storica. Perciò realmente possiamo vedere sintetizzato in questa visione la storia dei martiri di un secolo e in questo senso anche la passione dei Papi in questo secolo, e non esclusivamente l'attentato del 13 maggio '81, ma certamente in questa storia delle sofferenze dei Papi questo attentato che veramente portava il Papa alla soglia della morte è

they might have kept a note then -- not the text, not the sealed envelope containing the manuscript from Sister Lúcia, that absolutely does not follow, because it was returned to the archive of the Holy Office [....] – that they kept a note reporting some part of the third secret, it may be, it may exist in a drawer, etc., but not the sealed envelope, according to our archives.

Ratzinger:

I can respond to the first part of the question briefly: naturally such a symbolic text allows a margin for interpretation and not one absolute historical identification. Because of that, we truly can see summarized in this vision the history of the martyrs of a century, and in that sense also the passion of the popes in this century, and not exclusively the attack of 13 May '81; but certainly, in this history of the sufferings of the Popes, this attack which truly brought the Pope to the brink of death is the culmination which is partic-

il punto culminante che va particolarmente identificato come nocciolo di questa visione.

Navarro-Valls:

Aura Miguel

Aura Miguel:

Sono Aura Miguel de Rádio Renascença, Portugal. Suor Lucía non ha mai fatto nulla "senza il permesso del cielo", come a lei le piace dire. Come mai questa data del 1960, cioè lei stessa in questo documento adesso pubblicato dice che ha scritto solo quello che ha visto e non ha interpretato, invece è stata lei stessa che ha scritto la data 1960: volevo capire un po' di più.

L'altra domanda riguarda la frase "In Portogallo rimarrà sempre il dogma della fede" che fino a questo momento noi tutti interpretavamo come appartenente alla terza parte del segreto; anzi non si è mai commentato riguardo la prima e la seconda perché tutti pensavano che riguardava la terza e ha suscitato

ularly identified as the kernel of this vision.

Navarro-Valls:

Aura Miguel?

Aura Miguel:

I am Aura Miguel from "Rádio Renascença", Portugal. Sister Lúcia has never done anything without the permission of Heaven, as she likes to say. Why this date of the 1960, that is, in this document being published now, she herself says that she only wrote what she saw and she did not interpret; on the other hand, it was she herself who wrote the date 1960. I wanted to understand a bit more.

The other question regards the sentence, "In Portugal the dogma of the faith will always remain", which up to this moment we all were interpreting as belonging to the third part of the secret; and yet no one has ever commented in regard to the first also and the second, because everyone thought that it related to

anche, anche tutte queste speculazioni sulla fine del mondo, eccetera; invece adesso capiamo che non c'entra nulla con la terza parte del segreto. Volevo sapere allora come dobbiamo considerarla, grazie.

Bertone:

Dunque, anzitutto nel colloquio con Suor Lucía non si poteva non porre la domanda sulla data 1960 perché era un po' la data che era ritenuta cruciale, decisiva.

Come ho scritto nella presentazione e poi nel testo preciso che riferisce il colloquio, ho chiesto a Suor Lucía "come mai la data 1960? È stata suggerita da nostra Signora direttamente?" Suor Lucía ha detto "no, sono stata io, ho avuto l'intuizione di mettere io quella data perché prima non si sarebbe capito, si sarebbe capito solo dopo". Rimane un po' un mistero il 1960, ma certamente rinvia a dopo, alla piena comprensione della visione dopo i fatti accaduti.

the third, and it also raised – all these speculations about the end of the world, et cetera. On the other hand, now we understand that it has nothing to do with the third part of the secret. I wanted to know then how we ought to think of it; thank you.

Bertone:

So, above all, in the conversation with Sister Lúcia, we could not fail to ask the question about the date 1960, because it was, a bit, the date considered crucial, decisive.

As I wrote in the presentation, and then in the specific text which refers to the conversation, I asked Sister Lúcia, "Where does the date 1960 come from? Was it suggested by our Lady directly?" Sister Lúcia said, "No, it was me. I had the intuition to put down that date, I, because earlier it wouldn't have been understood; it would only have been understood later." The [date of] 1960 remains a bit of a mystery, but certainly it points to a later time, to the full understanding of

E poi riguardo a quell'altro problema: ecco questo è un po' un problema particolare, questo della – come diceva [incomprehensible] – del Portogallo: è difficile dire se si riferisce alla seconda parte, o alla terza parte. Certamente è una aggiunta che ha fatto Suor Lucía in quella famosa redazione, in una nuova redazione, con i puntini, eccetera, che lascerebbero supporre chissà che cosa, mentre invece poi quando inizia nel testo preciso, come avete visto, che è un testo staccato dalla prima e dalla seconda parte, inizia a riferire sulla terza parte del segreto non fa più nessuna sutura, non mette più nessun riferimento a quella espressione "Il Portogallo conserverà la fede", e quindi è difficile dire se appartiene alla seconda o alla terza parte, sembra di più che appartiene, appartenga alla seconda parte.

the vision after the events have taken place.

And then regarding that other problem: see, that is a bit of a particular problem, the problem of, as you were saying, [*incomprehensible*], about Portugal: it is hard to say if it refers to the second part, or to the third part. Certainly it is an addition which Sister Lúcia made in that famous version, in a new version with the dots, etc. – which would let people suppose who-knows-what – while, on the other hand, with-- when it begins with the precise text, as you all have seen, it is a text detached from the first and from the second part; it starts by referring to the third part of the secret there's not another stitch [of connection], it makes no further reference to that expression "Portugal will preserve the faith"; and hence it is hard to say if it belongs to the second or the third part. It seems more that it belongs – it may belong to the second part.

Navarro-Valls:

Marco Politi

Marco Politi:

Marco Politi di Repubblica. Eminenza, chiederei conforto su due punti nella lettura del documento. Il primo: in nessuna parte della sua spiegazione, mi pare, del suo commento, mi pare che lei metta direttamente in comunicazione la visione di questa persona che cade colpita da pallottole e da frecce con l'attentato del 1981. Lei semplicemente con un punto interrogativo mostra di comprendere che il Papa vi abbia riconosciuto il proprio destino, cioè mi pare che non c'è comunque, diciamo, con questa spiegazione ufficiale della Chiesa, un parallelo diretto dicendo "la visione si riferisce a, all'attentato".

Seconda questione: se ho ben capito, le visioni descritte a Fátima non sono state percepite dai sensi umani, non erano visibili dai sensi umani, ma erano una percezione interiore. È giusto? Grazie.

Navarro-Valls:

Marco Politi?

Marco Politi:

Marco Politi from "Repubblica". Eminence, I am going to ask for some assistance on two points in reading the document. The first: in no part of your explanation, it seems, of your commentary, it seems that you do put directly into contact the vision of this person who falls, struck by bullets and arrows, with the attack of 1981. You simply show, with a question mark, that you understand that the Pope had acknowledged in it all his own destiny; that is, it appears that with this official explanation from the Church, there isn't somehow, let's say, a direct parallel saying "the vision refers to the attack."

Second question: if I have understood correctly, the visions described at Fátima were not perceived by human senses; they were not visible to human senses but were an interior perception: is that right? Thank you.

Ratzinger:

Sì, cominciamo con l'ultimo, parlo di sensi interiori, non è una cosa che è presente come qui, questo microfono è presente da toccare: è una realtà che si rende visibile, nell'interno, con le capacità di percezione che sono presente nell'interno dell'uomo così che appaiono anche in una certa visibilità ma tuttavia non è quella di cose che sono presenti come realtà, oggetti sensibili nello spazio, questo mi sembra evidente che le realtà: il Papa, la città distrutta, eccetera, non erano presenti come era presente forse un albero – è una presenza diversa che nell'interno tuttavia si rivela come una presenza che non viene dalla mia fantasia.

Politi:

Mi scusi: e la Bianca Signora, a sua volta? Dove si colloca?

Ratzinger:

Forse non dobbiamo anda-

Ratzinger:

Yes, let's begin with the last part. I am speaking of interior senses. It's not a thing which is present like this microphone here – it's present to the touch, it's a reality that makes itself visible, in the inner side, with the capabilities of perception that are present in man. This way, they also appear with a certain visibility, but in any case, it is not the visibility of things that are present as realities, sensible objects in space. It seems evident to me that the real things: the "Pope", the "destroyed city", etc., were not present in the way perhaps a tree was present; it's a different presence that reveals itself, nonetheless, interiorly, as a presence that does not come from my imagination.

Politi:

Sorry, and what about the White Lady? Where can we locate her?

Ratzinger:

Maybe we should not go

re troppo avanti con queste definizioni ma anch'io direi è una presenza molto reale, ma è una presenza distinta da oggetti di questo mondo, di questa materia, della fisica, per così dire.

Al primo punto, come ho già accennato nell'altra risposta, non esiste una definizione ufficiale o interpretazione ufficiale, della Chiesa, di questa visione. La visione si apre con il progresso della storia del secolo scorso, nel '60 evidentemente o '60, sì, quando il Santo Padre Giovanni, Giovanni XXIII, ha aperto, ancora non c'era da vedere la corrispondenza storica a questa visione. Nello svilupparsi si vede come, si vede sempre più come è una sintesi molto profonda della storia di un secolo, almeno di un mezzo secolo e proprio con l'attentato si vede ancora il punto culminante di questa storia che va molto oltre del punto ma che appare come punto centrale.

Così nella luce della storia sviluppatasi, adesso passata,

too far ahead with these definitions, but I would also say it is a very real presence, but it is a presence distinct from objects of this world, this matter, of the physical, so to speak.

On the first point, as I indicated in the other response, there is no official definition or official interpretation of this vision by the Church. The vision opens with the progress of the history of the past century. In '60 evidently or – '60, yes, when the Holy Father John, John XXIII, opened [it], again there was no way to see the historical correspondence to this vision. In the way things developed, we can see how – we can see more and more how it is a very profound synthesis of the history of a century, at least of a half century; and with the attack itself, we can see again the culminating point of this history, that it goes well beyond that point, but that it appears as the central point.

So, in the light of the history that developed, which is

possiamo decifrare questa visione e capire che cosa la Madonna ci voleva dire con queste, con questa visione, ma non è intenzione della Chiesa di imporre una interpretazione. Mi sembra, la storia stessa, la corrispondenza tra visione e realtà vissuta e sofferta: indica che questa è la linea da seguire, e se io ho detto "il Papa ha capito che si trattava della sua sorte", mi identifico con questa percezione del Papa nel mondo della grande sofferenza, mi sembra, era proprio il momento nel quale nessuno più poteva capire di che cosa realmente parla l'immagine.

Navarro-Valls:

Marco Tosatti, poi andiamo a Svidercoschi.

Marco Tosatti:

Marco Tosatti, La Stampa. Eminenza, se dovessimo spiegare perché per 50 anni la Chiesa non ha rivelato questo segreto, a una persona molto semplice, Lei che cosa direbbe? Grazie.

now past, we can decipher this vision and grasp what the Madonna wanted to say to us with this, with this vision; but it is not the intention of the Church to impose an interpretation. It seems to me, the history itself, the correspondence between vision and lived and suffered reality, it shows that this is the line to follow, and if I said, "The Pope understood that it was about his fate," I am identifying with this perception of the pope, in the world, of great suffering, to me [it seems] it was right the moment in which no one could understand better what the image is really speaking about.

Navarro-Valls:

Marco Tosatti, then Svidercoschi.

Marco Tosatti:

Marco Tosatti, "La Stampa". Eminence, if you had to explain why the Church has not revealed this secret for 50 years, to a very simple person, what would you say? Thank you.

Ratzinger:

Dunque fino al '60 abbiamo avuto questo, per così dire, "embargo" da parte della veggente stessa. La domanda si pone dal momento del '60. Come risulta dalla nostra documentazione, Papa Giovanni ha parlato anche con il suo confessore che cosa fare e in coscienza ha deciso di non pubblicarlo, lo stesso Paolo VI.

Io non potevo parlare né con l'uno né con l'altro, ma immagino che in questo momento l'immagine ancora non parlava, e non aveva senso adesso offrire all'umanità una immagine indecifrabile, che avrebbe creato solo speculazione, forse anche insulti, non so. Si doveva aspettare realmente il momento nel quale si dischiudeva la realtà dietro questa visione. Quindi, penso, era una riflessione pragmatica, non dobbiamo presentare all'umanità una cosa ininterpretabile: era necessario aspettare lo svilupparsi della storia nella quale man mano si rende comprensibile il conte-

Ratzinger:

Well, until '60 we had had this "embargo", so to speak, from the seer herself. The question arose immediately at 1960. As emerged from our documentation, Pope John even spoke with his confessor about what to do, and in conscience he decided not to publish it; and Paul VI did the same.

I couldn't speak to either one or the other, but I imagine in that moment the image was still not speaking, and it made no sense to offer to humanity an undecipherable image that would have created only speculations: perhaps even insults, I don't know. It was necessary to really wait for the moment in which the reality behind this vision disclosed itself. Hence, I think it was a pragmatic reflection: we mustn't present humanity something [un]interpretable, and it was necessary to wait for the development of history in which gradually the content of

nuto di questa visione e la beatificazione dei pastorelli si offriva come momento giusto, per dire finalmente, anche alla fine di un secolo, di un millennio, "adesso abbiamo capito in grandi linee in ogni caso che cosa è il contenuto" e così con un significato positivo era possibile proporre all'umanità e alla Chiesa questo testo.

the vision becomes comprehensible, and the beatification of the little shepherds offered itself as the right moment to say, finally, even at the end of a century, of a millennium, "now we have grasped, in broad outline anyway, what the content is", and so, with a definite meaning, it was possible to present this text to humanity and to the Church.

Navarro-Valls:

La Croix, poi Svidercoschi, poi Kramer.

Navarro-Valls:

La Croix, poi Svidercoschi, poi Kramer.

Guillaume Goubert:

Guillaume Goubert, journal La Croix. Vorrei sapere se si può affermare che questo messaggio concerne solo il passato, che la visione è ormai compiuta e che non c'è, per così dire, pericolo per il futuro.

Guillaume Goubert:

Guillaume Goubert, "La Croix" newspaper. I would like to know if it is possible to state that this message only concerns the past: that the vision is complete by now and that there is, so to speak, no danger for the future.

Ratzinger:

Penso di sì perché naturalmente il martirio è una realtà presente in tutti i secoli, e in questo senso concerne naturalmente anche il futuro.

Ratzinger:

I think so, because naturally martyrdom is a reality present in every century, and in this sense it naturally concerns the future also.

Non c'è secolo senza martirio, ma qui si tratta di una storia molto specifica, di una storia di persecuzione, di una storia di violenza, di una storia di distruzione delle città, dell'essere umano. Penso che questo mondo delle distruzioni, delle violenze, delle guerre culminante finalmente nell'attentato al Papa attuale è il contenuto concreto, positive, di questa vision, che non indica il percorso della storia future: ci indica il martirio come fatto di questo secolo, e ci indica che la corrispondenza al martirio deve essere la penitenza, la conversione, dare forza all'amore contro la forza della violenza. Altri avvenimenti certamente non indica: indica una cosa in questo senso anche permanente per la storia, che il martirio ci sarà sempre perché l'odio ci sarà sempre e l'amore è sempre l'unica forza che può affrontare questo problema e superare le forze dell'odio.

There is no century without martyrdom, but here it is a matter of a very specific history, a history of persecution, a history of violence, a history of destruction of cities, of the human being. I think that this world of acts of destruction, of acts of violence, of wars culminating finally in the attack on the current pope, is the concrete, definite content of this vision, which does not show the course of future history: it shows us martyrdom as a fact of this century; it shows us that the counterpart to martyrdom must be penance, conversion, giving power to love against the power of violence. It certainly does not show other events; it shows one thing, in this sense, that is also permanent through history, that there will always be martyrdom because there will always be hate, and love is always the only force that can face up to this problem and overcome the forces of hate.

Navarro-Valls:

Crista Kramer, poi Svider-

Navarro-Valls:

Crista Kramer, poi Svider-

coschi, poi Orazio La Rocca.

Crista Kramer:

Sono Crista Kramer [von Reisswitz] del giornale Neue Bildpost e voglio sapere se nel terzo segreto viene detto che il vescovo cade in terra, è morto e cammina tra i morti, se questo potrebbe essere collegato anche ad una visione di una terza guerra mondiale, come è stato nelle speculazioni. Perché Einstein per esempio ha detto in riguardo a una possibile guerra atomica, "se ci fosse un'altra guerra ci sarà solo una guerra con le frecce". Come si potrebbe vedere questa cosa? Cioè si potrebbe fare un'interpretazione dicendo "potrebbe essere stato una visione di una terza guerra mondiale nel momento in cui c'era la minaccia di una guerra atomica in quanto non c'erano ancora gli accordi che dopo sono stati fatti nel 60'-'70"

coschi, poi Orazio La Rocca.

Crista Kramer:[2]

I am Crista Kramer [von Reisswitz] from the newspaper "Neue Bildpost", and I want to know if – in the third secret it says that the bishop falls to the ground, dies, and walks among the dead – if this could also be linked with a vision of a third world war, as it has been in speculations, because Einstein, for example, said in regard to a possible atomic war, "if there were another war, it would only be a war with arrows"; how could we see this? That is, could one make an interpretation saying, "this may have been a vision of a third world war at the moment when there was the threat of an atomic war, inasmuch as the agreements

---

2   Crista Kramer composed a book about the third part of the secret: *Das letzte Geheimnis von Fátima: Johannes Paul II. bricht das Schweigen.* (München: Pattloch, 2000). The book title translates as: "The third secret of Fátima: John Paul II breaks the silence."

which were made later, eh, in the 60s and 70s, didn't exist yet."

Ratzinger:

Io direi di no, non si dovrebbe troppo storicizzare, per così dire, queste visioni. Ci sono, come sappiamo, anche interpretazioni dell'Apocalisse dove volevano già trovare l'indicazione delle bombe atomiche, tutti i titani degli armamenti futuri. E si trova sempre qualche espressione per far capire, coincide con queste nuove scoperte terribili ma sono applicazioni sbagliate del genere "apocalisse", del genere "profezia" il quale non intende dare dettagli dei possibili terrori del mondo ma intende dare solo, da una parte, la sofferenza, il pericolo, la minaccia, come tale, senza strumentalizzare in dettagli e poi anche la risposta possibile. E l'accento è sulla risposta, anche in questo cosiddetto "terzo segreto": le minacce, le crudeltà vanno indicate per svegliare la coscienza dell'umanità e per chiamarci alla forza dell'amore e della fede, e così direi, da tut-

Ratzinger:

I would say no, we mustn't historicize these visions, so to speak, too much. There are, as we know, also interpretations of [the book of] the Apocalypse in which people want to find signs of atomic bombs already – all the titans of future armaments. There is always some expression to make this understood: it coincides with these new terrible discoveries, but they are mistaken applications of the genre of apocalypse, of the genre of prophecy, which does not intend to give details of possible terrors to the world, but only intends to give, on one hand, suffering, danger, menace, as such, without making use of it in detail; and then also giving the possible response. And the accent is on the response, in this so-called "third secret" too. The threats, the cruelty are shown to wake up the conscience of humanity, and to call us to the power of love

ti questi testi, non solo da questa terza visione, si deve tener lontane interpretazioni storicistiche che vogliono identificare avvenimenti o realtà delle invenzioni umane. Si tratta di una cosa molto più generale, [della] del nostro pericolo, delle minacce che pesano su di noi e anche del cammino da prendere, e soprattutto far coraggio che c'è sempre, anche in un mondo mezzo distrutto, una forza superiore e che quindi la morte non ha l'ultima parola.

and of faith, and so I would say about all these texts, not only about this third vision, we have to keep away from historicist interpretations that want to identify events or realities of human inventions. It's about something much more general, our danger, the threats that weigh on us, and also about the path to take, and above all to take courage that there is always, even in a half- destroyed world, a superior power, and that hence death does not have the last word.

Navarro-Valls:

Svidercoschi e poi andiamo a La Rocca.... Un momento...

Navarro-Valls:

Svidercoschi and then La Rocca.... One moment...

Gian Franco Svidercoschi:

Per ritornare sul discorso del perché, diciamo, del ritardo, di questo allungamento della prudenza della Chiesa dal '60 ad oggi, Lei in qualche modo ha già risposto parlando giustamente della evoluzione della storia, e poi mi permetto anche di ripetere quella sua bellissima frase "l'immagine non parlava"

Gian Franco Svidercoschi:

To get back to the discussion of the "why", let's say, for the delay, for this prolongation of the Church's caution from '60 to today, you have, in a way, already responded, speaking rightly of the evolution of history, and so I take the liberty of repeating your very nice phrase "the image was not speaking" then, at that time.

allora, a quei tempi. Ha ripetuto anche e anche c'è la relazione di Monsignor Bertone, della diversa sensibilità, delle scelte diverse che hanno fatto i papi, è cambiata la situazione storico-politica e indubbiamente questo. Ma io Le chiedo: non è che la Chiesa abbia pagato un prezzo troppo alto per questo lungo silenzio, questo lungo segreto sul segreto?

In fin di conti la terza parte del segreto non contiene altro, a parte l'accenno al vescovo bianco, non è nient'altro che, diciamo, un po' la, il corollario di quello che è già stato detto nelle precedenti parti, cioè questo martirio esisteva già nel 1960.

Allora, dicevo: non c'è una maniera diversa per, da parte della Chiesa, non soltanto anche per Fátima, ma per affrontare le rivelazioni private, che non entrano nel deposito della fede e quindi forse si potrebbe anche non provocare tutta quella serie di strumentalizzazioni e di scandali invece che ci sono stati proprio perché questo segreto è

And repeated also and in the report of Monsignor Bertone, it also spoke of the different sensibility, of the various choices the popes made; the historical-political situation has changed, and this undoubtedly. But I ask you, has the Church not paid a price too high for this long silence, this long secret about the secret?

When all is said and done, the third part of the secret doesn't contain anything else, apart from the reference [to the] white bishop, there's nothing else but, let's say, somewhat the corollary of what has already been said by the preceding popes; that is, this martyrdom existed already in 1960.

Then, I was saying, there's no different approach on the part of the Church, not only for Fátima, but for dealing with private revelations: that they are not part of the deposit of the faith; and so perhaps would it be possible to not even provoke all that series of exploitations and scandals which took place, really, because this secret was kept that

durato così a lungo? Grazie.

Ratzinger:

Certamente la decisione dei tre Papi di non pubblicare il segreto, perché anche il Papa attuale nell' '81 non voleva pubblicarlo, era una decisione non dogmatica ma prudenziale, e si può sempre discutere su la prudenza di una decisione se politicamente un'altra prudenza sarebbe stata preferibile, quindi non è da dogmatizzare questo atteggiamento dei Papi.

Tuttavia, in retrospettiva, direi, certo, abbiamo pagato un prezzo per queste speculazioni che abbiamo avuto in questi ultimi decenni, ma dall'altra parte penso che era anche giusto aspettare un momento di retrospettiva. Nel '60 siamo alla soglia del Concilio, questa grande speranza di trovare una nuova relazione positiva tra mondo e Chiesa e anche di aprire un po' le porte chiuse del Comunismo, e lo stesso ancora nel tempo di Papa Paolo VI ancora siamo in digestione, per così dire, del

way so long? Thank you.

Ratzinger:

Certainly, the decision by three popes not to publish the secret – because even the current pope, in '81, did not want to publish it – was not a dogmatic but a prudential decision, and it's always possible to debate [the] prudence of a decision, if politically a different prudence would have been preferable, so we shouldn't make this attitude of the popes a dogma.

In retrospect, I would say, certainly we have paid a price for these speculations that we have had in these last decades, but on the other hand, I think it was also right to wait for a moment of retrospection. In '60 we were on the threshold of the Council, this great hope of finding a new positive relation between the world and the Church, and also to open up a bit the doors closed by Communism, and still the same in the time of Pope Paul VI, we were still digesting the Council, so to speak,

Concilio con tanti problemi che questo testo non avrebbe avuto il suo collocamento corretto. Lo stesso subito dopo l'attentato, adesso uscire immediatamente con questo testo non avrebbe prodotto, mi sembra, la comprensione sufficiente. Io penso:

Senza dogmatizzare questa decisione ma personalmente con una sincera, sincera convinzione, penso, che era tutto sommato bene aspettare un po' la fine del secolo per avere una visione più globale e per poter capire meglio il vero imperativo e le vere indicazioni di questa visione.

with so many problems, that this text would not have had a proper context of its own; the same [was true] right after the attack: to go out right away with this text then, it seems to me, would not have produced enough understanding, I think.

Without making this decision a dogma, but personally with a sincere, sincere conviction, I think that it was good, all things considered, to wait a little for the end of the century, in order to have a more global vision, and to be able to understand the true imperative and the true content of this vision better.

Navarro-Valls:

La Rocca, e poi finiamo qua.

Navarro-Valls:

[*calls out the next couple of journalists*] La Rocca, and then we'll finish here.

Orazio La Rocca:

Orazio La Rocca di Repubblica. Eminenza, perché si parla di, espressamente, di Russia atea, e non si fa riferimento nel segreto a, per esempio, al Nazismo che ha fatto ben altri

Orazio La Rocca:

Orazio La Rocca from "Repubblica". Eminence, why does the secret speak expressly of atheistic Russia and not refer to, for example, Nazism, which also brought other troubles? Then, it

guai pure? Poi, si parla di vescovo bianco e con tutto il rispetto e l'affetto per Papa Wojtyla c'è stato un vescovo bianco che è stato purtroppo ammazzato durante la messa: parlo di Oscar Romero. Potrebbe essere anche lui il vescovo bianco? Poi ultima domanda: Suor Lucía dichiara secondo alcuni articoli di stampa che sta avendo anche in questo periodo delle visioni, è prevedibile che un domani la sua congregazione possa intervenire ancora a spiegare nuove visioni? Grazie.

Ratzinger:

Su questo testo?

Orazio La Rocca:

No, no, leggendo la stampa, ha annunciato che sta avendo ancora delle visioni, com'è possibile?

Ratzinger:

Allora darei ancora mezza risposta, poi Monsignor Bertone, tenendo conto del suo ultimo colloquio con Suor Lucía, aggiungerà qualcosa.

speaks of the white bishop, and with all respect and affection for Pope Wojtyla, there was a bishop in white who was slain during the Mass: I'm speaking of Oscar Romero; could he also be the white bishop? Then, a last question: Sister Lúcia says, according to some articles in the press, that she has also been having visions in the present time. Is it foreseeable [that] someday your Congregation may make a statement again to explain some new visions? Thank you.

Ratzinger:

About this text?

Orazio La Rocca:

No, no. Reading the newspapers, she announced that she was still having visions, how is it possible?

Ratzinger:

Well, *[a few words from LaRocca, unclear, are mixed in]* I would give a partial answer again, and then Monsignor Bertone, will add something, taking

Qui dobbiamo tener presente quanto avevo detto sulla limitazione della capacità di comprensione e una visione del tipo da me spiegato, cioè si può parlare solo nel limite e nei limiti della capacità comprensiva del soggetto in questione: in realtà, Suor Lucía ha detto che "non sapevamo niente dalla Russia, neppure la parola Russia ci era conosciuta". Hanno capito che si tratta di qualcosa di pericoloso.

E naturalmente non si riferiva, la Madonna, tramite questo organo limitato che era la mente, l'anima dei tre pastorelli, alla Russia come un paese con tanti cristiani, ma a un sistema anticristiano. Non è una condanna della Russia, conosciamo la grande fede del popolo russo: ma di un sistema ateo, quello classico, per così dire, che minacciava l'umanità.

Che, in realtà, altri sistemi,

into account his last conversation with Sister Lúcia.

Here we have to keep in mind what we have said about limitations in the capacity for understanding, and about a vision of the type which I explained. That is, we can only speak within the limit and – the limits of the capacity for understanding on the part of the subject in question. In reality, Sister Lúcia said that: "we didn't know anything about Russia, not even the word Russia was known to us". They did understand that it was about something dangerous.

And naturally the Madonna only made reference, through the limited organ which is the mind, the soul of the three little shepherds, to Russia, as a country with many Christians but an anti-Christian system. That is not a condemnation of Russia – we know the great faith of the Russian people – but of an atheistic system, the kind that, so to speak, threatened humanity.

It is obvious that in reality

particolarmente il Nazismo, erano radicalmente antideistici e minacciosi per l'umanità e per la Chiesa è evidente, e non c'è nessuna esclusività, direi, in questa parola, come ho detto: non ogni parola di una tale visione ha una corrispondenza storica esatta. Dall'altra parte ogni parola ha anche una ampiezza e si deve anche andare oltre il limite della parola per capire tutta la visione in questione, quindi esige, come si diceva prima, la capacità comprensiva dell'organo del bambino, del pastore, della pastorella, così anche la nostra capacità comprensiva che può vedere adesso più esattamente nell'ambito di una parola la realtà, le realtà minacciose, in queste parole. Adesso lascio la parola a Monsignor Bertone.

Bertone:

Forse potrei dire qualcosa sul vescovo bianco e sulle altre visioni. Sul vescovo bianco nel testo stesso originale di Suor Lucía risulta che i tre pastorelli

other systems, particularly Nazism, were radically anti-deistic and threatening for humanity and for the Church, and, I would say, there's no exclusivity in this message in which every word of such a vision has an exact historical correspondence, as I said. On the other hand, every word also has a breadth, and it's even necessary to go beyond the limits of the word to grasp the whole vision in question; so, as I was saying before, it requires the capacity for understanding of a child's mind: the mind of the little shepherd girl; and it also requires our capacity for understanding, which now can see more exactly the reality in the range of a word, the menacing realities in these words. Now I'll give the floor to Monsignor Bertone.

Bertone:

Maybe I would be able to say something about the white bishop and about other visions. On the white bishop in Sister Lúcia's original text itself, it is

hanno intuito subito che si trattava di un Papa, loro non sapevano di quale Papa si sarebbe trattato, specialmente dell'attentato, ma certamente i vescovi erano altri, cioè assieme al Papa, il Papa che prega per tutti i martirizzati, vescovi, sacerdoti, religiosi, religiose, laici, di ogni età, sesso, posizione – dice, no – quindi hanno escluso subito che fosse un vescovo di per sé, questo lo dice proprio la confessione, direi la rievocazione della testimone sopravvissuta: si trattava di un Papa, l'individuazione del Papa è stata possibile, come è già stato detto da Sua Eminenza, dopo l'attentato, direi così, micidiale, del 1981, per cui mi sembra che l'interpretazione qui è obbligatoria, in questo senso, non senza diminuire tutto il valore degli altri martiri e degli altri sacrifici che sono stati anche ricordati proprio il 7 maggio ultimo scorso.

clear that the three little shepherds intuited right away that it was about a pope. They didn't know which Pope it was supposed to be about, especially about the attack, but certainly the bishops were others, that is, together with the Pope, the pope who is praying for all the people martyred, the bishops, priests, religious men and women, lay people, of every age, sex, position. Therefore, let's say, no: right away they excluded the possibility that it was one bishop as such. That is what the testimony says, I would say the recollection of the surviving witness: it was about a pope. It became possible to identify the pope, as was already said by your Eminence, after the attack, I would say the deadly attack, of 1981. Because of that, it seems to me that the interpretation here is obligatory in this sense: without diminishing all the value of other martyrs and of other sacrifices that were also recalled just on the past 7th of May.

Riguardo ad altre visioni, certamente Suor Lucía ha avuto diverse, adesso le chiamiamo "visioni", non saprei dire se "apparizioni" ma nemmeno locuzioni ma comunicazioni speciali, con la Madonna dopo il '17, certamente il '25, '27, '29, '35, ancora negli anni '80, perché essa ha scritto tante lettere ai Papi, soprattutto a Paolo VI e a Giovanni Paolo II, dove rievoca dei messaggi speciali, e soprattutto insiste sulla pratica della devozione al Cuore Immacolato di Maria, sulla consacrazione di tutto il mondo al Cuore Immacolato di Maria. Adesso confesso che non mi ha detto che ha ancora visioni, apparizioni adesso, quindi ciò che dicono i giornali non so di dove lo derivino, ma ha avuto dopo il '17 certamente dei momenti di particolare comunicazione, e da, anche da comunicare, da trasmettere alle autorità competenti, questo è indubbio.

In regard to other visions, certainly Sister Lúcia has had various – now we call them visions, I wouldn't know to say if they were apparitions or even locutions, but special communications with the Madonna after '17; certainly in '25, '27, '29, '35; again in the '80s, because she wrote many letters to the Popes, especially to Paul VI and to John Paul II, in which she recounts the special messages, insists above all on the practice of devotion to the Immaculate Heart of Mary, and on the consecration of the whole world to the Immaculate Heart of Mary. Now I admit that she didn't tell me that she is still having visions, apparitions now; so what the newspapers say, I don't know where they are deriving that from; but she certainly has had moments of particular communication after '17, and also of communicating, sending them to the competent authorities, there's no doubt about that.

Navarro-Valls:

Siamo alle 12 e mezza, mi pare adesso finisce la diretta: un saluto alle persone che ci hanno seguito fin qua e continuiamo, Eminenza, con qualche domanda da sviluppare. Finiamo in quel settore, poi andiamo avanti ...

Claudia:

Claudia [incomprehensible] in Español. Su Eminenza, esta una pregunta in español: ¿porque la iglesia si esparar tanto tiempo para revelar la tercera parte del secreto? ¿Hay una razon en especial y cual es el mensaje que quiere transmitir la iglesia hoy?

Navarro-Valls:

Se vuole, può rispondere in Italiano.

Ratzinger:

Sì, non sono in grado di aggiungere molto. Era, come detto, una decisione prudenziale, e ci sono i momenti nei quali

Navarro-Valls:

We are at 12:30; it seems to me the live feed is ending now. Greetings to the people who have remained with us up to now. And we continue, Her Eminence, with some additional questions. Let's finish up in this area, and then we'll go...

Claudia:

Claudia [incomprehensible] in Spanish. Your Eminence, this is a question in Spanish: why has the Church waited so much time to reveal the third part of the secret? Is there a reason in particular, and what is the message that you want to convey to the Church today?

Navarro-Valls:

[speaking sottovoce to Ratzinger] If you want, you can answer in Italian.

Ratzinger:

Yes, I'm not in a position to add much. It was, as I said, a prudential decision; and there are moments in which a word

394

una parola parla e non parla. E, mi sembra, anche dopo l'attentato era necessario un tempo di riflessione e la maturazione del processo dei pastorelli ha un po' anche indicato il cammino da prendere. Questa maturazione di un processo importante, connesso con questi avvenimenti, ha avuto i suoi tempi necessari, e uscire prima forse sarebbe stato anche poco conveniente. Così penso che oltre le ragioni già dette, anche la pazienza che lasciava maturare il processo e così arrivare il momento giusto indica un motivo per questa... questo ritardo.

Navarro-Valls:

Vediamo un po', Orazio Petrosillo, poi Alessandra Stanley - subito, qui, o Alessandra Stanley o Orazio Petrosillo, è lo stesso, OK.

Orazio Petrosillo:

Sono Orazio Petrosillo del Messaggero. Due domande: ad alimentare le fantasie ha concorso quell'incontro del Papa a

speaks and doesn't speak. And it seems to me, even after the attack, a time of reflection was necessary; and the maturation of the [beatification] process for the little shepherds also showed, a little, the way to take. This maturation of an important process connected with these events took its necessary time, and going out early perhaps not might have been very suitable either. Thus, I think that besides the reasons already mentioned, the patience which allowed the process to mature and thus the right moment to arrive, shows a motivation for this delay.

Navarro-Valls:

Let's see a bit, Orazio Petrosillo, then Alessandra Stanley, ... quickly, here, Alessandra Stanley or Orazio Petrosillo, it's the same, OK.

Orazio Petrosillo:

I am Orazio Petrosillo from the "Messaggero". Two questions: one thing that contributed to feeding imaginations was that

Fulda il 17 novembre dell' '80, incontro, dialogo, con un gruppo di cattolici tedeschi che si dice registrato. Ora, il Papa avrebbe fatto allusione a una versione apocrifa del terzo segreto. Ora, o è apocrifo il dialogo tout-court o è apocrifo il riferimento, o il Papa faceva riferimento a una versione apocrifa del messaggio, tanto più che lui avrebbe visto il messaggio 7-8 mesi dopo il colloquio. Questa è una domanda su Fulda.

Una seconda domanda: perché queste due prudenze del Cardinale Sodano, il 13 maggio il Papa ucciso nel segreto e invece viene detto come morto, si fa riferimento implicitamente alla Russia, ergo al Comunismo come sistema ateo, e invece il Cardinale parla al plurale, quindi facendoci intendere anche il Nazismo, e quindi chi ci dice che il terzo segreto ormai è chiuso con il XX secolo? Perché

meeting of the Pope at Fulda on 17 November in '80; meeting, conversation with a group of German Catholics, which is said to have been recorded. Now the Pope reportedly alluded to an apocryphal version of the third secret. Now, was either the conversation apocryphal *tout court*, or was the reference apocryphal, or did the Pope really make reference to an apocryphal version of the message; all the more because he reportedly saw the message 7-8 months after the conversation. That is a question about Fulda.

A second question: why were there these two hedges by Cardinal Sodano: on 13 May, [there is] the pope killed in the secret, and instead he is said to be "as though dead". It implicitly makes reference to Russia and thus to Communism as an atheistic system, and instead the Cardinal speaks in the plural, so that we hear it as including Nazism also, and therefore, who is telling us that the third se-

forse il Comunismo è caduto in Europa nell' '89? Grazie.

cret is closed now with the 20th century? Maybe because Communism fell in Europe in '89? Thank you.

Ratzinger:

Al primo punto, secondo le mie informazioni, questo incontro è realmente apocrifo, non ha avuto luogo e non parlano, il Papa non ha mai detto queste cose.

Secondo punto: io non oso adesso interpretare il Cardinal Sodano. Le due, i due elementi da Lei indicati, non essendo ancora accessibile il testo al popolo e tutte le possibilità di interpretare bene un testo, ha preferito, così capisco io, di parlare nella luce dell'avvenimento stesso dove il Papa era quasi morto ma non morto. È vero che nel testo stesso si parla della morte, ma è vero anche che un tale testo che parla esplicitamente della necessità di conversione, di penitenza, lascia la possibilità di un cambiamento dei fatti previsti che non sono fotografati ma sono

Ratzinger:

On the first point, according to my information, that meeting is really apocryphal: it didn't take place, and they didn't speak; the pope never said those things.

Second point, I don't dare to give an interpretation of Cardinal Sodano. The two, two elements which you indicated, inasmuch as the text wasn't accessible to the people yet, and all the possibilities of interpreting a text well: he preferred, or so I understand, to speak in the light of the event itself, in which the pope was almost dead but not dead. It is true that the same text speaks of death, but it is also true that such a text that speaks explicitly of the need for conversion, for penance, allows for the possibility of a change to the events foreseen, which are not photographed but are an indication of

the maximum. At the maximum, it is important above all that human freedom always remains. It is important in this vision that they are not making a film of an absolutely irreversible fate, but that they indicate the potentialities of history, the dangers of history; [they] also indicate the human freedom which is able to change these things. Thus, the plural "atheisms" seems to me a totally correct interpretation: that is: in one word for the little shepherds with little content, "Russia", we can see, we must see not only an atheistic system [he pauses] essentially, immediately indicated, but it is about the problem of atheisms generally. In this sense, it seems to me, it is an interpretation that goes beyond the text but corresponds to the profound intentions of the text.

Navarro-Valls:

Alessandra?

Alessandra Stanley:

Sì, grazie. New York Times. Volevo sapere, il Papa quando ha chiesto il testo del terzo segreto, quando stava in ospedale, perché l'ha chiesto? Volevo sapere se qualcuno, se è un'intuizione o se forse Lei l'aveva già visto il segreto? Due domande: se Lei l'aveva visto prima e perché il Papa l'ha chiesto nell' '81.

Navarro-Valls:

Lei chi?

Alessandra:

Il Cardinale.

Navarro-Valls:

Aveva visto prima il Papa o il testo?

Alessandra Stanley:[3]

Yes, thank you, "New York Times". I wanted to know: the Pope, when he asked for the text of the third secret, when he was in the hospital, why did he ask for it? I wanted to know if anyone, if it was an intuition, or if perhaps you had already seen the secret? Two questions: had you seen it before, and why did the Pope asked for it in '81?

Navarro-Valls:

Who?

Alessandra:

To the Cardinal.

Navarro-Valls:

Had you seen the Pope before, or the text? [*Navarro-Valls asks to clarify because Stanley's request could have referred to either "him" or "it".*]

---

3   Stanley composed this article for the *New York Times*: <http://www.nytimes.com/2000/06/27/world/vatican-issues-text-of-third-secret-of-Fátima.html> (Accessed 2 August, 2016).

Alessandra:

Volevo sapere se il Cardinal Ratzinger aveva già visto il segreto e poi volevo sapere perché il Papa l'aveva chiesto nell' '81 se non l'aveva letto.

Ratzinger:

No, io sono arrivato a Roma in – un po' troppo – ufficialmente in novembre '82, ma di fatto in febbraio '83, e ho visto il testo in '83, quindi dopo questi avvenimenti.

Navarro-Valls:

[incomprehensibile]

Bertone:

Adesso il perché. Certamente dopo l'attentato, questo è storico, dopo l'attentato già ancora dall'ospedale Gemelli, il Santo Padre ha mandato a chiedere il testo della terza parte del segreto, il perché lo lasciamo a ... [al] Signore e al Papa stesso e poi il 13 maggio è una data, una coincidenza eccezionale, no: i 13 maggio hanno diverse coincidenze, come sapete, anche

Alessandra:

I wanted to know if Cardinal Ratzinger had already seen the secret, and then I wanted to know why the Pope had asked for it in '81 if he hadn't read it.

Ratzinger:

No, I arrived in Rome in – maybe a bit too [*laughing*] – officially in November '82, but in fact in February '83, and I saw the text in '83, therefore after these events.

Navarro-Valls:

[*incomprehensible*]

Bertone:

Now the why. Certainly, after the attack – this is history – after the attack, while still in the Gemelli hospital the Holy Father gave an order to ask for the text of the third part of the secret. Let's leave the why to, to the Lord and to the Pope himself, and then [*incomprehensible words by the journalists*] the 13th of May is a date, an exceptional coincidence, no, thirteenths of

la ordinazione episcopale di Pio XII che è stato molto devoto di Fátima, ha compiuto tanti atti ma ha mai letto il testo della terza parte del segreto, il Papa ha chiesto la terza parte e poi, come dico anche, ha subito cercato, ha pensato subito alla consacrazione della Russia e del mondo al Cuore Immacolato di Maria e difatti il primo gesto di consacrazione è stato compiuto a Santa Maria Maggiore ma assente il Papa, mentre lui era all'ospedale.

May have various coincidences, as you know: it was also the episcopal ordination of Pius XII who was very devoted to Fátima, who carried out so many acts, but who never read the text of the third part of the secret. The pope asked for the third part of the secret, and then, [as] I'll also say, he immediately sought, he immediately thought of the consecration of Russia and of the world to the Immaculate Heart of Mary and in fact the first gesture of consecration was carried out at St. Mary Major but in the absence of the Pope, while he was in the hospital.

Navarro-Valls:

Eh, vediamo qua.

Navarro-Valls:

Eh, let's see here.

Padre Marchesi:

Padre Marchesi de "La Civiltà Cattolica". Una prima domanda volevo farla a Monsignor Bertone: Sua Eccellenza l'ha appena chiarito, riguardava Pio XII e il terzo segreto di Fátima; invece a Sua Eminenza il Cardinal Ratzinger vorrei chiedere,

Padre Marchesi:

Padre Marchesi de "La Civiltà Cattolica". I wanted to pose a first question to Monsignor Bertone: your Excellency just clarified it, with regard to Pius XII and the third secret of Fátima. In turn, I would like to ask Cardinal Ratzinger: does

non Le sembra, Eminenza, che ci sia stata forse, anche in ambito ecclesiale, un accostamento da un punto di vista teologico troppo stretto tra la profezia biblica propriamente detta, e l'aspetto profetico di questa terza parte del segreto, sottolineando forse troppo che è proprio della profezia quello di essere come veggente e preveggente appunto del futuro, indicando cose future, cose nascoste? Lei nel suo intervento, anche qui in aula, ha chiarito questo aspetto, però forse una Sua parola ancora chiarificatrice ci può aiutare a decantare un po' tutta l'attesa e la potenzialità che si è voluta dare anche in ambito mass-media e nell'opinione pubblica a questa rivelazione apocalittica di Fátima.

Ratzinger:

Dire "segreti" di per sé provocano speculazioni e se è un segreto che, è ascritto alla Madonna, è un segreto che non va pubblicato, il fatto della segretezza nutre le speculazioni.

it not seem to you, Eminence, that there had perhaps been an overly strict association, from the theological point of view, even in the ecclesiastical milieu, between biblical prophecy properly speaking and the prophetic aspect of this third part of the secret, perhaps emphasizing too much what is proper to prophecy: that is, being like a seer, or more precisely, a foreseer of the future, showing future things, hidden things? Your intervention, including here in the hall, has clarified this aspect, but perhaps yet another clarifying word from you could help us to settle somewhat all the expectation and potential that is being given to this apocalyptic revelation of Fátima in the mass media and in public opinion.

Ratzinger:

To say "secrets" – by itself – they provoke speculations; and if it is a secret that is ascribed to the Madonna, [and] it's a secret that is not published, the fact of the secrecy feeds speculations.

Il secondo punto è che realmente è diffusa l'idea che "profezia", nel senso biblico, sarebbe soprattutto indicazione di avvenimenti futuri e un concetto preciso e corretto di profezia manca, mi sembra, in tanti ambient, che la profezia biblica certamente ha aperto l'orizzonte per l'arrivo del Messia, di Cristo, in questo senso ha aperto l'orizzonte del future, ma tuttavia lo ha fatto preparando le anime per il cammino verso il Cristo, era sempre e soprattutto una chiamata al presente, alle persone del presente, e solo dichiarando e dischiudendo i segni del tempo nel presente ha anche aperto la grande visione del futuro.

Tanto più nel momento nel quale conosciamo Cristo, la profezia non si occupa di speculazione e la vera profezia non ha come oggetto la curiosità nostra di conoscere qualche cosa di un tempo che per noi è inaccessibile ma di chiarire la nostra strada da prendere e così anche di trovare il vero significato del futuro. Mi

The second point is the idea is really widespread that prophecy in the biblical sense would especially be the showing of future events; and a precise and correct concept of prophecy is lacking. It seems to me, in so many spheres, that biblical prophecy certainly opened the horizon for the arrival of the Messiah, of Christ; in this sense it opened the horizon of the future, but nonetheless it did so to prepare souls for the journey toward the Christ: it was always and especially a call to the present, to the people of the present, and only declaring and disclosing the signs of the times in the present, it also opened the great vision of the future.

All the more in the moment in which we recognize Christ, prophecy is not occupied with speculations; and real prophecy does not have, as its object, our curiosity to know something about a time that is inaccessible for us, but to clarify the way for us to take, and so also to find, eh, the real meaning of the future. It

sembra che chiarire il concetto di profezia, capire meglio così anche il cuore della sacra scrittura è molto importante, questo può essere un momento propizio per farlo.

Navarro-Valls:

Cerchiamo di fare le due ultime domande purtroppo. Giancarlo Zizzola, poi, così copriamo tutta la sala.

Giancarlo Zizzola:

Per alzata di mano?

Navarro-Valls:

Venite.

Giancarlo Zizzola:

Temevo ormai l'invisibilità. Anzitutto vorrei chiedere che se affermare che solo la Russia necessita di conversione non appaia forse offensivo nei confronti dell'animo religioso del popolo russo, che ci sia sempre bisogno di fedeltà evangelica è una cosa ma che dal punto di vista della conversione il popolo russo non si debba convertire

seems to me that to clarify the concept of prophecy, and so to understand the heart of sacred scripture better, is very important: this could be a propitious moment to do so.

Navarro-Valls:

Let's try to do the last two questions. Giancarlo Zizzola, next, and so we'll cover all the hall.

Giancarlo Zizzola:

By raising a hand?

Navarro-Valls:

Go ahead.

Giancarlo Zizzola:

I was afraid I was invisible *[laughing]*. First of all, I would like to ask that, if affirming that only Russia [is in] need of conversion might [such] not perhaps appear offensive, in view of the religious soul of the Russian people; it is one thing that there is always need for faithfulness to the gospel, but from the point of view *[he pauses]* of conversion,

tanto quanto quello italiano, o americano, o portoghese, o tedesco, eccetera. Mi sembra una questione che può essere illuminante in questa conferenza stampa. E se si tratta piuttosto di una conversione dal Comunismo, dal sistema comunista, e posto dall'esegesi di pezzi di segreto già rivelato, il problema come la Vergine, potè, di Fátima potesse introdurre questa idea nel luglio del '17 prima della Rivoluzione di ottobre di quell'anno.

La seconda questione è, riguarda precisamente l'idea del divino che non esce, mi pare, troppo purificata da questo coacervo di castighi divini, e rivela forse una visione terroristica un po' reificata del religioso, dell'uso politico improprio della devozione della Madonna del Magnificat. Tutto ciò non va finalmente criticato nello spirito penitenziale del Giubileo.

the Russian people doesn't need to be converted as much as the Italian, or American, or Portuguese and German, etc. It seems to me a question that could be illuminating in this press conference, and if it is, rather, about a conversion from Communism, from the Communist system – it [the question] has been posed in the exegesis of parts of the secret already revealed – the problem of how the Virgin, from Fátima, could introduce this idea in July of '17, before the October Revolution of that year.

The second question is, precisely regards the idea of the divine, which doesn't come out, it seems, too purified by that jumble of divine chastisements, and perhaps reveals a terroristic vision, a bit reified, of the religious, of the improper political use of the devotion of the Madonna of the *Magnificat*. Finally, all this is not being critiqued in the penitential spirit of the Jubilee.

Ratzinger:

Io rispondo alla seconda questione e lascio la prima a Monsignor Bertone.

Io penso che non c'è qui il tipo di abuso dell'angoscia dell'uomo per guidarlo al religioso. C'è sempre il realismo della sofferenza, del martirio che è il contrassegno di questo secolo scorso, nessun secolo ha conosciuto tanti martiri, tanta violenza, tanta crudeltà, tante nuove dimensioni della opposizione al vero umanesimo; e attirare l'attenzione a questa realtà che risulta finalmente dalla versione dell'uomo da Dio e nello stesso tempo mostrare che questo non è un fatto inevitabile ma che c'è la libertà, che c'è la forza di amore che può opporsi con successo a questo: dirci, nonostante tutto questo, che vedrete, e lo abbiamo visto, rimane vero che l'amore è più forte che l'odio: mi sembra, è un messaggio di grande ottimismo che ci aiuta in mezzo al realismo di, degli innegabili mali di questo tempo e

Ratzinger:

I'll respond to the second question, which springs from the first one for Monsignor Bertone.

I think that here this is not the type, of abuse of man's anguish to guide him to the religious. There is always the realism of suffering, of martyrdom, which is the counter-sign of this past century: no century has known so many martyrs, so much violence, so much cruelty, such new dimensions of opposition to dialogue with humanism; and to draw attention to this reality, which finally results from man's turning away from God, and at the same time to show that this is not an inevitable fact but that there is freedom; that there is the power of love that can oppose it, and with success. To tell us, notwithstanding all that, that you will see – we have seen it -- it remains true that love is stronger than hate: it seems to me, it is a message of great optimism that helps us in the midst of realism, of the undeniable evils of this

perciò tutt'altro che creare angoscia è un messaggio che dice "in mezzo alle angosce che esistono avete coraggio, il Signore è più forte". Allora alla prima domanda.

Bertone:

Mi sembra che Sua Eminenza aveva già parlato di questo tema, che non si tratta di una condanna sul male del popolo russo. Tra l'altro il popolo russo è uno dei popoli più devoti della Madonna, quindi la Madonna certamente non se la prende con il popolo russo, e anzi, il popolo russo ha sofferto tanto proprio per l'oppressione di un sistema ateo che è nato dalla Russia. Il fatto che nel '17 si preveda questo sistema ateo insieme ad altri sistemi, è la prova un po' della profezia, di una vera profezia con l'accezione, con l'ampiezza di interpretazione della profezia di cui ha parlato Sua Eminenza. È un appello anche al popolo russo per la conversione, ma a coloro che hanno oppresso l'anima religiosa del popolo russo,

time; and thereby, quite opposite from creating anguish, it is a message that says, "in the midst of the anguishes that exist, have courage, the Lord is stronger". Now to the first question.

Bertone:

It seems that your Eminence has already spoken on this topic, that it is not a matter of a condemnation about the evil of the Russian people. Among other things, the Russian people is one of the peoples most devoted to the Madonna; hence the Madonna certainly is not offended with the Russian people; and rather, the Russian people has suffered so much, precisely from oppression by an atheistic system that was born from Russia. The fact that in '17, this atheistic system is foreseen, along with other systems, [which is] a bit of proof of the prophecy, of a true prophecy with the meaning, with the breadth of interpretation of prophecy of which his Eminence spoke. It is also a call to the Russian people for conversion, but

to those who oppressed the religious soul of the Russian people, and it is also a gift of hope to the Russian people because, as the Cardinal Prefect said now, it is stated together with the prediction of so much sufferings, with the description of such great sufferings, the prediction of the presence of the healing power of God who in his sovereign freedom intervenes in history and guides history and even changes history – and this is true, the Lord can change history and in fact has changed it, even at the turn of this 20th century.

Navarro-Valls:

The last question, unfortunately,

Director of the Catholic Information Center:

I am Father [*incomprehensible*], director of the Catholic Information Center in Lebanon. Can I speak in English or French?

Navarro-Valls:

Sì.

Il direttore del Centro Cattolico per l'informazione [Francese]:

Bien. Depuis une vingtaine d'années, le père Nicolas Gruner du Canada a demandé au Vatican par plusieurs moyens de déclarer ce secret. Même en 1992 dans un congrès à Fátima il a été battu et chassé de l'église. Il a été rejeté. J'étais présent à ce congrès. Je me demande pourquoi le père Nicolas Gruner - je ne le défends pas - a été rejeté parce qu'il demande une chose très normale que vous déclarez maintenant, et pourquoi le moment est venu maintenant pour déclarer le troisième secret qui a défendu au père Nicolas d'en parler. Merci.

Ratzinger:

È una lunga storia quella di Padre Gruner e penso che non è il luogo adesso qui di entrare in questa storia perché non vorrei violare la privacy di Padre Gruner. Vero è che certamente ha

Navarro-Valls:

Yes.

Director of the Catholic Information Center [in French]:

Good. For twenty years, Father Nicholas Gruner of Canada has asked the Vatican by various means to declare this secret. Even in 1992 in a congress at Fátima he was struck and chased from the church. He was rejected. I was present at that congress. I wonder why Father Nicholas Gruner – I don't defend him – was rejected because he is asking for a very normal thing, which you are declaring now, and why has the moment come now to declare the third secret, which Father Nicholas was forbidden to talk about? Thank you.

Ratzinger:

The history of Father Gruner is a long one, and I think this is not the place now to go into that history, because I would not want to violate the privacy of Father Gruner. It's true that he

buona intenzione ma i mezzi scelti da lui non sono sempre ugualmente buoni: queste crociate che fa portano un po' con sé, mi sembra, il tipo adesso rimproverato da Zizzola, cioè, lavorano un po' con l'angoscia.

In ogni caso penso dovrebbe conformarsi con il magistero della Chiesa, riconoscere che la consacrazione della Russia è fatta come voluta dalla Madonna e dovrebbe anche lasciare al magistero della Chiesa di trovare il momento giusto. Poteva fare questa proposta, e, ma dovrebbe anche essere capace e sufficientemente generoso per accettare che il magistero ha avuto le sue ragioni per non farlo subito ma per aspettare ancora un po', soprattutto la maturazione del processo dei pastorelli.

Navarro-Valls:

Grazie Eminenza, grazie Eccellenza. Grazie a voi per il vostro interesse.

certainly has good intentions, but actions he has chosen are not always equally good; these crusades he makes seem to present, a bit, the type just criticized by Zizzola, that is: they work a little with anguish.

In any case I think he should conform to the magisterium of the Church, recognize that the consecration of Russia has been done as wished by the Madonna, and should also leave to the magisterium of the Church to find the right moment. He could have made this proposal, eh, but he should also be able and sufficiently generous to accept that the magisterium has had its reasons for not doing it right away, but for waiting a while yet, especially the maturation of the process of the little shepherds.

Navarro-Valls:

Thank you, Eminence; thank you, Excellency. Thank you all for your interest.

—Appendix D—
Transcript of the May, 2007 Episode of Porta A Porta With Cardinal Bertone

This transcript was made by the same company that rendered the Q&A session of the June 26, 2000 press conference. This author and two others have gone through the transcript and made emendations or notes where appropriate.

[Notes from the transcriptionist and the translator are in brackets.]

[Screens in the studio display the words: "The fourth secret of Fátima does not exist"]

Bruno Vespa:

Buonasera al pubblico di Porta a Porta, buonasera al Segretario di Stato Vaticano Tarcisio Bertone, buonasera a Giulio Andreotti, senatore a vita, e a Giuseppe De Carli autore con Bertone di un libro, "L'ultima veggente di Fátima". È una serata speciale questa perché, come vi abbiamo annunciato negli spot che hanno

Bruno Vespa:

Good evening to the viewers of "Porta a Porta" good evening to the Vatican Secretary of State Tarcisio Bertone, good evening to Giulio Andreotti, senator for life, and to Giuseppe De Carli, author together with Bertone of a book, "The Last Seer of Fátima". This is a special evening because, as we announced in the

preceduto questa trasmissione, il cardinal Bertone ha con sé un documento. Il cardinal Bertone ha, come racconta in questo libro, ha incontrato per tre volte Suor Lucía, l'ultima veggente, come si dice anche nel titolo del libro. Fu la pastorella che il 13 maggio del 1917 a Fátima vide la Vergine, incontrò la Vergine, e allora ricordiamo, anche a chi ci ascolta oltre che a chi vi parla, che cosa successe quel 13 maggio 1917. Manuela Orrù...

Manuela Orrù:

"Non abbiate paura". È il 13 maggio 1917, una signora vestita di bianco più splendente del sole appare nella cavità campestre di Cova da Iria, frazione di Fátima, a tre pastorelli, Giacinta e Francesco Marto e Lucía dos Santos. Siamo nel pieno

promo before this broadcast, Cardinal Bertone has a document with him. Cardinal Bertone, as he relates in this book, has met three times with Sister Lúcia, the last seer, as the title of the book says. She was the little shepherd girl who, on May 13, 1917 saw the Virgin at Fátima, met the Virgin, and now we are remembering, in addition to who was listening and who was speaking, what happened that May 13, 1917. Manuela Orrù...

Manuela Orrù:

[pre-recorded video, including images from an old film depiction of Fátima, and historical video showing figures named in the following narration: Sister Lúcia, Pope Pius XII, Pope John Paul II, Cdl. Ratzinger]

"Be not afraid". It is May 13, 1917. A woman clothed in white, more brilliant than the sun, appears in the country hollow of Cova da Iria, in the village of Fátima, to three shepherd children, Jacinta and Francisco Marto and Lúcia dos

della prima guerra mondiale. Da quel giorno il fenomeno si ripete il 13 di ogni mese fino al mese di ottobre, giorno in cui 70.000 persone assistono al miracolo del sole; ma è il 13 luglio che la Signora rivela il segreto.

La prima parte riguarda la visione dell'inferno che Lucía descriverà come un grande mare di fuoco che sembrava stare sotto terra dove cadono le anime dei peccatori.

Nella seconda parte si prevede la fine della prima guerra mondiale ma se ne annuncia una seconda, durante il pontificato di Pio XI, se gli uomini non smetteranno di offendere Dio e si chiede di consacrare la Russia al cuore immacolato di Maria perché se si convertirà; si avrà la pace. Altrimenti la Russia spargerà i suoi errori per il mondo promuovendo guerre e persecuzioni alla Chiesa. I buoni, continua il messaggio, saranno martirizzati, il Santo Padre avrà molto da soffrire, varie nazioni saranno distrutte.

Santos. We are in the middle of the First World War. From that day, the phenomenon repeats on the 13th of every month until the month of October, a day in which 70,000 people are present at the miracle of the sun; but it is July 13 when the Lady reveals the secret.

The first part relates to the vision of Hell which Lúcia will describe as a great sea of fire that seemed to be on the ground where the souls of sinners fell.

In the second part, the end of the First World War is predicted, but a second one is announced, during the pontificate of Pius XI, if man does not cease offending God; and there is a request to consecrate Russia to the Immaculate Heart of Mary, because Russia will be converted; there will be peace. Otherwise, Russia will spread its errors through the world, promoting wars and persecutions of the Church. The good men — the message continues — will be martyred; the Holy Father will

Il 2 dicembre 1940, 10 anni dopo l'autorizzazione del vescovo di Leira al culto ufficiale della Madonna di Fátima, dal convento delle Dorotee Lucía scrive a Pio XII manifestando il desiderio di rivelare il messaggio della Madonna ma Papa Pacelli non risponde. 17 anni dopo, il 4 aprile 1957, la busta sigillata contenente il segreto finisce nell'archivio segreto del Santo Uffizio: secondo le indicazioni di Suor Lucía, il contenuto non deve essere reso noto prima del 1960. La terza parte del segreto verrà divulgata solo quarant'anni dopo, il 13 maggio 2000, dal Segretario di Stato Vaticano Angelo Sodano in occasione della cerimonia di beatificazione a Fátima dei due pastorelli Francesco e Giacinta Marto, officiata da Giovanni Paolo II. Nell'anticipazione del cardinale Sodano, a cui seguirà un mese e mezzo dopo la conferenza stampa e il commento teologico dell'allora

have much to suffer; various nations will be destroyed.

On December 2, 1940, ten years after the bishop of Leiria gives authorization for official devotion to the Lady of Fátima, from the convent of the Dorothean Sisters, Lúcia writes to Pius XII making known her desire to reveal the message of our Lady, but Pope Pacelli does not respond. 17 years later, on April 4, 1957, the sealed envelope containing the secret ends up in the secret archive of the Holy Office: according to the instructions of Sister Lúcia, the contents must not be made known before 1960. The third part of the secret will be divulged only forty years later, on May 13, 2000, by the Vatican Secretary of State Angelo Sodano, on the occasion of the beatification ceremony at Fátima for the two little shepherds Francisco and Jacinta Marto, with John Paul II presiding. In Cardinal Sodano's anticipation – which was to be followed a month and a half

Prefetto della Congregazione per la Dottrina della Fede Joseph Ratzinger, il vescovo vestito di bianco che cade a terra come morto è Karol Wojtyla colpito da Ali Ağca.

later by the press conference and the theological commentary by then-Prefect of the Congregation for the Doctrine of the Faith Joseph Ratzinger – the bishop clothed in white who falls to the ground as though dead is Karol Wojtyla, struck by Ali Ağca.

Bruno Vespa:

Signor Cardinale, posso chiederle che impressioni ha avuto la prima volta che ha incontrato Suor Lucía?

Cardinal Bertone:

Ho avuto l'impressione, come avete visto anche voi adesso fissandola in volto, di una donna straordinariamente luminosa, pacata, tranquilla, ricca di spiritualità, anche gioiosa, quasi sul suo volto non c'erano i segni di tutti i drammi, di tutte le vicende storiche che si sono un po' – rivolte anche dentro di lei, e che ha portato con sé per tante diecine di anni nel secolo ventesimo: quindi certamente una amica di Dio, una de-

Bruno Vespa:

Cardinal, may I ask you: what impressions did you have the first time you met Sister Lúcia?

Cardinal Bertone [*speaking by remote video from the Apostolic Palace*]:

I had the impression, as you also saw now, looking her into the face, of a woman extraordinarily luminous, calm, tranquil, rich in spirituality, also joyful: there practically wasn't a sign on her face of all the drama, of all the historic events that had unfolded, even within her, somewhat; and who carried that with her for so many decades in the 20th century; so she was certainly a friend of God, an ex-

vota straordinaria di Maria ed una grande amica dell'umanità.

traordinary devotee of Mary and a great friend of humanity.

Bruno Vespa:

Suor Lucía quindi ha vissuto tutte le tragedie che erano state anticipate dalle apparizioni della Vergine ...

Bruno Vespa:

Thus, Sister Lúcia lived through all the tragedies that had been anticipated in the apparitions of the Virgin ...

Cardinal Bertone:

Senza dubbio, e le ha vissute soprattutto nella preghiera, le ha vissute ripensandole, direi, rimuginandole nel suo cuore, nella sua mente, nella contemplazione di Dio e in una lunga perseverante intercessione secondo la parola di Maria, preghiera, penitenza. Ha sofferto molto anche nei due conventi in cui è stata dopo la vicenda straordinaria delle apparizioni di Maria.

Cardinal Bertone:

Without a doubt, and she lived through them, above all, in prayer; she lived through them, reflecting on them, I would say, turning them over in her heart, in her mind, in the contemplation of God, and in a long persevering intercession according to the word of Mary, prayer, penance. She also suffered a lot in the two convents in which she lived after the extraordinary event of the apparitions of Mary.

Bruno Vespa:

Senatore Andreotti, Lei ha conosciuto molti pontefici, è stato vicino anche a Giovanni Paolo II che a sua volta Le è sta-

Bruno Vespa:

Senator Andreotti, you have known many Popes; you have also been close to John Paul II, who in turn was very close to

to molto vicino in un momento molto difficile della, della sua vita. Che immagine ha avuto Lei, sempre di questa pastorella che poi è vissuta tanto a lungo da poter vedere tutto quello che la Vergine le aveva anticipato?

Giulio Andreotti:

Io devo dir la verità, siccome sono stato battezzato e ho vissuto da ragazzo nella parrocchia romana di Santa Brigida, dove c'è la prima immagine della Madonna di Lourdes pervenuta a Roma, allora sono sempre stato più attratto - per essere esatti - dalla Madonna di Lourdes e Bernadette Soubirous che non da Fátima, però certamente quello che ha fatto poi impressione era di vedere attraverso la grande attenzione che dava verso di lei, insomma, i Papi, insomma, di vedere che cosa ha significato questa presenza di una donna umile che irradiava però questo grande fascino e che ha profetizzato, cosa che è veramente importante e credo che

you in a very difficult time of your life. What image have you always had of this shepherd girl, who then lived so long as to see everything the Virgin had foretold to her?

Giulio Andreotti:

To tell you the truth: since I was baptized and lived as a boy in the Roman parish of Santa Brigida, where there is the first image of Our Lady of Lourdes that came to Rome, then I have always been more attracted, to be exact, by Our Lady of Lourdes and by Bernadette Soubirous than by Fátima. But, certainly, what made an impression then was to see, through the great attention that was given to her, well, the Popes; well: to see what it meant, this presence of a humble woman, but who radiated this great fascination and who prophesied, something that is truly important, and I believe it still can bear a certain emotion now for us to reflect on.

417

porti ancora adesso una certa emozione a rifletterci.

Bruno Vespa:

Prima di arrivare a De Carli e al libro che lui ha scritto con il cardinal Bertone, pregherei la regia di inquadrare i due madonnari, Nedo Consoli che è il presidente dell'Associazione Madonnari d'Italia e Federico, Federico Pillan. [*applause*] Da, da quanto tempo esistono madonnari? Forse da sempre…

Nedo Consoli:

Stabilirlo, stabilirlo è difficilissimo, anche perché è un'arte effimera, quindi non ha mai lasciato un segno indelebile nel tempo…

Bruno Vespa:

I posti preferiti sono sempre le strade, i marciapiedi, le…

Nedo Consoli:

Sempre, sì, sempre. Ecco, diciamo che testimonianza potrebbe essere una lettera di Isabella d'Este che dalla stanza

Bruno Vespa:

Before we go to De Carli and to the book he's written with Cardinal Bertone, I would ask the director to bring into view the two "*madonnari*" [*religious street artists*], Nedo Consoli, who is the president of the Association of *Madonnari* of Italy, and Federico Pillan. [*applause*] How long have there been *madonnari*? Probably since forever…

Nedo Consoli:

To establish that – it's very difficult, especially because it's an ephemeral art, so it has never left a mark that's indelible in the time …

Bruno Vespa:

The favorite places are always the streets, the sidewalks, the –

Nedo Consoli:

Yes, always. You know, we say that one witness might be a letter by Isabella d'Este *[the Renaissance art patron]* who

del bagno scriveva che sarebbe scesa sul listone, quindi sul marciapiede a portare le polveri al dipintore, però poteva anche essere Mantegna ...[*laughing*] non è detto che fosse un madonnaro...

Bruno Vespa:
Beh, un bravo madonnaro Mantegna, devo dire...

Nedo Consoli:
[*laughing*]... bravissimo, chiaramente.

Bruno Vespa:
... ha avuto un certo successo.

Bruno Vespa:
Si ferma molta gente?

Nedo Consoli:
Sì, sì, si ferma molta gente e per rimanere in tema con la puntata di Porta a Porta il soggetto che da sempre, son 35 anni che lo faccio, quindi da sempre che attrae di più e, se me lo permettono, che ci dà anche qualche soldino in più, perché la gente paga di più è proprio la

wrote that she went down to the ground-level, that is, to the sidewalk, to bring the painter some powder – but it also might have been *[the painter]* Mantegna; *[laughing]* we can't say that he was a *madonnaro*...

Bruno Vespa:
Well... Mantegna, a great *madonnaro*, I must say...

Nedo Consoli:
[*laughing*]... great, clearly.

Bruno Vespa:
... he had a certain success.

Bruno Vespa:
Do a lot of people stop?

Nedo Consoli:
Yes, yes; a lot of people do stop; and to stay on the topic of today's "Porta a Porta", the subject that has always – I've been doing this for 35 years – so what has always attracted people the most, and if I may say so, what has brought in the most money, because people pay more, is the

Madonna.

Bruno Vespa:
La Madonna.

Bruno Vespa:
State ritraendo una Madonna del '700, credo...

Nedo Consoli:
Sì, sì, di un anonimo del '700, una Madonna col bambino.

Bruno Vespa:
Perché, Eminenza, c'è questa devozione così massiccia e credo anche abbastanza incrollabile per la Vergine?

Cardinal Bertone:
Eh sì, perché la Vergine è una creatura affascinante, è la madre di Dio ma è una donna profondamente immersa nella storia dell'umanità e nella vita di ogni famiglia, di ogni persona, in qualche modo si identifica con le aspettative, le attese, lo sviluppo, la crescita, le aspirazioni di ogni persona buona che

Madonna herself.

Bruno Vespa:
The Madonna.

Bruno Vespa:
You're recreating a Madonna from the 1700s, I believe

Nedo Consoli:
Yes, it's by an anonymous painter from the 1700s, a Madonna with the Child.

Bruno Vespa:
Eminence, why is there such a solid and, I think also, unshakeable devotion for the Virgin?

Cardinal Bertone:
Oh, yes; because the Virgin is a fascinating creature. She is the Mother of God, but she is a woman profoundly immersed in the history of humanity and in the life of every family, of every person. In some way she identifies with the expectations, the waiting, the development, growth, aspirations, of every

vive nel mondo e allora la Madonna è sentita molto vicina, basta pensare a tutte le poesie che l'hanno celebrata, è colei che in qualche modo ci da la mano per congiungerci a Dio, con una mano ci lega a sé, come ha detto tante volte "vi porto accanto a me, accanto al mio cuore, nel mio cuore" e con l'altra mano ci indica Dio, ci lega a Dio.

Bruno Vespa:

Allora, De Carli," L'ultima veggente di Fátima", in che cosa questo libro ha portato delle novità?

Giuseppe De Carli:

Mah, le novità sono essenzialmente direi quattro: innanzitutto io quando avevo fatto questa proposta al cardinale Bertone che era impegnato ed era appena diventato Segretario di Stato, poi prenderà possesso della sua carica il 15 settembre, anzi pensavo che

good person who lives in the world, and now we feel the Madonna is very close to us. We just need to think of all the poems that have celebrated her: she's the one who, in a way, gives us her hand to join us to God, and with one hand connects us with herself. As she has said so many times, "I bring you close to myself, close to my heart, into my heart", and with the other hand which points to God, connects us to God.

Bruno Vespa:

Now, De Carli, "The last seer of Fátima": in what aspect has this book brought some news?

Giuseppe De Carli:

Well, the news are, essentially, I would say, four. First of all, when I had made this proposal to Cardinal Bertone who was very busy and had just become Secretary of State, and then he was going to take up his new duties on September 15: I thought he would say no, to tell you the

mi dicesse di no, a dir il vero, e poi invece sono stato sorpreso di questa sua disponibilità, era quello che io ero intrigato dalla figura di Suor Lucía, come tutti noi, cioè di questa suora cocciuta, di questa suora controversa, di questa suora che andava controcorrente, una spina nel fianco per ben cinque papi e la quale non era mai riuscita ad arrivare al Sommo Pontefice e a farsi sentire, poi ha trovato un papa che finalmente, l'ha sentita

Bruno Vespa:

Un momento solo...

Giuseppe De Carli:

Era Papa Giovanni...

Bruno Vespa:

Un momento solo, scusi... Eminenza, scusi, ma come fa un papa a non essere se non altro curioso di ricevere una suora che ha visto la Madonna?

Cardinal Bertone:

Be', Lei sa che tante persone, forse anche tante suore, dicono di aver visto la Madonna,

truth, and then instead I was surprised by his willingness to be available. It was that – I was intrigued by the figure of Sister Lúcia, as we all are, that is: by this stubborn sister, this controversial sister, this sister who went against the current, a thorn in the side for some five Popes, who never succeeded in reaching the Supreme Pontiff and being heard; and then she found a pope who finally heard her.

Bruno Vespa:

Just a moment...

De Carli:

It was Pope John –

Bruno Vespa:

Just a moment, excuse me... Excuse me, Eminence, how can a Pope not be, if nothing else, curious to receive a sister who has seen the Madonna?

Cardinal Bertone:

Well: you know that a lot of people, maybe even a lot of sisters, say that they've seen the

di aver avuto rivelazioni personali, locuzioni interiori. Allora se il Papa, i Papi, ricevessero tutte queste persone certamente ci sarebbe un surplus di lavoro, ecco, di udienze. E poi c'è sempre nella storia della Chiesa, nella prudenza della Chiesa, c'è sempre una serie di filtri che magari si possono discutere ma che seguono queste persone e in qualche modo verificano la verità delle loro affermazioni prima di arrivare alla suprema autorità che è il papa.

Bruno Vespa:

Eh, converrà però Eminenza che il santuario di Fátima non l'ha fatto Suor Lucía, l'ha fatto la Chiesa...

Cardinal Bertone:

Be', evidentemente...

Bruno Vespa:

... quindi un minimo di, di credibilità gliel'ha dato perché se no...

Madonna, that they have had personal revelations, interior locutions. Now, if the Pope, if the Popes, were to receive all these people, certainly there would be a surplus of work, I mean, of audiences. And then, in the history of the Church, in the prudence of the Church, there is always a series of filters that maybe can be debated, but which follow these people and in a way, verify the truth of their statements before coming to the supreme authority which is the Pope.

Bruno Vespa:

Eh, but your Eminence will agree that Sister Lúcia didn't make the shrine at Fátima; the Church did that...

Cardinal Bertone:

Well, obviously ...

Bruno Vespa:

... therefore a minimum of credibility which it gave her, because if not,

Cardinal Bertone:

...certo gliel'ha dato...

Bruno Vespa:

...gliel'ha dato, perché se no, non avrebbe fatto il santuario...

Cardinal Bertone:

Dopo, dopo tutte le verifiche a cominciare dal vescovo locale...

Bruno Vespa:

...certo...

Cardinal Bertone:

...com'è noto, come è ovvio, no, in tutte le apparizione ecco la prima autorità, il vescovo locale, il vescovo locale che poi informa a Roma. Quando io ero segretario alla Congregazione per la Dottrina della Fede ricevevo molte informative di eventi presuntamente soprannaturali, poi incominciava tutta l'opera di discernimento e di preghiera anche per verificare la veridicità dei messaggi, delle apparizioni, degli eventi in modo da catalo-

Cardinal Bertone:

... certainly it gave her ...

Bruno Vespa:

... it gave it to her, because if not, it wouldn't have built the shrine...

Cardinal Bertone:

After, after all the verifications, starting with the local bishop...

Bruno Vespa:

... certainly ...

Cardinal Bertone:

... as we all know, as is obvious, in all apparitions, you see, the first authority [is] the local bishop, the local bishop who then informs Rome. When I was secretary at the Congregation for the Doctrine of the Faith, I used to receive a lot of reports about allegedly supernatural events; then we would begin all the work of discernment and prayer to verify the authenticity of the messages, the apparitions, the events, by way of cataloguing

garli, ecco, nel giudizio della Chiesa.

Bruno Vespa:
Bene, arriviamo, torniamo a De Carli.

Giuseppe De Carli:
Sì, dai, allora prima, prima, la curiosità era questa, quella di conoscere questa Suor Lucía che era una donna cocciuta e determinata, che aveva cominciato a scrivere a vent'anni e che poi ha scritto moltissimo, non è vero che a lei hanno messo il silenziatore oppure la Chiesa ufficiale ha messo il silenziatore, la gran parte dei suoi settant'anni di vita da quando lei ha incominciato a scrivere ed è vissuta fino ai 97 anni, li ha passati a scrivere, a scrivere e non ha scritto mai per sua volontà ma sempre per comando degli altri perché era il vescovo diocesano oppure era il padre spirituale o erano altri sacerdoti che erano incuriositi da questa sua esperienza del divino, del soprannaturale.

L'altro elemento che mi

them, you see, according to the judgment of the Church.

Bruno Vespa:
Good, we're getting there; let's return to De Carli.

Giuseppe De Carli:
Yes; say – now first, the curiosity was this: knowing this Sister Lúcia, who was a stubborn, determined woman, who had started to write at the age of twenty and then wrote a lot – it's not true that they silenced her, or that the official Church silenced her; for most of the seventy years after she began to write – and she lived to the age of 97 – she wrote and wrote, but she never wrote of her own will, but always when ordered by someone else, because it was the diocesan bishop or her spiritual father, or there were other priests who had become curious about her experience of the divine, the supernatural.

The other element that had

aveva molto colpito di Suor Lucía era collegato alla figura di Papa Paolo Giovanni II. Nel libro, secondo me soprattutto perché è stato il cardinal Bertone ad illuminarmi, c'è tutta una reinterpretazione del pontificato alla luce del mistero di Fátima. Ma devo dire che fa venire i brividi, fa accapponare la pelle come Giovanni Paolo II sia entrato nel gorgo di questo mistero e abbia assunto su di sé quello che è il soprattutto il terzo segreto di Fátima.

Poi c'è un terzo elemento che mi ha colpito ed è la figura, perché è qua collegato con noi ed è il cardinal Tarcisio Bertone che io conoscevo, sapevo che era una persona diretta, che era che è una persona effervescente, che è un Segretario di Stato abbastanza singolare nella storia della Chiesa e lo si rivela ancor di più...

Bruno Vespa:
Il primo Segretario di Stato

struck me greatly about Sister Lúcia was connected with the figure of Pope Paul John II [*sic*, Pope John Paul II]. In the book, in my opinion particularly – because it had been Cardinal Bertone who enlightened me – there was a whole reinterpretation of his pontificate in the light of the mystery of Fátima. But I have to say, what makes me tremble, what gives me goose-bumps, is how John Paul II entered into the whirlpool of this mystery and had taken this upon himself: which is, above all, the third secret of Fátima.

Then there is a third element that struck me, and it is the figure – because he is connected here with us, it is Cardinal Tarcisio Bertone, whom I knew already, I knew he was a direct person, he was and is a sparkling person, he is quite a unique Secretary of State in the history of the Church and is revealing himself even more –

Bruno Vespa:
The first Secretary of State

che è stato anche un buon tele-
cronista…

Giuseppe De Carli:

È stato un ottimo telecroni-
sta, e che affronta, affronta questa vicenda proprio con lo spirito
di un attaccante, proprio, di una,
di una grande squadra.

Bruno Vespa:

… prego…

Giulio Andreotti:

Credo, è salesiano…questa
è una caratteristica importante…

Giuseppe De Carli:

È un salesiano… dunque…
e il quarto ed ultimo elemento
io credo che sia proprio questo
cammino, eh, che noi abbiamo fatto all'interno del divino,
cioè c'è all'interno della storia
della Chiesa, ci sono delle persone che improvvisamente sono
toccata, cioè, ci possono essere
tutte le spiegazioni psicologiche
che vogliamo ma ad un certo
punto nella coscienza irrompe il

who has also been a good TV
commentator –

Giuseppe De Carli:

He's been a great commen-
tator, and he is taking on these
events really with the spirit of a
football striker, of a great team.

Bruno Vespa (to Senator Andreotti):

… pardon?…

Giulio Andreotti:

I believe, he's a Salesian –
that's an important characteristic…

Giuseppe De Carli:

He's a Salesian… then;
and the fourth and last element
I believe belongs to this, uh,
journey we have taken into the
divine, that is, into the history of
the Church, there are people who
unexpectedly are touch – that is,
there can be all the psychological explanations you want, but at
a certain point the sacred breaks
into our awareness; if we are attentive, this sacred touches us -

sacro, se noi stiamo attenti questo sacro ci tocca -

Bruno Vespa:

Allora, vediamo un momento con Paolo Mielitic il ritratto di Suor Lucía e i suoi incontri con il cardinale Tarcisio Bertone che era stato inviato dal pontefice proprio come segretario della Congregazione per la Dottrina della Fede che, lo ricordiamo, era diretta dal cardinale Joseph Ratzinger.

Paolo Mielitic:

Una carmelitana tenace, caparbia, esuberante, protagonista nel lontano 1917 di una meravigliosa avventura nella Cova da Iria nei pressi di Fátima, in Portogallo, in compagnia dei due piccoli cugini. Dei tre pastorelli Lucía, con i suoi 10 anni, è la più grande, l'unica in grado di cogliere l'intera ricchezza e drammaticità del messaggio di Fátima. Morti prematuramente Francesco e Giacinta, Lucía rimane l'unica testimone; così la

Bruno Vespa:

Now, let's look for moment, along with Paolo Mielitic, at the portrait of Sister Lúcia and her meetings with Cardinal Tarcisio Bertone, who was sent by the Pope precisely as secretary of the Congregation for the Doctrine of the Faith, which, let us recall, was directed by Cardinal Joseph Ratzinger.

Paolo Mielitic [*pre-recorded segment with voiceover*]:

A Carmelite nun, strong, stubborn, exuberant, the protagonist long ago in 1917 of a marvelous adventure in the Cova da Iria in the village of Fátima, in Portugal, in the company of her two younger cousins. Of the three little shepherds, Lúcia, at age 10, is the oldest, the only one in a position to grasp the whole richness and drama of the message of Fátima. After Francisco and Jacinta died prematurely, Lúcia remains the only

descrivono alcune note dell'epoca "Di bassa statura, mani grosse da lavoro, vivace, intelligente ma modesta e senza pretese". Comincia per lei una lunga missione cui si manterrà fedele fino alla fine della sua vita, quasi centenaria, assume una nuova identità per sottrarsi alla curiosità opprimente di fedeli e curiosi, impara a leggere e scrivere, segue la propria vocazione religiosa ed entra come suora carmelitana nel monastero di Santa Teresa a Coimbra, una vita normale, fedele al motto "All'esterno come tutte, all'interno come nessuna". In realtà una carmelitana scomoda, circondata da un alone di mistero e di santità, per decenni bussa alla porta dei papi trovandola quasi sempre sbarrata ma a partire dal 2000 il cardinale Tarcisio Bertone, allora segretario della Congregazione per la Dottrina della Fede, fa la spola fra il Vaticano e Coimbra, per tre volte incontra Suor Lucía, l'ultima veggente di Fátima, per verificare con lei l'autenticità

witness. Some notes from that time describe her thus: "Small in stature, her hands large from work, lively, intelligent but modest and unpretentious". A long mission begins for her, to which she will keep faithful until the end of her life, almost a century. She assumes a new identity to withdraw from the oppressive curiosity of the faithful and the curious, learns to read and write, follows her own religious vocation and enters as a Carmelite sister in the monastery of Santa Teresa at Coimbra, a normal life, faithful to the motto: "Outside like everyone else, inside like no one else." In reality, an uncomfortable Carmelite, surrounded by a halo of mystery and sanctity: for years she knocks at the door of the popes, finding it almost always barred, but starting in 2000 Cardinal Tarcisio Bertone, now secretary of the Congregation for the Doctrine of the Faith, goes back and forth between the Vatican and Coimbra; three times he meets Sister

del cosiddetto "terzo segreto", lo spinge l'ansia di Papa Wojtyla che ha deciso di abbandonare la segretezza perché fra le tante cerimonie del Giubileo è prevista la beatificazione dei due pastorelli Giacinta e Francesco. A questo punto protrarre il silenzio sul terzo segreto verrebbe interpretato come un'omissione inspiegabile, imperdonabile, così quella donna minuta, umile, obbediente ma anche tenace per la prima volta dopo decenni prova l'immensa gioia di essere ascoltata dal papa, sia pure per il tramite del legato pontificio. I suoi ricordi sono ancora precisi, le immagini incisive, chi aveva atteso eccitanti rivelazioni apocalittiche sulla fine del mondo o sul futuro corso della storia deve rimanere deluso: come conferma Suor Lucía, la profezia consiste nella descrizione del vescovo vestito di bianco che cade ai piedi della croce e nel pressante invito alla conversione, alla penitenza e alla preghiera.

Lúcia, the last seer of Fátima, to verify with her the authenticity of the so-called "third secret". He is driven by the anxiety of Pope Wojtyla, who has decided to abandon the secrecy, because among the many ceremonies of the Jubilee, the beatification of the two little shepherds Jacinta and Francisco is expected. At this point, to continue the silence about the third secret would be interpreted as an inexplicable, unpardonable, omission; so this little woman, humble, obedient but also stubborn, for the first time after decades feels the immense joy of being heard by the Pope; be it only through the papal legate. Her recollections are still precise, the images incisive. Anyone who had expected exciting apocalyptic revelations about the end of the world or about the future course of history has to remain disappointed: as Sister Lúcia confirms, the prophecy consists in the description of the bishop clothed in white, who falls at the foot of the cross, and in the

pressing invitation to conversion, to penance, and to prayer.

Bruno Vespa:

Posso chiederLe, Eminenza, con quale tipo di linguaggio Suor Lucía le parlava della Madonna? Come la chiamava, come la…?

Cardinal Bertone:

L'ha, l'ha sempre chiamata "Nostra Signora" e come nello scritto e negli scritti di Suor Lucía e nella descrizione dei segreti e in modo speciale nella descrizione del terzo segreto, della terza parte del segreto, ha sempre detto "Nostra Signora" e naturalmente avete visto anche quando prega il rosario si illumina, anche parlando della Madonna è quasi rivivendo una presenza che non l'ha mai abbandonata, come sappiamo, anche interiormente soprattutto e probabilmente anche visibilmente ha avuto probabilmente altre apparizioni, anche lungo la sua vita.

Bruno Vespa:

Can I ask You, Eminence, with what type of language did Sister Lúcia speak to you about the Madonna? What did she call her, how did she –

Cardinal Bertone:

She, she always called her "Our Lady", and as in the writing, in the writings of Sister Lúcia and in the description of the secrets and especially in the description of the third secret, the third part of the secret, she always said, "Our Lady", and naturally you have also seen, when she prays the Rosary, she is radiant; and when she's speaking about the Madonna, it's as though she were reliving a presence that has never abandoned her, as we know, including interiorly above all, and probably also visibly: she probably had other apparitions, through the length of her life.

Bruno Vespa:

Glien'ha parlato?

Cardinal Bertone:

Eh, non me n'ha parlato ma indirettamente io ho chiesto delle verifiche, ho cercato di fare delle verifiche e per esempio dopo la famosa, il famoso atto di consacrazione di Papa Giovanni Paolo II al cuore immacolato di Maria lei mi ha detto "è nostra Signora" – mi ha detto che quella era la consacrazione che lei attendeva e che era contenta e siamo nel 1984.

Bruno Vespa:

Buonasera Marco Politi. [*applause*] Marco Politi è il vaticanista, vaticanista di Repubblica. A me fa una certa impressione sentir parlare, insomma, di una, di una suora che dice "Nostra Signora mi ha detto" e alla quale è stata data una credibilità indiscussa visto che il santuario di Fátima c'è da, da un bel po' di tempo. A te?

Bruno Vespa:

Did she tell you about that?

Cardinal Bertone:

Well, she didn't tell me about that, but indirectly I asked for evidence; I tried to look for evidence, and for example, after the famous act of consecration by Pope John Paul II to the Immaculate Heart of Mary, she told me "it's Our Lady" – she told me that this was the consecration that She was waiting for and She was pleased – and we are in 1984.

Bruno Vespa:

Good evening, Marco Politi [*applause*]. Marco Politi is the Vatican reporter of the "Repubblica" [*newspaper*]. It gives me a certain impression to hear someone speaking – in short – about a sister who says "Our Lady told me", and who was given an undisputed credibility, seeing that the shrine of Fátima has been there, for quite a long time. And you?

Marco Politi:

Eh! No, a me non fa tanta impressione, in questo senso: io ho un enorme rispetto per quello che è il mondo della fede e quando il cardinale Segretario di Stato diceva che Suor Lucía era amica di Dio e donna di grande preghiera, evidentemente c'è qualche cosa di molto profondo che va sempre rispettato. Però ricordiamoci, qui non siamo di fronte a un fatto uguale a quello di dire "Papa Benedetto XVI ieri è partito per il Brasile". Quando noi vediamo il filmato, non è che questa apparizione è come abbiamo visto nel filmato che risale a un vecchio film perché il cardinale Ratzinger stesso, nella sua relazione del 2000, dice non è avvenuto niente di esterno, come un fatto, come una bianca figura che appare accanto a un albero, lui definisce questo teologicamente una percezione interiore, quindi un rapporto strettissimo fra un soggetto che è Suor Lucía e un mistero, naturalmente per la Chiesa Cattolica

Marco Politi:

Heh! No, it doesn't make so much of an impression on me, in this sense: I have an enormous respect for what the world of faith is, and when the Cardinal Secretary of State was saying that Sister Lúcia was a friend of God and a woman of great prayer, evidently there's something very profound, and that is always respected. But let's remind ourselves, we aren't in front of a event that is on par with saying, "Pope Benedict XVI left for Brazil yesterday." When we see the clip – it's not as though this apparition is like what we saw in the clip from the old movie, because Cardinal Ratzinger himself, in his report in 2000, says that nothing external happened, like an event, like a white figure that appears next to a tree. He defines this theologically as an interior perception: therefore, a very close relation between a subject, who is Sister Lúcia, and a mystery. Naturally for the Catholic Church it is the

è il mistero divino, il mistero di Dio. La Chiesa Cattolica autorizza anche tutte queste manifestazioni di culto, però non obbliga a credere a questo fatto, è molto importante, quindi diciamo, un già molti credenti non sono obbligati a credere e molti credenti non si interessano di Fátima, altri credenti invece moltissimi vanno, vanno in pellegrinaggio e quindi a maggior ragione, diciamo, non possiamo considerarlo come un fatto storico uguale a quello che noi leggiamo sui giornali. È chiaro che però è un evento che ha segnato moltissimo diverse epoche.

Bruno Vespa:

Eminenza, Lei è d'accordo su questa analisi?

Cardinal Bertone:

Sì, io non direi che non c'è stato anche un'apparizione. È chiaro che il Papa, cioè il cardinale Ratzinger allora, nel commento a questa rivelazione privata, la analizza sotto il criterio, alla luce del criterio delle

divine mystery, the mystery of God. The Catholic Church also authorizes all these manifestations of devotion, but does not oblige anyone to believe in this event. It's very important, and so we say: although there are many believers, they are not obligated to believe, and many faithful are not interested in Fátima; on the other hand, very many faithful do go there on pilgrimage, and so for good reason, we say, we can't consider it as a historical fact on par with what we read in the newspapers. But it is clear that it is an event that left a great mark on various eras.

Bruno Vespa:

Eminence, are you in agreement with this analysis?

Cardinal Bertone:

Yes. I wouldn't say that there wasn't also an apparition. It's clear that the Pope – that is, Cardinal Ratzinger then – in the commentary on this private revelation, analyzes it according to the criteria, in light of the cri-

apparizioni private, delle locuzioni interiori, delle rivelazioni interiori e infatti certamente la la percezione di Suor Lucía è una percezione che è difficile da fotografare ma è una percezione che le ha dato esattamente quelle coordinate che lei ha memorizzato, che ha memorizzato per sempre perché lei ha avuto questa apparizione di una figura straordinaria, della figura di nostra Signora e la percezione delle parole dal 1917 al 1944 perché lei ha scritto il terzo segreto nel gennaio del 1944, quindi ha memorizzato e registrato indelebilmente nella sua memoria questa percezione e questa rivelazione o questa locuzione interiore.

Bruno Vespa:

Eh, come ricorda Lei l'incontro tra Giovanni Paolo II e Suor Lucía?

Cardinal Bertone:

Io personalmente? Io ricordo l'incontro che è avvenuto a Fátima, io non ero presente allora a Fátima ma l'incontro è stato

teria for private revelations, for interior locutions, for interior revelations; and certainly in fact the perception of Sister Lúcia is a perception that is difficult to photograph, but it is a perception that gave her exactly those coordinates which she committed to memory, committed to memory forever because she had this apparition of an extraordinary figure, the figure of our Lady; and the perception of the words from 1917 to 1944, because she wrote the third secret in January of 1944. So, she memorized and indelibly recorded this perception and this revelation, or this interior locution, in her memory.

Bruno Vespa:

How do you remember the meeting between John Paul II and Sister Lúcia?

Cardinal Bertone:

Me personally? I remember the meeting that took place at Fátima; I wasn't present at Fátima then, but the meeting was a

un incontro di due persone che si ritrovavano e che si ritrovavano depositarie di un grande mistero e ricordo che il Papa l'ha presa per mano, ha parlato brevemente con lei, ma poi ha detto, aveva già detto a Suor Lucía che..., perché Suor Lucía voleva parlare, Suor Lucía era una donna che quando usciva dal recinto del monastero contemplativo e quando quindi poteva anche parlare con me, io ho parlato, come ho scritto, anche per diverse ore con lei, di tanti problemi, di tante cose, di tante, non solo di questi problemi specifici. Era una donna esuberante nel parlare, allora il Papa le disse "parlerà poi dopo a suo tempo". E, difatti fissò poi il gli altri incontri eccetera per spiegare eccetera, no...

Bruno Vespa:

Buonasera Paola Rivetta. Paola Rivetta, giornalista del TG5, è stata uno dei volti del Family Day, è stata parecchie volte a Fátima. Con quale ritorno, con quale ricordo, con quale...?

meeting of two people who found themselves custodians of a great mystery, and I remember that the Pope took her hand, spoke briefly with her, but then he said he had told Sister Lúcia – because Sister Lúcia wanted to speak: Sister Lúcia was a woman who, when she went out of the enclosure of the contemplative monastery – and so when she was able to talk with me, I spoke with her for several hours, as I've written, about many problems, about many things, about many, not just about these specific problems. She was a woman exuberant in speaking, and then the Pope said to her, "we'll talk later at the right time". And, in fact, he scheduled the other meetings, etc., to explain, etc.

Bruno Vespa:

Good evening Paola Rivetta. Paola Rivetta, journalist from TG5 [*daily news program*], was one of the faces of the Family Day, and she has been to Fátima numerous times. What do you

bring back from there, what do you remember...?

Paola Rivetta:

Mah, io devo dire che il primo incontro con la Madonnina di Fátima è stato in Vaticano, nel nell'ottobre del 2000, quando in occasione del Giubileo dei vescovi Giovanni Paolo II volle portare la statua in Vaticano. Io sono andata per lavoro, perché per più di dieci anni ho seguito il Vaticano con il responsabile di questo servizio del TG5 che è Marina Ricci e in quell'occasione ero andata io con un operatore, era pieno di fedeli in Vaticano che si raccoglievano ai piedi della Madonnina per pregare e noi abbiamo avuto il privilegio di saltare quella coda perché eravamo lì per lavoro, io mi sono inginocchiata davanti a questa statua, attraversavo un momento molto difficile della mia vita e ricordo di essere rimasta in ginocchio, in preghiera davanti a questa statua per credo un tem-

Paola Rivetta:

Ah, I have to say that the first meeting with the little Madonna of Fátima happened in the Vatican, in October of 2000, when John Paul II wanted to bring the statue to the Vatican on the occasion of the jubilee of bishops. I went there for work, because for over ten years I've covered the Vatican together with the director of the TG5 service, Marina Ricci, and on that occasion I had gone with a cameraman. The Vatican was full of the faithful who were gathering at the feet of the Madonna to pray and we had had the privilege of skipping the line because we were there for work. I knelt in front of the statue – I was going through a very difficult time in my life – and I remember that I stayed there on my knees, praying before the statue for, I think, an infinite amount of time.

po infinito, ero completamente attraversata da quello sguardo ed è, eh, voi me lo confermerete, è una statuina di 60 cm che non ha una, non ha una particolare bellezza artistica, non ha un particolare pregio artistico eppure emana un potere, un magnetismo infinito, ha uno sguardo così soave che mi ha aiutato molto, devo dire quell'incontro ha segnato un prima e un dopo, l'operatore che era con me dopo mi confidò di non essere riuscito a zumare, ad avere il primo piano della statua perché appena zumava l'immagine quasi si sfocava, quindi abbiamo ancora conservato in redazione un'intera cassetta di immagini di quel giorno in Vaticano, inutilizzabili perché l'immagine non era mai a fuoco. Anni dopo sono tornata a Fátima quando è nato mio figlio che si chiama Andrea Maria e aveva 10 mesi quando l'ho portato a Fátima con mio marito.

I was completely transfixed with that gaze, and – you'll confirm this for me – it's a little statue, 60 centimeters tall, that doesn't have a, any particular artistic beauty; it doesn't have particular artistic value, and yet it gives off a power, an infinite magnetism; it has such a sweet gaze that it helped me a lot. I have to say that encounter marked a before-and-after. The cameraman who was with me confided to me later that he wasn't able to zoom in, to have a close-up of the statue, because as soon as he zoomed, the image sort of went out of focus; so, we still have a whole cassette saved in the production department, full of images from that day in the Vatican, but unusable because the image was never in focus. Years later I went to Fátima when my son was born; he name is Andrea Maria, and he was ten months old when I took him to Fátima with my husband.

Giuseppe De Carli:

E c'era anche un particolare che forse Paola dimentica, che a condurre il rosario collegati con Coimbra era proprio Suor Lucía. Eh questo, questo fatto mi dice che, eh, durante il Giubileo il papa sia stato quasi ispirato da Suor Lucía perché ci sono stati alcuni eventi che ci hanno anche impressionato, ad esempio la celebrazione dei martiri del XX secolo, non sapevamo come Giov... come fosse arrivato a quel punto Giovanni Paolo II. Leggendo il terzo segreto si legge di un papa vestit, di un vescovo vestito di bianco che cammina tra i cadaveri dei carbonizzati, ecco, questo legame di Suor Lucía con il papa è stato così forte da indurre il papa a pensare ad una strategia pastorale mariana proprio su indicazione, su suggerimento di Suor Lucía.

Bruno Vespa:

Be'...

Paola Rivetta:

Ho un ricordo bellissimo

Giuseppe De Carli:

And there's also a detail that Paola may have forgotten: that leading the rosary was Sister Lúcia herself, connected from Coimbra. And this, this fact tells me that during the Jubilee the Pope was sort of inspired by Sister Lúcia, because there were a few events that also made an impression: for example, the celebration of the martyrs of the 20th century; we didn't know how John – how John Paul II had come to that. Reading the third secret, we read about a pope clothed – a bishop clothed in white who is walking among the corpses of the burnt; you see, Sister Lúcia's connection with the pope was strong enough to induce the pope to think of a Marian pastoral strategy, precisely at the suggestion of Sister Lúcia.

Bruno Vespa:

Eh –

Paola Rivetta:

I have a beautiful memory...

Bruno Vespa:

Prego, prego…

Paola Rivetta:

Ho un ricordo bellissimo dell'arrivo a Fátima perché stavano – sono andata il 16 ottobre del 2003 e stavano recitando nell'anniversario dell'elezione di Giovanni Paolo II al soglio pontificio, stavano recitando il rosario per il Papa in portoghese e nelle altre lingue del mondo ed erano tutti raccolti intorno alla cappellina delle, delle apparizioni ed era molto bello, una una fede molto, molto composta, un po' sommessa, direi, a Fátima.

Bruno Vespa:

Allora, voleva dire qualcosa Senatore?

Giulio Andreotti:

Be', vorrei dire questo, non vorrei cantare fuori del coro, però mentre senza dubbio c'è grande fascino verso quest'immagine, però Lourdes è qualche cosa di

Bruno Vespa:

Please, please…

Paola Rivetta:

I have a beautiful memory of arriving in Fátima because – I went on October 16, 2003 – and they were reciting – on the anniversary of the election of John Paul to the Papal See, they were reciting the rosary for the Pope in Portuguese and in the other languages of the world and they were all gathered around in the Chapel of the Apparitions; and it was very beautiful: a faith that is very composed, a bit gentle, I would say, at Fátima.

Bruno Vespa:

Now, did you want to say something, Senator?

Giulio Andreotti:

I'd like to say this; I wouldn't want to sing apart from the choir, but while no doubt there's great fascination with this image, but Lourdes is something much more attractive, probably

molto più attraente, probabilmente per questa serie di ammalati che sono lì, questa serenità degli ammalati che non guariscono ma che ripartono contenti da Lourdes, io devo dire, forse sono stato sfortunato, sono stato a Fátima una sola volta, era un giorno di tempo cattivo, non c'era quasi nessuno, insomma, allora, non che con questo non senta un grande fascino, ma devo dire lo sento più per Madre Teresa per esempio che non per Suor Lucía, spero di essere perdonato.

because of the many sick who are there, the serenity of the sick who aren't cured but who leave Lourdes content. I have to say, maybe I was unlucky, I've only been to Fátima once, and it was a day with bad weather; there was almost no one there, so it's not – I don't feel a great fascination with it, but I have to say I felt it more for Mother Teresa, for example, than for Sister Lúcia; I hope you'll forgive me.

Giuseppe De Carli:

Sì, c'è una sorta però di passaggio di consegne tra i novant'anni di Lourdes ed entriamo nei cent…, tra i novant'anni di Fátima ed entriamo nei 150 anni di Lourdes.

Giuseppe De Carli:

Yes; yet there's a sort of handover between the ninety years of Lourdes and we're getting to a hundred – between the ninety years of Fátima and we're getting into 150 years of Lourdes.

Marco Politi:

No, diciamo che ognuno si sceglie la Madonna che preferisce.

Marco Politi:

No, let's say that everyone chooses the Madonna he prefers.

Giulio Andreotti:

Ah, sì, sì.

Giulio Andreotti:

Yes, yes.

Marco Politi:

This motherly figure is so strong, and is so widespread. We say that it is something new introduced in Christianity, in comparison to the Jewish religion, which was so rigorous in the relationship between believers and God, and the figure of the Madonna, historically, breaks in. There's also certainly a confluence of many images of the mother goddess, which were present in the Mediterranean when Christianity was born, and thus this need to have not only a God, but also a mother within reach. I know atheists too who sometimes, when they don't know what to do, take a moment to think about the Madonna to resolve a problem: I know people who – but there to some extent everybody chooses the mother he wants in various places in the world.

Bruno Vespa:

Would it be an impertinent question to ask the Secretary of State which shrine he prefers? Which one do you feel closer to,

in qualche modo…

Cardinal Bertone:

Adesso, certamente, una volta a Lourdes, io sono andato più volte al santuario di Lourdes che non al santuario di Fátima, anche come vescovo, ma una volta a Lourdes ho parlato di Fátima, della Madonna di Fátima, proprio accanto alla grotta di Massabielle e sono stato subito rimproverato, mi hanno detto dopo la messa "ma come hai fatto, sei qui a Lourdes a parlare della Madonna di Fátima".

Bruno Vespa:

Ah, perché c'è concorrenza…

Cardinal Bertone:

C'è concorrenza [*laughing*]…

Bruno Vespa:

C'è concorrenza … c'è un po' di campanilismo.

Cardinal Bertone:

Però, volevo, scusi, vole-

in some way?

Cardinal Bertone:

For now, certainly – one time at Lourdes – I've been to the shrine at Lourdes more times than to the shrine at Fátima, including as a bishop, but one time at Lourdes I spoke there about Fátima, about Our Lady of Fátima, right next to the Grotto of Massabielle, and someone rebuked me right away after the Mass: they said, "but how can you do this? You're here at Lourdes to talk about Our Lady of Fátima?"

Bruno Vespa:

Ah, maybe there's competition…

Cardinal Bertone:

There is competition … [*laughing*] …

Bruno Vespa:

There's competition… there's a little hometown rivalry.

Cardinal Bertone:

But I wanted, excuse me, I

vo solo sottolineare brevemente a ciò che ha detto Marco Politi, no…

Bruno Vespa:

Prego…

Cardinal Bertone:

… che ci sono tante persone anche non cristiane che invocano la Madonna, la Madonna di Fátima, noi nel viaggio a Efeso, nel viaggio del papa in Turchia, abbiamo visto proprio a Efeso centinaia di mussulmani che sono venuti alla celebrazione del papa, era un po' ai bordi di quella piccola area nella quale celebrava il papa e ci hanno raccontato che molte donne mussulmane, soprattutto in difficoltà di maternità, vanno a pregare al santuario di Efeso e poi portano il loro ex voto alla Madonna quando hanno avuto il figlio e portano il figlio, come ha fatto la signora, a Fátima in omaggio alla Madonna.

Bruno Vespa:

Allora, il cardinal Bertone

only wanted to underscore briefly what Marco Politi said…

Bruno Vespa:

Please do…

Cardinal Bertone:

… that there are so many people, even non-Christians, who call on Our Lady, Our Lady of Fátima. In the journey to Ephesus, in the Pope's journey in Turkey, we saw hundreds of Muslims right at Ephesus who came to the Pope's celebration. It was right up to the edge of the little area, where the Pope was celebrating Mass, and they told us that many Muslim women, especially if they are having difficulties in maternity, go to pray at the shrine in Ephesus and then they bring their ex-voto to Our Lady when they have their child, and they bring the child, as the lady did [*referring to Paola Rivetta*] in homage to the Madonna.

Bruno Vespa:

So, Cardinal Bertone first

prima ha ricordato che Suor Lucía ha imparato a leggere e a scrivere, insomma, ha scritto nel '44 il terzo segreto ma ce n'è stato un quarto? Ecco, qui, su questo c'è stata una grande polemica e come vedremo, il cardinal Bertone esclude recisamente che ci sia un quarto segreto di Fátima ma vediamo com'è nata questa polemica. Manuela Orrù.

Manuela Orrù:

Il testo del segreto di Fátima è stato pubblicato integralmente o ne è stata omessa una parte? Ad avanzare tali dubbi sembrano non essere solo i lefreviani o i fatimiti ma anche alcuni cattolici ortodossi che sospettano che sia stata celata quella parte del segreto in cui si annuncia l'apostasia e la lotta interna alla Chiesa. A questi dubbi ha dato voce Antonio Socci attraverso una complessa indagine condotta in un libro di recente pubblicazione intitolato Il quarto segreto. La sua tesi è che la parte rivelata del messaggio, la

recalled that Sister Lúcia learned to read and write; well, in '44 she wrote the third secret, but wasn't there a fourth? You see, there has been a great argument about that and, as we shall see, Cardinal Bertone, flatly excludes that there is any fourth secret of Fátima, but we'll see how this argument came to be. Manuela Orrù:

Manuela Orrù

[pre-recorded segment with historical and other footage]:

Has the text of the secret of Fátima been published in its entirety, or has part of it been omitted? Not only are Lefebvrians or followers of Fátima raising such questions, but also some orthodox Catholics who suspect that part of the secret has been concealed, which foretells apostasy and internal struggle in the Church. Antonio Socci has given voice to these questions by a complicated inquiry presented in a recently published book titled "The Fourth Secret". His thesis is that the part of the message which has been revealed,

visione del vescovo vestito di bianco prostrato in ginocchio ai piedi della grande croce, ucciso da vari colpi d'arma da fuoco e frecce sia autentica ma costituisca solo un frammento. Il messaggio integrale preannuncerebbe invece una terribile crisi della fede, una lotta interna alla Chiesa tra il bene e il male, lo scontro finale tra il drago e la donna vestita di sole a cui si fa riferimento anche nell'Apocalisse di Giovanni. Suor Lucía chiese di rivelare il segreto nel 1960. Secondo Socci, Giovanni XXIII e Paolo VI ne avrebbero impedito la pubblicazione per evitare di fornire argomenti ai critici del Concilio Vaticano II. Giovanni Paolo II e l'allora prefetto della Congregazione per la Dottrina della Fede Joseph Ratzinger sarebbero stati influenzati dai predecessori e soprattutto sarebbero stati fermati dal rifiuto di gran parte dell'episcopato alla consacrazione della Russia chiesta dalla Vergine. Nel 2000 si arrivò probabilmente ad un

the vision of the bishop who is clothed in white, kneeling at the foot of the great cross, and is killed by gunshots and arrows, is authentic but only constitutes a fragment. The entire message, he says, foretells a terrible crisis of the faith, an internal struggle in the Church between good and evil, the final confrontation between the dragon and the woman clothed in the sun, to whom the Apocalypse of John refers. Sister Lúcia asked to reveal the secret in 1960. According to Socci, John XXIII and Paul VI had blocked the publication of the secret in order to avoid furnishing arguments for the critics of the Second Vatican Council. John Paul II and then-Prefect of the Congregation for the Doctrine of the Faith Joseph Ratzinger supposedly had been influenced by their predecessors and above all were stopped by the refusal of a great part of the episcopate for the consecration of Russia requested by the Virgin. In 2000 they probably came

compromesso, decidendo che quel 13 maggio, alla fine della messa di beatificazione dei due pastorelli a Fátima, una figura politica, quella del Segretario di Stato Angelo Sodano, avrebbe annunciato la pubblicazione del testo della visione mentre i contenuti essenziali del messaggio della Madonna sarebbero stati resi noti implicitamente nell'omelia che Giovanni Paolo II tenne in quella messa. Questo escamotage avrebbe permesso alla Chiesa di poter dire in coscienza che tutto il terzo segreto era stato rivelato ma senza un'integrale pubblicazione esplicita che avrebbe provocato un grande shock nella comunità cristiana.

Bruno Vespa:

Allora, Eminenza…

Cardinal Bertone:

Mi sembra una ricostruzione fantasmagorica, io non voglio entrare in polemica, però accusare i papi Giovanni XXIII e Paolo VI di aver impedito la pubblicazione, Giovanni XXIII

to a compromise, deciding that on May 13, at the end of the beatification Mass for the two little shepherds at Fátima, a political figure, the Secretary of State Angelo Sodano, would announce the publication of the text of the vision, while the essential content of Our Lady's message would be made known implicitly in the homily John Paul II gave in that Mass. This sleight of hand would let the Church say in good conscience that all of the third secret had been revealed, but without a complete explicit publication which would have provoked a great shock in the Christian community.

Bruno Vespa:

So, your Eminence…

Cardinal Bertone:

That seems to me a phantasmagorical reconstruction. I don't want to get into an argument, but accusing Popes John XXIII and Paul VI of having blocked the publication – John

XXIII and Paul VI read the text of the secret, the entire authentic, unique text written by Sister Lúcia – I repeat it, I will show it – and they decided not to publish it. It's a judgment. Sister Lúcia herself said in one of the conversations "I offer what I heard, what I perceived, and what I recorded, what I have written; I look to the Pope for the decision about this text, and also for the decision about everything that relates to me," because she also desired the famous publication of a book of hers, to respond, globally as it were, to all the letters which the faithful were writing to her; and then the two Popes decided not to publish it, because at that moment, they probably didn't consider the publication of the third secret that meaningful for the life of the Church.

Bruno Vespa:

Perhaps in a way they were afraid of that image of the pope bloodied, well, of that figure…

Cardinal Bertone:

Può darsi, può darsi, adesso bisognerebbe interrogare loro ed è difficile, non hanno lasciato traccia di una giustificazione di questa volontà, Giovanni XXIII, come si ricorda nel suo diario, dice "io ho avuto la copia del terzo segreto, ho deciso di leggerlo con il mio confessore" che era Monsignor Cavagna, l'ha letto con il confessore e poi a deciso di rimandarlo all'archivio segreto del Santo Uffizio. E così ha fatto Paolo VI. Giovanni Paolo I non l'ha avuto in mano, ha avuto, come si sa, un lungo colloquio con Suor Lucía nel 1977 e poi Giovanni Paolo II ha ripensato al segreto dopo l'attentato del 13 maggio del 1981, questo numero 13 che ritorna insistentemente, che martella un po' tutti i collegamenti e le connessioni misteriose su Fátima, del segreto delle profezie di Fátima.

Quindi io non andrei a indagare. Giovanni Paolo II e il cardinale Ratzinger furono condizionati dai predecessori per

Cardinal Bertone:

It may be, it may be; now we'd need to ask them, and it's not easy: they didn't leave any trace of a justification of such an intention. John XXIII, as he recorded in his diary, says, "I had the copy of the third secret; I decided to read it with my confessor", who was Monsignor Cavagna. He read it with his confessor and then he decided to send it back to the secret archive of the Holy Office. And Paul VI did the same. John Paul I never had it in his hand. He did have, as is known, a long conversation with Sister Lúcia in 1977, and then John Paul II reconsidered the secret after the attack of May 13, 1981 – this number 13 that keeps returning insistently: it hammers a bit on the mysterious links and connections about Fátima, the secret of the prophecies of Fátima.

So, I wouldn't go investigating: were John Paul II and Cardinal Ratzinger conditioned by their predecessors to not pub-

non pubblicare il fantomatico quarto segreto? Mi sembra quando prese la decisione Giovanni Paolo II di pubblicare il segreto, prese la decisione, io ero presente, quando nella riunione in cui prese questa decisione pubblicare tutto ciò che esisteva effettivamente nell'archivio del Santo Uffizio e portato da Suor Lucía da Coimbra, no, e in modo che non esisteva nulla di segreto, tra l'altro poi il famoso terzo segreto era stato letto e commentato dalla plenaria dei cardinali del Santo Uffizio, proprio negli anni '60, dopo che Papa Giovanni XXIII l'aveva visto, aveva posto ai cardinali anche questo quesito, si pubblica, non si pubblica? I cardinali hanno deciso di non pubblicarlo ma non c'è quest…, purtroppo c'è questa attesa un po' spasmodica di una profezia sull'apostasia della Chiesa e c'è una ostinazione nell'attesa di questa profezia sull'apostasia della Chiesa.

Mi sembra anche un po' problematica questa attesa, qua-lish the phantom fourth secret? It seems to me, when John Paul II made the decision to publish the secret – he made the decision, I was present…. In the meeting in which he made the decision to publish everything that there was in the archive of the Holy Office at the time – brought from Sister Lúcia, from Coimbra, hm? And in such a way that there was no more secret. Among other things, the famous third secret had been read and commented on by the plenary meeting of the cardinals of the Holy Office, actually in the '60s, after Pope John XXIII had seen it. He had also posed a *quaesito* to the cardinals: should it be published, or not? The cardinals decided not to publish it, but there's this, unfortunately, there's this expectation – it comes back spasmodically – of a prophecy about apostasy in the Church; and there's a stubbornness about expecting this prophecy on the apostasy of the Church.

To me, it seems a bit problematic also, this expectation, al-

si questa aspirazione che esista una profezia della Madonna madre della Chiesa, colei che stende proprio come, sentiamo ripetere tante volte, il suo manto materno sulla vita della Chiesa e l'accompagna, l'ausiliatrice che l'accompagna nel suo cammino pellegrinante nel tempo, che esista una profezia sull'apostasia della Chiesa.

most this hope that there exists a prophecy from the Madonna, the Mother of the Church: especially her, who – as we hear it repeated so many times – extends her motherly mantle over the life of the Church and accompanies her; the helper who accompanies the Church in her journey on pilgrimage within time – that there exists a prophecy on the apostasy of the Church.

Bruno Vespa:

Allora, prima di proseguire, perché ci son domande anche qui in studio, vediamo un momento il rapporto che con la Madonna di Fátima per le note vicende dell'attentato ha avuto Giovanni Paolo II. Roberto Arditti.

Bruno Vespa:

Now, before we go on, because we have questions here in the studio also, for a moment let's see the relation that there is between Our Lady of Fátima and the known events of the attack on John Paul II. Roberto Arditti.

Roberto Arditti:

Sono innumerevoli e concordanti le fonti che ci permettono di comprendere il pensiero di Giovanni Paolo II sulla dinamica dell'attentato di Piazza San Pietro. Ecco ad esempio la lettera all'episcopato italiano del maggio '95: "Fu una mano

Roberto Arditti [*pre-recorded segment with voiceover*]:

There are countless and consistent sources that allow us to understand the thinking of John Paul II on the dynamics of the attack in St. Peter's Square. For example, here is the letter to the Italian bishops in May '95: "It

451

materna a guidare la traiettoria della pallottola e il papa agonizzante si fermò sulla soglia della morte".

Torniamo a quel drammatico mese di maggio dell' '81, poco dopo le 17 del giorno 13 Ali Ağca spara al papa, la ferita all'addome è gravissima, il papa perde conoscenza mentre arriva al Gemelli, il suo medico personale Buzzonetti chiede a Don Stanislaw, segretario di Wojtyla, di amministrare l'estrema unzione, invece il Papa ce la fa, quando si sveglia ascolta i racconti dell'accaduto, a cominciare da quello di Stanislaw che era sulla jeep bianca con lui. Ed è proprio il suo più fedele collaboratore a fargli notare la coincidenza con il giorno dell'apparizione a Fátima, il papa vuole saperne di più, inizia a studiare. Quando il suo vecchio amico cardinale argentino Pironio va a trovarlo in ospedale, lo trova attorniato da documenti sulla storia del santuario portoghese, poi il papa chiede di vedere il terzo segreto,

was a motherly hand that guided the trajectory of the bullet, and the pope, in his agony, stopped at the threshold of death."

Let us turn to that dramatic month of May of '81, a little after 5 p.m. on the 13th. Ali Agca fires at the pope, the wound to his abdomen is very serious; the pope loses consciousness while he arrives at the Gemelli [hospital]. His personal doctor Buzzonetti asks Don Stanislaw, Wojtyla's secretary, to administer extreme unction. But the Pope recovers. When the Pope awakens, he is able to listen to the accounts of the event, starting with Stanislaw's, who was in the white Jeep with him. And it's precisely his most faithful collaborator who brought to his attention the coincidence with the day of the apparition at Fátima. The Pope wants to know more; he begins to study. When his old friend the Argentinian Cardinal Pironio goes to see him in the hospital, he finds him surrounded with documents about the history of

è il 18 luglio dell' '81 durante il secondo ricovero al Gemelli, Monsignor Martinez Somalo porta in ospedale due buste, uno con l'originale scritto da Suor Lucía e l'altra con la traduzione, da quel momento il papa non ha più dubbi, una mano ha sparato e un'altra ha guidato la pallottola, ripeterà infinite volte.

Passano le settimane, a febbraio dell' '82 Giovanni Paolo II annuncia che il 13 maggio sarà a Fátima, a un anno dall'attentato, a 65 dall'apparizione. Non c'è soltanto la volontà di ringraziare la Madonna ma c'è anche uno degli aspetti più misteriosi e delicati della testimonianza di Suor Lucía: la consacrazione alla Vergine Madre della Russia con tutte le enormi implicazioni del caso. Il papa non si ferma, nonostante i molti pareri contrari all'interno della Curia, il 24 marzo dell''84 riceve a Roma la statua della Madonna di Fátima, trascorre la not-

the shrine in Portugal; then the Pope asks to see the third secret. It's July 18 of '81, during the second admission to the Gemelli. Monsignor Martinez Somalo brings two envelopes to the hospital, one with the original, written by Sister Lúcia and the other with the translation. From that moment, the Pope has no more doubts, one hand fired and another guided the bullet: he will repeat this infinitely many times.

The weeks pass; in February of '82 John Paul II announces that on May 13 he will be at Fátima, a year from the attack, and 65 years from the apparition. It's not just the wish to thank the Madonna, but it's also one of the more mysterious and delicate aspects of the testimony of Sister Lúcia: the consecration of Russia to the Virgin Mary with all the enormous implications of the case. The Pope does not stop, despite the many contrary opinions within the Curia. On March 24 of '84 he receives the statue of Our Lady of Fátima at Rome,

te in preghiera nella sua cappella privata dove è stata sistemata, il giorno dopo incontra il vescovo portoghese di Leiria e gli affida una scatoletta con lo stemma papale, contiene la pallottola che stava per ucciderlo, quella pallottola che è ora incastonata nella corona della statua. Ecco allora che la memoria deve andare al 27 dicembre dell' '83, il papa va nel carcere di Rebibbia per incontrare Ali Ağca, il killer gli si fa incontro e gli chiede "perché lei non è morto?"

Bruno Vespa:

Politi…

Marco Politi:

Mah, io ho due testimonianze personali che mi rimangono molto in mente. Intanto l'anno seguente all'attentato quando papa Wojtyla va a Fátima, eh lui rimane vittima di un altro attentato, ci fu un pazzo con una baionetta che tentò di raggiungerlo e fu bloccato all'ultimo momento e questo è rimasto un fatto simbolico molto forte. E poi,

spends the night in prayer in the private chapel where it was placed. The next day he meets the Portuguese bishop of Leiria and entrusts him with a little box bearing the papal coat of arms: it contains the bullet that was meant to kill him: the bullet that now is encased in the crown of the statue. And so now memory has to turn to December 27 of '83: the Pope goes to the Rebibbia prison to meet Ali Agca; the killer does meet with him and asks him: "Why didn't you die?"

Bruno Vespa:

Politi…

Marco Politi:

I have two personal testimonies that are still very much on my mind. During the year following the attack, when Pope Wojtyla went to Fátima, he was still the victim of another attack: there was a crazy man with a bayonet who tried to get to him and was blocked at the last moment; and this has remained a powerful symbolic event. And

proprio per quello che riguarda il rapporto fra la Madonna di Fátima e la Russia, io mi ricordo che l'anno, il dicembre in cui finì l'impero sovietico, era il dicembre, il capodanno fra il '91 e il '92, fu una festa di popolo sulla Piazza Rossa, si ballava, si cantava, si aprivano bottiglie e non c'era più la bandiera rossa sul Cremlino ma c'era il tricolore russo, tra la folla si fece strada un uomo che portava la statuetta della Madonna di Fátima e la portò esattamente davanti alla tomba di Lenin, al mausoleo di Lenin come per dire "ha vinto la Madonna...

Bruno Vespa:

...ha vinto lei...

Marco Politi:

...e hai perso tu".

Però in tutta questa vicenda, io sono, credo bisogna dare credito assolutamente a quello che ha detto il cardinale Bertone sul fatto che non esistono altri documenti, però ci sono del-

then, specifically as regards the relation between the Madonna of Fátima and Russia, I remember that in the year, the December in which the Soviet empire ended: it was December, the turn of the year from '91 to '92; there was a public festival in Red Square: people were dancing, singing, they were opening bottles, and the red flag was no longer over the Kremlin, but rather the Russian tricolor. In the crowd, a man was making his way through, carrying the little statue of Our Lady of Fátima, and he brought it precisely in front of the tomb of Lenin, the mausoleum, as if to say: "Our Lady has won..."

Bruno Vespa:

... she really won ...

Marco Politi:

"... and you've lost".

But in that whole event, I am – I believe we absolutely need to give credit to what Cardinal Bertone said about the fact that no other documents exist; but there are some strange

things that also appear in the excellent book De Carli has written: that is, Cardinal Ottaviani said that – in terms of the composition of the secret of Fátima – it was 25 rows long, while there's a text of 62 rows. Pope Wojtyla, when he went to Germany in 1980 to speak to a group of German intellectuals, mentioned the third secret of Fátima, and spoke of great trials that were waiting for Christianity, and the people who were present there had the impression – they referred to it later and, let's say, they were able to know something: that it was about powerful catastrophes, cataclysms, while then on the other hand, reading the text of the third secret, we see that it's a vision which, in a sense, photographs the persecutions of the Church that already belonged to the past. These strange things remain.

Giuseppe De Carli:

Yes, Marco; but you may have forgotten that right after this utterance from the Pope, which certainly was a sibylline utterance, but somehow a strong

prove ci attendono", ci fu un'interpretazione allora del cardinale Ratzinger che era arcivescovo di Monaco il quale spiegherà che non si riferiva tanto a previsioni catastrofiche ma alla situazione della Chiesa in quel momento, non dimentichiamo che eravamo durante la guerra fredda, la Chiesa si sentiva assediata da tutte le parti, avviata, avevamo anche la Chiesa del silente, poi noi per quel che riguarda un po' il terzo segreto dobbiamo metterci un po' nell'animo di coloro che lo leggevano quando ancora non era avvenuto l'attentato del 13 maggio 1981. Dei papi che si trovano di fronte ad una profezia di questo genere, con un vescovo vestito di bianco, cioè probabilmente un papa, lo capivano anche loro, che veniva ammazzato tra montagne di cadaveri di carbonizzati, be' questo doveva fare una impressione fortissima sia sui papi sia sui prefetti della Congregazione della Dottrina della Fede che leggevano il testo ma loro pensavano che fosse

statement: "great trials await us." There was an interpretation then from Cardinal Ratzinger, who was archbishop of Munich, which would explain that it wasn't referring so much to catastrophic forecasts, but rather to the situation of the Church at that time – let's not forget that we were in the Cold War then; the Church felt itself besieged from all sides: that was already in place; and we also had the Church of silence. Then as far as the third secret is concerned, we have to put ourselves into the mindset of the people who were reading it, when the attack of May 13, 1981 had not happened yet. As for the popes who found themselves looking at a prophecy of this genre, with a bishop clothed in white, that is, probably a pope, they also understood that this bishop was killed amid mountains of corpses of people burnt to death. Well, that had to make a most powerful impression both on the popes and on the prefects of the Congregation for the Doctrine of the Faith who were reading the

lo scritto di una visionaria, non probabilmente non credibile.

text; but they thought that it was the writing of a visionary, not likely, not credible.

Bruno Vespa:

Cardinal Bertone, di quante righe è questo terzo segreto?

Bruno Vespa:

Cardinal Bertone, of how many rows is this third secret?

Cardinal Bertone:

Mah, io ho detto, dunque, tre paginette di sedici righe, poi vedremo, e la prima pagina di 9 righe, quindi a me stupisce un po' che il cardinal Ottaviani abbia detto categoricamente un foglio di 25 righe, perché il cardinal Ottaviani che allora era segretario, perché era il cardinal segretario della congregazione del Santo Uffizio, ha avuto in mano proprio materialmente e diverse volte perché l'ha fatto vedere egli stesso nella plenaria dei cardinali del Santo Uffizio, ha avuto in mano il foglio e quindi può darsi che abbia fatto un calcolo così sommario, si sia sbagliato. Non credo che questo elemento sia così cogente per dire che esiste un un foglio di 25

Cardinal Bertone:

Um, as I said, three little pages of sixteen rows, we'll see later, and the first page of 9 rows; so it surprises me that Cardinal Ottaviani had said categorically, one page of 25 rows, because Cardinal Ottaviani, who was secretary then, since he was the cardinal secretary of the Congregation of the Holy Office, physically held it in his hands, and, various times, because he had had it shown in the plenary meeting of the cardinals of the Holy Office: he had the page in his hands, and hence it's possible that he may have made such a rough calculation, made a mistake. I don't think this element is so persuasive as to say that there is one page of 25 rows in contrast

righe rispetto all'altro di, di circa 60 righe, ecco, capito?

Bruno Vespa:

Lei...

Cardinal Bertone:

E poi mi stupisce un po' anche nel servizio che è stato presentato, si dice che nell' '84 o quando il papa Giovanni Paolo II ha voluto portare la Madonnina di Fátima a Roma c'era molta resistenza e avversione da parte della Curia, di portare la statua della Madonna di Fátima a Roma, io non, non riesco a capire questa avversione, non so, ero qui a Roma nell' '84, siamo venuti in molti, sacerdoti, i fedeli, a pregare, a dire il rosario davanti alla statua della Madonna di Fátima, non ho visto che, non ho percepito che c'erano delle resistenze così forti da parte della Curia, non so come mai.

Bruno Vespa:

Chi portò quella statua? Chi, come nasce quella statua?

with the other of, of about 60 rows, you see: is that clear?

Bruno Vespa:

You...

Cardinal Bertone:

And then I'm also a bit surprised in the report that was presented: it says that in '84, or when Pope John Paul II wanted to bring the little Madonna from Fátima to Rome there was a lot of resistance and aversion to this from the Curia: to bringing the statue of the Madonna from Fátima to Rome. I – I cannot understand this aversion; I don't know: I was here in Rome in '84, we came together in great numbers: priests, the faithful, to pray, to say the Rosary before the statue of Our Lady of Fátima. I didn't see – I didn't perceive that there such strong resistance on the part of the Curia: I don't know why.

Bruno Vespa:

Who brought that statue? Who – how did the statue come to be?

Cardinal Bertone:

Hm, I think the bishop of Leiria had it made....

Bruno Vespa:

... back then? Shortly after the apparition?

Cardinal Bertone:

Afterward, but not right away: it was further on. I don't remember the date now, but there's a....

Bruno Vespa:

Now I'll ask Cardinal Bertone if he could kindly talk to us about that white envelope; but meanwhile, picking up on what Politi said about the amazing collapse -- that's probably the right word – of the Soviet empire.

At the time you [*Senator Andreotti*] were President of the Council when the flag was lowered: the Communist flag was lowered from the Kremlin. I remember a live television feed with great emotion: it seemed –

sembrava, mi sembrava un film perché non pensavo che nell'arco della mia vita avrei visto niente di simile. Lei si meravigliò?

it seemed like a movie because I didn't think that I would have seen anything like it in my whole life. Were you amazed?

Giulio Andreotti:

Mah, io potrei dire l'impressione che qualche settimana fa ho avuto andando a Mosca al funerale di Eltsin che era il terzo funerale di capo dello Stato russo che andavo ma gli altri due niente di religioso, tutto semplicemente...

Giulio Andreotti:

Uh, I could tell you the impression that I had some weeks ago, going to Moscow for the funeral of Yeltsin; it was the third funeral for a Russian head of state that I went to, but at the other two there was nothing religious: everything simply...

Bruno Vespa:

Quali erano stati gli altri due?

Bruno Vespa:

Who were the other two?

Giulio Andreotti:

...parata militare, parata civile...

Giulio Andreotti:

... military parade, civilian parade...

Bruno Vespa:

Gli altri due quali erano?

Bruno Vespa:

The other two, who were they?

Giulio Andreotti:

be', vedere la basilica del Salvatore...

Giulio Andreotti:

Uh, to see the Basilica of the Holy Savior...

Bruno Vespa:

Gli altri due quali erano?

Bruno Vespa:

The other two, who were they?

Giulio Andreotti:

Eh?

Bruno Vespa:

… gli altri due capi di stato?

Giulio Andreotti:

Be', erano [*laughing*] scusi …

Bruno Vespa:

Brezniev?

Giulio Andreotti:

…c'ero andato anzi ci andammo con Pertini, anzi si doveva fare una giostra perché eravamo in Argentina…

Bruno Vespa:

Ah…fu la fam…

Giulio Andreotti:

mmhhh

Bruno Vespa:

Posso dire, posso dire un pettegolezzo?

Giulio Andreotti:

Prego…

Giulio Andreotti:

Eh?

Bruno Vespa:

… the other two heads of state?

Giulio Andreotti:

Uh, they were [*laughing, shrugging*] excuse me… --

Bruno Vespa:

Brezhnev?

Giulio Andreotti:

… I'd gone there, or rather, we'd gone, with Pertini; that is, we had to make a U-turn because we were in Argentina…

Bruno Vespa:

Ah… there was the –

Giulio Andreotti:

Uh-huh.

Bruno Vespa:

Can I – can I tell a rumor?

Giulio Andreotti:

Go ahead…

462

Bruno Vespa:

Era, era, Pertini interruppe la visita in Argentina perché voleva avere la riconferma come capo dello Stato e insomma pensò che essere andato a Mosca, be', ma questa devozione se no come se la spiega?

Giulio Andreotti:

No, io credo, guardi…,

Bruno Vespa:

No?

Giulio Andreotti:

…siccome ero lì: voleva solo che non fosse Craxi a rappresentare l'Italia ma voleva essere lui [*laughing*]

Bruno Vespa:

Ah ecco…va bè

Giulio Andreotti:

…sì, sì

Bruno Vespa:

Voleva andarci, voleva andarci [*laughing*]… allora diceva, i primi due li aveva visti ma ve-

Bruno Vespa:

It was – Pertini interrupted the visit to Argentina because he wanted to be reconfirmed as head of State, and, in short, he thought he would go to Moscow, well, But this polite paying of respect: if that's not the reason, how can you explain it?

Giulio Andreotti:

No, I think – look…

Bruno Vespa:

No?

Giulio Andreotti:

…since I was there: he only wanted that it wouldn't be Craxi representing Italy; he wanted it to be him [*laughing*]

Bruno Vespa:

Ah, I see… that's good

Giulio Andreotti:

…yes, yes

Bruno Vespa:

He wanted to go, he wanted to go there [*laughing*]… so I was saying: you saw the first

dere la basilica con Eltsin?

Giulio Andreotti:

Be', vedere la basilica con questa grande cerimonia religiosa, con un discorso lungo senza traduzione simultanea, nemmeno un foglio, quindi immagino che abbia detto bene del defunto, insomma, però con questa solennità del rito bizantino e nella basilica del Salvatore, be', si vede veramente l'espressione di qualche cosa che è cambiato e che doveva cambiare e questo allora penso che in un certo senso noi abbiamo avuto l'avventura di appartenere ad una generazione che ha visto questo cambiamento.

Bruno Vespa:

Nemmeno Lei s'aspettava la caduta del muro (*muro di Berlino*), vero, in quel, in quei giorni?

Giulio Andreotti:

No, no, ma precipitavano le co', fortunatamente ma insomma in un modo anche insperato mmh lo stesso Kohl [*lau-*

two, but with Yeltsin, you saw the basilica?

Giulio Andreotti:

Ah, to see the basilica, with that great religious ceremony, with a lengthy address without any simultaneous translation, not even a sheet of paper; so I imagine he spoke well of the deceased; but with that solemnity of the Byzantine rite and in the Basilica of the Savior, well, you really see the expression of something that has changed and had to change, and this – now I think, in a certain sense, we have had the adventure of belonging to a generation that has seen this change.

Bruno Vespa:

And you didn't expect to see the fall of the wall [*the Berlin wall*] either, in those days?

Giulio Andreotti:

No, no, but things precipitated; luckily but also in an unexpected way, hm, the same Kohl [*laughing*] was on a visit

ghing] era in in visita in Polonia e insomma quando glielo dissero rimase piuttosto meravigliato.

Bruno Vespa:

Secondo Lei, il papa Giovanni Paolo II gliel'ha data una spallatina a quel muro?

Giulio Andreotti:

Be', senza dubbio insomma, ba basta vedere la manifestazione che ci fu in Polonia nel primo viaggio del Papa: insomma, quel milione di persone che furono sulla piazza e che applaudivano e che esprimevano grandissima gioia, eh be' non a caso questo poi è dimostrato anche nella commissione Mitrokhin. Abbiamo visto dei documenti, la preoccupazione enorme che suscitava a Mosca il fatto di...

Bruno Vespa:

Eh be' non a caso qualche tempo dopo

Giulio Andreotti:

di avere la nomina, la nomina del papa

in Poland, and, in short, when they told him, he was rather amazed.

Bruno Vespa:

According to you, Pope John Paul II also gave the that wall a shove?

Giulio Andreotti:

Well, no doubt, it was enough to see the demonstration there was in Poland at the first visit by the Pope; well, that million people that was in the square, applauding and expressing great joy,and, well, not by chance, this was shown later by the Mitrokhin commission. We've seen the documents, the enormous worry that this raised for Moscow, the fact that...

Bruno Vespa:

It was no accident sometime later, after...

Giulio Andreotti:

...to have the naming, the naming of the Pope...

Bruno Vespa:

… qualcuno gli sparò…

Giulio Andreotti:

mmhm la nomina, la nomina del Papa polacco, insomma, be' insomma, la Chiesa qualche volta i suoi tempi sono diversi da quelli nostri che dobbiamo far le programmazioni a breve termine però se una programmazione… prima è stato ricordato il cardinale Ottaviani, vede Eminenza, forse può darsi che non l'abbia visto bene, il cardinale Ottaviani non ci vedeva molto bene, c'è una definizione io che mi è rimasta impressa di Giovanni XXIII, disse "Alfredo bravissimo ma è un po' ciecuziente" [*laughing*] que, questa frase…

Bruno Vespa:

Ah, eccolo qua, allora abbiamo scoperto le ragioni per le quali il cardinale Ottaviani ha visto…

Marco Politi:

a lui, ciecuziente per l'analisi del mondo e della Chiesa…

Bruno Vespa:

… someone shot him …

Giulio Andreotti:

…hm, the naming of the Polish Pope. Well, well sometimes the Church's time is different from ours. We have to make plans in the short term, but if a plan … but first I remember Cardinal Ottaviani: Your Eminence, it was probably the case that he wasn't able to see very well – Cardinal Ottaviani couldn't see well. There's a definition from John XXIII that has stuck in my memory: he said, "Alfredo, wonderful; but it's a little blinding…" [*laughing*] That expression….

Bruno Vespa:

Ah, there it is, now we've discovered the reasons why Cardinal Ottaviani …

Marco Politi:

going blind due to his analysis of the world and the Church…

Giulio Andreotti:

...però è stato...

Marco Politi:

il cardinale Ottaviani era un grande frenatore

Bruno Vespa:

non c'è dubbio, però il senatore Andreotti credo l'abbia conosciuto benissimo il cardinale Ottaviani, quindi se diceva che non ci vedeva tanto bene...

Marco Politi:

Però Bruno c'è c'è...

Giulio Andreotti:

...be', però è stato una figura splendida...

Bruno Vespa:

Sì, scherzavo...

Giulio Andreotti:

...perché veramente insomma, be', tutti i cardinali lo sono ma insomma era un uomo di Dio anche visibilmente.

Marco Politi:

No, su Wojtyla e la Russia

Giulio Andreotti:

... but he was ...

Marco Politi:

Cardinal Ottaviani was a great brake-man.

Bruno Vespa:

There's no doubt, but I believe Senator Andreotti knew Cardinal Ottaviani very well, so if he says that he couldn't see well...

Marco Politi:

But Bruno, there's...

Giulio Andreotti:

... well, but he was a splendid figure ...

Bruno Vespa:

Yes, I was kidding.

Giulio Andreotti:

... because really, uh, all the cardinals are, but well, he was a man of God, even visibly.

Marco Politi:

About Wojtyla and Russia,

c'è una frase sua di Wojtyla proprio sul crollo dell'impero molto interessante, lui disse "l'albero era marcio, io gli ho dato solo una scossa"

Bruno Vespa:

E infatti…

Giuseppe De Carli:

C'è comunque una concatenazione secondo me prodigiosa di avvenimenti, dopo l'atto di affidamento del, di papa Giovanni Paolo II di … al cuor…della Russia al cuore immacolato di Maria del 1984 cadono Andropov e Cernenko e subito dopo viene Gorbaciov con la sua perestrojka e la sua glasnost.

Bruno Vespa:

Allora, Eminenza, la busta.

Cardinal Bertone:

Ecco, allora prima faccio vedere la busta arancione …

Marco Politi:

Ah, ce ne sono du…[*laughing*]

there's a very interesting expression from Wojtyla himself about the collapse of the empire; he said: "the tree was rotten, I just gave it a jolt."

Bruno Vespa:

And in fact…

Giuseppe De Carli:

Somehow there was a miraculous succession of events, in my opinion, after the act of entrustment by… by Pope John Paul II to the Heart – of Russia to the Immaculate Heart of Mary in 1984. Andropov and Chernenko fell, and suddenly Gorbachev came in with his perestroika and his glasnost.

Bruno Vespa:

Now, Eminence, the envelope.

Cardinal Bertone:

Here it is; first I'll show the orange envelope …

Marco Politi:

Ah, there are two [*laughs*]

Bruno Vespa:

Che cos'è?

Cardinal Bertone:

La busta arancione è la busta che è stata citata prima anche nel servizio. È la busta che contiene la traduzione italiana della redazione del terzo segreto di Fátima...

Bruno Vespa:

Leggo una data, 6 marzo

Cardinal Bertone:

la busta antica [incomprehensible]

Bruno Vespa:

6 marzo '67

Cardinal Bertone:

'67, esatto, quindi siamo ai tempi di Papa Paolo VI. Ecco la traduzione, questa è una busta che si accompagna sempre alla

Bruno Vespa:

What is that?

Cardinal Bertone:

The orange envelope is the envelope that was mentioned first during the segment. It's the envelope that contains the Italian translation of the redaction of the third secret of Fátima.

Bruno Vespa:

I see a date: March sixth.

[*The television image shows the envelope marked with the date "6-III-1967" and with the Italian inscription "Secret of Fátima in Italian translation (manuscript)".*]

Cardinal Bertone:

... the old envelope [*incomprehensible*]...

Bruno Vespa:

March 6, '67

Cardinal Bertone:

'67, exactly. So we are in the time of Pope Paul VI. Here is the translation. This is an envelope that always accompanies the

bustapiù antica, autentica che contiene l'originale del terzo segreto che è stata citata nel servizio, mentre veniamo alla busta bianca.

Ecco una prima busta più grande, la vedete, con la scritta di Cosé boh di José Bispo de Leiria. È una busta scritta dal vescovo di Leiria che contiene le altre buste, fino alla busta autentica che contiene il terzo segreto, una busta con i sigilli.

Apro questa busta, estraggo un'altra busta semplice di color giallognolo già con la calligrafia di Suor Lucía "Eccellentissimo, reverendissimo Senhor Don Cosé o José Alvez Da Silva bispo de Leiria"

Bruno Vespa:
Il vescovo.

Cardinal Bertone:
…indirizzata al vescovo di

older, authentic envelope, which contains the original of the third secret, which was mentioned in the segment. Meanwhile we come to the white envelope.

Here's a first larger envelope, as you can see, with the handwriting of José *[pronounced as if Spanish]*, oops – of José *[pronounced as Portuguese]*, Bishop of Leiria. This is an envelope with writing from the Bishop of Leiria that contains the other envelopes, up to the authentic envelope which contains the third secret; an envelope with seals.

I am opening this envelope, and I extract another simple envelope, yellowish in color, now with the calligraphy of Sister Lúcia: "Eccellentissimo, reverendissimo Senhor Don José *[pronounced as if Spanish]* o José Alvez da Silva, Bispo de Leiria"

Bruno Vespa:
The Bishop.

Cardinal Bertone:
…addressed to the bishop

Leiria, scrittura di Suor Lucía. Apro ed estraggo, questa è senza sigilli perché era messa nella grande busta sigillata, un'ulteriore busta con i sigilli e con la scritta di Suor Lucía, la scritta autentica di Suor Lucía dove parla dell'anno 1960 – ecco "por orden", voi riuscite a vedere…

Bruno Vespa:

Sì, sì, riusciam a vederla

Cardinal Bertone:

"…espressa de nossa senhora este", quindi per ordine espresso di nostra Signora, "este envelope se pode ser aberto en 1960"

Bruno Vespa:

Questa busta può essere aperta nel 1960…

Cardinal Bertone:

…nel 1960 por sua Eminenza o Signor Cardinal Patriarca de Lisboa, o dal patriarca di Lisbona o dal vescovo di Leiria, va bene, la scrittura di Suor

of Leiria, writing by Sister Lúcia. I am opening it and pulling out – this one has no seals because it was placed within the large sealed envelope – a further envelope with seals and with the handwriting of Sister Lúcia, the authentic handwriting of Sister Lúcia, where she speaks of the year 1960: there it is: "por orden…", you can see it…

Bruno Vespa:

Yes, we are able to see it.

Cardinal Bertone:

"…espressa de nossa senhora este", thus by express order of our Lady, "este envelope se pode ser aberto en 1960"

Bruno Vespa:

This envelope can be opened in 1960…

Cardinal Bertone:

…in 1960 "por sua Eminenza o Senhor Cardinal Patriarca de Lisboa," – either by the patriarch of Lisbon or by the bishop of Leiria. that's fine: the

Lucía.

Apro ancora questa busta ed ecco finalmente la piccola busta che è larga 9 centimetri come hanno scritto diversi autori e larga 14 centimetri, la piccola busta che ripete le parole che abbiamo già letto, "per ordine di Nostra Signora", e che contiene il foglio, ecco, l'unico foglio autentico, l'unico foglio in cui è contenuto il terzo segreto, l'unico foglio.

Quando io ho portato a Suor Lucía queste buste, l'abbiamo aperte davanti al vescovo di Leiria che assisteva al primo colloquio del 27 aprile del 2000 prima della decisione di pubblicare il terzo segreto, Suor Lucía ha toccato bene la carta, le buste, i sigilli, ha detto "sì, questa è la mia busta" e poi toccando la carta dice "questa è la mia carta", vedete, una carta da lettera che si piega, quattro paginette, no, e ha detto "questa è la mia carta", e poi guardando bene con una lente eccetera perché era già anch'essa un po' ciecuziente ma

writing of Sister Lúcia.

Again, I'm opening this envelope and here it is finally, the little envelope, which is 9 centimeters tall, as many authors have written, and 14 centimeters long: the little envelope that repeats the words that we have just read, "by order of our Lady," and which contains the sheet: here, the one authentic sheet, the one sheet on which the third secret is contained: the one sheet.

When I brought these envelopes to Sister Lúcia, we opened them in front of the bishop of Leiria who was present at the first conversation on April 27, 2000, before the decision to publish the third secret, Sister Lúcia touched well the sheet of paper, the envelopes, the seals, quite well, and she said, "yes, this is my envelope", and, then, touching the paper, she said, "this is my paper" – you see, a sheet of letter paper that folds up, four little pages, hm?, and then looking at it thoroughly with a lens and so on, because she was already losing her sight a bit -- but

non troppo perché ci vedeva ancora abbastanza bene, prima con gli occhiali e poi con una lente dice "questa è la mia scrittura, sì, sì, questo è il testo che ho scritto io" e incomincia proprio "a terzera parte do segredo revelado" il 13 luglio 1917, la terza parte del segreto rivelato e c'è solo questo foglio.

Nell'archivio del Santo Uffizio nel 1957 quando per ordine di Nostra Signora e del vescovo di Leiria Suor Lucía ha accettato di che il terzo segreto fosse portato a Roma dall'archivio del patriarca di Lisbona, c'era solo questa busta e questo foglio, non c'era altro.

Bruno Vespa:

Ma Eminenza, però eh sono quattro fogli scritti fitti...

Cardinal Bertone:

Sì, sì, sì, sì

Bruno Vespa:

...e quindi allora torniamo alle, non sono 23 righe come diceva Ottaviani...

not too much, because we could still see each other well enough – at first with glasses, and then with a lens; she said, "this is my writing, yes, yes, this is the text that I wrote". And it actually begins "a terzera parte do segredo revelado" July 13, 1917, "the third part of the secret revealed," and there is only this sheet.

In the archive of the Holy Office in 1957 when by order of our Lady and of the bishop of Leiria, Sister Lúcia agreed that the third secret should be brought to Rome from the archive of the patriarch of Lisbon; there was only this envelope and this sheet; there was nothing else.

Bruno Vespa:

But Eminence, but, uh, the four pages are written closely?

Cardinal Bertone:

Yes, yes; yes, yes.

Bruno Vespa:

... and so now we turn to the – there's not 23 rows as Ottaviani said ...

Cardinal Bertone:

No, no, no

Bruno Vespa:

Sono 62 righe

Cardinal Bertone:

62 righe, esatto…

Bruno Vespa:

… ma, ma come fa Ottaviani a dire che sono 62 righe?

Cardinal Bertone:

Mah, pazienza, io non lo so…

Bruno Vespa:

Eh, appunto, questa mi pare la prova documentale che non è…

Cardinal Bertone:

No, questa è la prova che eh il cardinale Ottaviani ha avuto questo testo perché lo conservava lui nell'archivio segreto del Santo Uffizio e abbiamo tutta una documentazione delle sue, è impossibile leggere, ripercorrere tutte le volte che questa busta è stata presa è stata aperta, è sta-

Cardinal Bertone:

No, no, no…

Bruno Vespa:

There are 62 rows…

Cardinal Bertone:

62 rows, exactly.

Bruno Vespa:

… but, but how did Ottaviani come to say that there are …

Cardinal Bertone:

Eh, patience, I don't know…

Bruno Vespa:

So, exactly, this seems to me the documentary proof that there is not ….

Cardinal Bertone:

No, this is the proof that – Cardinal Ottaviani had this text because he preserved it in the secret archive of the Holy Office, and we have a whole documentation about his – it's impossible to read, to review all the times this envelope has been taken, it's been opened, it's been examined

ta vagliata dai cardinali, dalla plenaria dei cardinali del Santo Uffizio che hanno deciso di non pubblicare il terzo segreto.

Bruno Vespa:

Questa, Eminenza, è la prima volta che questa busta e il suo prezioso contenuto vengono mostrati in pubblico…

Cardinal Bertone:

La prima volta assolutamente.

Bruno Vespa:

Ecco, io sono, guardando sia pur a distanza questa, questa è stata scritta nel '44, se non…

Cardinal Bertone:

Nel '44.

Bruno Vespa:

Perché lei ha aspettato tanto per scrivere?

Cardinal Bertone:

Be', perché aveva la proibizione, il terzo segreto doveva conservarlo dentro di sé e non rivelarlo a nessuno, questo era l'ordine di Nostra Signora, poi

by the Cardinals, by the plenary of the Cardinals of the Holy Office, who decided not to publish the third secret.

Bruno Vespa:

This, Eminence, is the first time that this envelope and its precious contents have been shown in public…

Cardinal Bertone:

The first time, absolutely.

Bruno Vespa:

You see, I'm – looking at it, even from this distance – this was written in '44, if not –

Cardinal Bertone:

In '44.

Bruno Vespa:

Why did she wait so long to write?

Cardinal Bertone:

Well, because she had a prohibition: she was supposed to keep the third secret within herself and not reveal it to anyone. That was the order of our

dopo la insistenza del patriarca di Lisbona, del vescovo di Leiria ha chiesto a Nostra Signora e Nostra Signora le ha detto che poteva scrivere e consegnare al vescovo.

Bruno Vespa:

Il 13 maggio del '17 quando Suor Lucía e gli altri due bambini hanno avuto l'apparizione era analfabeta, ha imparato a scrivere più tardi…

Cardinal Bertone:

Più tardi.

Bruno Vespa:

…forse molto più tardi?

Cardinal Bertone:

Ha imparato a scrivere molto più tardi.

Bruno Vespa:

Più tardi. Quello che mi colpisce, seppur vedendo a distanza questa busta, è una calligrafia apparentemente elegante.

Cardinal Bertone:

Molto elegante, molto, per-

Lady; then after the insistence of the Patriarch of Lisbon, of the bishop of Leiria, she asked our Lady, and our Lady said she could write it and entrust it to the bishop.

Bruno Vespa:

On May 13, of '17, when Sister Lúcia and the other two children had the apparition, was she illiterate; did she learn to write later…

Cardinal Bertone:

Later.

Bruno Vespa:

… probably much later?

Cardinal Bertone:

She learned to write much later…

Bruno Vespa:

Later. What strikes me, even seeing this envelope at a distance, is an apparently elegant calligraphy.

Cardinal Bertone:

Very elegant; very, because

ché lei è stata quando è entrata, anzitutto prima ancora di entrare nel monastero, nel convento delle Dorotee in Spagna…

Marco Politi:

è stata educata …

Cardinal Bertone:

… perché lei voleva già entrare tra le carmelitane ma non le è stato permesso, non è stato possibile. Ha dovuto soffrir molto e lì nel convento delle Dorotee poi ha sofferto molto tanto che, confidandosi con il suo confessore, il confessore a un certo punto ha deciso di farla trasferire, secondo il suo antico desiderio, nel convento delle carmelitane a Coimbra. Non so, adesso posso raccontare qualche piccolo episodio, però prima ancora di entrare in convento Lucía, la ragazza Lucía, è stata affidata a delle nobildonne che le hanno insegnato a leggere e a scrivere e per questo che ha una scrittura così bella, così perfetta, io penso un po' alla scrittura di Papa Paolo VI, non so se qualcuno ricorda un una…

she was – when she entered – rather, before entering the monastery of the Dorothean Sisters in Spain…

Politi:

she was educated…

Cardinal Bertone:

… because she already wanted to enter the Carmelites but she wasn't permitted; it wasn't possible. She had to suffer a lot, and in the convent of the Dorotheans, then, she suffered so much that, admitting it to her confessor, the confessor at a certain point decided to have her transferred into the convent of the Carmelites at Coimbra. I don't know, now I can relate a little episode, but before going into the convent Lúcia, the girl Lúcia was entrusted to some noblewomen who had her taught to read and write and because of this, she has such a beautiful handwriting, so perfect I think a bit of the writing of Pope Paul VI; I don't know if anyone remembers a …

Bruno Vespa:
Ehi...

Cardinal Bertone:
...i manoscritti di Paolo VI erano perfetti, erano...

Bruno Vespa: (58:01)
Eh, Eminenza, li ricordiamo purtroppo perché nella nostra memoria c'è incancellabile la lettera

Cardinal Bertone:
anche la lettera

Bruno Vespa:
... agli uomini delle Brigate Rosse

Cardinal Bertone:
... alle Brigate Rosse certamente

Bruno Vespa:
...arrivò una domenica mattina questa calligrafia perfetta

Cardinal Bertone:
... perfetta proprio

Bruno Vespa:
Eh ...

Cardinal Bertone:
... the manuscripts of Paul VI were perfect; they were ...

Bruno Vespa:
Eh, Eminence, we remember that, unfortunately because there was the letter – indelible in our memory –

Cardinal Bertone:
also the letter

Bruno Vespa:
... to the men of the Red Brigades...

Cardinal Bertone:
... to the Red Brigades, certainly...

Bruno Vespa:
... this perfect calligraphy came in one Sunday morning...

Cardinal Bertone:
... really perfect ...

Bruno Vespa:

... nuda che fece una impressione veramente drammatica

Cardinal Bertone:

... drammatica

Bruno Vespa:

... si vedeva la disperazione di di...

Cardinal Bertone:

Suor Lucía ha imparato a scrivere molto bene e poi ha scritto, ha scritto migliaia di lettere, oltre le sue memorie, le tre parti del segreto di Fátima ha scritto migliaia di lettere che sono diffuse in tutto il mondo perché molta gente le scriveva e lei rispondeva e poi ha poi chiesto di pubblicare quel libro famoso nel 1982, l'ha chiesto...

Bruno Vespa:

Allora, avete visto per la prima volta questa immagine, torneremo a parlare di questo straordinario documento tra due minuti.

[*applause*]

Bruno Vespa:

... plain, which made a really dramatic impression.

Cardinal Bertone:

... dramatic ...

Bruno Vespa:

... you could see the desperation of ...

Cardinal Bertone:

Sister Lúcia learned to write very well, and then she wrote, she wrote thousands of letters, in addition to her memoirs, the three parts of the secret of Fátima. She wrote thousands of letters that went out into all the world, because a lot of people wrote to her, and she answered and then; then she asked to publish that famous book in 1982; she asked –

Bruno Vespa:

Now you've seen this image for the first time; we'll come back to talk about this extraordinary document in two minutes.

[*applause*]

[*program break*]

Bruno Vespa:

Riprendiamo allora "Porta a Porta", il Segretario di Stato Vaticano Tarcisio Bertone ci ha appena mostrato in assoluta anteprima un documento straordinario, la lettera con la quale, la lettera, il documento, il foglio di diario, non sappiamo come definirlo, a chi è indirizzata, Eminenza, questa? È una sua, è una specie di diario, di testimonianza, di dichiarazione? Come la possiamo chiamare?

Cardinal Bertone:

Sì, una dichiarazione.

Bruno Vespa:

Una dichiarazione.

Cardinal Bertone:

Non è indirizzata a nessuno, in alto c'è "i emme I" Jesus Maria Joseph come si usava mettere una volta nelle lettere e poi parte subito con la intitolazione, il la terza parte del segreto rivelato a id 13 luglio 1917 a Cova da Iria eccetera no…

Bruno Vespa:

We're returning to "Porta a Porta". The Vatican Secretary of State Tarcisio Bertone has just shown us, absolutely for the first time ever, an extraordinary document: the letter with which – the letter, the document, the diary page, we don't know how to define it: to whom is it addressed, Eminence? Is it her – is it a sort of diary, a testimony, a declaration? What should we call it?

Cardinal Bertone:

Yes, a declaration.

Bruno Vespa:

A declaration.

Cardinal Bertone:

It's not addressed to anyone. At the top there are "I, m, I", the initials of Jesus, Mary, and Joseph, as we used to put them on letters, and then it goes directly to the title: the third part of the secret revealed July 13, 1917 at the Cova da Iria, etc.

Bruno Vespa:

E difatti…

Cardinal Bertone:

No, eh

Bruno Vespa:

È il terzo segreto di Fátima

Cardinal Bertone:

No, una piccola un tentativo di spiegazione di quella affermazione del cardinal Ottaviani forse si può trovare se noi calcoliamo nella prima pagina del foglio, prima e ultima, magari il cardinale Ottaviani la teneva in mano così e si vede che sono, di per sé sarebbero 16 righe più 9, vi ricordate che nella prima pagina son 9 righe scritte del segreto, allora 16 più 9 fa proprio 25 senza contare quella seguente, ecco può darsi che il cardinale Ottaviani ricorda dice, forse sono 25 righe…

Bruno Vespa:

Probabilmente si riferiva ad una…

Cardinal Bertone:

Può essere una spiegazione

Bruno Vespa:

And in fact…

Cardinal Bertone:

No, eh

Bruno Vespa:

It is the third secret of Fátima.

Cardinal Bertone:

No – a little attempt to explain that statement by Cardinal Ottaviani. Maybe we can find, if we calculate from the first page of the sheet, first and last, maybe Cardinal Ottaviani held it in hand this way, and he saw there were 16 rows plus nine: you remember that on the first page where are 9 rows of the secret written; then 16 plus 9 does make 25 without counting what follows; so it may be that Cardinal Ottaviani remembered – said, probably there are 25 rows.

Bruno Vespa:

Probably he's referring to a …

Cardinal Bertone:

It may be an explanation…

Bruno Vespa:

… esiste una versione datti-loscritta anche probabilmente, non lo so, voi l'avrete, immagino ci saranno state delle copiature evidentemente, no, di questo documento…

Cardinal Bertone:

Oh sì, certamente…

Bruno Vespa:

mmh, forse si riferisce

Cardinal Bertone:

È stata trascritta, poi è stato questo documento è stato poi tradotto in italiano per comodità anche dei padri cardinali della plenaria eccetera, no.

Bruno Vespa:

Guardi, io guardando seppur a distanza, lo dicevo durante l'intervallo pubblicitario, ho, lo confesso, sarò un'anima semplice ma ho provato una grande emozione a vedere un documento di questo genere. Senatore Andreotti?

Giulio Andreotti:

No, scusa…

Bruno Vespa:

… probably a typed version exists also: I don't know, you would have it. I imagine that copies were obviously made of this document, hm?

Cardinal Bertone:

Oh, yes, certainly.

Bruno Vespa:

Hm: maybe he's referring…

Cardinal Bertone:

It was transcribed, and then it was – then that document was translated into Italian, also for the convenience of the Cardinal fathers of the plenary meeting, etc., hm?

Bruno Vespa:

Look, even looking from a distance, I was saying during the commercial break: I admit it, I may be a simple soul, but I felt a great emotion at seeing a document of this kind. Senator Andreotti?

Giulio Andreotti:

Uh, sorry?

Bruno Vespa:

Dicevo, io ho provato una grande emozione a vedere questo documento seppure a distanza, non so se…

Giulio Andreotti:

…no, no…

Bruno Vespa:

… anche lei

Giulio Andreotti:

no, no

Bruno Vespa:

… Paola Rivetta avete avuto la stessa sensazione.

Giulio Andreotti:

… no, no, anche io insomma, prima ho detto, insomma, provo maggior devozione per Lourdes perché la vedo collegata con gli ammalati e con il pellegrinaggio militare che è una cosa stupenda che c'è a Lourdes ogni anno, tutte queste rappresentanze di tutti i paesi NATO che vanno in pellegrinaggio, però, ecco, da adesso in poi sarò più attento [*laughing*] a Fátima insomma…

Bruno Vespa:

I was saying, I felt a great emotion at seeing this document, even if only from a distance: I don't know if …

Giulio Andreotti:

… no, no ..

Bruno Vespa:

… you also …

Giulio Andreotti:

… no, no ..

Bruno Vespa:

… Paola Rivetta, had you had the same feeling?

Giulio Andreotti:

… no, no; I, well, I said before, I feel more devotion for Lourdes I see it connected with the sick and with the military pilgrimage, which is an amazing thing that takes places at Lourdes every year: all these representatives from all the NATO countries who come in pilgrimage, but, see, I'll be more attentive in the future [*laughing*] to Fátima, uh …

Bruno Vespa:

… anche a Fátima, anche a Fátima.

Bruno Vespa:

Guardi, anche a me Lourdes ha fatto una straordinaria impressione… [female voice in background]

Bruno Vespa:

Quando andai la prima volta perché era morto lì sul sagrato il cardinal Dell'Acqua…

Giulio Andreotti:

Ah, sì…

Bruno Vespa:

… l'impressione è invece, forse perché la visita fu troppo rapida, insomma fu un'impressione negativa perché vedevo queste bancarelle, queste cose che non mi piacquero, son tornato con con mia madre, son tornato con gli ammalati e francamente l'impressione è stata assolutamente diversa e di uno straordinario coinvolgimento, mi mi ha veramente commosso il coinvolgimento del-

Bruno Vespa:

… to Fátima also; to Fátima also.

Bruno Vespa:

Look, Lourdes also made an extraordinary impression on me [*female voice in background*]

Bruno Vespa:

When I went there the first time because Cardinal Dell'Acqua had died at the churchyard…

Giulio Andreotti:

Ah, yes…

Bruno Vespa:

The impression, on the other hand, was – perhaps because the visit was too hurried: it was a negative impression because I saw those stalls, those things which I didn't like. I went back with my mother, I went back with the sick, and frankly the impression was absolutely different: the impression of an extraordinary involvement of the people, of so many people

la gente, di tanta gente che sa che molto difficilmente guarirà ma che proprio la fede è veramente vista e toccata con mano. Paola?

Paola Rivetta:

È un luogo, Lourdes, dove davvero hai la sensazione che lì ci sia Dio. Arrivare a Lourdes, lasciarsi alle spalle tutto quello che è il bazar, indubbiamente, però entrare all'interno del recinto del santuario è veramente un dono…

Bruno Vespa:

e sulla …poi parleremo dei santuari se faremo in tempo. Ma la lettera, il documento…di Suor Lucía…

Paola Rivetta:

… no, no, un'emozione enorme, un'emozione infinita: ora fino ad ora l'avevo vista soltanto stampata…

Bruno Vespa:

Un vaticanista disincantato come Marco Politi?

who know that many will hardly be cured but there you can see the faith and touch it with your hands. Paola?

Paola Rivetta:

Lourdes is a place where you really have the sense that God is there. Arriving in Lourdes, leaving aside everything in the bazaar, without a doubt, but going into the enclosure of the shrine is really a gift…

Bruno Vespa:

and on the … later we'll talk about the shrines if there is time. But the letter, the document of Sister Lúcia…

Paola Rivetta:

… no, no, a tremendous feeling, an infinite feeling: now, and when I had first seen it just in print….

Bruno Vespa:

A jaded Vatican reporter like Marco Politi?

Marco Politi:

Eh, no, un vaticanista disincantato avrebbe dato l'ira di Dio per avere quel documento...

Paola Rivetta:

Esatto

Marco Politi:

... prima del 2000 [*laughing*], assolutamente [*laughing*], no, devo dire, però devo dire che se poi entriamo nel merito del documento, lì c'è una cosa molto strana perché in queste righe che poi sono appunto pubblicate nel libro dove si parla di questa visione apocalittica che assolutamente è generica perché avere una processione di vescovi, religiosi e suore attraverso un paesaggio bombardato di guerra e che poi sotto la croce finiscono uccisi da frecce, da fucilate è una visione assolutamente generica che secondo me, proprio tirata per i capelli, si collega poi all'attentato contro Giovanni Paolo II ma c'è una stranezza nel documento. Nelle righe scritte da Suor Lucía viene elencata questa

Marco Politi:

Well, a jaded Vatican reporter would have given the wrath of God to have that document...

Paola Rivetta:

Exactly.

Marco Politi:

... before 2000 [*laughing*], absolutely [*laughing*], no, I have to say, but I have to say that if we get into the merits of the document there, there's something very strange because in these rows precisely that were published later in the book, where it speaks about this apocalyptic vision, which is absolutely is generic – because to have a procession of bishops, religious brothers and sisters crossing a countryside bombed by war, and that they end up at the foot of the cross slain by arrows and gunshots: that is a vision absolutely generic that, in my opinion, pushing things a bit, then gets connected to the attack against John Paul II, but there's a strangeness in the document. In the rows written by Sister Lúcia

visione apocalittica e si parla di un vescovo vestito di bianco; poi Suor Lucía apre delle virgolette e dice "e io avevo il presentimento che fosse il papa" chiuse le virgolette. Quindi quasi nella visione della Madonna c'è un inserimento diretto di Suor Lucía scritto 25 anni dopo. Ora che una analfabeta di dieci anni che in quel momento ascolta o crede di ascoltare o di vedere questa visione e lei già ha il presentimento che questo figura vestita di bianco è il papa, secondo me è difficile da digerire.

Giuseppe De Carli:

Eh, posso permettermi di non essere

Bruno Vespa:

Sì, sentiamo, sentiamo la risposta...

Giuseppe De Carli:

Posso permettermi di non essere d'accordo con l'amico Marco, con quello che hai detto. Intanto non mi sembra che questo terzo segreto sia generico

this apocalyptic vision is listed out, and it speaks of a bishop clothed in white; then Sister Lúcia opens quotation marks and says "and I have the presentiment that it's the Pope", closes the quotation marks. So in the vision from the Madonna, sort of, there's an insertion direct from Sister Lúcia written 25 years later. Now, that an illiterate ten-year-old, who at that time hears, or believes she hears, or sees this vision, and she already has the presentiment that this figure clothed in white is the Pope: in my opinion it's hard to stomach that.

Giuseppe De Carli:

Ah, may I take the liberty of not to be

Bruno Vespa:

Yes, let's hear, let's hear the answer ...

Giuseppe De Carli:

May I take the liberty of not being in agreement with my friend Marco, with what he said: inasmuch as it doesn't seem to me that this third secret is ge-

perché quando si parla dei cadaveri dei martirizzati se tu consideri quello che è stato il XX secolo è stato il mattatoio della storia, pensa solo che nel XX secolo ben 20 milioni di cristiani sono stati ammazzati per la loro fede e quindi…

Marco Politi:

Ho detto la visione generica, non…

Giuseppe De Carli:

Be'

Marco Politi:

… i morti no…

Bruno Vespa:

Scusate…

Giuseppe De Carli:

Intanto l'altra cosa, devo dire che questa, questa visione che ho avuto anch'io della, della busta, ne avevamo parlato tante volte con il cardinal Bertone proprio per la stesura di questa sua, di questa sua memoria. È stato anche per me il grande oggetto del desiderio, vederla mi ha fatto una certa emo-

neric, because when it speaks of cadavers of the martyred, if you consider what the 20th century was: it was the slaughterhouse of history. I only think that in the 20th century some 20 million Christians were martyred for their faith and so….

Marco Politi:

I said that the vision was generic, not…

Giuseppe De Carli:

Well--

Marco Politi:

… not the deaths …

Bruno Vespa:

Excuse me…

Giuseppe De Carli:

Inasmuch – the other thing I need to say – that this viewing, which I've also had, of the envelope: we had spoken many times about it with Cardinal Bertone, just in drawing up this, this memoir of his. For me it was also the thing I desired greatly; to see it gives me a certain emo-

zione. Ecco, l'unica cosa che può presentare un problema è quella data, 1960. Perché Suor Lucía ha scritto 1960? Il cardinal Bertone dà una spiegazione anche perché con Suor Lucía aveva un concetto della temporalità che era completamente diverso dal nostro.

Bruno Vespa:

Ma no, ma prima, scusi Eminenza, Lei ha detto "Suor Lucía dice che Nostra Signora le ha detto non prima del '60"…

Cardinal Bertone:

Sì.

Bruno Vespa:

Quindi una prescrizione della, della Vergine.

Cardinal Bertone:

Sì, della Vergine però io ho chiesto "ma è stata proprio la Madonna che ha ordinato di non aprire la busta prima del '60 o è stata lei che ha messo questa data?" e Suor Lucía mi ha risposto letteralmente così "son stato io che ho messo questa data, la

tion. You see, the only thing that can present a problem is that date, 1960. Why did Sister Lúcia write 1960? Cardinal Bertone gives an explanation: because with – Sister Lúcia had a concept of temporality completely different from ours.

Bruno Vespa:

But no: first – excuse me, Eminence: you said, Sister Lúcia said that our Lady told her not before '60…

Cardinal Bertone:

Yes…

Bruno Vespa:

Therefore: an instruction from, from the Virgin.

Cardinal Bertone:

Yes, from the Virgin, but I asked: "But was it the Madonna herself who gave the order not to open the envelope before '60, or was it you who set that date?" and Sister Lúcia literally answered me this way: "It was I who set the date; the Madonna didn't want

Madonna non voleva che si conoscesse il segreto", questo è un punto fermo, no, anche se lei si è decisa a scriverla con il permesso della Madonna, poi si è decisa a scriverlo e a consegnarlo come segreto che non venisse pubblicato, no, ma disse "son stato io perché pensavo che il 1960 fosse un termine sufficiente per poter aprire poi la busta" e disse anche "io pensavo già magari di essere morta e allora devo essere più coinvolta nel terzo segreto", queste sono le parole che ha detto Suor Lucía.

Bruno Vespa:

Allora, a proposito del vescovo vestito di bianco…

Cardinal Bertone:

Sì…

Bruno Vespa:

… vi leggerei la prima parte del, di questa testimonianza così poi sentiamo il Cardinal Bertone che interpretazione ne dà.

Allora, dopo le due parti

the secret to be known," this is an established point, hm? Even if she decided to write it, with the permission of the Madonna, she decided to write it, then, and entrust it as a secret that would not be published, hm? But she said "it was me, because I thought that 1960 would be a sufficient period of time to be able to open the envelope then," and she also said, "I was already thinking maybe I would be dead: and now, I have to be more involved with the third secret." Those are the words Sister Lúcia said.

Bruno Vespa:

Now on the topic of the bishop clothed in white…

Cardinal Bertone:

Yes…

Bruno Vespa:

… I will read to you the first part of, of this testimony; then we'll hear Cardinal Bertone, who is giving an interpretation of it.

Now, after the two parts

che ho già esposto, scrive Suor Lucía, abbiamo visto al lato sinistro di Nostra Signora un poco più in alto un angelo con una spada di fuoco nella mano sinistra, scintillando emetteva fiamme che sembrava dovessero incendiare il mondo ma si spegnevano al contatto dello splendore che Nostra Signora emanava dalla sua mano destra verso di lui. L'angelo, indicando la terra con la mano destra, con la voce forte disse: penitenza, penitenza, penitenza e vedemmo in una luce immensa che è Iddio, aperte virgolette, qualcosa di simile a come si vedono le persone in uno specchio quando vi passano davanti, chiuse virgolette, un vescovo vestito di bianco, aperte virgolette, abbiamo avuto il presentimento che fosse il Santo Padre e poi prosegue.

Allora quando, ve, ve lo leggo tutto.

Vari altri vescovi, sacerdoti, religiosi e religiose salire in una montagna ripida in cima alla quale c'era una grande croce di

I have already presented, Sister Lúcia writes, we saw at our Lady's left side, a little bit higher, an angel with a sword of fire in his left hand, sparkling: it gave off flames that seemed they would have to burn up the world, but they went out when they came into contact with the splendor that our Lady gave off from her right hand in his direction. The angel, pointing to the earth with his right hand, said in a strong voice: penance, penance, penance, and we saw in an immense light that is God, (open quotation marks) "something like what people see in a mirror when they pass before it" (close quotation marks), a bishop clothed in white, (open quotation marks) "we had the presentiment that it was the Holy Father"

and then it continues. So then, I'll read it all to you:

Various other bishops, priests, religious men and religious women, are climbing a steep mountain to the summit

491

tronchi grezzi, come se fosse il sughero con la corteccia, il Santo Padre prima di arrivarvi attraversò una grande città mezza in rovina e mezzo tremulo con passo vacillante, afflitto di dolore e di pena, pregava per le anime dei cadaveri che incontrava nel suo cammino; giunto alla cima del monte, prostrato in ginocchio ai piedi della grande croce, venne ucciso da un gruppo di soldati che gli spararono vari colpi di arma da fuoco e frecce e allo stesso modo morirono gli uni dopo gli altrivescovi, sacerdoti, religiosi e religiose e varie persone secolari, uomini e donne di varie classi e posizioni. Sotto i due bracci della croce c'erano due angeli, ognuno con un innaffiatoio di cristallo nella mano nei quali raccoglieva il sangue dei martiri e con esso irrigavano le anime che si avvicinavano a Dio. 3 gennaio 1944.

Allora Eminenza, c'è del simbolismo in questa, il San-

where there was a great cross in rough sections, as if it were of cork-tree with the bark. The Holy Father, before reaching there, crossed a great city half in ruins, and half shaking, with unsteady steps, afflicted with sorrow and pain; he was praying for the souls of the corpses he met on his way. Reaching the summit of the mountain, prostrate on his knees at the foot of the great cross, he is killed by a group of soldiers who fire several shots with firearms and arrows, and in the same way, the other bishops, priests, religious men and religious women, and various lay people, men and women of various classes and positions, die, all one after another. Under the two arms of the cross, there were two angels, each with a sprinkling-bottle in hand, made of crystal, with which they collected the blood of the martyrs, and with it they irrigated the souls that were drawing nearer to God. January 3, 1944.

Now, Eminence, there is some symbolism in this: the

to Padre, quando dice il Santo Padre, il Santo Padre è un'interpretazione di Suor Lucía o la Madonna gli ha parlato, secondo quanto ha capito lei, di Santo Padre, gli ha parlato espressamente del papa?

Cardinal Bertone:

Io credo che sia una interpretazione di Suor Lucía ma un'interpretazione ispirata di Suor Lucía. C'è molto simbolismo in questa descrizione. Nelle profezie in genere, se noi analizziamo i testi profetici, non c'è mai una descrizione così precisa, rigorosa, geografica, circostanziata e nemmeno una successione temporale e precisa, c'è un misto di visione, di simbolismo, di eventi che devono accadere, che vengono descritti con un linguaggio, eh con un linguaggio, noi diciamo, profetico, apocalittico ma che vuole esprimere dei messaggi, delle verità da comunicare e le verità forti sono la descrizione, come abbiamo detto, del martirio del XX secolo e l'invito pressante alla

Holy Father – when it says "the Holy Father", is "the Holy Father" an interpretation by Sister Lúcia, or did the Madonna speak to her of the Holy Father, as you understand it: did she speak expressly of the Pope?

Cardinal Bertone:

I believe that this is an interpretation by Sister Lúcia, but it is an inspired interpretation by Sister Lúcia. There's a lot of symbolism in that description. In prophecies in general, if we analyze prophetic texts, there's never such a precise, rigorous, geographical, detailed description; nor is there a temporal, precise succession. There's a mixture of vision, of symbolism, of events that have to happen, that are described with a language – eh, with a language, we call prophetic, apocalyptic, but which desires to express messages, truths to be communicated; and the strong truths are the description, as we have said, of the martyrdom of the 20th century, and the pressing invitation to penance

penitenza e alla preghiera, è anche consolante, molto consolante come dice il papa nel suo commento, che su questa visione così catastrofica veglia la Madonna con la mano destra, no, che emana uno splendore, una luce che rischiara, che illumina e i due angeli che raccolgono il sangue dei martiri e in qualche modo innaffiano, nutrono gli amici di Dio che continuano a camminare verso la croce e che vogliono affermare la loro fede, quindi mi sembra, bisogna poi interpretare la profezia e è ciò che ha tentato di fare, ciò che ha fatto, molto profondamente, il cardinale Joseph Ratzinger nel suo commento teologico.

Bruno Vespa:

Infatti. Visione, apparizione del '17, scritta nel '44, quindi direi abbastanza in tempo per essere profetica, in qualche modo, nella seconda parte del secolo anche, no?

Marco Politi:

Anche per esser influenzata però da quello che suc-

and prayer. It is also consoling, very consoling, as the Pope says in his commentary, that in this vision, which is so catastrophic, the Madonna watches over this with her right hand, hm?, which gives off a splendor, a light that shines, that illuminates, and the two angels who gather the blood of the martyrs and sprinkle it in some way, nourish the friends of God who continue to walk toward the cross and who want to affirm their faith. So it seems to me, we need to interpret the prophecy then, and this is what I have tried to do, what Cardinal Joseph Ratzinger has done, very profoundly, in his theological commentary.

Bruno Vespa:

Indeed. The vision, the apparition of the 1917, written in '44; so I would say it's on time enough to be prophetic, in some sense, in the second part of the century, too, hm?

Marco Politi:

But it's also on time enough to be influenced by what happened

cede nel secolo, perché qui il grande problema è quello che a dieci anni, questi tre pastorelli sentono, avvertono, che Suor Lucía ricorda e che poi dopo quarant... nel quaranta... dopo un quarto di secolo scrive e nel frattempo sono già, nel frattempo c'è stata la rivoluzione russa, nel frattempo ci sono le persecuzioni.

Però prima quando dicevo che la visione è assolutamente generica è perché è la classica visione di una persecuzione della Chiesa che avviene attraverso delle rovine, quindi in questo senso può essere collocata in varie situazioni, certamente non è collegata all'attentato al papa e io credo che d'altra parte poi vada tenuta anche presente una... io sono rimasto sempre colpito, una volta ho stuzzicato Monsignor Dziwisz il segretario di Giovanni Paolo II sul terzo segreto, ancora non era stato pubblicato, eravamo in un aeroporto, e e lui mi ha detto solo due parole, mi ha ditto "ci vuole

during the century, because the big problem here is that at the age of ten these three little shepherds heard, they say, what Sister Lúcia remembers, and that then after forty – in forty – after a quarter of a century she writes it and in the meantime, there's already been – in the meantime there's been the Russian revolution, in the meantime there have been persecutions.

But before when I was saying that the vision is absolutely generic, that's because it's the classic vision of a persecution of the Church, that takes place amid ruins; so in this sense it can be placed in various situations. Certainly it's not tied to the attack on the pope, and I believe that, on the other hand, there is also present a – I am always struck by this: one time I prodded Monsignor Dziwisz, the secretary of John Paul II, about the third secret; it hadn't been published yet, we were in an airport, and, and he said to me just two words: he said, "it takes a lot of prudence to understand what Sister Lúcia says and what the

molta prudenza per capire cosa dice Suor Lucía e cosa dice la Madonna".

Bruno Vespa:

Cioè secondo te quindi il Papa ha arbitrariamente immaginato che si riferisse al Papa Giovanni Paolo II, dico, ha arbitrariamente immaginato di essere ritratto in questo racconto?

Marco Politi:

No, io dico, non dico che ha arbitrariamente perché poi, come dico, sul piano di quello che è il mondo religioso intimo ci vuole sempre un grande rispetto. È chiaro che, rispetto a quello che Wojtyla ha vissuto, Giovanni Paolo II ha vissuto, di essere colpito proprio a Piazza San Pietro cioè nel cuore simbolico della cristianità, è questo che giustamente gli ha scatenato tutta la curiosità, la voglia di capire il segreto di Fátima, poi lui stesso era profondamente convinto, come ha detto, che la Vergine, la sua madre a cui lui sempre si è rivolta, lo abbia salvato dall'attentato, questo

Madonna says."

Bruno Vespa:

So, in your view, that is, the Pope has arbitrarily imagined that it refers to Pope John Paul II: I mean, he arbitrarily imagined that he was described in this story?

Marco Politi:

No, I'm saying: I'm not saying that he arbitrarily did, because then – as I say, on the level of the intimate world of religion we always want a great respect. It is clear that, with respect to what Wojtyla lived through, John Paul II lived through, being struck right in St. Peter's Square, that is, in the symbolic heart of Christendom, that is what rightly sparked all his curiosity, his wish to understand the secret of Fátima; then he himself was deeply convinced, as he said, that the Virgin, his mother to whom he always turned, had saved him from the attack: this

conta sul piano storico perché è ciò che lui sente.

Bruno Vespa:

Sentiamo Paola Rivetta e poi Giuseppe De Carli... Paola, prego...

Paola Rivetta:

Sì, no, volevo dire soltanto questo: intanto è un ricordo che non è un normale ricordo, come può essere il tuo, il mio o quello di Giuseppe che si riferisce, tu dici, ma a vent'anni prima, venticinque anni prima, qui parliamo di un incontro con il divino, un incontro che, che è assolutamente in una sfera soprannaturale ed è un ricordo ispirato perché se noi non crediamo a questo, chiaramente allora si può dire tutto il contrario di tutto...

Marco Politi:

No, no, ricordati che un cattolico non è obbligato a crederci...

Paola Rivetta:

No, ma infatti non è dogma

counts on the historical level because it's what he felt.

Bruno Vespa:

Let's hear Paola Rivetta and then Giuseppe De Carli. Paola, please.

Paola Rivetta:

Oh, I just wanted to say this: inasmuch as it's a memory which is not a normal memory, as yours or mine or Giuseppe's might be, but referring, as you say, to twenty years before, twenty-five years before, here we are talking about an encounter with the divine, an encounter that – that is absolutely in a supernatural sphere and it's an inspired memory, because if we don't believe in it, clearly then it can say completely the opposite of everything...

Marco Politi:

No, no; let's remember that a Catholic is not obliged to believe in it...

Paola Rivetta:

No; indeed, it is not a dogma.

Giuseppe De Carli:

Lo dice anche il cardinale Ratzinger…

Marco Politi:

Lo so, proprio perché lo dice il cardinale Ratzinger

Paola Rivetta:

Lo so, ci mancherebbe, chiaro che… però dico se noi vogliamo analizzare il, il segreto di Fátima e quello che racconta Suor Lucía, dobbiamo pensare comunque ad un ricordo ispirato, anche perché, come il cardinal Bertone racconta e spiega, le visioni e gli incontri di Suor Lucía con la Vergine sono state frequenti negli anni e non si sono fermate nel 1917. Poi devo dire che, al di là di tutto questo, la visione assolutamente terrificante, impressionante che è contenuta nel terzo segreto, quindi non so che cosa ci potrebbe essere di più apocalittico di una cosa del genere, mah è è veramente la descrizione di Papa Wojtyla già con la sua sofferenza, addirittura già con la sua sofferenza fisica.

Giuseppe De Carli:

Cardinal Ratzinger says that too.

Marco Politi:

I know it, precisely because Cardinal Ratzinger says it.

Paola Rivetta:

I know, we all should – it's clear that – but I'm saying, if we want to analyze the, the secret of Fátima and what Sister Lúcia relates, we have to think of it as an inspired memory – also because, as Cardinal Bertone relates and explains, the visions and the encounters of Sister Lúcia with the Virgin have been frequent during the years and did not stop in 1917. Then I have to say that, beyond all that, the absolutely terrifying, disturbing vision which is the content of the third secret – so I don't know what could be more apocalyptic than something like this, but it's, it's really the description of Pope Wojtyla already with his suffering, and specifically with his physical suffering.

Bruno Vespa:

De Carli?

Giuseppe De Carli:

Ho capito che Paola abbia proprio toccato il punto perché noi diciamo che il terzo segreto no è una questione di carattere generico, io mi permetto sempre, caro Marco, di essere in disaccordo con te su questa interpretazione [incomprehensible words by Marco Politi] ma in realtà, in realtà invece è qualcosa di cupo, di apocalittico, cioè se si legge il terzo segreto, chi lo leggeva prima che accadesse il fatto, come dico sempre, del 13 maggio 1981, da tener conto di un'altra cosa, che la versione del cardinale Bertone coincide perfettamente; e noi non conoscevamo il contenuto del libro del, di Monsignor Dziwisz "La mia vita con Karol", coincide proprio perfettamente con quanto il segretario allora del di Papa Giovanni Paolo II scrive nel suo libro. Sono due testi, guardate, che sembrano quasi uguali, li abbiamo scoperti dopo che era stato pubblicato il libro del cardinale Dziwisz con le bozze che

Bruno Vespa:

De Carli?

Giuseppe De Carli:

I understand that Paola has put her finger right on the point, because we say that the third secret is not a question of generic character. I'm still taking the liberty, dear Marco, of not agreeing with you about this interpretation [*incomprehensible words by Politi*] but in reality, in reality, on the other hand, it's something obscure, apocalyptic, that is: if you read the third secret, as I always say, whoever read it before the events of May 13, 1981 came to pass, to take another thing into account, Cardinal Bertone's version matches perfectly; and we didn't know the contents of Monsignor Dziwisz's book "My life with Karol" – it just matches perfectly with what the then-secretary of Pope John Paul II writes in his book. There are two texts, you see, which seem almost the same – we discovered this after Cardinal Dziwisz's book was published – with the proofs we

avevamo noi, non avevamo toccato neanche una riga. Ecco

had; we didn't touch a line. So, there it is….

Bruno Vespa:

Possiamo sentire anche il cardinal Bertone? Prego.

Bruno Vespa:

Can we also hear from Cardinal Bertone? Go right ahead.

Cardinal Bertone:

Sì, mah, vorrei dire il, non, non so se si può affermare come afferma categoricamente il Dottor Politi che questo terzo segreto non ha nessun riferimento all'attentato, ma come fa a dire questo? Ha proprio riferimento all'attentato, al vescovo vestito di bianco, abbiamo presentito, abbiamo avuto il presentimento che fosse il Santo Padre, io ho interrogato Suor Lucía, adesso dobbiamo stare anche a ciò che ha detto Suor Lucía, poi possiamo discutere finché vogliamo ma voi, quando lei ha sentito la notizia dell'attentato al papa il 13 maggio e tutto il convento è stato in subbuglio, hanno pregato tutta la notte, ha pensato che questo fosse il momiento proprio purtroppo della realizzazione di quella terribile profezia e che

Cardinal Bertone:

Yes, uh, I'd like to say – I don't know if I can affirm what Doctor Politi affirms categorically, that this third secret has no reference to the attack, but how can you say this? It really does have reference to the attack, to the bishop clothed in white. We've sensed it, we had the presentment that it was about the Holy Father; I questioned Sister Lúcia; now we have to stay with what Sister Lúcia said; then we can discuss it as long as we want, but you – when she heard the news of the attack on the Pope on May 13 and the whole convent was in turmoil, they prayed all night, had she thought that this really was the moment, unfortunately, for the realization of that terrible prophecy, and that he was the pope of the third

fosse il papa del terzo segreto, ha detto "sì, io ho pensato a quello" e quindi, cioè c'è una un suffragio, ecco una prova ulteriore della bontà dell'interpretazione che è stata poi data, che abbiamo scritto anche non è un'interpretazione infallibile ovviamente, non chiede la fede di nessuno però la logica, la dinamica delle cose e l'interpretazione della successione della profezia, dell'evento porta a queste conclusioni.

Tra parentesi, poi devo dire anche, il Dottor Politi dice "mah, Suor Lucía può aver sentito della rivoluzione russa, dell'inizio della guerra", non so, anche della guerra in Abissinia, supponiamo e via, ma ricordiamo che Suor Lucía era in un convento, né riceveva giornali né ascoltava la radio, non c'era la televisione, non era così informata di tutti questi eventi, no? E quindi la descrizione, anche se viene fatta nel 1944, è una descrizione, a mio parere dopo averla interrogata, che registra perfettamente una memoria di un evento, di un'esperienza,

secret? She said, "Yes, I thought of that", and so, that is, there's a support, there's a further proof of the goodness of the interpretation that was given then, which we also wrote. It's not an, an infallible interpretation, obviously, it does not demand faith from anyone, but the logic, the dynamic of things and the interpretation of the unfolding of the prophecy, of the event, leads to these conclusions.

In parenthesis, then, I also have to say: Dr. Politi says, "well, Sister Lúcia may have heard of the Russian revolution, of the beginning of the war," and I don't know, the war in Abyssinia too, let's suppose, and so on, but let's remember that Sister Lúcia was in a convent; she neither received newspapers nor listened to the radio; there was no television yet: she wasn't so informed about all these events, hm? And so the description, even if it is made in 1944, it is a description, in my opinion after having questioned her, that

di rivelazione soprannaturale in quel momento del 13 ottobre del 1917.

Bruno Vespa:

Questo è realistico, diceva Politi: è realistico perché anche la gran parte dell'opinione pubblica che non viveva in un convento del Portogallo, ricordiamoci poi cos'era il Portogallo allora, un paese arretratissimo, un convento di clausura in un paese arretratissimo ma anche chi viveva nei nostri paesi europei, soltanto alla fine della guerra ha capito completamente le dimensioni di quello che era successo, per esempio l'Olocausto, per esempio tante altre cose, quindi è abbastanza verosimile, insomma, è difficile che Suor Lucía nel '44 avesse una visione storica di quello che era successo tra il '17 e il '44, diciamolo

Marco Politi:

No certo.

Bruno Vespa:

This is realistic, Politi was saying: it's realistic because even most of public opinion – the public that wasn't living in a convent in Portugal – let's remember what Portugal was then, a very backward country – a cloistered convent in a very backward country, but she was also living among our European countries; only at the end of the war did she completely understand the dimensions of what had happened: for example, the Holocaust, for example, so many other things, so is it plausible enough, in short, is it difficult that in '44 Sister Lúcia had a historical vision of what had happened between 1917 and 1944, let's say…

Marco Politi:

No, certainly.

Bruno Vespa:

… diciamolo è improbabile, eh?

Marco Politi:

Sì, ma quello che io volevo solo dire è che da un lato già il documento del cardinale Ratzinger dice che queste visioni sono sempre molto anche nella parte descrittiva colorate dalla soggettività, anche da ciò che si vede in libri devozionali, questo l'ha detto il cardinale Ratzinger. Secondo, la visione apocalittica di per sé cioè di una città distrutta, di soldati che uccidono preti, suore e vescovi è generica in questo senso, che ci sono chili nelle biblioteche del '900 di altre visioni, magari non riconosciute ma comunque di mistici, che raccontano episodi del genere, perché raccontano episodi di persecuzione, noi abbiamo avuto nell'arco di due secoli oltre duecento apparizioni [words]. Caterina Emmerich che è la mistica che ha fatto scoprire la casa di Efeso della Madonna, che è stata scoperta proprio da questa

Bruno Vespa:

… let's say it's improbable, hm?

Marco Politi:

Yes, but what all I wanted to say is that, on one hand, the document by Cardinal Ratzinger has said that these visions are always colored, very much in their descriptive part, by subjectivity, including by what can be seen in devotional books: that's what Cardinal Ratzinger said. Second, the apocalyptic vision per se, that is, of a destroyed city, of soldiers who are killing priests, sisters, and bishops, is generic in this sense: that there are kilos of books in the libraries from the 1900s, from other visions, maybe not recognized but mystics anyway, who tell episodes of this kind, because they tell episodes of persecution. In the arc of two centuries we have had over 200 apparitions. Catherine Emmerich, who is the mystic who caused our Lady's house in Ephesus to be discovered – it was discovered there precisely

mistica bavarese, a sua volta ha pubblicato libri di visioni in cui per esempio ci sono lotte intestine nella Chiesa terribilissime, cioè c'è una letteratura apocalittica.

Bruno Vespa:

Eminenza?

Cardinal Bertone:

Sì, però mi sembra una dimensione... prima si parlava di Lourdes, de, dei messaggi di Lourdes, una dimensione così coinvolgente della vita della Chiesa, della storia della Chiesa perché qui si uccidono un papa, vescovi, sacerdoti, suore, gente di ogni età, classe e posizione eccetera, una visione così coinvolgente è rara se non unica e quello che qualifica un po' il segreto di Fátima, il messaggio di Fátima, il mistero di Fátima nell'ultimo secolo.

Bruno Vespa:

Allora vediamo un momento con Fabio D'Alfonso il reportage su com'è Fátima oggi.

because of this Bavarian mystic – for her part she published books of visions in which there are the most terrible internecine struggles in the Church: that is, there is an apocalyptic literature.

Bruno Vespa:

Eminence?

Cardinal Bertone:

Yes, but it seems to me, a dimension – earlier we were talking about Lourdes, about the messages of Lourdes, a dimension so involved with the life of the Church, with the history of the Church – because here a pope, and bishops and priests, sisters, people of every age, class, and position, etc., are killed, a vision involving so much is rare if not unique; that is what characterizes somewhat the secret of Fátima, the message of Fátima, the mystery of Fátima in the last century.

Bruno Vespa:

Now for a moment let's watch the report with Fabio D'Alfonso about how Fátima is today.

Fabio D'Alfonso:

"Cerchiamo la pace, è una grande gioia essere qui, siamo venuti solo per la pace..." "Sono venuta qui in primo luogo a pregare per la mia famiglia, per miei fratelli, le mie sorelle, per tutto il mondo"

Fabio D'Alfonso:

Sono passati poco più di novant'anni da quel 13 maggio del 1917 quando su questa spianata dove ora sorge il santuario, una signora vestita di bianco apparve ai tre pastorelli di Fátima. Da allora in questo luogo che è divenuto il centro più importante del culto mariano arrivano ogni anno milioni di pellegrini che si recano qui in auto, a piedi o in ginocchio per chiedere una grazia o recitare il rosario.

Fr. Cesare Cuomo:

Qui a Fátima ogni anno vengono tra i quattro e i cinque milioni di pellegrini, da tutto il

Fabio D'Alfonso:

[*Prerecorded feature: scenes of pilgrims at Fátima*]:

"We are looking for peace: it is a great joy to be here; we came only for peace..." [*Female voice, translating Spanish speaker*:] "I came here, in the first place, to pray for my family, for my brothers, my sisters, for the whole world"

Fabio D'Alfonso:

A little more than ninety years have passed since that May 13th of 1917 when in this clearing where the Shrine now rises, a lady dressed in white appeared to the three little shepherds of Fátima. Since then, in this place which has become the most important center of Marian devotion millions of pilgrims arrive every year, making their way here by car, on foot, or on their knees to ask for a favor or to recite the rosary.

Fr. Cesare Cuomo:

Here at Fátima every year between four and five million pilgrims come from all over the

world, and we know that God is present everywhere; our Lady is also working everywhere, but there are places that we call graced in a particular way, and Fátima is one of these; and the Shrine receives many letters about favors received, and they are not only extraordinary favors, but also sometimes ordinary favors. The person may ask for a favor for their own work or some other thing, and for the good of their own family members, or for themselves, and really there is a great increase, you see of this devotion to the little shepherds.

Fr. Luis Kondor, SVD:

[*vice-postulator of the cause for the canonization of Bl. Francisco and Jacinta—voice of translator:*]

What happened in St. Peter's Square on May 13, 1981 has already been retold in detail: the Pope had suffered an attack. Monsignor Dziwisz, then secretary of His Holiness John Paul II, who was accompanying the Holy Father in those days, was

ni, era presente in ospedale quando il Santo Padre aprì la busta e lesse la terza parte del segreto, fu allora che il Santo Padre comprese ed esclamò "Questo sono io", poi Sua Santità Giovanni Paolo II aggiunse "C'è stata una mano che ha diretto la pistola e un'altra mano che ha deviato il proiettile". Quel proiettile in seguito è stato collocato qui, nella corona di Nostra Signora perché il Santo Padre era convinto che si fosse trattato di un intervento speciale di Nostra Signora di Fátima. A partire da quel momento tutto il messaggio di Fátima è entrato nel cuore del papa e tutto l'amore del papa è entrato nel messaggio di Fátima.

Bruno Vespa:

Senatore Andreotti, ho visto che Lei annuiva prima quando il cardinal Bertone riaffermava, direi con molta convinzione, che questo fosse il ritratto anticipato dell'attentato al Papa…

Giulio Andreotti:

Sì, perché ricordo la sera

present in the hospital when the Holy Father opened the envelope and read the third part of the secret; it was then that the Holy Father understood and exclaimed "That's me"; then the Holy Father John Paul II added: "There was one hand directing the pistol and another hand that diverted the bullet". As a result, that bullet is now located here, in the crown of our Lady, because the Holy Father was convinced that there had been a special intervention by our Lady of Fátima. From that moment on, the message of Fátima entered into the Pope's heart, and all the love of the Pope entered into the message of Fátima.

Bruno Vespa:

Senator Andreotti, I saw that you were nodding earlier when Cardinal Bertone was affirming, I'd say, with great conviction, that this was the portrait of the attack on the Pope which he expected.

Giulio Andreotti:

Yes, because when I re-

che il Santo Padre andò al Regina Coeli e visitò Ali Ağca, fece subito il giro questo quesito: Ali Ağca gli ha detto "ma scusi Lei che c'entra con Fátima, perché ha detto che è stato salvato da Fátima?" Ma lui non pensava certamente a Suor Lucía, questo mi ha sempre colpito perché io credo che certo come si è detto prima, non so, dogmi di fede però c'è un inserimento storico di questa menzione della Madonna di Fátima e del fatto che il Santo Padre sia sopravvissuto, ora Ali Ağca credo che sappia fare poche cose ma a sparare sa fare, insomma, …

Bruno Vespa:

Ah, su questo non c'è dubbio, lui è veramente un grande killer professionista. Prima parlavamo di Lourdes e di Fátima, ciascuno poi ha il suo santuario di riferimento, tra chi crede ovviamente. Abbiamo chiesto a Saverio Gaeta che è uno specialista

member the evening when the Holy Father when to Regina Coeli and visited Ali Ağca, this question suddenly came up: Ali Ağca said to him, "But excuse me: how this has to do with Fátima – why did you say that you were saved by Fátima?" But certainly he was not thinking of Sister Lúcia: that always struck me, because-- I think, it's certain, as was said before, these aren't dogmas of the faith, but …. There's a historical insertion of this mention by our Lady of Fátima – and from the fact that the Holy Father survived – now, I believe Ali Ağca didn't know a lot of things, but he knew how to fire a gun, so…

Bruno Vespa:

Ah, there's no doubt about that, he is really a big professional "killer". Before, we were talking about Lourdes and Fátima, and then each of us has a shrine he prefers, that is, for those who believe, obviously. We asked Saverio Gaeta, who is a specialist on these matters for

di queste cose per "Famiglia Cristiana" di parlarci dei santuari e delle apparizioni mariane.

Saverio Gaeta:

È una vera e propria geografia della fede quella disegnata in ogni angolo d'Italia dai santuari che ricordano le tante manifestazioni mariane avvenute durante i duemila anni di storia cristiana. Spesso si tratta di apparizioni che affondano le radici in secoli lontani e che sono state tramandate attraverso suggestive narrazioni d'epoca come quella del XV secolo a Caravaggio in Lombardia. Altre volte lo spunto per la costruzione di una basilica è stato un evento portentoso come la traslazione della casa della Madonna da Nazareth a Loreto, oppure il verificarsi di un prodigio quale la lacrimazione a Siracusa di un bassorilievo raffigurante il cuore immacolato di Maria. In altre circostanze è stata la devozione

Famiglia Cristiana [magazine], to talk to us about shrines and Marian apparitions.

Saverio Gaeta [*prerecorded segment, with title: "Geography of Faith, around the Madonna"*]:

There is a real geography of the faith, drawn in every corner of Italy, from the shrines that record the many manifestations of Mary that have taken place during the two thousand years of Christian history. Often they are cases of apparitions whose roots sink into distant centuries, and have been handed on through evocative narratives of the time, such as those from the 15th century at Caravaggio in Lombardy. Other times the impulse for the construction of a basilica was a portentous event, such as the transfer of the house of our Lady from Nazareth to Loreto; or even the verification of a miracle, like the lacrimation at Siracusa from a bas-relief depicting the immaculate Heart of Mary. In other circumstances, popular devotion

popolare a volere l'edificazione di una cappella per onorare un particolare titolo della Vergine, tipico esempio quello della Madonna del Rosario a Pompei o per commemorare la protezione da lei attuata in favore di persone in difficoltà, è il caso della Madonna del Divino Amore a Roma. Ma sicuramente l'apparizione più strettamente correlata a quella di Fátima, almeno sotto l'aspetto del messaggio, è quella del 1947 nella località romana delle Tre Fontane. La Madonna si presentò come la Vergine della Rivelazione, un termine che fa correre la mente al testo biblico dell'Apocalisse. Il veggente Bruno Cornacchiola, che in quel tempo era uno sfegatato anticattolico desideroso di uccidere il papa, ricevette fra l'altro un segreto che aveva a che fare con i segni della persecuzione contro la Chiesa. A suggello della veridicità della visione anche qui, come trent'anni prima in Portogallo, si ebbe il prodigio del sole rotante.

wanted a chapel built to honor a particular title of the Virgin; a typical example is that of our Lady of the Rosary at Pompeii, or to commemorate the protection she provided for the benefit of people in difficulty: this is the case for the Madonna of Divine Love in Rome. But surely the apparition most closely correlated to that of Fátima, at least under the aspect of its message, is the 1947 apparition in the Rome neighborhood of Tre Fontane. The Madonna presented herself as the Virgin of Revelation, a term that brings to mind the biblical text of the Apocalypse. The seer Bruno Cornacchiola, who at the time was a fanatical anti-Catholic who wanted to kill the Pope, received, among other things, a secret that had to do with signs of persecution against the Church. Here too, as in Portugal thirty years earlier, as a seal of the authenticity of the vision, the miracle of the spinning sun took place.

Bruno Vespa:

E a proposito di sole rotante, Eminenza, sabato scorso proprio a Caravaggio che veniva la località in provincia di Bergamo, che veniva citata nel servizio e che è sede di un santuario mariano, alcuni turisti hanno visto, dicono di aver visto un disco di luce fortissima che rotava intorno al sole, proprio come quello che si dice sia apparso a Fátima e erano parecchie persone. Naturalmente il rettore del santuario, come sempre si usa nella Chiesa, è molto prudente, eccetera, come valutate voi queste testimonianze e come si arriva a stabilire che in una certa località, una certa località è meritevole di un santuario?

Cardinal Bertone:

Prima di tutto normalmente ecco si chiede una relazione accurata, rigorosa dei fatti avvenuti, poi una relazione sulle persone che son state protagoniste, cioè sulla qualità delle persone, se son delle persone, direi, usiamo la parola psichicamente a posto, persone mature la cui testimonianza

Bruno Vespa:

Your Eminence, in regard to the spinning sun, last Saturday right at Caravaggio, which was the town in the province of Bergamo which was cited in the report, and which is the home of a Marian shrine, some tourists saw, or said they saw, a disk of powerful light rotating within the sun, just like what is said to have appeared at Fátima; and there were several people. Naturally the rector of the shrine is very cautious, etc., as the Church always is. How do you evaluate these testimonies and how do you come to establish what, in some particular place, deserves a shrine?

Cardinal Bertone:

First of all, normally, you ask for an accurate, rigorous report on the events that took place. Then a report on the people who were the protagonists, that is, about the qualities of the people; I would say, to put it simply, let's use the word, psychologically mature people whose testimony

can be considered credible. And then an interpretation is given, I would say a historical-critical interpretation; also a medical interpretation, if a miraculous event appears, a precise medical judgment and then a theological interpretation, because these facts and these events must have a meaning, to be judged authentically supernatural events, a supernatural meaning, a connection with a truth of the faith and a message to communicate to the believing community. It's stated many times that private revelations or these supernatural events that happen here and there can be, should be, a help to faith, an illustration of a truth of the faith which is already held and believed by the Christian people.

Bruno Vespa:

When you hear someone say they have seen the Madonna weeping, does caution prevail, or a little dismay, or some emotion?

Cardinal Bertone:

Di per sé prevale la prudenza. Io credo come primo sentimento, come primo elemento, specialmente negli organi della Chiesa preposti alla tutela della vera fede, della fede teologica, della fede integrale, prevale la prudenza e prevale una ricerca accurata di documentazioni. Io ricordo il processo che ci ha portato per esempio all'approvazione dell'apparizione di Kibeho in Ruanda che sono le ultime apparizioni della Madonna giudicate autentiche sia dalla Chiesa locale e sia dalla Congregazione per la Dottrina della Fede, si è proceduto attraverso tutta una serie di elementi, di constatazione, di verifiche eccetera, di interrogatori, naturalmente, dei testimoni e di interrogatori di verifica dei vescovi locali, dei vescovi della conferenza episcopale ruandese e poi la Congregazione per la Dottrina della Fede ha posto il suo sigillo dicendo "ecco, queste apparizioni sono documentate e possono ritenersi eventi soprannaturali con un messaggio per la Chiesa del nostro tempo".

Cardinal Bertone:

Caution prevails, per se. I think, as the first sentiment, the first element, especially in the organs of the Church designated for the protection of the true faith, theological faith, integral faith, caution prevails, and an accurate search of the documentation prevails. For example, I remember the process that led to the approval of the apparitions at Kibeho in Rwanda, which were the last apparitions of the Madonna judged authentic both by the local bishop and by the Congregation for the Doctrine of the Faith. It took place by means of a whole series of elements, of confirmations, verifications, etc., interviews, naturally; verification interviews by the local bishops, the bishops of Rwandan Bishops Conference, and then the Congregation for the Doctrine of the Faith put its seal on it, saying "here, these apparitions are documented, and can be considered supernatural events with a message for the Church in our time."

Bruno Vespa:

Now we are going to close; do we want to add something? Briefly, because we are about to close.

Marco Politi:

For example, the Madonna of Civitavecchia shed male tears, so – absolutely inadmissible. But I think it's right, from this point of view, that the Church is extremely cautious, as Cardinal Bertone said, because anything can happen…

Bruno Vespa:

A little like with miracles, hm?

Marco Politi:

And the, and the story of the spinning sun, for example, the spinning sun which thousands of people saw at Fátima, including famous anti-clerical journalists: on the other hand, Lúcia the seer saw the sun still, and next to the Madonna; and the astronomical observatory of

mosferico, quindi quando poi ci sono questi fenomeni di massa può succedere di tutto.

Bruno Vespa:

Allora chiudiamo con un nuovo dizionario sulla figura di Maria scritto da un notissimo mariologo, Stefano De Fiores. Lo ha intervistato per noi Ester Vanni.

Ester Vanni:

Questo nuovissimo dizionario è il risultato di trent'anni di studi e di approfondimenti sulla figura della Madre di Dio.

Stefano De Fiores:

Tutta la teologia contemporanea si può concentrare in questa visione di Maria come una sintesi, diremmo che è come un diamante dalle molte sfaccettature, che riceve la luce di Dio e la rimanda verso gli altri con una sua colorazione particolare, cioè guardando Maria, creatura relazionale, noi pensiamo a tutto il mistero della salvezza.

Lisbon didn't record any atmospheric change, so then, when there are these mass phenomena, anything can happen.

Bruno Vespa:

Now we'll close with a new dictionary on the figure of Mary, written by a noted Mariologist, Stefano De Fiores. He was interviewed by our Ester Vanni.

Ester Vanni [*Prerecorded segment*]:

This brand-new dictionary is the result of thirty years of in-depth study on the figure of the Mother of God.

Stefano De Fiores:

All of contemporary theology can be concentrated in this vision of Mary as a synthesis; we'll say she is like a diamond with many facets, that receives the light of God and gives it to others with a particular coloration; that is; looking at Mary, the relational creature, we think of the whole mystery of salvation.

Ester Vanni:

Lei ci invita a cogliere le novità della donna Maria?

Stefano De Fiores:

Maria sconfigge alcuni pregiudizi, soprattutto questo: che la donna non debba agire nella società, anzi Maria con il suo consenso all'angelo ha partecipato alla storia della salvezza, è divenuta causa di salvezza per tutto il genere umano.

Ester Vanni:

La prima voce del dizionario dedicato alla Vergine di Nazareth è "affidamento".

Stefano De Fiores:

Affidiamo alla Vergine Maria questa grande causa della pace nel mondo attraverso questi atti di affidamento che sono, diciamo, una manifestazione della potenza salvifica di Cristo attraverso Maria.

Ester Vanni:

Alcune voci sono una

Ester Vanni:

Are you inviting us to take in something new about Mary the woman?

Stefano De Fiores:

Mary defeats several prejudices, especially this one: that woman is not supposed to act in society, but Mary with her consent to the angel participated in the history of salvation. She became the cause of salvation for the whole human race.

Ester Vanni:

The first entry in the dictionary dedicated to the Virgin of Nazareth is *"affidamento"* (entrustment).

Stefano De Fiores:

We entrust to the Virgin Mary the great cause of peace in the world, through these acts of entrustment which are, we say, a manifestation of the saving power of Christ through Mary.

Ester Vanni:

Some of the entries are a

mano tesa alle nuove generazioni, per esempio giovani, pace, vita.

Stefano De Fiores:

La figura di Maria svolge una funzione terapeutica perché li porta ad impegnarsi per sempre, superando non solo il pensiero debole ma anche l'amore debole.

Ester Vanni:

L'ultima voce del dizionario, "volto".

Stefano De Fiores:

Il volto è la rivelazione dell'io profondo, la rivelazione dell'anima. Nel volto di Maria noi vediamo il volto materno di Dio perché Dio si fa vicino, non è un'immagine, diciamo così, ide idealizzata, è una creatura umana, un'ebrea, una galilea, una donna mediterranea.

Bruno Vespa:

Chiudiamo, vedete che i nostri madonnari Nedo Consoli e Federico Pillan nell'ora e mez-

hand stretched out to the new generation: for example: youth, peace, life.

Stefano De Fiores:

The figure of Mary carries out a therapeutic role, because she leads people to commit themselves for ever, overcoming not only weak thinking, but also weak love.

Ester Vanni:

The last entry in the dictionary: *"volto"* (face).

Stefano De Fiores:

The face is the revelation of the deep ego, the revelation of the soul. In the face of Mary, we see the maternal face of God, because God draws near. She is not an image, as we say, an idealized idea; she is a human creature, a Jew, a Galilean, a Mediterranean woman.

Bruno Vespa:

Now we're closing; you can see that our *madonnari* Nedo Consoli and Federico Pil-

za di "Porta a Porta" hanno completato il loro magnifico lavoro, hanno copiato [*applause*] devo dire molto brillantemente questa dolcissima Madonna con il bambino da un dipinto del del '700, di un anonimo del '700, ringraziamo il Segretario di Stato Vaticano per averci dato,

lan, in the hour and a half of *Porta a Porta* have completed their magnificent work, have copied, [*applause*] I must say brilliantly, this very sweet Madonna with the Child from a painting of the 1700s, by an anonymous artist of the 1700s. Again, we thank the Vatican Secretary of State for having been with us...

Cardinal Bertone:
Grazie.

Cardinal Bertone:
Thank you.

Bruno Vespa:
... per averci concesso il privilegio di vedere in anteprima questo straordinario documento, la lettera, la dichiarazione di Suor Lucía sul terzo mistero di Fátima, grazie, grazie a tutti, buona notte.

Bruno Vespa:
... for having given us the privilege of previewing this extraordinary document, the letter, the statement of Sister Lúcia on the third mystery of Fátima. Thank you, thanks to all, good night.

Cardinal Bertone:
Grazie, a voi e buona notte.

Cardinal Bertone:
Thanks to you, and good night.

—APPENDIX E—

ACCOUNT OF FR. AGUSTÍN FUENTES OF HIS MEETING WITH SR. LÚCIA (SPANISH & ENGLISH) 1958-1959

The following texts concern the account of a meeting between the Mexican priest Fr. Agustín Fuentes and Sr. Lúcia that took place in December, 1957 at her convent in Coimbra, Portugal. The Spanish text is the lengthy citation provided by Fr. Joaquín María Alonso in 1976. The English is the English translation published in June, 1959. The paragraphs are herein numbered and indicated in brackets for the sake of easy referencing and comparison. They correspond to the numbers provided in chapter five.

Spanish:[1]

[1] «La encontré en su convento muy triste, pálida y demacrada; y me

---

1   Joaquín María Alonso, C.M.F., *La Verdad sobre el Secreto de Fatima: Fátima sin mitos.* (Madrid, Espana: Centro Mariano, 1976), 103-106. Owing to the generosity of the nephew of Fr. Fuentes, this author was able to obtain some scans of the November-December, 1958 edition of *Hacia los Altares* (pages 48-52). There appeared in this edition an article entitled *Las Conferencias del Padre Fuentes* by Arturo Eloy, C.M.F. He provides what appears to be quotations from the Conferences that provide some variant readings from Alonso's text. These areas will be noted in the following text as notes in brackets. No speculation is herein given as to why these are variant readings.

dijo:[2] "Padre, la Santísima Virgen está muy triste, porque nadie hace caso a su Mensaje, ni los buenos ni los malos. Los buenos, porque prosiguen su camino de bondad; pero sin hacer caso a este mensaje. Los malos, porque no viendo el castigo de Dios actualmente sobre ellos, a causa de sus pecados, prosiguen también su camino de maldad, sin hacer caso a este Mensaje. Pero, créame, Padre, Dios va a castigar al mundo, y lo va a castigar de una manera tremenda. El castigo del cielo es inminente.[3] ¿Qué falta, Padre, para 1960; y qué sucederá entonces?[4] Será una cosa muy triste para

---

2   [Fr. Eloy's text here reads:

"Esta religiosa, dice el P. Fuentes, me recibió llena de tristeza, demacrada y triste; tiene 51 años, pero representa muchos menos, representará unos 24 años, quizás porque la Santísima Virgen, dijo: "A FRANCISCO Y A JACINTA ME LOS LLEVARE EN BREVE; PERO TU TE QUEDAS ALGUN TIEMPO MAS, JESUS QUIERE SERVIRSE DE TI PARA HACERME CONOCER Y AMAR. EL QUIERE ESTABLECER EN EL MUNDO LA DEVOCION A MI INMACULADO CORAZON".]

3   [Fr. Eloy's text here reads:

"Cuando Lucía me vió, —continúa el Padre Fuentes—me dijo: "Padre, la Santísima Virgen está muy triste porque nadie hace caso a su mensaje, ni los buenos, ni los malos: los buenos porque prosiguen su camino de virtud a apostolado pero sin unir su vida a este mensaje: y los malos también porque prosiguen su camino de maldad, porque no ven el castigo actual sobre ellos y no hacen caso. Pero, créame, Padre, Dios va a castigar al mundo y muy pronto, el castigo del cielo es inminente.]

4   [Fr. Eloy's text starts a new paragraph for this thought and reads as follows:

Qué falta, Padre ¡1960! Menos de dos años y el castigo del cielo vendrá y vendrá muy grande. Pero dígales a las almas que no teman solamente el castigo material que vendrá sobre nosotros, si nosotros no hacemos oración y penitencia; que teman sobre todo, las almas que se irán al infierno, las almas que se perderán para siempre. Eso es lo que causa la tristeza de la Virgen Santísima, lo que causa la tristeza de Nuestro Señor. Dígales que la Santísima Virgen repetidas veces me dijo:]

todos; y no una cosa alegre si antes el mundo no hace oración y penitencia. No puedo detallar más, ya que es aún secreto que, por voluntad de la
Santísima Virgen, solamente pudieran saberlo tanto el Santo Padre como
el señor Obispo de Fátima; pero que ambos no han querido saberlo para no
influenciarse. Es la tercera parte del Mensaje de Nuestra Señora, que aún
permanece secreto hasta esa fecha de 1960. Dígales, Padre, que la Santísima Virgen, repetidas veces, tanto a mis primos Francisco y Jacinta, como
a mí, nos dijo: Que muchas naciones de la tierra desaparecerán sobre la
faz de la misma, que Rusia sería el instrumento del castigo del Cielo para
todo el mundo, si antes no alcanzábamos la conversión de esa pobrecita
Nación (…)".[5]

[2] Sor Lucía me decía también: "Padre, el demonio está librando
una batalla decisiva con la Virgen; y como sabe qué es lo que más ofende
a Dios y lo que, en menos tiempo, le hará ganar mayor número de almas, está tratando de ganar a las almas consagradas a Dios, ya que de esta
manera también deja el campo de las almas desamparado, y más fácil-
mente se apoderará de ellas.

[3] Dígales también, Padre, que mis primos Francisco y Jacinta se
sacrificaron porque vieron siempre a la Santísima Virgen muy triste en todas sus apariciones. Nunca se sonrió con nosotros, y esa tristeza y angustia
que notábamos en la Santísima Virgen, a causa de las ofensas a Dios y de

---

5   [Fr. Eloy's text here reads:

"Muchas naciones de la tierra desaparecerán des castigo del cielo si
todos nosotros con la oración y el sacrificio, no alcanzamos la conversión de esa pobrecita nación". Dígales, padre, que el demonio está
librando una batalla decisiva con la Virgen, así la llama "LA VIR-
GEN"; y como sabe qué es lo qué más lastima el Corazón Inmaculado
de la Santísima Virgen y el Corazón Sacratísimo de Jesús, y qué cosa
es lo que hará ganar más almas en más poco tiempo, trata ahora de
ganar las almas consagradas a Dios tanto en la vida religiosa como
en la vida secerdotal [sacerdotal?]. Pero todavía es tiempo, podemos
detener el castigo del cielo. Las dos armas que la Santísima Virgen
nos ha dado son la ORACION Y EL SACRIFICIO.]

los castigos que amenazaban a los pecadores, nos llegaba al alma; y no sabíamos qué idear para encontrar en nuestra imaginación infantil medios para hacer oración y sacrificio (…).

[4] Lo Segundo que santificó a los niños fue la visión del infierno (…).

[5] Por esto, Padre, no es mi misión indicarle al mundo los castigos materiales que ciertamente vendrán sobre la tierra si el mundo antes no hace oración y penitencia. No. Mi misión es indicarles a todos el inminente peligro en que estamos de perder para siempre nuestra alma si seguimos aferrados al pecado".

[6] "Padre —me decía Sor Lucía—, no esperemos que venga de Roma una llamada a la penitencia, de parte del Santo Padre, para todo el mundo; ni esperemos tampoco que venga de parte de los señores Obispos para cada una de sus diócesis; ni siquiera tampoco de parte de las Congregaciones Religiosas. No; ya Nuestro Señor usó muchas veces estos medios, y el mundo no le ha hecho caso. Por eso, ahora, ahora que cada uno de nosotros comience por sí mismo su reforma spiritual; que tiene que salvar no solo su alma, sino salvar a todas las almas que Dios ha puesto en su camino (…).

[7] Padre, la Santísima Virgen no me dijo que nos encontramos en los últimos tiempos del mundo, pero me lo dio a demostrar por tres motivos: el primero, porque me dijo que el demonio está librando una batalla decisiva con la Virgen y una batalla decisiva es una batalla final, en donde se va a saber de qué partido es la Victoria, de qué partido es la derrota. Así que ahora, o somos de Dios, o somos del demonio; no hay término medio. Lo Segundo, porque me dijo, tanto a mis primos como a mí, que dos eran los últimos remedios que Dios daba al mundo: el Santo Rosario y la devoción al Inmaculado Corazón de María; y, al ser los últimos remedios, quiere decir que son los últimos, que ya no va a haber otros. Y tercero, porque siempre en los planos de la Divina Providencia, cuando Dios va a castigar al mundo, agota antes todos los demás medios; y cuando ha visto que el mundo no le ha

hecho caso a ninguno de ellos, entonces, como si dijéramos a nuestro modo imperfecto de hablar, nos presenta con cierto temor el ultimo medio de salvación, su Santísima Madre. Porque si despreciamos y rechazamos este último medio, ya no tendremos perdón del cielo; porque hemos cometido un pecado, que en el Evangelio suele llamarse pecado contra el Espíritu Santo; que consiste en rechazar abiertamente, con todo conocimiento y voluntad, la salvación que se presenta en las manos; y también porque Nuestro Señor es muy buen hijo; y no permite que ofendamos y despreciemos a su Santísima Madre, teniendo como testimonio patente la historia de varios siglos de la Iglesia que con ejemplos terribles nos indica cómo Nuestro Señor siempre ha salido a la defensa del honor de su Santísima Madre.

[8] Dos son los medios para salvar al mundo, me decía Sor Lucía de Jesús: la oración y el sacrificio (…).

[9] Y luego, el Santo Rosario. Mire, Padre, la Santísima Virgen, en estos últimos tiempos en que estamos viviendo, ha dado una nueva eficacia al rezo del Santo Rosario. De tal manera que ahora no hay problema, por más difícil que sea, sea temporal o sobre todo spiritual, que se refiera a la vida personal de cada uno de nosotros; o a la vida de nuestras familias sean familias del mundo o Comunidades Religiosas; o la vida de los pueblos y naciones; no hay problema, repito, por más difícil que sea, que no podamos resolver ahora con el rezo del Santo Rosario. Con el Santo Rosario nos salvaremos, nos santificaremos, consolaremos a Nuestro Señor y obtendremos la salvación de muchas almas.

[10] Y luego, la devoción al Corazón Inmaculado de María, Santísima Madre, poniéndonosla como sede de la clemencia, de la bondad y el perdón; y como puerta segura para entrar al cielo. Esta es la primera parte del Mensaje referente a Nuestra Señora de Fátima; y la segunda parte, que, aunque es más breve, no es menos importante, se refiere al Santo Padre.»

(No transcribimos esta así llamada «Segunda Parte» porque se refiere a los sufrimientos personales de Pío XII ante la situación del mundo y de la Iglesia.)

English:[6]

[1] Most esteemed Mothers and Sisters in Christ our Lord, I bring you a message of great urgency from Fatima and from Rome. I have had the opportunity to speak to Sister Lucy of Jesus, the only living witness of the apparitions of Fatima. I was given the opportunity because of the fact that I had been given charge of the causes of Beatification and Canonization of Jacinta and Francisco, cousins of Sister Lucy of Jesus.

[2] Sister Lucy has been a discalced Carmelite for the past nine years. She resides in the Convent of St. Theresa in Coimbra, Portugal. Anterior to this she was a member of the Institute of Spanish Teaching Sisters. She herself was directed by the Bishop of Fatima who passed away last year, December 4th. Sister Lucy changed to the Carmelite order under the guidance of the Holy Father (Pope Pius XII). The following are some of the words of a letter she wrote to him: "Most Holy Father, I would like to live a life of greater austerity. I would like to be less known. I wish people would not surround me with such an environment of veneration which fills me with confusion." The Holy Father answered her by not only allowing her to change to another religious order but he himself chose the order she was to enter.[7]

[3] When I visited Sister Lucy, she received me full of sadness. She is 51 years old but appears to be only about 24.

[4] The first thing she said to me was: "Father, the Blessed Virgin is very sad because no one heeds her message; neither the good nor the bad.

---

6   *Fatima Findings* (June, 1959), 1-2, 6.

7   [Author's Note: From the Carmelites' biography of Sr. Lúcia, we know that she indeed wrote to Pius XII and asked to join the Carmelite Order. However, according to the same biography, Fuentes was mistaken when he claimed that Pius XII chose the order that she was to enter (cf. Carmelo de Santa Teresa – Coimbra, *Um Caminho sob o Olhar de Maria: Biografia da Irmã Lúcia de Jesus e do Coração Imaculado, O.C.D.* (Coimbra, Portugal: Edições Carmelo, 2013), 328-333).]

The good continue on with their life of virtue and apostolate, but they do not unite their lives to the message of Fatima. Sinners keep following the road of evil because they do not see the terrible chastisement about to befall them. Believe me, Father, God is going to punish the world and very soon. The chastisement of heaven is *imminent*. In less than two years, 1960 will be here and the chastisement of heaven will come and it will be very great. Tell souls to fear not only the material punishment that will befall us if we do not pray and do penance but most of all the souls who will go to hell;" many times she repeated to me: "Many nations will disappear from the face of the earth and Russia will be the instrument of chastisement unless all of us, by prayer and sacrifice, obtain the conversion of that poor nation. Father, tell souls that the devil is carrying on a decisive battle with the Virgin Mary."

[5] But there is still time! We can still avoid the chastisement of heaven. The two weapons Our Lady has given us, said Sister Lucy, are prayer and sacrifice. She explained them to me in her own way. "Prayer," she said, "is a conversation with God, our Heavenly Father. But it is not necessary to be in Church or before a holy picture to converse with Him. We can pray everywhere, in the street, at school, in the office, the workshop—everywhere. The devil, who suffers the immense sadness of never seeing God again, will do everything in his power to keep us away from prayer and sacrifice.

[6] "All of us, regardless of our state in life, must suffer. We must suffer because of original sin and also as true followers of Christ. Everyone has some kind of affliction, contrariety, illness or problem to bear. Our Lord offers His Cross to all; we should love it then and embrace it. But we should not only accept the sufferings He sends us—we should also have the generosity to make many sacrifices. Every Christian is "*another Christ*" and as such he should be willing to pray and suffer for souls. Now as never before we should put selfishness to one side. We have to save our souls or lose them along with many other souls. Many souls depend upon our correspondence to grace. If we lose our souls we will likewise lose many other souls."

[7] Let us think, venerable Sisters of these two powerful weapons we have at our disposal. Let us keep in mind that heaven is preparing to chastise but that we can still keep back that tremendous punishment. I give you this message. It is a sign of divine predestination on the part of Our Lord Who has permitted that it reach you. How many souls would love to know of this message; it depends upon you to make it fructify. You can spread it to other souls. You can open heaven to many souls and likewise shut hell to many souls. Remember that the devil is struggling against consecrated souls. He sees that time is getting short and he is making every effort to fill hell with souls. He wants to get hold of consecrated souls.

[8] Sister Lucy said to tell souls that the two things which sanctified the souls of her cousins, Jacinta and Francisco, were to see Our Lady so full of sadness and the sight of the vision of hell. Our Lady never smiled during the apparitions. She always showed her arms extended in the form of the miraculous medal and luminous rays came forth from her hands.[8] Once when Our Lady crossed her hands over her heart, the earth was opened and the three children saw the vision of hell.[9] "What a terrible thing hell is, Father! How many souls fall into it and are tormented by the devils! Oh, how many souls go to hell!" Sister Lucy said that Our Lady's sadness and the vision of hell sanctified Jacinta and Francisco so rapidly that she has never seen souls run so generously along the road to prayer and sacrifice for sinners as these two children, and she has seen more than one soul die in the odor of sanctity since.

[9] Lucy said that Our Lady did not tell her openly that we are living

---

8   [KJS Note: Sr. Lucia never described Our Lady's position as always being like this. In fact, when she was giving instructions to Fr. Thomas McGlynn for the statue of Our Lady of Fatima, Lucia described another posture (cf. Fr. Thomas McGlynn, O.P., *Vision of Fatima*. (Boston, Massachusetts: Little Brown and Company, 1948), 62-70, 88, 112.]

9   [KJS Note: Our Lady never did this. Cf. Dr. Antonio Maria Martins, S.J., *Memórias e Cartas de Irmã Lúcia*. (Porto, Portugal: Simão Guimarães, Filhos, LDA, 1973), 339.]

in the last epoch of the world but she did give her to understand it in three ways: *First*, because she said we are going through a decisive battle, a battle at the end of which we will be either of God or of the evil one. There will be no middle way. *Second*, because Our Lady said to Lucy: "The last means that God will give to the world for its salvation are the Holy Rosary and My Immaculate Heart." The words "last means" indicate that there will be no others. *Third*, because whenever Our Lord, in the plans of His divine Providence, determines to chastise the world, He first uses every means to save us and when He sees we have not made use of them, He gives us the last anchor of salvation, His Mother.

[10] Sister Lucy emphasized the fact that all this is not for the purpose of filling souls with terror but to make souls realize the reality of the circumstances in which we are living.

[11] The second part of the message refers to the Holy Father (Pope Pius XII). He himself does not deny that in 1956 he was miraculously cured by Our Lord. He was gravely ill and praying the *"Soul of Christ, sanctify me"*. When he came to the words, *"and bid me come to Thee,"* he heard Our Lord say to him, "No, your hour has not yet come." The Holy Father arose from his bed and said Mass. Since then he has given everyone the impression of someone who is working with little time life and is making known his last desires with great urgency. He does not deny that he has seen the Blessed Virgin. He also witnessed the miracle of the sun the day before the Proclamation of the Dogma of the Assumption. The Holy Father suffers very much at the present time. A proof of this is the following incident. He recently received the primate Cardinal of Poland, Stephen Wyszynski, in private audience. They spoke over an hour and a half at the end of which he took the Cardinal by the hand to a group who were conversing together. The Holy Father then said: "I love Poland very much because all through the ages she has given proofs of her staunch faith with the blood of her bishops and priests, of her faithful of every category and in these times with the sufferings of the Cardinal Primate. How much the

Church has suffered! But the Vicar of Christ suffers all these trials in his heart, these and the trials of the entire world. The Pope suffers from all the hate and rancor of humanity and his cross is becoming so heavy that his weak shoulders can no longer carry it." On saying these words he let go of the Cardinal's hand and, burying his face in his hands, he wept bitterly. Is not this a proof of how much the Holy Father needs our support and our prayers, he who carries the Cross of Christ, the cross of the entire human race on his shoulders?

[12] My dear Sisters, now that you have heard my message, a grave responsibility rests on you. It is a personal responsibility. Sister Lucy of Jesus said to me, "Father, let us not expect the Holy Father to make a general summons to do penance, nor let us expect a general summons from our Bishops and Superiors.[10] Let each one begin himself to reform. It is a personal responsibility towards God. With prayer and penance we will not only save ourselves but others. Let us remember that we must enter heaven with many souls and that if we lose our souls, we shall also hear other souls say to us: "Through your fault, I am in hell."

[13] Beloved Sisters, let us realize that this struggle is against each one of us but also that Our Lord has given us a powerful weapon, the Holy Rosary. Sister Lucy said to me: "Father, with the new efficacy Our Lady has given to the Rosary, there is no problem in the life of anyone which cannot be solved by frequently praying the Rosary." For this reason the devil will make every effort to keep us from saying the Rosary. He will suggest a thousand excuses for neglecting it: fatigue, duties, distractions, but we must pay no need to him. Our means of salvation which is offered us is most brief and easy: the Holy Rosary! With the Rosary we will keep the Commandments, make use of the Sacraments, carry out our duties of

---

10   [KJS Note: Here the *Fatima Findings* publication inverted the lines. The uncorrected text read, "...nor let us expect a general summons from our begin himself to reform. It is a per- Bishops and Superiors. Let each one sonal responsibility towards God...." The error is herein corrected.]

state and do all that God requires of each of us.

[14] Let us save our souls. You who have heard the message have a tremendous responsibility. Be aware, venerable Sisters, that the devil will do all in his power to snatch your religious vocation from you. He will try to discourage you. His idea is that by depriving you of your vocation, he is taking away from your mission which is the *Mission of Christ*. He is full of hate and wants to take all souls to hell. Don't let him! Take the Rosary into your hands. Take this message into your hearts, carry it out and you will see how you have opened wide the gates of heaven to all souls, how you have closed the gates of hell, consoled the Heart of Christ and dried the tears of the Blessed Virgin. Then we can also say to Our Lady as Christ said to the widow of Naim, "Weep not. My Mother, week not for with my life of *prayer and sacrifice* I will lead many souls to you. I will console your heart and the Heart of your Divine Son." Amen.

—APPENDIX F—
"IS THERE A 'FOURTH SECRET' OF FATIMA?"
KEVIN J. SYMONDS
FEBRUARY, 2015

Recently, I read a copy of a magazine with an article that claimed there was new information that (allegedly) proved that there was another text of the third part of the secret of Fátima. While reading this article and checking it against the text of a Portuguese book reference in the article, I noticed some discrepancies. The present article will discuss this claim of another text and the discrepancies.

For those who need a quick refresher, the following is an outline of events relative to the discussion at hand.

From May, 1917-October, 1917, Our Lady appeared to three Portuguese children in Fátima, Portugal. Their names were Lúcia, Jacinta and Francisco. The latter two died within three years of the apparitions' end (October, 1917). Lúcia became a nun (first a Dorothean, then a Carmelite in 1948) and lived until February, 2005. During which time she wrote and explained the message of Fátima.

During the apparitions in general, Our Lady made two specific requests—that Russia be consecrated to the Immaculate Heart of Mary, and the spread of a new devotion in reparation to the Immaculate Heart called the Five First Saturdays. Also, during the July 13, 1917 apparition, Our Lady communicated a secret in three parts to the children. The first was a

vision of hell, the second the prediction of World War II and the third was of the persecution of the Church and of the Holy Father.

The first two parts of the secret were published around 1941. The third part was not committed to writing until 1944. Under obedience to her religious superiors, and at the command of Our Lady, Sister Lúcia wrote the secret down on paper, sealed it in an envelope, and communicated it to the competent ecclesiastical authority. She wrote that at the command of Our Lady, the secret was not to be opened until 1960 or upon Sister's death (she was ill at the time).

The contents of that sealed envelope remained shrouded in mystery and Catholics around the world eagerly anticipated the secret's revealing in 1960. They were shocked, however, when Pope John XXIII opened, read it and decided against publishing it. This decision led to many theories as to why this was, but such are unnecessary to recount here in this brief history.

For forty years (1960-2000) the contents of that envelope became the subject of much speculation. People stepped forward and offered various reasons as to why this was. In May, 2000, at the order of Pope John Paul II, Cardinal Angelo Sodano announced in Fátima the nature of the third secret and that Sister's full document was going to be disclosed in June of that year. This was indeed done and through the then Prefect of the Congregation for the Doctrine of the Faith, Joseph Cardinal Ratzinger (later Pope Benedict XVI).

Regretfully, the theories and speculation surrounding the document did not end with the disclosure of Sister's text. People read the text, asked questions, and did not receive answers to their satisfaction. Some have gone so far as to accuse the Holy See of covering up an alleged, as yet undisclosed, second text of the third secret. For years now these theories and accusations have dominated the discussion on the third part of the secret of Fátima and influenced countless people.

The above is the basic history. Let us now get into the heart of the matter: is there an alleged second text of the third secret?

In 2013, a biography of Sr. Lúcia was published in Portuguese entitled *Um Caminho Sob o Olhar de Maria* (A Pathway under the Gaze of Mary). This biography was drawn from the primary source texts, i.e. the public and private writings of Sr. Lúcia. In chapter 13 of this book are some truly revelatory texts that discuss how the third part of the secret came to be written down.

Within the English-speaking world, this biography went unnoticed until August, 2014. It was at this time that an article was published in Italian in which it is claimed that the new biography backs the thesis of a second text. The relevant texts were quoted in Italian translation, accompanied with some commentary. This article was translated from Italian into English and published in the above-mentioned magazine.[1]

A look at the Portuguese text of chapter 13, however, demonstrates that a closer look at the "two texts" theory is necessary. Before I explain how this is so, I am pleased to announce that the above-mentioned biography will be published by the World Apostolate of Fátima in March of this year. The title will be *A Pathway under the Gaze of Mary*. English-speaking readers will have the opportunity to read the text and decide the facts for themselves.[2]

I obtained the text of chapter 13 and had the entire chapter translated (before I knew of the impending English translation). I discussed one of the more troublesome passages with the translator in order to understand better the meaning. Between my own language background, the wise insights of the translator, and a friend who understands Portuguese culture, I came to understand clearly the text.

What chapter 13 contained was a gold mine of information that clarified some important elements of the Fátima story, and even revealed some

---

1   *The Fatima Crusader*, Issue 110, Fall 2014, pages 22-26.

2   I am not permitted by the Carmelite Sisters to use my English translation, so instead I make reference to the Portuguese text and allow the readers to check my understanding against the official English edition when it is published.

new facts—though just what they are, I will let readers see for themselves in March. I will say this much: we learn more of why Sister put the date of 1960 on the envelope containing the third secret.

To begin clarifying the text of chapter 13, there is an important distinction to make. This is between a "general" argument and a "specific" argument of those who advance a "second text" theory.

First, there is a "general" claim since the year 2000 that there is more to the third secret than what was disclosed in June, 2000. The argument went further, however to be more "specific" to say that there is a deliberate cover-up on the part of the Holy See of the existence of a second text. It is allegedly being covered up because it is so "terrifying."

Chapter 13 of the 2013 biography indicates that indeed had the *general* theory been argued alone, it would have been correct. This is because the biography quotes from the private diary of Sr. Lúcia entitled *O Meu Caminho* ("My Way") in which she records how she came to write down the third secret. It is in fact true that Sr. Lúcia wrote that there was more to the third secret than what she wrote down in 1944 and communicated to the competent ecclesiastical authority.

Where it seems an oversight has been made though is a neglecting of something that Our Lady said to Sr. Lúcia. According to Sister's diary, Our Lady appeared to her and told Sister that she was to write down what her superiors commanded of her, *but not what she was given to understand of its meaning*. This is understood to mean that Our Lady made a distinction between what Sister saw in the vision on July 13, 1917 and how she was made to understand said vision, i.e. its interpretation.

What is most peculiar is that though Our Lady's distinction is acknowledged by those who advance the "two texts" theory, there is a failure to understand the distinction at face value.[3] The words of Our Lady are

---

3   Perhaps the journalist failed to understand the text because some of the Portuguese words of Our Lady are omitted in the Italian? The Portuguese text is, "*Não temas, quis Deus provar a tua obediência, Fé e humildade, está*

taken to mean that they support the thesis of a cover-up of a second text. In fact, a simple observation disproves this claim: if Our Lady told Sister she was *not* to write down the interpretation, then *Sister did not write it down.* Moreover, if Sister had not written it down, then there can be no cover-up over a document that doesn't exist.

The above is, of course, subject to whether or not Sister later wrote the interpretation down and with Our Lady's permission. The burden of proof then is for someone to prove beyond doubt that in fact Sister wrote down the interpretation at some later point in time. If such is proven, I will be more than happy to admit my observation is incorrect. Until such a time though, the *status quaestionis* (state of the question) is going to revolve around this point.

I suspect that people might be tempted to respond to the above observation by appealing to the fact that there *was* an attempt to contact the Sisters in Coimbra but no answer was given. One must consider though that to argue for the "two texts" theory after the publication of this new biography of Sr. Lúcia puts one in a quandary.

If someone were to continue advancing the "two texts" theory, then one simultaneously argues that the Sisters are deliberately misleading the public. The Sisters would be, in fact, publishing information that leads the public one way, all the while knowing that it is not true. This is defamation of untold proportions towards cloistered nuns and ought not to be tolerated, much less countenanced.

One final point concerns the alleged writing down of the "second

---

em paz e escreve o que te mandam, não porém o que te é dado entender do seu significado..." (*Um Caminho Sob o Olhar de Maria*, pg. 266). In the Italian-English translation, the Italian word *comandano* is mistranslated, which is itself a translation of the Portuguese word *mandam* ("they command"). Both are third person plural verbs in the present tense. The translator renders *comandano* as a first person singular verb in the perfect tense ("I have commanded") and makes it sound like Our Lady commanded something/someone when it is, in fact, Sister's religious superiors being referenced.

text." There is a finer aspect that needs to be addressed and to do so it is necessary to back up and go over the history of how Sister came to write down the third part of the secret.

The reason why Sr. Lúcia wrote down the third part of the secret was because her religious superiors feared that Sister would die without revealing it and the world would lose a great grace. They ordered her to write it down. As the biography indicates, Sister was torn between obeying Our Lady who had ordered her in 1917 not to tell the secret to anyone (except Francisco), and obeying her superiors who represented the will of God.[4]

Being so torn, Sister sought guidance through prayer in late December 1943/early January 1944 and it is at this time that Our Lady appeared to Sr. Lúcia. Our Lady told Sister that her faith, humility and obedience were being tested by God, but that now she was to write down what her religious superiors commanded, but not what she was given to understand of its meaning.

It is clear that as of 1944, Sr. Lúcia would not have written a second text. Our Lady had commanded her against writing down the interpretation of the vision. Those who advance the second text theory have to address an objection. As the known history recalls, Sister Lúcia only wrote down the vision in obedience to her religious superiors. When she did, this would have satisfied their demands. One must ask what cause would they have had to "prime the pump" with Sister to ask if there was anything further?

It is possible that Sr. Lúcia's religious superiors did prime the pump.[5]

---

4   Incidentally, this fact is clearly addressed in *Um Caminho Sob o Olhar de Maria*. It also answers a claim of the "two texts" theorists that Sister was so terrified of the third secret that she could not write it down. It is clear that it was not an alleged terrifying nature of the vision that was difficult for Sister, it was her being torn on who to obey.

5   The historical record tells of one story involving a Jesuit priest named Fr. Schweigl. Under orders from Pius XII, Father went to Coimbra in 1952 and spoke with Sr. Lúcia privately and in secret. One of Schweigl's colleagues wrote a private letter to a French author who quoted it in a book. The colleague

However, the biography indicates that Sister never expressed her opinion on the interpretation of the vision. Once again, the problem still comes down to the above-mentioned *status quaestionis*. In response to this, those who advance the "two texts" theory must of necessity rest their laurels on an alleged cover-up. However, the recorded history is being widened and starting to work against the theory. It will be very interesting to see how well received the English translation of the biography will be.

In conclusion, had the discussions on the third part of the secret of Fatima revolved around the general claim that there was more to the third secret then the 2013 biography on Sr. Lúcia indicates the correctness of this position. The fact however that the claim became convoluted means the evidence now works against it. It is hoped that the English translation of the biography will go a long way to dispel these theories.

---

claimed that Schweigl distinguished the Pope from the words of Our Lady in the third secret. If this is true, then it is clear that Church authorities had opportunity to know of a distinction between the vision and its interpretation. This does not necessarily prove that a second text exists.

—Appendix G—
Book Review: *A Pathway Under the Gaze of Mary*
Kevin J. Symonds
April 13, 2015 A.D.

Shortly after Sr. Lúcia of Fátima died ten years ago, I remember remarking to someone, "Her death means we will only now come to know of things about Fátima that were previously unknown." Knowing the beautiful story of Fátima, its message, and the unfortunate controversies surrounding it, I also knew that there was a treasure to be uncovered. This treasure was guarded—and well—by Sister herself and intended by God to be known only after her death.

What is this "treasure?" This is the treasure of the interior life of Sr. Lúcia. In these ten years since her death, we have waited patiently for this treasure to be made manifest. I am happy to say that it is now becoming known in the book entitled **A Pathway Under the Gaze of Mary** published by the World Apostolate of Fátima, USA, Inc.

A Pathway Under the Gaze of Mary is destined to become an invaluable book in the literature on Fátima as it provides an in-depth look at Sister Lúcia herself. Previously, a gap existed in this area because Sister Lúcia was the source for most of what we know on Fátima. She only explained herself insofar as was necessary to spread Our Lady's message or to clarify some aspect of it. Her humility would not allow for much else, but her death provided the opportunity to fill in this lacuna and allow for a fresh perspective on the message of Fátima.

Knowing of this gap in the literature, Lucia's sisters in religion, the Carmelites of St. Teresa monastery in Coimbra, Portugal have stepped in to fill the gap. In 2013, the Sisters published the book in Portuguese under title **Um Caminho Sob a Olhar de Maria**. It is based upon public and private documents of Sr. Lúcia (among other sources) and provides an in-depth biographical—though not critical—look into Sister's life and work written by the women who lived closely with Sr. Lúcia and knew her intimately.[1] Sr. Lúcia's own words are distinguished from the commentary and narrative provided by the Sisters in italicized text.

For its part, **A Pathway Under the Gaze of Mary** can be divided into two sections. The first is Lúcia's life from birth (1907) to her entrance to the Coimbra monastery in 1948. The second half encompasses 1948 to her death in 2005 and subsequent transfer of her remains to the Fátima basilica in 2006. Some 300+ pages of the 440 given to this book are devoted to the first half of Lúcia's life and the rest are her life in the Carmel monastery.

The emphasis on the first half of Sr. Lúcia's life can be a little off-setting to the reader. This is until one realizes that it is entirely consistent with the battle that was waged within Sr. Lúcia's soul over her desire to become a Carmelite—a previously little-appreciated fact. The Carmelite Sisters do an excellent job in building up this drama, drawing from Sister's own writings. This comes across as the Sisters making Lúcia's entrance into Carmel the climax of the book and her life in it the falling action.

The theme chosen by the Carmelite Sisters for the book is fundamentally Marian, namely Our Lady's "yes" (**fiat**) to the Archangel Gabriel. Just as Mary said "yes" to the Will of God, no matter what the cost, so too did Sr. Lúcia and this provides some excellent material for prayer, meditation and theological study. This theme begins with the "yes" of Lúcia and her two cousins to Our Lady's request in May, 1917 to suffer for God.

---

1   It is also my hope that there will be efforts to have a critical edition of Sister's life and perhaps even one or more volumes of Sister's "collected letters" for the faithful.

It then runs throughout all the events of Sr. Lúcia's life and is specifically highlighted in several key moments by the Sisters, leaving no doubt as to an appropriate interpretation of events.

In choosing this theme, the Sisters are not creating a hagiography of Lúcia. In fact, the Sisters portray her in a very human way. I found myself laughing in some scenes from her life and then wanting to cry in others. The Sisters are careful to point out that though Sr. Lúcia was favored with intimate communications from heaven she still walked in the light of faith common to all in this valley of tears. Not only this, but that Lúcia also lived a simple life of prayer and sacrifice, never expecting special treatment as the "seer of Fátima." Such moments are highlighted by the Sisters, making it easier for the reader.

In addition to the above, Lúcia is also shown as having lived the interior life of virtue to a heroic degree, demonstrating a powerful and attractive supernatural current that underlay Sister's life, thoughts, and deeds. She was utterly devoted to the Holy Father and the conversion of poor sinners, praying as she was taught by the Angel of Portugal and fulfilling her promise to Our Lady. She offered up all her sufferings and mortifications for these ends and attained a high level of sanctity that is inspiring to read. One is struck by her simplicity but also her holiness.

In a sense, **A Pathway Under the Gaze of Mary** is "dangerous" because the reader is, at the same time, making an examination of conscience. This happens while he or she is drawn into an awareness of their own sinfulness and need for God's mercy as seen through the life events of Sr. Lúcia. If the reader finds him or herself caught up within this dynamic, it should be welcomed as it draws him or her closer to the true message of Fátima, namely prayer and penance.

It is to be noted that **A Pathway Under the Gaze of Mary** also offers new insights into old controversies and has potential to start new ones. As I have written previously, one will learn that there were words of Our Lady that explained the vision of the third part of the secret and why Sr.

Lúcia never revealed them. We see that there is discussion of the date of 1960 on the envelope containing said secret that calls into question the "official" narrative on the subject. We also learn that Sister was never really "silenced" by the Vatican and go deeper into what Our Lady meant when she said in 1917, "I shall appear here yet a seventh time."

The reader, however, does a disservice first to God and then him or herself if this book is read in order to satisfy curiosity over more private revelations. In fact, the relative paucity of such material will cause nothing but disappointment to the curious. This is, dare I say, deliberate and reflects Sr. Lúcia's own life and desires to escape such people in order to be with God—a facet admirably illustrated by the Carmelite Sisters. It is this dynamic of Sister's interior life that provides the necessary context for many of the controversies surrounding Fátima. We owe a debt of gratitude to the Carmelite Sisters for clarifying it, as well as for the book itself.

Simply put, **A Pathway Under the Gaze of Mary** is intended to help people become saints by giving them the example of the beautiful soul of Sr. Lúcia. It is the story of a shepherdess transformed by grace under the gaze and protection of the Immaculate Heart of Mary who promised to be a refuge and the path that leads to God. These words, spoken by Our Lady to and for Sr. Lúcia, also speak to all who follow the path of prayer and penance as outlined in the message of Fátima. Everything else within this book is secondary, as it should be, to the context of Sister's life and the obedience under which she lived faithfully for many decades.

In the end, if the reader picks up this book with a mind towards wanting to be holy, then he or she reads in a good spirit. **A Pathway Under the Gaze of Mary** will show them heights of holiness that are needed in a world where we are bringing punishment upon ourselves by not amending our lives and falling further into sin. Let us then follow the example of Sr. Lúcia and always give our "yes" to God and accept that which He sends us for our sanctification.

—APPENDIX H—
In Defense of the World Apostolate of Fátima
Kevin J. Symonds
July 5, 2015 A.D.

The World Apostolate of Fatima, USA Inc. recently published a biography of Sr. Lúcia—the last surviving visionary of Fátima (†2005)—entitled **A Pathway Under the Gaze of Mary**. The book itself was a translation of a Portuguese biography entitled **Um Caminho Sob o Olhar de Maria** and was published in 2013 by the Carmelite Sisters of Coimbra, Portugal. This translation was critiqued recently, and I would like to respond to the critique as a whole.

The critique makes two particular assertions for our consideration here. The first is an observation and the second is an erroneous claim. The observation concerns the translation of a key text within the new biography of Sr. Lúcia. The claim is that the publisher is "hiding" the "real" text. Before I respond, let me first briefly explain the matter at hand.

Background

Back in February, I wrote an article entitled **Is There a "Fourth Secret" of Fatima**. In this article, I discussed the apparitions of Our Lady of Fátima within the context of some theories surrounding her message and the publication of a new biography of Sr. Lúcia. The principle theory

identified in the article is what I labeled the "two-text" theory.[1] Those who subscribe to this theory were identified as "two-text theorists."

After the publication of the Portuguese text of **Um Caminho Sob o Olhar de Maria**, the World Apostolate of Fatima, USA Inc. (WAF-USA) was given the rights from the Coimbra convent to publish the book in English translation. Unfortunately, the existence of the Portuguese biography was not announced too well in the English-speaking world.

The above changed when an Italian journalist learned of the biography and wrote about it in August, 2014. Said journalist wrote an article in which he discussed a revelatory piece of information from chapter 13 of the biography. This article was read and translated from Italian into English and published.[2]

The new "revelation" in the biography is an indication that the third part of the secret of Fátima was comprised of what I will here call "visual" and "interpretative" components. The "visual" component was a supernatural vision and the "interpretative" one appears to be an as yet unknown explanation of the vision (it is presumed to have been given by Our Lady).

The biography states that the Virgin Mary appeared to Sr. Lúcia on January 3, 1944. This was after Sister had been ordered by her religious superiors to write down the third part of the secret. Sister was torn over obedience. Our Lady had said in 1917 not to tell the secret to anyone (except her cousin Francisco), but Sister's religious superiors were ordering the contrary. Our Lady appeared to Sr. Lúcia in 1944 and said, "….be at peace and write what they command you, not, however, what is given to you to understand of its significance."[3]

In the above quotation, we see that Our Lady made the distinction

---

1   The theory states that the third part of the secret of Fátima has two parts. The first was revealed in the year 2000 by the Holy See, but, says the theory, it is allegedly covering up another text purported to be from Sr. Lúcia.

2   **Fatima Crusader** (Fall 2014, Issue 110, pages 22-26).

3   I am here using my own translation of the Portuguese.

between the "visual" and the "interpretative" components. She told Lúcia to write down what she saw, i.e. the "vision," but not what she was given to understand of its meaning.[4]

This was truly a revelation because for years it was debated whether or not there were words of Our Lady that explained the vision (which was published in the year 2000). Having the confirmation in Sr. Lúcia's own handwriting that an interpretation did, in fact, exist—but which was not intended by Our Lady in 1944 for public consumption—was as valuable as it was remarkable. As remarkable as it is, the effort from two-text theorists has been rejuvenated.[5]

The "Observation"

The recent critique makes the observation that there was a mistranslation of the above key text. On this simple point, I agree that the text was mistranslated. The WAF-USA's translation is, "Be at peace and write what they order you, but do not give your opinion of its meaning." A more literal rendering of the Portuguese text is what I gave above, namely, "....be at peace and write what they command you, not, however, what is given to you to understand of its significance."

---

4   This phrase is largely being interpreted to mean that there was some understanding of the vision given to Sr. Lúcia at an unspecified point in time. "Two-texts" theorists are interpreting the meaning given to Sr. Lúcia as continuing the debated phrase, "In Portugal, the dogma of the faith shall always be preserved..." from July, 1917. Here, Sister broke off the narration with a simple "etc." hence the debate over whether there were more words of Our Lady. That there were more words of Our Lady is not necessarily a foregone conclusion at this time and is still a matter of debate.

5   The critique against WAF-USA accuses the Apostolate of mistranslating the Portuguese text in the key area already discussed. The reader is reminded of the salient observation made in endnote 3 of my article **Is There a "Fourth Secret" of Fatima**? Though we respectfully disagree on some finer points, I **do** respect the professional accomplishments of this particular writer.

The mistranslation is particularly questionable because it makes the discourse of Our Lady to be about Sister's **opinion** as opposed to an actual **interpretation** given to her by heaven. This mistranslation lends itself to the belief of two-text theorists that there is a cover-up of the third part of the secret of Fátima. This is why the critique in question states that WAF-USA is trying to "hide" something.

The Erroneous Claim

While it is true that an error was made in translation, does it follow that there was a mistranslation with means to "hide" the truth? Just how did the text in question come to be mistranslated? I am in a position to address this matter and shall do so presently. WAF-USA has issued its own response. To shed further light, I would like to share my own personal story with WAF-USA's roll-out of **A Pathway Under the Gaze of Mary**.

For research purposes, I had contacted WAF-USA in February of this year (2015). I requested of the National Coordinator of WAF-USA, to read the Apostolate's translation of chapter 13. To make a long story short, I was directed to the editor of the biography translation. We spoke at some length between phone and E-mail correspondence beginning on February 27. As the correspondence developed, I asked if it would be possible to read the entire book in advance to write a review for **Catholic Stand**.

At first, I was given permission to read chapter 13 only.[6] This was given on Wednesday, March 4, 2015. This was the same day that the book had gone to the printer. By March 12, I had read the chapter and noted the above discussed mistranslation. I pointed it out to the editor and this was submitted to WAF-USA officials.

Simply stated, the answer that I received was that it was now very

---

6   I later received the entire book in PDF format on March 24 for the purpose of my review.

late in the editorial process; it was too late to make any changes. According to a notice by the Carmelite Sisters, the publishing date was slated for March 22, but this ended up being delayed until April 13. Those familiar with the publishing world know that a printing company needs a final copy in order to print. Once the final seal of approval is given, any further changes incur a fee.

Based on the above, WAF-USA was going to go with the translation "as is" but with the caveat that there was going to be a second edition. Moreover, if I understood correctly what I was told, there were already plans for a second edition even before I pointed out the error on March 12.

In sharing the above, I make no excuses for WAF-USA, nor am I trying to throw it under the bus. I share the story because the above-mentioned critique assigns a negative characterization to the intentions of WAF-USA. This is inaccurate simply because the Apostolate did not know of the mistranslation until it was essentially too late. They had every intention of correcting this error in the second edition.

Moreover, one should ask a very important question: was WAF-USA contacted prior to the publication of the critique? Consider also that for the last several months, I myself have made 3-4 attempts to contact the author of the critique, including once on E-mail. In the times that I called, message was left with a gentleman whose name escapes me. The past two calls in particular were to discuss important matters related to recent remarks on Fátima made by the critique's author. **None** of my communications have received a response, written or verbal.

Conclusion

I think that everything written above boils down to people needing to be more careful and diligent. **All** of us are duty-bound to inform ourselves. Moreover, people must consider that we are dealing with the simple reality of the messiness that is humanity and its being prone to making mistakes.

It is a fact that **Um Caminho Sob o Olhar de Maria** largely went unnoticed in the English-speaking world. This changed when the Italian journalist's August 2014 article was publicized in that world. One can express a wish or desire for a better roll-out of the biography, but the fact is that we are dealing with some unique realities. First, there is the simple fact of working with cloistered nuns. Second, said book is in a foreign language and culture that, in my experience, is not too well understood in the English-speaking world.

For their part, all the Carmelite Sisters wanted was to tell the world of the beautiful soul of their fellow sister in religion, Lúcia of Fátima. Their primary goal is to show people a beautiful pathway to God through Mary as reflected in the life of Sr. Lúcia. Their aim is the interior life and Carmelite religious observance, **not** marketing strategies. They left the latter to the competency of others. This focus on the spiritual as opposed to the temporal has always been a terribly misunderstood, or at least little-appreciated, aspect of the history of Fátima and it is time that we give it its due. Let us be mindful of the fact that God uses poor instruments and that God's power is made perfect in infirmity (2 Corinthians 12:9).

Having been privy to a part of the roll-out of **A Pathway Under the Gaze of Mary** with the World Apostolate of Fatima, I can state that the folks at the Apostolate that I have met are honest and simple people who just want to serve God and Our Lady. Moreover, I understand that the Apostolate's staff is very small and limited and that this affected the roll-out. Mistakes were made, but I am sure that any questions posed to the Apostolate are received and answered charitably.

Finally, let us also keep everything in proper perspective. We are discussing a sentence from a book wherein it is explicitly indicated by the Virgin Mary herself that at least as of January 3, 1944, certain information was **not** to be given to the public. Unless the Will of God ordained it to be communicated at a later time—**and irrefutable evidence of this fact is provided to the public**—one might just be arguing the Will of God and

this can only displease the Almighty. This is the "state of the question," all else notwithstanding.

Update: 8-31-15 A.D.

I have updated Endnote iv to reflect more carefully the current terms of the debate on Fátima and the **status quaestionis** of the third part of the secret and Sr. Lúcia's understanding thereof.

—Appendix I—
Our Lady of Fátima and the Reality of Hell
Kevin J. Symonds
November 19, 2015 A.D.

The following article is included in the Appendices as it offers a reflection upon the consequence of not heeding Our Lady's call at Fátima to conversion.

In the apparitions of Our Lady of Fátima, there are 2 striking aspects. These aspects are the miracle of the sun and the famous three-part secret. Recently, I had cause to think about one of the parts of the secret, namely the vision of hell. There are some intriguing questions about Fátima and hell in relation to some contemporary theological views that deserve some treatment.

To begin treating these questions, it is first necessary to state the contents of the three-part secret of Fátima.

The Three-Part Secret: the Vision of Hell

In July, 1917, Our Lady gave a revelation to the three little seers—Bls. Francisco and Jacinta Marto, and Lúcia Santos who later entered the religious life and is best known as "Sr. Lúcia." This revelation was composed of three parts and known as "the secret." These parts are: 1) a vision of hell, 2) a prediction of World War II, and 3) a prediction of Russia spreading its errors.

While the secret is meant to be seen as an integral whole, I will focus here upon the vision of hell. Here is how Sr. Lúcia described the vision in her *Fourth Memoir*:

> [Our Lady said:] "Sacrifice yourselves for sinners and say many times, especially when you make some sacrifice: Jesus, it is for Your love, for the conversion of sinners and in reparation for the sins committed against the Immaculate Heart of Mary."
>
> When the Lady spoke these words She opened Her hands as She had in the two months before. The radiance seemed to penetrate the ground and we saw something like a sea of fire. Plunged in this fire were the demons and the souls, as if they were red-hot coals, transparent and black or bronze-colored, with human forms, which floated about in the conflagration, borne by the flames which issued from it with clouds of smoke falling on all sides as sparks fall in great conflagrations without weight or equilibrium, among shrieks and groans of sorrow and despair that horrify and cause people to shudder with fear....
>
> The devils were distinguished by horrible and loathsome forms of animals, frightful and unknown, but transparent like black coals that have turned red-hot. Frightened and as if we were appealing for help, we raised our eyes to our Lady who said with tenderness and sadness.
>
> "You saw hell, where the souls of poor sinners go. To save them God wishes to establish in the world the devotion to my Immaculate Heart. If they do what I will tell you, many souls will be saved, and there will be peace... (Memórias e Cartas de Irmã Lúcia. Porto: 1973, 340-341).

This terrible sight shocked Lúcia so much that it caused her to cry out during the vision and was overheard by onlookers. The vision that the

three children saw deeply affected them for the rest of their lives. Francisco and Jacinta would not live long after the miracle of the sun in October, 1917, but Lúcia went on to live until February 13, 2005—just shy of her 98th birthday.

About a month after the vision of hell, in August, 1917, Our Lady appeared once more to the children. Still, perhaps, feeling deeply the effects of the vision of hell from the previous month, the three children were reminded once more of the gravity of hell. Writing of this particular encounter with Our Lady in August, 1917, Sr. Lúcia writes:

> And then in a more sad way, the Lady said, "Pray, pray a great deal, and make sacrifices for sinners, for many souls go to hell because they have no one to sacrifice and pray for them" (*Memórias e Cartas de Irmã Lúcia*. Porto: 1973, 345).

It is this last statement about how "many souls go to hell" that deserves some discussion.

Many Souls Go to Hell

This statement is perhaps very stark. Does not the Church teach about grace, repentance and final perseverance? Can we not hope that men will be saved? Moreover, how can we know the number of people who are in hell, much less the rate at which they do so?

It is true that people can repent up to the moment that they draw their last breath. It is also true that the Church cannot pronounce in a solemn manner on the number of souls in hell. These truths of our faith, however, are not in question with the statement at hand from Our Lady. To focus upon said truths would be, I humbly submit, a distraction from the reality of the consequences of man's actions against God and His Church that Our Lady was impressing upon the visionaries, and by extension, to us. I am

speaking of the rejection of God and His Church by revolutionaries, liberals (in the classical 19th century definition given in the book *Liberalism is a Sin*), etc.

Though I believe it to be a distraction, I also recognize that many people today will remain unconvinced of the above observation. Thus I will, for the sake of edification, offer a discussion on the above-mentioned truths of our faith.

We know souls go to hell, Christ Himself affirms this (Matthew 5:22, 29-30; 7:13; 25:41), but just how many go and how many are present there is beyond our knowledge. This fact is limited though as it is only true for this present age. It is not now the time of the *eschaton* when such knowledge is manifested. In this, the present age, the number of the people of God is not yet complete. It would thus be foolish for the Church to give a figure on the number of souls in hell. This number has the potential to change at any given second![1]

The knowledge of who is damned is remote from the intellect of man, thus a prophetic utterance by supernatural means is necessary if we are to know anything about what happens beyond the veil of this life to the next. This process was expounded upon by St. Thomas Aquinas (ST II:II, q. 171 a. 3). If, in August of 1917, Our Lady revealed to the three seers that "many souls go to hell," then this is an act of prophecy. As such, the most we can do this side of heaven is to see if such prophetic utterances contradict the Deposit of Faith. From even the most cursory glance at the New Testament, one can see that the utterance in question does not contradict the Deposit.

---

1   The number of world-wide deaths for the past several years has consistently been around 55 million people per year.... This statistic should impress more deeply the reason why the Church cannot pronounce on the number of people in hell.

Help the Faithful Live the Gospel

It is important to make two observations on the use of the adjective "many" by Our Lady. The first is that the word is not qualified with a statement of time. Our Lady does not say "in all epochs of human history, many souls go to hell." If, as Joseph Cardinal Ratzinger pointed out in his June, 2000 Theological Commentary in the *Message of Fatima*, the purpose of private revelation is to help the faithful live the Gospel at a particular moment in history, then it is fair to understand Our Lady could be referring *at the very least* to a period of time before, during and after her apparitions in Fátima.

Moreover, on this last point, given the atrocities of the twentieth century (to say nothing of events from the nineteenth and the present century thus far), if "many souls go to hell," it is not all that surprising. In the twentieth century alone, there were two World Wars, countless genocides, the Korean & Vietnam Wars, Atheistic Communism trampling upon the rights of God and man, secularism/laicism, etc. Numerous Papal statements from Leo XIII to St. John Paul II easily testify to and deplore these and other atrocities.

The reality of the twentieth century, however, is not very popular due to various trends in contemporary theology built upon atheistic and integral humanism. There is a tendency to take the ignorance provided by the veil between time and eternity and claim the hope that all men might be saved. I do not intend to get into the finer points of this position, but I will point out an underappreciated side-effect. It has cooled devotion and piety within souls resulting in a healthy fear of hell and its horrors not being communicated, which Jesus and the Apostles clearly saw as necessary through their preaching and teaching. Why else would they preach on it? Hell is very real and an equally very real trend exists today to downplay it. I myself have seen terrible things to this effect.

The second observation is that (and without prejudice to the first

observation) there is something to be said for the *reason* why Our Lady stated "many souls go to hell...." She said there is no one to pray and make sacrifices for them. Surely prayer and sacrifice for the conversion of sinners is a timeless Christian practice, applicable in any day and age (the question of whether a few or many souls go to hell notwithstanding)? Here, Our Lady is putting the emphasis upon us by reminding us of *our duty and responsibility* to pray for sinners. To get caught up in a squabble over the adjective "many" could very well serve as a distraction from the onus of the request to pray and make sacrifices.

One final consideration concerns the nature of private revelation vs. public revelation. It is true that the apparitions of Our Lady at Fátima belong to the theological category of private revelation. As such, they are not part of the Deposit of Faith to which all Catholics must adhere with Divine and Catholic Faith. Private revelation is taken on the level of human faith, according to the teaching of Cardinal Lambertini/Pope Benedict XIV in his famous treatise *De Servorum Dei*. Based on these principles, one is free to accept or reject an authentic private revelation without fear of apostasy.

Conversely, one is wise to use a "help which is offered" even if he or she is "not obliged" to use it (cf. Joseph Cardinal Ratzinger's *Theological Commentary* on *The Message of Fatima*, June 26, 2000). The place of prophecy within the life of the Church is valid and must always work *in tandem* with the juridical authority of the Church. There is also the Apostolic mandate not to despise prophecy (1 Thessalonians 5:19-20). If a person decided not to live the message of Fátima this must not be done with scorn, hatred or malice. While it is true that no act of apostasy is performed in rejecting the message, if done in scorn, hatred or malice then such might very well reveal an "apostasy" already present in one's heart.

The Appeal of Our Lady

In the end, Our Lady's statement at Fátima in August, 1917 is in-

tended to impress upon the Church the reality and gravity of hell. This impression, however, is not for its own sake. The other half of the statement is a clarion call for all of us to pray and make sacrifices for sinners so that they *do not* end up in hell. This is the point of reminding us about hell and we should take this seriously. To this effect, we have the Five First Saturdays devotion Our Lady requested at Fátima, recitation of the Holy Rosary, and our other prayers and sacrifices.

Finally, let us remember the words of Pope St. John Paul II. He stated that, "The appeal of the Lady of Fatima is so deeply rooted in the Gospel and the whole of Tradition that the Church feels committed to this message" (*Il contenuto dell'appello della Signora di Fatima è così profondamente radicato nel Vangelo e in tutta la Tradizione, che la Chiesa si sente impegnata da questo messaggio*). Thus, one cannot state that the question of hell within the message of Fátima is contrary to Divine Revelation.

—Appendix J—
On the Third part of The Secret of Fátima
A Presentation by Kevin J. Symonds

Delivered in Fátima during the 24th Mariological Congress
September 8, 2016 A.D.

Good afternoon: Very reverend Fathers, religious brothers and sisters, ladies and gentlemen, esteemed colleagues and devotees of Our Blessèd Lady. It is truly an honor to be with you at this prestigious Conference in Fátima—the place blessed by Our Lady's presence nearly 100 years ago. I hope that you find the talk to be thought-provoking and challenging. Our topic, *On the Third Part of the Secret of Fátima*, is written from the heart but with scholarly perspective.

Much mystery, suspense, intrigue and sensational speculation have surrounded the third part of the secret for several decades. Regretfully, these issues have caused discussions on the overall secret to become mired in seemingly endless controversy, resulting in an utterly tragic misunderstanding of Our Lady's message. In the light of the upcoming centenary of Fátima, I intend in this paper briefly to make some observations concerning these distortions. Let us begin by pointing out the present *status quaestionis* of the discussions.

Currently, there are two considerable points of view on the message

of Fátima in relation to the present. The first is expressed by Cardinals Josef Ratzinger and Angelo Sodano in the Congregation for the Doctrine of the Faith's booklet entitled *The Message of Fatima*. It states that the "events [of the third part of the secret] now seem to pertain to the past."[1] The second point of view, which enjoys support within the Anglo- and Francophone worlds, holds a contradictory position, namely that there are unfulfilled or undisclosed prophecies and/or revelations.[2] The tension created between these two contradicting positions places us at a crossroad, a turning point, and the direction in which we go could affect the future of how we understand *and live* the message of Our Lady of Fátima. In order to demonstrate this reality, let us examine, briefly, the two positions, beginning with the first one mentioned above.

In the booklet *The Message of Fatima*, the Holy See released the text of the third part of the secret. The text's general portrayal of the suffering of the Holy Father, persecution of the Church, and the spread of Russia's errors was accompanied by supporting documentation which included a *Theological Commentary* from Cardinal Ratzinger. This *Commentary* discussed the text within the context of the Church's theology of Public and private revelation as well as treated the individual symbols and images contained within the vision. At the time of its publication, certain circles of Catholics were incredulous of the booklet and immediately questioned the Vatican, believing there to be more revelatory text than what was published.

A particular point, as stated earlier, was that the events to which the text refers now seem to pertain to the past, specifically the twentieth century. Owing in part to events since the beginning of the twenty-first centu-

---

1   Congregation for the Doctrine of the Faith, *The Message of Fatima*. (Vatican City: Libreria Editrice Vaticana, 2000), 31, 43.

2   Cf. Christopher A. Ferrara, *The Secret Still Hidden*. (Pound Ridge, New York: Good Counsel Publications, 2008). Hereafter *The Secret Still Hidden* followed by page number.

ry, many of the faithful are dissatisfied with the Vatican's position.[3] They see many ills plaguing the Church and seek supernatural enlightenment in order to understand the "signs of the times" that are about them. Among them is a general tendency to be distrustful of ecclesiastical authority, and to turn to private revelation (I speak here specifically on this occasion of Fátima in this regard) for supernatural enlightenment and vision.[4]

On a pastoral level, one can understand these sentiments as there are many issues within the Church that need to be addressed by the competent ecclesiastical authorities. The question before us is whether or not Fátima and its secret may be used to interpret these issues. Concerning this question, some recent information has been published that affords us an opportunity to re-assess matters. This information is contained in a biography of Sr. Lúcia, compiled by the Carmelite Sisters of the convent of St. Teresa in Coimbra, and entitled *Um Caminho sob o Olhar de Maria*.[5] Published in 2013 in Portuguese and released in English translation (April, 2015) as *A Pathway Under the Gaze of Mary*, their biography is a gift to the Church as it offers *much* clarity on various issues. Above all else, the biography affords to both scholars and devotees of Our Lady a piercing glance into the interior life of Sr. Lúcia—a noticeably neglected component in the history and literature of Fátima.[6] As the principal interlocutor of Our Lady

---

3   Ibid. See also Fr. Paul L. Kramer, *The Devil's Final Battle: Our Lady's Victory Edition*. (Good Counsel Publications, 2010). See also the earlier edition of this book from the year 2002 under the same title (without the subtitle).

4   For more information on this phenomenon, see my article entitled *The Greatest of Pastoral Care*: <http://www.catholiclane.com/the-greatest-of-pastoral-care/> (Accessed 31 August, 2016).

5   Carmelo de Santa Teresa – Coimbra, *Um Caminho sob o Olhar de Maria: Biografia da Irmã Lúcia de Jesus e do Coração Imaculado, O.C.D.* (Coimbra, Portugal: Edições Carmelo, 2013). Hereafter *Um Caminho sob o Olhar de Maria* followed by page number.

6   Cardinal Bertone once relayed that Sr. Lúcia spoke of herself as being the "last obstacle" to the secret (Tarcisio Cardinal Bertone, *The Last Secret of Fatima*. [New York: Doubleday, 2008], 80). This remark received some criticism

and her messenger, it is *imperative* that the life and person of Sr. Lúcia be understood; truly, a debt of gratitude is owed to the Carmelite Sisters in Coimbra for their labor of love.

One of the more notable events revealed in *Um Caminho* is the apparition of Our Lady to Sr. Lúcia in early January, 1944 wherein Sister received permission to write down the third part of the secret. This apparition was known to Fátima scholars, but a description of the event penned by Sr. Lúcia herself appears not to have been provided to the public, or at least not in the English-speaking world.[7] We now possess Sister's own account of the apparition wherein a most startling fact is revealed: Our Lady ordered Sr. Lúcia to "write down what they [Sister's religious superiors] command you, not, however, what is given to you to understand of its significance."[8] This revelation is "startling" because it indicates that Sr. Lúcia knew something more about the third part of the secret. Whether or not she ever revealed it is uncertain at this time, though we know she gave some general indications in her May, 1982 letter to Pope John Paul II.

These facts have the potential to make scholars ponder the relationship between this new revelation and the characterizations and/or interpretations given in *The Message of Fatima* booklet. When this booklet was published, Ratzinger stated to Italian journalist Marco Politi that the Church did not wish to impose an interpretation on the faithful.[9] This fact

---

(*The Secret Still Hidden*, 103-106), but was vastly misunderstood. For more information on the importance of knowing the interior life of Sr. Lúcia, see my book review of *A Pathway Under the Gaze of Mary*: <http://www.catholicstand. com/book-review-pathway-gaze-mary/> (Accessed 31 August, 2016).

7   Cf. Frère Michel de la Sainte Trinité, *The Whole Truth About Fatima. Volume III: The Third Secret.* (Buffalo, New York: Immaculate Heart Publications, 1990), 46-48.

8   *Um Caminho sob o Olhar de Maria*, 266.

9   Taken from the Q&A section of the June 26, 2000 Press Conference which introduced the publication of the text. Ratzinger stated, "…[M]a non è intenzione della Chiesa di imporre una interpretazione…" (But it is not the

leaves freedom for scholars who wish to pose—and answer—various questions which need to be addressed. Indeed, we have seen this need, for example, since 2014 from articles that were published first in Italian, then English.[10] These articles demonstrate that *immediate* clarity is necessary so as to lessen the opportunities for distraction against and distortion of the message of Our Lady of Fátima.

I noted earlier that scholars should ponder this new revelation with the information presented in the booklet *The Message of Fatima*. How should scholars go about addressing this matter? Along what interpretive lines ought they to follow? To answer these questions, let us ask two things: first, have we *truly* reflected upon and understood well the contents of the booklet *The Message of Fatima*, especially Cardinal Ratzinger's *Theological Commentary*? Secondly, was the point of view expressed in *The Message of Fatima* correct or is there room to question it, charitably and respectfully? To both of these questions, let us consider the words of French author and writer Yves Chiron. Earlier this year, Chiron stated "to re-read [Ratzinger's] Theological Commentary would be more useful and profitable, intellectually and spiritually, than [to] listen to the 'pure inventions, absolutely false'" of various people.[11] When one examines and studies the *Commentary* more closely, a beautiful, intricate world and picture of Fátima is discovered. This world possesses a depth and richness into

---

intention of the Church to impose an interpretation...).

10   See the Italian article entitled *Novita' Apocalittiche da Fatima (L'Ultim Mistero: Il Silenzio delle Suore, ma Chi Tace...)* by Antonio Socci. This article was published on his personal web site on 17 August, 2014 and is available via the *Internet Archive Wayback Machine*: <https://web.archive.org/web/20140820000910/http://www.antoniosocci.com/2014/08/novita-apocalittiche-da-fatima-lultimo-mistero-il-silenzio-delle-suore-ma-chi-tace/> (Accessed 31 August, 2016). For the English article, see Christopher Ferrara's article in *The Fatima Crusader*, Issue 110, Fall 2014, pages 22-26.

11   See <https://kevinsymonds.com/2016/06/08/chiron-and-fatima/> (Accessed 31 August, 2016).

theological systems and formulae with roots in the Patristic Age. Indeed, a deeper study of the *Commentary* is necessary.

It is truly saddening, in reading various pieces of literature, to see otherwise well-meaning but (in my opinion) woefully misguided writers attack and misrepresent the *Theological Commentary* either in part, or its whole. It is precisely this sort of literature which has successfully managed to bind the hearts and minds of many of the faithful into a false conception of the message of Fátima—particularly the third part of the secret. Who among us has not heard some modicum of wild theories and accusations presently available for free on the Internet or elsewhere? In the light of the upcoming centenary, when many eyes are on Fátima, it seems fitting that an objective, fact-based and in-depth assessment addressing these speculations be undertaken. To this end, for the past year or so, I have endeavored to research several areas of note and attempt to put conspiracies behind us and focus upon the truth of Our Lady's message. The fruit of this research is being organized into book format, a rough bound copy of which is present here, and tentatively titled *On the Third Part of the Secret of Fátima*.

In concluding, I would like to highlight the Apostolic Voyage of Pope Benedict XVI to Portugal in 2010 and the challenge it offers us. While at the Lisbon airport the Holy Father stated that Our Lady "came from heaven to remind us of Gospel truths that constitute for humanity – so lacking in love and without hope for salvation – the source of hope."[12] Later, he famously remarked that Fátima's prophetic mission is not complete.[13] It remains for us, as devotees of Our Lady, to learn at her feet, contemplating the Divine Mysteries of Her Son, from the one who "treasured all these things in her heart" (Luke 2:19) in order to make a place for Jesus in

---

12   *Acta Apostolicae Sedis* 102 [2010], 339-340. English translation courtesy of the Vatican's web site: <http://w2.vatican.va/content/benedict-xvi/en/speeches/2010/may/documents/hf_ben-xvi_spe_20100511_accoglienza-ufficiale.html> (Accessed 23 May, 2016).

13   *Acta Apostolicae Sedis* 102 (2010), 327.

our hearts. From there to go out—*as prophets*—to re-evangelize a world *deeply* impacted by the errors of Russia and which is much in need of the Gospel of Jesus Christ. This is the true message of Our Lady, and is how we bring about the Triumph of the Immaculate Heart of Mary—by repentance, doing penance, making reparation, and inculcating the devotion to her Immaculate Heart (the path which is held out to us at Fátima) thereby opening us to the purity of heart by which we see God (Matthew 5:8).[14] May the upcoming centenary of Our Lady's apparitions in Fátima ignite in our hearts, as Pope Benedict XVI stated, the desire for the "sweet joys" of God.[15] Thank you.

---

14   These thoughts were expressed by Cardinal Ratzinger in his *Theological Commentary*.

15   <http://w2.vatican.va/content/benedict-xvi/en/homilies/2010/may/documents/hf_ben-xvi_hom_20100513_fatima.html> (Accessed 26 May, 2016).

—Bibliography—

A

Alonso, Joaquín María. "O Segredo de Fátima: Conjuro de Uma Palavra." *Fatima 50* (May, 1967): 30-31, 38-39.

------------ "Fatima y la Critica." *Ephemerides Mariologicae* 17 (1967): 392-435.

------------ "O Segredo de Fátima: A Economia da Sua Progressiva Manifestação." *Fatima 50* (September, 1967): 23, 28.

------------ "O Segredo de Fátima: A Terceira "Coisa" do Segredo." *Fatima 50* (October, 1967):11.

------------ "O Segredo de Fátima: O Conteúdo." *Fatima 50* (November, 1967): 14-16.

------------ "O Segredo de Fátima: Gravidade e Seriedade." *Fatima 50* (December, 1967): 4-5.

------------ *História da Literatura sobre Fátima*. Fatima, Portugal: Edições Santuário, 1967.

------------ *La Verdad sobre el Secreto de Fatima: Fátima sin mitos*. Madrid, Espana: Centro Mariano, 1976.

------------ *The Secret of Fatima: Fact and Legend.* Cambridge, Massachusetts: The Ravengate Press, 1979.

------------ *La Vérité sur le Secret de Fatima.* Paris: Téqui, 1979.

------------ "De Nuevo el Secreto de Fátima." *Ephemerides Mariologicae* 32 (1982): 93.

Anderson, Wendy Love. *The Discernment of Spirits: Assessing Visions and Visionaries in the Late Middle Ages.* Tübingen, Germany: Mohr Siebeck, 2011.

Armstrong, April and Armstrong, Martin. *Fatima: Pilgrimage to Peace.* [Garden City, New York: Hanover House, 1954.

B

Barreto, José. "Edouard Dhanis, Fatima e a II Guerra Mundial." *Brotéria* 156 (January, 2003): 13-22.

Benedict XVI, Pope. "Interview of the Holy Father Benedict XVI with the Journalists During the Flight to Portugal." Last modified Unknown. Accessed May 14, 2016. http://w2.vatican.va/content/benedict-xvi/en/speeches/2010/may/documents/hf_ben-xvi_spe_20100511_portogallo-interview.html.

------------ "Homily of His Holiness Benedict XVI. May 13, 2010." Last modified unknown. Accessed May 26, 2016. http://w2.vatican.va/content/benedict-xvi/en/homilies/2010/documents/hf_ben-xvi_hom_20100513_fatima.html.

------------ *Light of the World: A Conversation with Peter Seewald.* San Francisco, California: Ignatius Press, 2010.

Bertone, Tarcisio con Giuseppe De Carli. *L'Ultima Veggente di Fatima: I Miei Colloqui con Suor Lucia.* Milano: Rai Eri Rizzoli, 2007.

------------ *The Last Secret of Fatima*. New York: Doubleday, 2008.

Bertone, Tarcisio con Giuseppe De Carli. *L'Ultima Segreto di Fatima*. Milano: Rai Eri Rizzoli, 2010.

Bogle, Joanna. "The Boring Third Secret of Fatima." Last modified unknown. Accessed August 13, 2016. http://www.catholicworldreport. com/Blog/4819/the_boring_third_secret_of_fatima.aspx.

------------ "No, Benedict XVI hasn't been brainwashed." Last modified unknown. Accessed August 13, 2016. http://www.catholicherald. co.uk/issues/july-29th-2016/no-benedict-xvi-hasnt-been-brain-washed.

Boland, Vivian. *St. Thomas Aquinas*. London: Continuum International Publishing Group, 2007.

Borelli Machado, Antonio. "Some Friendly Reflections for the Clarification of a Debate." *Lepanto Foundation*. Last modified Unknown. Accessed December 5, 2015. https://web.archive.org/ web/20140211073510/http:/www.lepantofoundation.org/wp-content/uploads/2010/05/Friendly-Reflections_Lepanto03.pdf.

------------ "Mensagem de Fátima: Por que o 3° Segredo de Fátima não foi divulgado em 1960?" *Catolicismo* N°790 (Outubro, 2016): 10-21. English translation: http://www.pcpbooks.net/email17.html.

Boyce, David. "Fatima Inquest – August 1990." Last modified unknown. Accessed 3 November, 2016. http://www.fatimacrusader.com/cr35/ cr35pg12.asp.

Brochado, Costa. *Fátima in the Light of History*. Milwaukee, Wisconsin: The Bruce Publishing Company, 1955.

Brown, Michael. "Around the World: From the Mail." *Spirit Daily*. Last modified unknown. Accessed August 3, 2016. http://www.spiritdaily.net/A69Popethirdsecret.htm.

C

Carlen, Claudia, edit. *The Papal Encyclicals 1878-1903. Volume II.* Raleigh, North Carolina: The Pierian Press, 1990.

------------ *The Papal Encyclicals: 1903-1922. Volume III.* Raleigh, North Carolina: The Pierian Press, 1990.

Carmelo de Santa Teresa – Coimbra. *Um Caminho sob o Olhar de Maria: Biografia da Irmã Lúcia de Jesus e do Coração Imaculado, O.C.D.* Coimbra, Portugal: Edições Carmelo, 2013.

Carmelo de Santa Teresa – Coimbra & James A Colson, trans. *A Pathway Under the Gaze of Mary.* Washington, New Jersey: World Apostolate of Fatima, 2015.

Carollo, David. "A Respectful Response to Mr. Christopher Ferrara." Last modified unknown. Accessed March 12, 2016. https://wafusa. org/a-respectful-response-to-mr-christopher-ferrara.

Carson, Thomas & Cerrito, Joann, edits. *The New Catholic Encyclopedia (Second Edition). Volume 10.* Detroit, Michigan: Gale, 2003.

Catholic News Agency. "Cardinal Bertone Shows Original Letter Containing Third Secret of Fatima on TV." Last modified unknown. Accessed August 4, 2016. http://www.catholicnewsagency.com/news/ cardinal_bertone_shows_original_letter_containing_third_secret_ of_fatima_on_tv.

Chiron, Yves. "À propos de quelques apparitions." Last modified unknown. Accessed August 3, 2016. https://www.academia.edu/24046882/ Fatima_LIle_Bouchard_Dozule.

Cirrincione, Joseph A. and Nelson, Thomas A., *The Rosary and the Crisis of Faith.* Rockford, Illinois: TAN Books and Publishers, Inc., 1986.

Collerton, Daniel, and Mosimann, Urs and Perry, Elaine, edits., *The Neu-*

roscience of Visual Hallucinations. Hoboken, New Jersey: John Wiley & Sons, Ltd, 2015.

Colquhoun, Iain. "The Impending World Crisis." *The Fatima Crusader* (Spring, 2010): 57.

Congar, Yves. *My Journal of the Council.* Collegeville, Minnesota: Liturgical Press, 2012.

Congregation for the Doctrine of the Faith. *The Message of Fatima.* Vatican City: Libreria Editrice Vaticana, 2000.

Congregazione per la Dottrina della Fede, *Il Messaggio di Fatima.* Citta del Vaticano: Supplemento a L'Osservatore Romano, numero 147 del 26-27 giugno 2000.

Cuneo, Michael W. *The Smoke of Satan.* New York: Oxford University Press, 1997.

D

Davies, Michael. *Pope John's Council.* Kansas City, Missouri: Angelus Press, 2007.

Dawson, Christopher. *The Movement of World Revolution.* New York: Sheed and Ward, 1959.

De Farias, José Jacinto Ferreira. "Les révélations privées dans la vie de l'Église, À propos du 'Message de Fatima' de la Congrégation de la Doctrine pour la Foi (26 Juin 2000). Analyse et Interprétation." *Apparitiones Beatae Mariae Virginis in Historia, Fide, Theologica.* Città del Vaticano, Pontificia Academia Mariana Internationalis, 2010.

De Fiores, Stefano. *Il Segreto di Fatima: Una luce sul futuro del mondo.* Milano: San Paolo Edizioni, 2008.

De la Fuente, Eloy Bueno. *A Mensagem de Fátima. A Misericórdia de*

Deus: o triunfo do amor nos dramas da história. Fátima, Portugal: Santuário de Fátima, 2014.

Delestre, Fr. Fabrice. "Revelation of the Third Secret of Fatima or Curtailed Revelation." Last modified unknown. Accessed July 17, 2015. http://www.sspxasia.com/Newsletters/2000/July-Aug/Delestre-3rd-Secret.htm.

De Jesus Crucificado, Maria Celina. *Our Memories of Sister Lucia.* Coimbra, Portugal: Carmelo de Coimbra, 2005.

De Mattei, Roberto. *The Second Vatican Council: An Unwritten Story.* Fitzwilliam, New Hampsire: Loreto Publications, 2012.

De Souza, Rodrigo Maria. "Comment." *Fratres in Unum.* Last modified unknown. Accessed August 7, 2016. https://fratresinunum.com/2016/05/23/onepeterfive-responde-ao-desmentido-da-sala-de-imprensa-da-santa-se-dollinger-confirma-dialogo/#comment-120365.

Dhanis, Edouard. "Bij de Verschijningen en de Voorzeggingen van Fatima." *Streven* (1944): 129-149, 193-215.

----------- *Bij de verschijningen en het geheim van Fatima: een critische bijdrage.* Brugge-Brussel: De Kinkhoren, 1945.

----------- "A propos de «Fatima et la critique »." *Nouvelle Revue Théologique* LXXIV (1952): 580-606.

----------- "Sguardo su Fátima e Bilancio di una Discussione." *La Civiltà Cattolica* (1953): 396-397, 399-401.

Dulles, Avery. *The Assurance of Things Hoped for: A Theology of Christian Faith.* New York: Oxford University Press, 1994.

E

Erlandson, Gregory and Bunson, Matthew. *Pope Benedict XVI and the Sexual Abuse Crisis*. Huntington, Indiana: Our Sunday Visitor, 2010.

Eternal Word Television Network. "Interview with Cardinal Ratzinger." Last modified unknown. Accessed October 19, 2016. https://www.ewtn.com/library/ISSUES/RATZINTV.HTM.

------------ "Answers to Journalists on the Flight to Lisbon." Last modified unknown. Accessed May 14, 2016. http://www.ewtn.com/library/papaldoc/b16portflght.htm.

F

Fellows, Mark. *Sr. Lucia: Apostle of Mary's Immaculate Heart*. Immaculate Heart Publications, 2007.

------------ "Reflections on the Silencing of Sister Lucia." *The Fatima Crusader*. (Summer, 2008): 36-38, 61.

Ferrara, Christopher. *The Secret Still Hidden*. Pound Ridge, New York: Good Counsel Publications, 2008.

------------ *The Secret Still Hidden: Epilogue*. Good Counsel Publications, 2010.

------------ "Fatima For Today: A Response." *The Fatima Crusader* (Summer, 2011): 43-55.

------------ *False Friends of Fatima*. Pound Ridge, New York: Good Counsel Publications, 2012.

------------ "Friendly Reflections?" *The Fatima Center*. Last modified unknown. Accessed December 22, 2015. http://www.fatima.org/news/newsviews/ferraraexpose.pdf.

------------ "Fatima for Today: A Response." *The Fatima Center*. Last modified unknown. Accessed October 31, 2016. http://www.fatima.org/news/newsviews/fatima-for-today-a-response.pdf.

------------ "Antonio Socci's Latest Evidence: Sister Lucy Biography Reveals Missing Third Secret Text." *The Fatima Crusader*. (Fall, 2014): 22-26.

------------ *"More Explosive News from the Convent in Coimbra."* The *Fatima Center*. Last modified unknown. Accessed December 22, 2015. http://www.fatimaperspectives.com/ts/perspective722.asp.

------------ "'World Apostolate of Fatima' Hides our Lady of Fatima's Words in English Translation of New Lucia Biography." Last modified unknown. Accessed March 12, 2016. http://fatima.org/perspectives/ts/perspective743.asp.

------------ "A Respectful Reply to David Carollo." Last modified unknown. Accessed March 13, 2016. http://www.fatimaperspectives.com/ts/perspective749.asp.

------------ "Bio-gate: Some Further Developments." Last modified unknown. Accessed March 13, 2016. http://www.fatimaperspectives.com/ts/perspective767.asp.

------------ "Update: Third Secret Still Silenced with Chris Ferrara." Last modified unknown. Accessed March 13, 2016. https://www.youtube.com/watch?v=7OIyqzjuiU8.

------------ "A Reply to Joanna Bogle Respecting the Third Secret of Fatima. Part I." Last modified unknown. Accessed August 13, 2016. http://fatimaperspectives.com/ts/perspective878.asp.

------------ "A Reply to Joanna Bogle Respecting the Third Secret of Fatima. Part II." Last modified unknown. Accessed August 13, 2016. http://fatimaperspectives.com/ts/perspective879.asp.

------------ "A Reply to Joanna Bogle Respecting the Third Secret of Fatima. Part III." Last modified unknown. Accessed August 13, 2016. http://fatimaperspectives.com/ts/perspective880.asp.

Ferrara, Christopher and Alban, Francis. *Fatima Priest*. Pound Ridge, New York: Good Counsel Publications, 2013.

Fox, Robert J. and Maria Martins, S.J., Antonio. *The Intimate Life of Sister Lucia*. Alexandria, South Dakota: Fatima Family Apostolate, 2001.

François de Marie des Anges. *Fatima Joie Intime Événement Mondial.* (aint-Parres Lès Vaudes, France: Éditions de la Contre-Réforme Catholique, 1991.

------------ *Fatima: Tragedy and Triumph*. Buffalo, New York: Immaculate Heart Publications, 1994.

Fülöp Miller, René. *Pope Leo XIII and Our Times*. London: Longmans, Green and Co., 1937.

G

Garrigou-Lagrange, Reginald. *The Three Ages of the Interior Life. Volume II*. Rockford, Illinois: TAN Books, 1989.

Graham, Robert. "Profezie di Guerra: Fatima e la Russia nella propaganda dei belligeranti dopo il 1942." *La Civiltà Cattolica* 132 (1981): 23.

Gregory the Great, Pope. *Moralia in Job. Volume I, Parts I and II*. Ex Fontibus Company, 2012.

Gruner, Nicholas, edit. *World Enslavement or Peace...It's Up to the Pope*. Ontario, Canada: The Fatima Crusader, 1988.

------------ edit. "The 3rd Secret Vision Explained." *The Fatima Crusader*. Last modified unknown. Accessed January 1, 2016. http://www.fatimacrusader.com/cr64/cr64pg18.asp.

------------ "Third Secret Revealed But Not All Of It!" *The Fatima Crusader*. Last modified unknown. Accessed January 1, 2016. http://www.fatimacrusader.com/cr64/cr64pg28.asp.

------------ edit. "Chronology of Four Cover-Up Campaigns: Suppression of the Third Secret." Last modified unknown. Accessed December 5, 2015. http://www.fatima.org/essentials/opposed/cvrup2.asp.

------------ edit. "Published Testimony: Pope John Paul II in Fulda, Germany (1980)." Last modified unknown. Accessed December 24, 2015. http://www.fatima.org/thirdsecret/fulda.asp.

------------ *Crucial Truths to Save Your Soul*. Buffalo, New York: Immaculate Heart Publications, 2014.

H

Hanisch, James and Gruner, Nicholas. "The Third Secret: A Recent Stunning Disclosure." *The Fatima Crusader*. (Spring, 2016): 30-39.

Hasson, Peter. "Leaked Soros Memo: Refugee Crisis 'New Normal,' Gives 'New Opportunities' For Global Influence." *The Daily Caller*. Last modified unknown. Accessed August 16, 2016.

Hickson, Maike. "Cardinal Ratzinger: We Have Not Published the Whole Third Secret of Fatima." *One Peter Five*. Last modified unknown. Accessed May 27, 2016. http://www.onepeterfive.com/cardinal-ratzinger-not-published-whole-third-secret-fatima.

------------ "Profile: The Life of Dr. Ingo Dollinger." *One Peter Five*. Last modified July 12, 2016. Accessed July 14, 2016.

------------ "Robert Moynihan Keeps Fatima Questions Alive." *One Peter Five*. Last modified August 8, 2016. Accessed 14 December, 2016. http://www.onepeterfive.com/robert-moynihan-keeps-fatima-questions-alive/.

------------ "A Private Letter to Pope Emeritus Benedict XVI Revealed." *One Peter Five*. Last modified November 18, 2016. Accessed November 19, 2016. http://www.onepeterfive.com/private-letter-pope-emeritus-benedict-xvi-revealed/.Holy See. *Acta Apostolicae Sedis* 29 (1937): 65-106.

------------ *Acta Apostolicae Sedis* 34 (1942): 10-21; 313-325.

------------ *Acta Apostolicae Sedis* 41 (1949): 334.

------------ *Acta Apostolicae Sedis* 44 (1952): 505-511.

------------ *Acta Apostolicae Sedis* 51 (1959): 65-69.

------------ *Acta Apostolicae Sedis* 54 (1962): 786-795.

------------ *Acta Apostolicae Sedis* 59 (1967): 885-928.

------------ *Acta Apostolicae Sedis* 80 (1988): 841-934.

------------ *Acta Apostolicae Sedis* 102 (2010): 324-327.

------------ *Acta Apostolicae Sedis* 104 (2012): 497-504.

------------ *Acta Sanctae Sedis* 40 (1907): 593-650.

------------ *Acta Sanctae Sedis* 12 (1879): 97-115.

------------ *L'Osservatore Romano* (May 16/17, 1983): 2.

------------ "Conferenza Stampa di Presentazione del Documento 'Il Messaggio di Fatima.'" Last modified unknown. Accessed August 4, 2016. http://press.vatican.va/content/salastampa/it/bollettino/pubblico/2000/06/26/0407/01462.html

------------ "Comunicato: a proposito di alcuni articoli relativi al 'Terzo Segreto di Fatima.'" Last modified unknown. Accessed May 27, 2016. http://press.vatican.va/content/salastampa/it/bollettino/pubblico/2016/05/21/0366/00855.html.

J

Jaki, Fr. Stanley. *The Sun's Miracle, or of Something Else?* New Hope, Kentucky: Real View Books, 2000.

K

Kondor SVD, Fr. Louis, edit. *Fatima in Lucia's Own Words: Volume One.* Fatima: Portugal: Secretariado dos Pastorinhos, 2005.

------------ *Fatima in Lucia's Own Words. Volume II.* Fátima, Portugal: Secretariado dos Pastorinhos, 2004.

Kramer, Paul L. *The Devil's Final Battle.* Terryville, Connecticut: The Missionary Association, 2002.

------------ "The Secret Warned Against Vatican Council II and the New Mass." *The Fatima Crusader* (Spring, 2009): 7-11.

------------ *The Devil's Final Battle: Our Lady's Victory Edition.* Terryville, Connecticut: The Missionary Association, 2010.

------------ "Reply to the Nonsensical Comments of Kevin Symonds." Last modified unknown. Accessed May 28, 2016. https://www.facebook.com/paul.kramer.1023611/posts/1216582278387181.

L

La Documentation Catholique 49 (March 19, 1967): 546-552.

------------ 66 (1969): 794-796.

League of Counter-Reform. "Fidei Defensor." Last modified unknown. Accessed January 1, 2016. http://crc-internet.org/our-founder/fidei-defensor.

------------ "The Founding of the League of the Catholic Counter-Reformation." Last modified unknown. Accessed January 1, 2016. http://crc-internet.org/our-doctrine/catholic-counter-reformation/for-the-church/3-founding-league-crc.

Lépicier, Alexio Maria. *Tractatus de Novissimis*. Parisiis: P. Lethielleux, 1921.

M

Martin, Malachi. *The Jesuits*. New York, New York: Simon & Schuster, 1987.

Martindale, C.C. *The Message of Fatima*. London: Burns Oates and Washbourne Ltd, 1950.

Martins, Antonio Maria. *Memórias e Cartas de Irmã Lúcia*. Porto, Portugal: Simão Guimarães, Filhos, LDA, 1973.

------------ "A Proposito del Secreto de Fatima." *Ephemerides Mariologicae* 36 (1986): 337-348.

------------ *Fatima: Way of Peace*. Chulmleigh, England: Augustine Publishing Company, 1989.

Martins dos Reis, Sebastião. *O Milagre do Sol e o Segredo de Fátima: Inconsequências e especulações*. Porto: Edições Salesianas, 1966.

------------ *Síntese Crítica de Fátima: Incidências e Repercussões*. Porto, Portugal: Edições Salesianas, 1967.

------------ *A Vidente de Fátima DIALOGA e responde pelas Aparições*. Braga, Portugal: Editorial Franciscana, 1970.

McGlynn, Fr. Thomas. *Vision of Fatima*. Boston, Massachusetts: Little Brown and Company, 1948.

Michel de la Sainte Trinité. *Toute la Vérité sur Fatima: Le Troisième Se-*

cret (1942-1960). Saint-Parres lès Vaudes, France: Renaissance Catholique Contre-Réforme Catholique, 1985.

----------- *Toute la Vérité sur Fatima: La Science et les Faits*. Saint-Parres lès Vaudes, France: Renaissance Catholique Contre-Réforme Catholique, 4ᵉ, 1986.

----------- *The Third Secret of Fatima*. Chulmleigh, United Kingdom: Augustine Publishing Company, 1986.

----------- *The Whole Truth About Fatima, Volume I: Science and the Facts*. Buffalo, New York: Immaculate Heart Publications, 1989.

----------- *The Whole Truth About Fatima. Volume II: The Secret and the Church*. Buffalo, New York: Immaculate Heart Publications, 1989.

-----------*The Whole Truth About Fatima. Volume III: The Third Secret*. Buffalo, New York: Immaculate Heart Publications, 1990.

Miguel, Aura. *Totus Tuus: Il segreto di Fatima nel pontificato di Giovanni Paolo II*. Castel Bolognese, Italia: Itaco, 2003.

Miranda, Salvador. "The Cardinals of the Holy Roman Church: Sodano, Angelo." Last modified unknown. Accessed December 21, 2016. http://webdept.fiu.edu/~mirandas/bios1991.htm#Sodano.

Mortensen, John and Alarcón, Enrique, edits. *Summa Theologiae: Prima Pars, 50-119*. Lander, Wyoming: The Aquinas Institute for the Study of Sacred Doctrine, 2012.

----------- *Summa Theologiae: Secunda Secundae, 92-189*. Lander, Wyoming: The Aquinas Institute for the Study of Sacred Doctrine, 2012.

Moynihan, Robert. "Letter #48, 2016: The Passing of Capovilla." *Inside the Vatican*. Last modified unknown. Accessed August 3, 2016. http://insidethevatican.com/news/newsflash/letter-48-2016-passing-capovilla.

----------- "Letter #40, 2016: Again, Russia...." *Inside the Vatican*. Last

modified unknown. Accessed August 3, 2016. http://insidethevatican.com/news/newsflash/letter-49-2016-russia.

N

Navarro-Valls, Joaquin. "Vi racconto il Papa che non si ferma mai." *Corriere della Serra*. Last modified unknown. Accessed October 31, 2016. http://navarro-valls.info/navarrovalls/wp-content/uploads/2016/09/VI_RACCONTO_IL_PAPA.pdf.

O

Ottaviani, Alaphridus (Alfredo). *Institutiones Iuris Publici Ecclesiastici. Vol. I. Ecclesiae Constitutio Socialis et Potestas [editio quarta].* Typis Polyglottis Vaticanis, 1958.

------------ "Mensagem de Fátima." *Lumen: Revista de Cultura do Clero* 19 (Maio-Junho,1955), 264-268.

P

Paolini, Solideo. *Fatima. Non Disprezzate le Profezie. Ricostruzione della Parte non Pubblicata del Terzo Segreto.* Segno, 2005.

Peers, E. Allison, trans. *Ascent of Mount Carmel.* Garden City, New York: Image Books, 1958.

Perrella, Salvatore M. "Il 'Messaggio di Fatima' della Congregazione per la Dottrina della Fede (26 giugno 2000). Interpretazioni contemporanee." *Marianum* 74 (2012): 283-356.

Pontificia Academia Mariana Internationalis. *Acta Pontificiae Academiae*

Marianae Internationalis vel ad Academiam quoquo modo pertinentia. Volume 4. Romae: Pontificia Academia Mariana Internationalis, 1967.

Poulain, Augustin, and Yorke Smith, Leonora L., trans. *The Graces of Interior Prayer: A Treatise on Mystical Theology.* 10[e] London: Routledge and Kegan Paul Limited, 1951.

R

Rahner, Karl. *Inquiries.* New York, New York: Herder and Herder, 1964.

------------ *Visioni e profezie: mistica ed esperienza della trascendenza.* Milano: Vita e Pensiero, 1995.

Ratzinger, Joseph. *The Theology of History in St. Bonaventure.* Chicago, Illinois: Franciscan Herald Press, 1971.

------------ *Eschatology: Death and Eternal Life.* Washington, D.C.: The Catholic University of America Press, 1988.

------------ "The Stations of the Cross." Last modified unknown. Accessed May 16, 2016. http://www.vatican.va/news_services/liturgy/2005/via_crucis/en/station_09.html.

------------ *Jesus of Nazareth: From the Baptism in the Jordan to the Transfiguration.* San Francisco: Ignatius Press, 2007. Ratzinger, Joseph and Messori, Vittorio. *The Ratzinger Report.* San Francisco, California: Ignatius Press, 1986.

Richardson, Elbert L. *et al.*, edits. *McKay's Modern Portuguese-English and English-Portuguese Dictionary.* New York: David McKay Company, Inc., 1943.

Ryan, John, edit. *Fatima Findings* (June, 1959): 1-3.

S

Santuário de Fátima, *Documentação Crítica de Fátima: I – Interrogatórios aos Videntes – 1917*. 2ᵉ. Fátima, Portugal: Santuário de Fátima, 2013.

Skojec, Steve, edit. "Alice von Hildebrand Sheds New Light on Fatima." Last modified unknown. Accessed May 14, 2016. http://www.onepeterfive.com/alice-von-hildebrand-sheds-new-light-fatima.

------------ "On Fatima Story, Pope Emeritus Benedict XVI Breaks Silence." *One Peter Five*. Last modified unknown. Accessed May 27, 2016. http://www.onepeterfive.com/on-fatima-story-pope-emeritus-benedict-xvi-breaks-silence.

Simpson, Victor L. "Vatican Finally Reveals 'Third Secret' of Fatima." *Associated Press*. May 14, 2000. Accessed November 10, 2016. http://thecabin.net/stories/051400/wor_0513000079.html#.WCRp-6forLIU.

Socci, Antonio. *Il Quarto Segreto di Fatima*. Rizzoli, 2006.

------------ *The Fourth Secret of Fatima*. Fitzwilliam, New Hampshire: Loreto Publications, 2009.

----------- "Novita' Apocalittiche da Fatima (L'Ultim Mistero: Il Silenzio delle Suore, ma Chi Tace…)." Last modified unknown. Accessed October 19, 2016. https://web.archive.org/web/20140820000910/http:/www.antoniosocci.com/2014/08/novita-apocalittiche-da-fatima-lultimo-mistero-il-silenzio-delle-suore-ma-chi-tace.

Society of Saint Pius X. "Fr. Gruner: Requiescat in pace." Last modified unknown. Accessed January 1, 2016. http://sspx.org/en/news-events/news/fr-gruner-requiescat-pace-8151.

Stanley, Alessandra. "Vatican Discloses 'Third Secret' of Fatima." *New York Times*. Last modified unknown. Accessed December 2, 2015.

http://partners.nytimes.com/library/world/global/051400pope-fatima-secret.html.

Symonds, Kevin. *Pope Leo XIII and the Prayer to St. Michael*. Boonville, New York: Preserving Christian Publications, 2015.

----------- "In Defense of the World Apostolate of Fatima." *Catholic Stand*. Last modified unknown. Accessed March 12, 2016. http://www.catholicstand.com/waf-usa-defense.

----------- "St. Michael and Spiritualism: A Hidden History?" *Catholic Stand*. Last modified unknown. Accessed July 13, 2016. http://www.catholicstand.com/michael-spiritualism-hidden-history.

----------- "Cardinal Ottaviani on the Third Secret of Fatima." *Catholic Stand*. Last modified unknown. Accessed December 6, 2015. http://www.catholicstand.com/ottaviani-fatima-secret.

----------- "Fatima and Fr. Dollinger: A Response." *The Personal Web Site of Kevin J. Symonds*. Last modified unknown. Accessed May 27, 2016. https://kevinsymonds.com/2016/05/17/fatima-and-fr-dollinger-a-response.

----------- "Fatima and Fr. Dollinger: A Response." *Academia.edu*. Last modified unknown. Accessed August 3, 2016. https://www.academia.edu/25807772/A_Response_to_Fr._Dollinger_on_F%C3%A1tima.

----------- "Chiron and Fatima." *The Personal Web Site of Kevin J. Symonds*. Last modified unknown. Accessed August 3, 2016. https://kevinsymonds.com/2016/06/08/chiron-and-fatima.

T

Thavis, John. *The Vatican Prophecies*. New York, New York: Viking, 2015.

Tosatti, Marco. *Il Segreto non Svelato*. Casale Monferrato, AL: Piemme, 2002.

TradiNews. "Pour en finir avec le «4e secret» de Fatima." Last modified unknown. Accessed August 3, 2016. http://tradinews.blogspot. com/2016/06/yves-chiron-aletheia-pour-en-finir-avec.html.

W

Weller, Philip T., trans. *The Roman Ritual. Volume II*. Boonville, New York: Preserving Christian Publications, 2013.

Westen, John-Henry. "On Fox News Fearless HLI Priest Takes on Sean Hannity over Contraception, Hannity 'Loses It.'" Last modified unknown. Accessed December 13, 2015. https://www.lifesitenews. com/news/on-fox-news-fearless-hli-priest-takes-on-sean-hannity-over-contraception-ha.

Y

Yzermans, Vincent A., edit. *The Major Addresses of Pope Pius XII. Volume II*. St. Paul, Minnesota: The North Central Publishing Company, 1961.